Fundamentals of Public Communication Campaigns

Fundamentals of Public Communication Campaigns

Jonathan Matusitz

WILEY Blackwell

Registered Offices
John Wiley & Sons, Inc., 111 River Street, Hoboken, NJ 07030, USA
John Wiley & Sons Ltd, The Atrium, Southern Gate, Chichester, West Sussex, PO19 8SQ, UK

Editorial Office
The Atrium, Southern Gate, Chichester, West Sussex, PO19 8SQ, UK

For details of our global editorial offices, customer services, and more information about Wiley products visit us at www.wiley.com.

A catalogue record for this book is available from the Library of Congress

Paperback ISBN: 9781119878070; ePub ISBN: 9781119878094; ePDF ISBN: 9781119878087

Cover image: © Hilch/Shutterstock
Cover design by Wiley

Set in 10/12.5pt STIXTwoText by Integra Software Services Pvt. Ltd, Pondicherry, India

SKY10035678_081222

Contents

Introduction

Divided into 16 chapters, this textbook describes the fundamentals of public communication campaigns for beginners; more specifically, for large audiences like undergraduate students and readers from both the United States and countries around the world. Unlike most works on that subject, this textbook has a considerably high international focus, a thorough description of over 700 basic concepts, and numerous real-life case studies—all of which being infused with communication theories. While this is not a perfect volume and there is still progress to be made, the author makes the point that successful public communication campaigns are ones that diversify their strategies and discard the notion that information alone is *the* solution to induce individual and/or social change. Effective campaigns are no longer based on the erroneous perception that society will improve if audiences acquire more information. Rather, campaigns are increasingly paying attention to context and combining their traditional media and behavior change strategies with social media and direct, face-to-face community action. In the end, this makes the social and human environment more supportive of the desired campaign outcomes.[1]

PUBLIC COMMUNICATION CAMPAIGNS

Public communication campaigns are typically large-scale initiatives designed, sponsored, and run by state actors or nonstate actors to alter people's behaviors, attitudes, social norms, and/or beliefs.[2] As Gültekin and Gültekin (2012) reason,[3] a campaign aims at mobilizing the public's conscience and sustaining this conscience with solid strategies on communication platforms. Campaigns can influence people at the individual, the social, and/or the institutional level. The majority of them seek to change behavior at the individual level, and must take specific individual factors into consideration—those factors that underlie behavioral intention and behavior within a given target audience.[4] Campaigns tend to be presented in different forms and serve various purposes, with the most prevalent ones created for promoting sociopolitical causes. Others are for public health, social programs, charitable causes, well-being, and safety. Most communication campaigns are supported by entities such as governments, private corporations, nonprofit organizations, communities, and social change promoters.[5]

In order to modify behavior, we need to understand people's behaviors when designing campaigns. Understanding the reasons that affect intention and behavior is important for laying the groundwork for the creation, implementation, and evaluation of effective public communication campaigns.[6] Communication scholars have devoted a great deal of attention

Fundamentals of Public Communication Campaigns, First Edition. Jonathan Matusitz.
© 2022 John Wiley & Sons Ltd. Published 2022 by John Wiley & Sons Ltd.

to the content and impacts of messages on audiences. Public health campaigns, in particular, are often addressed in books and scholarly studies, arguably due to their purported intent to champion social good instead of harm. Nevertheless, other types of public communication campaigns—like those of terrorist movements or campaigns for Islamophobia—have been understudied for their potential to produce undesirable effects. In addition to social change, public communication campaigns can be an instrument of self-insight and remedy. Whether it is meant for good or bad purposes is contingent upon us and our value system—the approaches that we take to change people's minds at work and at home, and how we consider the practice of persuasion with strangers and loved ones.

CHANGES IN THE MEDIA LANDSCAPE

All communication is humankind's fundamental symbolic resource for regulating the environment.[7] Today, communication brings together media and persuasion to change social conditions. Mass media campaigns are often designed to expose high volumes of people to messages through regular uses of traditional media, such as TV, radio, and newspapers. However, exposure through existing media like these is generally passive.[8] This is why a combination of traditional media, social media, interpersonal relationships, segmented communication, and culturally tailored messaging to audiences are more likely to make a public communication campaign efficient and thriving.[9] Large-scale public communication programs today necessitate mass communication campaign strategies, as marked by the investments of time, money, and other resources in most of contemporary initiatives. Success or failure in campaigning depends mainly on campaign managers' skills in crafting effective communication (including social media) campaigns. The strategies include opposition research, segmented targeting of audiences, continual adaptation of messages, and step-by-step tracking of issues. In this new era of digital communications and around-the-clock news cycles, undivided attention must be given to message delivery, audience feedback, and unintended consequences.[10]

The media landscape has metamorphosed since the dawn of the twenty-first century. Although long-established methods of communication are still important, new platforms of public communication are constantly emerging through digitalization, the internet, and social media.[11] The media landscape in modern societies has gradually been saturated with a proliferation of media outlets and options, presenting audiences with alternatives to fulfill their media-related needs.[12] Audiences frequently use a *mélange* of media and content types to absorb issues raised by public communication campaigns.[13] Publics have split into subgroups across platforms to come into contact with various online communities around certain niche interests, politics, ideologies, or hobbies like music and sports.[14] Online communities consist of cultures of participation in which members' activities form a collective type of sense-making.[15] Taken as a whole, owing to the changes in the media landscape, public communication campaigns need to be aware that they have to grow more sophisticated and strategic.

WHAT THIS TEXTBOOK OFFERS

It is important to understand that, for a college textbook to be successful in the social sciences, particularly if it is intended for international audiences, it must meet five main criteria: A comprehensive focus, an easy focus, an international focus, a practical focus, and a theoretical focus.

A Comprehensive Focus

This textbook is divided into four parts: (1) Introducing Public Communication Campaigns, (2) Health Communication Campaigns, (3) Communication Campaigns for Social Justice and Social Change, and (4) Terrorist, Extremist, and Anti-Terrorist Communication Campaigns. Each of the four parts contains four chapters. Most major works that have been available in the past and current literature only cover one or two parts. Under existing circumstances, it is important to teach students and practitioners alike how to create and implement public communication campaigns from a wide array of perspectives—including those produced by organizations like Black Lives Matter. Enter the last topic of the fourth part of the book: antiterrorist communication campaigns. Not only are counterradicalization communicators moving to the online space to counter (would-be) terrorists, but they can also assist volunteers or authorities in designing messages that help societies win the war of ideas against enemies (both external forces and enemies from within). Even communication campaigns against female genital mutilation (FGM) and honor killing are addressed. In a nutshell, this textbook is the most comprehensive one on public communication campaigns.

An Easy Focus

To date, no major textbook on public communication campaigns has been written for large audiences like undergraduate students and readers from both the United States and countries around the world. As will be explained in the next section (on the competition with other books), the few major volumes that have been published on that subject are certainly well written and thought-out, but the content is not written with the intention of explaining the fundamentals of public communication campaigns to beginners. Rather, the language is too elevated and theoretical for large publics or these volumes focus too much on one part of the world or other topics that fall outside the scope of this textbook. More importantly, this textbook includes over 700 fundamental concepts of campaigns that are in bold writing and clearly defined for readers. Each chapter is markedly different and includes case studies to which both young and older audiences can relate. For example, there are case studies on COVID-19 campaigns in several nations, LGBTQ+ initiatives in South America, and Hollywood celebrity health campaigns. At the end of this textbook, readers can look through a glossary that lists and defines all key terms and concepts used across the 16 chapters.

An International Focus

Most books on that subject tend to overly concentrate on projects in the United States. Although it is true that, for message designers and common citizens alike, the immense accessibility of both mainstream and social media in the United States facilitates the creation and impact of campaigns, most books tend to overlook the efforts made in other countries. As such, this volume includes public communication campaigns from both the United States and a whopping 25 other countries. These countries are Australia, Brazil, Canada, Chile, China, Colombia, Egypt, Hungary, India, Israel, Jamaica, Jordan, Nepal, Norway, Pakistan, Poland, Rwanda, Saudi Arabia, Singapore, Somalia, South Africa, South Korea, the United Kingdom, Uganda, and Vietnam. It is the author's hope that this international focus will open the reader's minds and perspectives in regards to public communication campaigns and how they become both a familiar and essential component of the civic culture of those nations and an important policy tool used by state actors and nonstate actors across six continents.

A Practical Focus

To make sound and educated choices and apply methods in the most optimal way, campaign designers need to be conscious of what is available and understand the fundamental principles and processes inherent to large-scale communication projects. Chapter 2, in particular, is on the 10 steps of public communication campaigns. It provides a detailed template for practitioners or scholars who need to create or adapt messages to scenarios in such areas as advertising, public relations, health, safety, personal well-being, entertainment, social justice, animal rights, and even terrorism and antiterrorism—among a myriad of others. Underlining the structure is the easy step-by-step process, which provides directions for all endeavors and suggestions for all types of messages. Chapter 2 explains how a public communication campaign is to be planned from start to finish by identifying what is to be done, for what purpose, by whom, for which audience, on what platform, within what time frame, and with what expected outcomes. The 10 steps show that substantial consideration must be exercised in crafting a campaign and that the key individuals involved in the implementation or supervision comprehend the overall purpose and the courses of action.

A Theoretical Focus

Many theories are integrated in this textbook because they help understand the procedures that actuate campaign effects and, especially for the discipline of communication, the theoretical foundations for the production of effective messages to inform, persuade, and inspire publics.[16] Theories serve a diversity of equally important purposes, all of which are geared towards cultivating the ability to think about and understand the issues in question. In addition, reinforcing a campaign with a theoretical foundation can both sustain its development and serve as a basis for its application and evaluation.[17] This textbook includes both mainstream communication theories and other essential theories that are often missing in the literature. The mainstream theories in this book include the Diffusion of Innovations (DoI) theory, framing theory, agenda-setting theory, social judgment theory (SJT), the Uses & Gratifications (U&G) theory, the Health Belief Model (HBM), the Transtheoretical Model, the Theory of Planned Behavior, the Elaboration Likelihood Model (ELM), self-efficacy theory, social cognitive theory (SCT), social learning theory (SLT), and social movement theory (SMT)—to name a few. In most cases, the theories were applied to specific case studies of public communication campaigns. Other essential theories, like self-determination theory (SDT) and media dependency theory, have surprisingly been rarely included in major volumes on that topic. This is why this textbook has filled this gap by developing entire case studies around them. Other theories include self-affirmation theory, attitude accessibility theory, the theory of responsive chord, selective perception theory, inoculation theory, the spiral of silence, and muted group theory—again, to name a few. Chapter 8, for example, applies SDT to health communication campaigns created through digital games.

SUMMARY OF ALL CHAPTERS

Chapter 1 provides definitions, strategies, and background information on public communication campaigns. It begins with a description of the communication process and the public sphere and then proceeds with a detailed account of the Diffusion of Innovations (DoI) theory. After giving examples of campaigns in history, it discusses current strategies like social marketing and social norms marketing.

Chapter 2 lays out the 10 steps of public communication campaigns. As such, the steps are (a) define and select your topic; (b) set goals and objectives; (c) analyze and understand the situation beforehand; (d) define your audience(s); (e) understand the timeline and budget; (f) choose appropriate media; (g) develop optimal message content; (h) avoid monologic communication and interact with your audience(s); (i) update the campaign with timely, relevant, and accurate information; and (j) evaluate the overall campaign.

Chapter 3 discusses the role of persuasion in public communication campaigns. A large section is devoted to Behavior Change Communication (BCC) and related theories such as self-affirmation theory and the Elaboration Likelihood Model (ELM). Another large section is devoted to attitudes and related theories such as social judgment theory (SJT) and attitude accessibility theory. Of particular relevance are the 10 ethical principles of public communication campaigns, the persuasive effects of such campaigns, and, conversely, their 12 negative effects.

Chapter 4 is on thought-provoking public communication campaigns. The Extended Parallel Process Model (EPPM), for example, explains how people's attitudes can be changed through fear appeals. At the same time, the effects of alarmist language are mentioned as well. A special focus is also placed on provocation, including the theoretical concept of shockvertising. The end of the chapter provides a detailed case study on two campaigns launched by People for the Ethical Treatment of Animals (PETA).

Chapter 5 offers readers general perspectives on health communication campaigns. After describing what "health" means and the different goals and strategies of such campaigns, the chapter continues with a thorough analysis of antismoking campaigns (like the truth initiative) and harm reduction campaigns. The chapter ends with a detailed case study that examines the social determinants of health (SDH) and ABC behaviors in Uganda.

Chapter 6 tackles the differences in literacy and culture in health campaigns. An important segment on eHealth and the digital divide highlights how communication technologies may fundamentally determine who has access to health information. What comes subsequently are the cultural barriers that audiences face when exposed to various public communication campaigns. This chapter ends with the key attributes of culture, cultural competency, and how ethnographic research can reduce cultural differences when designing campaigns.

Chapter 7 addresses public communication campaigns during the COVID-19 pandemic. After introducing fundamental concepts such as risk communication, a comprehensive section on the strategies for COVID-19 communication campaigns illustrate how campaign designers can concentrate on issues such as social distancing. Also significant is the information on both vaccination campaigns and countercampaigns like those of anti-vaxxers.

Chapter 8 looks at Entertainment–Education, digital games, and celebrity campaigns as alternatives to traditional health communication campaigns. Of particular interest to readers are the multiple case studies contained within one chapter and the theoretical framework of narrative involvement. Equally important are the section on Games for Change (GfC), serious games, and persuasive games, and the section on self-determination theory (SDT). Lastly, an interesting point is the impact of celebrity health disclosure.

Chapter 9 is about communication campaigns for social justice and social change. After reading the list of important terms, including seven manifestations of social change, readers can learn about case studies on campaigns against female genital mutilation (FGM) in Africa and honor killing in Pakistan. The second part of this chapter focuses on campaigning for environmental policies and what nongovernmental organizations are.

Chapter 10 addresses the #MeToo campaign. After an understanding of what constitutes sexual misconduct, one can see how the initiatives around the world have created a positive impact on both the United States and other countries. Long-established theories like the spiral of silence and muted group theory explain how minority groups are now part of the mainstream in their struggles against injustice. Other theories such as critical race feminism and social identity theory (SIT) are also included.

Chapter 11 is dedicated to public communication campaigns for LGBTQ+ communities. Three case studies—the GLAAD campaign in the United States (with an application of agenda-setting theory as well), the campaign against homophobia in Poland, and LGBTQ+ campaigns in Brazil—illustrate how grassroots initiatives and social media platforms can make waves even in countries with traditional beliefs that sexual rights are only for heterosexuals.

Chapter 12 discusses Black Lives Matter (BLM) campaigns, particularly how BLM started and has evolved to what it is today. The two large sections on campaigns against police brutality and systemic racism will inform anyone interested in policy solutions for societal reform. What comes next is a description of the role of intersectionality and standpoint theory, critical race theory, and critical social justice.

Chapter 13 presents readers with two major case studies of terrorist communication campaigns. The first one is about the FARC in Colombia since 1964; this Marxist–Leninist terrorist group used various forms of communications to spread their ideology to peasants and lowly educated workers. The author shows how speech act theory has great value here. The second one is about the Rwanda Genocide in 1994. The role of "Radio Machete," the genociders' main vehicle for spreading hatred and propaganda (including numerous euphemisms for killing), is something to behold.

Chapter 14 is about public communication campaigns of White supremacism. The concept of "manosphere"—a collection of groups and online sites that advocate male supremacy and subjugation of women—plays a crucial part for both recruitment and campaigning. Case studies on the "It's Okay to Be White," the Proud Boys, and the "2020 voter fraud" campaign exemplify the ability of social media platforms to amplify feelings of victimhood against what they call the "Evil Left."

Chapter 15 deals with public communication campaigns of Islamophobia and anti-semitism. A particular focus is placed on hashtag-driven Islamophobia campaigns in India and political campaigns that are antisemitic in Hungary. Both types of campaigns are immersed in historical events. The application of Terror Management Theory (TMT) to the case of Islamophobia serves to explain how campaigns are conducted to ensure the survival and growth of "natives."

Chapter 16 ends on a positive note. It discusses antiterrorist public communication campaigns and strategies on how to win the war of ideas through clever messaging. The battle is more likely to be won when campaigns are moved to the online space. Multiple case studies are offered, including the US government's initiative on how to build community resilience within Somali communities in the United States. Of particular interest are the antiterrorist public communication campaigns in the Middle East and the reparation campaigns in Australia.

NOTES

1. Julia Coffman, *Public Communication Campaign Evaluation: An Environmental Scan of Challenges, Criticisms, Practice, and Opportunities* (Cambridge, MA: Harvard Family Research Project, 2002).
2. Janet A. Weiss and Mary Tschirhart, "Public Information Campaigns as Policy Instruments," *Journal of Policy Analysis and Management* 13, no. 1 (1994): 82–119. https://doi.org/10.2307/3325092.
3. Bilgehan Gültekin and Tuba Gültekin, "Importance of Public Communication Campaigns and Art Activities in Social Education," *World Academy of Science, Engineering and Technology* 64 (2012): 708–24.
4. Lourdes S. Martinez and Nehama Lewis, "The Moderated Influence of Perceived Behavioral Control on Intentions Among the General US Population: Implications for Public Communication Campaigns," *Journal of Health Communication* 21, no. 9 (2016): 1006–15. https://doi.org/10.1080/10810730.2016.1204378.
5. Elizabeth Crisp Crawford and Charles C. Okigbo, "Strategic Communication Campaigns," in *Strategic Urban Health Communication*, ed. Charles C. Okigbo (New York: Springer, 2014): 11–23.
6. Martin Fishbein, Harry C. Triandis, Frederick H. Kanfer, Marshall Becker, Susan E. Middlestadt, and Anita Eichler, "Factors Influencing Behavior and Behavior Change," in *Handbook of Health Psychology*, ed. Andrew Baum, Tracey A. Revenson, and Jerome E. Singer (Mahwah, NJ: Lawrence Erlbaum, 2001): 3–16.
7. Ian Somerville, "Agency versus Identity: Actor-Network Theory Meets Public Relations," *Corporate Communications: An International Journal* 4, no. 1 (1999): 6–13. http://dx.doi.org/10.1108/13563289910254525.
8. Melanie A. Wakefield, Barbara Loken, and Robert C. Hornik, "Use of Mass Media Campaigns to Change Health Behaviour," *The Lancet* 376, no. 9748 (2010): 1261–71. https://doi.org/10.1016/S0140-6736(10)60809-4.
9. Richard M. Perloff, *The Dynamics of Persuasion: Communication and Attitudes in the 21st Century* (2nd Ed.) (Mahwah, NJ: Lawrence Erlbaum, 2003).
10. Crawford and Charles C. Okigbo, "Strategic Communication Campaigns," 12.
11. Christopher Laurell, Christian Sandström, Klas Eriksson, and Rasmus Nykvist, "Digitalization and the Future of Management Learning: New technology as an Enabler of Historical, Practice-Oriented, and Critical Perspectives in Management Research and Learning," *Management Learning* 51, no. 1 (2020): 89–108. https://doi.org/10.1177/1350507619872912.
12. John L. Sherry, "Media Saturation and Entertainment–Education," *Communication Theory* 12, no. 2 (2002): 206–24. https://doi.org/10.1111/j.1468-2885.2002.tb00267.x.

13. Harsh Taneja, James G. Webster, Edward C. Malthouse, and Thomas B. Ksiazek, "Media Consumption across Platforms: Identifying User-Defined Repertoires," *New Media & Society* 14, no. 6 (2012): 951–68. https://doi.org/10.1177/1461444811436146.

14. Grant Blank and Bianca C. Reisdorf, "The Participatory Web: A User Perspective on Web 2.0," *Information, Communication & Society* 15, no. 4 (2012): 537–54. https://doi.org/10.1080/1369118X.2012.665935.

15. Neta Kligler-Vilenchik and Kjerstin Thorson, "Good Citizenship as a Frame Contest: Kony2012, Memes, and Critiques of the Networked Citizen," *New Media & Society* 18, no. 9 (2015): 1993–2011. https://doi.org/10.1177/1461444815575311.

16. Joseph N. Cappella, "Editor's Introduction: Theoretical Approaches to Communication Campaigns," *Communication Theory* 13, no. 2 (2003): 160–3. https://doi.org/10.1111/j.1468-2885.2003.tb00286.x.

17. Thomas W. Valente, "Evaluating Communications Campaigns," in *Public Communication Campaigns* (3rd Ed.), ed. Ronald E. Rice and Charles C. K. Atkin (Thousand Oaks, CA: Sage, 2001): 105–24.

PART I

INTRODUCING PUBLIC COMMUNICATION CAMPAIGNS

CHAPTER 1

Definitions, Strategies, and Background Information

WHAT ARE PUBLIC COMMUNICATION CAMPAIGNS?

Public communication campaigns are found everywhere and it is nearly impossible to elude them in our modern-day environment of traditional communication and social media. By and large, a **campaign** is a comprehensive and organized attempt at shaping the behavior, attitude, or decision-making status within a community of people. It is a strategic course of action carried out during a specific time limit and for a precise outcome.[1] A **public communication campaign** consists of a set of coordinated messages or other communicative efforts aimed at accomplishing predetermined goals and objectives: to sway a high number of people's beliefs, attitudes, and behaviors.[2] Atkin (1981)[3] defines "public communication campaign" as a method that uses "promotional messages in the public interest disseminated through mass media channels to target audiences." Public communication campaigns tend to be waged by state or nonstate actors who seek to inform or affect behaviors in large audiences through an organized set of communication processes. They are designed with two phases in mind. The first phase generates awareness about a certain topic. Thus, a campaign has a purpose; the desired outcomes can be diverse—ranging from individual-level cognitive impacts to social or systemic change. The second phase uses that awareness to instill behavior change and shape the thoughts or actions of the audience; it is typically aimed at a large audience. "Large" is an important concept here because it helps differentiate campaigns from interpersonal persuasive endeavors by one—or a few—person that seek to influence a handful of others.[4]

A Method of Reform and Governance

The element of reform is inherent in all public communications campaigns. **Reform** refers to action that improves society or the lives of individuals. In the eyes of campaign designers, change within the audience's behavior will make life better. "**Better**" is aligned with emerging values in society during each historical era.[5] "Better" implies that one group intends to influence other groups' beliefs, attitudes, or behaviors on the basis of communicated appeals.[6] Campaigns should also be viewed as a governance strategy. **Governance** is "conduct of conduct." It motivates a group of people to govern themselves in a novel manner. Since requests for behavior change are usually not mandatory in modern societies, public communication campaigns need to employ the cleverest appeals to self-governance. This kind of strategy, "turning us into decent people," can have moral and normative effects on a whole class of citizens.[7] Overall, the concept of governance illustrates how public communication campaigns are prosocial in their efforts to influence behavior towards desirable social outcomes. The consequences of those behaviors may be that individuals, families, and communities are healthier, or that particular policy results bring about better outcomes for those individuals, families, and communities.[8]

Public Communication Campaigns vs. Advertising

Most public communication campaigns are not made to attain financial outcomes, even in commercial organizations. Rather, such campaigns are undertaken to raise awareness (i.e., of an issue, policy, or law), to transform attitudes, and/or to improve reputation. Almost half of public communication across the globe is undertaken by public-sector and non-profit corporations that do not have financial interests.[9] As Atkin and Rice (2012)[10] put it, public communication campaigns contain "an array of mediated messages in multiple channels generally to produce noncommercial benefits to individuals and society." The objectives and processes inherent in commercial advertising are not appropriate for public communication campaigns. The fundamental differences between advertising and public communication lie in the kind and quality of issues, the procedures involved in promotion and, evidently, in the type of audiences. In general, advertising by itself does not cause fundamental changes in behavior. It does not produce substantial effects on potential consumers, as some critics might believe. Nevertheless, incremental changes in market share for a specific product that are achieved as a result of advertising may lead to significantly higher sales and profits.[11]

Two Main Types of Public Communication Campaigns

There are two main types of public communication campaigns: (1) Individual behavior-change campaigns and (2) public will campaigns. **Individual behavior-change campaigns** attempt to change individual behaviors that create problems in society or promote behaviors that better individual or social well-being. Also known as **public information campaigns** or **public education campaigns**, they shape beliefs and information about a behavior and its impact. They influence attitudes in favor of behavior that will be perceived positively among one's peers. In other words, they create social norms about the acceptability of a desired behavior (and the intentions to perform it). They are more likely to induce behavior change if complemented by supportive program elements. Effective campaigns of this type target behaviors such as smoking, using drugs, recycling, driving responsibly, using the seat belt, and preventing fire and crime. Many are found within the public health arena. This type of campaign has also evolved into other sectors like education, criminal justice, and early childhood.[12]

Public will campaigns serve to muster public action for policy action and change. Although less understood, they are growing in numbers. As long as they spread visibility of a social issue and its magnitude, they can shape perceptions of such issues—and identify who is responsible—and criteria that the audience needs to judge policies and policymakers. Hence, they impart knowledge about solutions (based on who is portrayed as responsible) and help determine what can be done for service introduction and public support. They engage and galvanize interested individuals into action. A public will campaign focuses less on the person who takes harmful actions (e.g., smoking, polluting, or doing drugs), and more on the public's duty to make decisions that will foster an environment conducive to behavior change.[13]

A public will campaign searches for the various factors that are hurting communities and builds on current efforts or develops new ones to heal those communities. By definition, **public will** is a manifestation of how the community feels and acts. For instance, public will on problems that concern children and families may constitute a shared sense of community-based ownership of the welfare and comfort of children and families, as well as a collective commitment to make the indispensable changes to improve it. Public will has more commonalities with public engagement than with education and awareness. This is why it is also called a **public engagement campaign**.[14] Public will entails more than public opinion or awareness. It entails the inclination to act in favor of how an individual feels about an issue. Effective communications campaigns want to be clear as to what actions people should take. As such, the actions should strengthen policy agendas and enable people to carry them out in their own backyards. Certainly, it is not unusual for campaigns to include both individual change and public will components within the same project.[15]

COMMUNICATION

Communication is the fundamental pillar of our society. John Dewey (1916)[16] famously said that "society exists... in communication." Williams (1976)[17] agreed with Dewey when he stated that "society is a form of communication." Human communication is an exceedingly more multifaceted, ambiguous, and variable process than many of us would admit. We are well aware that communication is a practice that all humans do, to varying degrees, from the cradle to the grave. However, to presuppose that attempts at communicating are automatically, or even frequently, effective is to disregard the conflicts, divorces, breakdowns of relationships, family feuds, miscommunications, and other disturbances that take place on a daily basis in human society.[18]

Definitions

Communication is the "process of exchanging information, imparting ideas and making oneself understood by others and understanding others in return."[19] It is the process of conveying a message from a sender to a receiver. The study of communication in Western civilization dates back to roughly 2,500 years and ostensibly originated in Ancient Greece with Aristotle's *Rhetoric and Poetics*.[20] He, too, thought that communication was an exchange of meanings represented by signs. The term "communicate" stems from the Latin *communicare* ("to make common"). Communication is an act that makes something common; it reflects the need to participate in shared or common action. What makes human communication exceptional among all species, and most likely not transferable to other species, is that it can take place through multiple media of transmission.[21]

Contemporary communication comprises both mass communication and networked communication. **Mass communication** diffuses information from a major source via consolidated media, like TV, newspapers, and radio. This category of mass-mediated exchange is regulated by big corporations, some of which are government-owned; it also disseminates information through mainstream vehicles of distribution.[22] **Networked communication**, on the other hand, sends information from a wide array of sources, including nontraditional ones (e.g., average citizens on the street) and, as such, reflects many different views. It can happen through a mixture of formats, such as email, teleconferencing, and social networking sites like Twitter and Facebook.[23] By the same token, a **network effect** develops when individuals or groups are more willing to use a particular medium of communication if other people have done it successfully (and are fully associated with that medium).[24] If truth be told, Devji (2005)[25] calls this network effect the **global media effect**, because no single actor will have total control over the effects of other individuals or actions.

Communication as a Mediator of Social Change

Since communication is the sharing and diffusion of information, it is also the enabler of the initiation of any contact and relationship within communities. From this perspective, communication is a mediator of social change because it must be theorized in terms of various parties involved in producing meanings, by way of dialogue.[26] Change is a communicative challenge and appropriate communication approaches can abate the resistance to change. Since change is a communicative challenge, serious consideration needs to be paid whenever a change "project" is to be undertaken. Communication procedures are components of change implementation itself.[27] Information technologies, media organizations, and effective media coverage contribute to the creation and preservation of such social change. Accordingly, communication plays a vital role on the social map.[28] It allows the obtaining of new knowledge (as well as the reusing of old knowledge) for audiences and the persuasive appeals, based on that knowledge, to change their beliefs, attitudes, and/or behaviors.[29]

Community-Based and Interpersonal Communication

It is clear, by now, that public communication campaigns are (1) an organized communication enterprise, (2) directed at large audiences during a specific period of time, (3) designed to achieve definite goals and objectives, and (4) and ultimately attempting to create change. Such campaigns rely on the media, messaging, and a variety of communication activities to produce desired outcomes.[30] To amplify their likelihoods of success, public communication campaigns often combine media efforts with a *mélange* of community-based and interpersonal communication means.[31] Examples of community-based channels include, but are not limited to, TV, radio, newspapers, billboards, email, and social media. Examples of interpersonal channels include, but are not limited to, face-to-face gatherings, home visits, and workshops. Printed materials, such as brochures and pamphlets, are sometimes considered mass media or can also be incorporated in interpersonal contexts.[32]

Public communication campaigns have become more sophisticated and strategic. Messages are crafted on the basis of both form and content, and care is taken as to what appropriate communication channels and media should be selected. By combining media efforts with a *mélange* of communication channels, campaign designers can expand the reach and frequency of the messages and increase the probability that they will successfully lead to change.[33] Campaigns will differ based on the types of communication activities used, including posters, handouts, public service announcements (PSAs), discussion forums, workplace meetings, in-school exhibitions, and even clinic-based counseling. Campaigns that include at least one category of media to diffuse their messages are termed **mediated campaigns**.[34]

Messaging

Messaging is essential to the success of public communication campaigns. **Messaging** refers to a system or practice of sending messages, through community-based or interpersonal communication channels. A **message** is a statement of a certain scope that tends to contain only one central idea and relates to the objectives stipulated by a specific communication intervention.[35] Messaging entails more than using words or phrases that sound appealing and instill a feeling of persuasiveness. In fact, when messaging includes suitable means and words (like facts), it is more likely to educate individuals or communities *per se*. Campaigns transmit one or a mix of categories of knowledge—namely, impact, procedural, and normative knowledge.[36] **Impact knowledge** is general information about a topic with the inclusion of facts and figures.[37] When campaigns want to prompt action, **procedural knowledge** is used. It is knowledge of how to do something. The goal of employing procedural knowledge is to keenly engage the audience.[38] **Normative knowledge** focuses on the norms of audiences, at a larger level.[39]

THE "PUBLIC" ASPECT OF CAMPAIGNS

The supreme goal of public communication campaigns is to influence the public so as to change its behavior or attitude. Therefore, it is important to define the "public" aspect of campaigns. **Public** refers to the overall entity of humankind, or of a country or community. It is the people, indefinitely. Put simply, the public is a particular body or aggregation of individuals.[40] The origins of the word "public" lie in *poplicus* ("of the people"), which evolved into *publicus*, seemingly under the effect of its restriction to *pubes* ("adult men"). The evolution of the term reflects a general notion of open access and, more specifically, interpretations of who can have membership in the public.[41] The concept of public also stems from Greek and Roman understandings of the rightful members of polities. In many Greek city-states, **polity** was a gathering of citizens who took part in the political process. Suffrage excluded women, slaves, serfs, and foreigners. The polity included only a minority of the adult men.[42]

A distinction should be drawn between public and publics. Coca-Cola, for instance, addresses its communication campaign to the general public because the company sells highly popular products for all. On the other hand, **publics** refers to particular audiences who are the intended target of a message (a distinction from the general public). They are based on more precise audience characteristics. For example, the American Diabetes Association tends to target individuals who have contracted that illness.[43] Coca-Cola's deliberate attempt to manipulate the public's perception of its products is called **publicity**. The subjects of publicity are people (e.g., youths or performing artists), products and services, all types of organizations, and works of art or entertainment—to name a few. A **publicist** is an expert whose task is to create and manage publicity for a product, public figure (like a celebrity), or a work such as a book or film. Publicists are often employed by large corporations that handle multiple clients.[44]

Public Communication

The study of **public communication** relates to the production and management of messages in public settings. It is the practice of delivering a message (or a piece of information) from which audiences can learn. Its purpose is to inform and persuade, develop relationships and connections, and cultivate networks. Public communication allows people to remain in touch with everything that happens in their environment. It is essential to be open to communicate and exchange information.[45] Public communication is more inclusive than mass communication in the sense that it is concerned with all channels employed for direct and mediated communication, and it is directed as a wide collection of audiences with various interests and views (instead of one "imagined" mass audience).[46] At the same time, public communication also includes more than media campaigns, especially traditional media. Online media like popular websites (often known as **information hubs**), telephone hotlines for support (e.g., smoking "quit lines"), and social networking sites are part of public communication. Public communication practitioners do, nonetheless, acknowledge the advantages of using direct audience engagement approaches—like meetings, events, and cooperative community-based projects.[47]

At a macro level, public communication needs to be viewed as the constant communicative interaction between organizations and their many audiences—and vice versa. Today, public communication occurs around the clock, not only within the semicontrolled boundaries of campaigns. It happens every time an official delivers a speech, every time a user posts a tweet or comment on Facebook, and every time a photo is uploaded on Instagram, or Pinterest. Even simple individuals use public communication on a regular basis. Examples include independent media reporters, people who file public complaints, protesters, petitioners, social media commentators, and various other individuals who express the "will of the people." Still, entities such as organizations and institutions are tasked with monitoring and assessing what others say.[48]

Public Sphere

As opposed to interpersonal communication between two people (dyads) and within small clusters, public communication entails communication activities that occur in the public sphere[49] rather than the private sphere[50]—albeit the demarcation between private and public can be blurred in modern-day societies.[51] The **public sphere** is the aspect of life in which a person interacts with others in society.[52] When discussing the public sphere, the role of public place is something to behold. **Public space** is a place open to anyone without exclusion, even if this may not necessarily be the case in the real world. One of the earliest examples of public spaces are **commons**. In the case of commons, no permission or registration is mandatory for entry; nor are people discriminated based on who they are.[53]

Those at whom public communication campaigns are aimed are commonly referred to as people in a public sphere or public place. With this said, not all individuals and groups have a vested interest in a public communication campaign or the entity that organizes it. Nor are they directly affected by the activities of that entity. Those who are, however, can be attentive citizens, customers, partners, affiliates, employees, and even entire communities. They are also referred to as **stakeholders** because they have an investment (i.e., moral or financial) in the entity.[54] When people influenced by a campaign interact and influence each other in the public sphere as a result of that campaign, they form rhetorical strands. **Rhetorical strands** are rhetorical dimensions that form among individuals as a consequence of public communication. Such strands emerge in the public sphere and expand as people interact in their homes, workplaces, and locations where they spend a significant portion of their time. The public sphere of communication campaigns can be a neighborhood, town, or any public place that a number of individuals share in common or visit frequently.[55]

SEGMENTED COMMUNICATION

When campaign designers locate specific (often at-risk) segments of the entire population (rather than attempting to reach the broad public), they tailor their communication based on the type of audience, a phenomenon called **segmented communication**.[56] Segmented communication comes from **segmented marketing**, whereby advertisers focus on the lifestyle approach. They strive to reach markets through finely targeted, personalized marketing campaigns that focus on demographics, attitudes, values, interests, and community activities. By extension, **lifestyle marketing** involves creating a resemblance or emotional attraction to a certain product or service by associating it with the favorite lifestyles of potential consumers.[57] There are two main benefits of subdividing the audience based on demographic characteristics, tendencies, personality traits, and social contexts. First, message efficiency can be enhanced if subsets of the audience are prioritized in accordance with their centrality in achieving the campaign's objectives as well as the likelihood to being influenced. Second, effectiveness can be enhanced if message content, genre, style, and routes are adapted to the characteristics and abilities of subgroups.[58]

Personal Messaging

The era of mass mailings is long past. Instead, citizens are now getting personally customized messages according to age, gender, and/or background history. These personalized messages help them take action and are sent via the internet, over the phone, and by snail mail. Communication campaigns select and define their intended targets in very much the same way. They can divide the potential audience into segments based on characteristics of social diversity—like age, income, gender, and education. Even a single segment of the campaign typified by one demographic variable may consist of several subgroups. For example, the target audience of a mammography campaign for older women will include various female groups based on race, income, education, age, family history, sexual orientation, and beliefs.[59] An effective approach for improving the impact of communication strategies is **tailoring**, whereby messages are designed in relation to the audience's knowledge, beliefs, circumstances, and past experiences on certain issues.[60] Tailoring often involves computer-assisted personalization of letters, brochures, websites, or smartphone apps, and gives audiences feedback and personal advice at a reasonable price.[61]

Information about audiences can be acquired through current national or local data or by performing formative research. These processes consist of data collection on a population's sociodemographic characteristics (e.g., age, education, gender, employment, race, marital status, sexual orientation), behavior predictors or backgrounds (e.g., audience beliefs, values, skills, attitudes), and existing behaviors. For instance, a nutrition campaign designed for Hispanics and non-Hispanic Whites from the Southwestern United States may further segment their targeting according to age, but organize the age groupings differently for the two ethnic populations—e.g., according to lifestyle differences. Single White youths not living with their parents can become a new segment for which particular nutrition messages are created. Conversely, young Hispanics, usually more likely to live with their parents, may be sent nutrition messages similar to the ones created for their parents. In this event, it would be wiser to segment communication based on variables like lifestyles, social values, or language when crafting a culturally-specific campaign.[62]

Focal Segments

A successful campaign design details focal segments of the audience whose habits are at issue and the main focal behaviors are what the campaign wants to influence. Most campaigns direct their messages at the **focal segments**, which are subgroups who benefit more from the campaign because they were targeted based on their at-risk situations or their need of assistance or improvement.[63] Within focal segments, there exist demographic, social, and psychologically-based subpopulations. Examples include higher- versus lower-income strata, high- versus low-sensation seekers, those undergoing psychological or social challenges in performing certain behaviors, and individuals of different cultures. One central audience segment includes those who have displayed the unwanted behavior and whose background characteristics indicate they are at risk in the short term; they tend to be more receptive to persuasive messages. In fact, campaigns normally yield the biggest impact when triggering or strengthening messages intended for those who are favorably predisposed. Another central audience segment consists of people who have yet to try the unwanted behavior but who, unfortunately, remain at risk in the short term.[64]

A judicious communication campaign acknowledges the importance of heterogeneity in its audience. All members of the audience do not have the same status *vis-à-vis* a behavior. For an antismoking campaign aimed at youths, the latter may be heavy smokers, casual smokers, recent quitters, and individuals who have never smoked but are curious about it. On the other hand, there are those who have never smoked and, irrespective of a campaign, are highly unlikely to become smokers. Each of these categories of the youth population may be subject of different interventions. The audience can be further subdivided based on existing behavior and the behavior objective that campaign designers might elaborate for each group. However, even for each of these behavioral subpopulations, there is additional heterogeneity. Even if a single message (e.g., smoking causes bad health) might influence all of these groups in similar ways, much past research on such campaign models suggests otherwise. Rather, it is important to assume that, if heterogeneity exists in the roots of audience behaviors and in what triggers behavior change, then there is a requirement for heterogeneity in message designs too. This is segmented communication.[65]

Experiential Identity

Experiential identity constitutes the characteristics of a person with respect to his or her culture of origin, language, age, and gender, along with life experiences and cultural practices. Therefore, an individual whose mother and father were raised in different cultural and linguistic groups may, in turn, have been raised in a multicultural city, lived in a rural location during college, and started to work in another city with a different cultural mix from the place of origin. All of these events, including the discovering of a new profession, contribute to the person's experiential identity. Experiential identity may be relevant when determining individual response to behavior change approaches. The individual is at the crossroads between multiple life experiences that are also shared by others. Many people are affected by intersecting strands of social and cultural routes. The strands, individual or group-based, rather than the individuals themselves, lay the groundwork for public communication efforts that transcend the individual level. Frequent grouping variables—like the ones mentioned previously (i.e., age, occupation, and gender)—suggest a higher likelihood of shared experiences among people, but the markers mostly direct attention. They do not represent the point of interest in and of themselves.[66]

DIFFUSION OF INNOVATIONS (DOI): AN INTRODUCTION

Created by Everett Rogers, **Diffusion of Innovations** (**DoI**) is a theory that describes how innovations (i.e., ideas, movements, or inventions) are diffused via selected channels over time across communities and cultures. DoI presents the notion of relative advantage and trialability of desired behaviors. It also introduces the procedure for personal adoption decision and opinion leadership that influences diffusion through interpersonal channels and social networks (i.e., via multistep flows).[67] When a public communication campaign seeks to encourage behavior change, the principles of DoI can clearly inform campaign design and analysis. DoI emphasizes the importance of local players and opinion leaders as points of reference in their communities.[68] This means that campaigns should first try to persuade those members of a target audience who exert the highest influence. Public communication campaigns are also an example of planned, rather than spontaneous, diffusion. **Planned diffusion** refers to active interventions that seek to change behavior by disseminating programs to targeted populations. **Spontaneous diffusion**, on the other hand, occurs when the proliferation of messages within a specific population is not planned.[69]

Five Steps of Diffusion

During the diffusion process, people accept innovations through five steps:[70] knowledge, persuasion, decision, implementation, and confirmation. Individuals decide whether or not to adopt an innovation during any of these five steps.

1. **Knowledge** occurs when a person is presented with an innovation for the first time. He or she has not been exposed to the innovation before and has yet to decide whether he or she needs to look for more information about the innovation.
2. **Persuasion** occurs when he or she is persuaded to look for more information on the innovation and to actively acquire this information.

3. **Decision** is the critical point at which the person evaluates the benefits and short-comings of the innovation and, then, chooses whether or not to adopt it.
4. **Implementation** occurs when the individual carries out the innovation, determines its actual practicality, and looks for additional information.
5. **Confirmation** happens when he or she makes his or her final decision regarding the adoption. If the person opts to fully embrace the innovation, then he or she will use it to his or her advantage.

Adopters of any new innovation or idea are categorized as (1) **innovators** (2.5%), (2) **opinion leaders** (13.5%), (3) **early majority** (34%), (4) **late majority** (34%), and (5) **laggards** (people who adopt the innovation much later) (16%), based on a bell curve. Each adopter's readiness and capacity to adopt an innovation depend on his or her knowledge, interest, assessment, trial, and adoption.[71]

Four Elements of DoI

The first element of DoI is the **innovation**. It is the idea, movement, or invention that is regarded as new by a person or other unit of adoption. The second element is the **communication channel**—the means by which a message gets diffused from one person to the next. Communication plays a vital part in the spread of innovations. DoI postulates that mass media are the most influential in increasing knowledge of the innovation, whereas interpersonal communication is the most effective in changing attitudes in regards to the innovation. Newspapers, television, and the internet have contributed tremendously to informing people of the dangers of unhealthy lifestyles. It should come to no surprise that many people are now aware that smoking causes cancer, wearing a seat belt saves lives, and unprotected sex can lead to HIV/AIDS. In like fashion, many people know they can reduce their cancer risk by quitting smoking, promote longevity through physical exercise, or prevent HIV/AIDS by using condoms. The media has informed us about these things. Although the media is criticized on a daily basis, it deserves credit for diffusing information about harmful lifestyles and how to live a healthier life.[72] The third element is **time**—the amount of time needed for an innovation to diffuse and be accepted, or rejected, by audiences. The fourth element is the **social system**: a set of interrelated units integrated into a collective problem-solving task to attain a common goal.[73]

Communication channels can be further categorized as either cosmopolite or localite. **Cosmopolite channels** connect potential adopters with sources external to their social system. **Localite channels** connect potential adopters with sources inside their social system. Information about innovations usually moves into a system thanks to mass-mediated, cosmopolite channels. However, as the innovation makes its way through the system, localite channels become increasingly used as well. It is important to note that all mass media channels are cosmopolite. Conversely, not all interpersonal channels are localite.[74] According to Rogers (2003),[75] "interpersonal channels may be either local or cosmopolite while mass media channels are almost entirely cosmopolite." And a potential adopter may have interpersonal communications with a person outside of his or her social system.

When a public communication campaign has successfully diffused its messages within specific audiences, as witnessed through their change of behavior or attitude, the diffusion is said to have reached **critical mass**, the moment in the diffusion process at which the increase in new adopters is magnified by communication within the aforementioned social system.[76] This moment may occur when there is a sense that most people in the system have adopted the innovation; the value added by the innovation becomes significant.[77] Rogers (2004)[78] argued that critical mass is the point where an abundant number of individuals have adopted an innovation that "further diffusion becomes self-sustaining." Before achieving critical mass, external organizations and institutions must devote their resources and energy towards driving adoption. This may entail creating and diffusing messages through campaigns. Once a point of critical mass is reached, additional interpersonal pressures (from friends, neighbors) drive even more adoption, while external attempts to urge adoption become less efficient.[79]

DIFFUSION OF INNOVATIONS (DOI): SOCIAL CAPITAL

Social capital is a key element of community-level adaptation in public communication campaigns. **Social capital** refers to "the social norms, networks of reciprocity and exchange, and relationships of trust that enable people to act collectively."[80] Social capital can be divided into two major construct dimensions, **structural capital** and **cognitive capital**. The former includes social networks, the latter includes norms, values, attitudes, and beliefs that influence factors like interpersonal or intergroup trust and readiness to exchange knowledge or resources.[81] Successful adaptation calls for social networks, in combination with leadership and trust, and is considered by some as "the glue for adaptive capacity and collaboration."[82] Strengthening social ties and assessing their impact on behavioral outcomes can be explained by Social Network Analysis.[83]

Social Network Analysis

Social Network Analysis predicates that **nodes** (people in a network) are connected to each other via clear or unclear relationships. Nodes and their impact are regarded as interdependent (rather than independent). These connections are created by such interdependent connections and form a "network." The network is mapped through a diagram and can be analyzed without looking at anything else.[84] Although the majority of nodes within the network are interconnected and interdependent, it is essential to recognize that a certain number of them fulfill roles that are more central to the missions of the network than others. Within a network, some individuals are charged with meeting the function of facilitator. These individuals are generally more visible, less discreet, and interconnected to varying degrees with the other nodes or **hubs** (i.e., the key nodes in the network). The position of facilitator is highly relevant because it links the network to other networks or entities of the outside world. It also allows nonconnected parts to become linked with each other within a network. As the famous phrase goes, "no man is an island." Rather than being islands of noninteracting units, there is a widespread interconnected network of individuals who have more influence than mere operational cliques. Facilitators also try to ensure that certain parts of the world have high levels of participation in the network through their simple presence.[85] The next section describes three examples of networks.

Centralized, Decentralized, and All-Channel Networks

Centralized networks are networks in which centrality keeps the flow of communication smooth. "Centrality" denotes the state of being the hub in the network, like a go-to node. It is expected to yield more impact and influence thanks to a higher volume of contact and access. Based on the principles of Social Network Analysis, the metric ascertains the frequency with which a node is on the shortest conduit with other nodes. Nodes with high volumes become hubs and perform the most central role in the network. This state explains why the hub is more important than nodes on the margin, even if the simple number of links stays the same. Thus, social capital depends on how many "friends" one has. Developing connections with those who have many connections is best.[86]

Decentralized networks are networks with the most efficiency because they not only consist of numerous direct communication lines among nodes; they also manage to balance the need to operate cooperatively and the need to maintain trust and secrecy within collaborative undertakings.[87] Such networks do not generally hasten their plans or magnify the likelihood of their interventions; rather, they avoid frequent communication and retain a low profile.[88] Actors with many connections to other actors are perceived as powerful. Like the centralized network, however, those who act as brokers between disparate groups will have sizeable control over the amount of knowledge (and/or resources) within the network.[89]

All-channel networks are networks that allow individuals to communicate with each other or with those involved in the same process. In an all-channel network, information exchange flows upward, downward, and laterally among all members. In this case, all nodes communicate with all others. An all-channel network is a system in which the influence of active players in the network is equivalent, and where every node communicates with every other node. This mode of communication nurtures an egalitarian and unobstructed participative culture and promotes cross-functional efforts. Communication is quick and accuracy is modest.[90]

Case Study: The Guy-to-Guy Project

Launched in 1999, the Guy-to-Guy Project is a DoI program conducted by PROMUNDO, a nongovernmental organization based in Rio de Janeiro. The project demonstrated how young men became involved as key nodes in communities with a high risk of gender-based violence and in need of sexual and reproductive health promotion interventions. The innovation created for PROMUNDO was education to challenge stereotypes of men as the "better" gender that is worthy of wielding power over women. In order to do so, the Guy-to-Guy Project recruited young men who were disseminated through all-channel networks within manifold communities in the Rio de Janeiro area. As peer mentors, these young men were trained to influence other young men. They mostly used interpersonal communication channels with the assistance of educational materials, condoms, a lifestyle magazine, and a short stage play with the theme of reducing violence against women.[91]

An important part of the Guy-to-Guy Project was designing and implementing a condom social marketing program for and with young men, with a distribution and sales initiative promoted by the young men themselves—both as a way to champion condom use and generate a constant income for the project. Young men joined forces with a graphics company to devise a logo for condoms that would diffuse the message of new, youthful, and safe pleasure. The message was pretested through one-on-one interviews and focus groups in the community. The Guy-to-Guy Project decided to publish a magazine that young men would sell one-on-one along with three condoms. The reasoning was that, by purchasing a magazine, the target audience would be less embarrassed than buying condoms. The magazine also contains tips on safer sex behaviors and communicates gender-equitable ideas.

The Guy-to-Guy Project also developed a series of rap songs about condoms and a short sketch to promote condom use, which they present to young audiences and schools in the community.[92] By the early 2000s, the public communication campaign bore its fruits. As innovators, the young trained men developed legitimate influence in the adoption process of less risky sexual behaviors by other young men. In fact, by now, more young Brazilian men became knowledgeable about gender equality and reproductive health issues.[93]

DIFFUSION OF INNOVATIONS (DOI): OPINION LEADERSHIP

Opinion leadership is the practice of using influential individuals to change people's beliefs, attitudes, or behaviors in a desired manner with relative frequency. An opinion leader acts as a **change agent**, a person who stimulates innovation decisions in a direction deemed appropriate by a campaign. A change agent enacts sociocultural or behavior change either purposefully or through his or her natural character. Campaigns that include giving away objects like caps or T-shirts that display the campaign logo can help standardize the message and keep it noticeable. Interpersonal connections through one-on-one or small groups give outreach staff an opportunity to adapt messages to the audience and address issues directly. Prompt interpersonal interventions have been successful in modifying a number of behaviors, even when staff members are insufficiently trained in the content area.[94]

Opinion leadership also exemplifies the **two-step flow of communication**, a two-step model that works on human agency. According to the model, mass media messages are diffused to the "masses" by way of opinion leadership. People with most access to media, and having a more informed grasp of media content, explain and spread the content to others.[95] The two-step flow model laid the groundwork for the DoI theory. Interpersonal diffusion of campaign messages can be just as effective without mass media messages. Opinion leaders can easily share what they have acquired, recommend messages, and increase the impact of the media endeavors. Interpersonal communication entails a great deal of participation where interaction and feedback are present.[96]

Friends and Colleagues as Opinion Leaders

A good approach for a campaign is to diffuse messages to prospective interpersonal influencers or opinion leaders who are in a position to influence individuals whom they know personally—friends and colleagues. Campaigns cherish the involvement of opinion leaders because they can be trusted to adroitly diffuse campaign messages within target audiences. Their kindled influences are likely to be more accepted than campaign messages that directly target the focal segment.[97] Interpersonal influencers can induce behavior change through activities like bestowing positive and negative reinforcement, wielding control through rule making and enforcement, enabling better behavior with reminders at opportune times, and acting as role models. A benefit of such interpersonal connections is that, since the influencer knows individuals personally, he or she can tailor the messages to the distinctive needs and values of those individuals. Communication, here, becomes more precise and context-relevant than most mass media messages. Change agent-oriented campaigns are helpful when targeted to friends and members of the influencers' circles.[98]

Opinion leaders have attempted to diffuse messages about an assortment of health behaviors throughout their communities. The shattering COVID-19 pandemic pushed a great many people to act as influencers in their attempt to convince others to wear a facial covering or take the vaccine. An opinion leader in a community could be the priest, rabbi, or imam whom people have known since their childhood. It has been ascertained that the community changes its overall attitude about protecting itself from HIV thanks to the influence exerted by community members. As a result of peer-to-peer conversations, opinion leaders correct misperceptions, address the value of HIV prevention, and offer the best strategies to decrease risk (e.g., always having condoms, avoiding sex when inebriated, and resisting pressure for unprotected sex). They express their personal appreciation of the desired risk-reduction behavior—by incorporating the "I" pronoun in their approval as a way to emphasize personal endorsement. By now, readers have come to realize that friends and colleagues can be opinion leaders. In fact, it is not unusual for colleagues to be more important sources of information and influence than the mass media.[99]

Social Influencers in the Internet Era

People can become social influencers by developing a reputation in their respective online media communities. Internet-based influencers post their own content and direct their followers to other relevant news items, photos, and videos.[100] Here, again, the role of such influencers is similar to that of opinion leaders in the classic two-step flow model; it is comparable to that of innovators and early adaptors in the DoI theory. In the pre-internet age of opinion leadership, mass-media influencers were the ones who introduced new ideas that trickled down to opinion leaders who, in turn, further diffused them to their peers via face-to-face or interpersonal communication. Today, many of these interactions take place online where influencers expose audiences to new issues, raise unanswered questions, and trigger conversations on a multiplicity of topics. As online communities intersect with offline social networks, they perform an increasingly important function in the circulation of ideas, norms, and practices in the world.[101] In scores of online communities, content-creating users have become so influential as opinion leaders that they can set the agenda for conversations in their giant social circles. It should not be surprising that these social media influencers have caught the attention of campaign managers. Collaboration with these change agents provides ample opportunities to engage with global audiences; for example, by exhibiting correct health behaviors, breaking taboos, and sparking conversations.[102]

PUBLIC COMMUNICATION CAMPAIGNS IN HISTORY

Public communication campaigns are fundamental pursuits, focused on using communication channels and persuasion to change current conditions in society. They have a long, proud chronicle in the history of humankind.[103] Of course, as this section will demonstrate, campaigns from past centuries were much less sophisticated than the ones today. Nevertheless, long before it became trendy to publicize one's antagonism towards smoking or drugs, activists were speaking from the pavement, preaching, and proselytizing. Health communication campaigns, in particular, have a long history in the United States (for three centuries). In fact, it is important to note that campaigns to improve individual and public health stem from a long-established practice of noncommercial, media-based persuasion.[104]

Case Study 1: The United States

In the early 1720s, the Reverend Cotton Mather fronted a community-based initiative to endorse inoculation and prevent the spread of smallpox in Boston. This was partly done by distributing leaflets that underlined the effectiveness of immunization.[105] In the 1830s, William Alcott and Sylvester Graham set up a health food store that delivered fresh fruits and vegetables. For them, a proper diet was made up of wheat bread, grains, vegetables, fruits, and nuts. As they continued, by eating healthy meals and shunning food that abused the body, people would enjoy longer, healthier lives. Alcott and Graham were dedicated health crusaders, but their campaign was about 200 years ago.[106] Born in the late eighteenth century, they were early promoters of health education, innovators of a clean-living campaign that has subsisted to this day. Alcott's publications can be located in various libraries across the country. Graham—or at least his name—is still known thanks to his graham cracker.[107]

In the 1840s, a woman named Dorothea Dix relied on books, newspapers, and published materials to campaign against the substandard treatment of mental patients in New England. By the 1870s, well-coordinated national campaigns against alcohol sales employed a mix of media, such as newspapers and publications, interpersonal communication (e.g., community meetings and church interventions), and the opinion leadership of the clergy, medical practitioners, public officials, and others to raise awareness of alcohol's harmful effects.[108] It was intended to sway public opinion, champion cultural change, and pass new legislation in a manner analogous to present-day public health communication approaches advanced by Wallack (1993)[109] and Wallack and Dorfman (2001).[110]

In the late nineteenth century, a myriad of social change organizations sought to move mass audiences through print media. The abolitionist movement to eliminate slavery had already printed materials *en masse* a few decades earlier. The intent was to change beliefs and attitudes towards slavery and it eventually succeeded, earning the ire of protesters who damaged printing facilities. Unquestionably, this clever use of media played a crucial role in shifting the narrative at that time.[111] In fact, the practice of producing and circulating content around a specific narrative can be interpreted as **narrative exchange**.[112] During the same epoch, the cholera epidemic resulted in immense changes in sanitation. It also galvanized public health campaign efforts in the United States. Over the course of the late nineteenth and early twentieth centuries, as a reaction to contagious diseases and public health problems, activists devised campaign after campaign. These included advocacy of "do-it-yourself," herb-based therapies for illnesses, religious restoration movements in the 1880s that associated physical fitness with moral fitness, and venereal disease education programs that began in the early twentieth century and have continued to this day.[113]

Public communication campaigns did not focus solely on health. Some of the most potent campaigns in the United States centered on political concerns. The Revolutionary Generation—Washington, Jefferson, Adams, and Revere—took advantage of newspapers and symbolic moves like the Boston Tea Party to persuade their peers to rebel against England. The nineteenth century experienced the emergence of antislavery abolitionists, the Women's Suffrage (Right to Vote) Movement, and—regrettably so—crusades to block "undesirable" immigrants (like Irish Catholics) from moving to the United States.[114] By the early twentieth century, the new tradition in US journalism recommended that journalists (and the mass media) exploit their potential to catalyze public awareness, boost social consciousness, and engender political pressure to create reforms, which encompassed improvements in public health. Although reform-minded journalists published on diverse socioeconomic issues, inadequate public health conditions proved by childhood employment, pitiable food safety, and disregard of occupational and urban hygiene were also frequent topics. The popularity of reform-minded journalism is widely understood as putting pressure on US legislators to adopt multiple public health changes during the first third of the 20th century.[115]

By the mid-twentieth century, campaign managers began using social scientific approaches to devise and evaluate their campaigns. Early opinions argued that mass media campaigns had very little effect on their targeted audience and those audiences did not pay attention. More recent theories advance the notion that well-designed campaigns are more able to generate moderate success if they employ a balanced *mélange* of social transformation, media support, community participation, audience segmentation, message design, channel use, and time frames.[116]

Case Study 2:   The Temperance Movement

In Anglo-Saxon countries, temperance societies began to emerge in the 1820s to campaign against alcohol. It was propagated by Christian temperance activists and among the middle classes. In the United Kingdom, for example, the **temperance movement** campaigned against the recreational use and sale of distilled spirits and advocated total abstinence. In the nineteenth century, high volumes of alcohol consumption and intoxication were viewed by social reformers as a threat to society's well-being, causing social problems like poverty, child neglect, moral depravity, and economic regression.[117] The movement also championed alcohol education and insisted on the adoption of new legislation against the sale of alcohol, regulations on the amount of alcohol in stores, or the total prohibition of it.[118]

In the United States, the Prohibition was a community-level movement that changed the face of the nation. Some of the Prohibition's dynamic campaigners included Carry Nation who carried her ax to break up saloons, and Frances Willard who spearheaded the Women's Christian Temperance Union. Another active objector was Purley Baker, the influential lobbyist who induced lawmakers into carrying out the plans of his movement, the Anti-Saloon League, and prohibit the sale and production of distilled liquor.[119]

Taken as a whole, temperance proponents regarded the alcoholism issue as the most dangerous one in Western civilization. Alcoholism was perceived as causing secondary poverty and all kinds of social problems. It was the enemy of goodness—anything that modernity and science could offer.[120] Temperance proponents thought that abstinence could alleviate crime, reinforce family values, and improve society at large. Although the temperance movement started as nondenominational, it consisted predominantly of church-goers. Temperance campaigners nevertheless communicated scientific arguments to support their views, even if the centerpiece of the temperance philosophy was moral and religious.[121]

One of the landmarks of the movement was the **temperance fountain**, a fountain usually built by a private donor and inspiring citizens not to drink alcohol by the provision of free, clean water. Beer was the main substitute for water, and commonly safer. The temperance societies found tea and coffee to be too expensive, so drinking fountains became highly popular.[122] In California, fountains had a pedestal that released water and were ornamented with decorative sculptures, particularly a statue of Henry Daniel Cogswell, one of the frontpeople of the temperance movement in that state and, later, in the rest of the country.[123]

Case Study 3:   Singapore

On August 9, 1965, Singapore seceded from Malaysia to become an independent and sovereign state. With a population of approximately six million people today, the island city-state can pretend to have implemented one of the longest and most successful public communication campaigns in the history of humankind.[124] The primary objective of the campaign led by then-Prime Minister Lee Kuan Yew and his People's Action Party was to stimulate social symbiosis, shared values, a common will, and a unified national identity among the Chinese, Malaysian, and Indian peoples. In the 1960s, the "anti-litter" and "lungs for Singapore" campaigns fostered not only a clean and green environment, but also a general feeling of belonging to the nascent city-state. Thousands of volunteers were involved in such campaigns. Overpopulation and unemployment issues also pushed program managers to implement a vigorous family planning education program.[125]

By the mid-1970s, public communication campaigns had become so effective that they uplifted the morale and civic dignity of the Singaporean people. The campaign strategies involved oral presentations and displays at community centers where projects were also directed at youths. The Singaporeans arguably embraced these campaigns because they embodied the institution of a national culture, with national pursuits being prioritized over group-based sectional, ethnic, or linguistic interests. The Singaporean people did not seem to object to the reality that the actual mode of communication was directive and one-way. Furthermore, as time passed, the citizenry acknowledged the economic advantages that they experienced thanks to fruitful family planning and health campaigns. The authenticity of the campaigns never wavered: the standard of living skyrocketed, in consort with a thriving economy and the rise of a consumer society.[126]

Lastly, the Singaporean government instituted a productive literacy and "learn English" campaign. Literacy levels rose meaningfully on account of well-financed public education projects. English quickly became the language spoken in education, in the business sector, and at government functions. These factors, along with the popularity of television, smoothed the progress for public communication campaigns. In point of fact, the mass media were so well adapted to the new forms of campaigns that they could induce both attitude and behavior changes. They included "accident-free road/safety," "seatbelt," "anti-drug abuse," and "safety in construction and shipyard industries." Consequently, as the economy transformed, so did the character and strategy of the nation-building campaigns.[127]

CURRENT STRATEGIES OF COMMUNICATION CAMPAIGNS

Strategy is the backbone of a successful campaign. Take strategy out of the campaign and you will see it fail. It devolves into a set of advertisements, commercials, or communication elements that may excite the audience without any durable impact.[128] Campaign message strategies belong to one of two broad categories: content strategies and executional strategies. **Content strategies** represent the type of informational content on which campaign messages should focus. An important phase in developing content strategies is recognizing certain beliefs that carry some weight for the campaign-targeted behavior change.[129] Frequently called target beliefs, these are principles strongly associated with the behavior or behavioral intention at hand. Nonetheless, it is also primordial that these beliefs be given enough room for change and be conducive to the production of strong messages.[130] **Executional strategies** are assessments about the presentation of the informational content of campaign messages so that they get positively received by the target audience. Creativity is a core component of these decisions, but serious research needs to be conducted so as to impart thinking and strategizing on this matter.[131] The best executional strategies typically consist of emotional arousals, message framing, narrative persuasion, and visualization of risk—among others. Whereas general conclusions about these message strategies may or may not always be convincing, evidence in specific contexts may sufficient to influence decision-making.[132]

Reaching agreement or concordance among disciplines with distinct philosophies and methodologies is easier said than done, but it can be done. Three principal approaches can be used to combine expertise from diverse disciplines: multidisciplinary, interdisciplinary, and transdisciplinary. **Multidisciplinary approaches** integrate involvement from different disciplines independently. The result may be an assortment of nonintegrated interventions, which may hypothetically clash with each other. In **interdisciplinary approaches**, individual disciplines collaborate to produce input, but participants remain within their respective disciplinary boundaries.[133] Without proper coordination, this approach may, too, give rise to flawed cohesion, integration, and incompetent use of resources. The **transdisciplinary approach** is synergistic through its employment of models, theories, research methods, analytical tools, and strategies for the explanation of findings so as to create shared conceptual frameworks that incorporate relevant concepts, theories, and knowledge from various disciplines. The main characteristics of this approach that make it distinct from the multidisciplinary and transdisciplinary approaches are that the transdisciplinary approach rests on the recognition that no one entity or discipline should monopolize information. Moreover, agreement or concordance must be reached not only between diverse disciplines, but also between all scattered stakeholders who have vested interests or expertise in the issue.[134]

SOCIAL MARKETING

Social marketing is "the process of designing, implementing, and controlling programs to increase the acceptability of a prosocial idea among population segments of consumers."[135] Social marketing is also defined as a program-planning procedure that implements commercial marketing models and techniques to bring about voluntary behavior change. This approach enables the recognition, rejection, adaptation, abandonment, or preservation of specific behaviors by groups of individuals—i.e., the target audience.[136] Social marketing strives to build and combine marketing concepts with other strategies for social change. The purpose is to present competition-sensitive and segmented social change initiatives that are productive, efficient, fair, and durable, and that, in due course, benefit citizens and communities.[137]

Social marketing has the fundamental objective of achieving social good.[138] Occasionally referred to as the **common good**, **commonwealth**, **general welfare**, or **public benefit**, **social good** refers to either what is common and beneficial for all or most individuals within a community, or what is attained through citizenship, collaboration, and active participation in the arena of politics and public service.[139] **Social choice theory** can explain social good by highlighting the procedures by which social good may or may not be achieved in societies. This is done through the analysis of collective decision rules. Social choice integrates essentials of welfare economics and voting theory; it takes penchants and behaviors of individuals into account.[140]

Marketing Perspectives

Social marketing has gained extensive popularity as a method of inducing behavior change in individuals for social good. It is viewed as a noncoercive method of persuasion and compatible with, or complementary to, marketing and behavioral economics.[141] However, a common misconception subsists: that social marketing only pertains to the use of mass media or "social advertising." Put another way, the misconception is that successful interventions are based on mass media advertising such as television to diffuse the desired messages. A second misconception is that social marketing concerns mostly the use of online media platforms, especially social networking sites. The latter phenomenon has spawned the term "social media marketing." In reality, social marketing tends to involve both social advertising and social media. It is not unusual to allude to mass media-based initiatives as "campaigns" and full social marketing-based ones as "interventions." Marketing is most effective when social objectives are not directly and immediately in line with people's self-interests. Yet, citizens' attitudes and behaviors can be made to change by turning consequences into more advantageous ones. Like education, marketing gives humans freedom of choice but, in contrast to education, it modifies the behavior outcomes instead of expecting them to surrender privileges, rights, or favorite habits on society's behalf.[142]

Five Types of Social Marketing

There are five types of social marketing: (1) Push social marketing, (2) pull social marketing, (3) upstream social marketing, (4) midstream social marketing, and (5) downstream social marketing.

1. **Push social marketing**: a promotional technique that vigorously advocates products/services/ideas to audiences through adapted distribution channels. Also known as **direct marketing**, push marketing is a type of general advertising. Intervention is concerned about what motivates individuals to engage willingly with the intervention, and what to offer them in return (i.e., something beneficial). The benefit may be immaterial (e.g., personal satisfaction) or material (e.g., rewards for taking part in the campaign and showing behavior changes).[143]

2. **Pull social marketing**: a promotional strategy that targets audiences by allowing them to pull the product/service/ideas. While push marketing takes it to the consumer, pull marketing brings the consumer to it. The purpose is to cultivate a base of loyal customers by employing marketing techniques that express what they are looking for. A downside to this approach is that campaign designers might cater to the wrong target audience. To be able to connect to the right consumers, it is vital to know who they are and what they want.[144]

3. **Upstream social marketing**: a broader approach to social marketing that operates at the macro level and that can influence policymakers.[145] Upstream social marketing is a method to stimulate policy and solution adoption, as it centers on structural leadership. A useful approach for an upstream social marketing enterprise occurs when marketers employ a long-term, well-thought-out strategy to get policymakers, for example, to change the physical environment for the advancement of society.[146]

4. **Midstream social marketing**: a social marketing approach that targets social groups, opinion leaders, business owners, or municipal employees for causing change of individual behaviors and attitudes within their own communities. These are changes towards progress and solutions to contemporary problems. Midstream social marketing can seek to understand how local retailers should sway and endorse individual behavior change goals.[147] An example would be asking retailers to abide by the minimum legal drinking age.[148]

5. **Downstream social marketing**: a social marketing approach that functions at the micro level to influence and change an individual or small group. Social marketing started as a downstream undertaking, targeting specific groups for behavior change. It is beneficial to base the social or attitude change not just within people themselves, but influencers as well (e.g., local leaders).[149] Downstream social marketing often implements a full marketing combination to go beyond simple messaging. It considers competition an interesting asset that can offer a valuable exchange for the target audience.[150]

SOCIAL NORMS MARKETING

Sometimes confused with social marketing, **social norms marketing** postulates that, after people correct the perceived norm to match the actual norm, they will modify their behavior accordingly.[151] Social norms campaigns employ traditional marketing approaches that focus on people who overestimate the true norm of use.[152] However, in any campaign, some members of the target audience will overestimate (i.e., the overestimators), whereas others will underestimate (i.e., the underestimators). And a small number will interpret the norm with accuracy.[153] Social norms marketing originated on US college campuses.[154] The approach has a theoretical basis supported by four principles.[155] First, perceived norms are steadily and positively linked to drinking. Second, individuals often overestimate the drinking habits of their peers (i.e., normative misperception). Third, this overestimation of peer drinking is correlated with even higher subsequent drinking. Fourth, successful correction of such misconceptions should cut drinking. The first three principles have been reliably established in peer-reviewed empirical studies among college students.[156] The fourth tenet has received moderate support in rigorous studies assessing the correlation between modifications in perceived norms and reductions in drinking.[157]

Social norms marketing also describes situations in which individuals continue to believe that their peers' behaviors are different from their own (when in reality it is not the case). This phenomenon has been termed **pluralistic ignorance**.[158] These misperceptions pertain to problematic or risky behaviors (which are generally overestimated) and to healthy or positive behaviors (which are generally underestimated). One of the corollaries of pluralistic ignorance is to get individuals to modify their own behavior to match the misperceived norm. This, in turn, can normalize problematic or risky behavior and, at the same time, inhibit or suppress healthy or positive behavior.[159] All individuals with those misperceptions develop a climate that allows those negative behaviors to occur, whether or not they enact such behaviors. Perkins (2002)[160] coined the term **carriers of the misperception** to characterize those individuals. Thus, social norms marketing campaigns strive to correct the misperceptions of all individuals on college campuses—even if they do not engage in problematic or risky behaviors. Social norms marketing campaigns have been used to develop interventions that center on three levels of prevention: universal, selective, and indicated prevention. **Universal prevention** targets all members of a community without specifying who is at risk of abuse. **Selective prevention** targets all members of a community who are at risk for a precarious behavior. **Indicated prevention** targets certain individuals who already show signs of the problem. Interventions at all three levels of prevention can be integrated and intersected to generate a comprehensive solution that is theoretically sound and has mutually strengthening program components.[161]

Social Norms

Social norms guide individual behavior by advising members of a community what behaviors the group expects from and requires of them. Social norms are important standards for behavior because they are enforced unofficially and socially (e.g., by dishonoring or blackballing norm violators). Therefore, social norms have profound consequences that are less resource-intensive, than, for instance, a judicial or incentive-based framework for preventing or penalizing unwanted behaviors.[162] Social norms are philosophies of conduct as to what others do and approve of. Enter the following example: "People around me go to church and people important to me expect me to do likewise." This statement is powerful: someone may go to church not because that is what he or she really aspires to (attitude), but because he or she meets the expectations of society.[163] People tend to look to social norms to acquire a sound understanding of social situations and effectively respond to them, particularly in times of uncertainty.[164]

Social norms are essential to manifold behavior change interventions, and it is true when the objective is massive-scale and sustained behavior change. Within the public sector, private industry, and academia, the concept of social norms is gradually perceived as a key factor of motivation and behavior and, therefore, a centerpiece of behavioral stimulus and change. Social norms are perhaps "one of the most central theoretical constructs in the social sciences including sociology, law, political science, anthropology, and increasingly economics."[165] Social norms shape situations that, among a myriad of possibilities, "others (as a group, as a community, as a society) think are the correct ones, for one reason or another."[166] By establishing the socially accepted ways of behaving in particular environments, social norms are a crucial element of social regulation, the process through which "other stakeholders regulate our activity."[167] In doing so, they also solidify our membership and place in a community, how we interpret social situations, and how we communicate with others.

Types of Social Norms

Past studies have revealed many types of social norms that motivate human action. Based on the postulate that behavior is determined by perceptions of individuals' actions in a social group, each of the types of social norms below provides a model for understanding behavior.

1. **Descriptive social norms** influence perceptions of the behaviors performed by individuals with whom one has affinities. They are efficient because they "describe" the desired behavior—enacted by a majority—and they push the minority in the desired direction. Descriptive social norms are a guide from which others should not deviate. Because people gauge the suitability of their behavior by how distant they are from the norm, deviance will be measured as above or below the norm.[168]

2. **Injunctive social norms** influence perceptions of what behaviors should be approved or disapproved by an individual's in-group. These norms can direct people's behavior irrespective of what most people do. They are efficient when people perceive the desired behavior as harmonious with their own selves and the nature of the in-group. Injunctive social norms are also called **subjective norms**. They constitute perceptions of what is normally acceptable or unacceptable within the culture.[169] Focus theory asserts that, if either descriptive or injunctive social norms are prominent in a person's consciousness, it will wield the stronger influence on behavior. Hence, in contexts where descriptive normative information would produce an unwanted boomerang effect, it may be the case that including an injunctive norm message that signals that the wanted behavior is approved may prevent that effect.[170] The present intersubjective agreement in academia is that interventions should target injunctive norms because they have the most accumulated theory and evidence to demonstrate that they can work. In a nutshell, social norms marketing campaigns that use injunctive norms should strive to replace an old norm with a new norm.[171]

3. **Collective norms** are maneuvered at the social level or at the level of the social network, whereas **perceived norms** are used at the individual level. The difference between these two norms matters for a specific reason. Collective norms may not be consistent with perceived norms. In fact, people's perceptions about collective norms in their communities may clash with actual collective norms.[172] Information overload in the media is partly to blame for this.

4. **In-group norms** are used when people come together in groups to cultivate a notion of what they share in common and the characteristics that differentiate them from other groups. People argue that the informational merit of a response or its "persuasiveness" is equivalent to the extent to which it is perceived as representative of certain in-group norms or agreements.[173]

Peer Groups

The term **peer group** includes four types of groups that share similarities with each other: (1) The **peer cohort** (students who are in the same age group), (2) the **reference group** (those students in the cohort with whom the student has the most affinities), (3) the **peer cluster** (a small clique of friends with similar values, beliefs, attitudes, and behaviors), and (4) the **dyad** (two best friends). Under these circumstances, it is hard to determine with which group (or groups) of peers students identify—i.e., in order to have valid social comparisons.[174] Studies[175] reveal that college students overestimate occurrence of sexual relations among peers and the average number of sexual partners, while underestimating the commonness of safe-sex practices like condom use and the morning-after pill. In regards to high-school students, Hillebrand-Gunn, Heppner, Mauch, and Park (2010)[176] report that the majority of boys overestimate their peers' support of rape conspiracies and rape-supportive attitudes. Other scholars report similar findings for college men with respect to attitudes about sexual assault, the inclination to behave in a way that ensures consent, the inclination to prevent a sexual assault, and/or peers' unwillingness to use inappropriate language and actions towards females.[177]

Because a social norms marketing campaign includes descriptive normative knowledge that can be used as a yardstick of measure for an individual's own behavior, the descriptive norm can be appealing to individuals whose behaviors are either above or below the norm. A social norms marketing campaign targeting alcohol consumption on campuses might encourage students who used to consume less alcohol than the norm to actually drink more. Consequently, although giving descriptive normative knowledge may moderate an unwanted behavior among individuals who behave above the norm, the same information presented to them may actually increase the unwanted behavior among those who enact that behavior at a rate below the norm. Although social norms marketing campaigns aim at decreasing problematic or risky behaviors—and, by the same token, increasing prosocial behavior—by conveying the message that harmful behaviors happen less frequently than most people think, for individuals who refrain from performing the undesirable behavior, such normative information can produce unintended consequences or dangerous long-term effects.[178]

Third-Person Effect

The **third-person effect** predicts that individuals have a tendency to perceive that mass media messages are more impactful on others than on themselves, because of personal biases. The third-person effect is evident when an individual overestimates the impact of a mass-mediated message on other people, or underestimates the effect of a mass-mediated message on themselves.[179] The third-person effect can enlighten the degree of perceived media influence on peers. Studies demonstrate that people tend to believe that others were more impacted than themselves by advertisements for liquor and beer.[180] Shin and Kim (2011),[181] in particular, found that teenagers perceived higher effects of alcohol product placement in movies made for youths on other people than on themselves. Third-person effects are particularly noticeable when the message is perceived as unwelcome—that is, when individuals infer that "this message may not be so good for me" or "it's not cool to admit you're influenced by this media program." Consistent with these predictions, people usually perceive content that is deemed to be antisocial to have a stronger impact on others than on themselves (e.g., violence in movie, pornography, and antisocial rap music).[182]

The Theory of Planned Behavior

Although many people, particularly teenagers, often see themselves as their own persons in their actions, a substantial degree of peer influence is constantly documented in laboratory experiments, social surveys, and examinations of crowd behavior. In public communication campaigns that emphasize antecedents of individual health-related behaviors, widespread evidence supports the **Theory of Planned Behavior**, which presents norms as an indicator of personal behavior in addition to personal attitudes and perceived behavior control.[183] The Theory of Planned Behavior integrates individual attitudes, perceived norms of charismatic others, and motivation to conform as predictors of intended behavior. A foundational mechanism rests on the **expectancy-value equation**, which posits that attitudes are predicted by beliefs about the probability that a given behavior results in certain consequences, amplified by one's assessment of those consequences.[184] Three major elements guide those intentions: (1) An individual's attitude towards the behavior, (2) an individual's subjective norms about the behavior, or (3) the principle that the people important to the individual think that he or she ought to perform the behavior. Attitudes and subjective norms are, in turn, shaped by behavioral and normative principles.[185]

The social norms that produce such mental pictures of proper behavior act become standard in daily life and can transcend a person's (rational) perceptions or attitudes.[186] The effect of social norms on behavior is what the Theory of Planned Behavior describes. Social norms, together with perceptions of a behavior and behavioral control, influence people's behavioral intentions and, as a result, actual behaviors.[187] A great deal of research[188] confirms that other people's behaviors in the social environment mold individuals' interpretations of, and reactions to, the situation. This is particularly the case under new, ambiguous, or uncertain circumstances. When consumers become aware that seven out of 10 individuals select one brand of automobile over another, that teeth-whitening toothpaste is now more popular than its less useful counterpart, and that many others at the local dining hall do not eat the "spamburger surprise" entrée, they are absorbing information about social norms. More precisely, they are obtaining information about descriptive norms and how they should behave in certain situations.[189]

An oft-cited field study on descriptive norms tells of the motivation of hotel customers to reuse their towels. The message was that reusing towels helps the environment by cutting laundry, thereby reducing water and energy.[190] As the experiment demonstrated, after reading the message indicating that previous hotel patrons had reused their towels (i.e., a descriptive social norm message), the new hotel guests felt more inclined to reuse their towels than after reading a message that simply stated that towel reuse is beneficial to the environment (i.e., an informational message).[191] With hotels adopting this environmental strategy, more and more customers are motivated to reuse their towels to help preserve environmental resources by reducing the volume of detergent-related pollutants discharged into the environment. In many instances, the persuasion is formatted through a strategically placed card in the hotels' bathrooms. On top of the intrinsic benefit to the environment and to society, such descriptive norms approaches are adopted by an increasing number of hotel chains owing to the substantial economic benefits.[192] In addition to the direct reductions of costs such as labor, water, energy, and cleansing agents, there is a growing portion of consumers who praise corporations that tackle environmental issues through their business practices.[193]

Another oft-cited field experiment demonstrated the impact of descriptive social norms on energy consumption. It was developed in 2008 by the American company Opower and its partnering energy providers.[194] Over 600,000 households were placed into a treatment group and a control group. The households in the treatment group were given frequent reports with numbers on their energy consumption as compared with their neighbors (i.e., a descriptive social norm). The households in the control group did not receive this data. The households in the treatment group decreased their energy consumption after being told that they consumed more than the normal household in their areas. The program offers additional evidence that nonprice interventions can significantly reduce costs and alter consumer behavior. The effect corresponds to that of a short-term increase (in the electricity bill) of 11% to 20%, and the cost effectiveness compares positively to that of conventional energy conservation plans. Lastly, because the experiment on the treatment group incorporated descriptive social norms, effects are mixed: households in the highest bracket of pretreatment consumption reduced usage by 6.3%, whereas consumption in the lowest bracket reduced it by only 0.3%.[195]

NOTES

1. Laure Paquette, *Campaign Strategy* (New York: Nova, 2006).
2. Elizabeth Crisp Crawford and Charles C. Okigbo, "Strategic Communication Campaigns," in *Strategic Urban Health Communication*, ed. Charles C. Okigbo (New York: Springer, 2014): 11–23.
3. Charles K. Atkin, "Mass Media Information Effectiveness," in *Public Communication Campaigns*, ed. Ronald E. Rice and William J. Paisley (Beverly Hills, CA: Sage, 1981): 256–80, 265.
4. Daniel Catalán-Matamoros, "The Role of Mass Media Communication in Public Health," in *Health Management: Different Approaches and Solutions*, ed. Krzysztof Smigorski (Rijeka, Croatia: InTech, 2011): 399–414.
5. William J. Paisley and Charles K. Atkin, "Public Communication Campaigns: The American Experience," in *Public Communication Campaigns* (4th Ed.), ed. Ronald E. Rice and Charles K. Atkin (Thousand Oaks, CA: Sage, 2012): 21–33, 23.
6. William J. Paisley, "Public Communication Campaigns: The American Experience," in *Public Communication Campaigns* (2nd Ed.), ed. Ronald E. Rice and Charles K. Atkin (Newbury Park, CA: Sage, 1989): 15–38, 16.
7. Michel Foucault, "The Subject and Power," *Critical Inquiry* 8, no. 4 (1982): 777–95.
8. Janet A. Weiss and Mary Tschirhart, "Public Information Campaigns as Policy Instruments," *Journal of Policy Analysis and Management* 13, no. 1 (1994): 82–119. https://doi.org/10.2307/3325092.
9. Jim Macnamara, *Evaluating Public Communication: Exploring New Models, Standards and Best Practice* (New York: Routledge, 2017).
10. Charles K. Atkin and Ronald E. Rice, "Theory and Principles of Public Communication Campaigns," in *Public Communication Campaigns* (4th Ed.), ed. Ronald E. Rice and Charles K. Atkin (Thousand Oaks, CA: Sage, 2012): 3–20, 3.
11. B. J. Elliott, *Effective Mass Communication Campaigns: A Source Book of Guidelines* (Sydney: Elliott & Shanahan Research, 1987).

12. Julia Coffman, *Public Communication Campaign Evaluation: An Environmental Scan of Challenges, Criticisms, Practice, and Opportunities* (Cambridge, MA: Harvard Family Research Project, 2002).

13. Ibid.

14. Ibid.

15. Douglas Gould, *The Funder's Guide to Successful Media Investments for Social Change* (Larchmont, NY: Douglas Gould & Company, 1996).

16. John Dewey, *Democracy and Education* (New York: Macmillan, 1916): 5.

17. Raymond Williams, *Communications* (Harmondsworth, England: Penguin, 1976): 10.

18. Macnamara, *Evaluating Public Communication*, 3.

19. Fraser P. Seitel, *The Practice of Public Relations* (9th Ed.) (Upper Saddle River, NJ: Pearson Prentice Hall, 2004): 53.

20. Jonathan Matusitz, *Terrorism & Communication: A Critical Introduction* (Thousand Oaks, CA: Sage, 2013).

21. Jonathan Matusitz, *Symbolism in Terrorism: Motivation, Communication, and Behavior* (Lanham, MD: Rowman & Littlefield, 2015).

22. Hayley Watson, "Dependent Citizen Journalism and the Publicity of Terror," *Terrorism and Political Violence* 24, no. 3 (2012): 465–82. https://doi.org/10.1080/09546553.2011.6 36464.

23. Gustavo Cardoso, "From Mass to Networked Communication: Communicational Models and the Informational Society," *International Journal of Communication* 2 (2008): 587–630.

24. Namkee Park, Jae Eun Chung, and Seungyoon Lee, "Explaining the Use of Text-Based Communication Media: An Examination of Three Theories of Media Use," *Cyberpsychology, Behavior & Social Networking* 15, no. 7 (2012): 357–63. https://doi.org/10.1089/cyber.2012.0121.

25. Faisal Devji, *Landscapes of the Jihad: Militancy, Morality, Modernity* (Ithaca, NY: Cornell University Press, 2005).

26. Brenda Dervin, "Audience as Listener and Learner, Teacher and Confidante: The Sensemaking Approach," in *Public Communication Campaigns*, ed. Ronald E. Rice and Charles K. Atkin (Newbury Park, CA: Sage, 1989): 67–86.

27. James Allen, Nerina L. Jimmieson, Prashant Bordia, and Bernd E. Irmer, "Uncertainty during Organizational Change: Managing Perceptions through Communication," *Journal of Change Management* 7, no. 2 (1997): 187–210. https://doi.org/10.1080/1469 7010701563379.

28. Jonathan Matusitz, "Collapsing the Global and the Local through Interscalar Strategies: A Glurbanization Perspective," *Planning Theory* 9, no. 1 (2010): 6–27. https://doi.org/10.1177/1473095209342608; Jonathan Matusitz, "Glurbanization Theory: An Analysis of Global Cities," *International Review of Sociology* 20, no. 1 (2010): 1–14. https://doi.org/10.1080/03906700903525651.

29. Cristina Archetti, "Narrative Wars: Understanding Terrorism in the Era of Global Interconnectedness," in *Forging the World: Strategic Narratives and International Relations*, ed. Alister Miskimmon, Ben O'Loughlin, and Laura Roselle (Ann Arbor, MI: University of Michigan Press, 2017): 218–45.

30. Everett M. Rogers and J. Douglas Storey, "Communication Campaigns," in *Handbook of Communication Science*, ed. Charles R. Berger and Steven H. Chaffee (Newbury Park: Sage, 1987): 419–45.

31. Weiss and Tschirhart, "Public Information Campaigns as Policy Instruments," 82–9.

32. Linda Aldoory and Sandra Bonzo, "Using Communication Theory in Injury Prevention Campaigns," *Injury Prevention* 11, no. 5 (2005): 260–3. http://dx.doi.org/10.1136/ip.2004.007104.

33. Coffman, *Public Communication Campaign Evaluation*.

34. Leslie B. Snyder, "Health Communication Campaigns and Their Impact on Behavior," *Journal of Nutrition Education and Behavior* 39, no. 2 (2007): 32–40. https://doi.org/10.1016/j.jneb.2006.09.004.

35. Sherry Ferguson, *Communication Planning: An Integrated Approach* (Thousand Oaks, CA: Sage, 1999).

36. Consuela Mădălina Gheorghe, Iuliana Raluca Gheorghe, and Victor Lorin Purcărea, "Public Awareness Campaigns: A Consumer-Oriented Perspective Regarding the Advertising on LGBT Minorities," *5th World Conference on Business, Economics and Management*, WCBEM (2015): 10–21.

37. Jan Willem Bolderdijk, Madelijne Gorsira, Kees Keizer, and Linda Steg, "Values Determine the (In)Effectiveness of Informational Interventions in Promoting Pro-Environmental Behaviour," *Plos One* 12, no. 8 (2013): 1–7. https://doi.org/10.1371/journal.pone.0083911.

38. Bilal Khan, Khaled S. Alghathbar, Syed Irfan Nabi1, and Muhammad Khurram Khan, "Effectiveness of Information Security Awareness Methods Based on Psychological Theories," *African Journal of Business Management* 5, no. 26 (2011): 10862–8. https://doi.org/10.5897/AJBM11.067.

39. Lee Edwards, Bethany Klein, David Lee, Giles Moss, and Fiona Philip, "Framing the Consumer: Copyright Regulation and the Public," *Convergence: The International Journal of Research into New Media Technologies* 19, no. 1 (2012): 9–24. https://doi.org/10.1177/1354856512456788.

40. John Dewey, *The Public and Its Problems* (Chicago, IL: Swallow Press, 1927).

41. J. Barton Scott and Brannon D. Ingram, "What Is a Public? Notes from South Asia," *South Asia: Journal of South Asian Studies* 38, no. 3 (2015): 357–70. https://doi.org/10.1080/00856401.2015.1052896.

42. Howard Itzkowitz and Lauren Oldak, "Restoring the Ex-Offender's Right to Vote – Background and Developments," *American Criminal Law Review* 11, no. 3 (1973): 721–70.

43. Available at https://study.com/academy/lesson/public-communication-definitions-techniques.html.

44. Kenneth R. Lord and Sanjay Putrevu, "Advertising and Publicity: An Information Processing Perspective," *Journal of Economic Psychology* 14, no. 1 (1993): 57–84. https://doi.org/10.1016/0167-4870(93)90040-R.

45. Robert Hackett and William Carroll, *Remaking Media: The Struggle to Democratize Public Communication* (New York: Routledge, 2006).

46. Benedict Anderson, *Imagined Communities: Reflections on the Origins and Spread of Nationalism* (London: Verso, 1991).

47. Macnamara, *Evaluating Public Communication*, 10.

48. Ibid, 4–6.

49. Jürgen Habermas, *The Structural Transformation of the Public Sphere: An Inquiry into a Category of Bourgeois Society* (Cambridge, MA: MIT Press, 1989).

50. Mats G. Hansson, *The Private Sphere: An Emotional Territory and Its Agent* (New York: Springer, 2007).

51. Leslie A. Baxter, *Voicing Relationships: A Dialogic Perspective* (Thousand Oaks, CA: Sage, 2011).
52. Jürgen Habermas, "Political Communication in Media Society: Does Democracy Still Enjoy an Epistemic Dimension? The Impact of Normative Theory on Empirical Research," *Communication Theory* 16, no. 4 (2006): 411–26. https://doi.org/10.1111/j.1468-2885.2006.00280.x.
53. Garrett Hardin, "The Tragedy of the Commons," *Science* 162, no. 3859 (1968): 1243–8. https://doi.org/10.1126/science.162.3859.1243.
54. R. Edward Freeman, *Strategic Management: A Stakeholder Approach* (London: Pitman, 1984).
55. Joseph S. Tuman, *Communicating Terror: The Rhetorical Dimensions of Terrorism* (Thousand Oaks, CA: Sage, 2003).
56. Giacomo Corneo and Olivier Jeanne, "Segmented Communication and Fashionable Behavior," *Journal of Economic Behavior & Organization* 39, no. 4 (1999): 371–85. https://doi.org/10.1016/S0167-2681(99)00046-3.
57. Mohan Agrawal, "Divided... We Stand: An Alliance Goes Sour in India," *Asian Journal of Management Cases* 1, no. 1 (2004): 61–80. https://doi.org/10.1177/097282010400100106.
58. Atkin and Rice, "Theory and Principles of Public Communication Campaigns," 5–12.
59. Institute of Medicine, *Speaking of Health: Assessing Health Communication Strategies for Diverse Populations* (Washington, DC: Institute of Medicine, 2002).
60. Kay Bartholomew Eldredge, Christine M. Markham, Robert A. C. Ruiter, Maria E. Fernández, Gerjo Kok, and Guy S. Parcel, *Planning Health Promotion Programs. An Intervention Mapping Approach* (4th Ed.) (Hoboken, NJ: Wiley, 2016).
61. Denise Astrid Peels, Hein de Vries, Catherine Bolman, Rianne Henrica Johanna Golsteijn, Maartje Marieke van Stralen, Aart N Mudde, and Lilian Lechner, "Differences in the Use and Appreciation of a Web-Based or Printed Computer-Tailored Physical Activity Intervention for People Aged over 50 Years," *Health Education Research* 28, no. 4 (2013): 715–31. https://doi.org/10.1093/her/cyt065.
62. Institute of Medicine, *Speaking of Health*, 46–7.
63. Atkin and Rice, "Theory and Principles of Public Communication Campaigns," 5–12.
64. Ibid, 5–12.
65. Institute of Medicine, *Speaking of Health*, 87.
66. Ibid, 36.
67. Everett M. Rogers, *Diffusion of Innovations* (5th Ed.) (New York: Free Press, 2003).
68. Adrea Pitman Harris and Jonathan Matusitz, "The Exile of Hansen's Disease Patients to Moloka'i: A Diffusion of Innovations Perspective," *Social Work in Public Health* 31, no. 4 (2016): 299–308. https://doi.org/10.1080/19371918.2015.1137514.
69. Roberta Ferrence, "Diffusion Theory and Drug Use," *Addiction* 96, no. 1 (2001): 165–73. https://doi.org/10.1046/j.1360-0443.2001.96116512.x.
70. Jennifer P. Lundblad, "A Review and Critique of Rogers' Diffusion of Innovation Theory as It Applies to Organizations," *Organization Development Journal* 1, no. 4 (2003): 50–64.
71. Cited in Kevin B. Wright, Lisa Sparks, and Henry D. O'Hair, *Health Communication in the 21st Century* (Malden, MA: Blackwell, 2008): 221.
72. Richard M. Perloff, *The Dynamics of Persuasion: Communication and Attitudes in the 21st Century* (2nd Ed.) (Mahwah, NJ: Lawrence Erlbaum, 2003).

73. Everett M. Rogers, "Diffusion of Preventive Innovations," *Addictive Behaviors* 27, no. 6 (2002): 989–93.
74. Ismail Sahin, "Detailed Review of Rogers' Diffusion of Innovations Theory and Educational Technology-Related Studies Based on Rogers' Theory," *Turkish Online Journal of Educational Technology* 5, no. 2 (2006): 14–23.
75. Rogers, *Diffusion of Innovations* (5th Ed.): 196.
76. Thomas W. Valente, "Diffusion of Innovations and Policy Decision-Making," *Journal of Communication* 43, no. 1 (1993): 30–45. https://doi.org/10.1111/j.1460-2466.1993.tb 01247.x.
77. Alwin Mahler and Everett M. Rogers, "The Diffusion of Interactive Communication Innovations and the Critical Mass: The Adoption of Telecommunications Services by German Banks," *Telecommunications Policy* 23, no. 10 (1999): 719–40. https://doi. org/10.1016/S0308-5961(99)00052-X.
78. Everett M. Rogers, "A Prospective and Retrospective Look at the Diffusion Model," *Journal of Health Communication* 9, no. 1 (2004): 13–9, 13. https://doi.org/10.1080/ 10810730490271449.
79. Henry Seeger and Robyn S. Wilson, "Diffusion of Innovations and Public Communication Campaigns: An Examination of the 4R Nutrient Stewardship Program," *Journal of Applied Communications* 103, no. 2 (2019): Article 7. https://doi.org/10. 4148/1051-0834.2234.
80. Derek R. Armitage, Ryan Plummer, Fikret Berkes, Robert Arthur, Anthony T. Charles, Iain J. Davidson-Hunt, and Eva K. Wollenberg, "Adaptive Co-Management for Social-Ecological Complexity," *Frontiers in Ecology and the Environment* 7, no. 2 (2009): 95–102, 96. https://doi.org/10.1890/070089.
81. Kristie L. Ebi and Jan C. Semenza, "Community-Based Adaptation to the Health Impacts of Climate Change," *American Journal of Preventive Medicine* 35, no. 5 (2008): 501–7. https://doi.org/10.1016/j.amepre.2008.08.018.
82. Carl Folke, Thomas Hahn, Per Olsson, and Jon Norberg, "Adaptive Governance of Social-Ecological Systems," *Annual Review of Environment and Resources* 30, no. 1 (2005): 441–73, 451. https://doi.org/10.1146/annurev.energy.30.050504.144511.
83. Christina Prell, Klaus Hubacek, and Mark Reed, "Stakeholder Analysis and Social Network Analysis in Natural Resource Management," *Society and Natural Resources* 22, no. 6 (2009): 501–18. https://doi.org/10.1080/08941920802199202.
84. Shandon Harris-Hogan, "Australian Neo-Jihadist Terrorism: Mapping the Network and Cell Analysis Using Wiretap Evidence," *Studies in Conflict & Terrorism* 35, no. 4 (2012): 298–314. https://doi.org/10.1080/1057610X.2012.656344.
85. Ibid, 302.
86. Eliane Tschaen Barbieri and Jytte Klausen, "Al Qaeda's London Branch: Patterns of Domestic and Transnational Network Integration," *Studies in Conflict & Terrorism* 35, no. 6 (2012): 411–31. https://doi.org/10.1080/1057610X.2012.675551.
87. Carlo Morselli, Cynthia Giguère, and Katia Petit, "The Efficiency/Security Trade-off in Criminal Networks," *Social Networks* 29, no. 1 (2007): 143–53. https://doi.org/10.1016/j. socnet.2006.05.001.
88. Valdis E. Krebs, "Mapping Networks of Terrorist Cells," *Connections* 24, no. 3 (2002): 43–52; Efstathios D. Mainas, "The Analysis of Criminal Terrorist Organizations as Social Network Structures: A Quasi-Experimental Study," *International Journal of Police Science & Management* 14, no. 3 (2012): 264–82. https://doi.org/10.1350/ijps.2012.14.3.285.

89. Stephen P. Borgatti, Martin G. Everett, and Jeffrey C. Johnson, *Analyzing Social Networks* (2nd Ed.) (Thousand Oaks, CA: Sage, 2018).

90. Christopher A. Jarmon and James M. Vanderleeuw, "City Leaders and Economic Development Networks: The All-Channel Star Network," *Journal of Political Science* 39 (2011): 1–31.

91. Muhiuddin Haider, Ranjeeta Pal, and Sarah Al-Shoura, "Diffusion of Innovations and FOMENT: A Synergistic Theoretical Framework in Health Communication," in *Global Public Health Communication: Challenges, Perspectives, and Strategies*, ed. Muhiuddin Haider (Boston, MA: Jones and Bartlett, 2005): 1–24; Heidi Lary, Suzanne Maman, Maligo Katebalila, and Jessie Mbwambo, "Exploring the Association between HIV and Violence: Young People's Experiences with Infidelity, Violence and Forced Sex in Dar es Salaam, Tanzania," *International Family Planning Perspectives* 30, no. 4 (2004): 200–6. https://doi.org/10.1363/3020004.

92. Communication Initiative Network, *Guy-to-Guy Project–Brazil* (Victoria, Canada: Communication Initiative Network, 2004).

93. Haider, Pal, and Al-Shoura, "Diffusion of Innovations and FOMENT," 6–8.

94. Snyder, "Health Communication Campaigns," 32–40.

95. Elihu Katz and Paul F. Lazarsfeld, *Personal Influence: The Part Played by People in the Flow of Mass Communications* (Glencoe, IL: Free Press, 1966).

96. Siti Faidul Maisarah Abdullah, Ilya Yasnorizar Ilyas, and Noor Ashmalia Mohd Ashraff, "Barriers Towards the Effectiveness of an Anti-Smoking Campaign Program in Malacca," *Journal of Education and Social Sciences* 3 (2016): 99–105.

97. Kar-Hai Chu, Anuja Majmundar, Jon-Patrick Allem, Daniel W. Soto, Tess Boley Cruz, and Jennifer B. Unger, "Tobacco Use Behaviors, Attitudes, and Demographic Characteristics of Tobacco Opinion Leaders and Their Followers: Twitter Analysis," *Journal of Medical Internet Research* 21, no. 6 (2019). https://doi.org/10.2196/12676.

98. Lorien C. Abroms and Edward W. Maibach, "The Effectiveness of Mass Communication to Change Public Behavior," *Annual Review of Public Health* 29 (2008): 219–34. https://doi.org/10.1146/annurev.publhealth.29.020907.090824.

99. See Jason Turcotte, Chance York, Jacob Irving, Rosanne M. Scholl, and Raymond J. Pingree, "News Recommendations from Social Media Opinion Leaders: Effects on Media Trust and Information Seeking," *Journal of Computer–Mediated Communication* 20, no. 5 (2015): 520–35. https://doi.org/10.1111/jcc4.12127.

100. Sascha Langner, Nadine Hennigs, and Klaus-Peter Wiedmann, "Social Persuasion: Targeting Social Identities through Social Influencers," *Journal of Consumer Marketing* 30, no. 1 (2013): 31–49. https://doi.org/10.1108/07363761311290821.

101. Brian Alleyne, *Narrative Networks: Storied Approaches in a Digital Age* (Thousand Oaks, CA: Sage, 2015); Sandra González-Bailón, *Decoding the Social World: Data Science and the Unintended Consequences of Communication* (Cambridge, MA: MIT Press, 2017).

102. Roel O. Lutkenhaus, Jeroen Jansz, and Martine P. A. Bouman, "Tailoring in the Digital Era: Stimulating Dialogues on Health Topics in Collaboration with Social Media Influencers," *Digital Health* 5 (2019): 1–11. https://doi.org/10.1177/2055207618821521.

103. Perloff, *The Dynamics of Persuasion*, 339.

104. Paisley and Atkin, "Public Communication Campaigns," 23–7.

105. Brian G. Southwell and Marco C. Yzer, "The Roles of Interpersonal Communication in Mass Media Campaigns," in *Communication Yearbook 31*, ed. Christina S. Beck (New York: Routledge, 2007): 420–52.

106. Perloff, *The Dynamics of Persuasion*, 302.

107. Ruth C. Engs, *Clean Living Movements: American Cycles of Health Reform* (Westport, CT: Praeger, 2000).

108. Manon S. Parry, "Dorothea Dix (1802–1887)," *American Journal of Public Health* 96, no. 4 (2006): 624–5. https://doi.org/10.2105/AJPH.2005.079152.

109. Lawrence Wallack, *Media Advocacy and Public Health: Power for Prevention* (Newbury Park, CA: Sage, 1993).

110. Lawrence Wallack and Lori Dorfman, "Putting Policy into Health Communications: The Role of Media Advocacy," in *Public Communication Campaigns* (3rd Ed.), ed. Ronald Rice and Charles Atkin (Thousand Oaks, CA: Sage, 2001): 389–402.

111. Southwell and Yzer, "The Roles of Interpersonal Communication," 425.

112. Wilma Clark, Nick Couldry, Richard MacDonald, and Hilde Stephansen, "Digital Platforms and Narrative Exchange: Hidden Constraints, Emerging Agency," *New Media & Society* 17, no. 6 (2015): 919–38. https://doi.org/10.1177/1461444813518579.

113. Perloff, *The Dynamics of Persuasion*, 303.

114. Michael Pfau and Roxanne Parrott, *Persuasive Communication Campaigns* (Boston, MA: Allyn & Bacon, 1993).

115. Edwon Emery and Michael Emery, *The Press in America: An Interpretive History of the Mass Media* (Englewood Cliffs, NJ: Prentice Hall, 1978); Arthur Weinberg and Lila Weinberg, *The Muckrakers* (Urbana, IL: University of Illinois Press, 2001).

116. Ronald E. Rice and Charles K. Atkin, "Public Communication Campaigns: Theoretical Principles and Practical Applications," in *Media Effects: Advances on Theory and Research*, ed. Jennings Bryant and Mary Beth Oliver (Hillsdale, NJ: Lawrence Erlbaum, 2009): 389–415.

117. Brian Harrison, *Drink & the Victorians, The Temperance Question in England 1815–1872* (London: Faber and Faber, 1971).

118. Holly Berkley Fletcher, *Gender and the American Temperance Movement of the Nineteenth Century* (New York: Routledge, 2007).

119. Richard Worth, *Prohibition: The Rise and Fall of the Temperance Movement* (New York: Rosen Publishing, 2020).

120. Mark Freeman, "Seebohm Rowntree and Secondary Poverty, 1899–1954," *The Economic History Review* 64, no. 4 (2011): 1175–94. http://dx.doi.org/10.1111/j.1468–0289.2010.00570.x.

121. Joseph R. Gusfield, *Symbolic Crusade: Status Politics and the American Temperance Movement* (Urbana Champaign: University of Illinois Press, 1986).

122. Carol Mattingly, "Woman's Temple, Women's Fountains: The Erasure of Public Memory," *American Studies* 49, no. 3 (2008): 133–56.

123. Frances Alida Hoxie, "Connecticut's Forty-Niners," *Western Historical Quarterly* 5, no. 1 (1974): 17–28. https://doi.org/10.2307/967187.

124. Amry Vandenbosch and Richard Butwell, *The Changing Face of Southeast Asia* (Lexington, KY: The University Press of Kentucky, 2021).

125. James K. Van Leuven and Cornelius B. Pratt, "Public Relations' Role: Realities in Asia and in Africa South of the Sahara," in *International Public Relations: A Comparative Analysis*, ed. Hugh M. Culbertson and Ni Chen (New York: Routledge, 1996): 93–105.

126. Ibid, 97–8.

127. Ibid, 98.

128. Don E. Schultz and Beth E. Barnes, *Strategic Advertising Campaigns* (4th Ed.) (Lincolnwood, IL: NTC Business Books, 1995).

129. Xiaoquan Zhao, "Health Communication Campaigns: A Brief Introduction and Call for Dialogue," *International Journal of Nursing Sciences* 7, no. 1 (2020): S11–5. https://doi.org/10.1016/j.ijnss.2020.04.009.

130. Robert C. Hornik and Kimberly Duyck Woolf, "Using Cross–Sectional Surveys to Plan Message Strategies," *Social Marketing Quarterly* 5, no. 2 (1999): 34–41. https://doi.org/10.1080/15245004.1999.9961044.

131. Daniel J. O'Keefe, *Persuasion: Theory and Research* (3rd Ed.) (Thousand Oaks, CA: Sage, 2016).

132. Zhao, "Health Communication Campaigns," S12.

133. John H. Holmes, Amy Lehman, Erinn Hade, Amy K. Ferketich, Sarah Gehlert, Garth H. Rauscher, Judith Abrams, and Chloe E. Bird, "Challenges for Multilevel Health Disparities Research in a Transdisciplinary Environment," *American Journal of Preventive Medicine* 35, no. 2 (2008): S182–92. https://doi.org/10.1016/j.amepre.2008.05.019.

134. Gary L. Kreps and Edward W. Maibach, "Transdisciplinary Science: The Nexus between Communication and Public Health," *Journal of Communication* 58, no. 4 (2008): 732–48. https://doi.org/10.1111/j.1460–2466.2008.00411.x; Louise C. Mâsse, Richard P. Moser, Daniel Stokols, Brandie K. Taylor, Stephen E. Marcus, Glen D. Morgan, Kara L. Hall, Robert T. Croyle, and William M. Trochim, "Measuring Collaboration and Transdisciplinary Integration in Team Science," *American Journal of Preventive Medicine* 35, no. 2 (2008): S151–60. https://doi.org/10.1016/j.amepre.2008.05.020; Thierry Ramadier, "Transdisciplinarity and Its Challenges: The Case of Urban Studies," *Futures* 36, no. 4 (2004): 423–39. https://doi.org/10.1016/j.futures.2003.10.009.

135. James W. Dearing, Everett M. Rogers, Gary Meyer, Mary K. Casey, Nagesh Rao, Shelly Campo, and Geoffrey M. Henderson, "Social Marketing and Diffusion-Based Strategies for Communicating with Unique Populations: HIV Prevention in San Francisco," *Journal of Health Communication* 1, no. 4 (1996): 343–63, 345. https://doi.org/10.1080/108107396127997.

136. Sonya Grier and Carol A. Bryant, "Social Marketing in Public Health," *Annual Review of Public Health* 26 (2005): 319–39. https://doi.org/10.1146/annurev.publhealth.26.021304.144610.

137. Gerard Hastings, *Social Marketing: Why Should the Devil Have All the Best Tunes?* (Oxford: Butterworth-Heinemann, 2007).

138. Jeff French and Gordon Ross, *Strategic Social Marketing* (Thousand Oaks, CA: Sage, 2015).

139. Elinor Ostrom, *Governing the Commons: The Evolution of Institutions for Collective Action* (Cambridge: Cambridge University Press, 1990); William Riker, *Liberalism against Populism: A Confrontation between the Theory of Democracy and the Theory of Social Choice* (Long Grove, IL: Waveland Press, 1982).

140. Wulf Gaertner, *A Primer in Social Choice Theory* (Oxford: Oxford University Press, 2006).

141. Michael L. Rothschild, "A Few Behavioral Economics Insights for Social Marketers," *Social Marketing Quarterly* 7, no. 3 (2001): 8–13. https://doi.org/10.1080/15245004.2001.9961157; Bill Smith, "Behavioral Economics and Social Marketing: New Allies in the War on Absent Behavior," *Social Marketing Quarterly* 16, no. 2 (2010): 137–41. https://doi.org/10.1080/15245001003796241.

142. Grier and Bryant, "Social Marketing in Public Health," 326.

143. Deanne Brocato, "Push and Pull Marketing Strategies," in *Wiley International Encyclopedia of Marketing*, ed. Jagdish N. Sheth and Naresh Malhotra (Hoboken, NJ: Wiley, 2010).

144. Ibid.

145. Sally Dibb, "Up, Up and Away: Social Marketing Breaks Free," *Journal of Marketing Management* 30, no. 11 (2014): 1159–85. https://doi.org/10.1080/0267257X.2014.943264.

146. Ann-Marie Kennedy, Joya A. Kemper, and Andrew Grant Parsons, "Upstream Social Marketing Strategy," *Journal of Social Marketing* 8, no. 3 (2018): 258–79. https://doi.org/10.1108/JSOCM–03–2017–0016.

147. Rebekah Russell-Bennett, Matthew Wood, and Jo Previte, "Fresh Ideas: Services Thinking for Social Marketing," *Journal of Social Marketing* 3, no. 3 (2013): 223–38. https://doi.org/10.1108/JSOCM-02-2013-0017.

148. Tanja Kamin and Daša Kokole, "Midstream Social Marketing Intervention to Influence Retailers' Compliance with the Minimum Legal Drinking Age Law," *Journal of Social Marketing* 6, no. 2 (2016): 104–20. https://doi.org/10.1108/JSOCM-05-2015-0030.

149. Matthew Wood, "Midstream Social Marketing and the Co-Creation of Public Services," *Journal of Social Marketing* 6, no. 3 (2016): 277–93. https://doi.org/10.1108/JSOCM-05-2015-0025.

150. Nuray Buyucek, Krzysztof Kubacki, Sharyn Rundle-Thiele, and Bo Pang, "A Systematic Review of Stakeholder Involvement in Social Marketing Interventions," *Australasian Marketing Journal* 24 (2016): 8–19. http://dx.doi.org/10.1016/j.ausmj.2015.11.001.

151. Shelly Campo, Kenzie A. Cameron, Dominique Brossard, and M. Somjen Frazer, "Social Norms and Expectancy Violation Theories: Assessing the Effectiveness of Health Communication Campaigns," *Communication Monographs* 71, no. 4 (2004): 448–70. https://doi.org/10.1080/0363452042000307498.

152. Henry Wechsler and Meichun Kuo, "College Students Define Binge Drinking and Estimate Its Prevalence: Results of a National Survey," *Journal of American College Health* 49, no. 2 (2000): 57–64. https://doi.org/10.1080/07448480009596285.

153. Campo, Cameron, Brossard, and Frazer, "Social Norms and Expectancy Violation Theories," 449.

154. H. Wesley Perkins, Jeffrey W. Linkenbach, Melissa A. Lewis, and Clayton Neighbors, "Effectiveness of Social Norms Media Marketing in Reducing Drinking and Driving: A Statewide Campaign," *Addictive Behaviors* 35, no. 10 (2010): 866–74. https://doi.org/10.1016/j.addbeh.2010.05.004.

155. H. Wesley Perkins, "The Emergence and Evolution of the Social Norms Approach to Substance Abuse Prevention," in *The Social Norms Approach to Preventing School and College Age Substance Abuse*, ed. H. Wesley Perkins (San Francisco, CA: Jossey-Bass, 2003): 3–17.

156. For example, see Melissa A. Lewis and Clayton Neighbors, "Optimizing Personalized Normative Feedback: The Use of Gender-Specific Referents," *Journal of Studies on Alcohol and Drugs* 68, no. 2 (2007): 228–37. https://doi.org/10.15288/jsad.2007.68.228.

157. H. Wesley Perkins and David W. Craig, "A Successful Social Norms Campaign to Reduce Alcohol Misuse among College Student Athletes," *Journal of Studies on Alcohol* 67, no. 6 (2006): 880–9. https://doi.org/10.15288/jsa.2006.67.880.

158. Hans Toch and John Klofas, "Pluralistic Ignorance, Revisited," in *Progress in Applied Social Psychology* (Vol. 2), ed. Geoffrey M. Stephenson and James H. Davis (New York: Wiley, 1984): 129–59.

159. Jacob Shamir, "Pluralistic Ignorance Revisited: Perception of Opinion Distributions in Israel," *International Journal of Public Opinion Research* 5, no. 1 (1993): 22–39. https://doi.org/10.1093/ijpor/5.1.22.

160. H. Wesley Perkins, "Social Norms and the Prevention of Alcohol Misuse in Collegiate Contexts," *Journal of Studies on Alcohol* 14 (2002): 164–72. https://doi.org/10.15288/jsas.2002.s14.164.

161. Alan D. Berkowitz, "From Reactive to Proactive Prevention: Promoting an Ecology of Health on Campus," in *A Handbook on Substance Abuse for College and University Personnel*, ed. P.C. Rivers and E. Shore (Westport, CT: Greenwood Publishing, 1997): Chapter 6.

162. Elizabeth Levy Paluck and Laurie Ball, *Social Norms Marketing to Reduce Gender Based Violence* (New York: International Rescue Committee, 2010).

163. Benjamino Cislaghi and Lori Heise, "Theory and Practice of Social Norms Interventions: Eight Common Pitfalls," *Globalization and Health* 14 (2018): Article 83. https://doi.org/10.1186/s12992-018-0398-x.

164. Robert B. Cialdini, *Influence: Science and Practice* (4th Ed.) (Boston, MA: Allyn & Bacon, 2001).

165. Tatsuya Kameda, Masanori Takezawa, and Reid Hastie, "Where Do Social Norms Come From? The Example of Communal Sharing," *Current Directions in Psychological Science* 14, no. 6 (2005): 331–4, 331. https://doi.org/10.1111/j.0963-7214.2005.00392.x.

166. Saadi Lahlou, *Installation Theory: The Societal Construction and Regulation of Behaviour* (Cambridge: Cambridge University Press, 2017): 124.

167. Ibid, 124.

168. P. Wesley Schultz, Jessica M. Nolan, Robert B. Cialdini, Noah J. Goldstein, and Vladas Griskevicius, "The Constructive, Destructive, and Reconstructive Power of Social Norms," *Psychological Science* 18, no. 5 (2007): 429–34. https://doi.org/10.1111/j.1467-9280.2007.01917.x.

169. Robert B. Cialdini, Reno, Raymond R., and Carl A. Kallgren, "A Focus Theory of Normative Conduct: Recycling the Concept of Norms to Reduce Littering in Public Places," *Journal of Personality and Social Psychology* 58, no. 6 (1990): 1015–26. https://doi.org/10.1037/0022-3514.58.6.1015.

170. Robert B. Cialdini and Noah J. Goldstein, "Social Influence: Compliance and Conformity," *Annual Review of Psychology* 55 (2004): 591–622. https://doi.org/10.1146/annurev.psych.55.090902.142015.

171. Paluck and Ball, *Social Norms Marketing*.

172. Maria Knight Lapinski and Rajiv N. Rimal, "An Explication of Social Norms," *Communication Theory* 15, no. 2 (2005): 127–47. https://doi.org/10.1111/j.1468-2885.2005.tb00329.x.

173. John C. Turner, Michael A. Hogg, Penelope J. Oakes, Stephen D. Reicher, and Margaret S. Wetherell, *Rediscovering the Social Group: A Self-Categorization Theory* (Oxford: Blackwell, 1987).

174. Michelle A. Miller, Janet Alberts, Michael L. Hecht, Melanie R. Trost, and Robert L. Krizek, *Adolescent Relationships and Drug Use* (Mahwah, NJ: Lawrence Erlbaum, 2000).

175. For example, see Matthew P. Martens, Jennifer C. Page, Emily S. Mowry, Krista M. Damann, Kari K. Taylor, and M. Dolores Cimini, "Differences between Actual and Perceived Student Norms: An Examination of Alcohol Use, Drug Use, and Sexual Behavior," *Journal of American College Health* 54, no. 5 (2006): 295–300. https://doi.org/10.3200/JACH.54.5.295–300.

176. Theresa L. Hillebrand-Gun, Mary J. Heppner, Pamela A. Mauch, and Hyun-Joo Park, "Men as Allies: The Efficacy of a High School Rape Prevention Intervention," *Journal of Counseling and Development* 88, no. 1 (2010): 43–51. https://doi.org/10.1002/j.1556-6678.2010.tb00149.x.

177. For example, see Amy L. Brown and Terri L. Messman-Moore, "Personal and Perceived Peer Attitudes Supporting Sexual Aggression as Predictors of Male College Students' Willingness to Intervene against Sexual Aggression," *Journal of Interpersonal Violence* 25, no. 3 (2009): 503–17. https://doi.org/10.1177/0886260509334400.

178. Schultz, Nolan, Cialdini, Goldstein, and Griskevicius, "The Constructive, Destructive, and Reconstructive Power of Social Norms," 430–1.

179. W. Phillips Davison, "The Third-Person Effect in Communication," *Public Opinion Quarterly* 47, no. 1 (1983): 1–15. https://doi.org/10.1086/268763.

180. Prabu David, Kaiya Liu, and Michael Myser, "Methodological Artifact or Persistent Bias? Testing the Robustness of the Third-Person and Reverse Third-Person Effects for Alcohol Messages," *Communication Research* 31, no. 2 (2004): 206–33. https://doi.org/10.1177/0093650203261513.

181. Dong-Hee Shin and Jun Kyo Kim, "Alcohol Product Placements and the Third-Person Effect," *Television & New Media* 12, no. 5 (2011): 412–40. https://doi.org/10.1177/1527476410385477.

182. Richard M. Perloff, "Mass Media, Social Perception, and the Third-Person Effect," in *Media Effects: Advances in Theory and Research* (3rd Ed.), ed. Jennings Bryant and Mary Beth Oliver (New York: Routledge, 2009): 252–68.

183. Icek Ajzen and Thomas J. Madden, "Prediction of Goal-Directed Behavior: Attitudes, Intentions, and Perceived Behavioral Control," *Journal of Experimental Social Psychology* 22, no. 5 (1986): 453–74. https://doi.org/10.1016/0022-1031(86)90045–4.

184. Icek Ajzen and Martin Fishbein, *Understanding Attitudes and Predicting Social Behavior* (Englewood Cliffs, NJ: Prentice Hall, 1980).

185. Icek Ajzen, Dolores Albarracin, and Robert C. Hornik, *Prediction and Change of Health Behavior: Applying the Reasoned Action Approach* (Mahwah, NJ: Lawrence Erlbaum, 2007).

186. Henk Aarts and Ap Dijksterhuis, "The Silence of the Library: Environment, Situational Norm, and Social Behavior," *Journal of Personality and Social Psychology* 84, no. 1 (2003): 18–28. https://doi.org/10.1037/0022-3514.84.1.18.

187. Icek Ajzen, "The Theory of Planned Behavior," *Organizational Behavior and Human Decision Processes* 50, no. 2 (1991): 179–211. https://doi.org/10.1016/0749-5978(91)90020-T.

188. For example, see William O. Bearden and Michael J. Etzel, "Reference Group Influence on Product and Brand Purchase Decisions," *Journal of Consumer Research* 9, no. 2 (1982): 183–94. https://doi.org/10.1086/208911; Vladas Griskevicius, Noah J. Goldstein, Chad R. Mortensen, Robert B. Cialdini, and Douglas T. Kenrick, "Going Along versus Going Alone: When Fundamental Motives Facilitate Strategic (Non)Conformity," *Journal of Personality and Social Psychology* 91, no. 2 (2006): 281–94. https://doi.org/10.1037/0022-3514.91.2.281.

189. Noah J. Goldstein, Robert B. Cialdini, and Vladas Griskevicius, "A Room with a Viewpoint: Using Social Norms to Motivate Environmental Conservation in Hotels," *Journal of Consumer Research* 35, no. 3 (2008): 472–82. https://doi.org/10.1086/586910.

190. Ibid, 472.

191. Gerdien de Vries, "Public Communication as a Tool to Implement Environmental Policies," *Social Issues and Policy Review* 14, no. 1 (2020): 244–72. https://doi.org/10.1111/sipr.12061.

192. Goldstein, Cialdini, and Griskevicius, "A Room with a Viewpoint," 472.

193. Les Carlson, Stephen Grove, and Norman Kangun, "A Content Analysis of Environmental Advertising Claims: A Matrix Method Approach," *Journal of Advertising* 22, no. 3 (1993): 27–39. https://doi.org/10.1080/00913367.1993.10673409; Ajay Menon and Anil Menon, "Enviropreneurial Marketing Strategy: The Emergence of Corporate Environmentalism as Market Strategy," *Journal of Marketing* 61, no. 1 (1997): 51–67. https://doi.org/10.2307/1252189.

194. Hunt Allcott, "Social Norms and Energy Conservation," *Journal of Public Economics* 95, no. 9 (2011): 1082–95. https://doi.org/10.1016/j.jpubeco.2011.03.003.

195. Ibid, 1082.

CHAPTER 2

The 10 Steps of Public Communication Campaigns

An effective public communication campaign is based on a clear structure. In this chapter, 10 steps lay the foundations for producing the most important ideas from which large-scale campaigns can develop. Research plays an essential role within each step. As such, the 10 steps are:

1. define and select your topic;
2. set goals and objectives;
3. analyze and understand the situation beforehand;
4. define your audience(s);
5. understand the timeline and budget;
6. choose appropriate media;
7. develop optimal message content;
8. avoid monologic communication and interact with your audience(s);
9. update the campaign with timely, relevant, and accurate information; and
10. evaluate the overall campaign.

This detailed template for public communication campaigns is adaptable to scenarios in such areas as advertising, public relations, health, safety, personal well-being, entertainment, social justice, animal rights, and even terrorism or antiterrorism—among a myriad of others. Understanding every step of the structure is key. It offers guidance for all kinds of enterprises and suggestions for what type of message needs to be used. A public communication campaign cannot be successful unless it recognizes what is to be accomplished, the

Fundamentals of Public Communication Campaigns, First Edition. Jonathan Matusitz.

reasons for doing so, by which actors, for what audience(s), through what channels, within what time frame, and with what outcomes. The 10 steps show that serious consideration must be paid when devising a campaign and that the key individuals used for the implementation or supervision must be fully aware of the purpose and the courses of action. As Crawford and Okigbo (2014)[1] explain, although research is critical at every step of the way, it should be the full foundation on which all steps are developed. This 10-step approach is inspired by past research, expertise from multiple disciplines, and recommendations that facilitate the identification and creation of strategies. It helps overcome difficult challenges to social and behavior change and can also help legislators realize more fully the benefits of their policies in bettering or exacerbating the well-being of people, communities, nations, and the larger environment.[2]

It is important to note that this 10-step approach was conceived as a template that campaign designers can follow to accomplish large-scale campaigns and enhance their effectiveness. With this said, the 10-step approach is the author's suggestion (based on manifold campaigns described in past and contemporary studies). It is not *the* panacea. In fact, rarely do strategists adhere to all 10 steps fully (if they adhere to most of the steps at all). This is often due to insufficient preparation, inexperience, or lack of funding. As Kincaid, Delate, Storey, and Figueroa (2012)[3] aptly point out, a single public communication campaign is generally only one phase in a sequence of campaigns and similar types of interventions aimed at reaching desired outcomes. Many public communication initiatives are incorporated within other ones, such as regulatory procedures (e.g., bigger fines for driving violations), enforcement actions, and other policies.[4] In a similar vein, as we will see in Part III of the book, some campaigns—like the #MeToo campaigns around the world—can be independent of any corporation or state institution and effectuated through online social media without organization, painstaking preparation, or funding.

STEP 1: DEFINE AND SELECT YOUR TOPIC

Before designing public communication campaigns, communicators need to reflect on the perceived relevance of their topic for their target audience. The core issue of the campaign does not automatically have to be a trending phenomenon that will thrill the public. Making the public happy should not be the objective. As such, communicators should not pull out all the stops with keyword searches or keyword planners to find out what subjects are popular, like those that show up the most in social media ad campaigns. Rather, the issue in question should be of a genuine concern to improve society at large. Not only does the topic of the campaign need to contain value for the target audience but, also, it needs to penetrate or convince that target audience in a successful manner. Put simply, the communicator must show the audience how the topic is relevant to them, their lives, and their well-being.[5]

Campaigns are most effective when some degree of tone and content is reflected within the topic itself.[6] This means that determining or setting down the parameters of the topic is of utmost importance. For example, health communication campaigns are topic- and behavior-specific. Thus, the same standard employed to predict a particular behavior within a framework or context may not be efficient in predicting other behaviors within other frameworks or contexts.[7] For any topic, campaign designers must consider whether it is even possible to increase exposure, credibility, and perceived relevance of that topic. **Topical relevance** is the extent to which information meets the needs of the public.[8] In line with these contentions, research[9] on topic relevance and on applicability of information[10] demonstrates that, if an issue is regarded as applicable, relevant, and consistent with people's goals, the audience is more likely to adhere to the subsequent message.[11]

STEP 2: SET GOALS AND OBJECTIVES

A distinction needs to be drawn between goals and objectives. **Goals** are broad targets. Campaign goals stipulate what the campaign seeks to accomplish within a time frame. Goals indicate desired outcomes and behaviors that the campaign is advocating. As explained in Step 4, the goals should clearly identify the target population.[12] On the other hand, **objectives** are more specific and open to actual assessment. Thorough statements of objectives pave the way for a clear picture of the desired situation—one that is realistic and achievable—with expectations in regards to completion time and evaluation. While some objectives are articulated with respect to program achievements or outcomes, others tend to emphasize communication output or activities. The true significance of public communication campaigns should lie in their impact or outcomes, and not merely in the communication tactics undertaken.[13]

Both goals and objectives necessitate strategic choices in terms of vision, purpose, and the external and internal analysis of the entity that is designing the campaign. Such entity should be willing to make strategic choices that will change people's behavior in the best possible way. A factual, informative explanation of the desired behavior can be sufficient to induce behavior change. An example is the "Reuse your hotel towels" campaign[14] described in the previous chapter. Providing an example demonstrating that previous guests successfully engaged in the desired behavior can be a massive motivator for behavior change. As such, "previous guests in this hotel room also reused their towels."[15] An action approach can boost perceptions of self-efficacy and effectiveness if it makes it clear to the population how they can help solve environmental issues. Telling others how they can curtail their carbon footprint (e.g., "take public transportation") can make them feel valued. Besides, it can decrease the likelihood of cognitive biases and cognitive dissonance.[16] **Cognitive dissonance** is a phenomenon whereby someone has contradictory beliefs, ideas, or values.

Fundamental questions need be mulled over: Whom do we need to persuade, on what issue, and when, where, and why? What will be the takeaways for the audience? Should we attempt to transform their behavior, teach them something, make them follow a trend, or diffuse the gospel about an issue? Such questions can create an impact (or, as a minimum, pave the way for it). It should be obvious why the campaign is important to the public and how managers can share a vision or message based on persuasive communication and of significance to society. Edwin M. Stanton, a lawyer and the Secretary of War during the American Civil War, developed the notion of **inverted pyramid** to reflect the notion that the aforementioned "who, what, when, where, and why" questions are the pillars of any serious enterprise and the launchpad for any meaningful campaign. This is generally underpinned by other important details and relevant information.[17]

Schultz and Barnes (1995)[18] explain that determining the goals and objectives of a campaign is like a roadmap that tells the whole group of players what "direction the campaign is going to take. It points the way in terms of what is important; what messages, information, or benefits need to come through; what is valuable; and what must be done if the campaign is to succeed." It is not unusual for campaigns to include intermediate goals, such as enhancing knowledge or awareness of an issue, with a supposition that people are more likely to consider taking action when they learn of a problem.[19] Yet, people do not necessarily make decisions on the basis of what they know—a phenomenon known as the **knowledge gap** or the **communication effects gap**.[20] Thus, even when campaigns incorporate knowledge, awareness, or belief change goals, they also ought to embrace behavior goals.

STEP 3: ANALYZE AND UNDERSTAND THE SITUATION BEFOREHAND

An important step in planning a public communication campaign is to examine the current situation or issue by dividing the whole into pieces. The purpose is to distinguish causes from symptoms and identify the root causes of the problem. As a general rule, campaign developers can search through basic office records like annual and project reports, periodic evaluations, and the documented opinions of people who have experienced the situation and can be interviewed through focus groups or be required to share their examinations of the situation. Part of this process consists of describing the history of the problem and previous endeavors that have been implemented on the issue. Exploring past failures and successes can inform the campaign in question. At this stage, it would be wise for campaign planners to assess the opportunities and problems that the audience(s) might encounter during the course of the campaign.[21] Taking the specific strengths, weaknesses, opportunities, and threats (SWOT)—regarding the issue—into account will generate additional desirable insights. **SWOT analysis** refers to a strategic planning approach to help an individual or institution identify strengths, weaknesses, opportunities, and threats with respect to any important endeavor or project planning.[22] It gives information that is useful in approximating the campaign strategists' resources and potential to the prevailing environment in which it can be carried out.

Planning

At this point during the campaign, strategists make tough but fundamental decisions. In addition to setting goals and objectives, they have to settle on whether to concentrate on creating cognitions or changing current ones. They reflect on whether to attempt changing attitudes or behavior.[23] The initial planning stage entails getting relevant information to establish preliminary behavioral objectives, identify target markets, and list viable behavioral determinants and strategies. At this stage, formative research is done to examine factors inherent to the initial planning phase in order to segment populations and choose what factors must be addressed to generate behavior change. Explained differently, this process involves the setting up of a realistic marketing plan that consists of specific, measurable objectives and a step-by-step agenda that will direct the development, application, and tracking of the project. The plan contains the overarching goals of the program, a description of the target population, explicit behaviors that will be promoted to them, and approaches for dealing with the critical factors inherent to the target behavior.[24]

Planning sometimes requires contacting institutions or individuals who have conducted similar public communication campaigns. It is imperative that campaigners share experiences from their previous campaigns with others. Project managers can also identify and collaborate with strategic partners. Public communication campaigns often address issues that strategic partners have touched on within communities themselves. Having the endorsement of partners like media outlets, governmental bodies, and relevant organizations is a huge bonus.[25] In like fashion, applying theory as a guide to campaigns would likely contribute to campaign success. Theory can be the keystone for a campaign and provide chief determinants upon which campaign messages might concentrate.[26] In addition to theories, models and concepts are the backbone of campaigns. It would be difficult to instigate a campaign without some theoretical basis as to what needs to be achieved and how best to accomplish objectives. In order to make hypotheses between two variables (e.g., "Increased knowledge regarding the dangers of smoking will decrease smoking"), campaign designers need to have a good grasp of theoretical concepts and have adequate breadth about them. Theory may be basic in and of itself, but appropriate, solid theoretical concepts are invaluable. In short, one element that separates effective campaigns from ineffective ones is that the former hinges on conscientious application of theoretical principles.[27]

Formative Research

It would be beneficial for campaign strategists to conduct formative research in order to explore audience perceptions; to identify the stance, knowledge, and needs of the target group *vis-à-vis* a specific issue. The essence is to have a clear picture as to where the audience stands on a problem. Formative research is often hailed as the most important factor in the design and implementation of a successful campaign. Such research can also enable campaign developers to understand the target audience's message preferences and what communication channels should be used.[28] For example, Witte, Cameron, Lapinski, and Nzyuko (1998)[29] conducted in-depth qualitative interviews through focus groups with various at-risk populations in Kenya as part of the preparation for an HIV/AIDS prevention campaign. They also included a process model as a theoretical guide. For these researchers, although it was important to stress the perceived threat of HIV/AIDS, formative research—along with pamphlets and posters—indicated that it leads to better outcomes. Nevertheless, the four scholars acknowledged to have omitted using important campaign materials such as negotiating condom use and self- and response efficacy for safer sex. This could have resulted in better outcomes. Any feedback from the population prior to launching the campaign itself should be taken into consideration because it can considerably strengthen campaign materials. Atkin and Freimuth (2012)[30] outlined two phases of formative research: (1) **Preproduction research**, where information on audience characteristics, the behavior in question, and message channels are acquired; and (2) **production testing**, or **pretesting**, where initial messages are tested with target populations in order to obtain their perceptions regarding the suitability and persuasive effects of those messages.

Communication Design

After formative research is conducted and a theory is selected, the type of communication design must be thought-out. The communication design must approximate the real world as closely as possible, almost like a down-to-earth communication approach.[31] Critical to this is the level of comprehension of messages. This includes an awareness of the level of the audience's functional literacy, the manner by which messages are constructed, the tone of message, and the potential inclusion of appropriate visual components.[32] Communication design rests on six principles: balance, proximity, alignment, repetition, contrast, and space. While **balance** offers stability and structure to the design, **proximity** generates connections between the included elements. This could be of significance when using visual imagery. **Aligning** the material produces visual relationships between elements of the design characteristics. **Repetition** of messages—whether through leaflets, posters, paper-based advertising, and websites where each page has certain recurring elements—can foster association and reliability and, in turn, trust. **Contrast** stresses central elements in the design, whereas **space** alludes to the zone around the other elements that creates space.[33]

STEP 4: DEFINE YOUR AUDIENCE(S)

An **audience** is a chosen group of individuals that should be large for a public communication campaign and to whom frequent communication is directed. The **sender** is the source of the message and the audience is the **receiver** (or recipient) of that message. The purpose and setting of a public communication campaign are referred to as the **occasion** (or event). The audience becomes involved in an event either passively (e.g., by merely attending to a message transmitted by the sender) or actively (e.g., by overtly taking part in the event or giving feedback to the message sender). Whether passive or active, the audience is the interpretive entity, responding to the campaign's communication. As the public character of an event, the audience can be both the **second party** (the immediate receiver of the message) and the **third party** (the receiver beyond the immediate receiver of the message) of an event. Lastly, the source of the message can be within, near, or physically removed from the audience.[34] No matter the distance, relation-building is a centerpiece of public communication endeavors, and provides a yardstick of measure for the success or failure of public campaigns.[35] The goals and objectives of campaigns are more achievable when creating and maintaining a successful relationship with the audience(s).[36] The first step towards relation-building is an analysis of relevant audiences and their environments.[37]

Audience Analysis

Audience analysis is the study of the intended public for the communication campaign. Audience analysis is essential because the receiver of the message may be influenced by the content of the campaign, the type of communication channels employed, the source(s) of the message(s), and the overall communication campaign itself. Questions such as "What language does the audience understand the best?" "What will they remember the most?" "What are their interpretations of the world?" "What could be inappropriate or attractive to them?" and "With what will they identify?" will establish the type of audience reaction during and after the public communication campaign. As a result, communication must be adapted so that the audience understands and accepts it. Of equal relevance are the style, structure, and supporting materials of the campaign.[38] Under these circumstances, taking **audience diversity** into account helps campaign strategists understand the cultural, demographic, and individual characteristics that vary among publics. **Cultural diversity** encompasses the manifold cultural dimensions within the target audience. Examples are power distance, collectivism vs. individualism, femininity vs. masculinity, uncertainty avoidance, long-term vs. short-term orientation. **Demographic diversity** has to do with age, gender/sex, race, country or region of origin, socioeconomic status, education, occupation, religion, and language. And **individual diversity** comprises belief systems, values, self-drives, attitudes, knowledge, expectations, and needs.[39]

Public communication campaigns, even when they seemingly target the general public, are usually aimed at particular segments of the public. A certain number of campaigns include more than one target audience and can include various groups of the socioeconomic ladder. Setting the parameters as to who should be included in the target audience(s) facilitates the identification of the best communication media to reach them and at what intervals or periods.[40] Gender/sex, age, ethnicity, race, education, and income—just to name a few—all factor in the degree of impact that public communication campaigns have on those audiences. If they see themselves at higher risk based on the group to which they belong, or if they feel that the messages are meaningful to their everyday lives, they will be more likely to heed to the messages or attempt to embrace new behaviors, attitudes, or beliefs.[41] Thus, for a campaign to be effective, the audience must not only be exposed to the communication and understand it, but also must find it realistic and significant. Some groups will find messages more credible and relevant than other groups. At the same time, certain groups may be excluded from the campaign, not necessarily because it is done intentionally, but because they more difficult to reach. Or it may be the case that certain groups are considered a priority because of their special needs. Of course, it would be unproductive to target audiences that are not predisposed towards embracing new behaviors, attitudes, or beliefs.[42]

Audience Beliefs

A **belief** is an individual or group-based principle about the properties or peculiarities of an object. It is an opinion that people have about the universe. It is not infrequent for humans to confuse beliefs with facts. Beliefs are **cognitions about the universe**—subjective prospects that an object has a certain attribute, or an action will result in a specific outcome.[43] There are five types of beliefs: descriptive, prescriptive, core, central, and peripheral beliefs. **Descriptive beliefs** are perceptions or hypotheses about the environment in which we live and that are anchored in our heads. **Prescriptive beliefs** are "ought" or "should" principles that reflect interpretations of preferred end-states. Prescriptive beliefs, such as "American citizens should vote for Joe Biden" or "The minimum wage should be increased to $20 an hour," are opinions that cannot be proved or falsified by science. They reflect our preferences and worldviews. Some scholars regard prescriptive beliefs as value-laden.[44]

Core beliefs are the least likely to change and can be broken down into two types: Type A and Type B Beliefs. Type A beliefs are primitive beliefs; we learn them through direct contact with the object of belief and they get reinforced through—often undisputed—social consensus. An example of primitive belief is that death is inevitable. Type B beliefs are zero consensus beliefs; they are grounded in direct experience but, unlike the previous type, do not require social consensus. These beliefs, too, are highly unlikely to change. For instance, "I like myself" is a type B belief; it is not supported by social consensus. **Central beliefs** are less resistant to change and come directly or indirectly from an authority (whether an object or a person). They can be broken down into two types: Type C and Type D Beliefs. Whereas Type C beliefs are authority beliefs (e.g., beliefs in the truth of the Bible, Torah, or the Qur'an), Type D beliefs are based on authority figures' beliefs (e.g., beliefs in what the Pope, a rabbi, or an imam says). **Peripheral beliefs** are the least important and the most likely to change; they are called Type E beliefs.[45]

Audience Values

Values are our most cherished beliefs about right and wrong. They reflect our strong feelings and are not open for discussion about what is good or bad, beautiful or ugly, just or unjust, fair or unfair, valuable or worthless, kind or cruel, and normal or abnormal. Values exist within the hearts and minds of most of the members of a culture—or at least for those who occupy key positions. As the things we hold dear, values are ideals, guiding philosophies and moralities in our lives, or overarching goals that we seek to obtain.[46] They reflect our wants and desires of the means and ends of action.[47] When crafting a campaign message, it is pivotal to consider the audience's values because they will automatically determine their initial position(s) on an issue. In this context, the question should not only be, "Should we attempt to create a new attitude, reinforce an existing attitude, or change an existing attitude?" but it should also be, "Is the attitude in harmony with the audience's values?" This last question should also take the audience's heroes and myths into account.

Indeed, esteemed within specific groups are their heroes and myths. **Heroes** are the real or imaginary individuals used as role models within a culture. A culture's heroes often appear in the culture's myths, which have been an inspiration for novels and other forms of popular culture (i.e., the adventurous cowboy in the United States). **Myth** is a morality in story form which has profound explanatory or symbolic power for a culture. For many groups today, myths maintain and treasure the wisdom of their elders through orality by the use of experienced storytellers. Every long-established culture has cultivated its own mythology, made up of legends, religious practices, and other routines. The magnificent power of the symbolic meaning of myths is a major reason why cultures endure as long as they do, occasionally for thousands of years. One of the most famous myths in Japan is that the emperor is a successor of the Goddess of the Sun.[48]

Audience Needs

An important factor of audience analysis is to understand the needs of the target audience. A **need** is a state in which a person, animal, or object must do or have something. Abraham Maslow (1943)[49] wrote that there are two sets of personal needs: deficiency needs and growth needs. **Deficiency needs** are fundamental human needs that must be fulfilled before higher-order needs can be satisfied. They include needs for personal health, physical safety, survival (i.e., food, water, oxygen, and shelter), belongingness, love, self-esteem, and social esteem. **Growth needs** are higher-order human needs which can be gratified only after deficiency needs have been satisfied. They include self-actualization (the method of fully accomplishing one's potential), knowledge, awareness, and aesthetic needs.

The Human Needs Theory exemplifies the consequence of ignoring deficiency needs in times of turmoil. Developed by Burton (1979),[50] the **Human Needs Theory** posits that people turn to violence when their fundamental human needs are insufficiently met, totally denied, or taken away from them. Basic human needs, both biological and psychological, can be declined to or not fulfilled for a group people for centuries before they are restored to them. The theory asserts that it causes people to be angry and insecure, which drives them to be violent. It provides justification for groups to be hostile and engage in acts of terrorism.[51] Public communication campaigns that focus on improving or providing the basic needs of a target audience may avert violent conflicts in the long run.

Audience Adaptation

Audience adaptation is the process of tailoring a public communication campaign to the diversity, beliefs, values, and needs of the audience. As described in Chapter 1, when discussing segmentation, campaign designers know that it would be very difficult to be "all things to all people." Rather, audience adaptation separates people into subgroups according to needs, desires, lifestyles, behavior, and values that increase their likelihood of responding similarly to public interventions. Campaign strategists have long acknowledged intragroup differences within audiences, but they typically use race, age, and other demographics as the benchmark for identifying dissimilar subgroups. They are also likely to break down populations into distinct segments based on recurring behavior (e.g., heavy versus light smoking), potential intentions, willingness to change, product loyalty, and/or psychographics (e.g., lifestyle, values, personalities). Successful public communication campaigns devote a great deal of attention and resources to segmented communication with their multiple audiences. They spot one or more segments as the target audience to be given the highest priority in program development, and development of differential marketing approaches (e.g., in how issues will be addressed) for selected population segments.[52]

Hence, campaign designers will divide the audience into meaningful segments on the basis of key characteristics such as demographic factors, risk characteristics, experience with the behavior, and personality traits.[53] The purpose, here, is to generate homogeneous groups whose message preferences are comparable to one another so that the efficacy of campaign messages within the target audience is maximized.[54] On the other hand, failure to engage in group segmentation (and subsequent message segmentation) is believed to be a major reason for failed campaigns in the past.[55]

It is important to understand that audiences can change during the course of the campaign. This is why some campaigns are ready to include plans to "flip" audiences (as part of their communication objectives). For example, in the United States, the Folic Acid Campaign employed a stage-market segmentation strategy, whereby it expanded its audience segments in gradual steps, progressively including all women who could bear children and focusing on the most at-risk ones. Experienced communication campaigners will reevaluate their intended audiences over time, as they acquire more information about their audiences. When campaign strategists notice that audiences do not respond adequately to the intended campaign communication strategies, they come up with separate or specialized campaigns for those audiences.[56] Two cases include the Back to Sleep Campaign and the National High Blood Pressure Education Program, both of which employed constant tracking and evaluation to make up for the gaps in audience knowledge and behavior and to shift campaign approaches. During the entire process of implementation, the National High Blood Pressure Education Program progressively targeted new and broadened audiences, such as African Americans, women, and particular age and income segments, among others.[57]

Audience Perception

Audiences have a natural aptitude to create order according to specific laws of perception. **Audience perception** is a phenomenon whereby the public filters and construes information from the five senses to conceive a meaningful picture of the environment in which they live. Audience members interpret and generate meaning based on signals of the sensory system: what they see, taste, smell, feel, or hear.[58] Perception is both the passive receipt of these signals and the main influencer of the recipient's awareness, learning, memory, beliefs, and experience. Message receivers decipher communication after it has been absorbed through their filter of senses, attention, and general experience. The public's response is part of a feedback loop that emerges and is sent back to the source of the message. This is where audience perception comes into play.[59] Audience perception can be complex as the three additional terms of perceived control, perceptions of self-efficacy, and perceptions of effectiveness illustrate below.

Perceived control increases a person's assessment of the controllability of a situation to bring out the necessary coping strategy.[60] Control perceptions can be distorted when members of the target audience incorrectly infer that they have low (or high) control of the message(s) in the public communication campaign. In this preconceived notion, two elements are key: perceptions of self-efficacy and perceptions of effectiveness. **Perceptions of self-efficacy** have to do with confidence in one's own capacity to realize a behavior outcome; these perceptions are good at predicting behavior.[61] Those who perceive low self-efficacy think they cannot do much to counter, for example, messages of danger related to climate change. Consequently, they might not be willing to feel responsible for tackling environmental problems, instead attributing blame to others, such as the government or other nations.[62] **Perceptions of effectiveness** pertain to evaluations of the usefulness of actions. As such, in regards to solving global environmental issues, people may consider their own sustainable actions as only a very small amount compared to what is expected. This partly explains why they might refrain from taking sustainable actions until others do.[63] This is a true social dilemma; if everyone is inactive because of a belief of having a minimal effect on the environment, the whole group will perpetuate such inaction. It is also easier to defect if there are no injunctions against defecting or when people are not sure as to what others can do.[64]

STEP 5: UNDERSTAND THE TIMELINE AND BUDGET

Contingent on the goals, objectives, and the types of actions, the entire campaign can last as little as a few weeks or as long as three years. Campaigns can be temporary, intermittent, or recurring every so often while others seem to be lengthy, steady, and undeviating from their initial objectives.[65] Social marketing stresses the importance of framing the campaign's communication within the sphere of competing messages, attitudes, fears, expectations, and norms. As we have seen, communication should also be oriented towards relevant and shifting audience segments.[66] Although positioning the message on a myriad of platforms may only take up to a week, the degree of attention that the campaign needs to get for widespread exposure may take several months. Consequently, timing is a significant factor and can pertain to seasonality, time of day, or **consumer aperture**, a concept that tackles the question, "when, where and under what circumstances is the audience's mind most receptive to the message?"[67] The media is generally phased; there is a departure point where the campaign is set in motion. It is not unusual for the launch to include the highest media presence. The second phase entails the body of the campaign. The media tends to be used gradually to remind the audience of the message.[68]

Allocating the Budget

Humans cannot be exposed to a campaign's communication if it is not available to them. Conceivably, the main factor that determines whether or not a message will be available is funding. Money can get the media a certain degree of time and space. Nevertheless, for most public messages, there is not enough funding for acquiring media time and space or outreach agents. Under these circumstances, a beneficial question for most communication interventions is to know what gets a message free distribution. Free distribution means more time or space in the media, whether through public service announcements (PSAs), health messages in Entertainment-Education, or reporting of a subject on news programs, in newspapers or periodicals, or on talk shows. Outside the mass media, free distribution may happen when community institutions adopt the campaign's message.[69]

Besides paying for consulting services, cost can be a substantial component of campaign planning, especially nowadays because financial problems for health and social services programs have increased worldwide. The difficulty is to come up with acceptable justification for budget demands and to be able to exploit all available free media, provided that this does not compromise the outcome. Campaign strategists ought to prove that they are distributing the funding efficiently. The budget tends to be divided into categories like promotional expenses, social media and internet payments, and use of traditional media. Over and above giving evidence for how the money will be spent, campaign strategists need to justify their choices.[70]

Government Funding

Government funding may be available. This could be at the national, regional, or local level in one's own country or from international governmental organizations. However, government funding may not be the correct path for some institutions, campaigns, or messages. Thus, it is crucial to consider how the amount of funding (or the lack thereof) could affect the outcome of the intervention and, thereby, one's credibility with the audience. For example, nongovernmental organizations or charitable and philanthropic groups can be a solid source of funding for counternarrative campaigns. They add credibility that governments can lack in certain situations and already possess established connections at the grassroots level. Academic or research funding can be an alternative in some cases—i.e., if the purpose is to conduct a new methodology or implement widespread testing and in-depth assessments. Finally, crowdfunding websites represent a viable opportunity for supporting one's campaign.[71]

Antismoking campaigns are considered a favorite by federal funders, especially since they focus on youths. The Florida Tobacco Pilot Program sprung up from the $200 million initially granted from Florida's $11.3 billion financial agreement with the tobacco industry. This pile of money was able to support the design and implementation of a state-run initiative to prevent and decrease youth tobacco use (Florida "truth" campaign).[72] In any case, the recommendation is that particular amounts for each aspect of the campaign (e.g., content production versus promotion and distribution) be bestowed appropriately and that detailed records of how much was spent be maintained. Campaign planners should also integrate flexibility and stay alert to changes in expenses or requirements in the course of the production process and campaigning phase.[73]

STEP 6: CHOOSE APPROPRIATE MEDIA

The plural of "medium," **media** are the vehicles of communication, as TV, radio, newspapers, etc., that influence or get a message to audiences widely. By extension, **media kit** is a broad-based news release that includes backgrounders, leaflets, photo shoots, fact sheets, and any other germane information on a subject. It can be both in printed or in digital form—either on the internet or on a DVD.[74] On a broader level, **media ecology theory** describes how media, technology, and communication impact the human environment.[75]

What Medium to Use?

An effective media strategy begins with consideration for traditional media sources to maximize reach and frequency—while remaining cognizant of the gains and downsides related to them. The determination on what medium to use will help identify the type of production methods that can generate impactful content. For instance, when a photo-based campaign was used in the past, planners often used a camera and tools like Photoshop or Instagram to manage content.[76] Wilcox, Cameron, and Reber (2014)[77] listed the following popular tactical communication tools to connect with target audiences through key messages: the World Wide Web, websites, webcasts, blogs, social networking sites (like YouTube, Twitter, and Flickr), Wikis, podcasts, texting, news releases, media kits, e-kits, mat releases, media alerts and fact sheets, e-news releases, internet-based newsrooms, media interviews, news conferences, media tours and press parties, PSAs, video news releases, television programming, magazine shows, product placements, issue placements, open houses, conferences, and promotional events. The profusion of media available to campaign developers requires the creation of a media flowchart.[78]

Readers know by now that the type of medium selected to convey the message is of utmost importance to the audience. Having a good idea of where and how people spend their time online will facilitate the selection of the best platforms for the campaign. It is also important to keep in mind that advertising capabilities are based on the type of platform available to campaigners. For example, if it is a video-based campaign, then it would be logical to host it on an online venue like YouTube, TikTok, Dailymotion, or Vimeo. If it is an image-based campaign, then Instagram or Pinterest would be a better fit. Online venues like Facebook and Twitter are still the most popular in the world, and they can be used for many other types of content.[79]

Message conduits in campaigns have included printed materials, billboards, news coverage of specific events, public service advertisements, face-to-face tutorials in the community with experts, home visits, and booths at local shopping areas operated by trained volunteers. In any case, it was established in Chapter 1 that campaigns that mix interpersonal, mass media, and printed sources will be more productive than those that include only one communication medium. Whereas mass media conduits can boost information and awareness, interpersonal relationships in the community are better at inspiring certain kinds of behavior like trial behavior and safety actions.[80]

Media Advocacy

Media advocacy is the planned use of mass media in conjunction with community organizing to promote public policies. Media advocacy adopts a citizen-oriented rather than a customer-oriented method for mass media. Rather than visualizing the audience as consumers of knowledge, media advocates conceive of them as actors in democracy. The main focus is on the role of news media with additional attention to the incorporation of paid advertising. The media advocacy strategy strives to frame public issues to highlight policy-related results rather than the traditional focus on personal responsibility for the social good.[81] Media advocacy overtly tries to link social problems to social structures and inequities, modify public instead of individual behavior, connect with opinion leaders and policymakers, collaborate with groups to enhance participation in the communication process, and decrease the power gap rather than merely providing more information.[82]

The four main activities involved in media advocacy are to (1) set up an overarching strategy, which entails articulating policy options, locating the stakeholders who have the clouts to produce relevant change, putting pressure to create change, and devising messages for these stakeholders; (2) determine the agenda, including using the mass media through anecdotes, news events, and editorials; (3) set the tone for the debate, including framing public issues as ones that are relevant to audiences, stressing social accountability, and providing support and statistics for the broader claims; and (4) champion any relevant policy, including keeping interest, pressure, and sufficient exposure over time.[83]

Media advocacy supports an assortment of perspectives to diffuse campaign messages, such as the use of authority figures and regular citizens as spokespeople. The mix of voices increases the chances of credibility, attention, and support for campaign objectives. The use of opinion leaders can be beneficial because they serve as gatekeepers to attitude and behavior change. Thanks to them, a community is more likely to embrace a campaign message. It would be good to invite these individuals to assist in the planning, development, and implementation of the campaign. This will increase commitment from communities as well as audience attention and intention to change behavior. Lastly, opinion leaders can also help audiences in understanding peer or social norms, which have sometimes been obstacles to behavior change.[84]

Audience Engagement on Social Networks

Enter the 90:9:1 rule. According to this rule, the percentage of the audience that actually takes part in or generates media content is minuscule: 1% intense contributors, versus 9% sporadic contributors and 90% passive users.[85] However, success does not hinge only on a group of active frontrunners directing the streams of media content. In addition to the intense and sporadic contributors, there are sizeable groups of lurkers who play an essential role in magnifying information flows. Clever use of social networks around this critical periphery can be amplified by the personalization algorithms with mouse clicks and likes and, in turn, personalization algorithms can enlighten these data to reveal which media content should be displayed, and which not, to whom.[86]

Multiple layers of source are available for a social network message: **visible sources** (those who are visible to the receiver to send the message), **technological sources** (the platform on which the knowledge is displayed), and **receiver-sources** (the actual online users).[87] In regards to campaigns on social networking sites, a visible source could be a health organization[88] or a health expert,[89] whereas a technological source could be Instagram or Twitter. After being introduced to the original message on social networking sites, viewers may click "Like," post comments, or send the link to others (who develop into receiver-sources). This process is public and is akin to one-to-many communication, instead of being private and using one-to-one communication—as was frequently the case with the traditional Katz's (1957)[90] "two-step-flow" model.

In like fashion, **telelogic communication** refers to computer-mediated dialogue. Digital technologies have the capacity to produce a new kind of dialogue that takes place between individuals who communicate electronically.[91] It is called "telelogic" because, like traditional mass media, it is available to many users and can connect with a large audience.[92] The role of networked framing is worth mentioning too. Audience engagement can have a deeper effect than intended, having an effect on how ideas disseminate and flow through communities. By purely clicking, liking, or sending information that embodies messages or frames that they espouse, viewers nurture personalization algorithms and contribute implicitly to the frequency of specific frames in the streams of their peers.[93] In this manner, members of online communities engage in a process called **networked framing**,[94] influencing the process of online conversations. Retweeting a comment on a social networking site is part of a process of increasing a message's salience through public opinion formation. As such, a "retweet count" on Twitter or Sina Weibo—a Chinese microblogging website—can be considered a measure of user influence. The conjecture is that when B retweets A's message, B implicitly agrees with A and seeks to diffuse the message more widely.[95]

Two stipulations need to be discussed: clutter and reframing. Whether campaign messages are spread through traditional or social media—or both, as it is usually the case, how can a campaign vie for attention amid the plethora of information? This plethora of information is referred to as **clutter**—the infinite number of messages to which we are exposed every day.[96] What has been confirmed is that messages with subtle appeals will probably not attract our attention and, therefore, will be ignored. The inclusion of strong appeals is more likely to break through the clutter. Additionally, in the present-day media environment, information users can redefine the meaning of campaign messages more than ever. It is called **reframing**—a communicative technique like commenting, reposting, or even parodying. Even though audience engagement is, in theory, a good sign for a campaign and can improve campaign reach and influence, unconventional or unanticipated user redefinition or reinterpretation could be counterproductive as well. Careful planning, meticulous monitoring, and quick adjustments are necessary to ensure message loyalty and keep audience engagement as initially planned by the campaign.[97]

Building a Website for the Campaign?

A website can benefit a campaign if the audience visits it. There are a great many different options for building campaign websites. Whether downloading free online tools such as Tumblr, using a low-cost and easy-to-use website builder like Squarespace, or paying a qualified website designer, it is possible to come up with a great campaign website. A good start would be looking at the Apps section to discover some of the options available. When building a website, it is important to consider Search Engine Optimization (SEO). **Search Engine Optimization** is a method of improving the visibility of one's website in a search engine's "unpaid," "organic," or "earned" results—i.e., as opposed to paid advertising. To learn how to use SEO to increase one's website's search engine rankings, one should take a look at Google's SEO Starter Guide or the Video Tutorials. Or one can hire professional SEO experts, but they can be expensive and not necessarily be valuable for smaller campaigns.[98] Would building a website still be better than doing an e-blast as a campaign?

E-blasts are mass emails sent out to a targeted list of addressees. A case in point are the emails that land in our spam folders; they can also land in our email mailbox and be used for fundraising efforts.[99]

Uses & Gratifications (U&G) Theory

Developed by Katz, Blumler, and Gurevitch (1973),[100] the **Uses & Gratifications (U&G) theory** assumes that (1) audiences are not passive consumers of media, (2) they have power over media consumption, and (3) they are responsible for selecting media that fulfill (i.e., gratify) their desires and needs—i.e., they take an active role in embracing favorite types of media into their own lives. Given these circumstances, to meet the audience's gratification, the media vies for visibility and survival against other information sources. U&G grants us power to observe what types of media should be best consumed, with the postulation that audience members have a clear intent and use. The compelling question inherent to U&G is, "Why do people use media and what do they use them for?" People actively select media that satisfy certain needs—e.g., higher knowledge, relaxation, social relationships/companionship, entertainment, or escape—and offer them some level of gratification.[101]

Whereas **gratifications obtained** are those gratifications that we actually feel through the use of a specific medium, **gratifications sought** (usually known as "needs" or "motives") are those gratifications that we expect to gain from a medium before we even have come into contact with it. Fundamental to the U&G theory is that obtained gratifications may digress from those sought and the ensuing difference can forecast the degree of satisfaction/dissatisfaction that we experience after using a particular medium.[102] When a medium meets or exceeds the anticipated gratifications initially sought, this results in frequent use of the medium and, in the end, to predictable consumption routines. A medium can be as simple as a personal media player.[103] When a medium does not satisfy the sought-after gratifications, people often become disappointed and, consequently, stop utilizing it. This causes them to look for a different medium that can meet the levels of gratifications to which they are aspiring. Understanding the difference between these two categories of gratifications is essential for investigating how different audience members utilize all sorts of media, the expectations that they hope to reach through their media habits, and the gratifications they realistically obtain from their contact with a wide assortment of media messages.[104]

U&G theory is an audience-focused theory with a classification of audience activities across two factors: (1) **Audiences' exposure status**, which pertains to audiences' activity before media exposure, during such exposure, and after it, and (2) **audiences' selectivity**, which has to do with their participation in and use of media. A frequent example of pre-exposure activities includes our choice of media channels, expectations of participation in media exposure, and incentives for media use. Likewise, **during-activity behaviors** include our selective interpretation, attention, parasocial interaction, and amplification of media use. **Postactivity behaviors** include selective recollection of media messages, assessment, and opinion leading.[105] Last of all, U&G is applicable to social media on account of its roots in the communication literature. Social media is a method of communication that enables people to get in contact with thousands, and perhaps millions, of others across the world.[106] The advent of the internet has signaled a shift from the era of the **broadcasting schedule**, where people adapted to broadcasting schedules to make sure that their favorite shows were not missed, to the era of the **stream**, where people choose from a constant stream of media content at any opportune time.[107]

STEP 7: DEVELOP OPTIMAL MESSAGE CONTENT

When attempting to create optimal message content (e.g., for a press release), campaign designers adopt a standard format because reporters and editors usually read messages rapidly and decide whether or not to publish these messages. A **press release** is a brief news item that broadcasts events to newspapers, magazines, or social media outlets. The press release comes with an eye-catching headline and the first sentence. The world is replete with messages, all competing to attract our attention. The headline is what allows the message to stand out. The first sentence is what journalists call the **lede** (or **hook**). It determines whether the whole text will be read, remembered, and acted upon. If campaign planners devote their time and energy to these aspects, it is time and energy well spent.[108] Below is a list of guidelines for creating an ideal press release:[109]

1. Place the most relevant information first and the less significant details last.
2. Insert an interesting catchphrase: Why should the audience pay attention? What will make them retain the information? No message should be unremarkable. People pay particular attention when message or issues are out of the ordinary.
3. Brainstorm keywords: What will people search to locate your website or article? It is judicious to come up with as many keywords and tags as possible—anything that will guide users to your campaign.
4. Include subheadlines, hyperlinks, and lists. Headlines should be laced with facts—not cute, impractical, or promotional details. Information should be made easy to locate and access, as will hyperlinks and lists.
5. Apply the **bite–snack–meal approach**, whereby the headline is the bite and serve as a hyperlink to a whole "meal" of a message. A "snack" underneath the headline provides the main points of the message in a few short sentences. In this manner, the audience can pick and choose how much detail they need.[110]
6. Be as straightforward as possible. The audience should know what issue is at hand within the first few sentences. If it does not happen, the campaign has already lost their attention.
7. Do not include more than a few hundred words in your message. Most people scan instead of reading, so it is crucial to keep it brief and straightforward.
8. Generate a salient **nutgraf** (a portmanteau of "nutshell paragraph"). The nutgraf is a paragraph after a lede that explains why the issue is worthwhile. It is informative.[111] **Saliency** alludes to how significant an issue is. Without a nutgraf, it can be ignored even if the issue is salient.[112]
9. Additional guidelines (described below) consist of keeping the message simple, emphasizing benefits over risks, and avoiding confusion.

Keep the Message Simple

Simple messages contain one core idea and exclude nonpertinent details. The language is easy (at the eighth-grade level) and sentences are short. Simplicity allows the audience to read, understand, and retain information about any issue or policy.[113] Hence, the audience processes the information more methodically, which can contribute to more persistent and stable behaviors.[114] Put simply, the campaign strategist should diffuse understandable and credible communication. At the same time, the most effective communication is one that does not lecture the audience. Rather, it is something to consider and reflect on. A campaign message is one with a purpose. At the most fundamental level, a good message speaks *with* the audience, not *at* them. Campaigners should strive to emphasize the helpfulness of information and post knowledge of general value to all audiences—e.g., on their websites. Websites should contain characteristics that make them magnetic for frequent visits. Good features include updated information, change of topics, and special forums.[115]

Emphasize Benefits over Risks

The benefits or rewards should be clearly described in campaign messages and need to be prioritized over risk or fear-inducing messages. This brings up the need for response efficacy, which has been ascertained to raise audience confidence about the appropriateness of prevention tactics. The effectiveness of fear appeals hinges on the degree of efficacy information.[116] Fear appeals or overtly scary messages will be counterproductive if they are presented alone. They must be associated with messages that improve personal efficacy, response efficacy, and perceived personalization or salience.[117]

Avoid Confusion

Enter public communication campaigns on the environment. When people read a message on environmental policy, they decide whether or not they will adhere to it. This is rarely a straightforward practice because environmental messages are abounding with uncertainty. The Dutch campaign "Energy Savings, Do It Now" is a good case study for this. The purpose of this multimedia campaign was to multiply the number of homes insulated for energy efficiency. The campaign aimed at alleviating the obstacles to energy savings and enhance the urgency expressed by homeowners to make their homes more sustainable.[118] Regrettably, but consistent with past public communication failures on environmental issues,[119] the campaign was counterproductive. Assessments revealed low communication value during the first year of the campaign because it did not reach many people. In addition, communications about the urgency of energy savings and the effortlessness of making decisions did not go well with the general public. Assessments also revealed that comparatively few homeowners knew about the funding available to compensate costs. A major reason for the campaign's failure lied in the audience's confusion about how and when to be environment-friendly, notwithstanding the fact that multiple campaign volunteers were diffusing messages about energy savings, stressing various aspects and values.[120] Another reason, which was omitted in evaluations but suggested by research as leading to uncertainty, was skepticism as to whether climate change is real.[121]

Copyright and Intellectual Property Issues

Copyright is a form of intellectual property, including original designs, patents, and trademarks. **Intellectual property** enables the originator or owner of an invention (material or immaterial) or original work to make use of, reproduce and distribute it. We need to keep in mind that copyright laws differ between countries and jurisdictions. If strategists intend to make the campaign content freely available to anyone, online or offline, then a copyright license can shield the content from being plagiarized or modified by others. If campaign planners want to use stock images, several websites provide content that is free to use thanks to the Creative Commons license. For example, one can have a look at Flickr's Creative Commons site or Shutterstock, although many other options are available in the public domain.[122]

STEP 8: AVOID MONOLOGIC COMMUNICATION AND INTERACT WITH YOUR AUDIENCE(S)

Before discussing monologic communication and related concepts, it is important to describe the approach of rhetoric. **Rhetoric** is a process of communicating effectively and persuasively through language (oral or written). More than just individual expression, rhetoric influences communication activities between people who exchange ideas with one another to address differences of opinions. The words chosen in the communication influence perceptions of issues.[123] This impact of language as a persuasive mechanism to prompt behavior change (directly or indirectly) can be subtle and imperceptible to recipients, owing to certain psychological processes.[124] One-sided rhetoric introduces one outlook on the issue. Two-sided rhetoric presents arguments on behalf of both the persuader's position and the other side. Allen (1998)[125] and O'Keefe (1999)[126] aver that two-sided messages affect attitudes more than one-sided ones, as long as one crucial condition is met: The message refutes opposition claims. When the communication addresses, but does not shoot down, an opponent's argument, a two-sided message is usually less powerful than a one-sided message. Monologic communication is an example of one-sided rhetoric.

Monologic Communication

Monologic communication is characterized by a form of communication that tries to command, compel, manipulate, defeat, confuse, misinform, or exploit. The audience is viewed as "an object" to be totally exploited for the rhetorician's self-serving purpose; the audience is taken for granted. Attention is to the communicator's message, not on people's genuine needs. The core values and objectives adopted by the communicator are impermeable to the influence exerted by the audience. Audience reaction is used only to buttress the communicator's agenda.[127] Under the monologic model, communication is a conduit to bring about change. Focus is on the speaker's messages and how successfully these messages diffuse in a downwards, linear manner. Viewing people as "targets of change" highlights a one-way street of dissemination and ignores the proactive and driver-like roles of change that those people seek in continual change efforts. When communicating multifaceted change, monologic approaches are mostly unproductive because they do not account for the uncertainty, vulnerability, and swift decision-making processes inherent to continuous change.[128] Again, communication becomes a top-down, one-way street of information.[129] It boils down to establishing a relationship characterized by power over the audience and considering them objects for enjoyment or as things from which to profit.[130]

Dialogic Communication

Dialogic communication is a two-way street, a form of two-way communication where audience members share their opinions or provide feedback to campaign communicators.

At the same time, both parties take note of each other's positions with the purpose of mutual understanding.[131] Under the dialogic communication approach, "people function as essential information and idea resources, creating solutions we have never seen before."[132] Dialogic communication is infused with more genuineness, inclusion, confirmation, a supportive climate, and an atmosphere of mutual equality.[133] Public communication campaigns can facilitate all this by setting up channels and processes for dialogic communication. Under this model, campaigners should be disposed to interact with audiences in straightforward and ethical ways so as to build effective public communication channels. In this context, dialogue is to be viewed as communicating about issues with people.[134]

When people share their consideration to and participation in a publicly mediated fashion, a public connection emerges. **Public connection** is defined as individuals' shared "orientation to a public world where matters of shared concern are [...] addressed."[135] The concept is "designed to capture an orientation to any of those issues affecting how we live together that require common resolution."[136] Although only a fraction of the population participates in, say, a campaign on health and nutrition, and although people frame the issue in different ways, and only a small percentage of the engaged audience may modify their health and nutritional habits as a result of the encounter, it is still the case that any degree of audience engagement in the campaign amounts to public connection.[137]

One clear demonstration of dialogic communication in a public communication campaign occurs when campaign developers test the content directly within the audience. It is considered wise to try and get audience feedback on message content to make sure it has reached the desired impact. Testing content can help confirm that the message came across positively and the audience engages effectively as well. A trial-and-error approach is best because it helps refine aspects of the campaign content. If possible, test the content with a focus group that reflects the audience's demographics and/or attitudes.[138] From this vantage point, dialogic communication is a type of **invitational rhetoric**, whereby the communicative situation fosters an "invitation to understanding as a means to create a relationship rooted in equality, immanent value, and self-determination."[139] Therefore, the usefulness of invitational rhetoric does not lie in the control over others (like monologic communication), but in the willingness to engage in dialogic communication for mutual acknowledgment of the audience's importance (and even the uniqueness of the audience members). Instead of "an observer or onlooker," the openness for mutual acknowledgment motivates communication actors to engage in communication processes.[140]

Communal Mindset

Fostering and maintaining a communal mindset between public communication campaigns and their audience(s) is primordial. The idea of a **communal mindset** reflects the need for collaboration within communities, not only for the entity or institution designing the campaign.[141] Martin Buber (1958),[142] an Israeli-born Austrian philosopher, stresses the orientation of mutuality to distinguish dialogue from monologue in dialogic theory. Buber looked at dialogue as an **I–Thou relationship** in which communicators have the orientation of mutuality, considering other parties as being part of a grand unity. On the other hand, monologue is reflected through the **I–It relationship**, a relationship of divisiveness and detachment. There is also a similarity between Buber's I–Thou relationship and Habermas' (1984)[143] theory of communicative action, as both represent "intersubjective, ethical, and dialogical" facets of communication.[144]

Both dialogic communication and the I–Thou relationship exemplify the concept of empathy and grounding. **Empathy** plays a crucial part in a communicator's indirect experience of others' feelings in dialogic communication.[145] Empathy is the ability to attend to and envisage other communicators' needs and feelings[146] to be "supportive."[147] **Grounding** refers to a mutual orientation of interactants to find common ground. To have effective dialogic communication, campaign planners should invite audiences to communicate, find common ground, and confirm that what has been communicated has been rightly understood by both parties. In the absence of effective grounding in communication, communication between multiple parties devolves in monologue.[148]

STEP 9: UPDATE THE CAMPAIGN WITH TIMELY, RELEVANT, AND ACCURATE INFORMATION

When public communication campaigns last for months or several years, they require constant up-to-date information because of unforeseen events in the social environment, other than the manipulated variables, that occur during the course of the campaign (and that likely affect the outcome). For example, if a campaign takes the form of a drug prevention intervention, and during the time of the campaign, admired celebrities lose their lives to drug overdoses, the effect on the audience(s) may have been caused by the group's reaction to the celebrities' deaths rather than the campaign itself. To be able to achieve positive outcomes, we must be mindful about events that occur during the course of the campaign that might impact the final goals/objectives. This is why timely, accurate, and relevant information is of utmost importance during such drug prevention intervention—i.e., in this case, information that transcends such sudden, unexpected tragedies.

Using a similar example, imagine that the campaign operates like a health education program in public schools to generate awareness about teenage pregnancy. During the program, some students become pregnant, quit school, and commit suicide. If these unpleasant occurrences become broadly publicized, they would unmistakably have a profound effect on the students' awareness. So, when we assess the effectiveness of a public communication campaign and we observe an increase in awareness, we must be sure to factor in the impact of surprising events and/or information. Thus, it would be clever to resort to thorough and unremitting gathering of "tracking" data about the target population's awareness of messages, changes in beliefs, social outlooks, and self-efficacy with respect to desired behaviors, as well as evaluations of those behaviors. This requirement is even more important in the context of initiatives that target heterogeneous audiences, when tracking research needs to enable assessment of differential trends across key population subgroups.[149]

Boost the Confidence to Make Changes

Many types of campaign messages are likely to be modified because of the erratic nature of the social environment. Audience members must have total trust in those messages and believe they can perform a recommended action. This will decrease their beliefs that such messages are not reliable. More often than not, inexperienced campaign planners lack sufficient confidence to make changes. The key is to do things in a timely fashion. News can only be timely for so long until it is a new story emerges. Upon trying to ensure that the messages be factual and newsworthy, campaign strategists should also ensure that they fact-check their own messages. It would be much better than being corrected by the public after errors are found because they can and they will. Campaigns should never fall back on using erroneous information for the sake of making the writing more interesting. Public communicators must also be attentive when formulating slogans. Their persuasiveness often depends on the perceived bearing of the issue communicated. Audiences respond positively to pushy requests, like "Keep the highway clean," if they consider the topic (i.e., clean roads) as one of great magnitude. However, if they find the topic irrelevant or out-of-date, they should use more suggestive—gentle—pleas to persuade them to act in a more sustainable way.[150]

Update Campaign Memes

In the *The Selfish Gene*, the British evolutionary biologist and author Richard Dawkins (1976)[151] introduced the term "meme" to apply the main tenets of Darwinian evolutionary theory to the progress of culture and society. Dawkins advanced the notion that genes, the most fundamental replicating units in biological systems, must have some counterparts or parallels during the course of cultural evolution, and therefore coined the term **meme** to define a unit of cultural transmission. Today, memes reflect various norms of digital culture, like peer-to-peer sharing, cooperation, and the reuse of cultural artifacts.[152] Naturally, like genes, memes change and grow. In contrast to genes, however, memes are not natural; they are created by people within their social environments. Campaign memes can be updated via official press releases or even through 140-character posts on Twitter. Online campaign memes make interactive behaviors easy and offer users a method to influence others through digital social networks and social movements. Besides, the instruments and channels of digital culture allow people to embrace, challenge, or reappropriate frames and meanings entrenched within campaign memes as they circulate through online media sources, to massive audiences, and back to online platforms again.

STEP 10: EVALUATE THE OVERALL CAMPAIGN

In spite of their substantial cost in terms of both time and money, large-scale public communication campaigns are not necessarily thoroughly evaluated, to some extent because of the flawed assumption that communication efforts will produce the desired outcomes. This ignores the reality that audiences may have different interpretations, beliefs, degrees of literacy, and sociocultural influences[153]—all of which are discussed in Chapter 6. When hundreds of thousands, or even millions, of dollars, euros, or other units of money are exhausted on public communication, advertising, public relations, or speaking engagements, it is imperative to bear in mind that the famous quote by marketing pioneer John Wannamaker is accurate: "Half of my advertising is wasted; the only trouble is I don't know which half."[154]

What Is Meant by "Evaluation"?

Evaluation is the passing of judgment about the value and relevance of findings and results within a framework and with respect to objectives set, and it puts these judgments into operation to both reporting and planning of future approaches. Measurement is part of the procedure of evaluation, but, in and of itself, measurement offers merely raw statistics (metrics) and explanations. Measures do not carry much weight without interpretation and context. Thus, it is more suitable to allude to the field of practice as evaluation—although informed by facts acquired through various forms of measurement—instead of simply as measurement.[155] The measures of performance must pertain directly to the goals of the campaign and should employ valid and consistent methods. A difference must be drawn between output (communication products) and outcome (results and effects of actions taken).[156]

Another distinction needs to be made between effect evaluation and outcome evaluation. **Effect evaluation** considers the actual outcome of a campaign. Does the campaign fulfill its objectives? As seen in the social sciences, this kind of evaluation research is divided into two groups. **Positivists** champion quantitative methods where randomized, controlled trials are viewed as the "gold standard." By randomly separating the audience of an intervention into an experimental group (for the actual intervention) and a control group (with no intervention or a placebo), it aims at confirming the efficacy and effects of interventions. This assumes a rather direct, linear correlation between intervention and effect, while ignoring social context.[157] Unlike positivists, **interpretivists** stress the role of interpretation and context. By employing interpretive approaches of data collection like in-depth interviews or participant observation, evaluators can come up with a "thick description" of a particular intervention. Nevertheless, interpretivists are disapproved of because they generally offer insight into the effectiveness of only one intervention, in one social context.[158] **Outcome evaluation** seeks to determine whether a campaign created its desired impact. Without a solid outcome evaluation, there is no way to tell whether a campaign accomplished its objectives—e.g., enhancing knowledge, producing positive attitudes, decreasing risky behaviors, and so forth.[159]

Regardless of the position or approach used for evaluation, contemporary public communication campaigns can be empirically assessed. This can be done in a myriad of ways, including memory tests, persuasion or motivation tests, and inquiry tests (which provide statistics as to the number of responses to a campaign).[160] Effects can be examined at the individual level, when evaluators compare those exposed to campaign messages with those who were not. If the campaign was productive, people who were exposed to, say, many PSAs are expected to modify their attitude in the desired direction (as compared with those who were not or who saw fewer PSAs). Campaign evaluators also operate at the community level. For instance, one village can be randomly selected as the treatment group; its residents are given promotional materials on seat belt use. A comparative analysis can also be done; an equivalent village is used as the control group—meaning that its inhabitants are not shown campaign messages. Then, researchers can compare the two villages by asking police officers to stand at intersections counting the number of drivers with their safety belts on. If a higher percentage of drivers in the treatment group wear safety belts than in the control group, the campaign can be deemed a success.[161]

Bonfadelli and Friemel (2005)[162] assert that the success of a public communication campaign can only be evaluated if a summative evaluation is implemented as an essential part of the campaign. **Summative evaluation** is the practice of answering questions in regards to exposure of the intended audience (size and features), as well as acceptance and assessment of campaign messages and effects (i.e., on knowledge, attitudes, and behavior). Test criteria can be used only if the evaluation is conducted by an external entity. More specifically, if the evaluation is operated on scientific principles like reliability and validity, and if it rests on a solid theoretical model of the campaign, then it is considered a fair, summative evaluation.

Beginning at the Outset of the Campaign

It is recommended to perform an evaluation during or even at the outset of the public communication campaign itself, especially if it will run over a long time, to determine whether activities are on their way to reaching success and whether it is necessary to adjust activities based on audience feedback. Keeping an eye on the progress of the campaign is a given, but it is not the same as evaluating it. This is why it is important not only once the campaign is completed, but also during its operation. Any piece of information as to how campaigners are doing can be used to fine-tune aspects of the content or strategies to ensure objectives are met. After the campaign is finished, evaluators can decide whether goals were met and what improvements should be made.[163]

Grier and Bryant (2005)[164] also promote evaluation for a social marketing intervention at the very beginning. Plans for assessing such intervention should begin with specific assessments. After they are implemented, each is scrutinized to determine its effectiveness, whether it should be sustained, and what activities should be identified for midcourse revision. It is a well-known fact that public health interventions engage in process and impact assessments; considerable resources are devoted to this activity and practices on a constant basis. Social marketers are regularly scrutinizing target audiences to measure their reactions to all facets of an intervention, from broad marketing approaches to specific messages and materials.

Two techniques that can be employed during the course of a campaign are process research and process evaluation. **Process research** evaluates the campaign as it develops to guarantee that the messages get across the target audience through the media.[165] If a message or a medium faces obstacles during the course of a campaign, certain points will be fine-tuned to make sure that there is a connection between the audience and the message. **Process evaluation** pertains to the regulation and gathering of data on fidelity and execution of campaign activities.[166] Such data can enhance the implementation of campaigns and inform campaign strategists as to why particular goals of a campaign were or were not accomplished.[167] Explained differently, a central focus of process evaluation is getting the audience to be exposed to campaign messages with frequent and ample reach, as even large-scale campaigns have had disappointing results in terms of audience exposure.[168]

Different Platforms for Evaluation

The type of data or metric for campaign evaluations depends on the type of platform. There is a wide assortment of metrics that can assist campaign designers in determining whom to reach, to what degree to engage the audience(s), and the impact of the campaign. By and large, these metrics can be classified into many types (four of which are listed below):[169]

- **Awareness**: metrics that show how many people are reached by a campaign (e.g., impressions, reach or video views) and demographic characteristics (e.g., age, gender, or geographic location) can offer insights as to whether the right audience is on target.
- **Engagement**: metrics that show the extent to which people interact with a campaign's message and the number of social media accounts or websites—including video retention rates, numbers of likes, posts, or shares—are examples of engagement. Comments disseminated through social networking sites as a result of content posted by campaigners are also an indicator of audience reception and reaction.

Comments can be made on a campaign's own social website, like Facebook pages and blogs that allow or even recommend comments.[170]

- **Impact**: metrics that help visualize if campaign goals are met will vary based on what the campaign was originally set out to do. Heated debates, discussions, critical thinking, and sustained online engagements within specific segments of the intended audience indicate that the campaign has a high impact. Nevertheless, measuring the impact of a campaign—whether or not it is changing people's attitudes or behaviors—is not an easy task and can seem inconclusive for a long period.

- **Google Analytics** is a free service that observes, measures, and gives an account of website traffic. It can be used for apps or the YouTube channel. It can assist in evaluating the audience of the campaign website and offer useful insights in terms of design and usability. It is important to be cautious about the so-called vanity metrics. **Vanity metrics** is a term that captures the measurement of how successful one is in the realm of social media. This concept implies an assessment of metrics regarding both the object of measurement and the capacity to measure discreetly or only to promote performance.[171] In many cases, vanity metrics may be impressive in terms of numbers, but it does not necessarily tell how effective the campaign is. For instance, if the campaign seeks to reach a very specific audience, even reaching 100,000 people is not a good result if it is not the right people.[172]

Another method to track online communication is **tagging content**. This entails embedding metadata in content. It enables to identify what online content has been accessed and for how much time. It also allows reactions to content like page views, video views, likes, and shares to be connected back to particular forms of content and messages. Thanks to tagging, the efficacy of platforms and types of content like advertisements or videos and messages can be measured. If posts and inquiries come from Facebook and not Twitter, focus should be placed on Facebook. Tagging of Facebook pages enables site owners to determine which pages are producing responses.[173]

NOTES

1. Elizabeth Crisp Crawford and Charles C. Okigbo, "Strategic Communication Campaigns," in *Strategic Urban Health Communication*, ed. Charles C. Okigbo (New York: Springer, 2014): 11–23.

2. Jonathan E. Fielding, Ross C. Brownson, and Larry W. Green, "Public Health: Moving from 'What' to 'How'," *Annual Review of Public Health* 31, no. 1 (2011): 1.

3. D. Lawrence Kincaid, Richard Delate, Douglas Storey, and Maria Elena Figueroa, "Closing the Gaps in Practice and in Theory," in *Public Communication Campaigns* (4th Ed.), ed. Ronald Rice and Charles Atkin (Thousand Oaks, CA: Sage, 2012): 305–19.

4. Jim Macnamara, *Evaluating Public Communication: Exploring New Models, Standards and Best Practice* (New York: Routledge, 2017).

5. Rudolph F. Verderber, Deanna D. Sellnow, and Kathleen S. Verderber, *The Challenge of Effective Speaking in a Digital Age* (17th Ed.) (Boston, MA: Cengage Learning, 2018).

6. Jaeho Cho, "Campaign Tone, Political Affect, and Communicative Engagement," *Journal of Communication* 63, no. 6 (2013): 1130–52. https://doi.org/10.1111/jcom.12064.

7. Ali Atıf Bir and Önder Yönet, "A Method Proposal for Determining Health Communication Campaigns' Messages," *European Journal of Interdisciplinary Studies* 2, no. 2 (2016): 48–72.

8. Rebecca Green, "Topical Relevance Relationships. I. Why Topic Matching Fails," *Journal of the American Society for Information Science* 46, no. 9 (1995): 646–53. https://doi.org/10.1002/(SICI)1097-4571(199510)46:9<646::AID-ASI2>3.0.CO;2-1.

9. See Edwin A. Locke and Gary E. Latham, "New Directions in Goal-Setting Theory," *Current Directions in Psychological Science* 15, no. 5 (2006): 265–8. https://doi.org/10.1111/j.1467-8721.2006.00449.x.

10. See John A. Bargh, "Attention and Automaticity in the Processing of Self-Relevant Information," *Journal of Personality and Social Psychology* 43, no. 3 (1982): 425–36. https://doi.org/10.1037/0022-3514.43.3.425.

11. Thijs Verwijmeren, Johan C. Karremans, Wolfgang Stroebe, and Daniël H. J. Wigboldus, "Goal Relevance Moderates Evaluative Conditioning Effects," *Learning and Motivation* 43, no. 3 (2012): 107–15. https://doi.org/10.1016/j.lmot.2012.06.002.

12. Leslie B. Snyder, "Health Communication Campaigns and Their Impact on Behavior," *Journal of Nutrition Education and Behavior* 39, no. 2 (2007): 32–40. https://doi.org/10.1016/j.jneb.2006.09.004.

13. Crawford and Okigbo, "Strategic Communication Campaigns," 15–6.

14. Gerd Bohner and Lena E. Schlüter, "A Room with a Viewpoint Revisited: Descriptive Norms and Hotel Guests' Towel Reuse Behavior," *PloS One* 9, no. 8 (2014). e104086. https://doi.org/10.1371/journal.pone.0106606.

15. Noah J. Goldstein, Robert B. Cialdini, and Vladas Griskevicius, "A Room with a Viewpoint: Using Social Norms to Motivate Environmental Conservation in Hotels," *Journal of Consumer Research* 35, no. 3 (2008): 472–82. https://doi.org/10.1086/586910.

16. Gerdien de Vries, "Public Communication as a Tool to Implement Environmental Policies," *Social Issues and Policy Review* 14, no. 1 (2020): 244–72. https://doi.org/10.1111/sipr.12061.

17. David T. Z. Mindich, "Edwin M. Stanton, the Inverted Pyramid, and Information Control," *Journalism Monographs* 140 (1993): 1–31.

18. Don E. Schultz and Beth E. Barnes, *Strategic Advertising Campaigns* (4th Ed.) (Lincolnwood, IL: NTC Business Books, 1995): 149.

19. Snyder, "Health Communication Campaigns," 35.

20. Prakash M. Shingi and Bella Mody, "The Communication Effects Gap: A Field Experiment in TV and Agricultural Ignorance in India," *Communication Research* 3, no. 2 (1976): 46–58. https://doi.org/10.1177/009365027600300205.

21. Crawford and Okigbo, "Strategic Communication Campaigns," 15.

22. Emet Gürel and Merba Tat, "SWOT Analysis: A Theoretical Review," *The Journal of International Social Research* 10, no. 51 (2017): 10–21. http://dx.doi.org/10.17719/jisr.2017.1832.

23. Martha C. Monroe, Elaine Andrews, and Kelly Bidenweg, "A Framework for Environmental Education Strategies," *Applied Environmental Education & Communication* 6, no. 3 (2008): 205–16. https://doi.org/10.1080/15330150801944416.

24. Sonya Grier and Carol A. Bryant, "Social Marketing in Public Health," *Annual Review of Public Health* 26 (2005): 319–39. https://doi.org/10.1146/annurev.publhealth.26.021304.144610.

25. Crawford and Okigbo, "Strategic Communication Campaigns," 16.

26. Seth M. Noar, "A 10–Year Retrospective of Research in Health Mass Media Campaigns: Where Do We Go from Here?" *Journal of Health Communication* 11, no. 1 (2006): 21–42. https://doi.org/10.1080/10810730500461059.

27. Monroe, Andrews, and Bidenweg, "A Framework for Environmental Education Strategies," 206–8.
28. Thomas W. Valente, "Evaluating Communications Campaigns," in *Public Communication Campaigns* (3rd Ed.), ed. Ronald E. Rice and Charles C. K. Atkin (Thousand Oaks, CA: Sage, 2001): 105–24.
29. Kim Witte, Kenzie A. Cameron, Maria Knight Lapinski, and Solomon Nzyuko, "A Theoretically Based Evaluation of HIV/AIDS Prevention Campaigns along the TransAfrica Highway in Kenya," *Journal of Health Communication* 3, no. 4 (1998): 345–67. https://doi.org/10.1080/108107398127157.
30. Charles K. Atkin and Vicki Freimuth, "Guidelines for Formative Evaluation Research in Campaign Design," in *Public Communication Campaigns* (4th Ed.), ed. Ronald E. Rice and Charles K. Atkin (Thousand Oaks, CA: Sage, 2012): 53–68.
31. Ibid, 55–61.
32. Nancy R. Lee and Philip Kotler, *Social Marketing: Behavior Change for Social Good* (6th Ed.) (Thousand Oaks, CA: Sage, 2019).
33. Lynne Eagle, Rachel Hay, and Marina Farr, *Harnessing the Science of Social Marketing and Behaviour Change for Improved Water Quality in the GBR: Background Review of Literature* (Cairns, Australia: James Cook University Press, 2016).
34. Jonathan Matusitz, *Terrorism & Communication: A Critical Introduction* (Thousand Oaks, CA: Sage, 2013).
35. John A. Ledingham, "Government-Community Relationships: Extending the Relational Theory of Public Relations," *Public Relations Review* 27, no. 3 (2001): 285–95. https://doi.org/10.1016/S0363-8111(01)00087-X.
36. Rachel S. Kovacs, "Relationship Building as Integral to British Activism: Its Impact on Accountability in Broadcasting," *Public Relations Review* 27, no. 4 (2001): 421–36. https://doi.org/10.1016/S0363-8111(01)00098-4.
37. Miejeong Han and Sei-Hill Kim, "South Koreans' Perceptions of North Koreans and Implications for Public Relations Campaigns," *Public Relations Review* 30, no. 3 (2004): 327–33. https://doi.org/10.1016/j.pubrev.2004.04.004.
38. Denis McQuail, *Audience Analysis* (Thousand Oaks, CA: Sage, 1997).
39. Verderber, Sellnow, and Verderber, *The Challenge of Effective Speaking*, 66.
40. Crawford and Okigbo, "Strategic Communication Campaigns," 16–7.
41. Linda Aldoory and Sandra Bonzo, "Using Communication Theory in Injury Prevention Campaigns," *Injury Prevention* 11, no. 5 (2005): 260–3. http://dx.doi.org/10.1136/ip.2004.007104.
42. Nurit Guttman and Charles T. Salmon, "Guilt, Fear, Stigma and Knowledge Gaps: Ethical Issues in Public Health Communication Interventions," *Bioethics* 18, no. 6 (2004): 531–52. https://doi.org/10.1111/j.1467-8519.2004.00415.x.
43. Martin Fishbein and Icek Ajzen, *Belief, Attitude, Intention and Behavior: An Introduction to Theory and Research* (Reading, MA: Addison-Wesley, 1975).
44. Richard M. Perloff, *The Dynamics of Persuasion: Communication and Attitudes in the 21st Century* (2nd Ed.) (Mahwah, NJ: Lawrence Erlbaum, 2003): 45.
45. Brydon, Steven R., and Michael D. Scott, *Between One and Many: The Art & Science of Public Speaking* (7th Ed.) (Boston, MA: McGraw Hill, 2011).
46. Gregory R. Maio and James M. Olson, "Values as Truisms: Evidence and Implications," *Journal of Personality and Social Psychology* 74, no. 2 (1998): 294–311. https://doi.org/10.1037/0022-3514.74.2.294.

47. Clyde Kluckhohn, "Values and Value-Orientations in the Theory of Action: An Exploration in Definition and Classification," in *Toward a General Theory of Action*, ed. Talcott Parsons and Edward Shils (Cambridge, MA: Harvard University Press, 1951): 388–433.

48. Fred Jandt, *An Introduction to Intercultural Communication: Identities in a Global Community* (5th Ed.) (Thousand Oaks, CA: Sage, 2006).

49. Abraham H. Maslow, "A Theory of Human Motivation," *Psychological Review* 50, no. 4 (1943): 370–96. https://doi.org/10.1037/h0054346.

50. John W. Burton, *Deviance, Terrorism and War: The Process of Solving Unsolved Social and Political Problems* (New York: St. Martin's Press, 1979).

51. Derek McGrath and Jonathan Matusitz, "Understanding Uighur Terrorism: The Human Needs Theory," *Asian Journal of Interdisciplinary Research* 3, no. 4 (2020): 48–57. https://doi.org/10.34256/ajir2045.

52. Melinda S. Forthofer and Carol A. Bryant, "Using Audience-Segmentation Techniques to Tailor Health Behavior Change Strategies," *American Journal of Health Behavior* 24 (2000): 36–43. https://doi.org/10.5993/AJHB.24.1.6.

53. Noar, "A 10–Year Retrospective of Research," 25.

54. Charles K. Atkin, "Theory and Principles of Media Health Campaigns," in *Public Communication Campaigns* (3rd Ed.), ed. Ronald E. Rice and Charles K. Atkin (Thousand Oaks, CA: Sage, 2001): 49–68.

55. Sonja L. Myhre and June A. Flora, "HIV/AIDS Communication Campaigns: Progress and Prospects," *Journal of Health Communication* 5, no. 1 (2000): 29–45. https://doi.org/10.1080/108107300126731.

56. Institute of Medicine, *Speaking of Health: Assessing Health Communication Strategies for Diverse Populations* (Washington, D.C.: Institute of Medicine, 2002): 95.

57. Edward J. Roccella, "The Contributions of Public Health Education toward the Reduction of Cardiovascular Disease Mortality: Experience from the National High Blood Pressure Education Program," in *Public Health Communication: Evidence for Behavior Change*, ed. Robert Hornik (Mahwah, NJ: Lawrence Erlbaum, 2002): 73–84.

58. Harrigan, Claire and Robin Capon, *Abstract and Colour Techniques in Painting* (London: Anova Books, 2007).

59. Douglas A. Bernstein, *Essentials of Psychology* (Boston, MA: Cengage Learning, 2010).

60. Lauren S. Kim, Irwin N. Sandler, and Jenn-Yun Tein, "Locus of Control as a Stress Moderator and Mediator in Children of Divorce," *Journal of Abnormal Child Psychology* 25 (1997): 145–55. https://doi.org/10.1023/A:1025783513076.

61. Anthony S. R. Manstead and Sander A. M. Van Eekelen, "Distinguishing between Perceived Behavioral Control and Self–Efficacy in the Domain of Academic Achievement Intentions and Behaviors," *Journal of Applied Social Psychology* 28, no. 15 (1998): 1375–92. https://doi.org/10.1111/j.1559-1816.1998.tb01682.x.

62. de Vries, "Public Communication as a Tool," 251.

63. Elke U. Weber, "Breaking Cognitive Barriers to a Sustainable Future," *Nature Human Behaviour* 1 (2017): Article 0013. https://doi.org/10.1038/s41562-016-0013.

64. de Vries, "Public Communication as a Tool," 251.

65. Crawford and Okigbo, "Strategic Communication Campaigns," 18.

66. Neil Bracht and Ronald E. Rice, "Community Partnership Strategies in Health Campaigns," in *Public Communication Campaigns* (4th Ed.), ed. Ronald E. Rice and Charles K. Atkin (Thousand Oaks, CA: Sage, 2012): 289–304.

67. Schultz and Barnes, *Strategic Advertising Campaigns*, 301.
68. Crawford and Okigbo, "Strategic Communication Campaigns," 18.
69. Institute of Medicine, *Speaking of Health*, 59.
70. Crawford and Okigbo, "Strategic Communication Campaigns," 18.
71. Henry Tuck and Tania Silverman, *The Counter-Narrative Handbook* (London: Institute for Strategic Dialogue, 2016).
72. Institute of Medicine, *Speaking of Health*, 95.
73. Tuck and Silverman, *The Counter-Narrative Handbook*, 14.
74. Morag White, *The Publicity Push: How to Build and Sustain a Media Profile* (Brighton, Victoria, Australia: Green Olive Press, 2012).
75. Marshall McLuhan, *Understanding Media* (New York: Mentor, 1964).
76. Tuck and Silverman, *The Counter-Narrative Handbook*, 19.
77. Dennis L. Wilcox, Glen T. Cameron, and Bryan H. Reber, *Public Relations: Strategies and Tactics* (11th Ed.) (Upper Saddle River, NJ: Pearson, 2014).
78. Crawford and Okigbo, "Strategic Communication Campaigns," 17.
79. Tuck and Silverman, *The Counter–Narrative Handbook*, 23.
80. Aldoory and Bonzo, "Using Communication Theory," 260–3.
81. Lori Dorfman, and Lawrence Wallack, "Putting Policy into Health Communication: The Role of Media Advocacy," in *Public Communication Campaigns* (4th Ed.), ed. Ronald E. Rice and Charles K. Atkin (Thousand Oaks, CA: Sage, 2012): 337–50.
82. Charles K. Atkin and Ronald E. Rice, "Theory and Principles of Public Communication Campaigns," in *Public Communication Campaigns* (4th Ed.), ed. Ronald E. Rice and Charles K. Atkin (Thousand Oaks, CA: Sage, 2012): 3–20.
83. Ibid, 5–15.
84. Aldoory and Bonzo, "Using Communication Theory," 260–3.
85. Nielsen Norman Group, *Participation Inequality: The 90-9-1 Rule for Social Features*. Retrieved on March 6, 2021 from https://www.nngroup.com/articles/participation-inequality.
86. Pablo Barberá, Ning Wang, Richard Bonneau, John T. Jost, Jonathan Nagler, Joshua Tucker, Sandra González-Bailón, "The Critical Periphery in the Growth of Social Protests," *PLoS One* 10, no. 11 (2015): e0143611. https://doi.org/10.1371/journal.pone.0143611.
87. Shyam Sundar and Clifford Nass, "Conceptualizing Sources in Online News," *Journal of Communication* 51, no. 1 (2001): 52–72. https://doi.org/10.1111/j.1460-2466.2001.tb02872.x.
88. For example, see Giuseppe La Torre, Silvia Miccoli, and Walter Ricciardi, "The Italian Alliance for Vaccination Strategies: Facebook as a Learning Tool for Preventive Medicine and Public Health," *Human Vaccines & Immunotherapeutics* 10, no. 10 (2014): 2910–4. https://doi.org/10.4161/21645515.2014.970497.
89. Gabrielle M. Turner-McGrievy, Charis R. Davidson, Ellen E. Wingard, and Deborah L. Billings, "Low Glycemic Index Vegan or Low-Calorie Weight Loss Diets for Women with Polycystic Ovary Syndrome: A Randomized Controlled Feasibility Study," *Nutrition Research* 34, no. 6 (2014): 552–8. https://doi.org/10.1016/j.nutres.2014.04.011.
90. Elihu Katz, "The Two-Step Flow of Communication: An Up-to-Date Report on a Hypothesis," *Public Opinion Quarterly* 21, no. 1 (1957): 61–78. https://doi.org/10.1086/266687.

91. David Russell Brake, "Who Do They Think They're Talking to? Framings of the Audience by Social Media Users," *International Journal of Communication* 6 (2012): 1056–76.

92. Sandra J. Ball-Rokeach and Kathleen Reardon, "Monologue, Dialogue, and Telelog: Comparing an Emergent Form of Communication with Traditional Forms," in *Advancing Communication Science: Merging Mass and Interpersonal Processes*, ed. Suzanne Pingree, Robert P. Hawkins, and John M. Wiemann (Newbury Park, CA: Sage, 1988): 135–61.

93. José van Dijck, "Users Like You? Theorizing Agency in User-Generated Content," *Media, Culture & Society* 31, no. 1 (2009): 41–58. https://doi.org/10.1177/0163443708098245.

94. Sharon Meraz and Zizi Papacharissi, "Networked Gatekeeping and Networked Framing on #Egypt," *The International Journal of Press/Politics* 18, no. 2 (2013): 138–66.https://doi.org/10.1177/1940161212474472.

95. Joyce Y. M. Nip and King-wa Fu, "Networked Framing between Source Posts and Their Reposts: An Analysis of Public Opinion on China's Microblogs," *Information, Communication & Society* 19, no. 8 (2016): 1127–49. https://doi.org/10.1080/1369118X.2015.1104372.

96. Herbert Jack Rotfeld, "Understanding Advertising Clutter and the Real Solution to Declining Audience Attention to Mass Media Commercial Messages," *Journal of Consumer Marketing* 23, no. 4 (2006): 180–1. https://doi.org/10.1108/07363760610674301.

97. Xiaoquan Zhao, "Health Communication Campaigns: A Brief Introduction and Call for Dialogue," *International Journal of Nursing Sciences* 7, no. 1 (2020): S11–5. https://doi.org/10.1016/j.ijnss.2020.04.009.

98. Tuck and Silverman, *The Counter-Narrative Handbook*, 19.

99. Lily R. Mundy, Karen Homa, Anne F. Klassen, Andrea L. Pusic, and Carolyn L. Kerrigan, "Normative Data for Interpreting the BREAST-Q: Augmentation," *Plastic and Reconstructive Surgery* 139, no. 4 (2017): 846–53. https://doi.org/10.1097/PRS.0000000000003186.

100. Elihu Katz, Jay G. Blumler, and Michael Gurevitch, "Uses and Gratifications Research," *Public Opinion Quarterly* 37, no. 4 (1973): 509–23. https://doi.org/10.1086/268109.

101. Werner J. Severin and James W. Tankard Jr., *Communication Theories: Origins, Methods and Uses in the Mass Media* (Boston, MA: Addison-Wesley, 2000).

102. Philip Palmgreen, Lawrence A. Wenner, and J. D. Rayburn, "Relations between Gratifications Sought and Obtained: A Study of Television News," *Communication Research* 7, no. 2 (1980): 161–92. https://doi.org/10.1177/009365028000700202.

103. John McCormick and Jonathan Matusitz, "The Impact on US Society of Noise-Induced and Music-Induced Hearing Loss Caused by Personal Media Players," *International Journal of Listening* 24, no. 2 (2010): 125–40. https://doi.org/10.1080/10904011003744565.

104. Philip Palmgreen and J. D. Rayburn, "Uses and Gratifications and Exposure to Public Television," *Communication Research* 6, no. 2 (1979): 155–80. https://doi.org/10.1177/009365027900600203.

105. Kimberly B. Massey, "Analyzing the Uses and Gratifications Concept of Audience Activity with a Qualitative Approach: Media Encounters during the 1989 Loma Prieta Earthquake Disaster," *Journal of Broadcasting and Electronic Media* 39, no. 3 (1995): 328–42. https://doi.org/10.1080/08838159509364310.

106. Anita Whiting and David Williams, "Why People Use Social Media: A Uses and Gratifications Approach," *Qualitative Market Research: An International Journal* 16, no. 4 (2013): 362–9. https://doi.org/10.1108/QMR-06-2013-0041.

107. Cited in Roel O. Lutkenhaus, Jeroen Jansz, and Martine P. A. Bouman, "Toward Spreadable Entertainment-Education: Leveraging Social Influence in Online Networks," *Health Promotion International* 35, no. 5 (2020): 1241–50, 1243. https://doi.org/10.1093/heapro/daz104.

108. David Spark and Geoffrey Harris, *Practical Newspaper Reporting* (Thousand Oaks, CA: Sage, 2010).

109. For example, see https://site.uvm.edu/tutortips/?page_id=1586.

110. Christina Manzo, "5 Lessons Library Websites Can Learn from Buzzfeed," *Weave* 1, no. 3 (2015): 10–21. https://doi.org/10.3998/weave.12535642.0001.302.

111. Paranjoy Guha Thakurta and Subi Chaturvedi, "Food and Nutrition Justice: How to Make it More Newsworthy?" *IDS Bulletin* 43, s1 (2012): 58–64. https://doi.org/10.1111/j.1759-5436.2012.00347.x.

112. Erika Falk and Kate Kenski, "Issue Saliency and Gender Stereotypes: Support for Women as Presidents in Times of War and Terrorism," *Social Science Quarterly* 87, no. 1 (2006): 1–18. https://doi.org/10.1111/j.0038-4941.2006.00365.x.

113. Gerdien de Vries, M. Rietkerk, and R. Kooger, "The Hassle Factor as a Psychological Barrier to a Green Home," *Journal of Consumer Policy* 43 (2020): 345–52. https://doi.org/10.1007/s10603-019-09410-7.

114. Richard E. Petty, Curtis P. Haugtvedt, and Stephen M. Smith, "Elaboration as a Determinant of Attitude Strength: Creating Attitudes That Are Persistent, Resistant, and Predictive of Behavior," in *Attitude Strength: Antecedents and Consequences*, ed. Richard E. Petty and Jon A. Krosnick (Mahwah, NJ: Lawrence Erlbaum, 1995): 93–130.

115. Tuck and Silverman, *The Counter-Narrative Handbook*, 9–11.

116. April Raneri and Jonathan Matusitz, "Source Representation in the Communication of Childhood Immunisation," *Child Care in Practice* 21, no. 2 (2015): 114–27. https://doi.org/10.1080/13575279.2014.966651.

117. Aldoory and Bonzo, "Using Communication Theory," 260–3.

118. Cited in de Vries, "Public Communication as a Tool," 249.

119. Gerald T. Gardner and Paul C. Stern, "The Short List: The Most Effective Actions US Households Can Take to Curb Climate Change," *Environment: Science and Policy for Sustainable Development* 50, no. 5 (2008): 12–25. https://doi.org/10.3200/ENVT.50.5.12-25; Folke Ölander and John Thøgersen, "Informing versus Nudging in Environmental Policy," *Journal of Consumer Policy* 37 (2011): 341–56. https://doi.org/10.1007/s10603-014-9256-2.

120. M. Schalkwijk, *Energie besparen doe je nu: Eindrapportage campagne–effectonderzoek* (Amsterdam: Kantar Public, 2017).

121. Robert Gifford, "The Dragons of Inaction: Psychological Barriers That Limit Climate Change Mitigation and Adaptation," *American Psychologist* 66, no. 4 (2011): 290–302. https://doi.org/10.1037/a0023566.

122. Tuck and Silverman, *The Counter-Narrative Handbook*, 20.

123. Jonathan Matusitz and Gerald-Mark Breen, "Consumer Dissatisfaction, Complaints, and the Involvement of Human Resource Personnel in the Hospitality and Tourism Industry," *Journal of Human Resources in Hospitality & Tourism* 8, no. 2 (2009): 234–46. https://doi.org/10.1080/15332840802269866.

124. Catalina Udani and Jonathan Matusitz, "Terrorism, Emotion, and Well-Being," in *Emotion, Well-Being, and Resilience: Theoretical Perspectives and Practical Applications*, ed. Rabindra Kumar Pradhan and Updesh Kumar (New York: Apple Academic Press, 2021): 425–38.

125. Mike Allen, "Comparing the Persuasive Effectiveness One- and Two-Sided Message," in *Persuasion: Advances through Meta-Analysis*, ed. Mike Allen and Raymond W. Preiss (Cresskill, NJ: Hampton Press, 1998): 87–98.

126. Daniel J. O'Keefe, "How to Handle Opposing Arguments in Persuasive Messages: A Meta-Analytic Review of the Effects of One-Sided and Two-Sided Messages," in *Communication Yearbook* 22 (1999): 209–49.

127. Richard L. Johannesen, *Ethics in Human Communication* (4th Ed.) (Prospect Heights, IL: Waveland Press, 1996): 69.

128. T. J. Larkin and Sandar Larkin, *Communicating Change: How to Win Support for New Business Directions* (New York: McGraw-Hill, 1994).

129. Stanley Deetz, *Transforming Communication, Transforming Business: Building Responsive and Responsible Workplaces* (Cresskill, NJ: Hampton Press, 1995).

130. Paul Capriotti and Hugo Pardo Kuklinski, "Assessing Dialogic Communication through the Internet in Spanish Museums," *Public Relations Review* 38, no. 4 (2012): 619–26. https://doi.org/10.1016/j.pubrev.2012.05.005.

131. Mikhail Bakhtin, "Forms of Time and the Chronotope in the Novel," in *The Dialogic Imagination: Four Essays by M.M. Bakhtin*, ed. Michael Holquist (Austin, TX: University of Texas Press, 1981): 84–283.

132. Eric M. Eisenberg, Linda Andrews, Alexandra Murphy, and Linda Laine-Timmerman, "Transforming Organizations through Communication," in *Organizational Communication and Change*, ed. Philip J. Salem (Cresskill, NJ: Hampton Press, 1999): 125–50, 142.

133. Michael L. Kent and Maureen Taylor, "Toward a Dialogic Theory of Public Relations," *Public Relations Review* 28, no. 1 (2002): 21–37. https://doi.org/10.1016/S0363-8111 (02)00108-X.

134. Michael L. Kent, Maureen Taylor, and William J. White, "The Relationship between Web Site Design and Organizational Responsiveness to Stakeholders," *Public Relations Review* 29, no. 1 (2003): 63–77. https://doi.org/10.1016/S0363-8111(02)00194-7.

135. Nick Couldry, Sonia Livingstone, and Tim Markham, *Media Consumption and Public Engagement. Beyond the Presumption of Attention* (London: Palgrave Macmillan, 2010): 3.

136. Ibid, 6.

137. Ibid, 3–8.

138. Tuck and Silverman, *The Counter-Narrative Handbook*, 21.

139. Sonja K. Foss and Cindy L. Griffin, "Beyond Persuasion: A Proposal for an Invitational Rhetoric," *Communication Monographs* 62, no. 1 (1995): 2–18, 5. https://doi.org/10. 1080/03637759509376345.

140. Richard L. Johannesen, "The Emerging Concept of Communication as Dialogue," *Quarterly Journal of Speech* 57, no. 4 (1971): 373–82. https://doi.org/10.1080/0033 5637109383082.

141. Loris Vezzalia, Małgorzata A. Gocłowska, Richard J. Crisp, and Sofia Stathi, "On the Relationship between Cultural Diversity and Creativity in Education: The Moderating Role of Communal versus Divisional Mindset," *Thinking Skills and Creativity* 21 (2016): 152–7. https://doi.org/10.1016/j.tsc.2016.07.001.

142. Martin Buber, *I and Thou* (translated by Ronald Gregor Smith) (New York: Charles Scribner's Sons, 1958).

143. Jürgen Habermas, *The Theory of Communicative Action, Vol. 1: Reason and the Rationalization of Society* (Boston, MA: Beacon, 1984).

144. Joohan Kim and Eun Joo Kim, "Theorizing Dialogic Deliberation: Everyday Political Talk as Communicative Action and Dialogue," *Communication Theory* 18, no. 1 (2008): 93–116, 96. https://doi.org/10.1111/j.1468-2885.2007.00313.x.

145. Sung–Un Yang, Minjeong Kang, and Heewon Cha, "A Study on Dialogic Communication, Trust, and Distrust: Testing a Scale for Measuring Organization-Public Dialogic Communication (OPDC)," *Journal of Public Relations Research* 27, no. 2 (2015): 175–92. https://doi.org/10.1080/1062726X.2015.1007998.

146. Sarah Trenholm and Arthur Jensen, *Interpersonal Communication* (4th Ed.) (Belmont, CA: Wadsworth, 2000).

147. Kent and Taylor, "Toward a Dialogic Theory of Public Relations," 27.

148. Herbert H. Clark and Susan E. Brennan, "Grounding in Communication," in *Perspectives on Socially Shared Cognition*, ed. Lauren B. Resnick, John M. Levine, and Stephanie D. Teasley (Washington, D.C.: American Psychological Association, 1991): 127–49.

149. Institute of Medicine, *Speaking of Health*, 265.

150. Ann Kronrod, Amir Grinstein, and Luc Wathieu, "Go Green! Should Environmental Messages Be So Assertive?" *Journal of Marketing* 76, no. 1 (2012): 95–102. https://doi.org/10.1509/jm.10.0416.

151. Richard Dawkins, *The Selfish Gene* (Oxford: Oxford University Press, 1976).

152. Bradley E. Wiggins and G. Bret Bowers, "Memes as Genre: A Structurational Analysis of the Memescape," *New Media & Society* 17, no. 11 (2015): 1886–1906. https://doi.org/10.1177/1461444814535194.

153. Macnamara, *Evaluating Public Communication*, 5.

154. Cited by Isabelle Albanese, *The 4Cs of Truth in Communications: How to Identify, Discuss, Evaluate and Present Stand-Out Effective Communication* (Ithaca, NY: Paramount Market Publishing, 2007): 10.

155. Macnamara, *Evaluating Public Communication*, 23–4.

156. Crawford and Okigbo, "Strategic Communication Campaigns," 19.

157. Marc Berg and Stefan Timmermans, *The Gold Standard: The Challenge of Evidence-Based Medicine and Standardization in Health Care* (Philadelphia, PA: Temple University Press, 2010).

158. Amy-Jane Gielen, "Countering Violent Extremism: A Realist Review for Assessing What Works, for Whom, in What Circumstances, and How?" *Terrorism and Political Violence* 31, no. 6 (2019): 1149–67. https://doi.org/10.1080/09546553.2017.1313736.

159. Seth M. Noar, Philip Palmgreen, Melissa Chabot, Nicole Dobransky, and Rick S. Zimmerman, "A 10-Year Systematic Review of HIV/AIDS Mass Communication Campaigns: Have We Made Progress?" *Journal of Health Communication* 14, no. 1 (2009): 15–42. https://doi.org/10.1080/10810730802592239.

160. Sandra Moriarty, Nancy Mitchell, and William D. Wells, *Advertising: Principles and Practice* (Upper Saddle River, NJ: Pearson, 2009).

161. D. Steve Roberts and E. Scott Geller, "A Statewide Intervention to Increase Safety Belt Use: Adding to the Impact of a Belt Use Law," *American Journal of Health Promotion* 8, no. 3 (1994): 172–4. https://doi.org/10.4278/0890-1171-8.3.172.

162. Heinz Bonfadelli and Thomas Friemel, "Using Communication Theory and Research Based Evidence to Improve Public Communication Health Campaigns," in *Tailoring Health Messages: Bridging the Gap between Social and Humanistic Perspectives on Health Communication*, ed. Sara Rubinelli and Joachim Haes (Monte Verità, Switzerland: International Conference of Monte Verità, 2005): 13–9.

163. Tuck and Silverman, *The Counter-Narrative Handbook*, 43.

164. Grier Bryant, "Social Marketing in Public Health," 325.

165. Atkin and Freimuth, "Guidelines for Formative Evaluation Research," 53–68.

166. Valente, "Evaluating Communications Campaigns," 105–24.

167. Noar, "A 10–Year Retrospective of Research," 30.

168. Leslie B. Snyder, Mark A. Hamilton, Elizabeth W. Mitchell, James Kiwanuka-Tondo, Fran Fleming-Milici, and Dwayne Proctor, "A Meta-Analysis of the Effect of Mediated Health Communication Campaigns on Behavior Change in the United States," *Journal of Health Communication* 9, no. 1 (2004): 71–96. https://doi.org/10.1080/10810730490271548.

169. See Tuck and Silverman, *The Counter-Narrative Handbook*, 44.

170. Macnamara, *Evaluating Public Communication*, 160–1.

171. Richard Rogers, "Otherwise Engaged: Social Media from Vanity Metrics to Critical Analytics," *International Journal of Communication* 12 (2018): 450–72.

172. Tuck and Silverman, *The Counter-Narrative Handbook*, 45.

173. Macnamara, *Evaluating Public Communication*, 160.

CHAPTER 3

Persuasion in Public Communication Campaigns

Persuasion began with the Ancient Greeks, who accentuated rhetoric and diction as the highest criteria for successful politicians. Trials were conducted before the Assembly, and both the prosecution and the defense depended—as it is still the case today—on the persuasive capabilities of the orator.[1] Contemporary scholars have described persuasion in various ways. The following nine definitions describe how different researchers approach the topic. Persuasion has been framed both as a form of influence (the first four definitions) and as a method of communication (the last five definitions). As such, **persuasion** is

- an attempt to manipulate an individual's beliefs, attitudes, objectives, motivations, or behaviors;[2]
- a deliberate attempt by someone to change another person or group of people through sending a specific message;[3]
- an active effort by advocates to "change the utility functions of other players to reflect some new normative commitment";[4]
- a conscious effort to change an individual's mental state through communication in a situation in which the persuader has some degree of freedom;[5]
- "a communicative activity; thus, there must be a message for persuasion, as opposed to other forms of social influence, to occur";[6]
- a communication practice whereby the communicator wants to obtain an expected response from his or her recipient;[7]
- a "communication strategy designed to satisfy the needs of the parties involved by influencing attitudes and beliefs, therefore, behavior";[8]

- the "transmission of a message. The message may be verbal or nonverbal. It can be relayed interpersonally, through mass media, or via the internet. It may be reasonable or unreasonable, factual, or emotional";[9]
- a symbolic pursuit of which the purpose is to influence the internalization or intentional acceptance of novel cognitive states or patterns of explicit behavior through the sharing of messages;[10]

Taken as a whole, persuasion takes place within a context of deliberate messages that are sent by a communicator in an attempt to influence the receiver, in addition to an awareness that the recipient has a mental state that is prone to change.[11]

Three Types of Messages

Public communication campaigns generally contain three types of messages: awareness, instruction, and persuasive messages. **Awareness messages** impart fairly simple content that shows people what to do, details who should do it, or offers cues as to when and where things should be done. Even on-the-surface messages can motivate the audience to identify richer, in-depth content from expounded informational resources like websites, books, and opinion leaders. The more complex **instruction messages** relay how-to information in campaigns that seek to generate knowledge gain or skills acquisition. Examples are increasing self-efficacy in strengthening peer resistance and gaining media literacy skills. However, the main form of content in campaigns includes **persuasive messages**.[12] With respect to persuasive messages, public communication campaigns incorporate persuasion appeals that highlight reasons why people should adopt the recommended action or keep away from the proscribed behavior. For individuals who are favorably prone, the campaign has the mission to reinforce current predispositions. This consists of amplifying a positive attitude, advocating postbehavior consolidation, and promoting behavior continuance over time. As long-lasting campaigns tend to diffuse a vast array of persuasive messages, planners will develop a myriad of appeals centered on motivational incentives made for shaping attitudes and behaviors.[13]

Three Paths of Persuasion

There are generally three paths that public communication campaigns use to persuade audiences. The first consists of exposing audiences directly to the persuasive messages of the campaign. This can be done through media advertisements and educational programs, among others. The second path rests on a dissemination of campaign themes to other social entities, like the mass media, the executive and legislative branches of government, the judicial system, law enforcement, and religious groups.[14] Some campaigns embrace a media advocacy factor created to attract media and policy attention to the campaign objectives,[15] whereas others are a magnet for institutional attention.[16] The third path of influence includes campaign-induced methods of social diffusion. Through social interaction with relatives, peers, or citizens in the community, the audience learns about recommended or proscribed behaviors in society. They also become familiar with the advantages and disadvantages of performing each behavior within a social context. This method of social diffusion, in turn, helps influence attitudes, behaviors, beliefs, and intentions.[17]

Irrespective of the path of persuasion, some campaigns may expect instant results while others anticipate delayed responses because the success of their messages depends on a social or institutional model of diffusion (instead of a direct-learning standard). As a rule of thumb, social or institutional diffusion takes longer than one-on-one persuasion. The reason campaigns may take longer lies in the way recommended behaviors are addressed within a deeper social or cultural environment, and people will need frequent convincing before they are willing to change. In like fashion, some of the impacts may take longer to come through because the occasions to undertake new behaviors are themselves delayed. It should be noted that assessments that measure results too prematurely may easily lead to false positives or wrong conclusions about the impacts.[18]

LOGOS, PATHOS, AND ETHOS

Logos, pathos, and ethos are three methods of persuasion to appeal to audiences. The three appeals, even if different, can be integrated to create an overall persuasive argument. These rhetorical techniques are used not only in public communication campaigns, but also in political debates, oral presentations, texts, newspaper articles, and even marketing.[19]

Logos

According to Aristotle, **logos** is an appeal to facts. It is the heart of an argument, the words that rhetors will include. Public communication campaigns are especially predominant in war, but as revolutions demonstrated throughout the twentieth century, firepower arguments (logos) in and of themselves do not contribute to victory in war, and will win only a few hearts and minds.[20] Logos consists of introducing the arguments in one's messages from various sources (instead of just one). This is more likely to boost message credibility. An efficient strategy is to reframe persuasive messages through reasonable repetition of solid arguments. This can be done by introducing or previewing strong arguments at the beginning of the communication or text, developing them later in the message, and restating them at the end of it.[21]

Supporting arguments with evidence can lead people to reach logical conclusions. Methods to enhance the logical appeal of a message include (1) being well organized, (2) ensuring that claims rest on credible evidence, and (3) being transparent in presenting that evidence. Whatever method is used, consistency is important. If we articulate a seemingly logical message with weak or inconsistent evidence, there is a chance that the audience becomes skeptical about the arguments and even the entire message. Logos can also be attained through axioms, descriptions, and demonstrations. An **axiom** is a declaration that is believed to be true. It is employed as a premise or starting point for additional reasoning and arguments.[22]

Pathos

Pathos is an appeal made to people's emotions. Pathos habitually incorporates detailed examples and stories. In essence, it tells the audience why the message is important to them.[23] Emotion plays a predominant role in persuasion and attitude change. A great deal of research has stressed the value of pathos in influencing receivers through emotional manipulation. Emotion works in tandem with our thought process regarding a topic or situation. Emotional appeals are evident in advertising, health campaigns, and political communiqués. This is particularly true for tobacco advertising (and, conversely, no-smoking health campaigns) and political campaigns using fear-mongering. Emotion-based attitude change is highly obvious in the cognitive process of serial killers who experience high levels of stress.[24] There is ample empirical support for the notion that strong emotions such as fear arousal, empathy, or great excitement increase attitude change under certain conditions.[25]

Ethos

Ethos is an appeal to credibility. It is the reliability of the source on persuasive communication. Ethos is constructed to establish trustworthiness for the audience. Generally, the most effective public communication campaigns are those perceived as trustworthy and expert-like in relevant domains.[26] Ethos influences the receiver's perception of a communicator's credibility, competence, trustworthiness, and benevolence. To improve acceptance of the message, the campaign must rely on credible representatives and/or entities that mix trustworthiness and expertise. The ideal ethos is the one where the campaign appears diligently prepared and organized, and one that projects itself as having a caring attitude towards the audience.[27]

The people who diffuse information from the campaign should demonstrate suitable behaviors during that campaign, which is pivotal in increasing the message's credibility. To have a messenger that the audience views as credible, think of the messenger (and message) like a song. The lyrics might be great, but the performer needs a great voice too. Keep in mind whom the audience will trust, be encouraged by, or listen to the most. A multitude of effective messengers can be selected for each audience: well-established organizations, charities, or projects germane to the type of audience to be reached; people respected by the audience (like popular athletes, musicians, or actors); or charismatic and respected faith, community, or youth leaders and advocates.[28]

For some audiences, the message originator is more important than the message presenter. This is why campaign developers themselves should, first and foremost, be credible too. They should measure up with the reliability of the source of the institution—the one promoting the campaign—as much as possible.[29] When choosing appropriate, effective sources of messages, it is essential to understand the multifaceted characteristics of the target audience. Key questions to be addressed include the following: Who are the best people to influence the relevant behaviors of the audience in a specific culture? Which types of people are seen as the most important role models in that culture? Whom do people trust for scientific information? Besides authority figures, professionals, peers, parents, role models, and celebrities, are there other people who could be a great new type of messenger too?[30]

BEHAVIOR CHANGE COMMUNICATION (BCC)

Behavior Change Communication (BCC) is a strategy that uses communication to motivate individuals or communities to change their behavior. It encourages people to embrace healthy, beneficial, and positive behavior habits.[31] Hence, BCC has the task to diffuse well-tailored messages to get people to modify their behaviors. It is an interactive method that seeks to equip individuals with the tools to sustain a new behavior, with a special focus on the environment in which the message is accepted or not. BCC's interactive process is often integrated within a broader program to create tailored messages and approaches based on diverse communication channels to promote and uphold individual, community, and societal behavior change.[32] There are four elements inherent to BCC: behavioral intention, belief change, priming, and repeated exposure.

Behavioral Intention

Behavioral intention is the degree of likelihood that an individual will perform a particular behavior.[33] BCC stipulates that talking about facts alone is not sufficient to ensure behavior change. This is why BCC strategies focus on behavioral intention to identify the motivational factors that inspire a certain behavior. Ultimately, the more one intends to perform the behavior, the more one will actually enact that behavior.[34] BCC can help adjust the stage of behavior adoption of people and develop skills required to allow and sustain change. From this vantage point, BCC is a useful approach for health communication campaigns against HIV and AIDS. For example, in Mexico, medical professionals collaborated with truck drivers, marginalized youths, and traveling female merchants to develop a radio campaign with HIV- and AIDS-related messages.[35]

In another example, Public Health England (2016)[36] used, and continues to use, a four-step BCC model in its campaigns aiming at (1) improving knowledge to inform audiences on risks, (2) transforming beliefs to encourage audiences to change, (3) offering support to help people to change, and (4) providing information and support to maintain new behavior. This is based on a widespread body of research with respect to behavior change.[37] The unequivocal accent on behavior change as the ideal solution signals the need for a systematic understanding of the possibility of influences (internal and external) that ascertain why people act the way they do and how to motivate changes in behavior.[38]

Belief Change

Hornik and Woolf (1999)[39] present three factors to take into account when targeting beliefs to be changed in a communication campaign and similar types of intervention. First, in the population in question, the belief should have a high correlation with the intention or behavior that needs modification. Second, there should a sufficient number of people whose beliefs need change (to justify trying to change them). An example is the belief that "smoking causes bad health." Because this belief is already shared by many smokers and nonsmokers alike, little can be done to try to change it. Therefore, one must realize whether a campaign designed to transform a belief has the ability to move enough individuals to make it worthwhile. Third, one must think about whether changing a belief is even doable. In other words, can a campaign target a belief with a reasonable argument based on solid evidence?

If 80% of people "strongly agree" that they should adopt the new behavior under consideration, then reinforcing this belief is appropriate for a campaign. Thus, it is essential to contemplate "belief strength" and to conclude whether intensifying current beliefs (i.e., getting people to shift from "quite likely" to "extremely likely") could have an effect on their intentions (and behavior). Communications that can move individuals from "quite" to "extremely" likely can considerably influence the possibility that these people will develop serious intentions to perform the behavior in question. At the same time, not all beliefs are necessarily subject to change, and almost nothing can be accomplished by targeting a belief that is very hard, if not impossible, to change.[40]

Priming

Priming is a phenomenon whereby exposure to one stimulus inspires a reaction to another stimulus later, without intention or deliberate guidance.[41] In a sense, priming is the reinforcement of the covariance between two variables. It may also entail a certain degree of belief change, although not always a change in mean behavior intensity. Put another way, the extent of the correlation depends on the association between two variables, in addition to the entire variance of each of the two variables. Changes in variance are caused by changes in one's behavior.[42] Instead of focusing solely on beliefs that clearly distinguish intenders from nonintenders (or players from nonplayers), it would be prudent to target beliefs that (1) favor a given behavior, (2) are shared to a certain extent by most of the population, and (3) have at least a low or reasonable connection with the intention or behavior at hand. Focusing on these beliefs could reinforce their relationships with attitudes, perceived norms, or self-efficacy. When increases in the relationships between variables occur, it is an illustration of priming.[43]

Repeated Exposure

Sometimes referred to as **argument from repetition,** *argumentum ad nauseam,* or *argumentum ad infinitum*, **repeated exposure** is a technique that uses constant repetition of a message. When a message is repeated time and time again, it is more likely to be recalled and applied.[44] A good question would be to know how many exposures to a message within a certain period of time are necessary to induce behavior change. Conversely, how many exposures can cause a message to be in a decreasing return, to the point of turning the audience off (i.e., rejection of the message)? Repeated exposure by a person gives more opportunities for learning and applying the content of the message. For instance, 10 exposures to a message that smoking cannabis will impair parent–child relations may create more awareness and belief change than, say, five exposures. Repeated exposure to a message also may have the aforementioned priming effect.[45]

Youngsters may already be aware that parents would be distressed if they smoked cannabis, but they may consider not smoking it if they get exposed to repeated messages on this issue. Repetition implies a message that the topic is critical for consideration in making a choice about drug use. When a message is diffused through a multitude of communication channels, repeated exposure may transmit an implied message about what is socially anticipated. Repeated messages about smoking cannabis may tackle particular troubles about the corollaries, but they will also carry meaning about the nature of social norms for the health behavior modification.[46]

Of equal relevance is the fact that repetition through various channels may communicate the meta-message that society is concerned about this health issue. Similarly, repeated exposure to a message in this manner may step up the probability of interpersonal conversations of the message, which, in turn, amplifies exposure and dissemination of a communication message. Finally, repeated exposure entails an implicit legitimization of the topic of the health message. It often increases the likelihood of paying attention to potential new policies regarding the problem. Politicians tend to like high-exposure issues.[47] The next three sections describe three theories of BCC: self-affirmation theory, the Elaboration Likelihood Model (ELM), and the Transtheoretical Model.

SELF-AFFIRMATION THEORY

Developed by Steele (1988),[48] **self-affirmation theory** hypothesizes that people's contemplations of values that are personally dear to them will make them less likely to undergo distress or react in a defensive manner when faced with information that challenges or jeopardizes their self-concept. Also called **self-construction**, **self-identity**, or **sense of self**, **self-concept** refers to a set of beliefs about oneself. Put simply, it is a cognitive or descriptive part of one's self. It also includes past, present, and future selves.[49]

The Three Components

As a psychological theory, self-affirmation theory focuses on how people become accustomed to information or situations that are threatening to their self-concept. The theory has three components. First, self-affirmations increase self-resources, implying that people are imbued with a flexible self-system, so much so that they can react to pressure in one sphere of life by avowing self-worth in other spheres. In social psychology studies, there have been experiments whereby individuals affirm fundamental values within the framework of self-threatening situations. Second, and as a consequence of all this, self-affirmations broaden the spectrum with which humans interpret information and events in their lives and may illustrate permanent effects by transforming the nature of continuing experience. Third, self-affirmations initiate a dissociation between the self and the threat, decreasing the threat's effects in influencing the self. This paradigm helps understand what happens when people affirm values in the context of threats.[50] The objective of these three components is to sustain a unique experience of the self that is capable, coherent, unwavering, and open to free choice—i.e., a competent self that controls outcomes.[51]

Self-Integrity

Self-affirmation theory postulates that people are motivated to protect their self-integrity. **Self-integrity** is one's perception of oneself as a good, moral human being, who acts in a manner consistent with cultural and social norms.[52] Self-integrity can be reflected through the state of being independent, clever, a helpful citizen, part of a community or family, and/or part of a few subgroups. Threats against one's self-integrity are situations or communications that carry the meaning that a person is not good or adequate in certain domains. According to the tenets of self-affirmation theory, when people experience threats to one of these domains, they are driven to uphold a positive image of themselves—e.g., in public, on social media, and so forth.[53] Public communication campaigns have more chances to succeed when an expected threat to one's self-integrity is clear to the audience.

On the other hand, we are more likely to refuse to accept the message when self-affirmation emerges in the same sphere as the threat. The reason is that the incongruity between what a person believes to be and what a message asks him or her to be is obvious. The challenge, here, for campaign planners is to come up with messages that do not affirm the audience in threat-related spheres but, rather, affirm them in spheres with no connections to the threat.[54] Research has shown that self-affirmation in the latter spheres contributes to more methodical, unbiased information processing[55] and augments accessibility of threat-related cognitions.[56] This leads to profound and unbiased processing of the message and enhances message acceptance, especially after messages are framed with respect to the consequences of the risky behavior.[57]

THE ELABORATION LIKELIHOOD MODEL (ELM)

Developed by Petty and Cacioppo (1986),[58] the **Elaboration Likelihood Model** (**ELM**) is based on the premise that people with motivation and ability are more prone to initiating elaborative processing. **Elaboration** is the level at which the audience scrutinizes a message. It is "the extent to which a person carefully thinks about issue-relevant information."[59] With elaboration, the person considers or mentally changes arguments inherent in the communication. **Likelihood**, alluding to the chance that an event will take place, recognizes that elaboration can be either likely or unlikely. Elaboration can be located along a wide spectrum, with one end typified by substantial cogitation on the fundamental merits of an issue, and the other by comparatively insignificant reflection. The model can inform us as to when individuals should be more likely to elaborate, or not elaborate, on campaign messages.[60] Knowledge is a highly important component. When we know a great deal about an issue, we process information thoroughly and competently. When examining a message, we become better at separating the wheat from the chaff than those with only a modicum of knowledge on the issue. We can better gauge the coherence of information and are skillful at pinpointing flaws within message arguments.[61] ELM explains two major routes to persuasion: the central route and the peripheral route.

Central Route

Under the **central route**, persuasion has more chances to succeed when coming from an individual's painstaking and thoughtful examination of the true merits of the information offered in support of an issue. The central route contains a high degree of message elaboration in which much cognition about the arguments is created by the message recipient. The outcome of attitude change is quite permanent, resilient, and predictive of behavior. **Central route processing**, then, is persuasion reached through the quality of the arguments in a message. The way of the central route is paved by extensive cognitive elaboration. Here, people devote much time and energy to the main features of the issue or message. When human beings process information centrally, they fastidiously assess message arguments, reflect on the implications of the communicator's ideas, and try to connect information to their own value system. This is the thoughtful individual's route to persuasion.[62]

Central route information processing is also referred to as **active information processing** and **active cognition**. The reason is that, in this framework of information processing, we rationally analyze and cogitate, taking empirical facts into consideration and contemplating an issue in great depth. The proper functioning of the central route is contingent upon a number of things. These include the degree of involvement, predominantly influenced by the importance of an issue or problem, self-inclination towards critical thinking, and the inspiration by other people like peers.[63]

Peripheral Route

Under the **peripheral route**, persuasion has more chances to succeed when coming from an individual's level of interest in an issue (without actually conducting a painstaking and thoughtful examination) or when he or she makes an easy inference about the merits of that issue. Under the peripheral route, the positive or negative cues received by the person do not necessarily have a correlation with the logical quality of the stimulus. These cues generally include factors like the reliability and appeal (i.e., ethos) of the source of the message or the quality of the message itself. In other terms, the audience gives a small amount of consideration to the message without elaborated thought. **Peripheral route processing**, then, is the influence of a message from factors external to the quality of the message. The peripheral route is totally different. Instead of analyzing issue-relevant arguments, the audience analyzes the message swiftly or concentrates on superficial cues to help them determine whether to accept the position championed in the message. Reasons that are not grounded in logos (but peripheral to message arguments) prevail. These can include a communicator's physique, smooth talking style, or friendly connection between the message and music playing in the surroundings. When processing peripherally, we regularly put our faith in uncomplicated decision-making rules or heuristics.[64]

Heuristics are any methods of problem-solving that may not be ideal or rational, but that are nevertheless adequate enough for reaching instant, short-term objectives or approximations.[65] Heuristics are mental shortcuts, mental blueprints, and, on some occasions, emotions.[66] Heuristics are experience-based "rules of thumb" that we use to interpret meaning and make quick decisions. Frequently applied heuristics include credibility (i.e., like source credibility), appreciating a person or thing (i.e., we often agree with those we like), and consensus (i.e., based on appeal to the majority or to popular opinion). Heuristics for information processing and decision-making also include habit (e.g., voting for the party line in elections) or purchasing a product brand to which we are accustomed.[67]

THE TRANSTHEORETICAL MODEL

Developed by Prochaska, DiClemente, and Norcross (1992),[68] the **Transtheoretical Model** is a model of behavior change that emphasizes the decision-making of the person. It has been useful for building successful campaigns that advocate health behavior change. The model explains how we change a problematic behavior or take on a positive behavior. Although we are aware that we need to make changes in our lives, we do it in steps and not through one major life transformation. As such, the Transtheoretical Model interprets change as a process that evolves through five main stages: (1) Precontemplation, (2) contemplation, (3) preparation, (4) action, and (5) maintenance. During these stages, we think about the problem, mull over what to do, and make a decision as to whether or not to take action.[69]

The Five Stages

Precontemplation is the stage during which we do not intend to change behavior in the immediate future. Many people in this stage are unaware or do not care for their problems. **Contemplation** is the stage during which we are aware of a problem and are seriously contemplating overcoming it. However, we have not made a decision to take action yet. **Preparation** is a stage that mixes intention and behavioral conditions. People in this stage want to take action in the foreseeable future, but have so far unsuccessfully done so. **Action** is the stage during which we change our behavior, experiences, or context in order to conquer our problems. Action entails the most explicit behavior changes and necessitates serious devotion of time and energy. **Maintenance** is the stage during which we make efforts to avoid relapse and consolidate the gains achieved during action. For addictive behaviors, for example, this stage goes from half a year to an undetermined period after the initial action.[70] The next section applies the Transtheoretical Model to the struggles of obesity. Given the current worldwide epidemic of obesity, there is a growing need for public communication campaigns with high impact.

Application to the Struggles of Obesity

The five stages of change can be applied to the struggle against obesity in the United States. To begin, in the precontemplation stage, regarding the domain of physical activity, an individual would not be active or considering becoming active at any point in the immediate future. An individual is now in the stage of contemplation when he or she becomes cognizant of a desire to modify a specific behavior. This stage usually involves a number of sedentary citizens in the United States, who have considered being physically active, but do not have enough commitment to change their behavior. When a person is in the preparation stage, he or she will change behavior for regular, moderate physical activity by looking for information on regular activity. The person will also call local gyms or muster support from relatives, friends, or colleagues for a lunchtime activity program. When taking physical activity into consideration, attitude translates into action such as changing routines, reworking our schedule around physical activity, and devising strategies to tackle the numerous environmental obstacles to engaging in physical activity.[71]

The fifth stage, maintenance, consists of continuous change of the behavior in question. However, people may experience a relapse to an earlier stage. The seasonal climate variations in many regions of the United States explain why relapse may be hard to avoid during maintenance. In the summer, the temperature is hotter and the days are longer, making outdoor activity easy. As the seasons become colder and the days are shorter, keeping levels of activity may be a challenge to people who have only a handful of indoor facilities available.[72] *Vis-à-vis* the last two stages (action and maintenance), we can also include higher food selectivity and impulse control as factors because they smooth the progress for the sustainability of behavior change.[73]

UNDERSTANDING ATTITUDE

Attitudes are evaluative cognitive structures that prompt us to behave in certain ways. They are a function of perceived attractiveness and likelihood of anticipated outcomes. They are also defined as learned predispositions to react in a consistently positive or negative manner in regards to a particular object.[74] Attitudes are not merely beliefs; they are also methods of reacting based, in some measure, on our beliefs. There are three dimensions to attitudes:[75]

- The **cognitive dimension** entails what we know about a subject. Attitude, then, is a psychological construct. It is a mental phenomenon that is peculiar to a person.[76]
- The **affective dimension** entails what we feel about a subject. Attitudes usually deal with affect and emotions. As Eagly and Chaiken (1998)[77] note, "attitudes express passions and hates, attractions and repulsions, likes and dislikes."
- The **behavioral dimension** entails what we believe should be done about an issue. Attitudes shape behavior. They guide our decision-making and maneuver us in the direction of doing what we think should be done. In many environments, connections between attitude and behavior are cherished, so we provide much effort to "practice what we preach." We often convert attitudes into behavior, but it is not always the case.[78]

Attitude Object

Attitude is a learned assessment of a phenomenon that guides our thoughts and actions. We are not born with attitudes, but we learn them through a gradual accumulation of experiences, which signifies that attitudes are primarily evaluations. Having an attitude implies that we have determined something and made a decision of its overall value or worth. We no longer remain neutral on the issue.[79] The notion around which an attitude develops and can transform in due course is called **attitude object**. Attitude object denotes an evaluative integration of both cognition and affect with respect to the attitude object. An illustration of an attitude object is an automobile. We can embrace a range of beliefs about automobiles— e.g., cognition that an automobile is fast—as well as assessments of those beliefs—e.g., affect; for example, we might appreciate or enjoy the fact that the vehicle is fast. Taken as a whole, these beliefs and affective evaluations of those beliefs symbolize an attitude towards the object of the automobile and leads us into temptation to purchase one.[80]

Attitude Change

Attitudes are not steady. They get altered by social influences, such as erratic patterns of communication and behavior by other people, as well as the person's drive to keep cognitive consistency when cognitive dissonance happens. As discussed in the previous chapter, cognitive dissonance is a phenomenon whereby two attitudes (or attitude and behavior) are incompatible. Attitudes and attitude objects also depend on affective and cognitive factors.[81] It has been postulated that the interstructural mechanism of an associative network can be modified by the initiation of a single node (part of the network). Therefore, by initiating an affective or emotional node, attitude change is likely, even if the affective and cognitive functions can be entangled.[82] There are three pillars for attitude change: compliance, identification, and internalization. These three processes represent the different levels of attitude change:[83]

- **Compliance** refers to behavior change according to consequences, such as someone's aspirations to obtain rewards or escape punishment from another group or individual. He or she does not necessarily change his or her beliefs or perceptions of an attitude object. On the contrary, he or she is inspired by the social outcomes of embracing behavior change.

- **Identification** describes someone's change of beliefs and affect in order to emulate a person that someone respects. This is why the person espouses the new attitude, not because of the particular content of the attitude object, but because it is mentally connected with the desired relationship. In general, children's perceptions of race or their political views are inspired by their parents' attitudes and beliefs. The apple does not fall far from the tree.
- **Internalization** refers to change of beliefs and affect upon realizing that the content of the attitude is inherently rewarding, and thus results in genuine change of beliefs or evaluations of an attitude object. The new attitude or behavior is in harmony with the person's value system, and is often mixed with the individual's current values and beliefs. Under these circumstances, behaviors espoused through internalization originate from the content of the attitude object.

Ego

Ego is defined as self-concept or the view that one has of one's self. Ego is revealed by "the characteristic feelings of continuity and permanence the individual has about himself."[84] A stimulus is ego-involving inasmuch as it helps us preserve our sense of self-identity. As Sherif and Cantril (1947) continue, "all attitudes that define a person's status or that give him some relative role with respect toother individuals, groups, or institutions are ego-involved."[85] Ego is highly correlated with attitude. Ostrom and Brock (1968)[86] aver that "the basic feature of an ego-involved attitude is its relation to the manner in which the individual defines himself. The individual defines himself primarily in terms of that 'distinct constellation of social and personal values' he has acquired." Attitudes and actions are influenced by values, and our favorite "mode of conduct and end-state of existence"[87] embody our values. This standpoint on ego involvement corresponds to Sherif and Cantril's (1947)[88] statement that "these contents of ego provide for the individuals the standards of judgment or frames of reference which determine to such an important degree his social behavior and reactions." The following three sections describe three attitude-centered theories so central to campaigns: social judgment theory (SJT), attitude accessibility theory, and expectancy theory.

SOCIAL JUDGMENT THEORY (SJT)

Developed by Sherif and Hovland (1961),[89] **social judgment theory** (**SJT**) rests on the premise that an idea is interpreted and deduced after comparing it with existing attitudes. A person gauges every new idea, stacking it up with his or her current perspective to conclude where it should be granted prominence on the attitude scale in his or her mind. This is also referred to as **reference point** or **anchor**; an individual's own attitude can be used as a reference point that shapes opinions on an issue. The reference point is a three-part latitude: acceptance, rejection, and noncommiment.[90] Research has demonstrated time and again that we place issues high on the attitude scale when we pay more attention to persuasive messages from communication campaigns.[91] We also undertake a higher level of elaboration[92] and our information processing is more objective and less partial.[93]

The Three-Part Latitude

According to the theory, attitudes consist of a **latitude of acceptance** (i.e., the scope of acceptable positions), a **latitude of rejection** (i.e., the breadth of objectionable positions), and a **latitude of noncommitment** (i.e., the range of viewpoints that are neither acceptable nor unpleasant).[94] When someone becomes more ego-concerned with an issue, the latitude of rejection goes up, whereas the latitudes of noncommitment and acceptance go down.[95] SJT is based on the notion that the impact of a persuasive message on a certain issue is contingent upon such latitude, on the way that the audience judges the position that the message advocates.[96] Sherif, Sherif, and Nebergall (1965)[97] argue that our attitudes towards a specific issue or behavior are not necessarily mirrored by a single alternative or opinion among those available. In SJT, each message recipient evaluates the range of alternatives on their own terms, and then these judgments can be merged "to reflect the consensus, defined by social norms, prevailing among given people." People frequently integrate statements that match their own attitudes and compare statements that are quite distant from their attitudes.[98]

Persuasion as a Two–Stage Process

In SJT, persuasion is regarded as a two–stage judgmental course of action. When exposed to a persuasive message, the receiver interprets the message with respect to their intended attitude position (i.e., the reference point). At first, if the message is likely to be accepted or rejected, the message's content is likely to be distorted too. Receivers will minimize the incongruity between the anchor and a message when the message falls in the range of acceptance. On the other hand, receivers maximize the incongruity when the message falls in the range of rejection. Afterwards, attitude change depends on the inconsistency between the message and the anchor.[99] Thus, messages that fall in the range of acceptance (i.e., because of an assimilation effect) will be viewed as resembling one's ideas or emotions more than they really are. Messages that fall in the range of rejection (i.e., because of a contrast effect) will be viewed as contradicting one's ideas or emotions more than they really are. In the end, messages that fall in either of these ranges (acceptance and rejection) would not be accepted at all. Conversely, "the messages that fall within the range (or latitude) of noncommitment should result in acceptance and behavior change."[100]

ATTITUDE ACCESSIBILITY THEORY

Developed by Fazio and Zanna (1978),[101] **attitude accessibility theory** postulates that attitudes towards more familiar objects are more developed and become more accessible than attitudes towards less familiar objects. Consequently, these attitudes are easily recovered from memory. There may be contending attitudes or beliefs about a target behavior or other attitude object. The most accessible attitudes from memory when a decision or evaluation is to be made will determine the outcome.[102] Attitudes may also be more accessible (1) due to related direct experience,[103] (2) for the reason that they fall within the context or cues in the environment when a decision is to be made,[104] or (3) owing to recent or coexisting exposure to interpersonal or mediated communication.[105]

Examples

Attitude accessibility theory is relevant to an oft-cited issue in health communication and behavior change: bridging the distance between intention and behavior.[106] There are scores of health behaviors that we agree we should do, want, and intend to do. However, it is usually not the case, or at least we do not in an adequately sustained manner. This is frequent both for primary prevention (e.g., as in people's goals and difficulties with respect to diet, exercise, and sunscreen use) and for secondary prevention (e.g., colon cancer checkups, Pap tests, mammography, and HIV/AIDS testing).[107] Likewise, based on this theory, our attitude *vis-à-vis* Budweiser is accessible, or likely to be promptly activated, from memory. Our favorable attitude *vis-à-vis* Bud Lite is a predictor of our purchasing habit. If we are in touch with our attitudes, we will act on them. If not, we will be influenced by salient aspects of the circumstances.[108] This corresponds to the core tenet of the theory that most of us are likely to have a low connection between an activity and our evaluation of it.[109] Accessible attitudes are more able to predict behavior than less accessible ones.[110] Individuals with more accessible attitudes regarding the topic of a message will more often process that message methodically.[111]

Biased Message Processing

Biased message processing refers to the selective use of information according to memory and experience, which may result in flawed subjective perception of information during the course of persuasion.[112] Ahluwalia (2000)[113] suggests three mechanisms for biased message processing: distorted assimilation, denial/minimization of impact, and relative weighting.

- **Distorted assimilation** is the selective acceptance of message content (or rejection of it) and prejudiced application of such content in ensuing message processing. Attitude-consistent information is regarded as more valid and accurate, whereas attitude-inconsistent content is regarded as less so (even if, in theory, both are just as valid), leading to resistance to persuasion. As a consequence, distorted assimilation will go in two directions: (1) The direction can be positive when message advocacy is attitude-consistent and the content is interpreted as more valid than it really is; and (2) the direction can be negative when message advocacy is attitude-inconsistent and the content is perceived as less valid.[114]
- **Denial or minimization of impact** depends on the extent to which a persuasive message influences people's beliefs about the attitudinal object. For instance, the American Legacy Foundation's "truth" campaign has some impact on teenagers' perceptions of the tobacco industry.[115] Yet, if teenagers distinguish the tobacco companies' untruthfulness from the dangers of tobacco smoking, the effects of industry-attack messages on attitudes regarding smoking will be negligible. Teenagers can also minimize the significance attributed to such information when the effects of anti-industry messages are not totally ignored. When either of these two processes happens, persuasion will likely fail.[116]
- **Relative weighting** is a prioritization tactic that takes both the advantages and the disadvantages of an action into account.[117]

EXPECTANCY THEORY

Developed by Victor Vroom (1964),[118] **expectancy theory** rests on the predication that individuals' behaviors or actions are guided by their motivations to choose a particular behavior of action over others. The reason is that the motivation to select the behavior or action is influenced by the appeal of the outcome. Thus, the theory places a heavy focus on motivation behind decision-making. **Motivation** is a phenomenon whereby choices are governed by various forms of voluntary activities. The process is always governed by the person. We make choices according to evaluations of how well the anticipated results of a certain behavior will correspond with or eventually result in the desired results.

Intrinsic and Extrinsic Motivation

Motivation is a result of the person's expectation that a particular endeavor will give rise to (1) the intended performance, (2) the instrumentality of this performance to attaining an outcome, and (3) the desirability of this result for the person—which is called valence.[119] Our motivation may be guided by external forces (extrinsic motivation) or by themselves (intrinsic motivation). The difference between intrinsic motivation and extrinsic motivation is a function of the type of actions behind it. **Intrinsic motivation** is motivation guided by an internal desire to perform a task and **extrinsic motivation** is motivation guided by the desire to accomplish a task so as to receive some type of reward.[120]

Let us take the example of our intrinsic motivation to earn good grades in college. Most of us are intrinsically motivated when we credit our educational results to factors under our own control, also known as autonomy or locus of control. This phenomenon also occurs when we believe that we possess the skills to be effective players in achieving our desired goals, also known as self-efficacy beliefs. And we are intrinsically motivated out of an interest in mastering an academic subject (not just to earn good grades) and when it is not from pressure, but from interest in that subject.[121] Extrinsic motivation comes from influences external to us. With extrinsic motivation, a difficult question to address is where do we obtain the motivation to continue acting and persevere. In general, extrinsic motivation is used to achieve results that we would not be able to do from intrinsic motivation. Frequent extrinsic motivations in a public communication campaign can be financial rewards if the main message is that hard and industrious work will reap more benefits. At the same time, the risk of negative outcomes as a consequence of misbehavior (i.e., neglecting to work hard and industriously) would motivate us to compete. Competition is an example of extrinsic motivation because it drives us to win and to defeat others, not merely to get pleasure from the activity's intrinsic reward.[122]

Three Components of Expectancy Theory

Expectancy theory is made up of three key variables: expectancy, instrumentality, and valence. The first one, **expectancy**, is the person's belief that efforts will lead to a desirable performance. This variable is influenced by our conviction of our ability to perform successfully, the challenge of the mission presented, and our perceived control over the anticipated result. The second variable is **instrumentality**. This is our belief that we will get a reward if we perform as anticipated. Instrumentality is guided by the trust that we have in people or external forces determining the outcome, in control over how the choice is made, and in the existing policies or factors regarding performance and outcome. The third variable in expectancy theory is **valence**, which is the value that we attribute to the expected reward. Valence is influenced by our needs, objectives, values, and sources of motivation. Motivations impact attitude and behavior change, and campaign communicators may use another person's motivations as an instrument to persuade them. One method to motivate others is by proposing a reward; something that we want accomplished as a result of compliance.[123] To further describe what valence entails, valence depends on what a person believes. If he or she believes that a high degree of performance is key to achieving other outcomes, then he or she expects that this performance will be rewarding (e.g., the above-referenced example of money). Likewise, if he or she thinks that a high degree of performance will be crucial to avoiding other outcomes that he or she wishes to avoid (e.g., making less money), then that person will ascribe a high valence on performing well.[124]

THE 10 ETHICAL PRINCIPLES OF PUBLIC COMMUNICATION CAMPAIGNS

Persuading an audience is one thing; being ethical about it is another thing. From an academic standpoint, **ethics** is a branch of philosophy that concerns itself with resolving issues of human morality by addressing concepts such as good and evil, and virtue and vice. From a human standpoint, ethics is a collection of moral principles established by a community, group, or person that make a distinction between right and wrong.[125] There are 10 ethical principles in public communication campaigns. The application of these principles to the design and implementation of campaigns is an acknowledgement that the purpose of changing behaviors or attitudes is an important one, but it is not the only one in the life of a community, group, or person. Therefore, the attempt at changing behaviors or attitudes must be balanced against other interests, particularly in this global era of diverse views, distinct cultures, and differences in interpreting the world.

1—Ethical Campaigners Are Factual

The target audience of a campaign expects facts to be true and proposals for behavior change to be reasonably grounded in evidence. Campaigners who present inaccurate information or half-baked ideas abuse their power. The content must also be information that is substantial and useful. Champions of inflated statistics or strong emotional appeals (i.e., strong pathos) will argue that these tactics are able to improve public response. However, the inclusion of such dubious morality in communication tactics is frowned upon by ethicists, who often describe campaigns like preventive health interventions as a marketing ploy replete with overstatements, crowd manipulation, or fear mongering.[126] People who need to make more imminent decisions in uncertain circumstances are particularly vulnerable to biased messages. In some cases, biased messages appear factual at face value, but they are actually cognitive biases. **Cognitive biases** are not factual because they systematically deviate from rationality in judgment.[127] Examples are belief biases and confirmation biases.

A **belief bias** is a pattern of reaching conclusions based on personal beliefs. It is a kind of **belief perseverance**—the persistence of hanging on to one's beliefs in the face of evidence to the contrary. One reason may reside in the mechanism of the human sensory system. Our brains and senses are patterned in such a way that they facilitate speedy assessments of social situations and others' states of mind. There is a personal advantage to judging significance and relevance promptly, instead of searching or providing a factual answer.[128] **Confirmation bias** is a phenomenon whereby people are used to actively seeking out and placing more emphasis on information that confirms their hypothesis. At the same time, information that could disconfirm our hypotheses is ignored or underweighted. As such, it can be viewed as a type of selection bias in presenting evidence.[129] Such a bias would be obvious during an anti-LGBTQ+ campaign of which the core message is that "you can't be born gay."

2—Ethical Campaigners Are Honest

Over and above presenting information carefully and accurately (i.e., all aspects of it), communicators should also supply the claims they make with sources and/or reference materials. In like fashion, they should not plagiarize or cyberplagiarize by passing others' ideas as their own. Rather, they ought to fully credit the ideas of others in their communications. The following are a few tips to keep in mind. If campaigners modify a few sentences at the beginning, in the middle, or at the end of their communications, but leave much of the rest of the original text intact and do not acknowledge the source, they are still committing plagiarism. In a similar fashion, if they paraphrase the entire original text but omit to credit it, they are still committing plagiarism too.[130]

3—Ethical Campaigners Act with Integrity

Campaigners should practice what they preach. Anyone who adheres to the philosophy of "Do what I say, not what I do" does not act with integrity. A communicator who promotes the value of civility but then interrupts and jeers others lacks integrity too. It is a violation of ethics for campaigners to champion principles that they themselves do not live up to.[131] Integrity, here, means that public communication campaigners should make it clear to publics what their true intentions are. A frequent problem in this context is crowd manipulation. **Crowd manipulation** is the deliberate use of techniques based on the core tenets of crowd psychology. These tenets consist of engaging, regulating, or swaying the desires of a population in order to direct its behavior towards an agenda—be it ideological, political, or religious (among many others). This phenomenon is frequent in the world of politics and business and can ease the approval, disapproval, or indifference towards a topic, individual, or product. The ethicality of crowd manipulation is subject to a great deal of reservations.[132]

4—Ethical Campaigners Balance the Message

Even if public communication campaigners include solid facts in their messages, do not plagiarize them, and practice what they preach, they can still be considered unethical if they do not balance their messages—as in concealing information about the negative long-term impact of smoking cannabis on a daily basis. Thus, for the target audience, balancing the message means considering all sides of the issue presented by the communicator, even when that evidence defies the ultimate purpose of the campaign. For example, balanced messages communicate both advantages and disadvantages of an environmental policy—and both of them should be treated with equal measures. A balanced message of an environmental policy that advocates the use of public transportation over driving automobiles may be the following: "The bus might not get you there as fast as an automobile, but it is good for the environment." This statement lists both an advantage and a disadvantage of taking the bus.[133]

Balancing is important because it lends credibility to both the message and the source. This is especially true for messages from sources that, in the eyes of the target audience, are perceived as more reliable and objective, like public agencies.[134] Academics have also conceptualized the notion that balanced messages are more likely to generate a positive long-term impact, such as enhanced faith in the integrity of a source.[135] This is why campaigns would better refrain from ignoring certain facts such as the negative consequences of smoking cannabis. Campaigns should refrain from doing these things even when these tactics would be more persuasive. Taken as a whole, offering a one-sided argument or selecting only positive supporting evidence is to be seen as unethical.[136]

5—Ethical Campaigners Demonstrate Respect

Demonstrating respect means demonstrating regard for the audience (or even competitors), including their opinions, interpretations, rights, and feelings. One way to show respect for the audience is using language and humor that is inclusive and not offensive.[137] Indeed, particular attention should be placed on content and messages that do not confound and/or offend populations. In some instances, messages sent in a tentative way or with unnecessary caveats can be viewed as baffling, culturally inappropriate, or even culturally irrelevant. Language and expressions that are meaningful to one population may have entirely different implications for another. The goal, here, is to demonstrate respect by promoting diversity and the cultural process, particularly in regards to the life experiences of the target audience that the campaign seeks to serve, and the sociocultural environment of those that the campaign wants to reach. This also means that planners should make sure that behaviors like stereotyping, victim-blaming, and using noninclusive or offensive messages be avoided.[138]

6—Ethical Campaigners Give Informed Choices

Rather than maneuvering the target audience towards a specific agenda, ethical campaigners should encourage listeners to make informed choices. Of course, it should be recognized that audience members, too, share the responsibility of acquiring information themselves on important issues. This also means to consider campaign arguments thoroughly and think critically about the facts presented. This approach is founded on the premise that an essential dignity of human beings lies in their ability to make rational choices and their right to do so.[139] An example of such unethical communication would be a situation in which the campaigners give off a high degree of optimism about the necessity of changing our daily habits in order to fight climate change because doing so, the campaigners argue, is the only way to make humankind happier and healthier. **Optimism bias**, in this case, occurs because communicators give the impression of being too optimistic about our future climate.[140] At the same time, they also convey the feeling to the audience that the only way to make humankind happier and healthier is to change our daily habits *vis-à-vis* the current climate.

7—Ethical Campaigners Do Not Violate Individuals' Autonomy

Respecting individuals' autonomy to avoid harm and treat them as citizens are core ethical principles, even if it is not the best route to maximize benefits. These principles are easily sanctioned, but not easily achieved. The application of ethical principles can be obscured by the campaigners' needs to consider manipulating the audience in order to maximize efficiency, cost, and improving the well-being of society at large. On some occasions, campaigners make choices under conditions of uncertainty, either with respect to uncertainty about the scientific evidence for an intervention or uncertainty about the impact of the intervention itself. In these conditions, a violation of the audience's autonomy will probably occur. Because they have been deceived, individuals may consider their roles in public communication campaigns as second-rate and powerless compared to the campaigner.[141] This situation calls for the ethical practice of beneficence. **Beneficence** looks at the balance between benefits and risks. The bottom line is that the benefits must offset or at least be equal to the risks the person is being asked to take.[142]

8—Ethical Campaigners Avoid Conflicts of Interests

Campaigners should avoid ulterior motives. Personal conflicts of interests are the best example of ulterior motives. Campaigners should not develop an outwardly innocuous public communication campaign to generate profits for their own personal dealings. This is why campaign websites should publish only essential links—in order to erase conflicts of interests—with clearly marked directions for viewers to return to the sites.

9—Ethical Campaigners Avoid Unnecessarily Privileging One Group over Another

Public communication campaigns can face obstacles when attempting to secure benefits for one part of the population versus another. This problem may be exacerbated when trying to reach heterogeneous audiences with a common denominator message. There is always the possibility that unintended consequences will occur (e.g., unprovoked confusion or anxiety on the part of the audience). This is true even with the most well-intentioned and well-organized public interventions. The dissemination of a segmented message—with systematic variations of meanings and linguistic strategies—will not only be more received by most populations, but it will also circumvent unnecessary favoritism or giving such impression. Public communication campaigns should target specific subgroups when past experiences or support from research suggest that significant differences exist in behaviors/attitudes/beliefs.[143] Treating groups with equal measures indicates that all individuals should be treated similarly and fairly in regards to the distribution of messages.[144]

10—Ethical Campaigners Are Responsible

Responsible campaigners understand the depth and power of communication. So, ethical communicators only promote issues that they know are in the best interest of the audience.[145] Whenever possible, program planners should use evidence-based programs that are grounded in facts or success from past campaigns. Upon looking at these 10 ethical princi-ples, it should be recognized that they are easily endorsed, but not effortlessly achieved. Applying them can be made harder by the temptation to consider tradeoffs among efficiency, cost, and improving the well-being of only certain populations (as opposed to trying to benefit all). To this point, it would be irresponsible for a campaign strategist not to make a clear choice between maximizing assistance for one segment of the population and benefiting all. Intentionally being unethical when trying to persuade an audience opens the floodgates for unintended consequences, even when public communication campaigns are well executed.

PERSUASIVE EFFECTS OF PUBLIC COMMUNICATION CAMPAIGNS

Research on the persuasive effects of public communication campaigns has yielded incon-sistent results. Early researchers[146] concluded that such campaigns had only partial persua-sive effects. This was due to the fact that audiences tended to look for messages that were harmonious with their current attitudes. Nevertheless, later researchers[147] contended that the impacts of public communication campaigns were moderate, rather than partial, and that media exposure had varying levels of efficiency depending on the circumstances and the types of audiences. For instance, whereas a certain number of health communication campaigns were found to have a positive impact on persuasive outcomes,[148] others had no impact[149] or even negative effects.[150]

The ability of interpersonal communication to boost the persuasive effects of public communication campaigns was discussed in Chapter 1, particularly in the section on the Diffusion of Innovation (Doi) theory. To further this point, Jeong and Bae (2018)[151] pub-lished a study on the impact of interpersonal communication in health campaigns. The authors found that conversations had considerable effects on knowledge, purpose, and behavior. In another study, Solovei and van den Putte's (2020)[152] reported that interpersonal communication plays a crucial role in justifying the persuasive impact of media exposure. Even though a small amount of direct effects of media exposure were established, results showed that interpersonal communication had a direct impact on many outcomes. Similarly, an indirect impact of media exposure through interpersonal communication was ascertained for online banners, television, and radio exposure in many models used in their study.

Five Positive Effects of Public Communication Campaigns

The Institute of Medicine (2002)[153] lists and describes five positive effects that public com-munication messages have on audiences, principally with respect to their beliefs and/or behaviors: (1) Immediate learning, (2) delayed learning, (3) generalized learning, (4) social diffusion, and (5) institutional diffusion. Without a doubt, there are other positive effects besides these five, but the ones below encapsulate a great deal of ideas about the affirmative impact of campaigns.

- **Immediate learning**: the audience can learn new knowledge in a straightforward manner from public communication messages. This immediate learning allows the audience to make diverse decisions. For instance, youths learn that smoking cannabis has negative consequences. Thus, they develop more negative attitudes and intentions and, in due course, are less likely to smoke cannabis. This new knowledge is supposed to have direct effects on their beliefs and behaviors. In this way, youths may learn about the negative and positive corollaries of using marijuana, about the social reverberations of drug use, and about aptitude, competence, and self-efficacy in avoiding drug use.

- **Delayed learning**: even if a message is diffused today, its effects may not be felt until sometime later. For example, antidrug communication campaigns for 12- and 13-year-old youths (who hardly ever smoke cannabis) might be projected to shape future behavior only during situations in which drug use is more likely to occur.

- **Generalized learning**: public communication campaigns provide immediate exposure to particular messages, but the audience may be convinced about similar concepts as well. As such, an anticocaine intervention might create messages postulating that cocaine has a long-term negative impact and that medical school of thoughts disagree with cocaine use. Individuals exposed to these messages may oversimplify these thought processes to an overarching negative perception of other classes of drug use. Therefore, even though the message emphasizes cocaine use, beliefs about cannabis use also change. This is generalized learning. Explained differently, the impact of exposure is not message-specific and does not unavoidably operate within only one sphere.

- **Social diffusion**: messages can kindle conversations among peers or between youths and their parents. In turn, these conversations can have an effect on what they have believed since their childhood. They may open up additional information about negative corollaries and social expectations, as well as new aptitudes and increased self-efficacy. Conversations may connect people who have been exposed to the campaign message with people who have not. Thus, the impact of a communication intervention would not be restricted only to people who have been directly exposed to the messages. If the messages pertain to drugs, conversations may generate or strengthen antidrug ideas, or they may create prodrug ones.

- **Institutional diffusion**: the inclusion of advertisements and similar intervention messages can lead to a general reaction from public institutions—e.g., school boards, state legislatures, and media outlets. In turn, these institutions may approve health policies or projects that influence thought processes and social expectations of the audience. Thus, an antidrug communication campaign may arouse concerns among school board administrators regarding drug use and push them to devote more school time to drug education. Faith, athletic, or private youth groups may heighten their antidrug initiatives. News outlets may cover drug problems more actively, and the character of their messages may be altered. Films, music, or entertainment television may shift their degree of attention to, and the content of, drug-related campaigns. Like the social diffusion path, institutional diffusion does not necessitate an individual-level connection between message exposure and beliefs or behavior modification. This sphere of influence is experienced at the level of community analysis. Moreover, institutional diffusion can be a lengthy process. There may be a rather long pause between exposure to parts of the communication campaign and a general reaction from institutions—sometimes, the pause can last for a few years. What is more, there may be an even longer pause until the impact on audience beliefs or behavior is felt.

Unintended Effects

Unintended effects can appear not only in intended audiences, but also in unintended ones, because media-based messages can be transmitted to all types of audiences. In point of fact, the third-person effect hypothesis, described in Chapter 1, rests on the examination of this very phenomenon.[154] It is clear, by now, that public communication campaigns influence a range of unintended social systems within society, and that their actions reconcile or assuage the impact of campaigns on the target audience. Systems, according to Bronfenbrenner (1979),[155] are analogous to a "set of nested structures, each inside the next, like a set of Russian dolls." For this reason, changes in a system (and its parts) may set off changes in other systems (and their parts). As Rogers (1995)[156] wrote, "a system is like a bowl of marbles. Move any one of its elements and the position of all the others are inevitably changed also."

The purposes of the actions of diverse societal groups—reporters, survey administrators, employers of the at-risk population, insurance companies, advocacy groups, and lawmakers—may or may not be compatible with those of the campaign strategists, but they can still act as mediators or moderators influencing the impact of campaigns and the subsequent changes in society.[157] Campaigns may inadvertently stimulate surrounding social systems by giving more power to the target audience and its social networks to manage support groups and advocacy organizations.[158] Exposure to campaigns may stimulate the press to publish news segments about the issue, scientists to analyze the issue, politicians to make promises to address the issue, the private sector to create preventative or remedial goods and services, and the general population to regard the issue as a socially important one—one worth showing their sympathy and concern.[159]

Indirect Routes

Behavior change may also happen through indirect routes. For example, mass media messages can develop an agenda for and boost the frequency, depth, or both, of interpersonal conversations about a specific health issue within a person's social network. This, in concert with personal exposure to messages, may add force to (or weaken) particular changes in behavior. In addition, because mass media messages are often aimed at large populations, behavior changes that become social norms within a person's network might sway his or her decisions even without direct exposure to or initial persuasion by the campaign. An illustration is televised antismoking campaign messages. After viewing several of these, a social group may be encouraged to set up a support group to help others quit smoking. Another person who has not been exposed to the TV campaign may still decide to join the support group and modify his or her own behavior. Media-based campaigns can induce public debates on health issues and bring about changes in public policy, thereby putting moral and social restrictions on people's behaviors. For example, a campaign against tobacco use that focuses on second-hand smoke may not be able to convince smokers to quit, but it may enhance public support to pass legislation that forbids smoking in certain places, which may induce the secondary effect of convincing smokers to quit.[160]

Gunther and Storey (2003)[161] reported that, in 1995, the Radio Communication Project (RCP), a Nepalese radio campaign aimed at clinic health workers, did not create a positive impact on the target audience. Yet, the general population thought that the clinic health workers had made positive changes thanks to the campaign. As a result, the Nepalese population cultivated more positive opinions towards the health workers and demonstrated higher self-efficacy in dealing with them. On this basis, Gunther and Storey proposed the alleged influence model, advancing the notion that communication campaigns can make unintended audiences to presume the impact on intended audiences, and the former can make behavior changes based on that presumption. In a similar vein, in the same nation of Nepal, there was a communication campaign, using Diffusion of Innovations (DoI), that sought to embellish the gardens of Nepali families by advocating the use of vitamin A. In this Nepali vitamin A initiative, a certain number of households began to grow kitchen gardens. These households showed that, as innovators, a significant improvement in well-being could be attained through higher vitamin A intake supplied by kitchen garden produce. The neighbors of the innovative homes noticed the changes resulting from the implementation of vitamin A-improved gardens, and began to cultivate kitchen gardens too. Within 12 months after the implementation of the communication campaign, the number of Nepalis cultivating kitchen gardens increased a hundredfold.[162]

THE 12 NEGATIVE EFFECTS OF PUBLIC COMMUNICATION CAMPAIGNS

Unintended consequences are not always positive. In fact, public communication campaigns have been known to cause problems that surface instead of, or in addition to, the initial goals and objectives of the campaign. For example, although campaigns can promote messages in favor of irrigation schemes (i.e., giving people water for agriculture), they may not take into account that those irrigation schemes may increase waterborne diseases with destructive health effects, such as schistosomiasis (a disease triggered by parasitic flatworms).[163] This section lists and describes the 12 negative effects of public communication campaigns. This list was influenced, in part, by the work of Cho and Salmon (2007):[164]

1—Low External Locus of Control

Having a **low external locus of control** means that people believe outside factors are beyond their influence and control, which deters them from considering the issue or trying to tackle it, notwithstanding powerful or factual campaign messages.[165] Fishbein and Ajzen (2010)[166] remark that although stronger intentions are more likely to get someone to perform a behavior, when behavioral control is low—e.g., being deficient in fundamental skills or facing barriers—people may be discouraged from fulfilling their intentions. This means that skills, capacities, environmental challenges, and facilitators ought to be considered in order to better predict when a behavior may occur.

Environmental constraints, for example, can represent situational factors that make performance of a behavior harder or impossible.[167] An illustration of this is people's desperate stance on climate change. Despite the high volume of public communication campaigns on that issue, the doomist view occupies the minds of certain groups. Their argument of having a low external locus of control over climate change is based on an unsubstantiated principle that is reflected through their "unstoppable tipping point-like responses" and a "runaway greenhouse effect." They respond to campaigns with indifference or hopelessness, advancing the argument that their endeavors are fruitless or too late because the damage to the environment has been done. They refuse any intervention on their part.[168]

Furthermore, a degree of psychological distress or discomfort may emerge when the audience senses that the targeted health state portrayed in a health communication campaign and their own states do not match and they feel powerless in decreasing that inconsistency.[169] Frameworks of behavior change hypothesize that, besides the desire to change, people must also possess the internal resources to act upon the recommended behavior. Consequently, when people want to change but feel that they do not have the required abilities (or necessary support), they can be distressed or turned off.[170]

2—Messages that Produce the Opposite Behavior

Public communication messages can actually produce the opposite behavior that the campaign was initially promoting. Starting with the concept of noise,[171] communication scholars have been wary of the potential of noise (i.e., interference) that was not accounted for at the beginning of the campaign. Noise alludes to a deviation of the result from its intention. Such communication impact stems from multiple forces, of which the campaign developer can only control one: the sender or the source.[172] In addition, upon articulating the first conceptual framework of mass communication, Westley and MacLean (1957)[173] noted that, in contrast to interpersonal settings, in most mass communication situations, the feedback from the recipient may not be promptly feasible or may be totally distorted. The latter is also referred to as the **boomerang effect**, whereby the response from the audience is contrary to the anticipated response of persuasion messages. Fear appeals continue to be the most notorious for their ability to produce boomerang effects. Janis and Feshbach (1953)[174] reported that, after being exposed to fear appeals, the receivers did not want to think or communicate about the danger portrayed in the message. Similarly, studies reveal that exposure to fear appeals leads to desires to increase smoking,[175] drinking,[176] and self-reported unsafe sex.[177]

In regards to the latter, unsafe sex, teaching youths about puberty, sexuality, menstruation, and pregnancy is primordial during their formative years. One important domain of sex education is safe sex conversation. A wide range of mass media campaigns and educational programs are set up to convince people to use condoms when having sex to protect themselves against pregnancy, HIV transmission, and sexually transmitted infections (SITs)—like genital herpes, gonorrhea (the most widespread sexually transmitted diseases worldwide), or syphilis.[178] However, in many countries, public communication campaigns against unsafe sex raise much contentious debate. In fact, they have been known to produce the opposite effect; that is, a higher incidence of unsafe sex, along with SITs and teenage pregnancy. Kay and Jackson (2008)[179] confirm that such campaigns are actually detrimental to women and girls. In the early twentieth century, the **social hygiene movement** was a massive-scale campaign in Europe and the United States to control STIs, regulate prostitution and sexual perversity, and diffuse sex education by including scientific research methods and modern media approaches. Yet, in the 1930s, Wilhelm Reich, an Austrian psychoanalyst, stated that such campaigns were counterproductive.[180]

Enter the "Captain Condom" campaign, a comic book produced by a US public health organization in 1990. Titled "Captain Condom," the book described a group of youngsters. It showed, through pictures and captions, how to correctly put on a condom. Likewise, in the same decade, a set of postcards created by another US public health agency sought to improve the health of gay men by depicting responsible young men who knew how to behave at parties and have proper casual sex. These two cases were tailored towards specific audiences. However, members of the larger population found these materials to be inappropriate and even immoral. Others have denounced the practices used by those US organizations—i.e., using comic books and postcards was not believed to be the proper communication medium. To this point, some people cling to the assumption that sexual intercourse is only for married adults. Therefore, they oppose delivering information to youths about contraceptives and safer sex practices. They put forward the notion that the mere diffusion of safe sex messages implies that sexual relations among youths are to be seen as acceptable and normal.[181]

3—Reactance

Reactance is a disagreeable motivational arousal that appears when we face a threat to or a decrease in our free behaviors. The degree of reactance is based on the significance of the threatened freedom and the apparent magnitude of the threat. **Internal threats** are self-inflicted threats that come from choosing particular alternatives and discarding others. **External threats** emerge either from impersonal situational circumstances that accidentally form an obstacle to a person's freedom or from social influence attempts aimed at a specific person.[182] Reactance can impede public communication messages. It is a powerful form of resistance that gets activated when someone feels compelled to embrace a particular view or to act in a certain way—i.e., their liberty to be or choose what they want is being restricted. A potential corollary is that the campaign audience may intensify a view or behavior that is opposite to what was intended. This is frequent for those who do not like "to be told what to do." What is casually referred to as reverse psychology is a simple approach that acknowledges this factor and uses strategies to combat reactance. Reactance is exacerbated by certain personal characteristics and predispositions, such as individuals who naturally resist authority.[183]

Unlike the boomerang effect, reactance does not necessarily result in actual opposite behavior. It is mostly a negative attitude towards what is perceived as a self-imposed threat. In fact, unlike the boomerang effect, when individuals experience too much pressure, they may fall back on inertia. **Inertia** is a tendency not to change our attitudes, behaviors, or beliefs.[184] This notion of doing nothing about ourselves rests on the idea that we want to maintain our attitude system in balance and will stand firm against persuasion in order to avoid dissonance. Inertia leads to selective avoidance of arguments that challenge our current attitudes, behaviors, or beliefs.[185]

For example, communication campaigns against obesity have had mixed reactions from the public. Launched on February 9, 2010, Michelle Obama's "Let's Move" campaign was designed to combat and, eventually, decrease the childhood obesity epidemic in the United States. The main strategies consisted of (1) convincing parents and companies to modify the nutritional content and labeling of products by the US Department of Agriculture, (2) increasing the nutritional norms of the National School Lunch Program, (3) providing more opportunities for childhood physical activity, and (4) offering more high-quality foods (at lower prices or for free) in the United States.[186] However, detractors and critics sensed that Michelle Obama's initiative reflected a "nanny state" approach from the US government that had no problem infringing on individual rights to choose their own diets. It was also an initiative that, to this day, has not yielded expected results. Rather, it has resulted in nothing more than a high-profile public relations campaign without any genuine substance.[187]

By nature, we like to think that we have certain freedoms to benefit from so-called free behaviors. Yet, in some cases, we cannot, or at least feel that we cannot, do so. Being persuaded to buy a specific product in the grocery store and being forced to wear a mask during a pandemic are two examples of threats to the freedom to act as desired, and this is where reactance comes into play. According to **psychological reactance theory**, people become defensive when they feel that they are manipulated; they want to make decisions independently from others. Public communication campaigns that shove people towards "correct" behavior can give them the impression that their freedom to choose or act the way they want is jeopardized.[188]

4—Widening Disparity

Even the most thought-out and well-designed public communication campaigns can pro- duce unintended disparities within nations. Negative consequences for diverse populations include uncertainty about the meaning of the message, particularly if the message was articulated in a language mainly geared towards the dominant or majority population. This can lead to widening disparity towards certain communities and, at the same time, stigma- tize them (or their cultural practices).[189] Explained differently, campaigns could inadver- tently create **social reproduction**, a phenomenon whereby public communication campaigns perpetuate current social distributions of knowledge, attitudes, and behaviors (instead of reform or improvement). Such widening disparity means that the campaigns' distribution of information on proper behaviors, and the steps to accomplish them, reflect the social distribution of education and income.[190]

Poor or underprivileged people tend to be less educated. Unavoidably, they know less about health issues than richer or privileged people with more education under their belts. A key objective of campaigns should be to reduce the gap between the advantaged and dis- advantaged members of society. Often, the opposite happens. Campaigns have been known to widen disparity, so much so that, in the end, the rich and better educated ones become more knowledgeable of the issue than their less privileged counterparts. These obstacles against behavior change should be taken very seriously. Campaigns should consider using strategies that seek to eliminate or minimize such obstacles.[191]

5—Opportunity Cost

The selection of a communication campaign to address a problem is generally contingent on cost. Can it be properly funded? Conversely, the primacy placed on certain issues over others will determine cost but, at the same time, may decrease the likelihood of improving society because the selection of those issues may not be the ideal one. Problems within society are in constant competition with one another in the public arena. Competition is inescapable because public arenas, being places of the public sphere, have a restricted carrying capacity. More precisely, citizens are limited in their capacity for attention, consideration, concern, time, and money that they can dedicate to issues. As a result, com- petition creates an uneven allocation of public attention and resources to the domain of social problems, regardless of their objective condition.[192]

6—Enabling

Campaigns empower individuals and institutions, just like they ameliorate the image and finances of industries. Campaigns may intentionally or inadvertently act as enablers to such institutions and industries. The designing and delivering of communication programs to improve personal well-being and society at large may contribute to the growth of big money-makers. Enabling can also occur in a less obvious manner.[193] For example, "green" campaigns, like the green car movement, advance the core message that they improve the environment by lowering emissions and increasing fuel economy. This, in turn, can pave the way towards energy independence and reduced oil imports. However, detractors are concerned that such campaigns would enable the power, influence, and wealth of industrialists like Elon Musk more than they would enable an improvement of the environment and humankind as a whole. By October 2021, Elon Musk was the wealthiest person on the planet, with a net worth of close to $300 billion.[194]

7—Loss of Self-Esteem

Public communication campaigns can become sources for stereotypes and social stigmas. Once stereotypes and social stigmas are enshrined within society, they solidify over time and create situations in which the Other is disliked, feared, shunned, perceived as deviant, and even blamed for so-called immoral behaviors that must have been the cause of their "punishment" or "affliction." This type of social atmosphere can be harmful to members of vulnerable groups who are already experiencing stigmatized medical conditions. This, in turn, can be the occasion of internalized or self-hatred and, in due time, erosion of self-esteem.[195] As a brief example, public communication campaigns that illustrate the dreadfulness of being confined to a wheelchair as a result of a drunk-driving car accident were interpreted by people with mobility disabilities as devaluing them and hurting their self-esteem and dignity.[196] Such high-consciousness messages over physical issues or health risks may generate unnecessary risks to self-esteem over the long term. They may also give rise to an unnecessarily high concern on the part of the general population, thereby chipping away at their sense of well-being.[197] Thomas (1983)[198] called this occurrence an **epidemic of apprehension**.

8—Less Enjoyment

Certain proposals laid out by public communication campaigns may deprive certain populations of behaviors or habits that they enjoy or that have been embedded within their identity and daily routine. These behaviors or habits, even if unhealthy, may be imbued with cultural significance or emotional importance. Smoking, for instance, gives members of certain groups not only pleasure, but also coping skills that cannot be replaced so easily.[199] The less privileged usually do not have a lot of options for healthier substitutions for practices they enjoy—again, even their practices are unhealthy. If truth be told, their quality of life may suffer from what commentators have termed "forceful, evangelistic health propaganda."[200]

One illustration of this is in an antismoking campaign targeting American-Vietnamese men who smoke on a daily basis and who offer cigarettes to friends in social encounters. Smoking together is an important social practice that buttresses social ties and solidarity within this immigrant group. Other minority groups, like Arab men in Israel, practice this type of togetherness as well. The well-intentioned messages adapted for American-Vietnamese men affirmed that giving someone a cigarette is like giving someone cancer. It clearly accentuated the obligation to protect others from life-threatening risks associated with smoking. Given the low rates of smoking cessation at that time (i.e., 1990s), its major effect may have actually been to instill a sense of guilt within those American-Vietnamese men.[201]

9—Culpability

When a public communication campaign stresses culpability, it often leads to what is called **blaming the victim**—that is, directing the causes of social problems at the person, not at the social environment.[202] Messages that highlight personal responsibility may de-emphasize the role of external or environment forces. Examples of such forces include insufficient resources to buy nutritious foods, poor work conditions, lack of access to healthcare, all of which are said to contribute to health problems at the broader societal level.[203] Associating health to individual responsibility may pigeonhole those who refuse to accept the proposed health-related practices as weak of character and to blame for particular medical conditions. This can make critics deduce that we should be held morally, and even legally, accountable for our behaviors.[204] The problem is that it frees society from covering certain healthcare costs, or requiring others to pay higher premiums.[205]

Results from a study on perceptions of breastfeeding in a low-income community indicated that feelings of guilt and shame were common among nonbreastfeeding mothers.[206] Culpability also adds force to the perception in the public's mind that we are accountable for the future of society or our own health. From this vantage point, we are responsible every time we get sick and, hence, we are culpable. Implied in communications that try to fashion a causal connection between our behavior and our health is a conjecture that our behavior can considerably affect our health and even that of others in our environment. Although such messages correspond to the concept of human agency, they are problematic because they do not account for the fact that we generally do not have a far-reaching impact on the social dynamics that affect our behavior. In fact, when public communication campaigns want to induce individual-level change, they may ignore key environmental or societal hurdles to change.[207]

10—Increased Danger to One's Health

The possible negative impact of public communication campaigns on the audience can raise ethical concerns when they endanger public health—even if the entire course of the campaign is filled with well-crafted, nonthreatening messages. There is ample disagreement as to what correct approach should be employed when tackling controversial or sensitive issues like obesity. The main bone of contention is centered on individual behavior-change campaigns, that do not seek to regulate or intervene in citizens' private lives, and public will campaigns, that advocate regulations on the same public grounds as the restrictions that are in place against tobacco products. Nevertheless, the danger emerges when public communication campaigns targeting the escalation of the obesity epidemic provide more justifications for campaigners to tell women to absolutely lose weight. To this point, the issue may cause unintended effects like eating disorders. Without a doubt, these types of public health messages can indirectly endorse unhealthy routines such as excessive dieting, anorexia, vomiting, excessive use of laxatives, and overexercising. A certain number of women are already preoccupied with their physique (e.g., being too thin), notwithstanding the health implications of weight loss. By placing a heavy emphasis on the "appearance of health," that is, trying to reach an ideal weight, public communication campaigns are unintentionally encouraging unhealthy behavior.[208]

11—Misunderstanding

Misunderstanding or uncertainty regarding risk and risk prevention processes may emerge during a public communication campaign. Interpreting messages in the direction of the campaign is a crucial step for behavior change. The notion of risks is a complicated one; yet, even professionals' risk assessments can be flawed, not to mention that of nonexpert citizens.[209] Messages targeting a subset of the population may generate misunderstanding among unintended audiences. On the other hand, messages aimed at the general public might unintentionally weaken risk information that is needed for high-risk populations.[210] In the 1980s, Gerber (a corporation that manufactures baby food and baby products) wanted to sell its products in Africa. The problem is that the company used the same packaging as in the United States. The packaging had a cute Caucasian baby photo on the label.[211] Later, Gerber was made aware that, in Africa, because many locals could not read English, companies regularly put pictures on the label to describe what content is inside the packaging. When Gerber started to campaign for its products in Africa, its packaging aimed at Western markets gave local Africans the impression that the US corporation was selling cute White babies. Unsurprisingly, the sales were low.[212]

12—Desensitization

Constant exposure to risk messages may turn the public into an apathetic entity over the long term. Long-term media reporting of a negative issue has been ascertained to cause desensitization and emotional burnout. This is especially true for issues like AIDS, homelessness, child domestic violence, and violent crime.[213] A term that captures the essence of this circumstance is **compassion fatigue**, whereby repeated exposure to a message can cause the audience to "switch off." Such people display a reduced ability to empathize or feel compassion for others or certain topics.[214] Negative emotions like fear are often used to convince people to reduce their carbon footprint. However, message recipients may become desensitized or express shame or guilt about their behavior or how they have an impact on the climate.[215] Srinivasan (2013)[216] confirmed that audience responses to campaigns on climate change and global warming are akin to "threat fatigue" and "unemotional pragmatism." As the author continues, this is probably caused by media saturation of these topics—unlike the first reason listed at the beginning of this section, which has to do with situations in which people have a low external locus of control.

Certain public communication campaigns can have a profound backlash. Two longitudinal, empirical studies on the impact of visual representations of climate change (e.g., melting ice) on the audience's feelings of engagement with the issue indicate that, although fear may be useful to attract people's attention, it is often more difficult to modify behavior. The authors of these two studies concluded that we can become easily desensitized by continuous exposure to repugnant images and lose our faith in the communication source if we believe that fear is used as leverage to manipulate us into taking action.[217]

NOTES

1. George A. Kennedy, *History of Rhetoric, Volume I: The Art of Persuasion in Greece* (Princeton, NJ: Princeton University Press, 2016).

2. Robert H. Gass and John S. Seiter, *Persuasion, Social Influence, and Compliance Gaining* (4th Ed.) (Boston, MA: Allyn & Bacon, 2010). 33.

3. Erwin P. Bettinghaus and Michael J. Cody, *Persuasive Communication* (4th Ed.) (New York: Holt, Rinehart & Winston, 1987): 3.

4. Martha Finnemore and Kathryn Sikkink, "International Norm Dynamics and Political Change," *International Organization* 52, no. 4 (1998): 887–917, 914. https://doi.org/10.1162/002081898550789.

5. Daniel J. O'Keefe, *Persuasion: Theory and Research* (1st Ed.) (Newbury Park, CA: Sage, 1990): 17.

6. Richard M. Perloff, *The Dynamics of Persuasion: Communication and Attitudes in the 21st Century* (2nd Ed.) (Mahwah, NJ: Lawrence Erlbaum, 2003): 11.

7. Kenneth E. Andersen, *Persuasion: Theory and Practice* (Boston, MA: Allyn & Bacon, 1971): 6.

8. Mohamed E. Bayou and Eric Panitz, "Definition and Content of Persuasion in Accounting," *Journal of Applied Business Research* 9, no. 3 (1993): 44–51, 44. https://doi.org/10.19030/jabr.v9i3.6034.

9. Perloff, *The Dynamics of Persuasion*, 11.

10. Mary John Smith, *Persuasion and Human Action: A Review and Critique of Social Influence Theories* (Belmont, CA: Wadsworth, 1982): 7.

11. Perloff, *The Dynamics of Persuasion*, 10.

12. Charles K. Atkin and Ronald E. Rice, "Theory and Principles of Public Communication Campaigns," in *Public Communication Campaigns* (4th Ed.), ed. Ronald E. Rice and Charles K. Atkin (Thousand Oaks, CA: Sage, 2012): 3–20.

13. Ibid, 3–20.

14. Itzhak Yanovitzky and Courtney Bennett, "Media Attention, Institutional Response, and Health Behavior Change: The Case of Drunk Driving, 1978–1996," *Communication Research* 26, no. 4 (1999): 429–53. https://doi.org/10.1177/009365099026004004.

15. Lawrence Wallack, "Media Advocacy: Promoting Health through Mass Communication," in *Health Behavior and Health Education: Theory, Research, and Practice*, ed. Karen Glanz, Frances Marcus Lewis, and Barbara K. Rimer (San Francisco, CA: Jossey-Bass, 1990): 370–86.

16. Everett M. Rogers, James W. Dearing, and Soonbum Chang, "AIDS in the 1980s: The Agenda Setting Process for a Public Issue," *Journalism Monographs* 126 (1991): 10–21.

17. Robert C. Hornik and Itzhak Yanovitzky, "Using Theory to Design Evaluations of Communication Campaigns: The Case of the National Youth Anti-Drug Media Campaign," *Communication Theory* 13, no. 2 (2003): 204–24. https://doi.org/10.1111/j.1468-2885.2003.tb00289.x.

18. Ibid, 205–11.

19. Anna E. Hartman and Erica Coslor, "Earning while Giving: Rhetorical Strategies for navigating Multiple Institutional Logics in Reproductive Commodification," *Journal of Business Research* 105 (2019): 405–19. https://doi.org/10.1016/j.jbusres.2019.05.010.

20. Jonathan Matusitz, *Terrorism & Communication: A Critical Introduction* (Thousand Oaks, CA: Sage, 2013).

21. Rudolph F. Verderber, Deanna D. Sellnow, and Kathleen S. Verderber, *The Challenge of Effective Speaking in a Digital Age* (17th Ed.) (Boston, MA: Cengage Learning, 2018).

22. Ibid, 10–5.

23. Matusitz, *Terrorism & Communication*, 185–6.

24. Deborah Lupton, "Risk and Emotion: Towards an Alternative Theoretical Perspective," *Health, Risk & Society* 15, no. 8 (2013): 634–47. http://dx.doi.org/10.1080/13698575.2013.848847.

25. Nancy Eisenberg and Richard A. Fabes, "Empathy: Conceptualization, Measurement, and Relation to Prosocial Behavior," *Motivation and Emotion* 14 (1990): 131–49. https://doi.org/10.1007/BF00991640.

26. Alice H. Eagly and Shelly Chaiken, *Psychology of Attitudes* (New York: Harcourt Brace Jovanovich, 1993).

27. Leslie B. Snyder, "Health Communication Campaigns and Their Impact on Behavior," *Journal of Nutrition Education and Behavior* 39, no. 2 (2007): 32–40. https://doi.org/10.1016/j.jneb.2006.09.004.

28. Henry Tuck and Tania Silverman, *The Counter-Narrative Handbook* (London: Institute for Strategic Dialogue, 2016).

29. Bilgehan Gültekin and Tuba Gültekin, "Importance of Public Communication Campaigns and Art Activities in Social Education," *World Academy of Science, Engineering and Technology* 64 (2012): 708–24.

30. Nedra Kline Weinreich, *Hands-On Social Marketing: A Step-by-Step Guide* (Thousand Oaks, CA: Sage, 1999).

31. Samuel Ngigi and Doreen Nekesa Busolo, "Behaviour Change Communication in Health Promotion: Appropriate Practices and Promising Approaches," *International Journal of Innovative Research & Development* 7, no. 9 (2018): 84–93. https://doi.org/10.24940/ijird/2018/v7/i9/SEP18027.

32. Robert Dreibelbis, Anne Kroeger, Kamal Hossain, Mohini Venkatesh, and Pavani K. Ram, "Behavior Change without Behavior Change Communication: Nudging Handwashing among Primary School Students in Bangladesh," *International Journal of Environmental Research and Public Health* 13, no. 1 (2016): 129–35. https://doi.org/10.3390/ijerph13010129.

33. Paul R. Warshaw and Fred D. Davis, "Disentangling Behavioral Intention and Behavioral Expectation," *Journal of Experimental Social Psychology* 21, no. 3 (1985): 213–28. https://doi.org/10.1016/0022-1031(85)90017-4.

34. Tressie Barrett and Yaohua Feng, "Effect of Observational Evaluation of Food Safety Curricula on High School Students' Behavior Change," *Journal of Food Protection* 83, no. 11 (2020): 1947–57. https://doi.org/10.4315/JFP-20-086.

35. Mary Freyder and John Hembling, *A Bi-National Partnership against HIV: USAID Legacy in Mexico* (Washington, D.C.: USAID, 2013).

36. Public Health England, "Change4Life Behaviour Change Model," in *Change4Life: Making It Easier for Families to Eat Well and Move More*, ed. Public Health England (London: Author, 2016).

37. For example, see Frederick Gibbons, Meg Gerrard, and David Lane, "A Social–Reaction Model of Adolescent Health Risk," in *Social Psychological Foundations of Health and Illness*, ed. Jerry Suls and Kenneth A. Wallston (Oxford: Blackwell, 2003): 107–36.

38. Karen Glanz, Barbara K. Rimer, and K. Viswanath, *Health Behaviour and Health Education: Theory, Research, and Practice* (4th Ed.) (San Francisco, CA: Jossey-Bass, 2008).

39. Robert C. Hornik and Kimberly Duyck Woolf, "Using Cross-Sectional Surveys to Plan Message Strategies," *Social Marketing Quarterly* 5, no. 2 (1999): 34–41. https://doi.org/10.1080/15245004.1999.9961044.

40. Institute of Medicine, *Speaking of Health: Assessing Health Communication Strategies for Diverse Populations* (Washington, D.C.: Institute of Medicine, 2002).

41. Endel Tulving and Daniel L. Schacter, "Priming and Human Memory Systems," *Science* 247, no. 4940 (1990): 301–6. https://doi.org/10.1126/science.2296719.

42. Institute of Medicine, *Speaking of Health*, 51.

43. Ibid, 51.

44. Ulrich de Balbian, "Philosophers' Thinking," *Logic & Argumentation* 5 (2017): 1–495.

45. James W. Dearing and Everett M. Rogers, *Agenda Setting* (Newbury Park, CA: Sage, 1994).

46. Institute of Medicine, *Speaking of Health*, 60–1.

47. Ibid, 60–1.

48. Claude Steele, "The Psychology of Self-Affirmation: Sustaining the Integrity of the Self," *Advances in Experimental Social Psychology* 21 (1988): 261–302. https://doi.org/10.1016/S0065-2601(08)60229-4.

49. Anthony Elliott, *Concepts of the Self* (4th Ed.) (Cambridge, England: Polity, 2020); Ellyn Lyle, *Identity Landscapes Contemplating Place and the Construction of Self* (Leiden: Brill, 2020).

50. David K. Sherman, "Self-Affirmation: Understanding the Effects," *Social and Personality Psychology Compass* 7, no. 11 (2013): 834–45. https://doi.org/10.1111/spc3.12072.

51. Steele, "The Psychology of Self-Affirmation," 261.

52. David K. Sherman and Geoffrey Cohen, "The Psychology of Self-Defense: Self-Affirmation Theory," in *Advances in Experimental Social Psychology*, ed. Mark P. Zanna (New York: Guildford Press, 2006): 183–242.

53. Joshua Correll, Steven J. Spencer, and Mark P. Zanna, "An Affirmed Self and an Open Mind: Self-Affirmation and Sensitivity to Argument Strength," *Journal of Experimental Social Psychology* 40, no. 3 (2004): 350–6. https://doi.org/10.1016/j.jesp.2003.07.001.

54. Sherman and Cohen, "The Psychology of Self-Defense," 184–7.

55. Correll, Spencer, and Zanna, "An Affirmed Self and an Open Mind," 352–3.

56. Guido M. van Koningsbruggen, Enny Das, and David R. Roskos-Ewoldsen, "How Self-Affirmation Reduces Defensive Processing of Threatening Health Information: Evidence at the Implicit Level," *Health Psychology* 28, no. 5 (2009): 563–8. https://doi.org/10.1037/a0015610.

57. Xiaoquan Zhao and Xiaoli Nan, "Influence of Self-Affirmation on Responses to Gain- versus Loss-Framed Antismoking Messages," *Human Communication Research* 36, no. 4 (2010): 493–511. https://doi.org/10.1111/j.1468-2958.2010.01385.x.

58. Richard E. Petty and John T. Cacioppo, *Communication and Persuasion: Central and Peripheral Routes to Attitude Change* (New York: Springer-Verlag, 1986).

59. Stephen W. Littlejohn and Karen A. Foss, *Theories of Human Communication* (9th Ed.) (Belmont, CA: Thomson-Wadsworth, 2008): 74.

60. Perloff, *The Dynamics of Persuasion*, 123.

61. Wendy Wood, Nancy Rhodes, and Michael Biek, "Working Knowledge and Attitude Strength: An Information-Processing Analysis," in *Attitude Strength: Antecedents and Consequences*, ed. Richard E. Petty and Jon Krosnick (Hillsdale, NJ: Lawrence Erlbaum, 1995): 283–313.

62. Debra G. Hutton and Roy F. Baumeister, "Self-Awareness and Attitude Change: Seeing Oneself on the Central Route to Persuasion," *Personality and Social Psychology Bulletin* 18, no. 1 (1992): 68–75. https://doi.org/10.1177/0146167292181010; Myung Ja Kim, Namho Chung, Choong-Ki Lee, and Michael W. Preis, "Dual-Route of Persuasive Communications in Mobile Tourism Shopping," *Telematics and Informatics* 33, no. 2 (2016): 293–308. https://doi.org/10.1016/j.tele.2015.08.009.

63. Littlejohn and Foss, *Theories of Human Communication*, 74.

64. James A. Forrest and Robert S. Feldman, "Detecting Deception and Judge's Involvement: Lower Task Involvement Leads to Better Lie Detection," *Personality and Social Psychology Bulletin* 26, no. 1 (2000): 118–25. https://doi.org/10.1177/0146167200261011; Anna R. McAlister and Danielle Bargh, "Dissuasion: The Elaboration Likelihood Model and Young Children," *Young Consumers* 17, no. 3 (2016): 210–25. https://doi.org/10.1108/YC-02-2016-00580.

65. Clark Moustakas, *Heuristic Research: Design, Methodology, and Applications* (Thousand Oaks, CA: Sage, 1990).

66. Em Griffin, *A First Look at Communication Theory* (7th Ed.) (New York: McGraw-Hill, 2009).

67. Shelly Chaiken, Akiva Liberman, and Alice H. Eagly, "Heuristic and Systematic Information Processing within and beyond the Persuasion Context," in *Unintended Thought*, ed. James S. Uleman and John Bargh (New York: Guilford Press, 1989): 212–52.

68. James O. Prochaska, Carlo C. DiClemente, and John C. Norcross, "In Search of How People Change: Applications to Addictive Behaviors," *American Psychologist* 47, no. 9 (1992): 1102–14. https://doi.org/10.1037//0003-066x.47.9.1102.

69. Bess H. Marcus and Laurey R. Simkin, "The Transtheoretical Model: Applications to Exercise Behavior," *Medicine & Science in Sports & Exercise* 26, no. 11 (1994): 1400–4. https://doi.org/10.1249/00005768-199411000-00016.

70. Available at https://www.ceceliahealth.com/the-five-stages-to-successful-behavior-change.

71. For example, see Matthew M. Clark, Vincent Pera, Michael G. Goldstein, Ronald W. Thebarge, and Barrie J. Guise, "Counseling Strategies for Obese Patients," *American Journal of Preventive Medicine* 12, no. 4 (1996): 266–70. https://doi.org/10.1016/S0749-3797(18)30323-4; Judy Gainey Seals, "Integrating the Transtheoretical Model into the Management of Overweight and Obese Adults," *Journal of the American Academy of Nurse Practitioners* 19 (2007): 63–71. https://doi.org/10.1111/j.1745-7599.2006.00196.x.

72. Ibid.

73. Patrícia Pinheiro de Freitas, Mariana Carvalho de Menezes, Luana Caroline dos Santos, Adriano Marçal Pimenta, Adaliene Versiani Matos Ferreira, and Aline Cristine Souza Lopes, "The Transtheoretical Model Is an Effective Weight Management Intervention: A Randomized Controlled Trial," *BMC Public Health* 20 (2020): 1–12. https://doi.org/10.1186/s12889-020-08796-1.

74. Lourdes S. Martinez and Nehama Lewis, "The Moderated Influence of Perceived Behavioral Control on Intentions Among the General US Population: Implications for Public Communication Campaigns," *Journal of Health Communication* 21, no. 9 (2016): 1006–15. https://doi.org/10.1080/10810730.2016.1204378.

75. Milagros Sáinz and Mercedes López-Sáez, "Gender Differences in Computer Attitudes and the Choice of Technology-Related Occupations in a Sample of Secondary Students in Spain," *Computers & Education* 54, no. 2 (2010): 578–87. https://doi.org/10.1016/j.compedu.2009.09.007.

76. Martin Fishbein and Icek Ajzen, *Predicting and Changing Behavior: The Reasoned-Action Approach* (New York: Psychology Press, 2010).

77. Alice H. Eagly and Shelly Chaiken, "Attitude Structure and Function," in *Handbook of Social Psychology* (4th Ed., Vol. 1), ed. Daniel T. Gilbert, Susan T. Fiske, and Gardner Lindzey (Boston, MA: McGraw-Hill, 1998): 269–322, 269.

78. Perloff, *The Dynamics of Persuasion*, 41.

79. Ibid, 39–40.

80. Martin Fishbein, "An Investigation of the Relationships between Beliefs about an Object and the Attitude toward that Object," *Human Relations* 16, no. 3 (1963): 233–9. https://doi.org/10.1177/001872676301600302.

81. Wendy Wood, "Attitude Change: Persuasion and Social Influence," *Annual Review of Psychology* 51 (2000): 539–70. https://doi.org/10.1146/annurev.psych.51.1.539.

82. Alice H. Eagly and Shelly Chaiken, "Attitude Strength, Attitude Structure and Resistance to Change," in *Attitude Strength*, ed. Richard E. Petty and Jon Kosnik (Mahwah, NJ: Lawrence Erlbaum, 1995): 413–32.

83. Herbert C. Kelman, "Compliance, Identification, and Internalization: Three Processes of Attitude Change," *Journal of Conflict Resolution* 2, no. 1 (1958): 51–60. https://doi.org/10.1177/002200275800200106.

84. Muzafer Sherif and Hadley Cantril, *The Psychology of Ego Involvement: Social Attitudes and Identifications* (New York: Wiley, 1947): 94.

85. Ibid, 96.

86. Thomas M. Ostrom and Timothy C. Brock, "A Cognitive Model of Attitudinal Involvement," in *Theories of Cognitive Consistency: A Sourcebook*, ed. Robert P. Abelson, Eliot Aronson, William J. McGuire, Theodore M. Newcomb, Milton J. Rosenberg, and Percy H. Tannenbaum (Chicago, IL: Rand McNally, 1968): 373–83, 375.

87. Milton Rokeach, *Beliefs, Attitudes, and Values: A Theory of Organization and Change* (San Francisco, CA: Jossey-Bass, 1968): 160.

88. Sherif and Hadley Cantril, *The Psychology of Ego Involvement*, 117.

89. Muzafer Sherif and Carl Hovland, *Social Judgment: Assimilation and Contrast Effects in Communication and Attitude Change* (New Haven, CT: Yale University Press, 1961).

90. Allison Ledgerwood and Shelly Chaiken, "Priming Us and Them: Automatic Assimilation and Contrast in Group Attitudes," *Journal of Personality and Social Psychology* 93, no. 6 (2007): 940–56. https://doi.org/10.1037/0022-3514.93.6.940.

91. For example, see Joy N. Rumble, Lisa K. Lundy, Brittany Martin, and Sandra Anderson, "Gender and GMOs: Understanding Floridians Attitudes toward GMOs through the Lens of Social Judgment Theory," *Journal of Applied Communications* 101, no. 4 (2017): 10–21.

92. Elizabeth M. Perse, "Involvement with Local Television News: Cognitive and Emotional Dimensions," *Human Communication Research* 16, no. 4 (1990): 556–81. https://doi.org/10.1111/j.1468-2958.1990.tb00222.x.

93. Anne P. Hubbell, Monique M. Mitchell, and Jenifer C. Gee, "The Relative Effects of Timing of Suspicion and Outcome Involvement on Biased Message Processing," *Communication Monographs* 68, no. 2 (2001): 115–32. https://doi.org/10.1080/03637750128056.

94. Carolyn W. Sherif and Muzafer Sherif, *Attitude, Ego-Involvement, and Change* (New York: Wiley, 1967).

95. Sherif and Hovland, *Social Judgment*, 3–9.

96. Carolyn W. Sherif, Muzafer Sherif, and Roger E. Nebergall, *Attitudes and Attitude Change: The Social Judgment-Involvement Approach* (Philadelphia, PA: W. B. Saunders, 1965).

97. Ibid, 10.

98. Yoori Hwang, "Selective Exposure and Selective Perception of Anti-Tobacco Campaign Messages: The Impacts of Campaign Exposure on Selective Perception," *Health Communication* 25, no. 2 (2010): 182–90. https://doi.org/10.1080/10410230903474027.

99. Ali Atıf Bir and Önder Yönet, "A Method Proposal for Determining Health Communication Campaigns' Messages," *European Journal of Interdisciplinary Studies* 2, no. 2 (2016): 48–72.

100. Sandi W. Smith, Charles K. Atkin, Dennis Martell, Rebecca Allen, and Larry Hembroff, "A Social Judgment Theory Approach to Conducting Formative Research in a Social Norms Campaign," *Communication Theory* 16, no. 1 (2006): 141–52, 144. https://doi.org/10.1111/j.1468-2885.2006.00009.x.

101. Russell H. Fazio and Mark P. Zanna, "On the Predictive Validity of Attitudes: The Roles of Direct Experience and Confidence," *Journal of Personality* 46, no. 2 (1978): 228–43. https://doi.org/10.1111/j.1467-6494.1978.tb00177.x.

102. Russell H. Fazio, Martha C. Powell, and Carol J. Williams, "The Role of Attitude Accessibility in the Attitude-to-Behavior Process," *Journal of Consumer Research* 16, no. 3 (1989): 280–8. https://doi.org/10.1086/209214.

103. Russell H. Fazio, Jeaw-mei Chen, Elizabeth C. McDonel, and Steven J. Sherman, "Attitude Accessibility, Attitude-Behavior Consistency, and the Strength of the Object-Evaluation Association," *Journal of Experimental Social Psychology* 18, no. 4 (1982): 339–57. https://doi.org/10.1016/0022-1031(82)90058-0.

104. Russell H. Fazio, "How Do Attitudes Guide Behavior?" in *The Handbook of Motivation and Cognition: Foundations of Social Behavior*, ed. E. Tory Higgins and Richard M. Sorrentino (New York: Guilford Press: 1986): 204–43.

105. Michael D. Slater, "Specification and Misspecification of Theoretical Foundations and Logic Models for Health Communication Campaigns," *Health Communication* 20, no. 2 (2006): 149–57. https://doi.org/10.1207/s15327027hc2002_6.

106. David M. Sanbonmatsu and Russell H. Fazio, "The Role of Attitudes in Memory-Based Decision-Making," *Journal of Personality and Social Psychology* 59, no. 4 (1990): 614–22. https://doi.org/10.1037//0022-3514.59.4.614.

107. Slater, "Specification and Misspecification," 152.

108. Cited in Perloff, *The Dynamics of Persuasion*, 96.

109. Michael J. Manfredo, Susan M. Yuan, and Francis A. McGuire, "The Influence of Attitude Accessibility on Attitude-Behavior Relationships: Implications for Recreation Research," *Journal of Leisure Research* 24, no. 2 (1992): 157–70. https://doi.org/10.1080/00222216.1992.11969883.

110. Russell H. Fazio and David R. Roskos-Ewoldsen, "Acting as We Feel: When and How Attitudes Guide Behavior," in *Persuasion: Psychological Insights and Perspectives* (2nd Ed.), ed. Timothy C. Brock and Melanie C. Green (Thousand Oaks, CA: Sage, 2005): 41–62.

111. Leandre R. Fabrigar, Joseph R. Priester, Richard E. Petty, and Duane T. Wegener, "The Impact of Attitude Accessibility on Elaboration of Persuasive Messages," *Personality and Social Psychology Bulletin* 24, no. 4 (1998): 339–52. https://doi.org/10.1177/0146167298244001.

112. Lijiang Shen, Jennifer L. Monahan, Nancy Rhodes, and David R. Roskos-Ewoldsen, "The Impact of Attitude Accessibility and Decision Style on Adolescents' Biased Processing of Health-Related Public Service Announcements," *Communication Research* 36, no. 1 (2009): 104–28. https://doi.org/10.1177/0093650208326466.

113. Rohini Ahluwalia, "Examination of Psychological Processes Underlying Resistance to Persuasion," *Journal of Consumer Research* 27, no. 2 (2000): 217–32. https://doi.org/10.1086/314321.

114. Charles G. Lord, Lee Ross, and Mark R. Lepper, "Biased Assimilation and Attitude Polarization: The Effects of Prior Theories on Subsequently Considered Evidence," *Journal of Personality and Social Psychology* 37, no. 11 (1979): 2198–3109. https://doi.org/10.1037/0022-3514.37.11.2098.

115. Jeff Niederdeppe, Kevin C. Davis, Matthew C. Farrelly, and Jared Yarsevich, "Stylistic Features, Need for Sensation and Confirmed Recall of National Smoking Prevention Advertisements," *Journal of Communication* 57, no. 2 (2007): 272–92. https://doi.org/10.1111/j.1460-2466.2007.00343.x.

116. Shen, Monahan, Rhodes, and Roskos-Ewoldsen, "The Impact of Attitude Accessibility," 106.

117. Laura J. Kray, "Contingent Weighting in Self-Other Decision Making," *Organizational Behavior and Human Decision Processes* 83, no. 1 (2000): 82–106. https://doi.org/10.1006/obhd.2000.2903.

118. Victor H. Vroom, *Work and Motivation* (San Francisco, CA: Jossey-Bass, 1964).

119. George Kominis and Clive R. Emmanuel, "The Expectancy-Valence Theory Revisited: Developing an Extended Model of Managerial Motivation," *Management Accounting Research* 18, no. 1 (2007): 49–75. https://doi.org/10.1016/j.mar.2006.10.002.

120. Richard M. Ryan and Edward L. Deci, "Intrinsic and Extrinsic Motivations: Classic Definitions and New Directions," *Contemporary Educational Psychology* 25, no. 1 (2000): 54–67. https://doi.org/10.1006/ceps.1999.1020.

121. Allan Wigfield, John T. Guthrie, Stephen Tonks, and Kathleen C. Perencevich, "Children's Motivation for Reading: Domain Specificity and Instructional Influences," *Journal of Educational Research* 97, no. 6 (2004): 299–309. https://doi.org/10.3200/joer.97.6.299–310.

122. Ryan and Deci, "Intrinsic and Extrinsic Motivations," 68–72.

123. Wadie Nasri and Lanouar Charfeddine, "Motivating Salespeople to Contribute to Marketing Intelligence Activities: An Expectancy Theory Approach," *International*

Journal of Marketing Studies 4, no. 1 (2012): 168–75; Stefania De Simone, "Expectancy Value Theory: Motivating Healthcare Workers," *American International Journal of Contemporary Research* 5, no. 2 (2015): 19–23.

124. Lyman W. Porter and Edward E. Lawler, *Managerial Attitudes and Performance* (Homewood, IL: Irwin-Dorsey, 1968).

125. Peter Singer, *Writings on an Ethical Life* (London: Harper Collins, 2000).

126. Nurit Guttman and Charles T. Salmon, "Guilt, Fear, Stigma and Knowledge Gaps: Ethical Issues in Public Health Communication Interventions," *Bioethics* 18, no. 6 (2004): 531–52.

127. Gerdien de Vries, "Public Communication as a Tool to Implement Environmental Policies," *Social Issues and Policy Review* 14, no. 1 (2020): 244–72. https://doi.org/10.1111/sipr.12061.

128. Henry Markovits and Guilaine Nantel, "The Belief-Bias Effect in the Production and Evaluation of Logical Conclusions," *Memory & Cognition* 17 (1989): 11–7. https://doi.org/10.3758/BF03199552.

129. Raymond S. Nickerson, "Confirmation Bias: A Ubiquitous Phenomenon in Many Guises," *Review of General Psychology* 2, no. 2 (1998): 175–220. https://doi.org/10.1037/1089-2680.2.2.175.

130. Adapted from Verderber, Sellnow, and Verderber, *The Challenge of Effective Speaking*, 5–6.

131. Ibid, 5–6.

132. Brian F. Kingshott, "Crowd Management: Understanding Attitudes and Behaviors," *Journal of Applied Security Research* 9, no. 3 (2014): 273–89. https://doi.org/10.1080/19361610.2014.913229.

133. Cited in de Vries, "Public Communication as a Tool," 264.

134. Gerdien de Vries, Bart W. Terwel, and Naomi Ellemers, "Perceptions of Manipulation and Judgments of Illegitimacy: Pitfalls in the Use of Emphasis Framing When Communicating about CO2 Capture and Storage," *Environmental Communication* 10, no. 2 (2016): 206–26. https://doi.org/10.1080/17524032.2015.1047884.

135. For example, see Gerdien de Vries, "How Positive Framing May Fuel Opposition to Low-Carbon Technologies: The Boomerang Model," *Journal of Language and Social Psychology* 36, no. 1 (2017): 28–44. https://doi.org/10.1177/0261927X16663590.

136. Richard L. Johannesen, *Ethics in Human Communication* (4th Ed.) (Prospect Heights, IL: Waveland Press, 1996).

137. Adapted from Verderber, Sellnow, and Verderber, *The Challenge of Effective Speaking*, 5–6.

138. Institute of Medicine, *Speaking of Health*, 246–9.

139. Ruth Edgett, "Toward an Ethical Framework for Advocacy in Public Relations," *Journal of Public Relations Research* 14, no. 1 (2002): 1–26. https://doi.org/10.1207/S1532754XJPRR1401_1.

140. Cited in de Vries, "Public Communication as a Tool," 250.

141. Institute of Medicine, *Speaking of Health*, 1–5.

142. Ibid, 243.

143. Ibid, 1–5.

144. Ibid, 243.

145. Adapted from Verderber, Sellnow, and Verderber, *The Challenge of Effective Speaking*, 5–6.

146. For example, see Herbert H. Hyman and Paul B. Sheatsley, "Some Reasons Why Information Campaigns Fail," *Public Opinion Quarterly* 11, no. 3 (1947): 412–23. https://doi.org/10.1093/poq/11.3.412; Joseph T. Klapper, *The Effects of Mass Communications* (Oxford: Free Press of Glencoe, 1960).

147. For example, see Edward Maibach, "Social Marketing for the Environment: Using Information Campaigns to Promote Environmental Awareness and Behavior Change," *Health Promotion International* 8, no. 3 (1993): 209–24. https://doi.org/10.1093/heapro/8.3.209; Garrett J. O'Keefe, "'Taking a Bite Out of Crime': The Impact of a Public Information Campaign," *Communication Research* 12, no. 2 (1985): 147–78. https://doi.org/10.1177/009365085012002001.

148. Philip Palmgreen, Lewis Donohew, Elizabeth Pugzles Lorch, Rick H. Hoyle, and Michael T. Stephenson, "Television Campaigns and Adolescent Marijuana Use: Tests of Sensation Seeking Targeting," *American Journal of Public Health* 91, no. 2 (2001): 292–6. https://doi.org/10.2105/AJPH.91.2.292.

149. Robert Hornik, Lela Jacobsohn, Robert Orwin, Andrea Piesse, and Graham Kalton, "Effects of the National Youth Anti-Drug Media Campaign on Youths," *American Journal of Public Health* 98, no. 12 (2008): 2229–36. https://doi.org/10.2105/AJPH.2007.125849.

150. Leslie B. Snyder and Deborah J. Blood, "Caution: Alcohol Advertising and the Surgeon General's Alcohol Warnings May Have Adverse Effects on Young Adults," *Journal of Applied Communication Research* 20, no. 1 (2012): 37–53. https://doi.org/10.1080/00909889209365318.

151. Jeong and Bae, "The Effect of Campaign-Generated Interpersonal Communication on Campaign-Targeted Health Outcomes: A Meta-Analysis," *Health Communication* 33, no. 8 (2018): 988–1003. https://doi.org/10.1080/10410236.2017.1331184.

152. Adriana Solovei and Bas van den Putte, "The Effects of Five Public Information Campaigns: The Role of Interpersonal Communication," *Communications* 45, no. s1 (2020): 586–602. https://doi.org/10.1515/commun-2020-2089.

153. Institute of Medicine, *Speaking of Health*, 61–3.

154. Hyunyi Cho and Charles T. Salmon, "Unintended Effects of Health Communication Campaigns," *Journal of Communication* 57, no. 2 (2007): 293–317. https://doi.org/10.1111/j.1460-2466.2007.00344.x.

155. Urie Bronfenbrenner, *The Ecology of Human Development* (Cambridge, MA: Harvard University Press, 1979): 22.

156. Everett M. Rogers, *Diffusion of Innovations* (New York: Free Press, 1995): 419.

157. Cho and Salmon, "Unintended Effects of Health Communication Campaigns," 307–8.

158. Robert C. Hornik, "Public Health Communication: Making Sense of Contradictory Evidence," in *Public Health Communication: Evidence for Behavior Change*, ed. Robert C. Hornik (Mahwah, NJ: Lawrence Erlbaum, 2002): 1–22.

159. Kasisomayajula Viswanath and John R. Finnegan, Jr., "Reflections on Community Health Campaigns: Secular Trends and the Capacity to Effect Change," in *Public Health Communication: Evidence for Behavior Change*, ed. Robert C. Hornik (Mahwah, NJ: Lawrence Erlbaum, 2002): 289–314.

160. Melanie A. Wakefield, Barbara Loken, and Robert C. Hornik, "Use of Mass Media Campaigns to Change Health Behaviour," *The Lancet* 376, no. 9748 (2010): 1261–71. https://doi.org/10.1016/S0140-6736(10)60809-4.

161. Albert C. Gunther and J. Douglas Storey, "The Influence of Presumed Influence," *Journal of Communication* 53, no. 2 (2003): 199–215. https://doi.org/10.1111/j.1460-2466.2003.tb02586.x.

162. Cited in Cho and Salmon, "Unintended Effects of Health Communication Campaigns," 303–13.

163. For example, see Alan Fenwick, "Waterborne Infectious Diseases—Could They Be Consigned to History?" *Science* 313, no. 5790 (2006): 1077–81. https://doi.org/10.1126/science.1127184.

164. Cho and Salmon, "Unintended Effects of Health Communication Campaigns," 293–317.

165. Julian B. Rotter, *Social Learning and Clinical Psychology* (New York: Prentice-Hall, 1954).

166. Fishbein and Ajzen, *Predicting and Changing Behavior*, 164–5.

167. Harry C. Triandis, *The Analysis of Subjective Culture* (New York: Wiley, 1972).

168. Cited in Alexandra Villarreal, "Meet the Doomers: Why Some Young US Voters Have Given Up Hope on Climate," *The Guardian* (September 21, 2020): A1. Retrieved on May 17, 2021 from https://www.theguardian.com/environment/2020/sep/21/meet-the-doomers-some-young-us-voters-have-given-up-hope-on-climate.

169. Leon Festinger, *A Theory of Cognitive Dissonance* (Stanford, CA: Stanford University Press, 1957).

170. Icek Ajzen, "The Theory of Planned Behavior," *Organizational Behavior and Human Decision Processes* 50, no. 2 (1991): 179–211. https://doi.org/10.1016/0749-5978(91)90020-T.

171. Claude Shannon and Warren Weaver, *A Mathematical Model of Communication* (Urbana Champaign, IL: University of Illinois Press, 1949).

172. Wilbur Schramm, "How Communication Works," in *The Process and Effects of Mass Communication*, ed. Wilbur Schramm (Urbana Champaign, IL: The University of Illinois Press, 1961): 3–26.

173. Bruce Westley and Malcolm S. MacLean, "A Conceptual Model for Mass Communication Research," *Journalism Quarterly* 34 (1957): 31–8.

174. Irving L. Janis and Seymour Feshbach, "Effects of Fear-Arousing Communications," *The Journal of Abnormal and Social Psychology* 48, no. 1 (1953): 78–92. https://doi.org/10.1037/h0060732.

175. Ronald W. Rogers and C. Ronald Mewborn, "Fear Appeals and Attitude Change: Effects of a Threat's Noxiousness, Probability of Occurrence, and the Efficacy of Coping Responses," *Journal of Personality and Social Psychology* 34, no. 1 (1976): 54–61. https://doi.org/10.1037//0022-3514.34.1.54.

176. Michael Kleinot and Ronald W. Rogers, "Identifying Effective Components of Alcohol Misuse Prevention Programs," *Journal of Studies on Alcohol* 43, no. 7 (1982): 802–11. https://doi.org/10.15288/jsa.1982.43.802.

177. Kim Witte, "Putting the Fear back into Fear Appeals: The Extended Parallel Process Model," *Communication Monographs* 59, no. 4 (1992): 329–49. https://doi.org/10.1080/03637759209376276.

178. Patricia Geist-Martin, Eileen B. Ray, and Barbara F. Sharf, *Communicating Health: Personal, Cultural, and Political Complexities* (Belmont, CA: Wadsworth Press, 2003).

179. Julie F. Kay and Ashley Jackson, *Sex, Lies & Stereotypes: How Abstinence-Only Programs Harm Women and Girls* (New York: Legal Momentum, 2008).

180. Lutz D. H. Sauerteig and Roger Davidson, "Shaping the Sexual Knowledge of the Young: Introduction," in *Shaping Sexual Knowledge: A Cultural History of Sex Education in Twentieth Century Europe*, ed. Lutz D. H. Sauerteig and Roger Davidson (New York: Routledge, 2009): 1–18.

181. Guttman and Salmon, "Guilt, Fear, Stigma and Knowledge Gaps," 545.

182. Mona A. Clee and Robert A. Wicklund, "Consumer Behavior and Psychological Reactance," *Journal of Consumer Research* 6, no. 4 (1980): 389–405. https://doi.org/10.1086/208782.

183. Jim Macnamara, *Evaluating Public Communication: Exploring New Models, Standards and Best Practice* (New York: Routledge, 2017).

184. Eric S. Knowles and Jay A. Linn, "The Importance of Resistance to Persuasion," in *Resistance and Persuasion*, ed. Eric S. Knowles and Jay A. Linn (Mahwah, NJ: Lawrence Erlbaum, 2004): 3–10.

185. Emily Moyer-Gusé, "Toward a Theory of Entertainment Persuasion: Explaining the Persuasive Effects of Entertainment-Education Messages," *Communication Theory* 18, no. 3 (2008): 407–25. https://doi.org/10.1111/j.1468-2885.2008.00328.x.

186. Alicia Batchelder and Jonathan Matusitz, "Let's Move" Campaign: Applying the Extended Parallel Process Model," *Social Work in Public Health* 29, no. 5 (2014): 462–72. https://doi.org/10.1080/19371918.2013.865110.

187. Steven Ross Johnson, "Gauging the Public Health Value of Michelle Obama's 'Let's Move' Campaign," *Modern Healthcare* (August 23, 2016). Retrieved on May 19, 2021 from https://www.modernhealthcare.com/article/20160823/NEWS/160829986/gauging-the-public-health-value-of-michelle-obama-s-let-s-move-campaign.

188. Jack W. Brehm and Sharon S. Brehm, *Psychological Reactance: A Theory of Freedom and Control* (New York: Academic Press, 1981).

189. Institute of Medicine, *Speaking of Health*, 246.

190. Phillip J. Tichenor, George A. Donohue, and Clarice N. Olien, "Mass Media Flow and Differential Growth in Knowledge," *Public Opinion Quarterly* 34, no. 2 (1970): 159–70. https://doi.org/10.1086/267786.

191. Perloff, *The Dynamics of Persuasion*, 309–10.

192. Stephen Hilgartner and Charles L. Bosk, "The Rise and Fall of Social Problems: A Public Arena Model," *American Journal of Sociology* 94, no. 1 (1988): 53–78.

193. Arthur J. Barsky, "The Paradox of Health," *New England Journal of Medicine* 318, no. 7 (1988): 414–8. https://doi.org/10.1056/NEJM198802183180705.

194. Available at https://www.forbes.com/sites/elizahaverstock/2021/10/26/elon-musk-nearing-300-billion-fortune-is-the-richest-person-in-history/?sh=1666c37e1933.

195. Nina Glick Schiller, Stephen Crystal, and Denver Lewellen, "Risky Business: The Cultural Construction of AIDS Risk Groups," *Social Science and Medicine* 38, no. 10 (1994): 1337–46. https://doi.org/10.1016/0277-9536(94)90272-0.

196. Caroline C. Wang, "Portraying Stigmatized Conditions: Disabling Images in Public Health," *Journal of Health Communication* 3, no. 2 (1998): 149–59. https://doi.org/10.1080/108107398127436.

197. Edward Tenner, *Why Things Bite Back: Technology and the Revenge of Unintended Consequences* (New York: Knopf, 1996).
198. Lewis Thomas, "An Epidemic of Apprehension," *Discover* 4 (1983): 78–80.
199. Walt Odets, "AIDS Education and Harm Reduction for Gay Men: Psychological Approaches for the 21st Century," *AIDS and Public Policy* 1, no. 9 (1994): 1–5.
200. T. Strasser, O. Jeanneret, and L. Raymond, "Ethical Aspects of Prevention Trials," in *Ethical Dilemmas in Health Promotion*, ed. S. Doxiadis (New York. Wiley, 1987): 183–93, 190.
201. Cited in Guttman and Salmon, "Guilt, Fear, Stigma and Knowledge Gaps," 550.
202. Paul R. Marantz, "Blaming the Victim: The Negative Consequence of Preventive Medicine," *American Journal of Public Health* 80, no. 10 (1990): 1186–7. https://doi.org/10.2105/ajph.80.10.1186.
203. David Blane, "Editorial: Social Determinants of Health—Socioeconomic Status, Social Class, and Ethnicity," *American Journal of Public Health* 85, no. 7 (1995): 903–5. https://doi.org/10.2105/ajph.85.7.903.
204. Lisbeth Sachs, "Causality, Responsibility and Blame – Core Issues in the Cultural Construction and Subtext of Prevention," *Sociology of Health and Illness* 18, no. 5 (1996): 632–52. https://doi.org/10.1111/1467-9566.ep10934515.
205. Hugh McLachlan, "Smokers, Virgins, Equity and Health Care Costs," *Journal of Medical Ethics* 21, no. 4 (1995): 209–13. https://doi.org/10.1136/jme.21.4.209.
206. Cited in Guttman and Salmon, "Guilt, Fear, Stigma and Knowledge Gaps," 544.
207. Marshall H. Becker, "A Medical Sociologist Looks at Health Promotion," *Journal of Health and Social Behavior* 34, no. 1 (1993): 1–6. https://doi.org/10.2307/2137300.
208. Available at https://www.news-medical.net/amp/news/2004/07/05/3080.aspx.
209. Paul Slovic, "Perception of Risk," *Science* 236, no. 4799 (1987): 280–5. https://doi.org/10.1126/science.3563507.
210. Cho and Salmon, "Unintended Effects of Health Communication Campaigns," 298–9.
211. Raquel de Pedro Ricoy, "Beyond the Words: The Translation of Television Adverts," *Babel* 42, no. 1 (1996): 27–45. https://doi.org/10.1075/babel.42.1.04ped.
212. Wasanti Argade, "'Think Local and Go Global' – A Key to Create a Successful Global Brand," *Journal of Management and Administration Tomorrow* 1, no. 2 (2013): 48–51.
213. Katherine N. Kinnick, Dean M. Krugman, and Glen T. Cameron, "Compassion Fatigue: Communication and Burnout toward Social Problems," *Journalism Quarterly* 73, no. 3 (1996): 687–707. https://doi.org/10.1177/107769909607300314.
214. Charles Figley, *Treating Compassion Fatigue* (New York: Brunner-Routledge, 2002).
215. Jonas H. Rees, Sabine Klug, and Sebastian Bamberg, "Guilty Conscience: Motivating Pro-Environmental Behavior by Inducing Negative Moral Emotions," *Climatic Change* 130 (2015): 439–52. https://doi.org/10.1007/s10584-014-1278-x.
216. Sunderasan Srinivasan, "Coldness to Global Warming, Threat Fatigue, or Unemotional Pragmatism: Investor Pattern Responses to Information Release," *Environmental Claims Journal* 24, no. 4 (2013): 277–90. https://doi.org/10.1080/10406026.2013.801190.
217. Saffron O'Neill and Sophie Nicholson-Cole, "'Fear Won't Do It' Promoting Positive Engagement with Climate Change through Visual and Iconic Representations," *Science Communication* 30, no. 3 (2009): 355–79. https://doi.org/10.1177/1075547008329201.

Thought-Provoking Public Communication Campaigns

A certain number of public communication campaigns disseminate thought-provoking messages to capture the attention of audiences or specific target groups. Such types of campaigns must come from reliable sources, have substance that attracts the audience's attention and, if feasible, try to impact social norms. Two exemplars of thought-provoking emotions are fear and provocation. Campaign strategists have been known to incorporate frightening, sexually-arousing, or crass humor as ways to capture the attention of intended populations. Dilemmas as to whether we should use such message appeals are something to behold. Messages found to be the most shocking but unforgettable to Vietnamese and Latino smokers were vivid depictions of cancerous tumors. Messages with fear appeals have more chances of raising awareness of the dangers of unhealthy practices like smoking, in hopes of reducing tobacco use. Nevertheless, some members of the audience may perceive such illustrations as distasteful or too creepy.[1] The first half of this chapter will discuss fear in detail, whereas the second half will tackle the concept of provocation.

By definition, **fear** is an unpleasant emotion that emerges in situations of seeming threat or danger to individuals or their environment. It often enables them to react to these situations in a flexible manner. In many instances, fear is activated automatically as a response; it is a type of unconscious mechanism.[2] Fear can be divided into serious fear (*metus gravis*), trifling fear (*metus levis*), and irrational fear. **Serious fear** is fear that permeates our psyche when facing immense peril. **Trifling fear** is fear that emerges when experiencing harm of inconsiderable dimensions. Even in the absence of facts or evidence, trifling fear can be disproportionate and unreasonably elevated.[3] **Irrational fear** is fear based on a non-existent threat or reality.[4] Regardless of the type of fear that

Fundamentals of Public Communication Campaigns, First Edition. Jonathan Matusitz.
© 2022 John Wiley & Sons Ltd. Published 2022 by John Wiley & Sons Ltd.

campaign developers try to induce within their audiences, the technique remains the same: fear mongering. **Fear mongering** refers to using fear to leverage the attitudes and actions of the audience towards a specific agenda. Fear mongering frequently works through repetition and different modes of communication in order to constantly underpin the intended effects of employing this technique in a self-reinforcing fashion.[5]

THE EXTENDED PARALLEL PROCESS MODEL (EPPM)

Developed by Witte (1992),[6] the **Extended Parallel Process Model** (**EPPM**) explains how people's attitudes can be modified through fear appeals; that is, when fear is exploited as a reason for persuasion. A **fear appeal** is a persuasive message that tries to stimulate fear in order to direct or switch our behavior through the threat of looming danger or harm. It presents a risk, our susceptibility to the risk, and then some type of protective action as a solution. Fear appeals are most effective (1) when we feel a concern regarding an issue or situation and (2) when we believe to be capable of handling that issue or situation. The success of fear appeals is increased by identifying the proper cognitive processes that regulate danger (as opposed to emotional processes). Cognitive processes regulate fear through denial or coping.[7]

Past Research

The EPPM can explain how campaigners charge themselves with (1) persuading the audience that, say, a health threat is to be taken seriously because it can affect personal lives and (2) instilling an intense belief in the personal achievability of the proposed protective action—e.g., by developing self-efficacy in connection to the recommended health action.[8] Past research confirms that fear appeals can greatly influence attitudes, beliefs, and behaviors. Large-scale campaigns have been dexterous in devising their messages through integration of fear appeals. For example, in a study conducted by Schmitt and Blass (2008),[9] subjects in high and low threat conditions watched suitably edited versions of a fear-arousing video produced by the American Lung Association's antismoking campaign. On the other hand, control condition subjects did not watch it. Threat condition subjects displayed higher antismoking behavioral intentions than the other participants. These results were part of the first effectiveness experiment of this widely used video.

In a number of studies evaluating the impact of the antitobacco "truth" campaign in Florida, which exposed the "predatory" and "manipulative" strategies of the tobacco industry, Zucker et al. (2000)[10] offered promising reports. Indeed, the researchers could establish that results of the campaign included a 92% brand awareness rate among adolescents, a 15% increase in adolescents who agreed with central attitude statements about smoking, a 19.4% decrease in smoking among middle-schoolers, and an 8% decrease among high-school students. However, it is important to acknowledge that fear appeals do not always work. As such, notwithstanding skillful exploitations of fear appeals in anti-skin cancer initiatives, skin cancer continues to rise in the United States, with more than one million cases reported annually. Likewise, traditional public health campaigns that employ scare tactics or passionate lectures telling adolescents to keep away from drugs are not necessarily successful because the directives seem like they are coming from an authority, and youngsters will naturally do the opposite.[11]

The EPPM as a Process Model

The EPPM is a process model, one that gives prominence to the manner by which we think and feel about persuasive messages.[12] Based on the principle that fear is an intricate emotion, Witte (1997)[13] discusses fear in detail and understands that we must consider other less obvious aspects of fear-arousing messages if we are to pinpoint their impact on attitudes. Fear-arousing communication contains two fundamental parts: threat and efficacy information, or a problem and solution. A message must first and foremost menace the audience, persuading them that dangers lie in wait. To achieve this, a message must include the following elements; more specifically, two information processes by which fear appeals can shape attitudes: severity information and susceptibility information. **Severity information** is information about the depth or magnitude of the danger ("Consumption of fatty food can lead to heart disease"). **Susceptibility information** is information about the probability that threatening results will take place ("People who eat a junk-food diet put themselves at risk for getting a heart attack before the age of 40").[14]

After threatening or alarming the audience, the message must offer a proposed solution—a method by which the audience can avoid the threat. It must include efficacy information or evidence about productive ways to face the danger in question. In turn, efficacy is made up of elements that give rise to two additional basics of fear appeals: response efficacy and self-efficacy information. **Response efficacy** is information regarding the effectiveness of the proposed action ("Maintaining a diet high in fruits and vegetables, but low in saturated fat, can reduce the incidence of heart disease"). **Self-efficacy information** is a set of arguments that the person needs to perform the recommended action ("You can change your diet. Millions have"). Each of these message parts can potentially spark a cognitive response in the person. Severity and susceptibility information should persuade the person that the threat is severe and will probably occur, on condition that no modification is made in the problematic behavior. By the same token, response efficacy and self-efficacy information should convince the person that these threatening results can be averted if the suggested actions are taken seriously.[15]

SENSATION SEEKING

Particularly useful for public communication campaigners are the roles of sensation for information processing. **Sensation seeking** is a personality attribute characterized by the search for experiences and feelings that are diverse, new, complex, and intense. Fear is not a deterring factor.[16] Zuckerman (1994)[17] defines sensation seeking as "the seeking of varied, novel, complex, and intense sensations and experiences, and the willingness to take physical, social, legal, and financial risks for the sake of such experience." Sensation seeking can moderately to strongly predict a range of risky behaviors like drug use, unsafe sexual intercourse, wrongdoing, law-breaking activities, drunk driving, and speeding, as indicated by a multitude of studies across four decades in different cultures.[18] Hoyle,

Fejfar, and Miller (2000)[19] discovered that sensation seeking is the personality trait with the strongest and steadiest associations with risky sexual behaviors including numbers of sexual partners, unprotected sex, and unusually risky sexual encounters. In many cases, risk is overlooked, allowed, or minimized; it may even be viewed as adding an extra-excitement to the activity.[20]

High-Sensation Seekers

High-sensation seekers are people who express a longing for freshness and stimulation, a personality feature that increase their chances of engaging in risky health behaviors like cannabis use.[21] Among teenagers, examples of first-time high-sensation seekers are those who voluntarily jeopardize their well-being by binge-drinking and smoking cannabis.[22] If a public communication campaign is set to engage the target audience, a message that brings forth some type of emotion may have higher impact. For some audiences, messages that include unusual content can increase their efficiency—unlike those that straightforwardly and dispassionately state facts. Taken as a whole, sensation seeking has been confirmed to be have a stronger association with seeking high levels of fear than other personality traits. This is why high-sensation-value messages will probably be more processed by and popular with high-sensation seekers than low-sensation-value messages.[23]

Farrelly, Niederdeppe, and Yarsevich (2003)[24] located a series of studies indicating that fear appeals can affect youths' attitudes towards smoking. A compilation of literature reviews of mass media campaigns seeking to decrease tobacco use included one study where a control group exposed to a thought-provoking mass media campaign modified their smoking behavior—more than a control group that was not exposed to the campaign.[25] Sensation seekers are apparently more vulnerable to high-emotion messages, and sensation seeking as a personality trait can more accurately predict drug and alcohol use. In a lab study that diffused several anti-marijuana messages to students and recorded their responses, Stephenson and Palmgreen (2001)[26] reported that high-sensation messages stimulated strong cognitive processing among sensation seekers.

Sensation Seeking Targeting (SENTAR)

Sensation seeking targeting (SENTAR) is a prevention method in the conception and placement of campaign messages, particularly resulting in a successful lessening in cannabis use among high-sensation seeking teenagers. A profound, biologically-based yearning for stimulation seems to make sensation-seeking youths more vulnerable to cannabis or hard drug abuse.[27] As a prevention approach, SENTAR is designed to expressly target high-sensation seeking students in high-school. High-schoolers represent an appealing population because of their psychobiological nature to participate in thrill-seeking behaviors. This urge for new, fresh, intricate, and intense sensations and experiences is often fulfilled through an increasingly higher level of social risks (e.g., impulsive activities and unsafe sex), physical risks (e.g., skydiving, bungee jumping, and driving far above the speed limit), legal risks (e.g., getting arrested and imprisoned), and financial risks (e.g., refusing to pay fines and making precipitate purchases).[28]

| Case Study |

SENTAR strategies entail adapting a public communication campaign to a specific target audience rather than the general public. Normally, "the audience [is]segmented into internally homogenous subgroups that may be more at risk than other segments and that can be reached through certain types of messages."[29] Researchers at the University of Kentucky conducted a new study that turned out to be efficient. Their campaign sought to get the attention of high-sensation seekers by diffusing highly novel messages on drug abuse prevention. The messages suggested that youths enjoy exciting activities instead of drug use. Put another way, they provided high-sensation seekers with stimulus substitutes for the high that those adolescents were longing for [from drugs].[30]

What the Kentucky scholars did was design a series of antidrug television advertisements that were stimulus-laden and that appealed to youths. One advertisement with high-sensation value, titled "Wasted," presented shocking metaphors for frequent terms used by drug users, such as "fried," "wasted," and "blasted." For instance, the word "fried" turned up on the screen backed by a heavy metal song. Then, the words, "With drugs you can get... Fried," turned up. This was right before black-and-white footage of a Vietnamese monk immolating himself and burning to death. Other appalling metaphors were used for the other terms. Then, the sentence, "Without drugs you can still get high," turned up, followed by color segments that showed exciting, high-sensation substitutes for drug use—like hang-gliding and rock climbing.

The theatrical and attention-grabbing antidrug public service announcements (PSAs) were broadcast during programs geared towards high-sensation seekers like action-packed TV shows. To attract high-sensation seekers, a PSA must be spectacular, extreme, and highly original. High-sensation seekers want to see that they can become wheelchair-bound, lose their job, or be dumped by their girlfriend or boyfriend as a consequence of drug use. The Kentucky scholars found that the fear of death is not a disincentive because high-sensation seekers do not think that dying from risky behavior is possible. More than 70% of the targeted age groups were exposed to at least three PSAs each week. Cannabis use was reduced substantially among high-school students.[31]

Sensation Value

Sensation value of televised communications is defined as "the degree to which formal and content audio–visual features of a televised message elicit sensory, affective, and arousal responses."[32] Messages have high-sensation value inasmuch as they possess the following attributes: (1) New, creative, or remarkably unique; (2) complex; (3) powerful stimuli that are passionately intense or physically stimulating; (4) graphic or explicit; (5) fairly ambiguous; (6) unorthodox; (7) fast-paced; and (8) filled with suspense.[33] It is not required for a message to possess all of these attributes. However, these attributes are "ingredients" that can be integrated into the conception of high-sensation-value messages.[34]

In a similar fashion, **perceived message sensation value** (**PMSV**) is the degree to which people view a message as possessing high-sensation-value traits.[35] A great many studies indicate that messages perceived as high-sensation-value messages are more fascinating to and more popular with high-sensation seekers, especially with respect to influencing changes in antidrug standpoints and behavioral intentions.[36] Public communication campaigns including televised PSAs and aimed at high-sensation seekers using a PMSV approach have also been the cause for behavior changes, most notably in the domain of cannabis use reduction among teenagers.[37]

EFFECTS OF ALARMIST LANGUAGE

From the early days of fear appeals, alarmist language has been used to attract attention and stir up motivation to get audiences to adhere to messages. In a world soaked with mediated messages, public communication campaigners must vie for our attention. This may involve **shock tactics**—powerful emotional appeals through both verbal and nonverbal communication.[38] Some think that to persuade audiences to embrace behaviors that they are not willing to embrace requires alarmist language. This includes exaggerations, oversimplifications, and the insincere use of statistics to magnify risk. Regarding the latter, on the basis of moral principles in communication, messages that intentionally misread or misinterpret statistics or that incorporate deep-seated emotional appeals may be unable to meet provisions for scientific honesty, sincerity, correctness, and precision.[39] Calls for personal responsibility are omnipresent in public health interventions and evocative of early exhortations to conquer vices like gluttony, sloth, and lust.[40] Messages can be unequivocal about the fact that disease or disability will be the outcome if one fails to embrace a "responsible" lifestyle and that people who behave recklessly—by not adhering to health messages—will be a liability to their surroundings and society at large.[41]

Negative Effects: Case Studies

Musarò and Parmiggiani (2017)[42] examined the role of promigration campaigns by media outlets that, in the end, contribute to negative stereotypes of the European migrant crisis—specifically concentrating on Italy—because of the media's alarmist language. Upon analyzing the coexistence of the humanitarian messages of saving lives and the criticism of militarized borders, the two researchers reported that the day-by-day diffusion of sensationalist and stereotyped narratives about migrants results in their turning into subjects and objects of fear. As a consequence, not only do those alarmist promigration campaigns cause migrants to face the fear of being unwanted and expelled, but, also, they instigate fear within the Italian population. This is why the authors called for a radical shift in the manner by which campaigners communicate about migrants. Migrants should be regarded not only as objects of policies, but also as collaborators of their own inclusion in modern nations like Italy.

What this case study demonstrates is that alarmist language is frequently used in the public sphere to accentuate the urgency of a message and convey the grave consequences of inaction. The results, however, can backlash. Part of the reason is that such approach can easily trigger negative emotions.[43] In another case study, a qualitative study conducted by Peters, Ruiter, and Kok (2014)[44] sought to examine experts' opinions about the impact of alarmist language. Expert participants included intervention strategists, lawmakers, politicians, scientists, and advertising specialists. They believed that hysterical or gloomy information would gain more attention to a campaign or stimulate self-reflection. The conclusions indicated that campaign developers have a tendency to erroneously assume that target audiences modify their behavior as a natural reaction to perceptions of higher risks, thereby ignoring the other impacts of communicating such risks.

Campaigners and lawmakers are known to elicit fear by employing alarmist language in environmental public communications. Their language can be in many forms. Using illustrations in campaigns about climate change, O'Neill and Nicholson-Cole (2009)[45] identified words and expressions like "dangerous climate change," "climate of fear," and "climate chaos." In another experimental study, led by Benjamin, Por, and Budescu (2017),[46] the phrase "global warming" was determined to elicit fear more often than the phrase "climate change," even in instances where these phrases were used interchangeably. More precisely, 457 participants were given a series of questions about either "climate change" or "global warming." To these participants, the phrase "climate change" suggested connections to changes in general weather patterns and the prospects of natural fluctuations, at the same time contributing to more frequent reported beliefs that the issue could have deep ramifications.[47] Therefore, careful selection of wording (i.e., framing) shapes perceptions of environmental issues. The impact of language as a persuasive instrument to prompt behavior change (directly or indirectly) can be subtle and imperceptible to audiences, owing to strong psychological processes.[48]

Nonconsequentialism: An Argument against Alarmist Language

Consequentialism is a worldview postulating that the outcomes of a specific action become the foundation for any viable moral judgment about that action. According to a consequentialist, then, a morally right action is one that yields good consequences. For the consequentialist, in theory, no inherently right or wrong actions exist. As long as the action has good consequences, it is always right.[49] Consequentialism implies **utilitarianism** (i.e., the end justifies the means) or **ethical egoism** (i.e., people should behave in their own self-interests).[50] For example, an egoistic organization might desire to attain professional fame by conducting a public communication campaign that does not heed the feelings or anticipated reactions from the audience. The designers of the campaign simply believe that it is acceptable to use alarmist language as a thought-provoking manner to induce change in people's attitudes or behaviors.

On the other hand, **nonconsequentialism** is a worldview according to which the end never justifies the means. It is a situation in which public communication actors or policymakers would not use any type of language that they deem inappropriate for public consumption. For the nonconsequentialist, an action is right if it is in harmony with accepted moral laws. The anticipated consequences do not matter at all. With nonconsequentialism, actions have fundamental moral values. Hence, alarmist or even deceptive communication is intrinsically wrong. Even if it is believed that some greater good could be produced (whether in the short or long term), it must first be ascertained that no other morally alternative exists that would be equally as effective.[51]

For the nonconsequentialist, using alarmist language could damage the credibility of communication campaigns overall. This is why this approach may not be the best solution to modify behaviors, attitudes, or beliefs. It would also be useful for campaign designers to seek advice from others, including a sample from the target audience. Douglas (1994)[52] describes how campaigns with alarmist language use rhetoric related to risk and liability. The language of risk becomes easily politicized too because it is socially constructed. In fact, some risk-taking actions may even be socially approved and even revered (e.g., risks associated with sports and firefighting), while others are outright rejected (e.g., riding a motorcycle without a helmet, smoking cigarettes, and unsafe sex). Some forms of risk-taking are encouraged because they are viewed as helping society and the Other, or they may be frowned upon because they are perceived as purely fulfilling personal gratification.[53]

VISUAL MATERIALS

Visual materials play an important role in the diffusion of messages. They enhance cognitive abilities when processed in concert with words.[54] They also communicate both literal (denotative) and symbolic (connotative) meanings.[55] They are internalized and processed faster than texts.[56] They more easily guide our attention, and manipulate exposure to, and connection with, information.[57] Visual materials can stimulate cognitive elaboration and ethical reasoning,[58] and contribute tremendously to higher emotions, engagement, and persuasion.[59] Depending on context, relevant images can improve learning and recollection of content.[60] They can shape audience reactions by implying, rather than openly expressing, associations between components of an image or between image and text. The ostensible objectivity of some types of images, particularly pictures and graphs, can also strengthen the relationship between the images and reality.[61]

Responsive Chord

Developed by Schwartz (1973),[62] the theory of **responsive chord** rests on the premise that the communication process is contingent on information with which people are already familiar. Visual materials are capable of producing intense feelings. It is not the visual itself that can achieve this, but it is its ability to elicit responses in individuals that are linked to their beliefs and values—i.e., the responsive chord. It is generally the case that political campaigns stir up voters' emotions by way of colorful visuals, a method that observers argue can warp the rational decision-making mechanism on which the democratic apparatus lies. Thus, campaigns attain their objectives, to some extent, by increasing emotional appeals thanks to visuals because they can promote desirable behavior more easily.

Color is a vital part of visual communication because of its attention-grabbing power. Color can also uphold the attention of audiences and reveal the details of the message to them. Artists are hired to use color by stressing certain characteristics of messages and disseminate desired messages. For health communication interventions, color is seen as essential to communicate health messages through posters to the target audience. It is efficient because color can effortlessly evoke emotions from people.[63] Visually-laden campaigns can transform the manner by which we participate and make decisions on the basis of images (and even music). Triggering interest and fervor through visual materials encourages participation and affirms existing loyalties. At the same time, triggering fear fuels vigilance, enhances reliance on current evaluations, and facilitates persuasion.[64]

Vivid Information

Information is considered vivid to the degree that it is visually appealing, imagery-provoking, emotionally tempting, and even close in a sensory, temporal, or spatial manner. Vivid information increases the chances of remembering campaign messages. The salience that it entails renders it particularly powerful. Psychological publications on social cognition abound with mental tactics whereby human beings interpret their worlds. One conclusion reveals that we have methodically biased perceptions whereby we overrate low-frequency vivid killers (and underrate high-frequency gentle killers).[65] Boholm (1998)[66] puts forward the notion that vivid messages based on visuals can wield a "positioning power" on the audience's imagination, which may be immune to arguments that defy the feelings they create. Visuals can be absorbed in an unmediated way because message recipients are rarely motivated to consider or deconstruct them in a manner that takes place in relation to verbal material. With respect to the association between persuasion and visuals, a solid chain of reasoning suggests that persuasion is influenced by pushing the audience into a state of emotion. In regards to campaigns, those who have been raised and educated mostly through texts are being increasingly exposed to visual-rich social marketing campaigns. This transformation speaks to a body of evidence that words alone are not sufficiently appealing to people—at least, not in a way that allows public communication campaigns to change behaviors, attitudes, and beliefs. Rather, people have to be "roped in" through visual materials.[67]

Case Study: Climate Communication Campaigns

Since the dawn of the twenty-first century, climate communication campaigns that incorporate visual materials are often hypothesized as facilitating the audience's understanding and absorption of information through well-designed or well-selected images or frames. This is especially true when the information or subject is complex. Visuals help bolster the objective truth value of the messages that they communicate; they can instill emotions that boost the urgency of risks and threats.[68] Under such circumstances, however, campaigners have employed imagery to evoke fear or anxiety, notwithstanding evidence that nonthreatening visuals related to common emotions and concerns (1) stimulate more efficient participation in climate change issues;[69] (2) neglect the visual competences or background knowledge necessary to make sense of imagery in the intended manner;[70] or (3) risk enabling the concreteness and objective truth linked to specific kinds of imagery to erode nuanced communication regarding uncertainty and risk. The use of such visual imagery to assist the audience in interpreting reality depends on persuasive communication approaches, which can render a message more credible and motivate the audience to take action (again, in the short or long term).[71]

PROVOCATION: DEFINITIONS

Provocation is the process of inciting people (not) to take actions on the basis of powerfully elicited emotions, such as anger, shock, and disgust, as a consequence of certain types of norm transgressions. Provocation is mostly cultural, as audiences have different perceptions of what constitutes appropriate and inappropriate phenomena.[72] In public communication, provocation can be classified into three main categories: distinctiveness, ambiguity, and transgression of norms and taboos.

- **Distinctiveness** in public communication is the ability to raise the audience's level of attention.[73] Going back to the subject of visual materials, distinctiveness works well in the domains of size, position, and color of messages. Distinctive stimuli bring a positive impact on the extent to which attention is generated and the message is remembered.[74] Irrespective of content, even when similar to other messages, if a message is not distinctive enough it could lose some of its provocative power. In fact, distinctiveness is at the core of the innovative nature of public communication campaigns. Provocation is a common route for being distinctive and can improve the impact of a strategy based—until audiences become accustomed to a certain type of provocation and begin to switch off. Part of the difficulty for a campaigner using provocation is the continuous reinvention of the campaign or update of messages to sustain originality.[75]

- **Ambiguity** in public communication attempts to elevate intrigue and make associations between variables that defy logic. These intrigues and associations have to be well executed, otherwise the message becomes confusing or too mystifying. Ambiguity can work when it encapsulates layers of meanings in an unforgettable slogan.[76] The degree to which a message leaves room for a range of interpretations matters. The fundamental principle behind message ambiguity is that a provocative message with no ambiguity is more expected to be ignored by those people who are shocked and, as a result, will not be processed at all. Put another way, the foundation of the provocative appeal of a message is generally the nonsense it purposely expresses.[77] According to Umberto Eco (1976),[78] attention is placed on the multiple meanings of messages, or "the multiple meanings engendered by the structural relation of signs" within the text.[79] It ultimately gives opportunity for an artistic or visual experience.

- **Transgression of norms and taboos** in public communication is anticipated to occur when the substance of a message alludes to something that is deemed by the audience as morally prohibited. Making sexual appeals in messages is often considered a case of transgression because the topic of sexuality is taboo—to varying degrees—in many cultures across the world.[80] More specifically, the exploitation of provocative stimuli like mild erotica is one example of such transgression, even though interpretations of the extent of transgression may differ across cultures.[81] Above and beyond the issue of sexuality, it could be claimed that other subjects could contain a similar level of shock value across the world. These topics include drugs, violence, and racial concerns.[82]

Of all three categories, transgression of norms and taboos elicits the most basic emotions, like disgust. **Basic emotions** are called "basic" because they are not composites or amalgamations of other emotions. Disgust occurs repeatedly when seeing, feeling, touching, smelling, or ingesting body waste or body matter. **Disgust stimuli** are also caused by death and poor hygiene.[83] Human reactions include vomiting, retching, recoiling, feeling nauseated, and taking offence. A certain number of modern-day health and safety initiatives, as well as those depicting natural and manmade disasters, use disgust-evoking imagery.[84] Although the use of transgression of norms and taboos has existed for many decades and continues to grow, the successes of this type of strategy are mixed.

Case Study: Antismoking Campaigns in England

The repeated use of intense fear evocation is manifest in the health and safety domain in England. From antismoking campaigns that display images of patients suffering from lung disease to "think—kill your speed" interventions to address speeding when driving, disgust stimuli are praised as convincing individuals to take on healthy and safe behaviors and to deter them from behaving in unhealthy and unsafe ways. Present-day health campaigns are heavily inspired by disgust-evoking visuals. Antismoking messages in the English mass media are showing cigarettes as arteries filled with cholesterol/fat and the smoker's human heart as one with smoke coming out of it. The intention seems to cause audiences to be disgusted by inviting them to look at body matter out of place. In the vein of previous antismoking campaigns that have depicted the smoker's mouth as an ashtray, present-day ones portray a beautiful young lady with highly visible wrinkles around her mouth, which the complementary text that reads "cat's-bum mouth." Another campaign depicts an attractive young lady with discolored and uneven teeth. Consistent with previous campaigns, smokers are depicted as quasi-dead, diseased humans. Such portrayals seem to reflect the notion—at least, from the perspective of campaign designers—that triggering sentiments of disgust will dissuade smokers from smoking and/or nonsmokers from trying it.[85]

SHOCKVERTISING

Also referred to as **shock advertising**, **shockvertising** is a type of advertising that "deliberately, rather than inadvertently, startles and offends its audience by violating norms for social values and personal ideals."[86] It is the inclusion of fear appeals, graphic visuals, and/or brusque slogans to promote a cause or issue (e.g., public service issue, health issue, and so forth). Shockvertising is intended mostly to grab people's attention and generate buzz.[87] As described previously, provocative messages are more likely to be recalled in comparison with nonprovocative ones. Shockvertising became notorious in antifur or antismoking campaigns a few decades ago. This type of campaign undoubtedly attracted the attention of various audiences worldwide, in spite of the fact that it came under heavy criticism on account of its offensive and "no holds barred" style. Products or issues that necessitate special attention have often been infused with negative shock values.[88]

Controversial, Troubling, Explicit, and Crass

Shockvertising in public communication campaigns is regularly controversial, troubling, explicit, and crass. It is imbued with audacious and provocative messages that challenge the audience's traditional conception of the social order. It not only causes offense to adults, but it also scares children, using fear tactics to diffuse a public service message, nevertheless creating a significant impact.[89] Shock campaigns can be appalling and distasteful for a number of reasons, and abuse of religious, sociocultural, and political mores happens in a multitude of ways. They can be framed as disrespect to tradition, law, or practice (e.g., vulgar or unsavory sexual references or obscenity), insolence towards the sociomoral code (e.g., crudeness, violence, nudity, body waste, or profanity) or the presentation of images or words that are gruesome, petrifying, or abhorrent (e.g., ghastly or revolting segments, or brutality).[90]

One category of such controversial, troubling, explicit, and crass type of communication is buzz campaigning. **Buzz campaigning** stems from the word **buzzy**, referring to the sound that instantly grabs attention or is infuriating to the point of drawing attention. Buzz campaigning, then, is a campaigning method that causes a stir and uproar about a product, service, or issue that pushed audiences to pay attention. To maximize the potential of a particular campaign, people will talk about it through word-of-mouth transmission or the diffusion of visuals on social media.[91]

Selective Perception Theory

The effects of shockvertising can also be explained through the theory of selective perception. **Selective perception theory** posits that people perceive whatever they wish to in mediated messages, at the same time paying no attention to opposing viewpoints. It is a broad concept that describes the behavior all human beings exhibit to perceive phenomena from their personal or cultural frame of reference. The theory also explains how we classify and make sense of sensory information in a manner that privileges one classification or interpretation over another. In other terms, selective perception is a type of bias because humans interpret information in a manner that is harmonious with their current values and beliefs. Psychologists assume that this process happens automatically.[92]

People are selective at varying degrees and at varying times. This is reflected (1) through the types and amounts of readings that they do, what they listen to, or what they watch (selective exposure); (2) in the degree of attention that they devote to content (selective attention); (3) in how they make sense of information and what they want to believe (selective perception); and (4) in what they remember (selective retention). Diverse levels of selectivity function as filters on texts and visuals that people consume.[93] Klapper (1960)[94] remarked that humans are inclined to give preferentiality to information that strengthens their preexisting views and to steer clear of contradictory information (that is, selective exposure). In addition to working in negative fashions, selectivity can work in positive ways. For example, in a 2003 study conducted for the Broadcasting Standards Commission, the BBC and other agencies in the United Kingdom determined that even "children are able to distinguish between fictional violence and violence that is 'real'."[95] This arguably gives reasons for the lack of evidence that on-screen scenes of violence are replicated in the real world.

Perceptual Defense and the Salience Effect

Selective perception is a matter of concern for advertisers, as audiences may identify with some advertisements and not others, depending on their preexisting beliefs about the brand.[96] From this vantage point, shockvertising works because people choose, arrange, and assess stimuli from the external environment to bestow meaningful experiences for themselves. Put simply, we focus on certain aspects of their environment to the detriment of others. We unconsciously select which information to pay attention to. This type of selection is based on various perceptual filters that come from our earlier experiences (sometimes, even from childhood). One category of this type of filter is perceptual defense. **Perceptual defense** is the propensity for people to shield themselves from ideas, objects, or circumstances that are threatening. If people see a certain message as threatening or upsetting, they will filter it out. An illustration of this is a heavy smoker who filters out an image of cancer-sick lungs because the content is viewed as disturbing and unpleasant.[97]

The **salience effect** is founded on the idea that, when individuals' attention is aimed at one aspect of the environment, they tend to remember and maintain it as central when making subsequent decisions. It answers the question, "To which elements are we the most attracted?" This is somewhat connected to the **availability heuristic**,[98] a foundation stone of social cognition. It rests on the premise that a phenomenon is deemed recurrent or plausible to the degree that instances of it can be extracted from memory without difficulty. Therefore, the point is that the emotional feature of visual materials nurtures its vividness. Vivid images or symbols leave a rich and intense memory trace where less vivid content would disappear gradually. This determines the salience of what it represents.[99]

FRAMING THEORY

Framing theory is based on the assumption that communicators employ schemas, mental images, or symbolic representations to describe "what exists, what happens, and what matters."[100] The concept of framing was first conceptualized by Erving Goffman (1974),[101] a Canadian-born sociologist, and later sharpened by Snow, Rochford, Jr., Worden, and Benford (1986). They characterized frames as "schemata of interpretation that enable individuals to locate, perceive, identify, and label occurrences within their life space and the world at large."[102] Framing theory was developed even further by Entman (1993),[103] who considered **framing** a form of social construction of an issue; framing can be done by media outlets, political or social movements, lawmakers, and other players and entities. Fluency in a language or knowledge community inevitably shapes our interpretations of the meanings assigned to concepts or phrases. Even though frames aid communicators in categorizing and structuring incoming stimuli, they can also act as political tools.[104] For example, they can be employed to depict the social order as positive or gloomy, normal or abnormal, and fair or harmful. Over time, repeated use of frames makes them enshrined into society; frames now operate as mainstream narratives. Audiences, then, embrace the values, lifestyles, and self-definitions intrinsic within those narratives.[105]

Framing a Campaign

In a public communication campaign, framing consists of building a central message or movement which encapsulates its shared characteristics and objectives. The central message is crafted as a narrative that covers the collective perceptions of the campaign's goals, values, features, and identity. The framing of an issue is a productive method to reveal this identity and express the movement's goals to the public at large. The construction of the frame and the narrative are essential in earning the public's support on an issue to fulfill a given agenda. Framing theory recognizes that, to guarantee success for a campaign's issue objectives, the issue needs to be framed in a way that correspond to the interests of their constituents. If done properly, the framing of the issue will eventually be the dominant frame in the discourse of society, gaining momentum for additional issues or policies.[106]

In health communication campaigns, for example, framing can be done through a process that presents information that is either more negative (i.e., losses, prevention, and unwanted outcomes) or more positive (i.e., gains, promotion, and desirable outcomes), whereas the various descriptions are comparable in informational substance. Despite being apparently subtle, message framing is confirmed to be a successful health communication approach for championing behavior change across a range of health behaviors. In health communication, a number of messages can be framed with respect to either the benefits of following the recommended behavior (gain-framed message) or the costs of not following the behavior (loss-framed message).[107] The differences between gain-framed messages and loss-framed messages are explained next.

Gain-Framed vs. Loss-Framed Messages

Gain-framed messages highlight the benefits or gains of abiding by messages. They accentuate the advantages of either following or not following a course of action.[108] A gain-framed message for a public health campaign may look as follows: "One in five lives could be saved in the US if people didn't smoke."[109] Or, as the major case study on the People for the Ethical Treatment of Animals (PETA)—in the next sections—will demonstrate, an example could be, "Be naked like animals, and you will live longer" or "Save animals to decrease the risk of mass extinction on Earth." **Loss-framed messages** emphasize the risks or costs of not following messages. They draw attention to the disadvantages of either following or not following a course of action.[110] A loss-framed message could look as follows: "One in five deaths occurs in the US because people smoke." Or, as PETA would say, "By killing animals, humans are also destroying themselves."

Gain-framed messages can be more influential than loss-framed messages when the results are more certain or obvious. As a rule, people like certain alternatives better than uncertain ones.[111] Gain-framed messages are more successful when aiming at prevention behavior, such as PETA's idea of preventing mass extinction on Earth by saving animals. In contrast, loss-framed messages are more successful when directed at detection or screening behaviors, such as PETA's idea of reporting any type of animal cruelty, the absence of which would destroy the human race in the process (i.e., because of decaying ethics, etc.). Along these lines, loss-framed messages may cause higher perceived threats (as well as reactance) from animal cruelty, while gain-framed messages may cause a higher decrease in positive feelings *vis-à-vis* animal cruelty than loss-framed messages.

Lastly, message framing is akin to **choice architecture**. Choice architecture means that the construction of different frames gives the audience choices. The framing of the actual presentation of choices also has an impact on decision-making. The number of choices offered, the way by which attributes are defined, and the existence of a flaw can all shape public choice. By the same token, choice architecture can be further explained through prospect theory.[112] **Prospect theory** describes how we choose between the likelihood of gains and losses.[113] Accordingly, it corresponds to the audience's reaction to gain-framed and loss-framed messages in regards to a variety of specific behaviors.

Case Study: People for the Ethical Treatment of Animals (PETA)

Early animal rights philosophy was a major discipline on the European continent, pointing the fingers at vivisection activists like René Descartes, who perceived animals as barely more than "mindless machines." Early advocates of human compassion (not rights) towards animals included Samuel Johnson, Emmanuel Kant, Henry Primatt, and Jeremy Bentham, who eminently said: "The question is not, Can they reason? Nor, can they talk? But can they suffer?"[114] Today, animal rights activists generally campaign for three major arguments:[115]

- Animals and humans are similar in many respects. They are conscious beings who have the benefit of life and who go through pain and suffering;
- Animals are innocent, unlike humans. They do not do anything to deserve abuse, exploitation, or cruelty on the part of humans;
- Treating animals fairly and acceptably helps fashion a more benevolent world, whereas abuse, exploitation, and cruelty contribute to moral bankruptcy.

Of all animal rights philosophers today, Peter Singer is arguably the most famous and is presently the Ira DuCamp Chair of Bioethics at Princeton University's Center for Human Values. Singer is a major voice for animal rights and his readings are familiar among activists. For Singer (1999),[116] all animals might not have the same levels of equality and interests, but many share some fundamental interests that ought to be cherished, according to their grade of "sentience." For Singer, "all sentient creatures are equal—are entitled to equal consideration of their interests, whatever those interests may be."

PETA as an Organization

People for the Ethical Treatment of Animals, or **PETA**, is an American animal rights organization headquartered in Norfolk, VA, established by Ingrid Newkirk and Alex Pacheco. Newkirk is still the president today. By June 2021, the nonprofit corporation boasted 6.5 million supporters. Its slogan is "Animals are not ours to experiment on, eat, wear, use for entertainment, or abuse in any other way."[117] PETA has laid out four principal issues—resistance to factory farming, fur farming, animal testing, and the exploitation of animals in entertainment. It also champions a vegan way of life and opposes eating meat, fishing, the slaying of animals considered pests, the maintenance of chained backyard dogs, cock fighting, dog fighting, beekeeping, and bullfighting.[118] In their early adulthood, Ingrid Newkirk was working on a career as a stockbroker, whereas Alex Pacheco was set to be a Catholic priest. In 1978, after visiting a slaughterhouse where his friend was employed, Pacheco was in deep shock and it became a turning point in his life. After witnessing the brutal carnage of dairy cows, pigs, and chickens, he was resolute to connect with the animal advocacy movement.[119] Already in the early 1980s, PETA quickly made a name for itself after the tragedy of the Silver Spring monkeys, during which Pacheco gained access to a laboratory to report the violations of animal protection laws.[120] Today, Newkirk and Pacheco are entirely associated with their PETA organization, still the world's largest animal advocacy group.

Techniques and Communications

Infiltration has remained an important tactic of PETA's catalog of strategies. The organization is frequently called on to obtain proof of carnage in laboratories, slaughterhouses, pig farms, roadside zoos, entertainment venues, and fur farms. Some of PETA's surreptitious activities have been quite triumphant and have managed to save a great many animals. In addition to infiltrations, PETA's repertoire includes an assortment of communicative tactics to save animals: protests, marches, online petitions, book publishing, leaflets and videos, the management of animal shelters, and lobbying. The organization also enjoys many celebrity endorsements and imaginatively uses erotic images to diffuse animal advocacy messages. Thanks to PETA, an increasing number of people are embracing the idea that it is ethically not acceptable to abuse animals.[121]

At the legal level, PETA has accomplished remarkable improvements in legislation, including the prohibition of gunning down live animals in military weapons training and of using live animals in automobile crash tests. The organization has successfully convinced important cosmetics companies to abandon testing on animals, fashion designers to stop manufacturing fur, restaurant chains to increase animal welfare standards, and retailers to no longer sell glue traps.[122] Today, PETA operates a seemingly unlimited source of websites, and all of them are unambiguous about communicating the organization's mission. Scientists who perform tests on live animals have come under scrutiny (marchofcrimes.com, stopanimal-tests.com), and, across the United States, partly thanks to PETA, the majority of investigators who use animals in laboratories—several thousands of them—are now hesitating to even to talk about their experiments in public.[123]

PETA's Campaigns

PETA is notorious for its provocative public communication campaigns, along with a broad base of celebrity support. Its honorary executives—Paul McCartney, Alicia Silverstone, Eva Mendes, Charlize Theron, Ellen DeGeneres, and a multitude of other international celebrities—have been featured in its campaigns.[124] Every week, Newkirk organizes what *The New Yorker* refers to as a "war council," with several key strategists who convene at a square table in the PETA conference room. During the meeting, no suggestion is deemed too outrageous.[125] By and large, organizations like PETA conduct two types of public communication campaigns: animal welfare initiatives and rights-oriented approaches.

Animal welfare initiatives are campaigns that promote healthier living conditions for animals during their treatment. Such initiatives are not directed at the instrumental use of animals, but attempt to enrich the quality of the lives enjoyed by animals (even though they remain subordinated to human ends).[126] On the other hand, **rights-oriented approaches** are concerned with both the quality of lives that animals enjoy and whether or not they benefit from liberty, autonomy, and other rights adapted to their capacities and needs. Animal rights advocates devote more time and energy to actions that will chip away at human endeavors that intentionally or unintentionally abuse animals by treating them as objects and as human commodities. Within the framework of justice for livestock and farm animals, what animal activists want are not larger cages, but no cages at all.[127]

CAMPAIGN #1: "I'D RATHER GO NAKED THAN WEAR FUR"

"I'd Rather Go Naked Than Wear Fur" was PETA's most notorious and visible communication campaign. Until February 2020, its campaign to outlaw the use, marketing, and selling of fur was promoted through advertisements that starred nude ladies who would prefer going naked than wearing fur. Sexualized pictures of female personalities relinquishing their taste for the hair of animals were meant to persuade other women—still the main consumers of fur today—to repudiate fur themselves. Those advertisements were actually directed at a widely female consumer base—a demographic regularly subject to harassment and intimidation as a consequence of the growingly normative character of women's sexual victimization.[128] "I'd Rather Go Naked Than Wear Fur" was an iconic enterprise that sought to make ethical fashion cool. The most famous supermodels of the globe posed naked for a string of antifur ads that became symbolic of the 1990s. Kate Moss, Naomi Campbell, Christy Turlington, Cindy Crawford, and Elle McPherson were all pictured under the banner "We'd rather go naked than wear fur."[129]

Women as Headline-Grabbers

PETA defended their nude campaign by saying that it had the power to constantly grab headlines. The exploitation of women's connection to nature as both nurturer and temptress was now profitable. As natural caretakers, women can easily be the representatives of animal rights. One component of their nurturer role is to fulfill the needs of both men and nonhumans (i.e., animals). Women personify the animal rights movement by being activists and performing its routine, but necessary, organizational work. Nevertheless, regarded as temptresses of the earthly realm, women have become sexualized objects used for sex and thirsty for power even in the social movement environment. By looking naked and victimized, women become essential tools of activism, thereby hoping to attract attention and men to the cause.[130]

The animal rights movement is usually perceived as a women's movement. Women dominated the first animal protection movements in the nineteenth century, when animals—together with children, inmates, and the downtrodden—became the targets of compassion. Increasingly, animals were adopted as relatives inside households.[131] Animal activism, in conjunction with other reform movements, gave women a conduit of participation in public life and expanded their status through their humanitarian efforts in the media—all of this during an era where women were excluded from many spheres of life (including the right to vote). Women identified themselves as caretakers against the callous realities of factory life and working-class hardships.[132]

Female Sexuality and Female Bodies

Based on the three-part element of provocation—distinctiveness, ambiguity, and transgression of norms and taboos—the latter was the most useful for PETA in drawing attention, recruiting volunteers and advocates, and producing income as it bestowed the moral shocks so needed for activism. It solidified the organization as even more distinct and unique in the world of reform movements.[133] The presence of female sexuality in PETA's campaign ought not to be interpreted as sexist or perpetuating female sexualization. Rather, the campaign spoke to a new genre of intersectional feminist ethic. PETA presented an intersectional feminist perspective, that is, a perspective reflecting the diversity of signs and symbols of identities and the corresponding structures of gender, race, and species that inform them.[134] Adams and Donovan (2000)[135] examined the gendered and racial ideologies of animal exploitation and the politics of sexist and racist customs towards species. The two authors made the point that the objectification and exploitation of women, racial groups, and animals actually intersect; they are highly connected and mutually sustaining. Adams (2003)[136] lays emphasis on the discursive links between images of animals and images of women. For Adams, the two intersect with each other as the common subordinated denominator in the social structure—i.e., dominating men commodify exchanges of meat-eating and heterosexist sexuality.

In January 2011, American actress Taraji P. Henson posed nude for PETA's "I'd Rather Go Naked Than Wear Fur" campaign. Forty years old at that time, Henson was photographed from the side completely naked and with her left arm hiding most of her breasts and her legs crossed to keep her vagina from view. As the ad read, "Animals killed for their fur are electrocuted, drowned, beaten, and often skinned alive." The message also read, "Be comfortable in your own skin" and "let animals keeps theirs."[137] The phrase "I'd rather go naked than wear fur" is now associated with pop culture icons—in varying degrees of undress—from Pamela Anderson to Eva Mendes, Pink, and Dennis Rodman. However, in February 2020, after almost 30 years of persuading countless celebrities to strip down for antifur ads, PETA abandoned its campaign. Owing to an increasing number of corporations, designers, and retailers who have refused to deal with animal skins in recent years, PETA deemed its long-running awareness campaign to be no longer needed.[138]

Beyond the antifur agenda, PETA's utilization of naked female bodies in their campaign also extended to other topics, including circuses, exotic skins, and veganism. In 2012, the organization set up a pornography website that matched their insufficiently clad female models with dreadful scenes of nonhuman animal suffering. To protect its image, PETA maintained that an .xxx domain name was primordial for gaining the public's attention. In London, the group organized a public demonstration in Trafalgar Square that featured two naked Playboy models in a bathtub to defend veganism as a way to conserve water.[139] In a commercial made specifically for Superbowl Sunday but rejected because of its sexual explicitness, PETA qualified the problem of meat-eating as pornographic pleasure and food porn. Speaking of food porn, PETA incorporated a soundtrack of sexual breathing and moaning to show how lingerie-clad women licked vegetables, rubbed their bodies against them, and bathed with these vegetables. They also masturbated with pumpkins, broccoli, and asparagus, with a line that read: "Studies show vegetarians have better sex."[140]

CAMPAIGN #2: "HOLOCAUST ON YOUR PLATE"

In 2003, PETA launched a new campaign, called "Holocaust on Your Plate," to compare the slaughter of animals for exploitation to the genocide of six million Jews in World War II. The campaign capitalized on the power of disgust stimuli: "Holocaust on Your Plate" juxtaposed 60-square-foot visual displays of animals in slaughterhouses with harrowing photos of emaciated Jews in Nazi death camps.[141] One photograph depicting a gaunt and sunken Jew was placed next to another of a starving cow. Another juxtaposed a heap of naked human bodies with a heap of pig remains. The exhibition started as a show in San Diego and at the

University of California, Los Angeles. PETA intended to take its "Holocaust on Your Plate" campaign on a tour of the United States and soon got its exhibition website, masskilling. com, up and running. PETA even called on the Jewish community for endorsement. In an open letter posted on the organization's website, it mentioned Isaac Bashevis Singer, a Jewish Nobel laureate who said of animals: "In relation to them, all people are Nazis."[142]

The first 60-square-foot visual display was called "Walking Skeletons." It portrayed a double line of famished victims, pallid with shaven heads, next to an equally pale and worryingly thin cow. Another visual display was named "Baby Butchers." On one side were young Jews in striped garments behind barbed wire; on the other were piglets looking at us from behind bars. Another visual bore the caption "To animals, all people are Nazis," featuring inmates lying on very narrow bunks on one side and rows of "broiler" chickens on the other. Nearby was a caption that read "the final indignity," showing a pile of pigs' carcasses. The set of displays ends with a final placard titled, "The Holocaust is on your plate: During the seven years between 1938 and 1945, 12 million people perished in the Holocaust. The same number of animals is killed every four hours for food in the US alone."[143]

Holocaust, Animals, and Himmler

Rarely is it acknowledged that the very term "Holocaust" inherently entails a comparison to animal exploitation. Sax (2000)[144] avers that "Holocaust" originally denoted "a Hebrew sacrifice in which the entire animal was given to Yahweh [God] to be consumed with fire." At some point in history, then, a repulsive genre of animal exploitation became the embodiment for what happened to the Jews in Nazi concentration camps. One could wonder if it is appropriate to compare the Holocaust with animal exploitation, despite the fact that the term itself involves such a comparison (although metaphorically). However, it is important to find out whether the Holocaust is analogous to contemporary methods of animal exploitation at large.[145]

PETA's "Holocaust on Your Plate" campaign focused on the animalistic aspect of the Holocaust and the related treatment of Jewish prisoners in death camps like Auschwitz. In the same way that Jews were on bunks, chickens are placed in rows in cages. Black-and-white photos of hungry victims were made to stand opposite hungry cattle. Likewise, rows of human bodies and rows of cattle corpses were juxtaposed to each other. The present-day treatment of "broiler" chickens—approximately nine billion of them are killed each year—was made to be connected symbolically to Heinrich Himmler, the main architect of the Holocaust. Himmler transferred his "interest in the breeding and killing of chickens... to the breeding and killing of humans."[146] Under the headline titled "Processing Lives," veal calves and laying hens are matched up to victims of the Holocaust, with both types of dead beings "dehumanized by overcrowding and mechanization." Additional Holocaust-inspired comparisons seem facile and bland, as echoed by the words of Costello: "The leather sofa and handbag are the modern equivalent of the lampshades made from the skins of the people killed in the death camps."[147]

Another key message intrinsic within PETA's campaign is that consumers tend to escape blame for the animal-based foods that they eat on a day-to-day basis, even just by not wanting to truly treat it as an issue. Just like locals who were aware of the tragedy at those camps in Germany and occupied lands (but did nothing about it, if they ever thought about it), many consumers treat animals in the same way in their daily diets.[148] They would rather follow the social order and let activists perform the "dirty work"—and the thinking—in their place. Claiming erroneously that we must eat meat may simply serve to cover up distressing choices in the matter. The notion of social order also implies that humans are habituated to be uninterested in animal suffering because it has become entrenched within our networks and social institutions. Even a number of scientists methodically employ objectifying language with respect to animals. Without a doubt, the refusal to identify with victims is reminiscent of Nazi rhetoric.[149]

Personhood

Peter Singer (1985)[150] has made the concept of "personhood" part of our vocabulary. For the philosopher, a "person" is an animal with a certain level of sentience and can be either a nonanimal human or a nonhuman animal. This conceptualization hypothetically allows great apes, cetaceans, and a certain number of higher mammals to enjoy many of the rights granted to humans. For Singer (1985), this new theorization of rights is of utmost importance because animals and humans share interests in common. For example, both species are interested in avoiding physical pain; "those interests are to be counted equally, with no automatic discount just because one of the beings is not human."[151]

For Charles Patterson (2002),[152] an American defender of animal rights, the emergence of the American industrial slaughterhouse became the reason for both the loss of personhood for animals and the machinery of death in Nazi Germany. Giant farming and meateating became important socializing mechanisms for committing genocide. To this day, cattle continue to be systematically branded by hot irons, sterilized, and tail-docked. Birds are routinely de-beaked—all without anesthesia. There is no credibility to contemporary practices which lawfully profess to avoid "unnecessary suffering." Patterson observes how the Nazis' conceptualization of personhood *vis-à-vis* their Jewish prisoners was confined to finding ways of killing them in the least stressful way possible. To this point, it was medically confirmed that, by gunning down Jews—so that they fall into mass graves— the SS were suffering from mental diseases.[153]

For Nazis, Jews were to be seen as animals or subhuman. Jews themselves complained that they were treated like animals, as many animals are treated today.[154] Patterson (2002)[155] calls Nazis uber-carnivores, meaning that their outward passion for meat-eating corresponded to their zeal as bloodless killers. Thus, we must deal with cheap throw-away comments: "Judging from letters and diaries of the killers in the camps, eating animals was one of their greatest pleasures."[156] His analysis of eating habits during World War II suggests that Wehrmacht and SS diets contained a lot of meat, as a way to make up for the "not very pleasant stuff" they were required to do. In his examination of letters describing massive meals in an environment of death and despair, Patterson noticed how the Nazi writers handled the abundance of food in front of them.

Criticism

"Holocaust on Your Plate" did not earn favor from Jewish organizations. Abraham Foxman, National Director of the Anti-Defamation League and a Holocaust survivor himself, said that PETA's campaign was "outrageous, offensive and takes chutzpah to new heights." He added that, although the exploitation of animals is appalling, "the effort by PETA to compare the deliberate systematic murder of millions of Jews to the issue of animal rights is abhorrent." "Rather than deepen our revulsion against what the Nazis did to the Jews, the project will undermine the struggle to understand the Holocaust and to find a way to make sure such catastrophes never happen again," he also added.[157]

Taken as a whole, Jewish communities in North America perceived the campaign as a controversial case of misusing hurtful historical images. PETA's exploitation of death camp photos to describe the conditions of factory farms and slaughterhouses also drew negative criticism from the Canadian Jewish Congress and many Holocaust survivors, groups, authors, artists, and museum supervisors and donors. Throughout PETA's entire initiative in 2003, the following statement by Manuel Prutschi, National Director of Community Relations for the Canadian Jewish Congress, made his position clear: "To equate what is truly one of the most monumental crimes in the history of mankind to the abusive treatment of animals is totally unconscionable."[158]

DESCRIBING PETA'S CAMPAIGNS THROUGH SELF-EFFICACY THEORY AND INOCULATION THEORY

Developed by Albert Bandura (1977),[159] a Canadian–American psychologist, **self-efficacy theory** predicates that all courses of psychological change operate through the modification of the person's expectancies of self-mastery or individual efficacy. This central construct emphasizes the role of the person's perceived ability to perform behaviors effectively. Those who are confident about implementing proposed actions are more likely to engage in and maintain behavioral enactment efforts. Put another way, **self-efficacy** is the belief that we have the skills and aptitudes required to accomplish the behavior under various circumstances. We are also motivated to perform the behavior required for behavior change. Logically, an individual has to believe that he or she can (1) act in a recommended way under various circumstances and (2) be motivated to do it.[160] As was discussed a few pages earlier with framing theory, with respect to PETA's campaigns, to achieve self-efficacy and an appropriate level of confidence and motivation, one could use a gain-framed message such as "Be naked like animals, and you will live longer" or "Save animals to decrease the risk of mass extinction on Earth." Similarly, one could adhere to a loss-framed message such as "By killing animals, humans are also destroying themselves."

Maddux and Rogers (1983)[161] and Sutton and Eiser (1984)[162] have established that self-efficacy has a significant impact on the ways that audiences react to provocation and fear. Snipes, LaTour, and Bliss's (1999)[163] study was based on an experiment that included a campaign in which women were pushed to purchase a stun gun for protection against assault or rape. Now, messages that elicit intense emotions like fear and disgust can cause defensive avoidance if they do not include sufficient information about self-efficacy (e.g., developing confidence in using contraceptives) and response efficacy (e.g., developing confidence in believing that contraceptives work effectively).[164] This defensive mechanism refers to "the allocation of attention away from threatening or unpleasant stimuli, and one's emotional reactions to those stimuli."[165] Explained differently, certain topics may evoke such high degrees of disgust that the audience may refuse to consider them, leading to selective avoidance of the issue.[166] Yet, as we have seen, PETA's campaigns have been made to influence or persuade audiences by making them aware of the supposed threat of looming danger or harm if animals keep being mistreated—just like the Nazis treated the Jews in death camps.

The other theory in this section is inoculation theory. Developed by William McGuire (1961)[167] and, later, Michael Pfau (1992),[168] **inoculation theory** postulates that persuasive arguments can inoculate (immunize) the audience to the influence of messages. For instance, a college student who has been exposed to a multitude of arguments against binge drinking is expected to defy attempts by their binge-drinking peers (more so than students who have not received such exposure). Inoculation theory operates on two principles: a perceived threat and refutational preemption. A perceived threat is crucial in developing resistance to persuasive messages. For the inoculation process to be successful, message recipients must perceive a threat to encourage them to reinforce their existing attitudes.[169] **Refutational preemptions** aid in the inoculation process by offering arguments and/or evidence to reject arguments included in attitude attacks, and by giving message receivers practice at defending their positions through counterarguing.[170]

Persuasion not only seeks to transform attitudes; it also means persuading people not to fall prey to immoral or unwelcome influence attempts. It is not unusual for campaign developers to try to persuade audiences to resist messages that are viewed as unhealthy or risky. For instance, health campaigns urge youths to "say no" to drugs, smoking, drunk drinking, and unsafe sex. In a world repleted with unscrupulous persuaders, inoculation provides audiences with a valuable technique to resist undesirable influence attempts. Inoculation theory advances that the ideal method to induce resistance to immoral persuasion is to offer people incremental information—i.e., a small piece of dangerous information that they learn to refute; if it works, the next small dose of information comes in. This presents a useful alternative to those who claim that parents should protect children from the world's troubles or from unpleasant realities.[171] As Pratkanis and Aronson (1992)[172] remark, "we cannot resist propaganda by burying our heads in the sand. The person who is easiest to persuade is the person whose beliefs are based on slogans that have never been seriously challenged."

In October 2011, PETA launched its "End Slavery" campaign to declare that animals must be free from slavery and involuntary servitude, as stipulated by the Thirteenth Amendment to the United States Constitution. In this groundbreaking lawsuit, PETA stated that SeaWorld Parks & Entertainment (hereinafter SeaWorld), the well-known marine theme park, despoiled Section 1 of the Thirteenth Amendment by holding five Orcas (i.e., killer whales) as "slaves"—i.e., by forcing them to perform in entertainment shows.[173] So, PETA created a moral equivalence between the perpetual threat to animals and the perpetual threat that African Americans endured during slavery. Not only did PETA lose in court, but the organization also came under heavy criticism for its analogies between animal management and slavery. Most of the public appeared to be inoculated against PETA's baseless and failed "anti-slavery" propaganda. The refutational preemption was based on the campaign's questionable ethicality regarding its political message—that race and species should be integrated as one hierarchical category that dictates social life. Such comparisons were seen as "inadmissible" because one struggle for social justice cannot be necessarily equated with another.[174]

NOTES

1. Fabio Sabogal, Regina Oterso-Sabogal, Rena J. Pasick, Christopher N. H. Jenkins, and Elisa J. Pérez-Stable, "Printed Health Education Materials for Diverse Communities: Suggestions Learned from the Field," *Health Education Quarterly* 23, no. 1 (1996): S123–41. https://doi.org/10.1177/109019819602301S10.

2. Jan Plamper, *Fear: Across the Disciplines* (Pittsburgh, PA: University of Pittsburgh Press, 2012).

3. Terrence Earl Maltbia and Anne T. Power, *A Leader's Guide to Leveraging Diversity: Strategic Learning Capabilities for Breakthrough Performance* (Burlington, MA: Elsevier, 2009).

4. Irena Milosevic and Randi E. McCabe, *Phobias: The Psychology of Irrational Fear: The Psychology of Irrational Fear* (Santa Barbara, CA: Greenwood, 2015).

5. Barry Glassner, "Narrative Techniques of Fear Mongering," *Social Research: An International Quarterly* 71, no. 4 (2004): 819–26.

6. Kim Witte, "Putting the Fear Back into Fear Appeals: The Extended Parallel Process Model," *Communication Monographs* 59, no. 4 (1992): 329–49. https://doi.org/10.1080/03637759209376276.

7. Kim Witte, "Fear as Motivator, Fear as Inhibitor: Using the Extended Parallel Process Model to Explain Fear Appeal Successes and Failures," in *Handbook of Communication and Emotion: Research, Theory, Applications, and Contexts*, ed. Peter A. Andersen and Laura K. Guerrero (Cambridge, MA: Academic Press, 1997): 423–50.

8. Robert A. C. Ruiter, Loes T. E. Kessels, Gjalt-Jorn Y. Peters, and Gerjo Kok, "Sixty Years of Fear Appeal Research: Current State of the Evidence," *International Journal of Psychology* 49, no. 2 (2014): 63–70. https://doi.org/10.1002/ijop.12042.

9. Carol L. Schmitt and Thomas Blass, "Fear Appeals Revisited: Testing a Unique Anti-Smoking Film," *Current Psychology* 27 (2008): Article 145. https://doi.org/10.1007/s12144-008-9029-7.

10. David Zucker, Richard S. Hopkins, David F. Sly, Jennifer Urich, Josephine Mendoza Kershaw, and Sebastian Solari, "Florida's 'truth' Campaign: A Counter-Marketing, Anti-Tobacco Media Campaign," *Journal of Public Health Management and Practice* 6, no. 3 (2000): 1–6. https://doi.org/10.1097/00124784-200006030-00003.

11. David J. Craig, "Students Adopt Mass Persuasion Techniques to Promote Good Health," *B.U. Bridge* 5, 20 (2002): 1–3.

12. Richard M. Perloff, *The Dynamics of Persuasion: Communication and Attitudes in the 21st Century* (2nd Ed.) (Mahwah, NJ: Lawrence Erlbaum, 2003).

13. Witte, "Fear as Motivator, Fear as Inhibitor," 424–30.

14. Monique Mitchell Turner, Vanessa Boudewyns, Rowie Kirby-Straker, and Jana Telfer, "A Double Dose of Fear: A Theory-Based Content Analysis of News Articles Surrounding the 2006 Cough Syrup Contamination Crisis in Panama," *Risk Management* 15 (2013): 79–99. https://doi.org/10.1057/rm.2012.13.

15. Perloff, *The Dynamics of Persuasion*, 191–2.

16. Marvin Zuckerman, "Sensation Seeking," in *Handbook of Individual Differences in Social Behavior*, ed. Mark R. Leary and Rick H. Hoyle (New York/London: The Guildford Press, 2009): 455–65.

17. Marvin Zuckerman, *Behavioral Expressions and Biosocial Bases of Sensation Seeking* (Cambridge: Cambridge University Press, 1994): 27.

18. Daniel Romer and Michael Hennessy, "A Biosocial-Affect Model of Adolescent Sensation Seeking: The Role of Affect Evaluation and Peer-Group Influence in Adolescent Drug Use," *Prevention Science* 8, no. 2 (2007): 89–101. https://doi.org/10.1007/s11121-007-0064-7.

19. Rick H. Hoyle, Michele C. Fejfar, and Joshua D. Miller, "Personality and Sexual Risk Taking: A Quantitative Review," *Journal of Personality* 68, no. 6 (2000): 1203–31. https://doi.org/10.1111/1467-6494.00132.

20. Marvin Zuckerman, *Biological Bases of Sensation Seeking, Impulsivity and Anxiety* (Hillsdale, NJ: Lawrence Erlbaum, 1983).

21. Marvin Zuckerman, *Sensation Seeking: Beyond the Optimal Level of Arousal* (Hillsdale, NJ: Lawrence Erlbaum, 1979).

22. James D. Sargent, Susanne Tanski, Mike Stoolmiller, and Reiner Hanewinkel, "Using Sensation Seeking to Target Adolescents for Substance Use Interventions," *Addiction* 105, no. 3 (2010): 506–14. https://doi.org/10.1111/j.1360-0443.2009.02782.x.

23. Michael T. Stephenson, "Examining Adolescents' Responses to Antimarijuana PSAs," *Human Communication Research* 29, no. 3 (2003): 343–69. https://doi.org/10.1111/j.1468-2958.2003.tb00843.x.

24. Matthew C. Farrelly, Jeff Niederdeppe, and Jared Yarsevich, "Youth Tobacco Prevention Mass Media Campaigns: Past, Present, and Future Directions," *Tobacco Control* 12, no. 1 (2003): 35–47. https://doi.org/10.1136/tc.12.suppl_1.i35.

25. Bhash Naidoo, Daniel Warm, Robert Quigley, and Lorraine Taylor, *Smoking and Public Health: A Review of Reviews of Interventions to Increase Smoking Cessation, Reduce Smoking Initiation and Prevent Further Uptake of Smoking* (London: Health Development Agency, 2004).

26. Michael Stephenson and Philip Palmgreen, "Sensation Seeking, Perceived Message Sensation Value, Personal Involvement, and Processing of Anti-Marijuana PSAs," *International Journal of Culture and Mental Health* 68, no. 1 (2001): 49–71. https://doi.org/10.1080/03637750128051.

27. Philip Palmgreen, Lewis Donohew, Elizabeth Pugzles Lorch, Rick H. Hoyle, and Michael T. Stephenson, "Television Campaigns and Adolescent Marijuana Use: Tests of Sensation Seeking Targeting," *American Journal of Public Health* 91, no. 2 (2001): 292–6. https://doi.org/10.2105/ajph.91.2.292.

28. Michael T. Stephenson, Susan E. Morgan, Elizabeth Pugzles Lorch, Philip Palmgreen, Lewis Donohew, and Rick H. Hoyle, "Predictors of Exposure from an Antimarijuana Media Campaign: Outcome Research Assessing Sensation Seeking Targeting," *Health Communication* 14, no. 1 (2002): 23–43. https://doi.org/10.1207/S15327027HC1401_2.

29. Maureen W. Everett and Philip Palmgreen, "Influences of Sensation Seeking, Message Sensation Value, and Program Context on Effectiveness of Anticocaine Public Service Announcements," *Health Communication* 7, no. 3 (1995): 225–48, 226. https://doi.org/10.1207/s15327027hc0703_3.

30. Palmgreen, Donohew, Lorch, Hoyle, and Stephenson, "Television Campaigns," 292.

31. Ibid, 292–6.

32. Philip Palmgreen, Lewis Donohew, Elizabeth Pugzles Lorch, Mary Rogus, David Helm, and Nancy Grant, "Sensation Seeking, Message Sensation Value, and Drug Use as Mediators of PSA Effectiveness," *Health Communication* 3, no. 4 (1991): 217–27, 219. https://doi.org/10.1207/s15327027hc0304_4.

33. Everett and Palmgreen, "Influences of Sensation Seeking," 225–48.

34. Lewis Donohew, Elizabeth P. Lorch, and Philip Palmgreen, "Sensation Seeking and Targeting of Televised Anti-Drug PSAs," in *Persuasive Communication and Drug Abuse Prevention*, ed. Lewis Donohew, Howard E. Sypher, and William J. Bukoski (Hillsdale, NJ: Lawrence Erlbaum, 1991): 209–26.

35. Philip Palmgreen, Michael T. Stephenson, Maureen W. Everett, John R. Baseheart, and Regina Francies, "Perceived Message Sensation Value (PMSV) and the Dimensions and

Validation of a PMSV Scale," *Health Communication* 14, no. 4 (2002): 403–28. https://doi.org/10.1207/S15327027HC1404_1.

36. Lewis Donohew, Elizabeth P. Lorch, and Philip Palmgreen, "Applications of a Theoretic Model of Information Exposure to Health Interventions," *Human Communication Research* 24, no. 3 (1998): 454–68. https://doi.org/10.1111/j.1468-2958.1998.tb00425.x.

37. Philip Palmgreen, Elizabeth P. Lorch, Michael T. Stephenson, Rick H. Hoyle, and Lewis Donohew, "Effects of the Office of National Drug Control Policy's Marijuana Initiative Campaign on High-Sensation-Seeking Adolescents," *American Journal of Public Health* 97, no. 9 (2007): 1644–9. https://doi.org/10.2105/AJPH.2005.072843.

38. Fabrizio Turoldo, "Responsibility as an Ethical Framework for Public Health Interventions," *American Journal of Public Health* 99, no. 7 (2009): 1197–202. https://doi.org/10.2105/AJPH.2007.127514.

39. Nurit Guttman and Charles T. Salmon, "Guilt, Fear, Stigma and Knowledge Gaps: Ethical Issues in Public Health Communication Interventions," *Bioethics* 18, no. 6 (2004): 531–52.

40. Lisa F. Berkman and Lester Breslow, *Health and Ways of Living* (New York: Oxford University Press, 1983).

41. Guttman and Salmon, "Guilt, Fear, Stigma and Knowledge Gaps," 542.

42. Pierluigi Musarò and Paola Parmiggiani, "Beyond Black and White: The Role of Media in Portraying and Policing Migration and Asylum in Italy," *International Review of Sociology* 27, no. 2 (2017): 241–60. https://doi.org/10.1080/03906701.2017.1329034.

43. Daniel Kahneman, *Thinking, Fast and Slow* (New York: Farrar, Straus and Giroux, 2011).

44. Gjalt-Jorn Y. Peters, Robert A. C. Ruiter, and Gerjo Kok, "Threatening Communication: A Qualitative Study of Fear Appeal Effectiveness Beliefs among Intervention Developers, Policymakers, Politicians, Scientists, and Advertising Professionals," *International Journal of Psychology* 49, no. 2 (2014): 71–9. https://doi.org/10.1002/ijop.12000.

45. Saffron O'Neill and Sophie Nicholson-Cole, "'Fear Won't Do It' Promoting Positive Engagement with Climate Change through Visual and Iconic Representations," *Science Communication* 30, no. 3 (2009): 355–79. https://doi.org/10.1177/1075547008329201.

46. Daniel Benjamin, Han-Hui Por, and David Budescu, "Climate Change versus Global Warming: Who Is Susceptible to the Framing of Climate Change?" *Environment and Behavior* 4, no. 7 (2017): 745–70. https://doi.org/10.1177/0013916516664382.

47. Cited in Gerdien de Vries, "Public Communication as a Tool to Implement Environmental Policies," *Social Issues and Policy Review* 14, no. 1 (2020): 244–72. https://doi.org/10.1111/sipr.12061.

48. Gerdien de Vries, Bart W. Terwel, and Naomi Ellemers, "Perceptions of Manipulation and Judgments of Illegitimacy: Pitfalls in the Use of Emphasis Framing When Communicating about CO2 Capture and Storage," *Environmental Communication* 10, no. 2 (2016): 206–26. https://doi.org/10.1080/17524032.2015.1047884.

49. Philip Pettit, "Non-Consequentialism and Universalizability," *The Philosophical Quarterly* 50, no. 199 (2000): 175–90. https://doi.org/10.1111/1467-9213.00178.

50. Jan Österberg, *Self and Others: A Study of Ethical Egoism* (Boston, MA: Kluwer Academic Publishers, 1988).

51. Gordon Davis, "Traces of Consequentialism and Non-Consequentialism in Bodhisattva Ethics," *Philosophy East and West* 63, no. 2 (2013): 275–305. https://doi.org/10.1353/

pew.2013.0015; Kurt L. Sylvan, "An Epistemic Nonconsequentialism," *The Philosophical Review* 129, no. 1 (2020): 1–51. https://doi.org/10.1215/00318108–7890455.

52. Mary Douglas, *Risk and Blame: Essays in Cultural Theory* (London: Routledge, 1994).

53. Ralph L. Keeney, "Decisions about Life-Threatening Risks," *New England Journal of Medicine* 331, no. 3 (1994): 193–6. https://doi.org/10.1056/NEJM199407213310311.

54. Jonathan Matusitz, "The Current Condition of Visual Communication in Colleges and Universities of the United States," *Journal of Visual Literacy* 25, no. 1 (2005): 97–112. https://doi.org/10.1080/23796529.2005.11674619.

55. Roland Barthes, "Rhetoric of the Image," in *Image, Music, Text*, ed. Roland Barthes (London: Fontana, 1977): 32–51; James M. Clark and Allan Paivio, "Dual Coding Theory and Education," *Educational Psychology Review* 3, no. 3 (1991): 149–210. https://doi.org/10.1007/BF01320076.

56. Annie Lang, Robert F. Potter, and Paul D. Bolls, "Something for Nothing: Is Visual Encoding Automatic?" *Media Psychology* 1, no. 2 (1999): 145–64. https://doi.org/10.1207/s1532785xmep0102_4.

57. Dolf Zillmann, Silvia Knobloch, and Hong-Sik Yu, "Effects of Photographs on the Selective Reading of News Reports," *Media Psychology* 3, no. 4 (2001): 301–24. https://doi.org/10.1207/S1532785XMEP0304_01.

58. Renita Coleman, "The Effects of Visuals on Ethical Reasoning: What's a Photograph Worth to Journalists Making Moral Decisions?" *Journalism & Mass Communication Quarterly* 83, no. 4 (2006): 835–50. https://doi.org/10.1177/107769900608300407.

59. Allison Lazard and Lucy Atkinson, "Putting Environmental Infographics Center Stage: The Role of Visuals at the Elaboration Likelihood Model's Critical Point of Persuasion," *Science Communication* 37, no. 1 (2015): 6–33. https://doi.org/10.1177/1075547014555997.

60. John D. Bransford and Marcia K. Johnson, "Contextual Prerequisites for Understanding: Some Investigations of Comprehension and Recall," *Journal of Verbal Learning and Verbal Behavior* 11, no. 6 (1972): 62–84. https://doi.org/10.1016/S0022-5371(72)80006-9.

61. Paul Messaris and Linus Abraham, "The Role of Images in Framing News Stories," in *Framing Public Life: Perspectives on Media and Our Understanding of the Social World*, ed. Stephen D. Reese, Oscar H. Gandy, Jr., and August E. Grant (Mahwah, NJ: Lawrence Erlbaum, 2001): 215–26.

62. Tony Schwartz, *The Responsive Chord* (Garden City, NY: Anchor Books, 1973).

63. Chukwuemeka Vincent Okpara, Anibueze U. Anselm, Talabi Olajide Felix, Adelabu Omowale, and Verlumun Celestine Gever, "The Moderating Role of Colour in Modelling the Effectiveness of COVID-19 YouTube Animated Cartoons on the Health Behaviour of Social Media Users in Nigeria," *Health Promotion International* (2021). https://doi.org/10.1093/heapro/daab001.

64. Ted Brader, "Striking a Responsive Chord: How Political Ads Motivate and Persuade Voters by Appealing to Emotions," *American Journal of Political Science* 49, no. 2 (2005): 388–405. https://doi.org/10.1111/j.0092-5853.2005.00130.x.

65. Hélène Joffe, "The Power of Visual Material: Persuasion, Emotion and Identification," *Diogenes* 55, no. 1 (2008): 84–93. https://doi.org/10.1177/0392192107087919.

66. Åsa Boholm, "Visual Images and Risk Messages: Commemorating Chernobyl," *Risk, Decision and Policy* 3, no. 2 (1998): 125–43. https://doi.org/10.1080/135753098348248.

67. Joffe, "The Power of Visual Material," 86.

68. Jennifer Peeples, "Imaging Toxins," *Environmental Communication* 7, no. 2 (2013): 191–210. https://doi.org/10.1080/17524032.2013.775172.

69. O'Neill and Nicholson-Cole, "'Fear Won't Do It'," 355–79.

70. Jean Trumbo, "Visual Literacy and Science Communication," *Science Communication* 20, no. 4 (1999): 409–25. https://doi.org/10.1177/1075547099020004004.

71. Stacy Rebich-Hespanha and Ronald E. Rice, "Dominant Visual Frames in Climate Change News Stories: Implications for Formative Evaluation in Climate Change Campaigns," *International Journal of Communication* 10 (2016): 4830–62.

72. Paisley Rekdal, *Appropriate: A Provocation* (New York: W. W. Norton & Company, 2021).

73. John R. Rossiter and Larry Percy, *Advertising and Promotion Management* (New York: McGraw-Hill, 1987).

74. Terry L. Childers and Michael J. Houston, "Conditions for a Picture-Superiority Effect on Consumer Memory," *Journal of Consumer Research* 11, no. 2 (1984): 634–54. https://doi.org/10.1086/209001.

75. Jennifer A. Zarzossa and Bruce A. Huhmann, "Measures of Aesthetic Dimensions and Reactions in Advertising," *International Journal of Advertising* 38, no. 2 (2019): 258–75. https://doi.org/10.1080/02650487.2018.1442632.

76. Renáta Machová, Erika Seres Huszárik, and Zsuzsanna Tóth, "The Role of Shockvertising in the Context of Various Generations," *Problems and Perspectives in Management* 13, no. 1 (2015): 104–12.

77. Richard Vézina and Olivia Paul, "Provocation in Advertising: A Conceptualization and an Empirical Assessment," *International Journal of Research in Marketing* 14, no. 2 (1997): 177–92. https://doi.org/10.1016/S0167-8116(97)00002-5.

78. Umberto Eco, *A Theory of Semiotics* (Bloomington, IN: Indiana University Press, 1976).

79. Edward F. McQuarrie and David Mick, "On Resonance: A Critical Pluralistic Inquiry into Advertising Rhetoric," *Journal of Consumer Research* 19, no. 2 (1992): 180–97, 184. https://doi.org/10.1086/209295.

80. Vézina and Paul, "Provocation in Advertising," 181–4.

81. Nigel K. L. Pope, Kevin E. Voges, and Mark R. Brown, "The Effect of Provocation in the Form of Mild Erotica on Attitude to the Ad and Corporate Image," *Journal of Advertising* 33, no. 1 (2004): 69–82. https://doi.org/10.1080/00913367.2004.10639154.

82. Vézina and Paul, "Provocation in Advertising," 181–4.

83. Paul Rozin and April E. Fallon, "A Perspective on Disgust," *Psychological Review* 94, no.1 (1987): 23–41. https://doi.org/10.1037/0033-295X.94.1.23.

84. Joffe, "The Power of Visual Material," 87.

85. Ibid, 87.

86. Darren W. Dahl, Kristina D. Frankenberger, and Rajesh V. Manchanda, "Does It Pay to Shock? Reactions to Shocking and Nonshocking Advertising Content among University Students," *Journal of Advertising Research* 43, no. 3 (2003): 268–80, 268. https://doi.org/10.1017/S0021849903030332.

87. Tareq N. Hashem, "The Role of Buzz Marketing in Increasing Attention towards Green Products, Moderating Role of 'Shockvertising'," *Journal of Contemporary Issues in Business and Government* 27, no. 2 (2021): 1785–98. https://doi.org/10.47750/cibg.2021.27.02.189.

88. Machová, Huszárik, and Tóth, "The Role of Shockvertising," 104–12.

89. Jonathan Matusitz, *Terrorism & Communication: A Critical Introduction* (Thousand Oaks, CA: Sage, 2013).

90. Dahl, Frankenberger, and Manchanda, "Does It Pay to Shock?" 268.

91. Iris Mohr, "Managing Buzz Marketing in the Digital Age," *Journal of Marketing Development and Competitiveness* 11, no. 2 (2017): 10–21.

92. Christopher M. Massad, Michael Hubbard, and Darren Newtson, "Selective Perception of Events," *Journal of Experimental Social Psychology* 15, no. 6 (1979): 513–32. https://doi.org/10.1016/0022-1031(79)90049-0; Charles Taylor, George R. Franke, and Hae-Kyong Bang, "Use and Effectiveness of Billboards: Perspectives from Selective-Perception Theory and Retail-Gravity Models," *Journal of Advertising* 35, no. 4 (2006): 21–34. https://doi.org/10.2753/JOA0091-3367350402.

93. Werner J. Severin and James W. Tankard, Jr., *Communication Theories: Origins, Methods and Uses in the Mass Media* (Boston, MA: Addison-Wesley, 2000).

94. Joseph T. Klapper, *The Effects of Mass Communication* (New York: Free Press, 1960).

95. Cited in David Gauntlett, *Moving Experiences: Media Effects and Beyond* (Eastleigh, England: John Libbey, 2005): 51.

96. Leda M. Cooks and Mark P. Orbe, "Beyond the Satire: Selective Exposure and Selective Perception in 'In Living Color'," *Howard Journal of Communications* 4, no. 3 (1993): 217–33. https://doi.org/10.1080/10646179309359778.

97. Predrag Jovanović, Tamara Vlastelica, and Slavica Cicvarić Kostić, "Impact of Advertising Appeals on Purchase Intention," *Management: Journal of Sustainable Business and Management Solutions in Emerging Economies* 21, no. 81 (2016): 35–45. https://doi.org/10.7595/management.fon.2016.0025; Michael R. Solomon, *Consumer Behavior: Buying, Having, and Being* (8th Ed.) (Upper Saddle River, NJ: Pearson Prentice Hall, 2008).

98. Amos Tversky and Daniel Kahneman, "Judgement under Uncertainty: Heuristics and Biases," *Science* 185 (1974): 1124–31.

99. Joffe, "The Power of Visual Material," 85.

100. Todd Gitlin, *The Whole World Is Watching: Mass Media in the Making and Unmaking of the New Left* (Berkeley, CA: University of California Press, 1980): 6.

101. Erving *Goffman*, *Frame Analysis: An Essay on the Organization of Experience* (Cambridge, MA: Harvard University Press, 1974).

102. David A. Snow, E. Burke Rochford, Jr., Steven K. Worden, and Robert D. Benford, "Frame Alignment Processes, Micromobilization, and Movement Participation," *American Sociological Review* 51, no. 4 (1986): 464–81, 464. https://doi.org/10.2307/2095581.

103. Robert Entman, "Framing: Toward Clarification of a Fractured Paradigm," *Journal of Communication* 43, no. 4 (1993): 51–8. https://doi.org/10.1111/j.1460-2466.1993.tb01304.x.

104. Jonathan Matusitz and David Ochoa, "Agenda-Setting Theory in the US Media: A Comparative Analysis of Terrorist Attacks in France and Nigeria," *Global Media Journal* 16, no. 31 (2018): 1–6.

105. Eric Swank and Breanne Fahs, "Students for Peace: Contextual and Framing Motivations of Antiwar Activism," *Journal of Sociology & Social Welfare* XXXVIII, no. 2 (2011): 111–36. https://doi.org/110.1.1.724.7592.

106. For example, see Doug McAdam, "Social Movement Theory and the Prospects for Climate Change Activism in the United States," *Annual Review of Political Science* 20 (2017): 189–208. https://doi.org/10.1146/annurev-polisci-052615-025801; Robert D. Benford and David A. Snow, "Framing Processes and Social Movements: An Overview and Assessment," *Annual Review of Sociology* 26 (2000): 611–39. https://doi.org/10.1146/annurev.soc.26.1.611.

107. Elsbeth D. Asbeek Brusse, Marieke L. Fransen, and Edith G. Smit, "Framing in Entertainment-Education: Effects on Processes of Narrative Persuasion," *Health Communication* 32, no. 12 (2017): 1501–9. https://doi.org/10.1080/10410236.2016.1234536.

108. Alexander J. Rothman, Roger D. Bartels, Jhon Wlaschin, and Peter Salovey, "The Strategic Use of Gain and Loss-Framed Messages to Promote Healthy Behavior: How Theory Can Inform Practice," *Journal of Communication* 56, no. 1 (2006): 202–21. https://doi.org/10.1111/j.1460-2466.2006.00290.x.

109. Wayne T. Steward, Tamera R. Schneider, Judith Pizarro, and Peter Salovey, "Need for Cognition Moderates Responses to Framed Smoking-Cessation Messages," *Journal of Applied Social Psychology* 33, no. 12 (2003): 2439–64, 2460. https://doi.org/10.1111/j.1559-1816.2003.tb02775.x.

110. Brusse, Fransen, and Smit, "Framing in Entertainment-Education," 1502.

111. Daniel J. O'Keefe and Jakob D. Jensen, "The Relative Persuasiveness of Gain-Framed Loss-Framed Messages for Encouraging Disease Prevention Behaviors: A Meta-Analytic Review," *Journal of Health Communication* 12, no. 4 (2007): 623–44. https://doi.org/10.1080/10810730701615198.

112. Michael David Thomas, "Reapplying Behavioral Symmetry: Public Choice and Choice Architecture," *Public Choice* 180 (2019): 11–25. https://doi.org/10.1007/s11127-018-0537-1.

113. Jack S. Levy, "An Introduction to Prospect Theory," *Political Psychology* 13, no. 2 (1992): 171–86.

114. Cited in Lyle Munro, *Compassionate Beasts: The Quest for Animal Rights* (London: Praeger, 2001): 12–7.

115. Dale Jamieson, *Morality's Progress: Essays on Humans, Other Animals and the Rest of Nature* (Oxford: Clarendon Press, 2002): 149–51.

116. Peter Singer, "Peter Singer: Reflections," in *The Lives of Animals*, ed. John Maxwell Coetzee (Princeton, NJ: Princeton University Press, 1999): 87.

117. Cited in László Erdős, *Green Heroes* (New York: Springer, 2019): 55–60.

118. *ESPN*, "Video Showed Pedro, Marichal at Cockfight," *ESPN* (February 7, 2008). Retrieved on March 23, 2021 from https://www.espn.com/mlb/news/story?id=3234767; also available at https://www.peta.org/about-peta.

119. Alex Pacheco and Anna Francione, "The Silver Spring Monkeys," in *In Defense of Animals*, ed. Peter Singer (New York: Basil Blackwell, 1985): 135–47.

120. Erdős, *Green Heroes*, 55.

121. Erdős, *Green Heroes*, 56–9.

122. Ibid, 56–9.

123. Michael Specter, "The Extremist: The Woman Behind the Most Successful Radical Group in America," *The New Yorker* (April 4, 2003): 52–67.

124. *Chicago Tribune*, "Pictures: PETA's Famous Faces," *Chicago Tribune* (March 25, 2021). Retrieved on March 25, 2021 from https://www.chicagotribune.com/lifestyles/sns-green-peta-famous-faces-photogallery.html.

125. Specter, "The Extremist," 61.

126. Gary Francione, *Animals, Property and the Law* (Philadelphia, PA: Temple University Press, 1995).

127. Tom Regan, *The Case for Animal Rights* (Berkeley, CA: University of California Press, 2004).

128. Corey Lee Wrenn, "The Role of Professionalization Regarding Female Exploitation in the Nonhuman Animal Rights Movement," *Journal of Gender Studies* 24, no. 2 (2015): 131–46. https://doi.org/10.1080/09589236.2013.806248.

129. *The Independent*, "Fur – The Fake Debate," *The Independent* (November 23, 2004): A1. Retrieved on March 26, 2021 from https://www.independent.co.uk/news/uk/this-britain/fur-the-fake-debate-534303.html.

130. Wrenn, "The Role of Professionalization," 137–9.

131. Richard D. French, *Anti-Vivisection and Medical Science in Victorian Society* (Princeton, NJ: Princeton University Press, 1975).

132. Susan Sperling, *Animal Liberators: Research and Morality* (Berkeley, CA: University of California Press, 1988).

133. Robert, Garner, "Defending Animal Rights," *Parliamentary Affairs* 51, no. 3 (1998): 458–69. https://doi.org/10.1093/oxfordjournals.pa.a028810.

134. Maneesha Deckha, "Disturbing Images PETA and the Feminist Ethics of Animal Advocacy," *Ethics & The Environment* 13, no. 2 (2008): 35–76.

135. Carol J. Adams and Josephine Donovan, *Beyond Animal Rights: A Feminist Caring Ethic for the Treatment of Animals* (New York: Continuum International, 2000).

136. Carol J. Adams, *The Sexual Politics of Meat: A Feminist-Vegetarian Critical Theory* (New York: Continuum International, 2003).

137. Shari Weiss, "Taraji P. Henson Poses Nude for PETA's 'I'd Rather Go Naked Than Wear Fur' Ad Campaign," *Daily News* (January 28, 2011). Retrieved on March 26, 2021 from https://www.nydailynews.com/entertainment/gossip/taraji-p-henson-poses-nude-peta-naked-wear-fur-ad-campaign-article-1.154292.

138. Oscar Holland and Fiona Sinclair Scott, "PETA Ends "I'd Rather Go Naked" Anti-Fur Campaign after Three Decades," *CNN* (February 5, 2020). Retrieved on March 26, 2021 from https://www.cnn.com/style/article/peta-naked-fur-campaign-ends/index.html.

139. Cited in Wrenn, "The Role of Professionalization," 137–9.

140. Cited in Chloë Taylor, "Foucault and the Ethics of Eating," *Foucault Studies* 9 (2010): 71–88, 84. https://doi.org/10.22439/fs.v0i9.3060.

141. David Sztybel, "Can the Treatment of Animals Be Compared to the Holocaust?" *Ethics and the Environment* 11, no. 1 (2006): 97–132.

142. Cited in David Teather, "'Holocaust on a Plate' Angers US Jews," *The Guardian* (March 3, 2003): A1. Retrieved on March 26, 2021 from https://www.theguardian.com/media/2003/mar/03/advertising.marketingandpr.

143. Cited in David B. MacDonald, "Pushing the Limits of Humanity? Reinterpreting Animal Rights and 'Personhood' Through the Prism of the Holocaust," *Journal of Human Rights* 5, no. 4 (2006): 417–37, 426. https://doi.org/10.1080/14754830600978208.

144. Boria Sax, *Animals in the Third Reich: Pets, Scapegoats, and the Holocaust* (New York: Continuum, 2000): 156.

145. Sztybel, "Can the Treatment of Animals Be Compared to the Holocaust?" 98.

146. Cited in MacDonald, "Pushing the Limits of Humanity?" 427–8.

147. Ibid.

148. Claire Jean Kim, "Moral Extensionism or Racist Exploitation? The Use of Holocaust and Slavery Analogies in the Animal Liberation Movement," *New Political Science* 33, no. 3 (2011): 311–33. https://doi.org/10.1080/07393148.2011.592021.

149. Sztybel, "Can the Treatment of Animals Be Compared to the Holocaust?" 115.

150. Peter Singer, "Prologue," in *Defence of Animals*, ed. Peter Singer (Oxford: Basil Blackwell, 1985): 1–11.

151. Ibid, 9.

152. Charles Patterson, *Eternal Treblinka: Our Treatment of Animals and the Holocaust* (New York: Lantern Books, 2002).

153. Ibid, 131–2.

154. Sztybel, "Can the Treatment of Animals Be Compared to the Holocaust?" 118.

155. Patterson, *Eternal Treblinka*, 129–31.

156. Ibid.

157. Cited in Teather, "'Holocaust on a Plate' Angers US Jews," A1.

158. Cited in Brian Delevie and Isshaela Ingham, "'Unconscionable' or Communicable? The Transference of Holocaust Photography in Cyber Space," *Afterimage* 31, no. 6 (2004): 7.

159. Albert Bandura, "Self-Efficacy: Toward a Unifying Theory of Behavioral Change," *Psychological Review* 84, no. 2 (1977): 191–215. https://doi.org/10.1037/0033-295X.84.2.191.

160. Albert Bandura, "Self-Efficacy Mechanism in Human Agency," *American Psychologist* 37, no. 2 (1982): 122–47. https://doi.org/10.1037/0003-066X.37.2.122; Albert Bandura, "Health Promotion by Social Cognitive Means," *Health Education & Behavior* 31, no. 2 (2004): 143–64. https://doi.org/10.1177/1090198104263660.

161. James E. Maddux and Ronald W. Rogers, "Protection Motivation and Self-Efficacy: A Revised Theory of Fear Appeals and Attitude Change," *Journal of Experimental Social Psychology* 19, no. 5 (1983): 469–79. https://doi.org/10.1016/0022-1031(83)90023-9.

162. Stephen R. Sutton and J. Richard Eiser, "The Effects of Fear-Arousal Communication of Cigarettes Smoking: An Experimental-Value Approach," *Journal of Applied Social Psychology* 15, no. 2 (1984): 13–33. https://doi.org/10.1007/BF00845345.

163. Robin L. Snipes, Michael S. LaTour, and Sara J. Bliss, "A Model of the Effects of Self-Efficacy of the Perceived Ethicality and Performance of Fear Appeals in Advertising," *Journal of Business Ethics* 19, no. 3 (1999): 273–85. https://doi.org/10.1023/A:1005822414588.

164. Ronald W. Rogers, "A Protection Motivation Theory of Fear Appeals and Attitude Change1," *The Journal of Psychology* 91, no. 1 (1975): 93–114. https://doi.org/10.1080/00223980.1975.9915803.

165. Stephen L. Brown, "Emotive Health Advertising and Message Resistance," *Australian Psychologist* 36, no. 3 (2001): 193–9, 194. https://doi.org/10.1080/00050060108259655.

166. Emily Moyer-Gusé, "Toward a Theory of Entertainment Persuasion: Explaining the Persuasive Effects of Entertainment-Education Messages," *Communication Theory* 18, no. 3 (2008): 407–25. https://doi.org/10.1111/j.1468-2885.2008.00328.x.

167. William J. McGuire, "The Effectiveness of Supportive and Refutational Defenses in Immunizing and Restoring Beliefs against Persuasion," *Sociometry* 24, no. 2 (1961): 184–97. https://doi.org/10.2307/2786067.

168. Michael Pfau, "The Potential of Inoculation in Promoting Resistance to the Effectiveness of Comparative Advertising Messages," *Communication Quarterly* 40, no. 1 (1992): 26–44. https://doi.org/10.1080/01463379209369818.

169. Gerald-Mark Breen and Jonathan Matusitz, "Preventing Youths from Joining Gangs: How to Apply Inoculation Theory," *Journal of Applied Security Research* 4, no. 1 (2008): 109–28. https://doi.org/10.1080/19361610802210285; Jonathan Matusitz and Gerald-Mark Breen, "Prevention of Sexual Harassment in the Medical Setting: Applying Inoculation Theory," *Journal of Health & Social Policy* 21, no. 2 (2005): 53–71. https://doi.org/10.1300/J045v21n02_04; Jonathan Matusitz and Gerald-Mark Breen, "Applying Inoculation Theory to the Study of Recidivism Reduction in Criminal Prison Inmates," *Journal of Evidence-Based Social Work* 10, no. 5 (2013): 455–65. https://doi.org/10.1080/15433714.2012.760929.

170. Gerald-Mark Breen and Jonathan Matusitz, "Inoculation Theory: A Theoretical and Practical Framework for Conferring Resistance to Pack Journalism Tendencies," *Global Media Journal* 8, no. 14 (2009): 1–24; Jonathan Matusitz and Gerald-Mark Breen, "Inoculation Theory: A Framework for the Reduction of Skin Cancer," *Journal of Evidence-Based Social Work* 7, no. 3 (2010): 219–34. https://doi.org/10.1080/19371910902911172.

171. Perloff, *The Dynamics of Persuasion*, 124–6.

172. Anthony Pratkanis and Elliott Aronson, *Age of Propaganda: The Everyday Use and Abuse of Persuasion* (New York: W. H. Freeman, 1992): 215.

173. Sheri Flannery, "The Thirteenth Amendment Won't Help Free Willy," *The Scholar* 15 (2013): 29–62.

174. Claire Jean Kim, "Moral Extensionism or Racist Exploitation? The Use of Holocaust and Slavery Analogies in the Animal Liberation Movement," *New Political Science* 33, no. 3 (2011): 311–33. https://doi.org/10.1080/07393148.2011.592021.

PART II

HEALTH COMMUNICATION CAMPAIGNS

CHAPTER 5

Health Communication Campaigns

General Perspectives

Health communication campaigns are defined as approaches designed to convince or encourage audiences to modify their behavior so as to improve their health. They are directed at diverse audiences by adjusting behavior change goals so that they become applicable, suitable, and appealing to each audience targeted. Health communication campaigns must stipulate, as accurately as possible, the health behavior change that is wanted from a target audience when its members are presented with persuasive messages.[1] The behaviors advocated by campaigners should fall within the range of what can be achieved realistically by the audience.[2] In general, health communication campaigns promote the adoption of health-boosting behaviors or the decrease or rejection of risky ones. The desired action is identified from a meticulous analysis of the audience's existing behaviors. To this point, apposite implementation of behavioral theories can help determine factors that can affect the targeted behavior change with respect to the current behavior.[3]

Health communication, in and of itself, is the discipline and application of communication strategies to inform and sway personal and community decisions that improve health. Health communication is a crucial method to inform the public about health issues and to keep them on the public agenda. The assistance of mass media and multimedia channels, and additional technologies to diffuse health information to the public, steps up awareness of certain aspects of personal and collective health.[4] A principal objective is to amplify our effectiveness as communicators in the healthcare environment.[5] People who participate in health communication activities are stakeholders. **Stakeholders** include

Fundamentals of Public Communication Campaigns, First Edition. Jonathan Matusitz.
© 2022 John Wiley & Sons Ltd. Published 2022 by John Wiley & Sons Ltd.

media commentators, campaign developers, doctors, patients, attorneys, teachers, law-makers, civil servants, policy analysts, patient advocates, parents, law enforcement officers, school administrators, pharmacists, nurses, activists, federal agents, drug company spokes-people, and celebrities—among many others.[6]

Perceptions of Health over Time

Health communication as a sociocultural custom can be traced back to the dawn of civiliza-tion and to the earliest interventions to inform and influence behaviors of people and soci-eties confronting public health problems.[7] To begin, however, it would be useful to define what health means. Definitions have evolved over several millennia. The Greek physician Hippocrates of Cos (460–377 BC) is hailed as the father of medicine in the Western world. He was also the founder of a school that taught how the human body was retained to contain four liquids—i.e., the humors. These were blood, phlegm, black bile, and yellow bile. Health was maintained through a state of equilibrium of these four liquids. Conversely, disease was caused by their imbalance. Health, as conceptualized by the Hippocratic School, was seen as a philosophical–naturalistic vanity.[8] In later times of antiquity, health as the balance bet-ween an individual and the environment, the harmony of soul and body, and the natural cause of disease, was the spinal cord of what health constituted.[9] Similar concepts were pre-sent in ancient Indian and Chinese medicine.[10]

In the Middle Ages, conceptions of health became heavily influenced by religion and the Catholic Church. After the Roman Empire collapsed, the Church was left as the only true apparatus that provided care for its citizens and that gathered and shared knowledge on cures—e.g., herbs from monastery gardens. The "forgotten" wisdom and learning from Antiquity reemerged during the Renaissance and shaped a certain number of health prac-tices still in use in the present day.[11] In the early contemporary era, the traditional approach to Western medicine defined **health** as the absence of disease.[12] Since the 1940s, the World Health Organization (2006)[13] has defined it as a condition of physical, mental, and social well-being in which disease and infirmity do not exist. In the late twentieth century, a more academic and accurate definition of health is "a state characterized by anatomic, physio-logic, and psychological integrity; ability to perform personally valued family, work, and community roles; ability to deal with physical, biological, psychological, and social stress."[14]

Public Health

Public health is a branch of health studies that pertains to population health, sanitation, epidemiology, disease prevention (including mental disorders), access to healthcare, and overall well-being. Extending longevity and enhancing quality of life through coordinated efforts and informed choices of communities—i.e., organizations (public and private) and citizens (in their places of residence, learning, work, and recreation)—are key objectives of public health. Similarly, evaluating the determinants of health of society and the risks it faces are also the backbone of public health.[15] **New public health** differs through its foundation in a larger understanding of the manners by which lifestyles and living condi-tions establish health status. New public health also recognizes the importance of mobi-lizing resources and making sensible decisions in terms of policies, programs, and services that produce, preserve, and protect good health—i.e., by endorsing healthy lifestyles and fostering supportive contexts for health.[16]

During the course of the twentieth century, health communication campaigns were designed to tackle essential public health problems, including a wide range of behavioral issues such as the initiation and maintenance of preventive health actions and the ceasing of behaviors that multiply the risk of negative health consequences. The goal of a public health campaign can be preventing rather than curing an illness through observation of cases and the support of healthy behaviors.[17] Vaccination plans and dissemination of condoms are examples of public health initiatives. One of the most pressing public health issues facing the world for the past few decades has been HIV/AIDS.[18] Tuberculosis, which took the life of Bohemian novelist Franz Kafka, continues to be a major concern too—owing to the increase of HIV/AIDS-related infections and the growth of strains immune to standard antibiotics.[19]

Communication Tools

Communication is a fundamental platform in healthcare awareness and education, and the campaign option is a requirement in health communication. With the emergence of newspapers, radio, and TV, media-driven health campaigns have been key to health promotion and disease prevention since the 1940s. At that time, media-driven health campaigns also used film, public service announcements (PSAs), basic print materials (e.g., posters, booklets, and information brochures), and billboard ads. Health communication campaigns have contributed tremendously to the expansion of public health across the world and are still regarded as crucial elements of widespread intervention efforts, such as cancer and tobacco smoking prevention.[20]

Since the late twentieth century, health communication campaigns have turned to an assortment of conduits to diffuse their messages. Examples include long-existing mass media (e.g., TV, radio, newspapers); social networking sites (e.g., Facebook, Twitter, and Instagram); collateral print media (e.g., brochures, posters, flyers); group-based interactions (e.g., workshops, community forums); and one-on-one interactions (e.g., peer counseling). Campaigns have championed a great many health behaviors, like wearing the seat belt, changing diet, using proper medication, exercising, enhancing social support, quitting substance use, family planning, and testing and screening for diseases. Taken as a whole, health communication campaigns are useful to tackle many of the most common problems in the United States and the world.[21]

GOALS AND STRATEGIES

If health communication is defined as the application of communication strategies to inform choices and promote better health and well-being,[22] health communication campaigns, then, must entail the strategic mechanisms for swaying audiences with messages aimed at advocating positive health-related information and decisions. To put an end to the numerous health-related problems of present-day societies through public enlightenment, it is essential to produce dependable messages that the audience can understand and adopt. A campaign strategy to health communication can assist the communicator in designing and propagating effective messages consistently and advantageously. Health communication campaigns can be in many shapes and forms, lay out diverse objectives, and employ various media.[23] According to Rogers and Storey (1987),[24] they are usually designed:

- To shape the audience's beliefs and actions towards their health or the health of communities.
- For particular target audiences, and barely for a whole population.
- For accomplishment within a certain time frame.
- To be incorporated with other media and communication efforts to educate people about a health-related matter.

Health communication campaigns use integrated goals to diffuse messages—directly or indirectly—to notify, influence, and convince audiences' behaviors, attitudes, or beliefs about modifying or keeping healthful lifestyles. Whereas such campaigns can be as straightforward as a simple media-based program, a campaign's advertising component is usually accompanied by public educational communications and services offered by healthcare institutions, like hospitals and managed care organizations, and government institutions. All of these are also complemented by interpersonal support from healthcare workers, or by local sources like schools, religious organizations, and community-based groups; they serve to strengthen the desired health behaviors in the campaign.[25]

Noncommercial Aims

While the ultimate objective of health communication campaigns is behavior, attitude, or belief change, they can be informative or persuasive in nature.[26] They are often noncommercial health education initiatives. An exemplary health communication campaign might attempt to inform underserved women and girls about the new accessibility to mammograms or the significance of screening to encourage the prevention, early detection, and effective cure of breast cancer. Some campaigns also attempt to modify the audience's attitudes or capacity to handle a disease or condition—e.g., giving more inspiration to underprivileged Hispanic women to get a periodic mammogram.[27] No matter how advanced or large-scale, a true health communication campaign does not create profits about an issue or a cause.

This is consistent with Rogers and Storey's (1987)[28] interpretation of public communication campaigns as meaningful attempts (1) to inform, convince, or inspire changes within a rather well-defined population, (2) for noncommercial profits to the people or communities targeted, and (3) often within a certain time frame. Hence, health communication campaigns want to influence an audience's inclinations to take a particular action—e.g., by developing steps to get a mammogram from a certified doctor or clinic. The most thought-out campaigns seek to modify particular clinical outcomes for a targeted audience. For example, the outcomes may serve to demonstrate that, as a result of controlling for potential confounding variables, the length for people's treatment will decrease greatly among the intervention (in contrast to a treatment group condition).[29]

How Effective Are Health Communication Campaigns?

In the United States, health communication campaigns driven by mass media channels and that do not use coercion have an effect size of approximately five percentage points (r.05). Coercion via legal or regulatory means is not usually applicable to many health campaigns (e.g., nutrition campaigns because it is simply not effective). If 60% of members of a population were adopting the desired behavior before the campaign, it is expected that about 65% will perform the health behavior after the campaign.[30] In regards to many health issues, campaigns that advocate the adoption of a behavior that is new to the audience or that replaces an old one (with the new) have a better success rate than campaigns pushing on ending an unhealthy behavior—i.e., one that individuals are already doing or intend to do.[31]

Health messages possess many characteristics that distinguish them from other categories of mediated messages. Among these are the level of health issues, the fear that health messages can elicit, feelings of resistance to certain types of health messages, and the multifaceted aspect of certain health problems. Many health messages concentrate on sensitive and personal topics like sexually transmitted diseases (STDs), drug use and addiction, abortion, and mental disorders. Because these topics are complex and emotional for a great many people, they can be particularly challenging when designing public communication campaigns.[32]

Notwithstanding decades of fine-tuning, sophistication, and expenses in the billions of dollars, health communication campaigns made to prevent or reduce problematic health behavior have yielded inconsistent results. Nevertheless, such campaigns remain fashionable and prevalent because of their potential to reach large audiences in a cost-effective fashion.[33] Enter cardiovascular diseases, still a major cause of death globally and a huge driver of healthcare expenditures in developed countries. Besides tobacco use, contributors to cardiovascular diseases include high blood pressure, high levels of blood cholesterol, malnutrition, sedentarism (i.e., physical inactivity), and obesity. Health campaigns do not always attain decent success.[34] In many underdeveloped nations, a large percentage of premature deaths (and related morbidity) occur before age five. In spite of ambitious health intervention campaigns, a catastrophic rate of poor child survival subsists, including substandard treatment of dehydration coming from diarrhea, nonvaccination for avoidable illnesses, and lack of breastfeeding.[35]

Perceptions of Mass Media Messages about Health

The perception of mass media messages about health are influenced by various dimensions that can be either distinct or common. Each dimension faces potential obstacles that could erode the impact of a campaign, or potentially give an explanation as to why health campaigns might not produce anticipated increases in a public's knowledge, attitudes, cognitions, and ultimate behaviors. A conceptual framework should materialize, to explain how likely health communication obstacles could be the outcome of the health messages' (1) source, (2) content, (3) media conduit, (4) the audience's postexposure, and (5) destination.[36] Although these interactive dimensions and obstacles appear to be comprehensive, the conceptual framework underpinning health communication campaigns should expand greatly if more effective goals and adapted sociocultural dimensions (with respect to audience receptivity to health campaign messages) are recognized. Three sociocultural concepts extensively used in health campaign studies include:

- **social influences** (the impact of peer pressure and for-profit advertising on health behaviors);[37]
- **cognitive behaviors** (the type of behavior that influences health behaviors through problem-solving, decision-making, and self-control skills);[38] and
- **life skills** (the experience, acquired skills, and personal education/training necessary to cultivate a healthier lifestyle and which can facilitate a commitment to a particular health behavior).[39]

McGuire (2001)[40] explains that source-based obstacles to an ideal public response to health messages include the number of different sources to which the public is exposed, the harmony or consistency between health messages, the apparent demographic similarity between the source and the audience, and the source's influence and ethos. Message-based obstacles include the message's perceived influence, the incorporation or leaving out of relevant facts or familiar narrative frames, the display and organization of words and graphics, a message's readability for its target audience, the incorporation of suitable images or graphics within a text-based story, and the adaptation of the content to the audience's culture. Channel-based obstacles could be the inclusion of print, radio, video, or interactive channels to diffuse messages.

Receiver-based obstacles to an ideal audience response to health messages include differences in interpretations of and interest in health based on sex, age, education, race, socioeconomic status, literacy, health literacy (i.e., the ability to grasp health information irrespective of education), personal attributes, lifestyle, and values. Other obstacles include one's access to media and the healthcare-delivery system (e.g., one's health insurance status and affordability of care as well as physical distance from healthcare facilities). Destination-based obstacles include timeliness of the audience's exposure to information, the message's adaptation to audience needs, whether messages are prevention- or cessation-focused, and whether messages recommend health behaviors with an instant or a delayed reward.[41]

Five-Step Strategy for Better Health Communication Campaigns

It has been shown that health communication campaigns do not always adopt the best strategies to reach their target audiences. In addition to the different types of barriers just mentioned, another reason lies in the broad-based or blanket approaches that have been adopted within specific countries or contexts. Such approaches are seldom effective. Wright, Sparks, and O'Hair (2008)[42] have laid out a five-step strategy for better health communication campaigns: (1) Audience segmentation, (2) differential communication strategy, (3) level of communication intervention, (4) media mix, and (5) media planning.

1. **Audience segmentation**: As a first step, it involves identification of the audience and breaking it down into smaller segments for easy message targeting. For instance, a communication strategy would divide the whole population into groups—e.g., teenagers, young couples, middle-aged couples; men and women; married and single; rural and urban, and so forth. The basic notion behind audience segmentation is to guide the flow of communication towards a particular segment and improve the focus of efforts in a specific direction to obtain a good effectiveness/success rate.

2. **Differential communication strategy**: After segmenting/dividing the audience into smaller groups, the next step is to identify characteristics (nodal points) of each group. These nodal points are entry points to infuse the group and shape their behaviors, attitudes, or beliefs. Because all groups are different, a different communication strategy will be necessary. Differential communication strategy is the adaptation of communication efforts to the needs of every group to generate desired changes.

3. **Level of communication intervention**: Society is heterogeneous; it is a complex *mélange* of people with immense diversity with respect to interpretation, understanding, reaction, and other psychosocial and individual qualities. Hence, before using a communication strategy, it is important to determine the level of communication intervention. Three levels of communication intervention should be used in major public communication endeavors: (**a**) Mass level, (**b**) group level, and (**c**) individual level. These three levels of communication also ought to be finalized. The idea behind the **mass-level** intervention is to gain the audience's attention towards some topics that are relevant for society at large or raise awareness/interest towards some current activities. For instance, a campaign may be conducted to raise awareness about the insanitary environment and its origins of diseases like malaria. This contributes to a degree of "attitudinal readiness" towards community problem-solving. The **group-level** intervention requires refining communication efforts and making them more meaningful to well-chosen groups. As such, popularization of science may be categorized into popularization of science among children, school-going children, university students. Other categorizations could be for rural areas, urban areas, farmers, businesspeople, and laborers (among others). The third level of communication intervention (i.e., **individual-level**) determines the prospective beneficiaries and develops the communication strategy. The strategy is need-based, purposive, and made for individual contact. For instance, popularization of bio-gas plants will concentrate on people/families who have sufficient space and keep the necessary number of livestock.

4. **Media mix**: After the levels of communication intervention are prepared and ready, the next step is to locate a mixture of media for message delivery. An ideal media strategy is one that chooses a mix of mass media and personal media that will complement each other, thereby boosting the efficacy of communication intervention. **Information density**—i.e., the ability of a medium to bear the information load and distribute the same successfully—of media varies. Mass media have lower information density than personal media. This is why treatment of the message to be diffused must be implemented accordingly. Inserting too much content in a message through mass media will be less effective and might not induce a positive reaction. It may even cause confusion in the audience's mind. Information overload cannot increase or maintain public interest. As a more potentially successful case, a family planning campaign should broadcast mass media messages like "small family, happy family" or "space the children, grace the children." The methods to realize these goals can be done through personal media because they have high information density.

5. **Media planning**: This step involves knowledge of efficient reach, scope, and quality of available media. Before developing a media plan and undertaking any media-based campaign, two points are considered: (1) Frequency of media exposure (i.e., number of occasions for message exposure or delivery through media, like television, over a specific period; how many times is it going to be per week or month?) and (2) intensity of media exposure (i.e., message repetition through several media (e.g., radio, TV, newspapers) over a specific period).

The detailed case study on the antismoking "truth" initiative is a prime example where the five-step strategy for better health communication campaigns can easily apply. First, it is essential to provide readers with general background information on antismoking campaigns.

ANTISMOKING CAMPAIGNS

Cigarette use remains the first preventable disease in the world and in the United States.[43] Some populations disproportionately suffer from tobacco-related diseases—in part, because the tobacco industry has deliberately directed their advertisements at these groups. Young adults are highly vulnerable to cigarette smoking because of aggressive tobacco marketing campaigns,[44] with about 20% of them smoking cigarettes—18- to 25-year-olds have the highest rate at 41%.[45] Among young adults, most tobacco experimenters either quit or move on to frequent smoking and addiction.[46]

College is a decisive time in a youth's life when it comes to smoking cigarettes; 11–24% of smokers do it for the first time in college.[47] Almost one-third of college students have already smoked; 9.2% of them report having smoked during the last 30 days; 8% use e-cigarettes; and 2.8% smoke hookah.[48] The effects of tobacco use among college students are worrying because of (1) the health implications of early tobacco initiation, (2) the influence of nicotine on youths' brain development, and (3) the higher likelihood of sustained tobacco use in their adulthood.[49] Smoking-related behaviors also directly affect the campus community, including decreased academic excellence, higher cigarette butt litter, and more exposure to second-hand smoke.[50] Owing to the fact that 99% of smokers did it for the first time before the age of 26, prevention approaches on college campuses are of utmost importance in attempts to diminish tobacco use initiation and resultant addiction.[51]

Antismoking campaigns by cancer charities and government health agencies have tried to resist the advertising of tobacco by developing their own public notices to stress the negative impact of smoking. The earliest advertisements predominantly focused on assisting in smoking cessation, the higher risk of lung cancer, and the problems of passive smoking. However, they have become more and more hard-hitting over the past few decades; several campaigns have focused on reduced physical appeal and the dangers of erectile dysfunction. These are more directed at younger smokers than past campaigns. The Centers for Disease Control and Prevention (2014)[52] suggests that mass media campaigns be used for tobacco prevention and tobacco control. The reason is that they are cost-efficient and are able to reach diverse audiences. They can also carry a huge impact on tobacco use and related health consequences.[53]

The Health Belief Model (HBM)

Developed by Becker (1974),[54] the **Health Belief Model** (**HBM**) posits that two main factors increase the likelihood that people embrace a proposed health-protective behavior change. First, people must fear that an illness or grave health consequences could afflict them. Second, they must believe that the benefits of following the proposed action prevail over the perceived hurdles to (and/or costs of) adhering to the preventive action. Key concepts from the HBM relate specifically to the strength of health threat appeals: susceptibility amplified by the gravity of consequences and the self-efficacy and reaction efficacy of following the proposed behavior. The HBM originates in the public health realm. The model has been applied to many public health campaigns that incorporate disgust or fear appeals to combat AIDS[55] and in global child health campaigns.[56] The HBM acknowledges that a multitude of events (e.g., knowing a sick person and exposure to media campaigns) can function as "cues to action." These cues can be seen as influencing "threat."[57]

Australia's National Tobacco Campaign (NTC) was directed at smokers aged 18–40 and included a cessation narrative. The campaign used mass media ads (mostly TV ads) to accentuate the health implications of smoking and sought to get smokers to quit cold turkey. In order to do this, new messages about the health risks of smoking for smokers aged 18–40 years were broadcast through graphic TV ads created to elicit a negative visceral reaction. This approach was rooted in health behavior change theories like the HBM.[58] Graphic photos of the health ramifications of smoking were employed considerably during the campaign. According to the HBM, if people see their existing behavior (smoking) as posing a serious risk to their well-being, and they know that a certain action will decrease this risk (that is, quitting), they will more likely change their behavior. The HBM postulates that graphic photos like the ones in the NTC ads help boost both the perceived gravity of the health risks associated with smoking and the probability of these events happening. Therefore, consistent with the HBM, the negative emotions triggered by the NTC ads should motivate the audience to adapt their smoking behaviors.[59]

The NTC is one of the longest-running antismoking campaigns in the world. It started in June 1997. However, the results were disappointing. After five years (1997–2002), adult smoking only decreased by 3.7%.[60] At some point, the NTC replaced graphic photos with more academic/scientific information. Nevertheless, Gilbert (2005)[61] reported that the NTC's use of medico-scientific knowledge in its later series of antismoking campaigns (circulated in New South Wales, Australia) resulted in antismoking messages that were perceived as too detached from smokers' daily circumstances and from the smoking decisions of young ladies in particular.

The Negative Effects of Stigmatizing Smokers in Campaigns

It is hypothesized that stigmatization encourages people to quit smoking by activating a state of emotional distress, like shame, in audiences.[62] Unfortunately, studies have demonstrated that this approach is mostly ineffective. In their qualitative study in Christchurch, New Zealand, Thompson, Barnett, and Pearce (2009)[63] examined the ways by which people reacted to antismoking campaigns and voiced concerns about the manner by which "fear appeal" campaigns may perpetuate the stigmatization of heavy smokers. On the whole, campaigns are effective and behavior change takes place for groups and people who show high degrees of self-efficacy. Those who do not believe that they are efficacious react in a multitude of ways to these campaigns. Those who cannot or do not want to modify their smoking behavior represent a group of heavy smokers who, in the long term, may not be able to quit.

In like fashion, Kim, Cao, and Meczkowski (2018)[64] corroborate the fact that antismoker stigmatization typifies many of present-day antismoking campaigns and is counterproductive as well. The three scholars methodically tested it among 136 current smokers. Results indicated that exposure to a stigmatizing message greatly decreased smokers' motivations to quit smoking. The conditional negative impact of the message was explained by shame felt by smokers. Using the case of Australia again, Mahoney (2010)[65] reports that, notwithstanding a high volume of antismoking messages highlighting the toxic effects and social shame surrounding smoking—i.e., these messages were shown in primary and secondary schools and through the mass media—many youths still smoke in Australia, where antismoking school education and media-based initiatives about the consequences of smoking have been developed longer than most of these students have been alive.

Case Study: The truth Campaign

truth is a long-standing antismoking campaign designed for youths in the United States. The campaign is run by the American Legacy Foundation and funded by diverse tobacco companies. Stylized as "truth" (to never be capitalized) or even truth®, the campaign seeks to eradicate teen smoking by creating TV and digital content to condemn tobacco use and unite youngsters against the tobacco industry. Initiated in 2000, it particularly targets at-risk youths aged 12–17 years, chiefly stressing the tobacco industry's misleading and covert marketing practices to encourage smoking. These ads are considered cost-effective and have led to a downward spiral in cigarette smoking among teens.[66] During the first year of the campaign, 75% of all 12-to 17-year-olds nationwide could correctly remember and explain at least one truth advertisement; campaign-related antismoking beliefs and attitudes increased.[67] The financial support for truth mass media campaigns comes from the settlement reached between many US states and the tobacco industry. The truth campaign was also successful in lowering smoking initiation among young people.[68]

"Finish It"

In August 2014, "truth" launched **"Finish It,"** a revamped campaign advocating that youths be the first generation to eliminate the concept of smoking. "Finish It" was constructed on health behavior change theories other than the HBM. The mission was to prove that changes in attitudes, in particular antitobacco attitudes, precede changes in motivation to smoke.[69] "Finish It" became *the* nationwide media-based smoking prevention campaign targeting teenage audiences.[70] "Finish It" sought to be a trade name with which youths could identify. In sharp contrast to the solemn "life or death" tone used by numerous antitobacco campaigns, the strategy behind "Finish It" was to stress the dangers of tobacco and industry marketing practices, without belittling or stigmatizing its audience.[71] The recurring theme was, and still remains, the manipulation of the tobacco industry. Overall, thanks to hard-hitting ads featuring boys and girls challenging the tobacco industry, "truth" devised a brand determined to empower youths to foster positive, tobacco-free identities. The campaign does not attempt to "speak" directly to youths (i.e., "Do not smoke"). Rather, it persuades them to make their own decisions regarding smoking and the tobacco industry.[72]

During that same year (2014), truth repositioned its campaign message by making it more relevant to a 15- to 21-year-old audience (though already targeted by previous antitobacco campaigns). Although most members of the audience were statistically not inclined to smoke, the purpose was to influence the collective power of the nonsmoking majority to influence, in turn, the smoking minority who, hopefully, would become the one generation that ends smoking as well. From 2014 to 2016, "Finish It" used an integrated marketing campaign model, with paid media, digital engagement practices, and in-person contact to engage with that 15- to 21-year-old audience.[73]

Methods

In its "Finish It" campaign, truth used a wide mix of mass communication and new media platforms to reach the level of resources essential for such a campaign and concerning the possible benefits of lowering smoking among youths (see Table 5.1):[74]

Table 5.1 Direct outputs of the *Finish It* campaign (2014–2016)

Output	Description	Number of Outputs
Advertisements Produced		
Video	Television and digital ads.	14
Cinema	Ads aired in movie theaters.	2
Radio	Ads aired on Pandora, Spotify, and Soundcloud, typically 8 ads per year.	24
Banners Produced	Digital display banner ads, typically 10 per year.	30
Content Integrations/Digital Partnership Ads	Custom integrated content pieces within entertainment media. Three integrations per partnership, occurring 2 times per year, with 10 partners per year.	60
Homepage Takeovers	Custom content about *Finish It* that are displayed on another publisher's homepage (e.g., BuzzFeed). Typically 12–15 takeovers per campaign with a total of 30 takeovers per year.	90
Search	Text ads that appear on Google results pages and across the Google Network, which includes the Search Network, search partners, and the Display Network.	70
Influencer Creative Content	Videos and other creative content created and posted by social media influencers about *Finish It*.	30
Website	The truth website was rebuilt in 2014 and in 2015.	2
Articles	Copy-text and images developed by staff.	45
Quizzes	Unique quizzes that promote the truth brand and/or the current campaign.	30
Activations	Activities on the truth website that engage and increase brand awareness (e.g., petitions, thank you cards, submit an idea).	15
Social Media Network	Truth-owned social media accounts (i.e., Instagram, Twitter, Snapchat, Facebook, and YouTube).	5
Social Media Posts	Unique social media posts (e.g., gifs, images) that truth published on truth-owned social media accounts.	4254
Owned and Operated Messaging	Truth created and sent out email blasts and/or text message campaigns to engage consumers.	156
Video Games	Truth incorporated custom content for an existing console game.	1
Partnerships	Partnerships with other brands (i.e., PetCo, Vans, Tyra Banks, and Coda).	4
Events	Tours, concerts, and other events, typically 100 per year.	300

What this table shows is that, along with a repositioned campaign, high web presence, a sequence of advertisements, and many additional methods of communication, truth includes a robust campaign theme: be the generation that ends smoking altogether. By carefully analyzing its target audience, campaign developers found out that contemporary adolescents do not want to protest against tobacco industry manipulation as much as drive positive collective action. "Finish It" was designed to fulfill this generation's aspiration to be agents of social change.[75] The initiative aims to embolden the 94% of adolescent nonsmokers, as well as the 6% of adolescent smokers, to actively kill the tobacco epidemic.[76]

Its "Finish It" approach exploits youths' rebellious nature and craving to ensure their freedom from tobacco control and manipulation. The heart of the strategy is to position its message as a brand, like other well-known brands (e.g., Nike, Sprite), to appeal to boys and girls at risk of smoking. "truth" TV and print ads include what advertising specialists call "edgy" youths (i.e., those youths who are ahead of everybody on trends), promotional products (e.g., T-shirts, stickers), street marketing, and a website (www.thetruth.com). Despite the fact that truth is a national multiethnic program, special efforts were made to increase its appeal to African Americans, Hispanics, and Asians.[77] truth even joined forces with Vine celebrities for the "Big Tobacco Be Like" video series. The Big Tobacco Be Like ads used pop idols from the Vine app to expose tobacco industry ploys with youths.[78]

truth's Most Recognized Media

The most recognized media created by "truth" are its advertisements on TV, social networking sites, and YouTube channels. For instance, the "truth" advertisement titled *1200* depicts a crowd of youths walking towards a big tobacco corporation building, then abruptly falling down as if dead while one youth is still standing with a sign that reads, "Tobacco kills 1,200 people a day. Ever think about taking a day off?"[79] In the *Body Bags* advertisement, youths make a heap of body bags on the sidewalk in front of Philip Morris's (now former) headquarters in New York City. One of them steps forward with a loudspeaker to yell at the employees inside the building, "Do you know how many people tobacco kills every day? This is what 1200 people actually looks like."[80]

Another truth commercial, *Singing Cowboy*, presents a cowboy with a breathing stoma (opening) in his neck singing, "You don't always die from tobacco, sometimes you just lose a lung," and other analogous lyrics.[81] A third advertisement, *1 out of 3*, uses "fantasized scenes such as an exploding soda can"[82] to propagate the idea that tobacco is the only substance that prematurely takes the life of one out of three users. Arguably one of truth's best-known campaigns, *Shards O' Glass*, was broadcast during Super Bowl XXXVII. The commercial depicted a senior manager for a popsicle company, "Shards O' Glass," that gave disclaimers for their merchandise—a popsicle with shards of glass in it, unmistakably hazardous and deadly—and asked the question, "What if all companies advertised like big tobacco?"[83]

On top of its most recognized media like TV ads, truth has a significant online presence and uses guerrilla "on-the-street" marketing. **Guerrilla "on-the-street" marketing** is an advertisement approach in which a corporation relies on surprise and/or *avant-garde* interactions to promote a product, brand, or service. One purpose of such interactions is to stir an emotional response in the clients, and the supreme goal is to get audiences to remember products, brands, or services in an unusual manner (different from what they are used to).[84] The concept was popularized in Jay Conrad Levinson's (1984)[85] book *Guerrilla Marketing*. For the truth campaign, this is a type of grassroots marketing that is performed by a team of "truth tour riders" who are dispatched to popular music and sporting events nationwide every summer. These include the Warped Tour, Mayhem Festival, and High School Nation events.[86]

Effects of the truth Campaign

Hair et al.'s (2017)[87] investigation of the effects of the truth campaign revealed that exposure to a popular televised event leads to higher likelihood of advertisement awareness and social engagement. The investigation also indicates that the extent of social media engagement for an event period is more significant than for a nonevent period. The results show that featuring ads during a popular, culturally relevant televised show is associated with higher awareness of the truth campaign overall, controlling for variables that may also determine the reaction to campaign messages. Attentiveness to six truth ads broadcast during popular televised events and self-reported social media participation were evaluated through cross-sectional online surveys of people aged 15–21 years. Social participation was measured using different Twitter and YouTube metrics. Logistic regression models could anticipate self-reported social participation and advertisement awareness; a negative binomial regression could anticipate overall engagement across social media platforms.

Costs of the Campaign

The costs of the truth campaign, based on its expenditure records, consisted of the following: (1) Development, production, and delivery of TV, radio, social media, and cinema components; (2) development, production, participation, and analytics of social media platforms and content; (3) development and delivery of guerrilla "on-the-street" marketing summer "Finish It" tours after youth music events throughout the nation; (4) formative, process, and summative assessments and research on the campaign's intended audiences; and (5) salaries of truth employees directly working on the campaign.[88] A study analyzed whether the $324 million venture into the truth campaign could be justified by its impact on public health results. Experts and practitioners alike determined that the campaign was financially successful because it saved up to $5.4 billion in healthcare costs to society between 2000 and 2002. From this vantage point, scholars aver that truth is truly a cost-efficient public health campaign.[89]

Bar-Based Interventions

Campaigns such as "Finish It" appeal to lower-risk groups, not just higher-risk ones. Nevertheless, peer crowds that include significantly more smokers (e.g., party animals, hip hop fans, and country music fans) may not identify with campaigns that stress low overall smoking rates. Bars are known to be an interesting venue to get through to these high-risk peer crowds, as up to 70% of smokers in these peer crowds go to bars (and clubs). Moreover, as bars attract particular types of customers who frequently hang out with specific folks, bar-based interventions can be effortlessly adapted to such peer crowds.[90] In their study, Ling et al. (2017)[91] reported that bar attendance and affiliation with specific peer crowds involve considerably higher smoking rates. Campaigns that target hip hop and country music fans could reach smokers in the process. In fact, peer crowd-segmented interventions have yielded lower rates of smoking (and binge drinking).

In Ling et al. (2017) study, young professionals (37.1% of the sample) had a low (8.2%) smoking rate, but comprised a higher number of smokers ($n = 8,000$). Bars are a less suitable venue to reach young professionals, as the odds of finding a young professional customer who smokes there are only 10% (=4,200 smokers). On the other hand, the hip hop target group (8.4% of the sample) had a significantly higher smoking rate (39.2%), consisting of about 8,500 smokers. Ling et al. estimated the odds of smoking among hip-hop fans at 47% (=5,600 smokers), implying that bars are a good venue to reach hip hop smokers. Similarly, the odds of smoking among country fans were 52% (=2,900 smokers).[92]

HARM REDUCTION CAMPAIGNS

Harm reduction is an approach to public health intended to be a progressive substitute for the ban of particular hazardous dangerous lifestyles. The main premise of harm reduction is the acknowledgment that certain types of individuals always have and always will undertake behaviors that involve risks, such as the behaviors previously described in the lengthy case study on smoking—but also drug use, binge drinking, unsafe sex, and prostitution. An important purpose of harm reduction is to alleviate the potential dangers and health risks inherent to the risky behaviors themselves. Another purpose is to moderate harm linked to, or caused by, the legal contexts in which the behaviors are performed—e.g., a proscription of certain acts or substances can engender unintended consequences, like the establishment of a black market where unlawful trade prospers.[93]

Harm reduction campaigns vary from widely embraced ideas, such as (1) designated driver programs, to more controversial ones, like (2) the distribution of condoms in high schools, (3) needle exchange programs or safer injection areas for recreational drug users, (4) legalization of drugs, and (5) heroin maintenance programs. Harm reductionists argue that no individual should be denied assistance, such as clinical care or social security, for the simple reason that they take risks or exhibit behaviors that are unlawful or are generally frowned upon by society at large.[94] Barbour, McQuade, and Brown (2017)[95] assert that needle exchange programs are harmless and highly productive programs for advocating health among those who inject drugs. This is why, the three authors add, harm reduction campaigns for promotion, education, and application of new needle exchanges are fundamental to enhancing public health and combating structural inequality.

Campaigns to Legalize Prostitution

Public communication campaigns that champion the legalization of prostitution—in spheres where it is not lawful—spread the message that there are three major benefits: (1) Legalization permits prostitutes to work independently from pimps and organized criminals; (2) legalization enables the creation of better public health procedures against sexually transmitted diseases; and (3) legalization eliminates a victimless crime.[96] Change agents who insistently push for legalizing prostitution profess that "prohibitionists" are in the wrong with their beliefs that prostitution is the embodiment of male domination and objectification of women; such beliefs are framed as self-evident, unconditional truth, without being grounded in facts. For change agents, prohibitionists look at prostitution in a one-dimensional mode, as a type of violence or, more simply, as intrinsically exploitative and detrimental to sex workers worldwide. This definition contradicts findings of manifold evidence-based studies.[97] Ronald Weitzer (2010)[98] has advocated for this kind of harm reduction campaign for several decades. According to him, the reasoning is that (1) the abundance of myths based on the oppression philosophy give rise to a revitalization mythology of prostitution and (2) prohibitionists themselves may unintentionally objectify women who serve as sex workers by treating them as objects (instead of people) providing sexual services. On the other hand, countercampaign activists like Janice Raymond (2013)[99] make it loud and clear that harm reduction initiatives to decriminalize prostitution are dangerous.

Case Study: DanceSafe

DanceSafe is a not-for-profit organization in the United States of which the mission is to support health and safety at raves and nightclubs. Besides offering free earplugs and condoms, DanceSafe also provides complimentary and anonymous testing of Ecstasy, so that users can know whether their Ecstasy has been contaminated or mixed with any unsafe chemicals. From an organizational perspective, DanceSafe uses volunteers as change agents who stand visibly at raves and similar venues to do free-of-charge tests on pills that patrons purchased on the assumption that they were Ecstasy. These tests are considered by proponents as a practical method of harm reduction because Ecstasy acquired on the black market is generally impure, infused with unknown chemicals that can be potentially harmful to users. DanceSafe does not put Ecstasy or any drugs up for sale. Instead, they perform chemical tests after being given a sample of a pill by its user.[100]

A study of more than 700 college students investigated whether people use or avoid ecstasy irrespective of DanceSafe's assistance at raves and whether DanceSafe actually increases potential risks—i.e., by removing the fear of hazardous additives—which may motivate nonusers to try Ecstasy. Roughly 20% of nonusers admitted that they may be more likely to try Ecstasy when DanceSafe are present.[101] The organization was also the first one to conduct a Youth Harm Reduction campaign at the ID&T/SFX Partnered "TomorrowWorld" festival held in Chattahoochee Hills, GA. DanceSafe displayed its habitual "testing" campaign messages and performed its usual tests. The first collaboration of its genre, it was distinguished by the festival's exceptionally low rate of medical emergencies and its zero incidence of deaths.[102]

Criticism of Harm Reduction Campaigns

Detractors and opponents to harm reduction campaigns state that harm reductionists approve and even facilitate behaviors that are precarious, socially destabilizing, or highly unethical.[103] For these reasons, harm reduction remains a controversial approach in the United States, where it faces more defiance than in Europe, Canada, Australia, and New Zealand. In the United States, deliberation about harm reduction is highly polarized.

Activists are frequently pigeonholed as pro-drug. Opponents tend to be condemned for (1) overlooking the realities, backgrounds, and contexts of addictions, (2) neglecting scientific evidence, (3) disenfranchising affected persons and their basic human rights, and (4) reacting from a place of moral panic. One of the challenges in making an allowance for harm reduction campaigns is that content is often framed as scantily based in evidence.[104]

Other critics of harm reduction campaigns are concerned that they are ineffective— rather than exacerbating the problem even more. This may be correct with respect to the issue of alcoholism. Wakefield et al. (2017)[105] remark that, to date, insufficient evidence exists as to whether alcohol harm reduction campaigns—often targeting youths—are effective. This limited success could be driven by many factors, including substandard reach, frequency, and duration, the absence of integration of public education with an all-inclusive approach involving related alcohol control policies (including price controls), and the unhindered presence of pro-drinking alcohol advertisements that chip away at sporadic educational efforts.

Nevertheless, it is important to acknowledge that there are several harm reduction campaigns that target alcoholism in a rigorous fashion. For example, Dunstone et al. (2017)[106] conducted a comprehensive analysis of English-language alcohol harm reduction advertisements suitable for transmission on TV. They identified 110 ads from 72 different public health campaigns broadcast between 2006 and 2014. The results indicated that, across all English-language nations, only eight alcohol harm reduction campaigns were produced and broadcast every year on average. One explanation for the restricted use of alcohol harm reduction campaigns may be the deficiency in available peer-reviewed studies that evaluate current campaigns—and, among those available studies, there is only limited evidence of efficiency. In the same Dunstone et al.'s study, one third of all commercials tried to persuade the public to act responsibly when drinking and/or to avoid binge drinking. This emphasis on responsible drinking behavior is critical to the extent that the majority of the short-term harms and the alcohol-attributable detriment to nondrinkers stem from the manners by which drinkers behave when inebriated.[107] However, one problem with advertisement-based campaign messages is that conceptions of "responsible drinking" or "responsible behavior" tend to be deficient in clarity and specificity. Therefore, they are open to personal or subjective interpretations.[108]

Case Study: HIV Campaigns in South Africa

With a population of over 60 million people, South Africa has the highest percentage of HIV-positive people in the world, and the fourth-highest percentage of HIV-positive adults.[109] According to a study conducted by Mabaso et al. (2019),[110] overall HIV prevalence was 16.6% for Black African males and 24.1% for Black African females, in comparison with only 0.2% and 0.5% for their White male and female counterparts, respectively, in that country. Among Black African males, higher prevalence of HIV was particularly significant for people in the 25–49 age bracket (as well as those 50 years and older), unlike young males between the ages of 15 and 25. Among men of all racial backgrounds, reported condom use at last sex was highly correlated with heightened risk of HIV. Conversely, high socioeconomic status and perceived risk of HIV contributed to a lower risk of HIV. In regards to females across the board, condom use at last sex and ever testing for HIV led to a higher prevalence of HIV for Black African females only.

HIV Campaigns

South African scholar and HIV/AIDS specialist S.M. Kang'ethe (2015)[111] notes that, at the beginning of the HIV/AIDS epidemic in South Africa, campaigns on that issue had a difficult time making a dent because stigmatization of infected people was ubiquitous and prevalent. Stigmatization was caused by (1) the unfair treatment of racial groups, owing to varying and conflicting information on HIV/AIDS (on the part of both tribal and biomedical healthcare providers); (2) substandard policy and campaign conceptualization at early phases of HIV campaigns (i.e., thereby making the virus look frightening, incurable, and untreatable); and (3) community education that was seriously lacking and flawed.

The first major HIV campaigns in South Africa emerged in the 1990s. For example, around 1995, AIDS awareness campaigns were implemented by the mining industry as trends in unsafe sex were rampant among gold miners. The programs included social marketing campaigns for behavior change and condom use targeted at miners and professional sex workers in the mining community.[112] By the turn of the twenty-first century, three successful multimedia HIV behavior change campaigns, called Love Life, Soul City, and Khomanani, addressed the social stigma that patients were facing in society and the public health system.[113] The initiatives drew on Entertainment–Education to target youths. Emphasis was laid on both the medium (e.g., soap operas and music videos) and the message itself.[114] Two additional campaigns, Soul Buddyz (aimed at adults and children through television series), and the 46664 campaign—which promoted HIV prevention by organizing events and activities driven by the philosophy and principles of then-President Nelson Mandela (1994–9)—reached a certain level of success as well.[115]

The most impactful HIV campaign in South Africa is arguably the **Treatment Action Campaign** (**TAC**). Founded by HIV-positive activist Zackie Achmat in 1998, TAC quickly established itself as a patient-driven, rights-based activist campaign that grew predominantly from antidiscrimination, gay rights activism in the late apartheid and transition-to-democracy era.[116] One of the hallmarks of TAC's activism was to promote access to antiretroviral medicines to all South Africans and free access to AIDS treatment through the public health system. Simply put, the campaign worked. Today, South Africa has one of the largest antiretroviral systems in the world.[117] In addition to producing *Equal Treatment*, a magazine devoted to HIV and health topics,[118] TAC's campaign media channels include smartphones, email, mailing lists, and the internet, notwithstanding lower access among the organization's poor activist base. New media technologies are also used to assist TAC in engaging with élites, professional consortia, and media outlets, and in taking advantage of regional and global movement networks.[119]

World AIDS Day

On World AIDS Day, December 1, 2018, the South African government implemented a multidisease nationwide campaign to speed up screening and testing for HIV, tuberculosis, STDs, and noncommunicable diseases, such as hypertension and diabetes. Called Cheka Impilo, the campaign was inspired by the demand made by the President of South Africa, Cyril Ramaphosa. In his first State of the Nation address in February 2018, Ramaphosa called for (1) HIV treatment of an additional 2,000,000 people by 2020, (2) the detection of close to 90,000 missing tuberculosis cases yearly, and (3) the screening of 7,000,000 people for noncommunicable diseases. Since 2010, South Africa has made substantial progress in its response to HIV/AIDS. As such, by the end of June 2018, over 4,500,000 people had already received life-saving antiretroviral therapy—which was equivalent to 20% of all people receiving such treatment worldwide. More importantly, as a result, the percentage of AIDS-related deaths in South Africa decreased from 200,000 in 2010 to 110,000 in 2017. Nevertheless, the fight against HIV/AIDS is far from over. In 2017, for instance, 270,000 new HIV infections were recorded, including about 77,000 infections among girls and women between the ages of 15 and 24 years old.[120]

Case Study: Examining Social Determinants of Health (SDH) and ABC Behaviors in Uganda

Social determinants of health (SDH) are the conditions in the areas where people are born, reside, interact, learn, work, play, worship, and grow old. These factors influence a variety of health, performance, and quality-of-life consequences and risks.[121] The US Department of Health and Human Services classifies SDH into five spheres: financial stability, education access and quality, healthcare access and quality, community and infrastructural environment, and social context.[122] Besides indicators like earnings, education, employment, and residence, SDH also consist of cultural atmosphere, neighborhood settings, social connections, transportation networks, and other social indicators. SDH function at two important levels: (1) Basic structural factors, like a nation's macroeconomic model; public policies on schooling, housing, social security, and other domains; and (2) larger cultural and institutional factors that affect the distribution of resources within society and residents' social statuses within it. Both levels of structural factors, in turn, influence more downstream social factors. Examples include access to proper healthcare, living and working conditions, and access to financial resources to purchase food, clothing, and other basic necessities, which become the underlying pillars of people's everyday lives. The intersections of all these factors contribute to health and health inequalities.[123]

SDH have direct, indirect, and intricate impacts on health. In many environments, not just poorer neighborhoods, substandard air quality can precipitously aggravate asthma symptoms.[124] Likewise, the types of day-to-day jobs and levels of earnings and education affect the scope of health outcomes, such as the pervasiveness of chronic illnesses and longevity, across the lifespan.[125] The combined impact of SDH on health is astounding. In the United States, the lowest 1% passes away between 10 and 15 years earlier than the top 1%.[126] Two types of risk factors fall under SDH: social risk factors and behavioral risk factors. **Social risk factors** are the unfavorable social conditions caused by poor health, such as lack of food and housing instability. An individual may face a myriad of social risk factors but fewer instant social needs. This explains why patient-centered care and getting people to discuss their unfulfilled social needs are critical to determining which need is the most urgent for a patient in each situation.[127] On the other hand, **behavioral risk factors** are unfavorable social problems that can be reduced or solved by citizens or physicians. Examples include better diet, physical exercise, reduced smoking or substance use, safer sexual activity, and adoption of screening guidelines (among others).[128]

Risky Sexual Behaviors

Risky sexual behaviors encompass STDs and unwanted pregnancies, both prevalent health concerns for youths across the globe. Sexual intercourse is the principal conduit of the human immunodeficiency virus (HIV) and the acquired immunodeficiency syndrome (AIDS) among youths, with intergenerational sex between female youths and older males as a key driver with respect to certain SDH such as low-income situations. Teenage pregnancies cause a decrease in socioeconomic welfare of the mother and her child.[129] Today, about 38 million individuals worldwide are living with HIV/AIDS and, owing to existing vulnerabilities, they may run a higher risk of contamination by severe acute respiratory syndrome coronavirus 2 (SARS-CoV-2), which causes COVID-19. To regulate the spread of COVID-19, governments have applied measures to curtail physical contact between people.[130]

There is a growing awareness that, although personally focused interventions have generated positive outcomes when it comes to lowering risky sexual behavior, their success rates are greatly improved when HIV/AIDS prevention addresses SDH such as broader structural factors. These factors can enhance or constrain individual factors, like poverty and wealth, gender, age, decision-making, and power. The understanding of such factors for prevention and control purposes (of HIV/AIDS) facilitates the task of prevention experts to design more suitable approaches to their health campaigns. Such approaches encompass actions carried out as important policies or programs that seek to alter the conditions in which individuals live and affect the manner by which services are offered through supporting collaboration and integration.[131] In some parts of Africa, the SDH of gender is an obstacle to effective policies regarding risky sexual behaviors. Seeking compliance to obtain agreement necessitates that at least one person starts the conversation about condom use. Past studies report that, in those regions, women are hesitant about initiating such discussions. They often fear that their male partners will condemn them for doing so.[132]

Counter to hypotheses that poverty is a major cause of HIV in sub-Saharan Africa, a growing body of evidence from both national data and personal narratives indicates that wealthier nations, and wealthier people within nations, are at higher risk of HIV.[133] The SDH at hand, here, is wealth. For example, in their examination of population-representative data from nearly 36,000 households in Kenya, Ethiopia, and Tanzania, Hadley, Maxfield, and Hruschka (2019)[134] evaluated increasing measures along the wage economy dimension as positively and significantly correlated with the HIV/AIDS infection. On the other hand, increasing achievement along the agricultural economy dimension tends to be negatively correlated with the HIV/AIDS infection, and has zero correlation with higher HIV/AIDS risk. Fox (2010),[135] too, analyzed the SDH of wealth in regards to HIV/AIDS serostatus in sub-Saharan Africa and found an inverse relationship between poverty and contraction of HIV/AIDS.

ABC Behaviors

ABC behaviors is a concept employed by HIV/AIDS prevention scholars and practitioners to allude to the three behaviors believed to be crucial in lowering the sexual transmission of HIV/AIDS: abstinence, being faithful, and using condoms, respectively.[136] On the face of it, these three behaviors appear clear-cut. Abstinence means refraining from sex inasmuch as one is not in an official, long-term, and committed relationship. For youths, this occurs when postponing sexual initiation. Being faithful entails the notion of remaining monogamous and reducing the number of sexual partners to one: one's official, long-term, and committed partner. Condom use is the unswerving and correct use of condoms during sexual intercourse.[137]

Condom use has been the most visible component of health intervention campaigns. When campaigns recommend that people use condoms to avoid HIV/AIDS infection, the behavior at hand seems sufficiently precise. Upon closer examination, however, it is easy to notice manifold behaviors—both before and after the actual use of condoms—that are pertinent for guaranteeing their consistent use. To use condoms during sexual intercourse, partners must be in harmony to do so, meaning that they need to gain the approval of the other person. They also have to make sure that condoms be accessible before sexual intercourse. Obtaining agreement and ensuring accessibility, in turn, are two different behaviors of which sociocognitive antecedents may vary.[138]

ABC Behaviors Campaign in Uganda

As of 2021, Uganda had 47 million inhabitants. It is one of the few African nations where rates of HIV/AIDS infection fell sharply after public communication campaigns were implemented in the 1990s. At about 15% in the early 1990s, the rate fell to 5% in 2001. At the end of 2005, UNAIDS reported that 6.7% of adults had contracted the virus. The reasons of Uganda's early success were extensively studied to motivate other nations to model the approaches that worked. Researchers credit the lower rate of HIV/AIDS to the successful implementation of the ABC behaviors campaign by the Ugandan government—particularly the first two (i.e., abstinence and fidelity). Uganda received funds from President George W. Bush's Emergency Plan for AIDS Relief, which advocated the ABC approach with a special focus on abstinence-driven interventions.[139] Public health campaigns unambiguously stated that behavior change was the objective because it would drive the designing of appropriate messages and campaign strategies. An investigation of the broad principle of stating behavior change goals was conducted in regards to HIV/AIDS campaigns in Uganda, which revealed that campaigns were of better quality when they clearly stipulated what the behavior change goals were—as opposed to a simple awareness of HIV or an overarching goal of reducing AIDS.[140]

ABC behaviors can be considered proximate determinants of the HIV/AIDS infection, i.e., methods of averting or decreasing the risk of infection. One conclusion from the Ugandan successful experiment seems to be the following: (1) Include ABC behaviors in multiple interventions and through the methods employed (and often pioneered) in Uganda; (2) empower women by making them participants in organizations like People Living with AIDS (PLWAs) and engage them in prevention interventions; and (3) combat stigma by involving faith-based groups and the like. Another important consideration with respect to the Ugandan successful experiment is arguably the planned policy of fear arousal to fight denial, to stress that HIV/AIDS is real, and to cause Ugandans to feel at serious risk of the HIV/AIDS infection.[141] It is also necessary to point out that the Ugandan government employed a multisector approach to diffuse its HIV/AIDS prevention message. As such, it cultivated robust relationships with government, community, and faith leaders who collaborated with grassroots organizations to teach ABC behaviors. Educational institutions integrated the ABC message into curricula, whereas religious-based communities trained change agents and community workers in ABC materials. The government also developed a campaign through print, billboards, radio, and television media to champion abstinence, monogamous relationships, and condom use.[142]

Tackling Gender Inequities

In the early stages of the campaign, condom use was not a key factor of the HIV/AIDS prevention message. ABC behavior changes occurred in Uganda (and a small fraction of Africa) not only because anxiety concerning HIV/AIDS contributed to protective measures by adults, but also because numerous initiatives directly tackled gender inequities. Heightened transparency about the risks of unprotected sex and challenges to women's culturally entrenched inferior role in sexual decision-making have fostered situations in which many more women are now able to refuse, decrease their number of partners, and/ or discuss condom use.[143] To this point, several reports confirm that the reduction in the HIV/AIDS rate in Uganda was mainly attributable to monogamy and abstinence. According to Edward C. Green (2009),[144] a medical anthropologist at the Harvard School of Public Health, advocating abstinence and faithfulness to one's partner was the main reason for Uganda's success because it upset the age-old practice of having multiple sexual partners at the same time.

Overall, an essential consideration is that ABC behaviors are the results of prevention strategies, not strategies in and of themselves. The explanation for the success of the ABC behaviors campaign in Uganda transcends the mere content of the messages themselves. Abstinence, being faithful, or lowering one's number of partners were the centerpiece message for the general public. Condom use was barely emphasized (only for high-risk groups). However, Uganda's ability to generate behavior change was mostly contingent on widespread social mobilization at every level and on robust governance from its president, Yoweri Museveni, who lay strong emphasis on fidelity.[145]

Situation Today

In spite of the successful ABC behaviors campaign in Uganda in the 1990s, the country today still has 1.5 million people living with HIV/AIDS. Young women are particularly affected by it, with close to 9% of adult women living with HIV/AIDS, unlike 4.3% of men.[146] There are still obvious SDH barriers, such as political and cultural obstacles, that have mired efficient HIV/AIDS prevention planning. As a consequence, additional HIV/AIDS infections are anticipated to emerge in coming years. Although serious efforts have been made to expand treatment initiatives in Uganda, too many people still live with the infection and cannot access the medicines to treat it. Retaliatory laws and stigmatizing mindsets towards men-on-men sexual intercourse, prostitution, and intravenous drug use have had the implications that these groups (most susceptible to infection) are less likely to participate in HIV/AIDS treatment.[147]

HIV/AIDS cases among sex workers were evaluated at 37% in 2015–6. It is believed that sex workers and their clients represented 18% of novel HIV/AIDS infections in Uganda during that period alone.[148] A 2015 datasheet review reported that between 33% and 55% of sex workers in Uganda complained about inconsistent condom use in the course of only one month, owing to the fact that clients were willing to give more money for sex without a condom.[149] The criminalization of prostitution and deep-rooted social stigma mean that sex workers tend to avoid taking advantage of health services or lie about their occupation to healthcare providers. Expressions of disgrace and hatred towards male prostitutes who have sex with men are aggravated by homophobia. Again, scores of sex workers in Uganda perceive social discrimination to be a huge obstacle to their motivation to test for HIV/AIDS.[150]

In the face of such legal and social hurdles, selling sex is a viable means of livelihood in a corrupt economy for countless women and men in Uganda. The number of commercial sex workers in Kampala, the capital city, was estimated to be up to 15,000, depending on how sex work is defined or even enumerated.[151] Men-on-men sex work is insufficiently reported. A 2017 study on that topic in Kampala revealed that high-risk behaviors are common, including 36% of participants reporting unsafe anal sex, 38% selling sex, 54% having steady partners on a regular basis, 64% having casual partners on a frequent basis, and 32% doing drugs.[152]

Fisheries

Fisheries are immense natural resources in Africa and crucial for the economy and subsistence of many communities in several African nations. Data from 2011 shows that the fisheries industry—such as inland fishing, artisanal marine fishing, and industrial marine fishing—added more than US$21 billion to local African economies, representing 1.11% of the gross domestic product of all African nations. In Uganda, fisheries are a fast-growing sector that guarantees better food security, employment, and profits from exports. Fish and fish products are the nation's second largest export. Investment in that industry was evaluated at US$200 million in 2008.[153]

Some of the youngest populations in sub-Saharan Africa (and in the world) live in Uganda. Consistent with the nation's demographic profile, fishing communities are also composed of young populations.[154] Unfortunately, fishing communities have been afflicted by the HIV/AIDS epidemic and to which ABC behaviors are suitable, along with other communities, like commercial sex workers, uniformed services, truck drivers, and gay male prostitutes.[155] If truth be told, in the entire sub-Saharan Africa region, fishing communities are arguably the most-at-risk communities for HIV/AIDS.[156] High mobility, repeated commercial sex, casual sexual partners, excessive binge drinking, inadequate health infrastructures, and low access to healthcare are thought to be the main reasons that contribute to the HIV/AIDS epidemic in fishing communities.[157]

Case Study: The "Clean India Mission" Campaign

Also called **Swachh Bharat Mission, Clean India Mission** is a nationwide campaign launched by the Government of India in 2014—more specifically, by Prime Minister Narendra Modi—to eradicate open defecation and develop solid waste management.[158] Phase 1 of the campaign lasted until October 2019. The objectives of Phase 1 also consisted of eliminating manual cleaning and disposing of human excreta, creating awareness and causing behavior change about sanitation practices, and enhancing capabilities at the local level.[159] Phase 2 is expected to be completed by 2025. Toilet construction is a crucial part. Under the program, more than 100 million toilets were added by the end of Phase 1. Virtually all states in India have been proclaimed as free from open defecation. Open defecation is a prevalent practice in India that propagates diarrheal disease, accounting for almost one eighth of all deaths in the country. It also produces dangerous living conditions for women and girls as well as community-acquired multidrug resistant infections in neighboring countries, thereby affecting the environment at large. By December 2015, over 60% of the nearly 900 million people worldwide still practicing open defecation were believed to be in the Republic of India.[160]

To this day, Clean India Mission is India's largest cleanliness campaign, with 3,000,000 government employees and students from all over the country participating in over 4,000 cities, towns, and rural villages. Volunteers, called *Swachhagrahis* (or "Ambassadors of cleanliness") have been employed to diffuse the practice of indoor plumbing and clever approaches to sanitation in rural areas. Prime Minister Modi referred to Clean India as *Satyagrah se Swachhagrah*, alluding to Mahatma Gandhi's satyagraha movement launched in 1916–7.[161] A term coined by Gandhi himself, **satyagraha** was a form of nonviolent resistance or civil resistance. It became a catalyst for the Indian independence movement to end the British Crown rule in India (which was eventually achieved in 1947).[162] Making India a cleaner place was, indeed, a form of resistance to regress and misery in order "to restore India's natural beauty by making the country cleaner and pollution-free."[163] Substantive changes have already been attained in the rural parts of the country. For example, Rajasthan, the largest state by area, where about 8,000,000 toilets were built in rural homes, was declared free from open defecation in March 2018.[164] Taken as a whole, by the end of 2019, Clean India Mission was able to achieve waste management in 200,000 villages.[165] Equally interesting is the fact that, by the summer of 2021, the number of Indians without a toilet went from 550 million to 50 million, according to statistics provided by UNICEF.[166]

NOTES

1. Institute of Medicine, *Speaking of Health: Assessing Health Communication Strategies for Diverse Populations* (Washington, DC: Institute of Medicine, 2002).
2. Nedra Kline Weinreich, *Hands-On Social Marketing: A Step-by-Step Guide* (Thousand Oaks, CA: Sage, 1999).
3. Institute of Medicine, *Speaking of Health*, 48.
4. Patricia Geist-Martin, Eileen B. Ray, and Barbara F. Sharf, *Communicating Health: Personal, Cultural, and Political Complexities* (Belmont, CA: Wadsworth Press, 2003).
5. Ibid, 8.
6. Ibid, 96–8.
7. Charles T. Salmon and Thanomwong Poorisat, "The Rise and Development of Public Health Communication," *Health Communication* 35, no. 13 (2020): 1666–77. https://doi.org/10.1080/10410236.2019.1654180.
8. Wesley D. Smith, *The Hippocratic Tradition* (Ithaca, NY: Cornell University Press, 1979).

9. Anna Lydia Svalastog, Doncho Donev, Nina Jahren Kristoffersen, and Srećko Gajović, "Concepts and Definitions of Health and Health-Related Values in the Knowledge Landscapes of the Digital Society," *Croation Medical Journal* 58, no. 6 (2017): 431–5. https://doi.org/10.3325/cmj.2017.58.431.

10. John D. Day, Jane Ann Day, and Matthew LaPlante, *The Longevity Plan: Seven Life-Transforming Lessons from Ancient China* (New York: Harper Paperbacks, 2018).

11. Luis García-Ballester, Jon Arrizabalaga, Montserrat Cabré, and Lluís Cifuentes, *Galen and Galenism: Theory and Medical Practice from Antiquity to the European Renaissance* (New York: Routledge, 2002).

12. Alberto Conti Andrea, "Historical Evolution of the Concept of Health in Western Medicine," *Acta Biomedica* 89, no. 3 (2018): 352–4. https://doi.org/10.23750/abm.v89 i3.6739.

13. World Health Organization, *Constitution of the World Health Organization—Basic Documents* (Geneva: World Health Organization, 2006).

14. Joseph Stokes III, Jay Noren, and Sidney Shindell, "Definition of Terms and Concepts Applicable to Clinical Preventive Medicine," *Journal of Community Health* 8, no. 1 (1982): 33–41. https://doi.org/10.1007/bf01324395.

15. See James F. McKenzie, Robert R. Pinger, and Denise Seabert, *An Introduction to Community & Public Health* (9th Ed.) (Burlington, MA: Jones & Bartlett, 2016); Mary-Jane Schneider, *Introduction to Public Health* (6th Ed.) (Burlington, MA: Jones & Bartlett, 2020).

16. Theodore H. Tulchinsky and Elena A. Varavikova, *The New Public Health* (3rd Ed.) (Cambridge, MA: Academic Press, 2014).

17. Myleea Hill and Marceline Thompson-Hayes, *From Awareness to Commitment in Public Health Campaigns: The Awareness Myth* (Lanham, MD: Lexington Books, 2020).

18. Thomas M. Harmon, Kevin A. Fisher, Margaret G. McGlynn, John Stover, Mitchell J. Warren, Yu Teng, and Arne Näveke, "Exploring the Potential Health Impact and Cost-Effectiveness of AIDS Vaccine within a Comprehensive HIV/AIDS Response in Low- and Middle-Income Countries," *PLoS One* (2016). https://doi.org/10.1371/journal.pone.0146387.

19. Izet Masic and Vjekoslav Gerc, "On Occasion of the COVID-19 Pandemic—One of the Most Important Dilemma: Vaccinate or Not?" *Medical Archives* 74, no. 3 (2020): 164–7. https://doi.org/10.5455/medarh.2020.74.164–167.

20. Xiaoquan Zhao, "Health Communication Campaigns: A Brief Introduction and Call for Dialogue," *International Journal of Nursing Sciences* 7, no. 1 (2020): S11–5. https://doi.org/10.1016/j.ijnss.2020.04.009.

21. Leslie B. Snyder, "Health Communication Campaigns and Their Impact on Behavior," *Journal of Nutrition Education and Behavior* 39, no. 2 (2007): 32–40. https://doi.org/10.1016/j.jneb.2006.09.004.

22. The Centers for Disease Control and Prevention, *Gateway to Health Communication and Social Marketing Practice* (Atlanta: The Centers for Disease Control and Prevention, 2011).

23. Elizabeth Crisp Crawford and Charles C. Okigbo, "Strategic Communication Campaigns," in *Strategic Urban Health Communication*, ed. Charles C. Okigbo (New York: Springer, 2014): 11–23.

24. Everett M. Rogers and J. Douglas Storey, "Communication Campaigns," in *Handbook of Communication Science*, ed. Charles R. Berger and Steven H. Chaffee (Newbury Park, CA: Sage, 1987): 419–45.

25. Cited in Robert A. Logan, "Health Campaign Research," in *Handbook of Public Communication of Science and Technology*, ed. Massimiano Bucchi and Brian Trench (New York: Routledge, 2008): 77–92.

26. Charles K. Atkin, "Theory and Principles of Media Health Campaigns," in *Public Communication Campaigns* (3rd Ed.), ed. Ronald E. Rice and Charles K. Atkin (Thousand Oaks, CA: Sage, 2001): 49–68.

27. Logan, "Health Campaign Research," 78–83.

28. Rogers and Storey, "Communication Campaigns," 420–5.

29. Robert C. Hornik, "Communication in Support of Child Survival: Evidence and Explanations from Eight Countries," in *Public Health Communication: Evidence for Behavior Change*, ed. Robert C. Hornik (Mahwah, NJ: Lawrence Erlbaum, 2002): 219–48.

30. Cited in Snyder, "Health Communication Campaigns," 33.

31. Leslie B. Snyder, Mark A. Hamilton, Elizabeth W. Mitchell, James Kiwanuka-Tondo, Fran Fleming-Milici, and Dwayne Proctor, "A Meta-Analysis of the Effect of Mediated Health Communication Campaigns on Behavior Change in the United States," *Journal of Health Communication* 9, no. 1 (2004): 71–96. https://doi.org/10.1080/1081 0730490271548.

32. Crawford and Okigbo, "Strategic Communication Campaigns," 11.

33. Eusebio M. Alvaro, William D. Crano, Jason T. Siegel, Zachary Hohman, Ian Johnson, and Brandon Nakawaki, "Adolescents' Attitudes toward Anti-Marijuana Ads, Usage Intentions, and Actual Marijuana Usage," *Psychology of Addictive Behaviors* 27, no. 4 (2013): 1027–35. https://doi.org/10.1037/a0031960.

34. Cited in Melanie A. Wakefield, Barbara Loken, and Robert C. Hornik, "Use of Mass Media Campaigns to Change Health Behaviour," *The Lancet* 376, no. 9748 (2010): 1261–71, 1265. https://doi.org/10.1016/S0140-6736(10)60809-4.

35. Robert E. Black, Saul S. Morris, and Jennifer Bryce, "Where and Why Are 10 Million Children Dying Every Year?" *The Lancet* 361, no. 9376 (2003): 2226–34. https://doi.org/10.1016/S0140-6736(03)13779-8.

36. Logan, "Health Campaign Research," 82–4.

37. Richard I. Evans and Bettye E. Raines, "Control and Prevention of Smoking in Adolescents: A Psychosocial Perspective," in *Promoting Adolescent Health: A Dialog on Research and Practice*, ed. Thomas J. Coates, Anne C. Petersen, and Cheryl Perry (New York: Academic Press, 1982): 101–36; Richard I. Evans and Bettye E. Raines, "Applying a Social Psychological Model across Health Promotion Interventions: Cigarettes to Smokeless Tobacco," in *Social Influence Process and Prevention: Social Psychological Applications of Social Issues*, ed. J. Edwards, R. S. Tindale, L. Heath, and E. J. Posavac (New York: Plenum Press, 1990): 143–57.

38. Brian S. Flynn, John K. Worden, Roger H. Secker-Walker, Gary J. Chir, Berta M. Badger, Ed. Geller, and Michael C. Costanza, "Prevention of Cigarette Smoking through Mass Media Intervention and School Programs," *American Journal of Public Health* 82, no. 6 (1992): 827–34. https://doi.org/10.2105/ajph.82.6.827; P. C. Kendall and S. D. Holon, *Cognitive-Behavioral Intentions: Theory, Research and Practice* (New York: Academic Press, 1979).

39. Gilbert J. Botvin, Anna Eng Christine, and L. Williams, "Preventing the Onset of Cigarette Smoking through Life Skills Training," *Preventive Medicine* 9, no. 1 (1980): 135–43. https://doi.org/10.1016/0091-7435(80)90064-X; Gilbert J. Botvin and Anna Eng Christine, "The Efficacy of a Multicomponent Approach to the Prevention of Cigarette Smoking," *Preventive Medicine* 11, no. 2 (1982): 199–211. https://doi.org/10.1016/0091-7435(82)90018-4.

40. William J. McGuire, "Input and Output Variables Currently Promising for Constructing Persuasive Communications," in *Public Communication Campaigns* (3rd Ed.), ed. Ronald E. Rice and Charles K. Atkin (Thousand Oaks, CA: Sage, 2001): 22–48.

41. Ibid, 30–6.

42. Kevin B. Wright, Lisa Sparks, and Henry D. O'Hair, *Health Communication in the 21st Century* (Malden, MA: Blackwell, 2008): 245–8.

43. Ursula E. Bauer, Peter A. Briss, Richard A. Goodman, and Barbara A. Bowman, "Prevention of Chronic Disease in the 21st Century: Elimination of the Leading Preventable Causes of Premature Death and Disability in the USA," *The Lancet* 384, no. 9937 (2014): 45–52. https://doi.org/10.1016/S0140-6736(14)60648-6.

44. Cited in Daniel K. Cortese, Glen Szczypka, Sherry Emery, Shuai Wang, Elizabeth Hair, and Donna Vallone, "Smoking Selfies: Using Instagram to Explore Young Women's Smoking Behaviors," *Social Media + Society* 4, no. 3 (2018): 1–8, 1. https://doi.org/10.1177/2056305118790762.

45. Amanda K. Richardson, Valerie Williams, Jessica Rath, Andrea C. Villanti, and Donna Vallone, "The Next Generation of Users: Prevalence and Longitudinal Patterns of Tobacco Use among US Young Adults," *American Journal of Public Health* 104 (2014): 1429–36. https://doi.org/10.2105/AJPH.2013.301802.

46. Pamela M. Ling, Louisa M. Holmes, Jeffrey W. Jordan, Nadra E. Lisha, and Kirsten Bibbins-Domingo, "Bars, Nightclubs, and Cancer Prevention: New Approaches to Reduce Young Adult Cigarette Smoking," *American Journal of Preventive Medicine* 53, no. 3 (2017): S78–85. https://doi.org/10.1016/j.amepre.2017.03.026.

47. Ruth R. Staten, Melody Noland, Mary Kay Rayens, Ellen Hahn, Mark Dignan, and S. Lee Ridner, "Social Influences on Cigarette Initiation among College Students," *American Journal of Health Behavior* 31, no. 4 (2007): 353–62. https://doi.org/10.5993/AJHB.31.4.2.

48. American College Health Association, *National College Health Assessment II: Reference Group Undergraduates Executive Summary* (Hanover, MD: American College Health Association, 2018).

49. Natalia A. Goriounova and Huibert D. Mansvelder, "Short- and Long-Term Consequences of Nicotine Exposure during Adolescence for Prefrontal Cortex Neuronal Network Function," *Cold Spring Harbor Perspectives in Medicine* 2 (2012): 10–21. https://doi.org/10.1101/cshperspect.a012120.

50. Cited in Melinda J. Ickes, Karen Butler, Amanda T. Wiggins, Sarah Kercsmar, Mary Kay Rayens, and Ellen J. Hahn, "Truth® Ads, Receptivity, and Motivation to Use or Quit Tobacco among College Students," *Journal of American College Health* 68, no. 4 (2020): 366–73, 366. https://doi.org/10.1080/07448481.2018.1549559.

51. US Department of Health and Human Services, *The Health Consequences of Involuntary Exposure to Tobacco Smoke: A Report of the Surgeon General* (Atlanta: US Department of Health and Human Services, 2006).

52. The Centers for Disease Control and Prevention, *Best Practices for Comprehensive Tobacco Control Programs* (Atlanta: The Centers for Disease Control and Prevention, 2014).

53. Xin Xu, Robert L. Alexander, Sean A. Simpson, Scott Goates, James M. Nonnemaker, Kevin C. Davis, and Tim McAfee, "A Cost–Effectiveness Analysis of the First Federally Funded Antismoking Campaign," *American Journal of Preventive Medicine* 48, no. 3 (2015): 318–25. https://doi.org/10.1016/j.amepre.2014.10.011.

54. Marshall H. Becker, *The Health Belief Model and Personal Health Behavior* (San Francisco, CA: Society for Public Health Education, 1974).

55. For example, see Martin Fishbein, Harry C. Triandis, Frederick H. Kanfer, Marshall Becker, Susan E. Middlestadt, and Anita Eichler, "Factors Influencing Behavior and Behavior Change," in *Handbook of Health Psychology*, ed. Andrew Baum, Tracey A. Revenson, and Jerome E. Singer (Mahwah, NJ: Lawrence Erlbaum, 2001): 3–16.

56. Ronald E. Rice and Dennis Foote, "A Systems-Based Evaluation Planning Model for Health Communication Campaigns in Developing Countries," *Public Communication Campaigns* (3rd Ed.), ed. Ronald E. Rice and Charles K. Atkin (Thousand Oaks, CA: Sage, 2001): 146–67.

57. Nancy K. Janz and Marshall H. Becker, "The Health Belief Model: A Decade Later," *Health, Education Quarterly* 11, no. 1 (1984): 1–47. https://doi.org/10.1177/109019818401100101.

58. Victoria M. White, N. Tan, Melanie Wakefield, and David Hill, "Do Adult Focused Anti-Smoking Campaigns Have an Impact on Adolescents? The Case of the Australian National Tobacco Campaign," *Tobacco Control* 12, no. II (2003): ii23–ii9.

59. Ibid, ii23.

60. Australian Government Department of Health, *National Tobacco Campaign* (Canberra, Australia: Australian Government Department of Health, 2021).

61. Emilee Gilbert, "Contextualising the Medical Risks of Cigarette Smoking: Australian Young Women's Perceptions of Anti-Smoking Campaigns," *Health, Risk & Society* 7, no. 3 (2005): 227–45. https://doi.org/10.1080/13698570500229655.

62. Jinyoung Kim, Xiaoxia Cao, and Eric Meczkowski, "Does Stigmatization Motivate People to Quit Smoking? Examining the Effect of Stigmatizing Anti-Smoking Campaigns on Cessation Intention" *Health Communication* 33, no. 6 (2018): 681–9. https://doi.org/10.1080/10410236.2017.1299275.

63. Lee Thompson, J. R. Barnett, and Jamie Pearce, "Scared Straight? Fear-Appeal Anti-Smoking Campaigns, Risk, Self-Efficacy and Addiction," *Health, Risk & Society* 11, no. 2 (2009): 181–96. https://doi.org/10.1080/13698570902784281.

64. Kim, Cao, and Meczkowski, "Does Stigmatization Motivate People to Quit Smoking?" 681.

65. James Mahoney, "Strategic Communication and Anti-Smoking Campaigns," *Public Communication Review* 1, no. 2 (2010): 33–48.

66. David R. Holtgrave, Katherine A. Wunderink, Donna M. Vallone, and Cheryl G. Healton, "Cost-Utility Analysis of the National truth® Campaign to Prevent Youth Smoking," *American Journal of Preventive Medicine* 36, no. (2009): 385–8. https://doi.org/10.1016/j.amepre.2009.01.020.

67. 6David F. Sly, Gary R. Heald, and Sarah Ray, "The Florida 'Truth' Anti-Tobacco Media Evaluation: Design, First Year Results, and Implications for Planning Future State Media Evaluations," *Tobacco Control* 10 (2001): 9–15.

68. Amanda K. Richardson, Molly Green, Haijun Xiao, Natasha Sokol, and Donna Vallone, "Evidence for truth®: The Young Adult Response to a Youth-Focused Anti-Smoking Media Campaign," *American Journal of Preventive Medicine* 39, no. 6 (2010): 500–6. https://doi.org/10.1016/j.amepre.2010.08.007.

69. Donna Vallone, Alexandria Smith, Tricia Kenney, Marisa Greenberg, Elizabeth Hair, Jennifer Cantrell, Jessica Rath, and Robin Koval, "Agents of Social Change: A Model for Targeting and Engaging Generation Z across Platforms," *Journal of Advertising Research* 56, no. 4 (2016): 414–25. https://doi.org/10.2501/JAR-2016-046.

70. Brian W. Weir, Jennifer Cantrell, David R. Holtgrave, Marisa S. Greenberg, Ryan D. Kennedy, Jessica M. Rath, Elizabeth C. Hair, and Donna Vallone, "Cost and Threshold Analysis of the FinishIt Campaign to Prevent Youth Smoking in the United States," *International Journal of Environmental Research and Public Health* 15 (2018): Article 1662. https://doi.org/10.3390/ijerph15081662.

71. National Cancer Institute, *The Role of the Media in Promoting and Reducing Tobacco Use* (Bethesda, MD: National Cancer Institute, 2008).

72. Jane Allen, Donna Vallone, Ellen Vargyas, and Cheryl Healton, "The truth Campaign: Using Countermarketing to Reduce Youth Smoking," in *The New World of Health Promotion: New Program Development, Implementation, and Evaluation*, ed. Bernard J. Healey and Robert S. Zimmerman, Jr. (Burlington, MA: Jones & Bartlett Learning, 2009): 195–215.

73. Elizabeth Hair, Lindsay Pitzer, Morgane Bennett, Michael Halenar, Jessica Rath, Jennifer Cantrell, Nicole Dorrler, Eric Asche, and Donna Vallone, "Harnessing Youth and Young Adult Culture: Improving the Reach and Engagement of the truth® Campaign," *Journal of Health Communication* 22, no. 7 (2017): 568–75. https://doi.org/10.1080/10810730.2017.1325420.

74. Available at Weir, Cantrell, Holtgrave, Greenberg, Kennedy, Rath, Hair, and Vallone, "Cost and Threshold Analysis of the FinishIt Campaign," Article 1662.

75. Andrew Adam Newman, "A Less Defiant Tack in a Campaign to Curb Smoking by Teenagers," *The New York Times* (August 10, 2014): A1. Retrieved on March 10, 2021 from https://www.nytimes.com/2014/08/11/business/a-less-defiant-tack-in-a-campaign-to-curb-smoking-by-teenagers-html.

76. Available at https://www.tobaccofreekids.org/press-releases/2014_08_12_truth_campaign.

77. Matthew C. Farrelly, Cheryl G. Healton, Kevin C. Davis, Peter Messeri, James C. Hersey, and M. Lyndon Haviland, "Getting to the Truth: Evaluating National Tobacco Countermarketing Campaigns," *American Journal of Public Health* 92, no. 6 (2002): 901–7. https://doi.org/10.2105/ajph.92.6.901.

78. Jo Yurcaba, "Vine Stars Hilariously Call BS On Social Smoking," *Bustle* (September 30, 2015). Retrieved on March 10, 2021 from https://www.bustle.com/articles/114030-truth-initiatives-big-tobacco-be-like-campaign-uses-vine-stars-to-show-why-saying-ill-quit.

79. Available at https://www.youtube.com/watch?v=gJTCWtcAews.

80. Available at https://www.youtube.com/watch?v=c4xmFcrJexk.

81. Available at https://www.youtube.com/watch?v=LP6vMbkx2hw.

82. National Cancer Institute, *The Role of the Media*.

83. Ibid.

84. Bernard Cova and Marcel Saucet, "The Secret Lives of Unconventional Campaigns: Street Marketing on the Fringe," *Journal of Marketing Communications* 21, no. 1 (2015): 65–77. https://doi.org/10.1080/13527266.2014.970820.

85. Jay Conrad Levinson, *Guerrilla Marketing* (Boston, MA: Mariner Books, 1984).

86. Elly Leavitt, "Anti-Smoking Organization Launches Tour to End Teen Tobacco Use," *USA Today* (July 22, 2015): A1. Retrieved on March 10, 2021 from https://www.usatoday.com/story/college/2015/07/22/anti-smoking-organization launches-tour-to-end-teen-tobacco-use/37404845.

87. Hair, Pitzer, Bennett, Halenar, Rath, Cantrell, Dorrler, Asche, and Vallone, "Harnessing Youth and Young Adult Culture," 568.

88. Weir, Cantrell, Holtgrave, Greenberg, Kennedy, Rath, Hair, and Vallone, "Cost and Threshold Analysis of the FinishIt Campaign," Article 1662.

89. Holtgrave, Wunderink, Vallone, and Healton, "Cost-Utility Analysis of the National truth® Campaign," 385–8.

90. Ling, Holmes, Jordan, Lisha, and Bibbins-Domingo, "Bars, Nightclubs, and Cancer Prevention," S78.

91. Ibid, S78.

92. Ibid, S81.

93. Patricia Geist-Martin, Eileen Berlin Ray, and Barbara F. Sharf, *Communicating Health: Personal, Cultural, and Political Complexities* (Belmont, CA: Wadsworth Press, 2003): 279.

94. Neil Hunt, "The Importance of Clearly Communicating the Essence of Harm Reduction," *International Journal of Drug Policy* 12 (2001): 35–6.

95. Kyle Barbour, Miriam McQuade, and Brandon Brown, "Students as Effective Harm Reductionists and Needle Exchange Organizers," *Substance Abuse Treatment, Prevention, and Policy* 12 (2017): Article 15. https://doi.org/10.1186/s13011-017-0099-0.

96. For example, see Noémi Katona, "Political Representation and Spokespersons in the Prostitution vs. Sex Work Debate," *Intersections* 6, no. 1 (2020): 10–21. https://doi.org/10.17356/ieejsp.v6i1.631; Ronald Weitzer, "Legalizing Prostitution: Morality Politics in Western Australia," *The British Journal of Criminology* 49, no. 1 (2009): 88–105. https://doi.org/10.1093/bjc/azn027.

97. Available at https://www.policeprostitutionandpolitics.com/pdfs_all/Academic_pro_decrim_articles_pdfs/Ron_Weitzer/2019_The_Prohibitionist_Critique_of_Prostitut.pdf.

98. Ronald Weitzer, "The Mythology of Prostitution: Advocacy Research and Public Policy," *Sexuality Research and Social Policy* 7 (2010): 15–29. https://doi.org/10.1007/s13178-010-0002-5.

99. Janice G. Raymond, *Not a Choice, Not a Job: Exposing the Myths about Prostitution and the Global Sex Trade* (Washington, DC: Potomac Books, 2013).

100. Becky Cox-White, Peggy Connolly, Lawrence Hinman, David R. Keller, Robert Ladenson, and Martin Leever, *DanceSafe* (Greencastle, IN: Association for Practical and Professional Ethics, 2002).

101. Lauren Dundes, "DanceSafe and Ecstasy: Protection or Promotion?" *Journal of Health & Social Policy* 17, no. 1 (2003): 19–37. https://doi.org/10.1300/J045v17n01_02.

102. Jessica Gentile, "At TomorrowWorld, DanceSafe Will Tell You about Your Drugs," *Vice News* (September 24, 2013). Retrieved on May 21, 2021 from https://www.vice.com/en/article/z45bjj/tomorrowworld-dance-safe-drug-test-harm-reduction.

103. Available at https://www.bionity.com/en/encyclopedia/Harm_reduction.html.

104. Fiona Hutton, "Harm Reduction, Students and Pleasure: An Examination of Student Responses to a Binge Drinking Campaign," *International Journal of Drug Policy* 23, no. 3 (2012): 229–35. https://doi.org/10.1016/j.drugpo.2011.10.001.

105. Melanie A. Wakefield, Emily Brennan, Kimberley Dunstone, Sarah J. Durkin, Helen G. Dixon, Simone Pettigrew, and Michael D. Slater, "Features of Alcohol Harm Reduction Advertisements That Most Motivate Reduced Drinking among Adults: An Advertisement Response Study," *BMJ Open* 7 (2017): e014193. https://doi.org/10.1136/bmjopen-2016-014193.

106. Kimberley Dunstone, Emily Brennan, Michael D. Slater, Helen G. Dixon, Sarah J. Durkin, Simone Pettigrew, and Melanie A. Wakefield, "Alcohol Harm Reduction Advertisements: A Content Analysis of Topic, Objective, Emotional Tone, Execution and Target Audience," *BMC Public Health* 17 (2017): Article 312. https://doi.org/10.1186/s12889-017-4218-7.

107. Ibid.

108. Adam E. Barry and Patricia Goodson, "Use (and Misuse) of the Responsible Drinking Message in Public Health and Alcohol Advertising: A Review," *Health Education & Behavior* 37, no. 2 (2010): 288–303. https://doi.org/10.1177/1090198109342393.

109. Available at https://databank.worldbank.org/reports.aspx?source=2&series=SH.DYN.AIDS.ZS&country=ZAF.

110. Musawenkosi Mabaso, Lehlogonolo Makola, Inbarani Naidoo, Lungelo Mlangeni, Sean Jooste, and Leickness Simbayi, "HIV Prevalence in South Africa through Gender and Racial Lenses: Results from the 2012 Population-Based National Household Survey," *International Journal for Equity in Health* 18, no. 167 (2019): 1–11. https://doi.org/10.1186/s12939-019-1055-6.

111. S. M. Kang'ethe, "An Examination of HIV and AIDS Campaign in South Africa towards Eliminating Stigmatisation," *Journal of Human Ecology* 49, no. 3 (2015): 317–26. https://doi.org/10.1080/09709274.2015.11906851.

112. Dominique Meekers, "Going Underground and Going after Women: Trends in Sexual Risk Behaviour among Gold Miners in South Africa," *International Journal of STD & AIDS* 11, no. 1 (2000): 21–6. https://doi.org/10.1258/0956462001914850.

113. Chris Bateman, "Teenage Pregnancies/HIV Prevention—Doctors Help Fill Official Hiatus," *South African Medical Journal* 102, no. 8 (2012): 643–5. https://doi.org/10.7196/SAMJ.6081.

114. Claudia Mitchell and Ann Smith, "Changing the Picture: Youth, Gender, and HIV/AIDS," *Canadian Woman Studies* 21, no. 2 (2001): 56–61.

115. Karl Peltzer, Warren Parker, Musawenkosi Mabaso, Elias Makonko, Khangelani Zuma, and Shandir Ramlagan, "Impact of National HIV and AIDS Communication Campaigns in South Africa to Reduce HIV Risk Behaviour," *The Scientific World Journal* 12 (2012): 1–6. https://doi.org/10.1100/2012/384608.

116. Mandisa Mbali, "The Treatment Action Campaign and the History of Rights-Based, Patient-Driven HIV/AIDS Activism in South Africa," in *Democratising Development*, ed. Peris Jones and Kristian Stokke (Leiden, The Netherlands: Brill, 2005): 213–43.

117. Mandisa Mbali, "From AIDS to Cancer: Health Activism, Biotechnology and Intellectual Property in South Africa," *Social Dynamics* 46, no. 3 (2020): 449–70. https://doi.org/10.1080/02533952.2020.1853954.

118. Available at https://www.tac.org.za/equal-treatment.

119. Melissa Loudon, "ICTs as an Opportunity Structure in Southern Social Movements: A Case Study of the Treatment Action Campaign in South Africa," *Information, Communication & Society* 13, no. 8 (2010): 1069–98. https://doi.org/10.1080/13691180903468947.

120. Available at https://www.unaids.org/en/resources/presscentre/featurestories/2018/december/south-africa-access-hiv-treatment.

121. Hugh Alderwick and Laura M. Gottlieb, "Meanings and Misunderstandings: A Social Determinants of Health Lexicon for Health Care Systems," *The Milbank Quarterly* 97, no. 2 (2019): 407–19. https://doi.org/10.1111/1468-0009.12390.

122. Available at https://health.gov/healthypeople/objectives-and-data/social-determinants-health.

123. World Health Organization, *A Conceptual Framework for Action on the Social Determinants of Health* (Geneva: World Health Organization, 2010).

124. Michael Guarnieri and John R. Balmes, "Outdoor Air Pollution and Asthma," *The Lancet* 383, no. 9928 (2014): 1581–92. https://doi.org/10.1016/S0140-6736(14)60617-6.

125. Nancy E. Adler and Judith Stewart, "Health Disparities across the Lifespan: Meaning, Methods, and Mechanisms," *Annals of the New York Academy of Sciences* 1186 (2010): 5–23. https://doi.org/10.1111/j.1749-6632.2009.05337.x.

126. Raj Chetty, Michael Stepner, Sarah Abraham, Shelby Lin, Benjamin Scuderi, Nicholas Turner, Augustin Bergeron, and David Cutler, "The Association between Income and Life Expectancy in the United States, 2001–2014," *Journal of the American Medical Association* 315, no. 16 (2016): 1750–66. https://doi.org/10.1001/jama.2016.4226.

127. Katie Green and Megan Zook, "When Talking about Social Determinants, Precision Matters," *Health Affairs* 12 (2019): 10–21. https://doi.org/10.1377/hblog20191025.776011.

128. Gavin J. Putzer and Juan R. Jaramillo, "Trends in Behavioral Risk Factors Resulting in Premature Death in US from 2000–2015," *International Journal of Research in Business Studies and Management* 4, no. 4 (2017): 8–12. http://dx.doi.org/10.22259/ijrbsm.0404002.

129. Lucie Dale Cluver, Frederick Mark Orkin, Franziska Meinck, Mark Edward Boyes, and Lorraine Sherr, "Structural Drivers and Social Protection: Mechanisms of HIV-Risk and HIV-Prevention for South African Adolescents," *Journal of the International AIDS Society* 19, no. 1 (2016): 2064–6. https://doi.org/10.7448/IAS.19.1.20646.

130. Cited in Sebastian Linnemayr, Larissa Jennings Mayo-Wilson, Uzaib Saya, Zachary Wagner, Sarah MacCarthy, Stewart Walukaga, Susan Nakubulwa, and Yvonne Karamagi, "HIV Care Experiences During the COVID-19 Pandemic: Mixed-Methods Telephone Interviews with Clinic-Enrolled HIV-Infected Adults in Uganda," *AIDS and Behavior* 25 (2021): 28–39. https://doi.org/10.1007/s10461-020-03032-8.

131. Hazel D. Dean and Kevin A. Fenton, "Addressing Social Determinants of Health in the Prevention and Control of HIV/AIDS, Viral Hepatitis, Sexually Transmitted Infections, and Tuberculosis," *Public Health Reports* 125, no. 4 (2010): 1–5. https://doi.org/10.1177/00333549101250S401.

132. Gorrette Nalwadda, Florence Mirembe, Josaphat Byamugisha, and Elisabeth Faxelid, "Persistent High Fertility in Uganda: Young People Recount Obstacles and Enabling Factors to Use of Contraceptives," *BMC Public Health* 10 (2010): 530–42. https://doi.org/10.1186/1471-2458-10-530.

133. Ashley M. Fox, "The Social Determinants of HIV Serostatus in Sub-Saharan Africa: An Inverse Relationship between Poverty and HIV?" *Public Health Reports* 125, no. 4 (2010): 16–24. https://doi.org/10.1177/00333549101250S405.

134. Craig Hadley, Amanda Maxfield, and Daniel Hruschka, "Different Forms of Household Wealth Are Associated with Opposing Risks for HIV Infection in East Africa," *World Development* 113 (2019): 344–51. https://doi.org/10.1016/j.worlddev.2018.09.015.

135. Fox, "The Social Determinants of HIV Serostatus," 16.

136. James D. Shelton, Daniel T. Halperin, Vinand Nantulya, Malcolm Potts, Helene D. Gayle, and King K. Holmes, "Partner Reduction Is Crucial for Balanced 'ABC' Approach to HIV Prevention," *British Medical Journal* 328, no. 7444 (2004): 891–93. https://doi.org/10.1136/bmj.328.7444.891.

137. Rajiv N. Rimal and Rupali Limaye, "Sociocognitive Approaches for AIDS Prevention: Explicating the Role of Risk Perceptions and Efficacy Beliefs in Malawi," in *Public Communication Campaigns* (4th Ed.), ed. Ronald E. Rice and Charles K. Atkin (Thousand Oaks, CA: Sage, 2012): 249–56.

138. Ibid, 249–56.

139. Elaine M. Murphy, Margaret E. Greene, Alexandra Mihailovic, and Peter Olupot-Olupot, "Was the 'ABC' Approach (Abstinence, Being Faithful, Using Condoms) Responsible for Uganda's Decline in HIV?" *PLoS Med* 3, no. 9 (2006): e379. https://doi.org/10.1371/journal.pmed.0030379.

140. Cited in Snyder, "Health Communication Campaigns," 34.

141. Edward C. Green, Daniel T. Halperin, Vinand Nantulya, and Janice A. Hogle, "Uganda's HIV Prevention Success: The Role of Sexual Behavior Change and the National Response," *AIDS and Behavior* 10, no. 4 (2006): 335–46. https://doi.org/10.1007/s10461-006-9073-y.

142. Norman Hearst, Phoebe Kajubi, Esther Sid Hudes, Albert K. Maganda, & Edward C. Green, "Prevention Messages and AIDS Risk Behavior in Kampala, Uganda," *AIDS Care* 24, no. 1 (2012): 87–90. https://doi.org/10.1080/09540121.2011.582478.

143. Murphy, Greene, Mihailovic, and Olupot-Olupot, "Was the 'ABC' Approach," e379.

144. Edward C. Green, "Condoms, HIV-AIDS and Africa—The Pope Was Right," *The Washington Post* (March 29, 2009): A1. Retrieved on March 7, 2021 from https://www.washingtonpost.com/wp-dyn/content/article/2009/03/27/AR2009032702825.html.

145. Green, Halperin, Nantulya, and Hogle, "Uganda's HIV Prevention Success," 335–46.

146. The data is available at https://www.afro.who.int/sites/default/files/2017–08/UPHIA%20Uganda%20factsheet.pdf.

147. Available at https://www.avert.org/professionals/hiv-around-world/sub-saharan-africa/uganda.

148. Available at http://uac.go.ug/sites/default/files/JAR%202016.pdf.

149. Katherine A. Muldoon, "A Systematic Review of the Clinical and Social Epidemiological Research among Sex Workers in Uganda," *BMC Public Health* 15 (2015): 1226–39. https://doi.org/10.1186/s12889-015-2553-0.

150. Available at https://www.avert.org/professionals/hiv-around-world/sub-saharan-africa/uganda#footnote17_gqbnd36.

151. Cited in Rachel Kawuma, Andrew Ssemata, Sarah Bernays, and Janet Seeley, "Women at High Risk of HIV-Infection in Kampala, Uganda, and Their Candidacy for PrEP," *SSM—Population Health* 13 (2021). https://doi.org/10.1016/j.ssmph.2021.100746.

152. Wolfgang Hladik, Enos Sande, Mark Berry, Samuel Ganafa, Herbert Kiyingi, Joy Kusiima, and Avi Hakim, "Men Who Have Sex with Men in Kampala, Uganda: Results from a Bio-Behavioral Respondent Driven Sampling Survey," *AIDS Behaviour* 21, no. 5 (2017): 1478–90. https://doi.org/10.1007/s10461-016-1535-2.

153. Cited in Patou Masika Musumari, Teeranee Techasrivichien, Kriengkrai Srithanaviboonchai, Rhoda K. Wanyenze, Joseph K. B. Matovu, Hemant Poudyal, S. Pilar Suguimoto, Saman Zamani, Arunrat Tangmunkongvorakul, Masako Ono-Kihara, and Masahiro Kihara, "HIV Epidemic in Fishing Communities in Uganda: A Scoping Review," *PLoS One* (2021). https://doi.org/10.1371/journal.pone.0249465.

154. Ibid.

155. Uganda AIDS Commission, *2013 Uganda HIV and AIDS Country Progress Report* (Kampala: Uganda AIDS Commission, 2014).

156. Zachary A. Kwena, Stella W. Njuguna, Ali Ssetala, Janet Seeley, Leslie Nielsen, Jan De Bont, Elizabeth A. Bukusi, and Lake Victoria Consortium for Health Research (LVCHR) Team, "HIV Prevalence, Spatial Distribution and Risk Factors for HIV Infection in the Kenyan Fishing Communities of Lake Victoria," *PLoS One* (2019). https://doi.org/10.1371/journal.pone.0214360.

157. Alex Smolak, "A Meta-Analysis and Systematic Review of HIV Risk Behavior among Fishermen," *AIDS Care* 26, no. 3 (2014): 282–91. https://doi.org/10.1080/09540121.2013.824541.

158. Giribabu Dandabathula, Pankaj Bhardwaj, Mithilesh Burra, Peddineni V. V. Prasada Rao, and Srinivasa S. Rao, "Impact Assessment of India's Swachh Bharat Mission—Clean India Campaign on Acute Diarrheal Disease Outbreaks: Yes, There Is a Positive Change," *Journal of Family Medicine and Primary Care* 8, no. 3 (2019): 1202–8. https://doi.org/10.4103/jfmpc.jfmpc_144_19.

159. Bindeshwar Pathak and Indira Chakravarty, "Sanitation and Health: A Movement Visualizing Gandhi's Dream," *Indian Journal of Medical Research* 149, no. 1 (2019): S73–5. https://doi.org/10.4103/0971-5916.251661.

160. Cited in Natalie G. Exum, Emma M. Gorin, Goutam Sadhu, Anoop Khanna, and Kellogg J. Schwab, "Evaluating the Declarations of Open Defecation Free Status under the Swachh Bharat ('Clean India') Mission: Repeated Cross-Sectional Surveys in Rajasthan, India," *BMJ Global Health* 5, no. 3 (2020): 1–11. http://dx.doi.org/10.1136/bmjgh-2019-002277.

161. *Business Standard*, "Satyagraha to Swachhagrah: Narendra Modi Addresses Rally in Champaran," *Business Standard* (December 4, 2019). Retrieved on October 7, 2021 from https://www.frombusiness-standard.com/article/current-affairs/champaran-satyagraha-118041000379_1.html.

162. Uma Majmudar, *Gandhi's Pilgrimage of Faith: From Darkness to Light* (Albany, NY: SUNY Press, 2005).

163. Perfecto G. Aquino, Jr., Mercia Selva Malar Justin, and Revenio C. Jalagat, Jr., "Clean India Mission and Its Impact on Cities of Tourist Importance in India," in *Strategies in*

Sustainable Tourism, Economic Growth and Clean Energy, ed. Daniel Balsalobre-Lorente, Oana M. Driha, and Muhammad Shahbaz (New York: Springer, 2021): 89–107.

164. Exum, Gorin, Sadhu, Khanna, and Schwab, "Evaluating the Declarations," 2–4.

165. Data available at https://www.recyclean.in/recyclean-news-the-government-of-india-released-40700-crore-funds-under-swachh-bharat-mission-for-achieving-waste-management-in-2-lakh-villages-71.html.

166. Data available at https://www.unicef.org/india/what-we-do/ending-open-defecation.

CHAPTER 6

Differences in Literacy and Culture in Health Campaigns

With the expanding circulation of information across the world, the age-old definition of literacy as the capacity of reading and writing seems insufficient to encapsulate all the aptitudes and skills necessary to allow people to achieve their objectives, to widen their knowledge and potential, and to contribute fully to their community and society at large.[1] According to the US Department of Education, in 2020, 54% of US adults between the ages of 16 and 74—approximately 130 million people—lacked aptitude and skills in literacy, being unable to read at the sixth-grade level. This is not only a shocking statistic. The financial corollaries are immense—up to $2.2 trillion annually—because inadequate literacy influences factors like personal earnings, employment opportunities, general economic growth and, more importantly, well-being and survival.[2]

A distinction needs to be made between marginal literacy and functional literacy. **Marginal literacy** is a grade above functional literacy in the sense that it allows people to understand the content of plain reading material for solving problems experienced daily, such as completing a form or applying basic arithmetic and quantitative measures. It is important to note that, although highly literate individuals can better grasp general information, those who are marginally literate still have a harder time applying the general to specific situations. **Functional literacy** is the aptitude and skill to (1) understand the content of reading material or arithmetic questions, (2) communicate and resolve issues by gaining general information, and (3) apply the content to definite circumstances experienced on a daily basis. Good functional literacy involves understanding simple writing, the capacity of filling out forms, and applying basic quantitative tasks (like arithmetic calculations) in everyday situations.[3]

In order to acquire, comprehend, manage, and communicate health messages, we must employ a range of skills. This includes print materials, numeracy, communication, and information-seeking abilities in the process.[4] We ought to be able to not only find our way through websites, but also to process other stimuli like print materials (e.g., brochures, fact sheets, and pamphlets). Occasionally called reading fluency, **print literacy** is the capacity of understanding and handling written content, including text (prose literacy), and of identifying and using information in documents. **Numeracy skills** are the skills that we possess to apply arithmetic techniques and the way we use numerical information in printed materials; it is also called **quantitative literacy**.[5]

Health Literacy

An important part of literacy that is crucial to our well-being and survival is our level of health literacy. **Health literacy** is the extent to which people have the ability to acquire, process, and grasp basic health information and services required to make proper health decisions.[6] More specifically, it is (1) the capacity of comprehending scientific concepts, information, and health research; (2) proficiency in spoken, written, and web-based communication; (3) critical thinking regarding mass media messages; (4) finding our way in the midst of intricate systems of healthcare and governance; (5) knowledge and application of community resources; and (6) understanding cultural and native/local knowledge in health contexts.[7] To this last point, a factor that aids in the enhancement of health literacy is experiential knowledge of vocabulary and facts outside one's own culture. Conceptual knowledge of health is also primordial.[8] People with more conceptual knowledge of health—e.g., how body parts work or how bacteria lead to infections—will have an easier time understanding a phenomenon that references their current knowledge base. As a result, both experiential knowledge and conceptual knowledge affect our abilities to cultivate and use our health literacy skills to interpret, store, and retrieve information.[9]

Health literacy has three levels: (1) **Functional health literacy**, which encompasses the fundamental level of reading and writing necessary to function properly in daily life, (2) **communicative** (or **interactive**) **health literacy**, which encompasses higher cognitive and literacy skills (that complement social skills to allow us to engage in diverse activities and utilize information to changing situations), and (3) **critical health literacy**, which consists of high-quality cognitive and social skills that we can employ to wield more control over our lives.[10]

Four Message Characteristics

Four message characteristics need to be taken into account when establishing the health literacy demand of a message: (1) The communication channel, (2) the message content, (3) the message source,[11] and (4) the sociocultural environment of the public.[12] With respect to the communication channel, health-related stimuli can be diffused through interpersonal or mediated conduits. When mediated channels are used, there exist a number of formats to disseminate health content—e.g., print materials, audio recordings, videos, radio communiqués, and so forth. The type of the message will vary based on language (e.g., official language versus jargon, and elevated versus simple messages) and orientation (e.g., healing versus disease prevention, costs versus profits, use of fear appeals, and narrative versus nonnarrative). Decisions on what orientation of the message and what language to use have long-term implications for message understanding.[13]

In regards to the message source, the demographic aspect of the source will have an impact on the public. Indicators such as gender and age can be important, depending on the type of campaign. A case in point is that a certain number of societies across the world consider young people as not the ideal "face" for any endeavor of public communication, as respect and admiration are earned with age—i.e., the older one gets, the better. Messages that young people impart to the audience will likely not be received favorably. Even appearance and brand recognition matter. Going back to the logos–ethos–pathos model described in Chapter 3, the source of the message or the messenger (i.e., ethos) is a major driver of influence for the audience's ability to understand and interpret health information. Credibility of the messenger is deemed highly central to the public's trust of health messages.[14]

With respect to the fourth characteristic, the sociocultural background of the audience, it is consistent with Evans, Lewis, and Hudson's (2012)[15] view on **cultural literacy**—i.e., the ability to comprehend and participate confidently in a given culture. A culturally literate individual can talk to, feel, and interact with others in that culture effortlessly.[16] In like fashion, the issue of an audience's primary language is worth mentioning too. In the United States, a significant minority of residents communicate in languages other than standard English. Hence, language proficiency is an aspect of diversity that ought to be considered. The 2020 decennial census counted about 331,500,000 Americans. Most people in the United States speak English fluently, and most federal and municipal functions are in English. However, 8.4% of the population barely speaks English or does not speak it at all. This is equivalent to almost 28 million people.[17]

Taken as a whole, the success of health literacy is grounded in evidence of a connection between health literacy and health outcomes. Research indicates that low health literacy skills are correlated with lower medical knowledge, irregular reception of preventive services through email, more instances of hospitalization, lower management of chronic diseases, inadequate health status, and higher mortality rates.[18] Atkin and Rice (2013)[19] substantiate that patients with lower health literacy skills experience more challenges related to written and oral communication, which restricts their awareness of preventive screening and signs of diseases like cancer, thereby unfavorably impacting their stage at diagnosis. This is why it is crucial for health communication campaigns to diffuse messages that present "how to do it" information. This type of information ought to generate knowledge gain or skills acquisition, including increasing self-efficacy in inducing peer resistance and gaining media literacy skills.

EHEALTH AND THE DIGITAL DIVIDE

Communication technologies have profoundly transformed access to health content and, in the process, the recognition of health-behavior risk factors and health status. eHealth, in particular, is fundamental to the sharing and circulation of health information electronically.[20] **eHealth** refers to the use of available or remote communication technologies in the healthcare environment and the application of highly developed information and communication technologies to fulfill the needs of citizens, patients, healthcare providers, and practitioners. eHealth concentrates on the widespread opportunities of service delivery. As such, eHealth provides internet-based services like WebMD.com, visited by a high number of users. Nonetheless, eHealth has also significant limitations, such as lower instances of face-to-face interactions between patients and providers, and the lower accessibility to eHealth by some disadvantaged and isolated groups.[21]

A certain number of health communication campaigns have been featured on WebMD.com, such as the $52-million campaign to promote COVID-19 vaccinations.[22] To this day, WebMD.com is still the world's most visited website for access to healthcare content. WebMD.com is a healthcare website that offers top services to assist healthcare providers, patients, and other visitors in making their way through the complex healthcare system. More precisely, it aids all these people in communicating with each other by web-based services like email and provides a plethora of healthcare information. Examples of such information include symptoms, diagnostic processes, treatments, and general healthcare suggestions. Based on these services, it follows that WebMD.com is a highly ranked eHealth service, ensuring that its products and services simplify administrative and clinical procedures, support efficiency, and lower costs by smoothing the progress of information sharing, communication, and electronic transactions between participants.[23]

Bridging the Digital Divide

The **digital divide** is the gap in access to communication technologies and/or training in how to use them. It exposes the gap between those with experienced access to digital and information technologies (like WebMD.com) and those without or much lower access. The notion of digital divide encapsulates both deficiency in physical access to technology and the ability or aptitude needed to reach adequate levels of health literacy.[24] Because eHealth is still not available to a certain number of groups, technological means to overcome the obstacles of low literacy can improve their health outcomes. Groups that are at the lower end of the digital divide include (1) residents of rural, remote, or inner-city regions; (2) members of certain racial and ethnic communities; (3) socioeconomically disadvantaged individuals; and (4) those with disabilities.[25]

The internet has been glorified as a great equalizer,[26] a revolutionary technological platform that remarkably facilitates effective exchange of information on an international scale. Yet, environmental, political, social, ideological, and cultural hurdles still persist in the present day, which makes it hard or impractical for public communication campaigns to offer support to a few billion people. As of January 2021, there were 4.66 billion active internet users worldwide, or 60% of the global population. This means that a whopping 40% of the world were still not able to access the internet.[27] The digital divide is more manifest at the global level. In fact, it is the most obvious between developed and developing countries. Immense disparities exist with respect to not only access to the internet, but also the acquiring of information or the skills required for optimal well-being and survival.[28] The global divide is to be distinguished from the digital one. The **global divide** is the gap that falls along what has been called the north–south divide (between northern wealthier countries or regions and southern poorer ones).[29]

E-Inclusion

Also called **digital inclusion, e-inclusion** is a philosophical movement to bring to an end to the digital divide, given that the world is somewhat divided into groups that do and groups that do not have access to—or the capability of using—modern technological media.[30] As the case study on UNICEF will demonstrate in the next section, campaigns for e-inclusion advocate for policies that benefit the achievement of an inclusive information society. The first step is to bring modern information platforms like the internet into all segments of the population, including individuals who are deprived in the domain of education (a category called **e-competence**),[31] age (called **e-ageing**),[32] disabilities (called **e-accessibility**),[33] as well as the domains of gender, race, and geography (i.e., those living in remote regions)—all of whom are known to be highly susceptible to the digital divide.

E-inclusion serves to fill the space created by the knowledge-gap hypothesis. The **knowledge-gap hypothesis** rests on the premise that each new technology widens the gap between the information-rich and information-poor, due to disparities in access to the medium, and regulation over its use, among other reasons.[34] Another consideration is that health messages are less likely to reach, or be emotionally and psychologically accepted by, disadvantaged people. Those who have been disenfranchised by society may be so concerned with material survival needs that they fail to concentrate on health issues that are of long-term consequences. Diffusion research suggests that, to offer support to low-income and/or low-educated groups, the news media can communicate health innovations through special programs. They can also increase media coverage with concentrated interpersonal efforts in the community.[35]

Case Study: UNICEF's Reimagine Education Campaign

The **United Nations Children's Emergency Fund**, or **UNICEF**, is a United Nations program charged with providing humanitarian and developmental assistance to children and adolescents around the world. One of the most well-known and recognizable organizations since World War II, UNICEF's activities include providing children with disease prevention, healthcare treatment, childhood and maternal food sustenance, proper hygiene, as well as education, literacy, and access to technology.[36] UNICEF's more recent campaign, **Reimagine Education**, is a campaign designed to transform and modernize learning and skills development for high-quality education for every child. This can be achieved through e-inclusion, digital learning, internet access, affordable data and devices, and the engagement of youths. By 2030, UNICEF seeks to support 3.5 billion children and adolescents. Along with dozens of private industry partners and régimes, its support includes many things, like providing textbooks to remote regions, funding educational radio broadcasts, and offering children modern styles of education (e.g., education via SMS, WhatsApp groups, and podcasts). UNICEF operates on the principle that the better the children's education and access to technology, the better their health and well-being.[37]

Bridging the Digital Divide

The Reimagine Education campaign urges psychological and financial commitment to bridge the digital divide, support every youth with remote learning, and, more importantly, place priority on the trouble-free reopening of schools. At least a third of schoolchildren around the globe could not access remote learning when COVID-19 forced their schools to close, according to a UNICEF report, as countries had to brace with their possible "back-to-school" plans. In late August 2020, Henrietta Fore, UNICEF's Executive Director said the following: "For at least 463 million children whose schools closed due to COVID-19, there was no such a thing as remote learning."[38] In fact, during the pinnacle of worldwide lockdowns, roughly 1.5 billion schoolchildren were impacted by school closures. The report detailed the limitations inherent to remote learning and exposed the profound inequalities in digital literacy as a result. The data came from a globally representative investigation of the availability of home-based technology and devices necessary for remote learning among schoolchildren of all grades (from elementary to secondary), with statistics from 100 nations. Data included access to television, radio, and online connectivity, and the range of curricula offered across these platforms when schools were shuttered.[39]

Examples across the World

UNICEF has concentrated most of its Reimagine Education campaign on the Middle East and North Africa, where 40% of schoolchildren could not benefit from remote learning, with rural areas being the most disproportionately affected. The percentage of schoolchildren in such precarious situations was 38% in South Asia and 34% in Eastern Europe and Central Asia. Not surprisingly, students from higher-income families (with more educated parents) were more successful studying at home, according to researchers around the world. This has raised concerns that school closures would exacerbate long-standing inequalities during future pandemics.[40] In Malaysia, UNICEF has collaborated directly with the Ministry of Education to reimagine education, particularly for the most marginalized boys and girls. A special delegate for UNICEF in Malaysia and a special representative to Brunei Darussalam, Rashed Mustafa Sarwar affirmed that the COVID-19 pandemic has devastated children's lives, upset familiar patterns, and negatively affected their education, health, and mental well-being.[41]

In Jamaica, a series of conferences with hundreds of high-school teenagers to obtain their opinions on how to enrich the education system began on November 20, 2020—World Children's Day. The Reimagine Education campaign worked with the National Secondary Students Council (NSSC) to assist students from rural to urban districts, as well as children with disabilities and those in State care. They were asked to contribute to virtual consultations to make sure that the voices of youths be heard in the negotiations of the National Education Transformation Commission (established by the prime minister in early 2020). In Jamaica, so far, UNICEF has endorsed the training of 1,200 instructors and mentors via the Virtual Instructional Leadership module by the National College for Educational Leadership (NCEL). UNICEF has also given 500 tablets to children with disabilities, in a partnership with the Ministry of Education, Youth and Information.[42]

FACING CULTURAL BARRIERS

Cultural barriers are visible and/or invisible differences that separate cultures, regions, traditions, habits, understandings, interpretations, and opinions.[43] They do not always correspond to the physical barriers of political entities like nation-states. In contemporary multicultural societies and in occurrences of global communication, campaign communicators are drawn against the challenge of meaning-making across cultures—cultures with separate values, philosophies, beliefs, and practices. Understanding of multicultural and intercultural communication is vital to campaign communicators,[44] because governing Western approaches and Americentrism/Eurocentrism increase the chances of communication failures, as well as offense and disengagement. Cultural competence should be part of educating society on health issues—i.e., competence in regards to race, ethnicity, language, nationality, religion, age, gender, sexual orientation, social status, wages, and employment.[45] On the other hand, even if a public communication campaign is well designed, training communicators in cultural competence and making serious attempts at improving, adapting, or even solving the issue of literacy may not be sufficient to persuade some cultural groups. Part of the reason is that these cultures have been established for centuries or millennia. So, any endeavor to change the behaviors, attitudes, or beliefs of a target audience may be met with indifference, disdain, or anger.

Antismoking Campaigns

Take, for instance, the antismoking campaigns described in Chapter 5. Although we know that, in the Western world, the costs and problems to society caused by tobacco use are far greater than the benefits that may be gained—especially when measured from the standpoint of socially desirable outcomes (i.e., with reference to a healthy people and a productive workforce)[46]—cultural or sociopolitical attitudes in other countries can restrict the effectiveness of campaign messages experienced in Western nations. Whereas a certain number of countries, by reason of aggressive reporting, regard tobacco corporations as evil, other countries consider them benevolent. Smokers look at them as genuine contributors of "quality" cigarettes. Even nonsmokers perceive tobacco corporations as an important source of economic investment and employment. In these environments, a public communication campaign that oozes negative feelings about tobacco corporations may either not be successful or may face intercultural challenges.

This perception of tobacco as a welcome contribution to society is, of course, flawed and outright dangerous. In Jordan, for example, a country of only 10 million people, and where smoking has been ingrained in society for over 100 years, the World Health Organization made it clear that tobacco cost Jordan an alarming fraction of its GDP and over 9,000 lives in 2015.[47] Yet, antismoking campaigns and antitobacco regulations have not succeeded there.[48] Jordan continues to have the highest smoking rate in the world and influence from global tobacco corporations is the highest it has ever been. In fact, health agencies accuse them of excessive political influence. A 2020 report found that over 80% of Jordanian men used nicotine.[49] The case of Jordan does not pertain to the way sociocultural factors affect the degree and improvement of health literacy skills, but it illustrates how audiences respond (or not) to health communication campaigns.

Understanding Culture-Specific Interpretations

Approaches to health and illness in the modern world are principally guided by the biomedical model of health. **Biomedicine** refers to the medical practices and ideas stemming from Western scientific conventions, including studies of germs, biology, biochemistry, and biophysics. It mostly concentrates on determining physical causes for disease. In contrast, **ethnomedical belief systems** are culturally distinct beliefs and knowledge about health and illness. Communication of health risks (e.g., the risk of HIV/AIDS) based upon Western cultural conjectures will, for instance, prioritize the individual over the group or culture—a notion that clashes with a collectivist culture. Likewise, sequential–linear thinking, rooted in the Western scientific tradition, may not work when communicating with individuals from distant regions and cultures, like those found in South America, Central America, the Caribbean, and Africa. Both providers and practitioners alike may lack ample training in understanding the ethnomedical belief systems of people from other nations and cocultures within the United States.[50]

In situations where both the sender and receiver of a message technically understand the same language, other issues may arise when it comes to culture-specific interpretations of events. For example, various cultures attribute disease to spiritual forces, a conception that is at odds with the Western biomedical approach that ascribes illness to microorganisms, like viruses or lifestyles. The Hmong in Southeast Asia tend to attribute illness to malicious spirits or ghosts that inflict them with ill health or to the absence of protective spirits from ancestors. A significant minority of Mexican immigrants in the United States display fervent cultural dispositions towards fatalism with respect to health issues. **Fatalism**, here, is the philosophy that health issues are meant to be or brought about by God/supernatural forces.[51]

People who have fatalistic interpretations of health believe that they do not have control over health issues, and they are far less motivated to seek healthcare or even think that they can influence their own health outcomes. For example, hearing voices may be a symptom of insanity to Anglo-Saxons, but a religious experience to Mexican immigrants in the United States. Unlike traditional beliefs, hearing voices is not automatically a sign of mental illness; many who hear voices do not ask for assistance and claim that the voices have an affirmative effect on their lives, soothing or inspiring them. Similarly, campaigners ought to be prudent with messages that accentuate religious values in favor of laws and regulations. Although they may be influential in religiously homogeneous environments, they may be perceived as offensive in secular and pluralistic contexts.[52]

The concept of culture stresses the overall potential for communities to learn via social means—i.e., by interacting with others and through mass media like print materials and television. Dependence on tools and symbolic communication, especially language, are hallmarks of culture. Language is essential for the functioning of society and the development of cultural knowledge. Language "provides the most complex system of the classification of experience" and is "the most flexible and most powerful tool developed by humans."[53] Language also encompasses subtleties of meaning. For example, one study showed that the word "trauma" signified "injury" to a doctor speaking with the Mexican mom of a child with seizure disorders. However, it was frequently interpreted as "emotional shock" by the mom. Many concepts do not have word-for-word translation (or even conceptual meaning) into another language due to subtleties of meaning.[54]

Case Study: Jamaica

With a population of three million inhabitants, Jamaica is a developing nation located in the northern part of the Caribbean region and covers an area of about 4,300 square miles. In Jamaica, there exist numerous social determinants of health (SDHs) that impact the daily life of many, like inequality, shortage, exploitation, aggression, and injustice. These are often the cause of ill health or the decay of the poor and marginalized.[55] Jamaica's experience with formal education started during the British colonization, which was developed mostly for the White minority. The formation of schools was established without reflection on the divergences between Jamaican and British cultures. In 1845, 12 years after of the Slavery Abolition Act, the Negro Education Grant was sanctioned. This led to the increased matriculation of Blacks in schools, but concerns remained about their level of literacy.[56]

Patois or Creole

As the English language made its way into Jamaican society, the locals gradually adopted it as their mother tongue. Although English has been, in theory, the official language in Jamaican schools, for classroom instruction, and for literacy, the educational system is still influenced by a Creole-speaking legacy. English-lexicon Creole remains the colloquial dialect known as **Patois** (or **Jamaican Patois**). Authorities are uneasy that attempts are being made at teaching locals a language (English) that they cannot even master at the eighth-grade level. Patois is viewed as the "bad or broken English" identified with the uneducated, the urban working class, poor rural farmers, and, by extension, the Black masses.[57] As Patois is the vernacular for most Jamaicans, it can be heard in most public spheres of Kingston and the rest of the country. These public spheres include the marketplace, radio stations, television programs, churches, and the Parliament. People use Patois to fulfill their needs and it has become part of the literacy development of a great many Jamaicans.[58] Beecher (2010) corroborates the fact that, while Jamaica is an English-speaking nation, its Patois dialect shares many characteristics with dominant languages (i.e., syntax, spelling, and so forth). However, a formal arrangement of the language is conspicuously lacking. Today, Patois is an essential facet of Jamaican identity and is transmitted from generation to generation through oral traditions.

The Health Literacy Problem

The literacy rate in Jamaica is 86%, according to a UNICEF report. This perspective on the Jamaican language is significant to the discussion on health literacy.[59] Health literacy is particularly problematic among elderly men.[60] Older adults are the fastest-growing demographic in Jamaica. With a growth from 10% (252,225) of the entire Jamaican population in 1995 to 11% (279,051) in 2005, the rate is predicted to increase to 25% by 2025. This is why it is necessary to have a good grasp of the health literacy problem there.[61] Solutions have been proposed to tackle the problems of literacy when it comes to Jamaica's older population. The best solution is the promotion of culturally sensitive training and low-literacy materials to enhance awareness of health issues and the regularity and priority of diagnosis at earlier stages. Gender- and age-specific programs should decrease gender disparities among the elderly in Jamaica.[62]

As this case study will demonstrate, culture is a deep-seated construct; it is a collection of past experiences that mold a people's identity. Groundbreaking literacy campaigns can function as a conduit for cultural retention. It can groom and prepare new mindsets without losing identities tied to one's culture and values.[63] Culturally sensitive training and low-literacy materials can not only enrich consciousness of illnesses; they can also improve self-efficacy and health-seeking behaviors. Jamaicans with a low level of health literacy—even without chronic diseases—can gain from campaigns focused on health education and disease management.[64]

Targeted Community Intervention (TCI) for HIV/AIDS

The Jamaican government is both a constitutional monarchy and a representative democracy in a parliament. The latter facilitates the creation of health policies in a unitary effort.[65] Acknowledgment of the role of culture and the meaning of the cultural environment of a disease (e.g., HIV/AIDS) has been incorporated into Jamaican governmental programs since 1986. The first public communication campaign was kicked off by the Jamaica Information Service at the solicitation of the Ministry of Health (MOH).[66] The mission was to devise an HIV/AIDS prevention program in Jamaica. The MOH had to remain mindful of the cultural environment in which behavior change was expected to take place. To achieve this, the MOH adopted the following strategy to integrate culture: **Targeted Community Intervention (TCI)**.[67]

TCI was an innovative approach to offer support to residents of low-income districts. The approach consisted of interpersonal street corner "reasoning," skits and sketches, community drama groups, comedy performances by trendy Jamaican humorists, and songs played or performed by well-known local DJs. Some of the Jamaican comedians included Owen "Blacka" Ellis and Claudette Richardson-Pious. Through the TCI health campaign, official endorsement of HIV/AIDS prevention strategies was made loud and clear by Beenie Man, Buju Banton, and Lady Saw (among others), all of whom were popular dancehall artists. Reggae artists like Tony Rebel and Nadine Sutherland participated in public service announcements (PSAs) broadcast on the country's two main TV stations (TV exposure did not cost money for the TCI campaign). Prerecorded prevention communiqués were also aired frequently in the dancehalls.[68] Those artists were used because people tend to be more receptive to messages diffused by role models sharing their values and national origins. As a volunteer in an unrelated AIDS prevention program directed at homosexual Native Americans remarked,

> I think this is pretty basic for us, the philosophy of Natives helping Natives, and we got 100% Native staff, 100% Native board, most of our volunteers are Native, and it's really about hearing the information coming from another Native gay man.[69]

It is important to include a note on cultural perceptions of sexuality in Jamaica. In that country, sexuality is traditionally associated with the longing to create children. For both men and women, views on self-identity and power are grounded in the expression of sexual ability—which is cemented by the procreation of children. Jamaican art, music, and theater articulate the life and energy of a society in which both men and women acquire social status through their own sexual actions. Conventional beliefs about fertility and sexuality in present-day Jamaica are rooted in centuries of ways of thinking and habits that are hard to wear down and that ignore STDs.[70] One clear illustration is the generally negative conception and attitude *apropos* modern contraceptive methods, which are not based on religion but on traditional culture. This includes attitudes about the body and how it should remain strong and clean. It is widely believed that copulation is indispensable to the physical and mental health of men, although it can also have a deteriorating effect. For women, copulation is essential to avoid the risk of blocking natural vitality. The internal part of the body is seen as mysterious and sacred. Therefore, the "fear of losing things up there" is prevalent among Jamaican women.[71] Condoms are "invasive" objects that can easily slip off and disappear, provoking disease, sterility, and even death by barricading the tubes.[72]

Interventions through Oral Culture

Sometimes called **oral tradition** or **oral lore**, **oral culture** is a genre of human communication in which knowledge, talent, thoughts, and cultural material are imparted, maintained, and transmitted orally from one generation to the next. The transmission occurs through speech, art, or music. It includes, but is not limited to, folktales, ballads, songs, prose, or poems. In this manner, it is possible for a culture to pass on oral history, oral literature, oral law, and other information to future generations without a complex writing procedure, or anything akin to a writing system.[73] Jamaica has a long-established oral culture. Storytelling is customary at social gatherings, particularly in the rural areas.[74] In many respects, the educational system and community leaders have encouraged boys and girls to perceive them selves as legitimate, accomplished creators of culture based on their ancestry from Western Africa.[75] Culturally sensitive public health campaigns can bear a great impact on oral audiences. Understanding the culture and society in which the campaign is to be conducted is central to its success.[76]

For more than two centuries, Jamaican culture has been highly reliant on oral history and customs to attain continuity. In fact, the idea of learning about culture through written communication is still foreign for many Jamaicans. The cultural landscape there follows a tradition where culture is a phenomenon that is lived. Learning about Jamaican culture is a life-experience journey instead of something learned through secondary knowledge (which can be no knowledge at all). Many of the verses, chants, and stories relayed to children have not been converted into books or other types of written materials. Yet, they have been transmitted through oral traditions like storytelling, poetry, and drama. This genre of folklore is an important part of Jamaican identity.[77]

In a predominantly oral culture like Jamaica, to efficiently resolve the issue of preserving and retrieving delicately articulated thought, one's thought must be in harmony with intensely rhythmic, balanced patterns, with repetitions, with Jamaican-based thematic settings, and with sayings with which locals are familiar because they come to mind so quickly.[78] The aforementioned dancehall DJs exert awe-inspiring influence on Jamaican society; their lyrics voice social attitudes and sway ideas and behaviors. Their impact is island-wide, especially for low-income urban areas from which dancehall DJs come, although they also draw attention from middle-class Jamaica, like adolescents and adults under the age of 35.[79] The Sound System Association of Jamaica, the regulatory and representative institution of the dancehall DJs, was asked and agreed to get its more influential artists to participate in PSAs (free of charge) for the TCI health campaign. Beenie Man remains a well-known disc jockey in Jamaica. He recorded two PSAs inspired by his popular hit, "Wickedest Slam," which promoted the use of condoms.[80]

THE FIVE ATTRIBUTES OF CULTURE

As Edward T. Hall (1959)[81] put it, "culture is communication and communication is culture." Clifford Geertz (1973)[82] defined **culture** as "a historically transmitted pattern of meanings embodied in symbols by means of which men communicate, perpetuate, and develop their knowledge about and attitudes towards life." As a system of shared values, morals, principles, norms, ways of life, and rules for human behavior, culture also dictates the symbols—both physical and nonphysical—that represent, evoke, and stimulate these values, morals, principles, and the like.[83] Not only is culture fluid, but it also differs from person to person or from collective to collective. Culture has five attributes. As such, culture is habitus, structure, socially constructed and historically transmitted, our software of the mind, and learned.

Habitus

Culture is habitus. **Habitus** is the notion that human beings live in a social sphere. Pierre Bourdieu (1990)[84] hypothesized that individuals individually and collectively "internalize their position in social space" on the principles, values, and attitudes of the social environment around them and embrace them as their daily life. For the French scholar, humans interact in cultural domains in which there are norms, traditions, conventions, classifications, designations, titles, and so forth. These domains, he continued, amass more or less cultural capital based on circumstances. Because people interact in cultural fields, culture depends on the presence of specific people; it is, by nature, social. In addition to requiring **social capital** (e.g., systems of relationships and status, like a senior position), Bourdieu argued that our ability to reason and behave is influenced by our **cultural capital**—e.g., the type of education, general knowledge produced by the culture, communication skills, identity, dress, and the kinds of groups. For some public communication campaigns, it is imperative to understand the cultural and social capital of publics to get them to adhere to messages such as "get fit," "stop smoking," "get out the vote," "send your kids to college," or "invest in the environment."[85]

Structure

Culture is structure. On occasion, structure and culture are used interchangeably. Like culture, structures are fluid and dynamic entities; they can take different forms, depending on how systems and resources interact over a period of time—again, among people or collectives. Unlike culture, however, **structure** employs both systems (of rules and norms for group activity) and resources (to cement power or attain objectives) in an interactive context.[86] English sociologist Anthony Giddens (1979)[87] developed the notion of **duality of structure**, which signifies that structures consist of both the means and the products of the practices which make up social systems. Whereas human beings shape structure, structure determines what humans do. It is a paradoxical situation. The role of communication is also a catch-22. Although structure is the outcome of communication processes, it also shapes future processes of communication.

Another consideration is that structure is both enabling and constraining. For culture to function properly, individuals need to have rules, but not too many. Enter fraternities or sororities. For a fraternity or a sorority to operate in an optimal way, a structure must be set in place, with clear rules. On the other hand, if too many rules are in the way or if the structure is markedly rigid, some of the members may quit. Max Weber, a German sociologist, analyzed the propensity of religious organizations to impose a structure with too many rules, thereby eroding some of the congregants' enthusiasm and spirit. With too little structure, an organization is less likely to succeed. However, a superabundant structure with doctrine and rules can also be more likely to fail.[88]

Socially Constructed and Historically Transmitted

Culture is a socially constructed and historically transmitted system. **Social construct** alludes to the way we interpret reality. Cultures construct a reality for each concept, a practice that shapes many facets of culture through the meanings that we ascribe to the constructs.[89] Sexual harassment is a social construct; it is defined in a particular way through a consensus that individuals reach within their sociopolitical realities. This is how it is also codified into law. Social construct is rooted in Berger and Luckmann's (1966)[90] **social construction of reality**, a theoretical concept that explains how **concepts** (mental representations of the world) are created through our interactions in society. Over time, meaning solidifies like water and ice; our knowledge and perception of reality become ingrained in the social fabric of our culture—a process called **institutionalization**.[91] What is now our reality in the environment becomes **consensus reality**; it is a way for us to address the question "What is real?" What we have seems like a "realistic" answer: reality is that on which we agree through consensus. An important deduction is that the description of any social construct depends on the social environment that created the reality for that social construct. It is also based on the time and location of the community.[92]

Because culture is socially constructed, it is also historically transmitted. As we have seen, culture is a system of principles, beliefs, values, rules, norms, and customs—but also constructs, meanings, signs, and artifacts—that are transmitted from generation to generation and are shared to a certain degree by interactants in a community. Culture is more than a simple tradition that can be discarded or altered like a set of clothes. Because it is historically transmitted, culture is difficult to change. What seems normal in our culture can be deemed provocative in others. In the Middle East and Thailand, it is considered provocative to point the soles of the feet towards others (even inadvertently; e.g., when crossing our legs). By extension, the Thai believe that spirits are present in everything—both living and not living. As a consequence, rural areas are replete with spirit houses and the Thai insert offerings in such spirit houses on a daily basis.[93]

Software of the Mind

Culture is our **software of the mind**, as Geert Hofstede (2010)[94] phrased elegantly. Our software of the mind is our way of thinking, our thinking pattern, or our mental program. It is embedded within the social environment in which we live and that has accumulated our collective experiences. Our mental software also encompasses the unwritten rules of the social game and can become a large collective programming for the mind. Culture is, in essence, such large collective programming that differentiates members of one group from others. Human beings have a distinct way of organizing life, of thinking, and of conceiving what the family, the state, the economic system, and even humankind itself should look like. Culture governs behavior in profound and persisting ways, many of which are outside of our consciousness and beyond our genuine control. Because culture is our software of the mind, it is also our **social glue**. What binds us together not only maintains values for future generations to come, but it also constructs what education and learning should be. Again, it controls mental processes, behaviors, and attitudes. Social glue denotes the idea that culture is a mold in which humans are cast in various unsuspected ways.[95]

The "binding" aspect of social glue also implies that culture creates some type of blueprint, determinism, or even fundamentalism. **Cultural blueprint** means that culture creates a blueprint that shapes the way we think, feel, and behave in our environment—i.e., a blueprint that may bear a resemblance to some other cultures, but that is generally distinct from most of them.[96] **Cultural determinism** is the belief that our culture shapes who we have become from an emotional and behavioral perspective.[97] For example, some Native American tribes teach their members to never cry or show anger. **Cultural fundamentalism** is a vehement adherence to a particular set of beliefs, even when these beliefs defy logic or are seen as extremely unpopular by other countries.[98] In some parts of Africa, tribes practice female genital mutilation (FGM) on women (i.e., whereby their clitoris is removed). Other African groups believe that the only way to cure AIDS is by having sex with a virgin.

Fundamentalism refers to clinging to a radical, unshakable position in spite of reasoned argument or contradictory evidence.

Learned

Culture is learned, not innate. Culture is not built within us but, rather, it is a phenomenon with which we become familiar through our personal experiences. It is a code that we grow up to learn and share. Learning and sharing would be void without communication (communication consists of coding and signs that must be learned and shared). Because culture is learned, it is **extrasomatic**; it is nongenetic and nonbodily. It consists of things that we can see, hear, touch, feel, and consider. As such, culture is made up of tools, instruments, garments, decorations, customs, institutions, faith, play, and innovations[99]—all of which gradually make their way into a community's accumulation of skills and knowledge, producing more sophisticated repertoires. This aspect of culture is a central component of human cognition underscoring the advancement that characterizes our species.[100]

In the same way that culture is extrasomatic, it is also **extragenetic**—it is not in our DNA. Because we have to learn a culture, our norms for acceptable behavior are culture-based; that is, they are taught.[101] Enter weaver ants. These are a type of ants that build nests made of leaves. Whereas some ants pull the edges of two leaves together and bind them for a while, others carry larva in their jaws and sew them together with their own silk.[102] This is an impressive engineering exploit, but it is not cultural. The behavior displayed by weaver ants is innate, built into these insects' behavior mechanisms. They would not change their plans or try to come up with new methods to join leaves. Nor can they teach or be taught to achieve such engineering exploits.[103] There are famous examples of animals that can be taught behaviors. Although dogs are not born with the idea of urinating or defecating indoors, they can learn how to do it. However, even if dogs can learn specific behaviors, they cannot teach other canines or animals to do so. In a nutshell, they cannot transmit culture.

Case Study:　Gerber in Africa

Health communication campaigns may amplify, rather than decrease, disparities between cultures.[104] After health information is diffused to audiences at large, people from higher socioeconomic ranks are more likely to have acquired knowledge germane to the health message and to have followed the proposed changes, even if motivation to do so may not differ across different socioeconomic ranks. It may not be an issue for commercial purposes, but is an ethical challenge in public health.[105] In the 1980s, Gerber (a company that sells baby food and baby products) wanted to advertise baby food in Africa.[106] Because a certain number of Africans could not read English at that time, corporations methodically put photos on the label of what was inside. When Gerber ventured in Africa, it failed to take the habitus and software of the mind of the local culture into account; rather, it relied on the same packaging used for Western audiences. This packaging featured the photo of a baby boy on the label. Astounded by disappointing sales, Gerber realized that, in Africa, the pictures on the packaging depict the content of the product. In other words, a significant minority of Africans believed that Gerber was selling baby boys.[107]

Differences within Africa

Presentation influences how the message appears. It can engender a vast difference between messages that are accepted and those that are discarded by the audience. Messages not only need to draw attention; they also need to be easily understood by the target population. As is the case with segmented communication, messages should be adapted to the culture and made simple because complication is more likely to be misconstrued. Africa is a collection of 55 sovereign states, with some parts of the continent more developed than others. In sub-Saharan Africa, about one third of the overall population cannot read. Even a country, in and of itself, can be both a developing and a developed nation, like South Africa. South Africa is celebrated for its advanced infrastructure, but it also has massive social and economic problems that render some regions "developing."[108]

In certain illiterate regions of Africa, the packaging needs to have a photo of what the product is—i.e., to show what is inside the packaging, otherwise locals will not understand what the product is. When Gerber began selling its baby food in Africa, the company did not cater its packaging to the African people. Instead, the managers used the one for the US market: the photo of a cute Caucasian baby on the label, a move that turned out to be a catastrophe. Audiences in Africa believed that the food itself was a baby boy. This was so appalling to them that they did not even want to look at the product. Gerber's example is a case study of how multinational corporations fail when they do not glocalize.[109] **Glocalization** refers to the strategies of adaptation used by organizations when venturing in foreign cultures.[110] This is why they need to engage in proper marketing and conduct research prior to investing in such a foreign market.[111] What this case study also demonstrates is that some parts of Africa follow their cultural blueprint; many people associate the picture on a container label with its content and it has been socially constructed and historically transmitted in this manner. Therefore, when Gerber started selling its baby food using the baby pictured on the jars, Africans interpreted the labels as jars of human babies.[112]

Considering the Broader Picture and Formative Research

Considering the larger community context is imperative. Supporting the concept of cultural processes is not enough. It also needs to be integrated into a framework that takes ways of learning (and how different people think, feel, and act) into account. Understanding processes of intercultural communication are important here. Intercultural communication scholarship explains that collective learning and shared group experience are the social fabric of cultural communities, not including other complex indicators like levels of literacy, employment experience, age, religion, language, gender, and even generation—all of which can complicate things. Indeed, these indicators may lead to intracultural variation because people take part in, or are exposed to, various cultural processes. Framing a campaign message should be grounded in understanding and acknowledging the salient characteristics of a recognized group, a subgroup, or even a collective based on other factors (like region or language). These, then, represent the community of relevance for a health concern, health condition, or communication goal. Understanding the target audience and the context inherent to the message should be a priority when undertaking health communication interventions.[113]

An investigation of the communication environment should tell whether publics could welcome drastically new or different messages so as to avoid opposite reactions (to what the campaign anticipated). In the past, campaigns have used a range of communication strategies to modify the behavior of target audiences. Examples are strategies that seek to change the context in which individuals are making decisions, strategies aimed directly at the publics (i.e., bypassing leaders or change agents), and strategies aimed at leaders or change agents (i.e., rather than communicating with the target population directly). The ability to choose a communication strategy should rely on a careful examination of the context for the audience's decision-making. This includes current patterns of communication regarding the behavior and obstacles to behavior change. It has been demonstrated that formative research with target audiences and/or decision-makers can yield critical data for public communication campaigns.[114]

In addition, requesting the participation of members of the target audience (and/or decision-makers) as part of the communication campaign could be useful. The call can be made online or through community boards. Staff from the target population can be hired to contribute to the campaign design. Developing ties with community organizations can also help establish a program within a culture for the long term.[115] All in all, it is highly recommended that public communication campaigns constantly examine their audiences in order to learn about the cultures of their target populations and, ultimately, avoid mistakes. It is possible that campaign strategists may have to identify audiences that are indifferent to the campaign in general (so as to create separate or more streamlined campaigns for them).[116]

Case Study: A Case for Cultural Competency

Cultural competency is the ability of people to understand and cope with cultural phenomena, like language, beliefs, and traditions, in a manner that does not interfere with the exchange or communication with such cultural phenomena. We must not presuppose that we are totally conscious of what we communicate to another person. There can always be colossal distortions in meaning as we attempt to communicate with one another.[117] Cultural competency encompasses more than language, beliefs, and traditions. It also includes the capacity of behaving appropriately in the context of everyday interactions with those who come from different cultures. In healthcare, providers can show cultural competency by being culturally aware and courteous towards their patients—i.e., by respecting the faiths, interpersonal styles, mindsets, and behaviors of patients.[118] After all, healthcare practitioners (physicians, nurses, public health employees), just like public communication campaign designers, can also demonstrate both low cultural competency and low health literacy skills. An example of this would be the failure to clearly describe health issues to patients or the public at large.

Cultural Awareness, Knowledge, and Skill

Cultural awareness is the intentional and cognitive process by which we come to appreciate and become receptive to the values, lifestyles, practices, and problem-solving approaches of people from other cultures. Having cultural awareness means abstaining from developing stereotypes and foregone conclusions based on one's own cultural lens.[119] **Cultural knowledge** is the practice of actively searching for information about other cultural and ethnic groups. For example, in the context of health communication campaigns, campaign planners could try to understand other groups' ways of thinking, health conditions, and customs, including their views on health and disease; perceptions of home cure and self-medication; diets; pregnancy and childbearing routines; interpretations of Western medicine and healthcare professionals; risk-taking and health-seeking attitudes; genetic differences and drug metabolism predispositions; and motives for migration and occupational hazards.[120] **Cultural skill** is the skill and talent to perceive values, beliefs, and customs in interpersonal encounters and knowing how to interpret cultural or group variations in clinical statistics and program data. Cultural skill is a kind of cultural assessment based on an open and objective outlook about people and their cultures, and based on openness to differences. Healthcare practitioners need to be nonjudgmental about cultural differences.[121]

Reducing Cross-Cultural Misunderstandings

Cross-cultural misunderstandings are frequent. A surface-level consideration of cultural features, principles, beliefs, and behaviors can already decrease such misunderstandings. It is essential and, without it, cross-cultural competence cannot flourish.[122] The campaigner should comprehend and value the deeper functioning of a culture. This may also be accompanied by changes in the campaigner's own actions and positions, to allow for more flexibility and openness.[123] By the same token, this would avert problems like **explanatory uncertainty**—a phenomenon whereby we cannot explain why others behave the way they do.[124] Our **Kulturbrille** ("cultural glasses;" i.e., entrenched beliefs and attitudes) eliminate some facts and steer us towards other facts. Some of our conceptions stem from our culture and become self-deceptions that comfort us. If a culture teaches its members that crocodiles eat only bad people who deserve it, the members will feel at ease if they follow the logic that "I have not sinned, so the crocodiles will not eat me." It lowers anxiety and makes life more enjoyable. This also contributes to the "just world" philosophy. "He was eaten by a crocodile, so he must have sinned."[125]

An approach to make us aware of our Kulturbrille is diversity training. **Diversity training** is offered within organizations (i.e., to students, employees, or staff members), generally with the aim of making diversity a rationale for personal growth and allowing people from various backgrounds to effectively collaborate and make a significant contribution to the mission of the organization. Diversity training employs, *inter alia*, **cross-cultural trainers**. These are trainers who teach organizational members how to identify and honor other cultural norms, and to maximize the efficiency of their interactions with those of different domestic and international backgrounds.[126] Cross-cultural trainers can also make trainees more versed in **culturespeak**—a term denoting the myriad of ways in which human beings talk about culture. It is a type of language that covers our disparities and similarities in how we live daily.[127]

ETHNOGRAPHIC CONSIDERATIONS FOR HEALTH CAMPAIGNS

The failure of the Gerber campaign in Africa points to the need of observing and, in due course, understanding other cultures. This is why this section suggests that ethnographic research is one useful method of accomplishing this objective. **Ethnography** is the direct observation, reporting, and description of people's behaviors within a culture. The ethnographer lives within the culture, or goes back there every day (or very frequently), for several months to several years. The ethnographer knows or gets to know the language of the cultural group, takes part in some of their activities, and employs an array of recording techniques.[128] Creswell (2009)[129] defines ethnography as "a strategy of inquiry in which the researcher studies an intact cultural group in a natural setting over a prolonged period of time by collecting, primarily, observational and interview data." As opposed to the oft-distant approach of the scientific method of research, ethnography uses deep observation and, on occasion, participation within the world of the people to be studied, as well as interviews. Interviews are face-to-face and in-depth. They may be open-ended conversations over a certain time frame, with data gathered through notes, audio or video recordings, journals, and additional documents (such as minutes of meetings, transcripts of discourses, and so forth).[130]

Participant Observation

Ethnography uses participant observation, rather than **complete observation** (watching people from afar) or **full participant observation** (blending in a group without revealing one's true identity and purposes). **Participant observation** is the process by which an ethnographer builds and upholds many-sided and comparatively long-term relationships with individuals in their environment in order to provide a cultural interpretation of that association.[131] The ultimate mission of the ethnographer is to understand the culture and investigate the cultural patterns so as to develop a framework of the rules for the behaviors within that culture. Ethnography is a "very detailed description of a culture from the viewpoint of an insider in the culture to facilitate understanding of it."[132] Hence, ethnographers do not operate in laboratories or artificial surroundings, but in natural settings.

Participant observation follows the process of **subjective soaking**. This occurs as the ethnographer relinquishes the idea of pure objectivity or scientific neutrality. Rather, he or she proceeds to merge himself or herself into the culture under observation.[133] Subjective soaking means taking advantage of the local knowledge provided by that culture in order to increase one's understanding of phenomena not available outside the ethnographer looking in.[134] A synonym for subjective soaking is **cultural immersion**, whereby the ethnographer may live within the culture for a few years.[135] Cultural immersion allows for thick descriptions. A **thick description** is an in-depth observation (and subsequent report) of a cultural site. The description includes many details; a high volume of notes are taken.[136]

In the end, participant observation enables the ethnographer to increase his or her understanding of four cultural concepts: cultural patterning, conceptual mapping, learning processes, and sanctioning processes. **Cultural patterning** is the observation of cultural patterns involving both physical and nonphysical symbols. This signifies that ethnographic research is integral; symbols should not be looked at in a vacuum (but, instead, as part of a whole). **Conceptual mapping** is the creation of a model or theoretical framework that helps understand how individuals within a culture think. This can be done by using and describing the terms used by members of the culture themselves. The general public, then, can have a better grasp of symbols and contexts.[137] **Learning processes** assist ethnographers in understanding how a culture conveys practices, content, and symbols that it deems important for next generations. **Sanctioning processes** explain how certain elements of a culture are both formally and informally sanctioned or prohibited.[138] These four cultural concepts will eventually generate nuggets of data because they are the product of an extensive range of information gathered over a long period of time.

Discovering Symbolic Cultures

Symbolism is the language of symbols or a system of representing semantic units (both verbal and nonverbal) through symbols. As a method of communication, symbolism allows both the interpretation and categorization of the universe around us. A **symbol** can be a physical or nonphysical entity that represents something else—i.e., a material item, a concept, a behavior, or an event that stands for something else. For instance, the crescent on most Muslim standards or logos symbolizes Islam. The Star of David is the embodiment of Judaism. Symbolism offers a plethora of ideas for creating meaning and communicating it within cultures. For the reason that a symbol stands for something else, it consists of both denotative and connotative meanings. **Denotative meanings** are the direct and more objective uses of a symbol, like a flag that represents a nation, institution, university, sports team, and so on. **Connotative meanings** are the expressive and more subjective uses of a symbol, like flags symbolizing law and order, nationalism, chauvinism, national pride, and so forth. From a denotative perspective, a cat is a four-footed mammal that can be befriended like a family relative. From a connotative perspective, a cat symbolizes good luck in some cultures, but bad luck in others. Connotations can differ sharply across cultures.[139]

Culture scholars encourage the understanding of symbols of another culture. In fact, symbols are a central focus of ethnographic research. If a health communication campaign originates from a Western country or organization, it may not be well understood by audiences of other cultural backgrounds because Western symbols may not be aligned with the symbols of those backgrounds. The aforementioned concept of cultural processes makes it easier to accentuate the relationships among life experiences, learning, and sharing. By learning about, becoming a member of, or taking part in social groups, ethnographers develop ways of thinking about the world and are more prepared to act and respond according to those ways. Culturally acquired knowledge may also stem from cultural products, like books, TV shows, and computer software. Symbols are intrinsic to cultural processes; they are socially founded methods of learning that play a role in how we think, feel, and act.[140] As Edward Sapir (1985),[141] an American anthropologist, remarked, "The true locus of culture is in the specific interactions of individuals and, on the subjective side, in the world of meanings which each one of these individuals may unconsciously abstract for himself from his participation in these interactions."

Implications for Health Communication Campaigns

It is clear, by now, that health communication campaigns need to recognize, analyze, and understand **cultural norms**—that is, the system of values, beliefs, practices, and the like of a target audience. Identifying an audience's cultural and religious values that are at odds with a health innovation is important to the acceptance of that innovation. Campaign designers must overcome these cultural barriers before exposing the community to the innovation. In the Philippines, developers of family planning initiatives must understand the clouts exerted by the Catholic Church, which stands against modern contraceptive methods.[142] Local interpretations, norms, and attitudes work to uphold cultural traditions in ways that may be challenging to campaign strategists for decoding culturally different contexts. It can be wasteful and costly to launch an honest public communication campaign that only caters to the cultural norms from the "outside." Without formative or ethnographic research, the consequences of such campaigns might be as detrimental as the practices it is intended to replace. Campaigners should attempt to devise research-driven interventions that help staff and volunteers change local norms and strategies from the "inside," in ways that are harmonious with local cultural contexts.[143]

It is important to recognize that cultural norms can be exceedingly self-protective. If truth be told, people who try to challenge the norm may face public shame or even punishment. Again, a health campaign's failed attempt to challenge the status quo may cause more harm than good. Other publics witnessing the negative repercussions may be further deterred from joining future movements for change. One solution for the ethnographer is to ask the participants (whom he or she is observing) to plan and lead the public communication campaign. This can be done by identifying change agents, training them, collaborating with them, and kicking off the campaign. Rather than scattering intervention efforts across geographical or social regions, concentrated interventions that are effective within change agents' social networks might be more beneficial and less likely to provoke backlash against those change agents (because they may be perceived as traitors or disloyal if venturing across other geographical or social regions).[144]

Ultimately, data gathered through ethnographic research and in-depth interviewing will enable campaign developers to adapt their messages to the right audiences. Tailoring messages is an ethical proviso for both proper communication and comprehensibility. The campaign messages ought to be thoroughly reviewed, complete, and culturally segmented to diverse audiences. On the other hand, campaign planners need to make sure that diffusing culturally appropriate messages to particular populations do not unintentionally exclude or dishonor other groups.[145]

NOTES

1. Nicola Diviani and Peter J. Schulz, "What Should Lay Persons Know about Cancer? Towards an Operational Definition of Cancer Literacy," *Patient Education and Counseling* 85, no. 3 (2011): 487–92. https://doi.org/10.1016/j.pec.2010.08.017.
2. Cited in Michael T. Nietzel, "Low Literacy Levels among US Adults Could Be Costing the Economy $2.2 Trillion a Year," *Forbes* (September 9, 2020). Retrieved on May 22, 2021 fromhttps://www.forbes.com/sites/michaeltnietzel/2020/09/09/low-literacy-levels-among-us–adults-could-be-costing-the-economy-22-trillion-a-year/?sh=620108ca4c90.
3. For example, see Mark V. Williams, Ruth M. Parker, David W. Baker, Nina S. Parikh, Kathryn Pitkin, Wendy C. Coates, and Joanne R. Nurss, "Inadequate Functional Health Literacy Among Patients at Two Public Hospitals," *Journal of the American Medical Association* 274, no. 21 (1995): 1677–82. https://doi.org/10.1001/jama.1995.03530210031026.
4. Squiers, Peinado, Berkman, Boudewyns, and McCormack, "The Health Literacy Skills Framework," 48.
5. Russell L. Rothman, Victor M. Montori, Andrea Cherrington, and Michael P. Pignone, "Perspective: The Role of Numeracy in Health Care," *Journal of Health Communication* 13, no. 6 (2008): 583–95. https://doi.org/1010.1080/10810730802281791.
6. Linda Squiers, Susana Peinado, Nancy Berkman, Vanessa Boudewyns, and Lauren McCormack, "The Health Literacy Skills Framework," *Journal of Health Communication* 17, no. 3 (2012): 30–54. https://doi.org/10.1080/10810730.2012.713442.
7. Helen Osborne, *Health Literacy from A to Z: Practical Ways to Communicate Your Health Message* (New York: Health Literacy Press, 2018).

8. David W. Baker, "The Meaning and Measure of Health Literacy," *Journal of General Internal Medicine* 21 (2006): 878–83. https://doi.org/10.1111/j.1525-1497.2006.00540.x.

9. Annie Lang, "Using the Limited Capacity Model of Motivated Mediated Message Processing to Design Effective Cancer Communication Messages," *Journal of Communication* 56, no. 1 (2006): S57–S80. https://doi.org/10.1111/j.1460-2466.2006.00283.x.

10. Jane Taggart, Anna Williams, Sarah Dennis, Anthony Newall, Tim Shortus, Nicholas Zwar, Elizabeth Denney-Wilson, and Mark F. Harris, "A Systematic Review of Interventions in Primary Care to Improve Health Literacy for Chronic Disease Behavioral Risk Factors," *BMC Family Practice* 5 (2012): 13–49. https://doi.org/10.1186/1471-2296-13-49.

11. Christina Zarcadoolas, "The Simplicity Complex: Exploring Simplified Health Messages in a Complex World," *Health Promotion International* 26, no. 3 (2010): 338–50. https://doi.org/10.1093/heapro/daq075.

12. For example, see Mustapha Abdulhamid Baba, Shehu Halilu, and Abubakar Bappayo, "The Competence and Effectiveness of Translation of Radio Gotel Yola, Adamawa State, Nigeria," *KIU Journal of Social Sciences* 4, no. 1 (2018): 311–20.

13. Alexander J. Rothman, Steven C. Mano, Brian T. Bedell, Jerusha B. Detweiler, and Peter Salovey, "The Systematic Influence of Gain and Loss-Framed Messages on Interest in and Use of Different Types of Health Behavior," *Personality and Social Psychology Bulletin* 25, no. 11 (1999): 1355–69. https://doi.org/10.1177/0146167299259003.

14. David E. Nelson, Bradford W. Hesse, and Robert T. Croyle, *Making Data Talk: Communicating Public Health Data to the Public, Policy Makers, and the Press* (New York: Oxford University Press, 2009).

15. Kiameesha R. Evans, M. Jane Lewis, and Shawna V. Hudson, "The Role of Health Literacy on African American and Hispanic/Latino Perspectives on Cancer Clinical Trials," *Journal of Cancer Education* 27 (2012): 299–305. https://doi.org/10.1007/s13187-011-0300-5.

16. Eric Donald Hirsch, Jr., *Cultural Literacy: What Every American Needs to Know* (Boston, MA: Houghton Mifflin, 1987).

17. United States Census Bureau, *Language Spoken at Home* (Washington, D.C.: United States Census Bureau, 2021).

18. David H. Howard, Tetine Sentell, and Julie A. Gazmararian, "Impact of Health Literacy on Socioeconomic and Racial Differences in Health in an Elderly Population," *Journal of General Internal Medicine* 21, no. 8 (2006): 857–61. https://doi.org/10.1111/j.1525-1497.2006.00530.x; Tetine Lynn Sentell and Helen Ann Halpin, "Importance of Adult Literacy in Understanding Health Disparities," *Journal of General Internal Medicine* 21, no. 8 (2006): 862–6. https://doi.org/10.1111/j.1525-1497.2006.00538.x.

19. Charles K. Atkin and Ronald E. Rice, "Advances in Public Communication Campaigns," in *The International Encyclopedia of Media Studies*, ed. Angharad N. Valdivia, John C. Nerone, Vicki Mayer, Sharon R. Mazzarella, Radhika E. Parameswaran, Erica Scharrer, Fabienne Darling-Wolf, and Kelly Gates (Oxford: Wiley-Blackwell, 2013).

20. Gerald-Mark Breen and Jonathan Matusitz, "An Evolutionary Examination of Telemedicine: A Health and Computer-Mediated Communication Perspective," *Social Work in Public Health* 25, no. 1 (2010): 59–71. https://doi.org/10.1080/19371910902911206.

21. Jonathan Matusitz and Gerald-Mark Breen, "E-Health: A New Kind of Telemedicine," *Social Work in Public Health* 23, no. 1 (2007): 95–113. https://doi.org/10.1300/J523v23n01_06; Jonathan Matusitz, Gerald-Mark Breen, Shriram S. Marathe, and Thomas T. H. Wan, "Nurses in Need of Additional Support: Web Sites Offering Information in Eldercare Nursing Environments," *Creative Nursing* 16, no. 3 (2010): 115–8. https://doi.org/10.1891/1078–4535.16.3.115.

22. Carolyn Crist, "$52 Million Campaign to Push COVID Vaccinations" *WebMD* (February 25, 2021). Retrieved on May 22, 2021 from https://www.webmd.com/vaccines/covid-19-vaccine/news/20210225/52-million-campaign-to-push-covid-vaccinations.

23. Jonathan Matusitz and Gerald-Mark Breen, "Telemedicine: Its Effects on Health Communication," *Health Communication* 21, no. 1 (2007): 73–83. https://doi.org/10.1080/10410230701283439; Jonathan Matusitz, Gerald-Mark Breen, and Thomas T. H. Wan, "The Use of eHealth Services in US Nursing Homes as an Improvement of Healthcare Delivery to Residents," *Aging Health* 9, no. 1 (2013): 25–13. https://doi.org/10.2217/ahe.12.75.

24. For example, see Maya Forrester and Jonathan Matusitz, "A Narrowing Digital Divide: The Impact of the Internet on Youth Political Participation," *Communicare* 9, no. 2 (2010): 85–98. https://doi.org/10.10520/EJC27742; Jonathan Matusitz and George Musambira, "Power Distance, Uncertainty Avoidance, and Technology: Analyzing Hofstede's Dimensions and Human Development Indicators," *Journal of Technology in Human Services* 31, no. 1 (2013): 42–60. https://doi.org/10.1080/15228835.2012.738561.

25. See Eric G. Benotsch, Seth Kalichman, and Lance S. Weinhardt, "HIV-AIDS Patients' Evaluation of Health Information on the Internet: The Digital Divide and Vulnerability to Fraudulent Claims," *Journal of Consulting and Clinical Psychology* 72, no. 6 (2004): 1004–11. https://doi.org/10.1037/0022-006X.72.6.1004; Shanyang Zhao, "Parental Education and Children's Online Health Information Seeking: Beyond the Digital Divide Debate," *Social Science & Medicine* 69, no. 10 (2009): 1501–5. https://doi.org/10.1016/j.socscimed.2009.08.039.

26. Peter Drucker, "The Next Society: A Survey of the Near Future," *The Economist* 246 (November 3, 2001): 3–10.

27. Available at https://www.statista.com/statistics/617136/digital-population-worldwide.

28. George Musambira and Jonathan Matusitz, "Communication Technology and Culture: Analysing Selected Cultural Dimensions and Human Development Indicators," *International Journal of Technology Management & Sustainable Development* 14, no. 1 (2015): 17–28. https://doi.org/10.1386/tmsd.14.1.17_1.

29. Angel Luis Lucendo-Monedero, Francisca Ruiz-Rodríguez, and ReyesGonzález-Relaño, "Measuring the Digital Divide at Regional Level: A Spatial Analysis of the Inequalities in Digital Development of Households and Individuals in Europe," *Telematics and Informatics* 41 (2019): 197–217. https://doi.org/10.1016/j.tele.2019.05.002.

30. Massimo Ragnedda and Bruce Mutsvairo, *Digital Inclusion: An International Comparative Analysis* (Lanham, MD: Lexington Books, 2018).

31. Doris Elster, "Learning Communities in Teacher Education: The Impact of E-Competence," *International Journal of Science Education* 32, no. 16 (2010): 2185–216. https://doi.org/10.1080/09500690903418550.

32. Natasha Watson, Alicia Massarotto, Lisa Caputo, Leon Flicker, and Christopher Beer, "E-Ageing: Development and Evaluation of a Flexible Online Geriatric Medicine

Educational Resource for Diverse Learners," *Australian Journal on Ageing* 32, no. 4 (2013): 222–8. https://doi.org/10.1111/j.1741-6612.2012.00622.x.

33. Ray Adams, "Decision and Stress: Cognition and E-Accessibility in the Information Workplace," *Universal Access in the Information Society* 5 (2007): 363–79. https://doi.org/10.1007/s10209-006-0061-9.

34. Patricia Geist-Martin, Eileen B. Ray, and Barbara F. Sharf, *Communicating Health: Personal, Cultural, and Political Complexities* (Belmont, CA: Wadsworth Press, 2003).

35. Fiona Chew and Sushma Palmer, "Interest, the Knowledge Gap, and Television Programming," *Journal of Broadcasting & Electronic Media* 38, no. 3 (1994): 271–87. https://doi.org/10.1080/08838159409364265.

36. See UNICEF, *For Every Child, Answers: 30 years of Research for Children at UNICEF Innocenti* (Florence, Italy: UNICEF, 2019); Irene M. Wohlman, "The Worldwide Digital Divide and Access to Healthcare Technology," in *Technology and Global Public Health*, ed. Padmini Murthy and Amy Ansehl (New York: Springer, 2020): 241–56.

37. Available at https://www.unicef.org/press-releases/covid-19-least-third-worlds-school children-unable-access-remote-learning-during.

38. Ibid.

39. Ibid.

40. *The New York Times*, "Almost 500 Million Children Are Cut Off from School in Pandemic, Report Says," *The New York Times* (August 26, 2020): A1. Retrieved on April 8, 2021 from https://www.nytimes.com/2020/08/26/world/covid-19-coronavirus.html.

41. *Malay Mail*, "UNICEF Teams Up with Education Ministry to Reimagine Education in Malaysia," *Malay Mail* (February 23, 201): A1. Retrieved on April 8, 2021 from https://www.malaymail.com/news/malaysia/2021/02/23/unicef-teams-up-with-education-ministry-to-reimagine-education-in-malaysia/1952176.

42. Cited in *Jamaica Observer*, "UNICEF Taps Students' Views on Improving Education System," *Jamaica Observer* (November 20, 2020): A1. Retrieved on April 8, 2021 from https://www.jamaicaobserver.com/news/unicef-taps-students-views-on-improving-education-system_208122?profile=0.

43. Young Yun Kim, *Becoming Intercultural: An Integrative Theory of Communication and Cross-Cultural Adaptation* (Thousand Oaks, CA: Sage, 2001).

44. Jonathan Matusitz and Jennifer Spear, "Doctor–Patient Communication Styles: A Comparison Between the United States and Three Asian Countries," *Journal of Human Behavior in the Social Environment* 25, no. 8 (2015): 871–84. https://doi.org/10.1080/10911359.2015.1035148.

45. Joanna Crossman, Sarbari Bordia, and Colleen Mills, *Business Communication for the Global Age* (North Ryde, Australia: McGraw-Hill Australia, 2011).

46. Victor U. Ekpu and Abraham K. Brown, "The Economic Impact of Smoking and of Reducing Smoking Prevalence: Review of Evidence," *Tobacco Use Insights* 8 (2015): 1–35. https://doi.org/10.4137/TUI.S15628.

47. *The Jordan Times*, "Tobacco Cost Jordan 6% of GDP, More Than 9,000 Lives in 2015—WHO," *The Jordan Times* (July 9, 2019): A1. Retrieved on May 21, 2021 from https://jordantimes.com/news/local/tobacco-cost-jordan-6-gdp-more-9000-lives-2015-%E2%80%94-who.

48. Suha Philip Ma'ayeh, *Jordan: Mass Media Campaign Combating Smoking Requires Serious Commitment and Not Just Words* (Geneva: World Health Organization, 2003).

49. Michael Safi and Jassar al-Tahat in Amman, "Jordan Smoking Rates Highest in World amid Claims of Big Tobacco Interference," *The Guardian* (June 23, 2020): A1. Retrieved on May 22, 2021 from https://www.theguardian.com/world/2020/jun/23/jordan-smoking-rates-highest-in-world-amid-claims-of-big-tobacco-interference.

50. See Kevin B. Wright, Lisa Sparks, and Henry D. O'Hair, *Health Communication in the twenty-first Century* (Malden, MA: Blackwell, 2008): 104.

51. Ibid, 104.

52. Ibid, 104–6.

53. Alessandro Duranti, *Linguistic Anthropology* (Cambridge: Cambridge University Press, 1997): 49.

54. Anna Long, Susan C. M. Scrimshaw, and Nyrma Hernandez, "Transcultural Epilepsy Services," in *Rapid Assessment Procedures: Qualitative Methodologies for Planning and Evaluation of Health Related Programmes*, ed. Nevin S. Scrimshaw and Gary R. Gleason (Boston, MA: International Nutrition Foundation for Developing Countries, 1992): 205–14.

55. Monique Ann-Marie Lynch and Geovanni Vinceroy Franklin, "Health Literacy: An Intervention to Improve Health Outcomes," *Intechopen* 1 (2019): 10–21. https://doi.org/10.5772/intechopen.86269.

56. S. Riley, "A High School Equivalence Program JAMAL Foundation," *Paper presented at the Regional Meeting for the Review of Strategies and Programmes for Young People and Adult Learning in Latin America and the Caribbean* (2002).

57. Hubert Devonish and Karen Carpenter, "Towards Full Bilingualism in Education: The Jamaican Bilingual Primary Education Project," *Social and Economic Studies* 56, no. 1 (2007): 277–303.

58. Beth Cross, "'Watch Mi Eyes': The Predicament of Visual and Scribal Literacy Choices, as Explored with Rural Jamaican Adolescent Boys," *Compare* 33, no. 1 (2003): 65–83. https://doi.org/10.1080/03057920302603.

59. Ibid, 65–83.

60. Paul A. Bourne, Chloe Morris, Christopher A. D. Charles, Denise Eldemire-Shearer, Maureen D. Kerr-Campbell, and Tazhmoye V. Crawford, "Health Literacy and Health Seeking Behavior among Older Men in a Middle-Income Nation," *Patient Related Outcome Measures* 1 (2010): 39–49. https://doi.org/10.2147/prom.s11141.

61. Heather F. Fletcher, *The Association of Health Literacy with Self-care Agency in Older Adults in Jamaica*, Unpublished Doctoral Dissertation (2014). Retrieved on May 5, 2021 from https://scholarsrepository.llu.edu/cgi/viewcontent.cgi?referer=https://scholar.google.com/&httpsredir=1&article=1286&context=etd.

62. Darry Coverson, "Health Literacy in Rural Jamaica: Visual Aides to Assist and Increase Medication Adherence," *MedCrave Online Journal of Public Health* 2, no. 5 (2015): 149–52.

63. Meeckel B. Beecher, "Oral Traditions: A View from Jamaica," *Panorama* 10 (2010): 10–21.

64. Coverson, "Health Literacy in Rural Jamaica," 149–52.

65. Rebekah Hershey and Amy Way, "A Preliminary Understanding of Healthcare Needs in Rural Jamaica," *Keystone Journal of Undergraduate Research* 4, no. 1 (2017): 16–21.

66. Heather Royes, *A Cultural Approach to HIV/AIDS Prevention and Care* (Paris: UNESCO, 1999): 1.

67. Ibid, 15.

68. Ibid, 15.

69. James W. Dearing, Everett M. Rogers, Gary Meyer, Mary K. Casey, Nagesh Rao, Shelly Campo, and Geoffrey M. Henderson, "Social Marketing and Diffusion-Based Strategies for Communicating with Unique Populations: HIV Prevention in San Francisco," *Journal of Health Communication* 1, no. 4 (1996): 343–63, 357.

70. Carol P. MacCormack and Alizon Draper, *Social and Cognitive Aspects of Female Sexuality in Jamaica* (New York: Routledge, 1987).

71. Royes, *A Cultural Approach to HIV/AIDS*, 1–15.

72. MacCormack and Draper, *Social and Cognitive Aspects*.

73. Jack Goody, *The Interface between the Written and the Oral* (Cambridge: Cambridge University Press, 1987).

74. Cherrell Shelley-Robinson, "The Voluntary Reading Interests of Jamaican 6th Graders," *School Libraries Worldwide* 7, no. 1 (2001): 72–81.

75. Beth Cross, "Communication Policy at the Chalk Face in Scotland and Jamaica: Complexity as a New Paradigm for Understanding Language Policy Interpretation and Implementation," *Scottish Educational Review* 35, no. 1 (2003): 14–26.

76. Royes, *A Cultural Approach to HIV/AIDS*, 16.

77. Beecher, "Oral Traditions," 10–21.

78. Walter J. Ong, *Orality and Literacy: The Technologizing of the Word* (2nd Ed.) (New York: Routledge, 2002).

79. Royes, *A Cultural Approach to HIV/AIDS*, 16.

80. Kathleen Henry, "Jamaicans Begin to Embrace Safer Sex," *Family Health International* 4, no. 1 (1997): 18–22.

81. Edward T. Hall, *The Silent Language* (Garden City, NY: Doubleday, 1959): 186.

82. Clifford Geertz, "Religion as a Cultural System," in *The Interpretation of Cultures: Selected Essays*, ed. Clifford Geertz (New York: Basic, 1973): 87–125, 89.

83. Wendy Griswold, *Cultures and Societies in a Changing World* (Thousand Oaks, CA: Pine Forge Press, 1994).

84. Pierre Bourdieu, *In Other Words: Essays towards a Reflexive Sociology* (Cambridge: Polity, 1990): 110.

85. Cited in Jim Macnamara, *Evaluating Public Communication: Exploring New Models, Standards and Best Practice* (New York: Routledge, 2017): 64.

86. William H. Sewell, "A Theory of Structure: Duality, Agency, and Transformation," *American Journal of Sociology* 98, no. 1 (1992): 1–29. https://doi.org/10.1086/229967.

87. Anthony Giddens, *Central Problems in Social Theory* (London: Macmillan Press, 1979).

88. Anthony Giddens, *The Constitution of Society: Outline of the Theory of Structuration* (Cambridge: Polity Press, 1984).

89. Varol Akman, "Rethinking Context as a Social Construct," *Journal of Pragmatics* 32, no. 6 (2000): 743–59. https://doi.org/10.1016/S0378-2166(99)00067-3.

90. Peter L. Berger and Thomas Luckmann, *The Social Construction of Reality: A Treatise in the Sociology of Knowledge* (New York: Anchor Books, 1966).

91. Lynne G. Zucker, "The Role of Institutionalization in Cultural Persistence," *American Sociological Review* 42, no. 5 (1977): 726–43. https://doi.org/10.2307/2094862.

92. Jonathan Matusitz, *Terrorism & Communication: A Critical Introduction* (Thousand Oaks, CA: Sage, 2013).

93. Fred Jandt, *An Introduction to Intercultural Communication: Identities in a Global Community* (5th Ed.) (Thousand Oaks, CA: Sage, 2006).

94. Geert Hofstede, *Cultures and Organizations: Software of the Mind* (3rd Ed.) (Boston, MA: McGraw-Hill, 2010).

95. Richard A. Peterson, "The Production of Culture: A Prolegomenon," *American Behavioral Scientist* 19, no. 6 (1976): 669–84. https://doi.org/10.1177/000276427601900601.

96. Urie Bronfenbrenner, "Toward an Experimental Ecology of Human Development," *American Psychologist* 32, no. 7 (1977): 513–31. https://doi.org/10.1037/0003-066X.32.7.513.

97. Melford E. Spiro, "Cultural Determinism, Cultural Relativism, and the Comparative Study of Psychopathology," *Ethos* 29, no. 2 (2001): 218–34. https://doi.org/10.1525/eth.2001.29.2.218.

98. Verena Stolcke, "Talking Culture: New Boundaries, New Rhetorics of Exclusion in Europe," *Current Anthropology* 36, no. 1 (1995): 1–24. https://doi.org/10.1086/204339.

99. Leslie A. White, "The Concept of Culture," *American Anthropologist* 61, no. 2 (1959): 227–51. https://doi.org/10.1525/aa.1959.61.2.02a00040.

100. Mark Nielsen, "The Social Glue of Cumulative Culture and Ritual Behavior," *Child Development Perspectives* 12, no. 4 (2018): 264–8. https://doi.org/10.1111/cdep.12297.

101. Lorenzo Magnani, "Beyond Darwin: Cognitive Niches and Extragenetic Information," *Science & Education* 27 (2018): 811–3. https://doi.org/10.1007/s11191-018-9994-7.

102. Rastogi Neelkamal, "Provisioning Services from Ants: Food and Pharmaceuticals," *Asian Myrmecology* 4 (2011): 103–20.

103. Richa Malhotra, "12 Nests You Won't Belive Were Made by Insects," *BBC* (January 13, 2016). Retrieved on May 22, 2021 from http://www.bbc.com/earth/story/20160113-12-nests-you-wont-believe-were-made-by-insects.

104. John F. Aruffo, John Coverdale, and Carlos Vallbona, "AIDS Knowledge in Low-Income and Minority Populations," *Public Health Reports* 106, no. 2 (1991): 115–9.

105. Charles T. Salmon, Karen Wooten, Eileen Gentry, Galen E. Cole, and Fred Kroger, "AIDS Knowledge Gaps: Results from the First Decade of the Epidemic and Implications for Future Public Information Efforts," *Journal of Health Communication* 1, no. 2 (1996): 141–55. https://doi.org/10.1080/108107396128112.

106. Raquel de Pedro Ricoy, "Beyond the Words: The Translation of Television Adverts," *Babel* 42, no. 1 (1996): 27–45. https://doi.org/10.1075/babel.42.1.04ped.

107. Wasanti Argade, "'Think Local and Go Global'—A Key to Create a Successful Global Brand," *Journal of Management and Administration Tomorrow* 1, no. 2 (2013): 48–51.

108. *Consumer Law Magazine*, "Gerber's Baby Food: Does It Contain Babies?" *Consumer Law Magazine* (May 3, 2017). Retrieved on May 4, 2021 from http://consumerlawmagazine.com/gerbers-baby-food.

109. For example, see Jonathan Matusitz, "Disneyland Paris: A Case Analysis Demonstrating How Glocalization Works," *Journal of Strategic Marketing* 18, no. 3 (2010): 223–37. https://doi.org/10.1080/09652540903537014; Jonathan Matusitz, "Disney's Successful Adaptation in Hong Kong: A Glocalization Perspective," *Asia Pacific Journal of Management* 28, no. 4 (2011): 667–81. https://doi.org/10.1007/s10490-009-9179-7; Jonathan Matusitz and Laura Lord, "Glocalization or Grobalization of Wal-Mart in the US? A Qualitative Analysis," *Journal of Organisational Transformation & Social Change*

10, no. 1 (2013): 81–100. https://doi.org/10.1179/1477963313Z.0000000007; Jonathan Matusitz, "Bharti-Wal-Mart: A Glocalization Experience," *Journal of Asian and African Studies* 50, no. 1 (2015): 83–95. https://doi.org/10.1177/0021909613512948; Jonathan Matusitz, "A Giant Retailer in Argentina: 'Glocalization' Perspectives," *Portuguese Journal of Social Science* 15, no. 1 (2016): 111–27. https://doi.org/10.1386/pjss.15.1.111_1.

110. For example, see Jonathan Matusitz and Maya Forrester, "Successful Glocalization Practices: The Case of Seiyu in Japan," *Journal of Transnational Management* 14, no. 2 (2009): 155–76. https://doi.org/10.1080/15475770903028696; Jonathan Matusitz and Kristin Leanza, "Wal-Mart: An Analysis of the Glocalization of the Cathedral of Consumption in China," *Globalizations* 6, no. 2 (2009): 187–205. https://doi.org/10.1080/14747730902854158; Jonathan Matusitz and Laura Lord, "Dialectical Tensions in the Wal-Martization of the United States," *Journal of Transnational Management* 20, no. 3 (2015): 172–89. https://doi.org/10.1080/15475778.2015.1058691; Elizabeth Minei and Jonathan Matusitz, "Diffusion and Glocalization: Dialectical Tensions for Wal-Mart de México," *Global Business Perspectives* 1, no. 2 (2013): 106–21. https://doi.org/10.1007/s40196-013-0012-9; Demi Simi and Jonathan Matusitz, "Glocalization of Subway in India: How a US Giant Has Adapted in the Asian Subcontinent," *Journal of Asian and African Studies* 52, no. 5 (2017): 573–85. https://doi.org/10.1177/0021909615596764.

111. *Consumer Law Magazine*, "Gerber's Baby Food".

112. Sanjeev Malhotra and Seema Mangrulkar, "Branding in the Last of the Unsaturated Markets," *Design Management Journal* 12, no. 4 (2001): 53–8. https://doi.org/10.1111/j.1948-7169.2001.tb00565.x.

113. Institute of Medicine, *Speaking of Health: Assessing Health Communication Strategies for Diverse Populations* (Washington, D.C.: Institute of Medicine, 2002): 235.

114. Cited in Leslie B. Snyder, "Health Communication Campaigns and Their Impact on Behavior," *Journal of Nutrition Education and Behavior* 39, no. 2 (2007): 32–40. https://doi.org/10.1016/j.jneb.2006.09.004.

115. James Kiwanuka–Tondo and Leslie B. Snyder, "The Influence of Organizational Characteristics and Campaign Design Elements on Communication Campaign Quality: Evidence from 91 Ugandan AIDS Campaigns," *Journal of Health Communication* 7, no. 1 (2002): 59–77. https://doi.org/10.1080/10810730252801192.

116. Institute of Medicine, *Speaking of Health*, 95.

117. Madeleine Leininger, *Transcultural Nursing: Concepts, Theories and Practices* (New York: Wiley, 1978).

118. Institute of Medicine, *Speaking of Health*, 241.

119. Josepha Campinha–Bacote, *The Process of Cultural Competence in HealthCare: A Culturally Competent Model of Care* (Wyoming, OH: Transcultural C.A.R.E. Associates, 1994).

120. Institute of Medicine, *Speaking of Health*, 241.

121. Ibid, 241.

122. Nigel J. Holden and Harald F. O. Von Kortzfleisch, "Why Cross-Cultural Knowledge Transfer is a Form of Translation in More Ways Than You Think," *Knowledge and Process Management* 11, no. 2 (2004): 127–36. https://doi.org/10.1002/kpm.198.

123. Carole P. Christensen, "Cross-Cultural Awareness Development: A Conceptual Model," *Counselor Education and Supervision* 28, no. 4 (1989): 270–89. https://doi.org/10.1002/j.1556-6978.1989.tb01118.x.

124. Patricia M. Duronto, Tsukasa Nishida, and Shin-ichi Nakayama, "Uncertainty, Anxiety, and Avoidance in Communication with Strangers," *International Journal of Intercultural Relations* 29, no. 5 (2005): 549–60. https://doi.org/10.1016/j.ijintrel.2005.08.003.

125. Cited in Matusitz, *Terrorism & Communication*, 150.

126. Derald Wing Sue, "A Model for Cultural Diversity Training," *Journal of Counseling & Development* 70, no. 1 (1991): 99–105. https://doi.org/10.1002/j.1556-6676.1991.tb01568.x.

127. Esther Miedema, "'Culturespeak' Is Everywhere: An Analysis of Culturalist Narratives in Approaches to Sexuality Education in Mozambique," *Comparative Education* 55, no. 2 (2019): 220–42. https://doi.org/10.1080/03050068.2018.1541658.

128. Jandt, *An Introduction to Intercultural Communication*, 15.

129. John W. Creswell, *Research Design: Qualitative, Quantitative, and Mixed Methods Approaches* (3rd Ed.) (Thousand Oaks, CA: Sage, 2009): 13.

130. Macnamara, *Evaluating Public Communication*, 259.

131. Bruce L. Berg and Howard Lune, *Qualitative Research Methods for the Social Sciences* (9th Ed.) (Upper Saddle River, NJ: Pearson, 2016).

132. William Neuman, *Social Research Methods: Qualitative and Quantitative Approaches* (6th Ed.) (New York: Pearson, 2006): 381.

133. Berg and Lune, *Qualitative Research Methods*, 172.

134. Macnamara, *Evaluating Public Communication*, 36.

135. Sandra J. Brennan and Mary W. Schulze, "Cultural Immersion through Ethnography: The Lived Experience and Group Process," *Journal of Nursing Education* 43, no. 6 (2004): 285–8. https://doi.org/10.3928/01484834-20040601-08.

136. Macnamara, *Evaluating Public Communication*, 33.

137. Devesh K. Sahu and Ankita Arya, "Ethnographic Method and Its Applications in Cultural and and Social Anthropological Research," in *Ethnographic Discourse of the Other: Conceptual and Methodological Issues*, ed. Panchanan Mohanty, Ramesh C. Malik, and Eswarappa Kasi (Newcastle: Cambridge Scholars Publishing, 2008): 247–53.

138. Nathalie Lazaric and Edward Lorenz, "Collective Learning and the Theory of the Firm," *European Journal of Economic and Social Systems* 14, no. 2 (2000): 111–7.

139. Jonathan Matusitz, *Symbolism in Terrorism: Motivation, Communication, and Behavior* (Lanham, MD: Rowman & Littlefield, 2015).

140. Linda C. Garro, "Remembering What One Knows and the Construction of the Past: A Comparison of Cultural Consensus Theory and Cultural Schema Theory," *Ethos* 28, no. 3 (2000): 275–319. https://doi.org/10.1525/eth.2000.28.3.275.

141. Edward Sapir, "Cultural Anthropology and Psychiatry," in *Edward Sapir: Selected Writings* (Berkeley: University of California Press, 1985 [1932]): 509–21, 515.

142. Donald P. Warwick, "Culture and the Management of Family Planning Programs," *Studies in Family Planning* 19, no. 1 (1988): 1–18. https://doi.org/10.2307/1966735.

143. Benjamino Cislaghi and Lori Heise, "Theory and Practice of Social Norms Interventions: Eight Common Pitfalls," *Globalization and Health* 14 (2018): Article 83. https://doi.org/10.1186/s12992-018-0398-x.

144. Ibid.

145. Nurit Guttman and Charles T. Salmon, "Guilt, Fear, Stigma and Knowledge Gaps: Ethical Issues in Public Health Communication Interventions," *Bioethics* 18, no. 6 (2004): 531–52. https://doi.org/10.1111/j.1467-8519.2004.00415.x.

CHAPTER 7

Public Communication Campaigns during the COVID-19 Pandemic

In early 2020, the fight against COVID-19 became a major concern for all affected nations worldwide. Traditionally, governments are seen as the main custodians of "crisismanship" (i.e., leadership, direction, and operations).[1] They use large-scale communication campaigns to influence the actions and behaviors of their populations when the risk continually grows. Communicating with such populations is a fundamental part of pandemic preparation and response. Based on the pandemic communication strategies and proposals provided by numerous sources from the past, three core messages directed at the public are the most common: (1) Promoting individual- and society-level infection control behaviors, (2) championing trust in government agencies and adherence to their directives, and (3) constantly keeping informed about expert, scientific, and medical knowledge.[2]

Our planet is more exposed to pandemics than ever before because of the fast-growing population, more opportunities for travel around the world, and large influxes of immigrants and refugees. The COVID-19 virus has been the most salient and widespread pandemic that we have faced since the dawn of the twenty-first century. A combination of the Greek words *pan* and *demos*, a **pandemic** is a global epidemic that can affect all (*pan*) people (*demos*) on the globe or, at least, across large regions. According to the World Health Organization, a pandemic spreads when three conditions are met: (1) The presence of a disease new to societies; (2) the virus infects people, causing grave illnesses; and (3) the virus spreads without difficulty and consistently among humans.[3] In turn, combining the Greek words *epi* and *demos*, an **epidemic** is a category of disease that emerges as new cases in a

Fundamentals of Public Communication Campaigns, First Edition. Jonathan Matusitz.
© 2022 John Wiley & Sons Ltd. Published 2022 by John Wiley & Sons Ltd.

human population, during a specific time frame, at a fast-paced rate, and based on recent experience—i.e., the percentage of new cases in a human population during a given time frame is called **incidence rate**.[4] An epidemic is occasionally referred to as an **outbreak**, which alludes to a swift increase in occurrences of a disease within a small, localized group of individuals or agents infected with a virus or illness. Such groups are generally restricted to a village or a small zone.[5]

Most pandemics and epidemics fall under the umbrella of **Rose's Theorem**—i.e., a model postulating that a large percentage of individuals at small risk may cause more new cases of a disease than a small percentage at high risk.[6] With this said, a virus or a disease should not be called a pandemic simply because it is widespread or takes the lives of many people; it must also be infectious. As such, cancer causes a high number of deaths, but it is not a pandemic, epidemic, or outbreak because it is not infectious or contagious. The actual study of pandemics, epidemics, and outbreaks is referred to as **epidemiology**. It studies the reasons behind the health and illness of societies or nations. It serves as the main pillar for interventions conducted in public health and preventive medicine. A virus or disease can be endemic. Combining the Greek words *en* and *demos*, **endemic** means that it stays in (or within) a population. In other words, inasmuch as no cure or vaccine can solve the issue, such a virus or disease remains within the population without the necessity for external inputs.[7] If it were not for aggressive vaccination campaigns, COVID-19 could have become a tragic case of a deadly endemic virus. Lastly, in the context of pandemics, a **case definition** is a mechanism by which public health experts determine who is to be included as a case (i.e., a person directly impacted by an epidemic, pandemic, or outbreak). This is grounded in criteria like the geographic area where individuals reside and work, their gender, their age, and the prevalence of the disease—among many others. By creating a case definition, public health practitioners are more able to study the disease, identify possible causes, and develop possible treatments.[8]

COVID-19: DEFINITIONS AND FACTS

Also called **coronavirus disease 2019**, **COVID-19** is a contagious disease produced by a severe and acute form of the respiratory syndrome coronavirus 2 (SARS-CoV-2). The first case was identified in Wuhan, Hubei Province of China, in December 2019. The disease quickly proliferated across the world, leading to a pandemic. COVID-19 was pronounced a pandemic by the World Health Organization Director–General on March 11, 2020. In the most impacted nations in 2020, case fatality rates were believed to be up to 15% (even 15.2% in Belgium). COVID-19 causes both a physical risk, owing to its contagiousness, and a psychological risk, because of the fear it triggers.[9] COVID-19 also affects obesity and diabetes.[10] Symptoms of COVID-19 vary, but often consist of fever, cough, exhaustion, breathing problems, and loss of smell and taste. Symptoms may begin between 1 and 14 days after infection by the virus. At least 30% of those who are infected do not show any noticeable symptoms.[11]

By late February 2022, COVID-19 had killed 6,000,000 people worldwide, including about 1,000,000 people in the United States, 650,000 in Brazil, 520,000 in India, and 210,000 in Peru. Peru is a nation that was deeply affected, but widely ignored by the mainstream media—especially considering that, in proportion to its overall population, Peru experienced the highest percentage of deaths (which was twice as many as the second-worst nation per capita: Bosnia and Herzegovina).[12] To boot, a staggering 430,000,000 across the world had already contracted the virus. Early during the pandemic, the virus was named 2019-nCoV, but later was officially turned into COVID-19. Within the first few weeks of 2020, the COVID-19 virus became a household name and began to dominate global news. As more and more cases emerged, governments proceeded to shut down borders and impose social distancing restrictions and lockdowns, in an attempt to curb the fast acceleration of the virus. Already before many of these governmental measures were taken, reports indicated that people chose to self-isolate, as mass panic began to spread like wildfire. Other reports of verbal and physical assaults in supermarkets and hoarding of products and supplies ramped up as fear took over the world.[13]

The Great Lockdown

To this last point, in 2020, the COVID-19 pandemic led to product and supply shortages aggravated by panic buying, agricultural interruption, and food scarcities, as well as lower emissions of pollutants and greenhouse gases. It also led to hefty international social and economic disruptions, including the largest global recession since the 1930s and 1940s. In fact, COVID-19 sparked the implementation of large-scale quarantine measures, resulting in massive closures of key sectors of the global economy, like tourism and travel.[14] The International Monetary Fund (2020)[15] predicted—rightfully so—that world economies would face the worst recession since the Great Depression, labeling this phenomenon the **Great Lockdown**.

The Great Lockdown is not necessarily predicated on evidence or consistency among nations or even regions within each nation. For example, in April 2021, the Centers for Disease Control and Prevention (CDC) used one mechanism for rating the risks by country, the US State Department used another, creating different travel alert levels for the same nations. Mexico, a famous vacation destination for American tourists, was estimated to be "level 4" by the CDC—i.e., all travel should be avoided—but "level 3" by the US State Department—i.e., "reconsider travel." The Bahamas was raised to "level 4" by the CDC but "level 3" by the US State Department.[16] Needless to say, lockdowns imposed by governments are not necessarily grounded in sufficient evidence for health-related dangers.

Suicides, Mental Health Disorders, and Alcoholism

It is widely believed that economic recessions are linked to increased suicides, especially for working age men.[17] Each year, in a population of 100,000 people, about 12 die by suicide. For every death caused by suicide, there are up to 20 reported suicide attempts. Suicide is among the top 10 causes of death in the world.[18] Émile Durkheim (1897/1952),[19] a French sociologist, argued that times of deep economic, social, or political upheaval are more likely to lead to anomic suicide. Because of a lack of social integration and increased concerns for self-interest, people's material and social conditions fail as compared with their anticipated living standards. **Anomic suicide** is a type of suicide caused by a rupture of social equilibrium, like a bankruptcy or after winning a lottery. Anomic suicide occurs in a circumstance which has surfaced unexpectedly. By and large, COVID-19 has generated a higher risk of mental health disorders like chronic trauma and stress, which eventually escalates rates of suicidality and suicidal behavior. More data is needed on the association between pandemics and suicides. Cases of suicides climbed during the protracted peak of COVID-19. Cases of profound mental disorder, obsessive compulsive disorder, and anxiety disorder often experience relapses and undesired hospitalization rates. All three categories of disorders have a high suicide risk.[20]

In Japan, the suicide rate decreased considerably during the first wave of COVID-19 (February to June 2020), but rose sharply during the second wave (July to October 2020). A rising suicide trend could be seen during the second wave, whereby the rate increased by 38% in October 2020.[21] In the United States, one in four young adults has contemplated suicide since the coronavirus afflicted the country (according to the CDC in November 2020). Nationwide surveys revealed that 40% of Americans were struggling with at least one mental health or drug-related issue. To boot, young adults were more affected than any other age category, with 75% having to cope with such problems. In Arizona's Pima County, officials released two health bulletins informing doctors and healthcare facilities about spikes in suicides. In Oregon's Columbia County, the rate of suicides by the summer of 2020 had already exceeded the total rate for 2019. In the Chicago area, DuPage County reported a 23% increase in comparison with 2019. In the Windy City itself, the rate of suicides among African Americans surpassed, by far, the total for 2019.[22]

A study conducted by Columbia University (2021)[23] reported a significant surge in alcohol use during the pandemic. More precisely, the researchers noted a $7.5-billion uptick in US liquor store sales between the first three quarters of 2019 and 2020. Uncontrolled drinking at home was attributed to a dysfunctional manner of combating stress related to social distancing and quarantines, along with uncertainty about the future. Not surprisingly, excessive drinking at home is more likely to lead to domestic violence, according to the same scientists. Additionally, the Research Triangle Institute (RTI) reported an increase in alcoholism among mothers with children, particularly since the pandemic facilitated the purchase of liquor through curbside pickup and home delivery.[24]

RISK COMMUNICATION

Risk communication refers to the exchange of real-time information, recommendations, and educated opinions between experts and audiences experiencing risks to their health or socioeconomic well-being. The chief purpose of risk communication is to allow at-risk individuals to make proper decisions in order to protect themselves and their friends/relatives. Risk communication employs many communication approaches, ranging from communications via social networking sites to mass communications and community participation. It hinges on a solid understanding of audiences' backgrounds, concerns, and beliefs (on top of their levels of knowledge and practices). It also requires early detection and control of rumors, misinformation, and other communicative obstacles.[25] Risk communication campaigns give a promise of addressing and disentangling public conflict during major crises and implementing safety campaigns steeped in science, technology, and health. The idea of communication that is "in the public interest" is regarded as central in satisfying the public's craving for information and education, or for advocating behavior change and protective measures, when facing a projected disaster.[26]

Risk communication should be considered a two-way process that develops as a pandemic makes its way into society. It should be employed as a strategy to minimize the proliferation of viruses by filling the gap that is often felt between what authorities think we should know and what we want to know.[27] The main component of risk communication is trust-inspired communication centered on community risk perception. The objective of risk communication is to reduce fear to the lowest level by addressing uncertainties as much as possible, ultimately helping society become prepared for changes in its daily life in time of pandemics.[28] Risk communication consists of three elements: (1) Discuss what we know and what we do not know frankly; (2) listen to people's concerns when tackling fears and perceptions (through online social media, etc.); and (3) control rumors and misinformation as quickly as possible.[29]

Risk Communication vs. Crisis Communication

Whereas risk communication has to do with the identification of risks to public health and tries to persuade audiences to adopt healthful and harmless behaviors, **crisis communication** deals with the public relations side of it and attempts to strategically manage and frame audience perceptions of a crisis—i.e., to make sure that harm is alleviated for both the state and those who are impacted.[30] Crisis communication is a sphere within the public relations discipline aimed at protecting and defending individuals, corporations, or organizations experiencing a public challenge to their reputation. Crisis communication strives to raise awareness of a specific threat, its magnitude, its potential outcomes, and what behaviors should be assumed to decrease the threat.[31] Risk communication is more about campaigning to lower risks, and in so doing, bettering society. An example would be a public communication campaign on the risks of tobacco smoking. Risk communication also entails disseminating information about harm mitigation resources and methods (e.g., going for e-cigarettes), and about the possibilities of additional harm (e.g., smoking and abandoning physical exercising altogether).[32]

Strategic Communication

An approach analogous to risk communication is strategic communication, a concept frequently applied to planned communication campaigns. **Strategic communication** comprises a range of communication-related specialties, such as risk communication, public relations, brand management, and corporate communication. Other subjects include community relations, constituent relationship management, health promotion, community outreach, public affairs, population health, strategic advertising, and strategic marketing.[33] Strategic communication employs message development with high degrees of planning and audience analysis and perceptions to accomplish an organization's or entity's mission. Messages are designed to target particular audiences and help identify communication goals or objectives. Strategic communication operates from a variety of sources, like press releases, social networking sites, radio and TV advertisements, internal communications, interviews, white papers, and so forth.[34]

Campaigns centered on strategic communication often apply the blueprint of skills and approaches from the discipline of public relations, though they are not termed "public relations" by their designers.[35] Brown and Campbell (1991)[36] remark that numerous Western nations acknowledge the necessity for successful strategic communication *apropos* health-related and technological risks. One key requirement is to be as factual, relevant, and timely as possible when informing audiences. Strategic communication campaigns involve professionals trying to persuade these audiences of the authenticity of any scientific risk assessments for a specific threat. As was the case with a great many COVID-19-related campaigns in 2020 and 2021, it is nonetheless unsurprising that many of these campaigns have not had a high level of success.

Effective strategic communication is a core element of preparation for emergencies—making or breaking the attainment of prevention and relief endeavors. The timely release of true facts about impending or current hazards helps accomplish the goals of emergency response: (1) Raising the probability that at-risk individuals will take safety measures, averting harm and saving lives, (2) decreasing anxiety levels and circumventing needless care-seeking by unthreatened groups, and (3) smoothing the progress of relief efforts. These goals are sufficiently testing under circumstances of natural disasters or accidents. The perilous dream of modern terrorists to use biological, chemical, or radiological weapons presents unique challenges too. As such, terrorist attacks create an increased potential for general angst and an astronomical level of uncertainty. The challenge in defining and communicating these public health threats attests to the urge for needs analysis and response approaches.[37] The purpose for an effective strategic communication campaign is also contingent on the outcome of risk management. **Risk management** is the evaluation of the magnitude of a particular risk and an estimation of how serious the risk is. Two factors are associated with this: **Risk assessment** (the evaluation of the risk from data to generate a risk probability) and **risk evaluation** (producing a measurable perception about the risks that a society faces and what measures can be taken against those risks).[38]

Infodemic Management

An **infodemic** occurs when blatantly erroneous or misleading information is diffused in both online social media and physical environments during an epidemic, pandemic, or outbreak. It results in confusion and risk-taking attitudes that can jeopardize one's health or well-being. It also produces mistrust in authorities and erodes adequate public health response. An infodemic can exacerbate epidemics when citizens are confused as to what they should do to protect their health and that of others. Thanks to the expansion of **digitization**—a combined growth of social media and internet use—information can be disseminated in a rapid fashion. Although it can help fill information voids, it can also intensify the volume of deleterious messages.[39] Against this backdrop, **infodemic management** seeks to methodically use risk communication, risk-based assessments, and evidence-based approaches to manage the infodemic and decrease its effects on health attitudes during crises and emergencies. Infodemic management attempts to allow good health practices through four categories of actions: (1) Listening to public concerns and answering questions; (2) encouraging understanding of risk and health professional advice; (3) creating resistance to misinformation; and (4) involving and empowering society to take appropriate actions.[40]

STRATEGIES FOR COVID-19 COMMUNICATION CAMPAIGNS

COVID-19 has caused a considerable set of challenges for practitioners in the course of planning, carrying out, and assessing public communication campaigns. That pandemic is unparalleled in modern times in terms of global reach of infections and the consequent morbidity, mortality, and toll on healthcare systems.[41] Governments worldwide have enacted a wide assortment of interventions to ensure adherence to social distancing regulations. These interventions were rooted in the concepts of education, persuasion, motivation, pressure, environmental reformation, restriction, and enablement. Constant exhortations to prevent COVID-19 (e.g., wearing a face covering and hand washing) and the campaign for social distancing (e.g., staying home and maintaining a six-foot distance from others) have helped change people's attitudes towards the pandemic more seriously. Transparent communication about millions of positive cases also helped fashion a genuine image of governmental action in regards to COVID-19.[42]

COVID-19 has put the notion of social distancing on a global map. It has placed social distancing regulations and postponement of nonessential services at an extraordinary scale. Although **social distancing** is now a household term, it refers more specifically to keeping a physical separation by decreasing the number of instances we come into close contact with others.[43] Social distancing also applies outside infection status and does not have the same meaning as quarantine, self-isolation, or seclusion from those with suspected or diagnosed viruses.[44]

Early Campaigns as Infodemic Management

During early COVID-19 communication campaigns, the emphasis was laid on infodemic management as communication with the public was a major challenge. Planners had a hard time devising campaigns due to a lack of information on the disease and too many sources of false or unfounded information on the issue. Hence, many campaigners limited their efforts to the production of eighth-grade–type question-and-answer videos. Immediately after COVID-19 was declared a pandemic by the World Health Organization, risk communication initiatives contributed to an information platform called WHO Information Network for Epidemics (EPI-WIN), with the purpose of using a series of amplifiers to dissipate false or misleading messages and impart tailored information to target groups. Preventive measures have consisted of social distancing, quarantining, ventilation of indoor areas, drawings showing how to cover coughs and sneezes, handwashing, avoiding touching one's mask, and keeping unwashed hands away from the face. The use of face coverings has been made required in public locations to curtail the risk of transmissions. Several vaccines were finally developed and made available, and subsequent mass vaccination campaigns were initiated in many countries.[45]

In addition, a few problems surfaced during such campaigns, such as inconsistencies in core messages. An example includes "Do not drink chlorine bleach." The reality is that chlorine is different from hydroxychloroquine. Arguably the most challenging aspect of the infodemic is how to effectively expose the public to peer-reviewed evidence. Some of the communication challenges pertain to complex scientific questions: Is hydroxychloroquine efficient to prevent or treat COVID-19? Are nonsteroidal antiinflammatory drugs harmful to those who have COVID-19? Should disease-modifying antirheumatic drugs be banned to avoid an infection or during a confirmed infection? These questions not only have evolving answers and have been the focus of ongoing studies; they also pose a problem when developing a campaign—i.e., the campaign may lose credibility as primary questions can still not be answered with even a 50% accuracy. Thoroughly designed public health interventions without enough hard data can be subject to heavy criticism.[46]

The 12 Principles of Social Distancing Campaigns

Bonell et al. (2020)[47] laid out principles to inform campaigns that advocate total population adherence to social distancing measures. These were grounded in expert knowledge, current theories, and evidence, instead of a simple review of the literature. Social distancing campaigns draw on constant communication and promote durable health-based, behavioral, and social changes. An important purpose of this list is to achieve **containment**, a conscious attempt at limiting the length of a crisis or preventing it from propagating to other regions that have afflicted a country. A few suggestions from other scholars were added to this list as well:

1. **Clear and specific guidance**: Facts are necessary, but insufficient, to induce total population behavior change, because the latter also needs motivation and the opportunity to instigate change.[48] With this said, facts still matter as long as they are complemented by clear and specific guidance for what behavior people should adopt to apply social distancing measures.[49] Information on how to manage COVID-19 should be via messages of self-efficacy. This signifies that authorities (and/or the media) should tell people what steps they should take to decrease harm. These messages will help assuage a portion of the uncertainty in a pandemic.[50]

2. **"Protect each other" messages**: Such messages are reassuring, especially when inspired by messages that champion social identity and supportive social norms. They should underscore how expected behaviors benefit society and protect its most vulnerable citizens, including loved ones. This will be improved by real-life examples, meaningful images, and the published testimonies of those who need protection—including the vulnerable, healthcare systems, and workers—associated with clear, specific recommendations on how to carry out social distancing.[51] Upon conveying such messages, it is crucial to acknowledge variation across population groups—for instance, according to age, socioeconomic status, and ethnic group—regarding what is sacrificed when following social distancing,[52] which might provide more ideas about segmented communication and enablement approaches. On the other hand, "protect yourself" messages will produce lower impact among the general audience because many see themselves at low risk of serious consequences from COVID-19 infection and will probably be less persuaded otherwise.[53]

3. **"Stand together" messages**: Such messages stress how our sense of self is ingrained within our attachment to groups like families, neighborhoods, communities, and homeland. This instills a consensus of responsibility, solidarity, and inclusion. Messages should emanate from individuals symbolic of and trusted by society rather than those regarded as partisan or self-serving.[54] Messages may be adapted to attract certain subgroups based on sex, age, regional, racial, or cultural memberships,[55] inspired by family and faith/interfaith voices (especially for certain class and ethnic groups).[56] In achieving this, it is important to use voices that are suitable to the group in question. The public is not a homogeneous unit, but a complex composite of people, families, and other groups influenced by circumstances, experiences, and aspirations. All of this happens in an assemblage of communities with different levels of health literacy, values, and anticipations.[57] Youths are mostly swayed by the voices of peers and others of their demographic (including public figures and social media influencers), who can be exploited to improve adherence.[58] It is also crucial to keep away from stereotypical or potentially contentious messages. Instead, by drawing on stirring concrete examples (like community and healthcare volunteers), it should be emphasized that a range of groups, with varying ethnic or socioeconomic backgrounds, can come together by collaborating and forming an integral part of a common society. Messages are weakened when social distancing measures are viewed as unequitable or socially divisive.[59]

4. **"This is who we are" messages**: Such messages should adhere to social norms and rules that direct behavior of groups.[60] Messages should be framed as mirroring and

valuing group culture (i.e., "This is who we really are") and group behavior (i.e., "This is what we are doing").[61] Messages which infer that people are taking inappropriate actions (e.g., "Don't panic buy" or "Don't cheat on adherence") may bring about unintended consequences by eroding descriptive norms.

5. **Honesty, truthfulness, and openness**: These concepts fall under an overarching range of elements. Honesty should be *the* policy and the bottom line across all situations; truthfulness operates on the principle of sharing the entire truth even when it may expose the government's or organization's flaws; and openness is availability and closeness that rises above a simple response. Now, it is essential to embrace uncertainty and ambiguity; in the vast majority of cases, there is some level of uncertainty. Therefore, it is pivotal to reframe messages when additional information is acquired. Campaign strategists need to work in tandem with credible sources; communicators ought to regularly search for validation that allows their sources to communicate and liaise effectively with all stakeholders. Taking these steps is imperative and should not falter during a pandemic.[62]

6. **No fear- or disgust-based messages in relation to other people**: Fear- and disgust-based messages may contribute to encouraging others to wash their hands but should not be incorporated in messages about other people's hygiene. These would end up being counterproductive in the control of COVID-19 because they would weaken social identity and efficacy, and may give rise to the stigmatization of affected citizens or groups.[63]

7. **No authoritarian messages**: Messages that sound authoritarian or coercive could yield significant changes in the short term, but could be harder to uphold in the long term. Evidence shows that people or groups interpret messages in markedly different ways when communications are perceived as authoritarian moral messages—e.g., when violating a lockdown is framed as civil disorder, especially when audiences perceive inequities in how these are handled.[64] This implies that campaigns should diffuse messages of empathy, concern, and responsiveness; empathy, concern, and responsiveness will enhance message credibility and the credibility of the source before and after the crisis.[65]

8. **A regular plan**: Such a plan is more likely to sustain behavior change by helping audiences become more ready for potential obstacles and enablers to adherence (and attend to these in advance).[66] Messages should include clear, precise, and calm recommendations, allowing households to work together on how to best apply social distancing skills (while still enjoying their income, food, social networks, and possibly physical exercise). Circumstances change easily, so householders should be emboldened to assess plans frequently. Planning guidelines should be provided in printed form, via social networking sites, or through smartphone app support.[67]

9. **"Make it possible" messages**: Rewards and incentives for fulfilling desired actions are usually more effective influences during a major crisis than punishment, disincentives, or warnings.[68] Given that behavior tends to be influenced by social context,[69] messaging will be more efficient if done through a clearly communicated proposal of timely and generous support for income, employment rights, access to food, availability of social networks, entertainment, schooling, parenting and mental health support, and access to more green or environmental spaces. Such support should be long-term to ensure adherence to desired behaviors and to adopt

progressive universalism—open to everybody but seeking to take full advantage of benefits for the downtrodden or disenfranchised.[70]

10. **Style of messaging**: It would be better if messages were diffused through carefully designed mass and social media campaigns. Campaigns should also cooperate with media organizations to invite popular spokespeople and to guarantee responsible coverage (e.g., by highlighting social adherence rather than social divisiveness).[71]

11. **Communication briefs**: Each campaign should be framed as an intervention with communication briefs, including the following: a precise behavioral goal (e.g., under "consumer objectives"), a message (e.g., under "focal insight"), a message source and channel (e.g., under "deliverables"), a target audience (e.g., under "target group") and the desired reach and indicators (e.g., under "objectives" or "outcomes").[72] Under a "support/evidence" rubric, campaigns should also specify what evidence and benchmark for behavior change will be used. Single interventions should be part of a consistent overarching program with reliable information. Campaigns should certainly anticipate potentially unintended consequences using prevailing theories to curtail these possibilities.[73]

12. **Codesign**: Campaigns should be codesigned and conducted with relevant target audiences through various methods, like online engagement, ethnography, and virtual focus groups.[74] They should be assessed by preconvened indicators of delivery, reach, and impact. The assessment should feed back into upcoming communications. Developers should use polling and quantitative and qualitative research data to evaluate the effects of the general communications program on movements in, for instance, (a) feelings of social identity, (b) feelings of responsibility of care to others, (c) incentives for social distancing, (d) behavior planning, and (e) behavior change.[75] Collaborations with the audience do matter. The audience is a worthy associate who should be regularly informed during the course of the pandemic. The audience is often more a resource than a burden if treated as a partner.[76]

Case Study: Vietnam

Vietnam is a lower-middle income nation of over 100 million inhabitants. In 2018, its GDP per capita was roughly US$2,600, and only US$150 per Vietnamese was spent on healthcare annually. The country has a 1,300-kilometer border with China, where the first cases of SARS-CoV-2 were detected. The COVID-19 pandemic was declared to permeate Vietnam on January 23, 2020. Despite sharing a colossal volume of trade with China, Vietnam appeared to have managed the spread of the virus.[77] In fact, at the end of 2020, Vietnam had faced only two acmes of community transmission (March–April and July–August). The experience that the country acquired from previous pandemics, like SARS-CoV-1 in 2003 and the bird flu (H5N1) in 2004, was central in responding effectively to COVID-19. It should come to no surprise that it became the first country to stop the SARS dissemination successfully in 2003. Despite a moderate coronavirus spike in summer 2021, the Vietnamese case study offers lessons that may be valuable for low-income and middle-income nations to maximize the efficacy of their COVID-19 response.[78]

Quick and Appropriate Response

On January 16, 2020, way ahead of the first case of COVID-19 in the country, the Vietnamese authorities released the first diagnostic and control guidelines for the virus. The guidelines comprised instructions about contact tracing and the 14-day quarantine for those with direct contacts with a confirmed case. These enabled authorities to successfully identify the first two epidemiologically related COVID-19 cases (a dad and his son) a week later. The father came from Wuhan, China, to see his son in the Mekong Delta, which constituted the first case of human-to-human transmission of COVID-19 outside China. Their contacts were traced, isolated, and confirmed; one tested positive.[79] Within the first two months of the pandemic, all patients successfully improved their health and were released from hospitals. From February 27 to March 5, 2020, no new cases were reported in the country, and it really looked like that it was winning the battle against the virus.[80]

The combination of early lockdowns, successful diffusion of health campaigns, promotion of health declarations, regulation of wearing face coverings, and national unity were efficient to manage this fatal virus. The Vietnamese authorities treated COVID-19 as a grave concern from day one. They informed Vietnamese citizens to become more prudent about worst-case scenarios of that public health crisis. This was also a good lesson for many Western nations, which tended to neglect COVID-19 during the first stage. This is why Vietnam took proper actions by using "the golden time" to control the spread of the new coronavirus.[81] The majority of Vietnam's boundaries are made up of jungles and rugged mountains, making it harder to regulate immigration. Therefore, unauthorized immigration presents a challenge to preventing and fighting the outbreak.[82]

"Jealous Coronavirus" Video

Rather than causing a stir or mass panic, the Vietnamese government produced a COVID-19 video as a prevention campaign. It rapidly went viral.[83] The video is essentially a song, the product of a joint effort between Vietnam's Health Ministry and artists. By the summer of 2021, it had garnered over 80 million views. The song brought up healthy habits to wash hands and avoid touching the face. The song was also transmitted through US and European channels. This was part of a national intervention to communicate health policy messages to Vietnamese audiences. Instead of compelling people to take proper actions or punish them for not following regulations, the Vietnamese government diffused nudging-behavior policies, which can boost the "virality" of the message.[84]

The translation of the animated music video was "Jealous Coronavirus." In its effort to raise awareness about the international health crisis, the government creates lyrics such as "Let's wash our hands. Rub rub rub rub them. Don't put your hands on eyes, nose and mouth and limit going to crowded places. Fight back against corona." These were the English subtitles of the video. The three-minute-long audiovisual also discussed how the virus first emerged, from its epicenter in Wuhan, and how it contaminated other regions. "Where is it from? Its hometown is Wuhan. All was calm, then came a sudden breakout," says the video to the harmony of Coronavirus awareness.[85] The original Vietnamese version was called *Ghen Cô Vy* (the "Washing Hand" song). During the first few seconds of the video, a couple are arguing but, at the end—after suggestions and tips are offered to viewers to conquer the virus—they happily get back together. The video was produced by the Vietnamese Institute of Occupational and Environmental Health, in concert with artists Khac Hung, Min, and Erik.[86] As the description says,

Through this project, we aim to empower and strengthen trust in the community, so that we can join hands to combat COVID-19 (aka nCoV-2019). In this critical moment of fighting the virus, we hope the song will ignite our spirits and reduce stress for the frontline fighters of this war: the team of experts, physicians, health workers and millions of other workers who are in the frontline of exposure and daily struggle with this disease.[87]

Social Cognitive Theory (SCT)

Developed by Albert Bandura (1986),[88] **social cognitive theory** (SCT) rests on the premise that we are more likely to embrace new behaviors when we observe others performing them. When it comes to watching cartoons, our knowledge acquisition can be directly associated with the observation of other people—particularly in terms of social interactions, experiences, and external media inspirations. This theory is an extension of Bandura's social learning theory (SLT). According to the main tenets of SCT, when we observe a model enacting a behavior and witness the results of that behavior, we recall the sequence of events and use this occurrence for subsequent behaviors. Observing a model can also stimulate the viewer to adopt behavior with which they were already familiar (to a certain extent).[89] SCT has a wider theoretical scope than SLT because SCT entails a conceptualization of people as agents able to influence their environment and a conceptualization of self-regulation. Described in Chapter 8, SLT is restricted to addressing the learning process in the social environment. It posits that learning happens by observing a behavior and that the expression of that behavior in the learner is guided by the triadic reciprocal causation between personal (cognitive) motives, the behavior itself, and by the context (reinforcement).[90]

SCT has several constructs which aid in explaining its presuppositions. One of these constructs is **self-efficacy**, which denotes the belief that we have concerning our abilities to effectively perform a certain behavior and obtain the desired results. Self-efficacy is a key element of behavior modification.[91] Task is another essential construct. Task alludes to the confidence that we have to execute an action. Other constructs of SCT consist of coping self-efficacy, goal setting, and outcome expectancy. **Coping self-efficacy** refers to the confidence that we have when performing a task during taxing circumstances. **Goal setting** refers to the desired outcome. It helps enhance self-regulation, which has an effect on self-efficacy. **Outcome expectancy** denotes the beliefs associated with a particular behavior, which leads to a definite outcome.[92]

Cartoons are often seen as a comic approach to tackle serious issues. They present an opportunity to diffuse messages to target audiences in a way that entertains them, teaches them, and informs them on any given subject.[93] Abraham (2009)[94] remarks that, thanks to cartoons, grave problems can be calibrated in ways that actually help the general public to better understand problems that are in the public interest. He also argues that cartoons provide people with an opportunity to undertake profound reflection on the issues described in the cartoon messages. Animated cartoons on COVID-19 have illustrated the desired health behaviors for social media viewers to learn by way of observation.[95] This stands in contrast to health messages like comic books or texts of still pictures. Bandura (2001)[96] avers that SCT is suitable to the examination of health behavior. This is due to the interactions between people, their environment, and behaviors, with a resultant implication for well-being.

Okpara et al. (2021)[97] analyzed the opinions of 470 social media users in Nigeria who had been exposed to COVID-19 animated cartoons on YouTube. The researchers discovered that color can greatly predict recollection of YouTube animated cartoons on COVID-19. The results of the study also revealed that color can temper the effects of YouTube COVID-19 animated cartoons on social media users' health behaviors. The study further demonstrated that exposure to COVID-19 YouTube animated cartoons can greatly predict viewers' knowledge of the virus. As the study explained, remembrance of key themes of COVID-19 messages in these YouTube animated cartoons can easily predict social media users' health behaviors. Lastly, the researchers were able to prove that self-efficacy, task self-efficacy, coping self-efficacy, and outcome expectancy greatly predict health behavior sustainability among social media users who watch COVID-19 animated cartoons on YouTube.

Consistent, Truthful Messages

Due to the troublesome experience of Wuhan, the Vietnamese authorities decided to implement a method of reliability, steadiness, and truthfulness in communicating information on the pandemic. Messages from political and social leaders were transparent, consistent, and univocal in explaining the gravity of the circumstances and the importance to honor and follow the regulations and guidelines. The mass media also coped univocally and decisively with the challenge of rumors and misinformation. The Vietnamese Prime Minister appeared daily on television to provide updates on and justification for guided actions. Providing reliable and unequivocal messages conflicted with what transpired in Europe and the United States, where political leaders seemed to issue contrasting or all too dangerous "reassuring messages" to audiences. News in these nations was often broadcast with a political undercurrent, because the media has become notorious for diffusing content that is heavily inspired by political conviction. In due course, this results in conflicting messages; the disparity in opinions becomes a slippery slope that creates confusion, frustration, and anger among audiences.[98]

The Prime Minister made clear exhortations about attitudes towards COVID-19, such as combating the pandemic is combating an enemy. The Vietnamese government was ready to sacrifice economic benefits in the short term for the benefit of the citizenry and operate on principles that leave no one behind. Anti-COVID-19 campaign messages persuaded an entire nation to fight against COVID-19.[99] The individual behind Vietnam's victorious control of the COVID-19 pandemic, Nguyen Xuan Phuc, was officially sworn in as President in Hanoi on April 5, 2021. Phuc, then 66 years old, was Vietnam's Prime Minister for the past five years, a period of prosperous economy. His administration's COVID-19 response earned praises at home and abroad.[100]

In addition, the Vietnamese government unceasingly informed its citizens through mobile phone messages. As stated by the Ministry of Information and Technology, by mid-2020, approximately six billion messages had been sent to the Vietnamese people to increase their awareness about social distancing, handwashing, self-quarantine, and self-checking behaviors.[101] Since the beginning of the pandemic, mobile phone communication was an innovative strategy that proved to be not only successful, but also safe. The authorities sent frequent updates on COVID-19 preventive responses via a mobile app called Blue Zone. It enabled users to determine whether they were in proximity to a confirmed case.[102] By August 20, 2021, Blue Zone had surpassed 20 million downloads.[103] National phone ringtones were adapted to inform people about COVID-19. In fact, the Vietnamese were mandated to upload NCOVI health notification software—the app of the Ministry of Health and the Ministry of Information and Communications—and gave daily reports on their own health status and that of family members'.[104]

Messages of Unity and Community Responsibility

Messages from the government and health agencies centered on community responsibility. Since the Fall of Saigon and the unification after the Vietnam War, it was the first time that the entire Vietnamese nation—including armed forces, academics, businesspeople, and other classes in society—took part in various types of contributions. Many universities and student dormitories became quarantine zones. Soldiers voluntarily became public servants to assist those who returned from epidemic zones in quarantine areas. Businesspeople were spearheading campaigns for private citizens to donate land and offer financial incentives to combat COVID-19. Vietnam did not consider imposing restrictions (due to COVID-19) as a challenge or violation of its citizens' freedom. Rather, what citizens gained from the pandemic was the meaning of the country's unity.[105]

Wearing face coverings and using hand sanitizers were highly recommended early on. By mid-March 2020, the Vietnamese authorities requested that every person wear a face mask in public for their own protection and that of others'. It was not only a reassuring message of unity, but also a mandate applicable to everyone. Even though the World Health Organization suggested that only positively confirmed individuals wear face masks to contain COVID-19 transmission, it is apparent that, in several Asian nations, adoption of masks seemed to correspond with reducing the speed of COVID-19 transmission.[106] The Ministry of Health did major contributions overall. At the onset of the pandemic, Vietnam took the liberty to implement early measures, which far exceeded the World Health Organization's guidelines. Taken as a whole, Vietnam was the first nation on the planet to put medical declarations into practice and lay so much emphasis on community-based behavior and spirit.[107]

Lastly, neighborhood commune health centers offered extensive healthcare services to COVID-19 patients. Their frontline workers played a crucial role in the prevention of the virus. They (1) gave health education on preventive procedures for all citizens in local areas; (2) listed those who had been in close proximity to COVID-19 cases (or those returning from highly infected areas) and directed them during the course of entire procedures; and (3) located isolation points or home isolation with medical surveillance, like temperature charts or health check-up, and sent for referral if needed.[108] Lockdowns, imposed in late March 2020, were motivated by those neighborhood commune health centers and resulted in a decrease of new cases by 55% (in comparison with the previous period).[109]

COVID-19 VACCINATION CAMPAIGNS

The human race entered a new phase in its fight against the COVID-19 pandemic. Vaccination was the new phase as it was seen as capable of containing the disease. Nevertheless, its efficacy depends on people's willingness to be vaccinated. Vaccination is a recommended measure to avoid infection and lower the mortality rate of many infectious diseases.[110] By definition, **vaccination** is the act of injecting a vaccine to assist the immune system in developing protection from a disease. Vaccines possess a microorganism or virus in an enfeebled, live, or killed condition, or proteins (or even toxins) from that microorganism. By invigorating the body's adaptive immunity, a vaccine counteracts illness from an infectious disease.[111] When an adequate percentage of a population has received a dose of vaccine, herd immunity follows. **Herd immunity** protects people whose immunity may be compromised and who cannot be vaccinated because a slight dose of it would harm them. Herd immunity is a type of indirect protection from infectious disease that can work against certain diseases when enough people within a community have become immune to an infection, either through vaccination or past infections. At the same time, it decreases the probability of infection for those who lack immunity.[112]

According to the World Health Organization,[113] by May 2021, over 80% of vaccine shots had been administered in high- and middle-income nations, as opposed to barely 0.3% in low-income nations. The mere availability of a vaccine is not a criterion for ensuring massive immunological protection. Enter the case of Chile. By March 2021, Chile was one of the most vaccinated countries in the world. The government had planned to administer almost 90 million doses of vaccine, which could have vaccinated its 19-million population more than twice. The government's lofty objective was to vaccinate 80% of its people by June 2021. Its largest order was a whopping 66 million doses from Sinovac, a Chinese corporation.[114] Yet, notwithstanding vaccination success, by April 2021, Chile had to mandate new lockdowns to contain a new COVID-19 wave. On March 26, 2021, the country recorded over 7,600 new cases over a one-day period—the highest at any time during the pandemic—and by mid-July 2021, it had over 1,500,000 cases. A significant percentage of Chileans erroneously believed that vaccination was sufficient, thereby causing them to do away with masks and social distancing. Into the bargain, as global travel was still permissible, many Chileans took advantage of low-cost flights to Brazil, the Dominican Republic, Florida, and other tourist destinations.[115]

Vaccination-Driven Campaigns

The obtainability of COVID-19 vaccines was an opportunity to moderate the impact of the pandemic. Attaining high media coverage on the importance of vaccination could be done through intense pro-vaccination campaigns and had the potential to significantly lower COVID-19-associated morbidity and mortality. Clinical trials have ascertained the effectiveness of COVID-19 vaccines in preventing both mild and severe COVID-19 in controlled environments.[116] Policymakers devote much time and energy to communications that make mandatory vaccination policies more salient and visible. Ultimately, such communications make these policies more able to lift vaccine coverage rates. Part of the success of a vaccination-driven campaign is to locate well-known symbols or key change agents who can persuade and contribute to higher uptakes in vaccine administration.[117] In Brazil, the message "Vaccine saves, United for vaccines" was displayed on the Christ Redeemer statue in a campaign led by the Unidos Pela Vacina (United by the Vaccine) movement. It was made as a joint effort with the Cristo Redentor Sanctuary and the Ogilvy Brazil advertising agency to raise awareness on the benefits of immunization. The movement Unidos Pela Vacina seeks to attract the attention of Brazilians on the long-term effects of immunization for both Brazil and the rest of the world. By mid-May 2021, over 4,000 people had been following the movement and its 85,000 volunteers were jumping through hoops of fire to remove obstacles and make vaccination accessible in all corners of Brazil.[118]

COVID-19 vaccination campaigns were massively influenced by the presence of several key suppliers. Healthcare practitioners often find themselves on the frontlines combating outbreaks, and a significant minority of them have to methodically carry out procedures with high risks of contracting dangerous diseases. Protecting healthcare practitioners from infection is imperative in containing nosocomial transmissions (i.e., originating in hospitals).[119] They constitute a high-risk group during the pandemic. Their risk of infection could be aggravated for a variety of reasons, including constant contact with patients, scarcities of supplies and personal protective equipment, and substandard infection control training.

During the 2003 severe acute respiratory syndrome (SARS) virus in Hong Kong, the first massive cases of transmission occurred at the Prince of Wales Hospital, where healthcare personnel represented a large proportion of infections, with over 43% of cases of hospital admissions.[120]

Avoiding Manufacturing Consent

Manufacturing consent is a concept describing how the mass media "are effective and powerful ideological institutions that carry out a system-supportive propaganda function."[121] In this context, it can involve deceptive communication practices that serve to develop support for vaccine requirements as public policy. Because manufacturing consent is connected to support for a policy instrument, instead of a medical technology or scientific knowledge, such consent for vaccine requirements is a weapon used in political communication.[122] As such, studies have demonstrated that audiences' perceptions of the legitimacy of vaccines is much more politically slanted than perceptions of vaccines themselves.[123] This is why public communication campaigns focused on vaccination should take the form of educational campaigns that stress the benefits of taking the vaccine, particularly with respect to the positive influence of individual vaccinations on herd immunity. Honesty and clarity about vaccine efficiency will likely boost trust in a vaccine, but messaging should make sure to avoid inadvertently overemphasizing the danger of side effects or rare adverse events.[124] "Manufacturing" should not be applied to consent; rather, it should focus on how to manufacture billions of doses of top-notch vaccines, advocacy for vaccine purchase, good organization of supply, measured allocations of vaccines, and smart logistics of global vaccine delivery. All of these measures pave the way for a successful vaccination campaign targeting all age demographics.[125]

The Threat of Vaccine Hesitancy

It is important to make a distinction between those who are totally against vaccination—anti-vaxxers (see last section of this chapter)—and those with limited or inaccurate health information. The latter have legitimate concerns and questions about vaccines in general, their efficacy, and the degree to which they are made available to the public out of a genuine interest—i.e., this situation reflects the concept of vaccine hesitancy.[126] **Vaccine hesitancy** is postponement in acceptance or refusal of vaccination regardless of availability of vaccination services. Vaccine hesitancy is complicated and context-specific, depending on the location, the period, and vaccines themselves. It is driven by factors like contentment, convenience, and confidence.[127] Vaccine hesitancy is thought to contribute to a reduction in vaccine coverage and a growing risk of vaccine-preventable infections and epidemics. It may be the result of an overemphasis on healthy lifestyles, the importance of personal responsibility, and the growth of "consumerism" in healthcare (i.e., patients' participation in their own healthcare decisions). The increase of informed patients has shifted the long-established locus of power from healthcare professionals as sole caretakers of patients to collaborative decision-making between those professionals and patients who want to be fully involved in the decision-making process regarding their health.[128]

Already in 2015, the World Health Organization (2015)[129] considered vaccine hesitancy a threat to global well-being. For the organization, there are three major contributors: (1) People who do not have enough confidence in or are frightened by vaccines, arguably due to the misconception that vaccines present a risk of infection; (2) people who do not believe they need to be vaccinated (e.g., owing to underestimation of the gravity of a virus) or do not see value in the vaccine; and (3) people or groups who may have a hard time accessing the vaccine. Parents opposed to childhood vaccines also pose problems for society at large. When not enough people are fully vaccinated, the rate of diseases can escalate socioeconomic costs, leading to higher loss of human life. Nonetheless, under-vaccination remains a multifaceted issue, as parental attitudes are far from being the only driver.[130] Hence, the subject of under-vaccination does not have any easy answers and opens opportunities for deep thinking; too many components are involved, each interacting in unanticipated ways.[131]

Those who have reservations about the essence of vaccines have traditionally stood against the idea of mass vaccination. One of the most pervasive misconceptions is that vaccination benefits do not offset risks, and that immunity generated through survival of a disease is better than immunity from vaccination.[132] Vaccines should also be welcome by both the healthcare community and society across all racial groups. Fu, Haimowitz, and Thompson (2019)[133] found that African Americans (in a sample of 110 people) expressed more trust in vaccine recommendations from race-concordant than race-discordant physicians. They also had more trust in race-concordant community advisors, disease survivors, school nurses, and other people from the same racial group. This insinuates that public communication campaigns should recruit cultural leaders who are not part of conventional medical and public health communities as mass vaccination advocates.

Case Study: Israel

The first case of COVID-19 in Israel was confirmed in February 2020. Nonclinical interventions have included three nationwide stay-at-home orders, several instances of school closures, limitations imposed on commercial activity and travel, and a mandate for face coverings—among others. The most recent stay-at-home order became effective on January 8, 2021, amid a national uptick in cases. Israel launched its massive vaccination campaign by promoting the Pfizer–BioNTech BNT162b2 (Pfizer–BioNTech) vaccine in December 2020, prioritizing those who were over 60 years of age, healthcare professionals, and people with severe medical conditions.[134] A rapid COVID-19 vaccination release and integration made Israel the nation with the highest percentage of vaccinated people per capita in the world.[135]

Indeed, a nation of 9.3 million inhabitants, Israel quickly became the world leader in vaccinating its people against COVID-19. By February 2021, two-dose vaccination coverage among those who were over 70 years of age was 84%.[136] By March 2021, 50% of Israel's inhabitants had been fully vaccinated, and 60% had been injected their first dose. At that time, the comparable statistics for the United States were 12% and 21%, respectively. Among Israelis in their seventies, 91% had received at least two doses of vaccine, and 96% had received at least one.[137] By October 2021, fewer than 8,000 Israelis had died of COVID-19.

Several synergistic drivers led to this success. These included Israel's small geographical area (about 8,500 square miles), its manageable population size, the accessibility to a large number of vaccine doses, outreach endeavors, previous experience in responding adequately to massive national emergencies, and a public health system supplied by only four health maintenance agencies, with numerous community-based nurses.[138] At the same time, Israel faced the same difficulties as many other countries. It was going through its third spike in infection rates, with an overall positive test rate of 6% (with certain communities reporting infections rates of up to 25%). Israel was in the midst of a tense political campaign and, like the United States, has subgroups and ethnic minorities, some of whom live in precarious circumstances, have a propensity to distrust authorities and science, ignore social distancing measures, and have been slower at being vaccinated.[139]

Public Communication Campaigns

Public communication campaigns consisted of well-adapted outreach efforts to persuade Israelis to commit themselves to vaccinations and show up at their vaccination appointments. These outreach efforts functioned as efficient frameworks for making decisions about vaccinations and supportive means for aiding in the operation of vaccination campaigns. The application of simple, clear, and easy standards for deciding who should be prioritized for receiving vaccines in the first phases of the distribution process went smoothly.[140] Outstanding was the regular communication of facts and studies by the mainstream mass media during the whole pandemic. *The Times of Israel*, for instance, cited a study extolling the virtues of COVID-19 shots as both helping the vaccines and providing "cross-protection" to the rest of the population.[141] The study, by Milman et al. (2021),[142] concluded that mass vaccination is able to restrain the COVID-19 pandemic by protecting the inoculated from the virus and possibly reducing the probability of transmission to the unvaccinated ones. The high efficiency of the largely administered BNT162b vaccine in averting not only the disease but also infection implies a possibility for a population-level impact—which is essential for disease eradication.

In February 2021, the Israeli authorities distributed the green pass, a vaccination certificate, in both digital and paper format, made for any individual who had received two doses of the COVID-19 vaccine at any of the four health maintenance agencies (or another valid vaccination service) in the country. Those who recovered from COVID-19 and showed acquired immunity were not eligible if they had not received two doses of the vaccine.[143] The green pass was available in Hebrew only and often displayed in a mobile phone app.[144] Admission to gyms, hotels, theaters, and concerts was now available thanks to that pass, because it simply proved that people were fully inoculated. Soon, the green pass proved to be helpful in that it motivated unvaccinated Israelis to get the injections.[145]

The communicative tactic, here, is to generate social appeal by motivating Israelis to be vaccinated more quickly when they see green pass holders access various sites that require the pass. This approach is called **bandwagoning**, or the **bandwagon effect**. It is an appeal to a popular trend—the observation that human beings generally follow a trend because many others do the same. The notion of "jumping on the bandwagon" is used in the sense of "joining an increasingly popular trend."[146] Likewise, *argumentum ad populum* is an "appeal to the people." It is an argument based on the premise that a phenomenon is real because many people believe they should go along with it. It asserts that "If many find it acceptable, it is acceptable."[147] This sort of strategy is known by multiple names, including appeal to belief, appeal to the majority, appeal to the people, argument by consensus, authority of the many, bandwagon fallacy, tyranny of the majority.[148]

Ultra-Orthodox Jews as Change Agents

The Israeli government stressed the value of community-based efforts. In Israel, the tradition of the government is to collaborate with hospitals, emergency care services, and grassroots leaders—particularly during times of crises and national emergencies—and establish the frameworks for facilitating that collaboration.[149] The predominant attitude towards inoculations is an optimistic one in Israel, due in large part to a massive education campaign led by public figures like then-Prime Minister Benjamin Netanyahu. However, as Israel has a manifestly layered society, to some groups, such as Ultra-Orthodox Jews and Arab communities, a different approach was required to ensure conformity with the vaccination program.[150]

Pro-vaccination slogans for Ultra-Orthodox Jews are something to behold. In front of a synagogue in Jerusalem's Ultra-Orthodox neighborhood Har Nof, a placard had the name of Osnat Ben Sheetrit on it, a pregnant mom of four who lost her life to COVID-19, and the sentence: "For the ascension of her soul, get vaccinated." The blunt message was part of a public health campaign directed at Israel's 1.2 million Ultra-Orthodox Jews, the group that was the most affected by the virus and condemned by a great many people for exacerbating the pandemic by flouting lockdown rules. The percentage of infections within the *Haredim*, as they are called in Israel, dropped precipitously below the national average after most of them began receiving doses of the BNT162b vaccine. The success was credited to a decree from the *Haredim*'s leading rabbis, who tend to have more clouts in their communities than the State of Israel itself. They could act as change agents and promote vaccination as Israel launched its national rollout in late December 2020.[151]

At the onset of the national rollout, Ultra-Orthodox healthcare workers and grassroots leaders voiced concerns that a significant minority within their community vehemently refused to heed their guidance. They were skeptical of the vaccine for the whole population because of anti-vaccine sentiments—which had already been expressed by leading Ultra-Orthodox rabbis during previous pandemics—and anxiety about the pace at which the vaccines were released and the politicization of COVID-19.[152] Spurning secular society, many Ultra-Orthodox Jews were reluctant to acquiring information about the virus, unlike other Israelis who were keeping abreast with the pandemic through television, newspapers, and the internet.[153]

As Israel experienced its third nationwide lockdown in the spring of 2021, social media were replete by photos of black-clad men shamelessly crowding schools, weddings, and other public venues, including a 20,000 gathering at a Jerusalem funeral of a prominent rabbi. Secular critics pigeonholed the Ultra-Orthodox as the ultimate superspreaders, a hurdle to the country's mission to vaccinate its way out of COVID-19.[154] The *Haredim* leaders' decision to act as change agents was a turning point for a community that was already wrecked by the virus. In fact, by February 2021, at least 1% of the Ultra-Orthodox Jews above the age of 60 had died of the virus—a rate that was nearly six times higher than their non-Orthodox counterparts. The *Haredim*, about 12% of Israel's 9.3 million population, comprised 28% of the recorded 800,000 COVID-19 cases, as per Eran Segal, data scientist at the Weizmann Institute of Science.[155]

Arab Communities in Israel

The differences between Israel's successful vaccination campaign within its own population and the dearth of vaccines for Palestinians in the occupied territories drew reproach from the United Nations and human rights organizations, which exposed the inequities between groups in getting access to vaccines. Critics insisted that Israel had the duty to vaccinate Palestinians, whereas Israel argued that, according to interim peace agreements, the State was not responsible to do so. Israel's vaccination campaign, however, included its own Palestinian population.[156] Both Israeli citizens of any background and Palestinian residents in East Jerusalem were qualified for the vaccine, with residents older than 60, healthcare professionals, and the medically vulnerable being prioritized. On the other hand, approximately five million Palestinians in the West Bank and the Gaza Strip (outside Israeli control) did not qualify because their healthcare system falls under the umbrella of the Palestinian Authority per the Oslo Accords.[157] Still, by late March 2021, Israel vaccinated over 100,000 Palestinians who crossed the border daily as laborers.[158]

By March 2021, over 60% of Arab Israelis had been administered at least one shot of the vaccine. Roughly 68% of Arab Israelis aged 16 and older had either received at least one dose or recovered from COVID-19, in comparison to 84% of the nation as a whole. Healthcare officials blame the diffusion of rumors on social media for the low vaccination rate among Arab Israelis. Approximately 60% of Israel's Bedouin people—some 175,000 of them—reside in unrecognized townships. Largely disconnected from services like running water and electricity, their settlements have constituted a bone of contention. The Israeli authorities, which consider those townships unlawful, want to relocate the Bedouin to planned towns with utilities. Yet, the Bedouin maintain that they have the right to live where they are.[159]

COUNTERCAMPAIGN: ANTI-VAXXERS

Misinformation is an offsetting pool of confusion against legitimate information. Conspiracy theories are effective because they provide solace during periods of uncertainty and anxiety. Their messaging centers on basic emotions and values, and warps the mental cues that we use to determine whether the source is reliable. The most widespread and detrimental conspiracy theories tend to include ounces of truth. Now, who benefits from misinformation? Claire Wardle, cofounder and director of FirstDraft News, a program to combat misinformation, lists three reasons: financial gain, political gain, and experimental manipulation. The anti-vaccination movement is a good example of the first: data from the Centre for Countering Digital Hate reveals that wellness and nutritional supplement corporations are huge supporters of anti-vaccination campaigns. These corporations make colossal profits based on these. Of equal significance is that anti-vaccination messages reached close to 60 million online followers and were purposely retained by social media moguls, which generated cumulative advertising proceeds of $1 billion.[160]

Anti-Vaxxers

Anti-vaxxers are people who oppose the use of vaccines for a multitude of reasons. With the popularity of anti-vaxxers' rhetoric towards the COVID-19 vaccine, the mission of certain vaccination campaigns was to curtail the spread of misinformation through specific measures (e.g., penalties or interventions from companies). Less emphasis was laid on tackling the underlying problems of the anti-vaxxer community.[161] In spite of clinical trial data confirming that the Pfizer and Moderna vaccines were safe and effective, by December 2020, less than 50% of US adults surveyed said that they would get vaccinated, according to a study by the CDC.[162] By late April 2021, the number of US anti-vaxxers decreased to 26%, according to a CNN poll.[163] Arguments that human beings have freedom of choice mirror suspicion of the medical community. Although many subpopulations express mistrust in general, the perspectives of African Americans, in particular, are crucial to consider as an issue of health equity. Early data from cities and states exposed the disproportionate infliction of COVID-19 on African–American communities. Studies have established a link between suspicion of the healthcare system and fears of getting treatment for a certain number of African Americans. This link is rooted in both historical and present-day disparities in healthcare.[164] In Belgium, authorities observed a resistance to vaccinations within the country's French-speaking population.[165]

The Role of Social Media

Largely influenced by anti-vaxxers, social media has posed significant problems to the diffusion of truthful or useful information on vaccinations. As such, on anti-vaxxer platforms, whether in person on or online, misinformation on the side effects of vaccinations being associated with autism and toxins in the vaccines themselves is magnified by so-called documented reports of side effects—e.g., like cases of narcolepsy after receiving doses of the H1N1 vaccine.[166] Upon examining the history of vaccinations in the United States and the United Kingdom, it is obvious that certain media platforms have contributed to vaccination scares and keeping them alive, even despite ascertained evidence that vaccines are safe and effective. Numerous scientific studies have established the toxic influence of media-based controversies on vaccine administration.[167]

Besides traditional media, social media provides an opportunity for energetic anti-vaccination activists to disseminate their message.[168] Many believe that the ubiquity of anti-vaccination content on the web results in massive and quicker propagation of rumors, myths, and erroneous beliefs regarding vaccines, all of which have produced negative effects on vaccine uptake.[169] Even though healthcare professionals are often consulted by most people with health concerns, social media remains an essential source of information for them.[170] With Web 2.0 software and operations which enable users to post and share content via social networking sites (e.g., Facebook, Twitter, and YouTube), anyone can share his or her own experiences of vaccination. These narratives provide a new angle to health information; an individual and embodied perspective of vaccine-preventable illnesses, vaccines, and their potentially negative corollaries.[171] Indeed, studies evaluating the content of websites and social media posts on vaccinations demonstrate that the quality of information varies and that inaccurate or negative content is prevalent.[172]

Taken as a whole, the COVID-19 infodemic has posed a serious challenge because of the extensive use of social media and communication technologies. The coronavirus was subject to a higher social media infodemic than past viral outbreaks.[173] The expansion of social media is certainly a promising field, potentially able to raise the level of clarity and fairness in acquiring scientific data. At the same time, it has drastically raised the level of credibility of personal viewpoints and beliefs, and caused them to spread like wildfire. Some perceive it as an assault on democracy. Unlike facts, viewpoints and beliefs should have no place in the realm of vaccination. The availability and exchange of scientific data have two important aspects: (1) The presence or absence of filters that can improve the reliability of information and (2) personal duty of making information public and diffusing. Both aspects should be heeded seriously by all members of the scientific community.[174] Lastly, information overload can overpower even experienced healthcare professionals, which does not facilitate the discernment of opinions from evidence-based facts and expert conjecture. Rapid and widespread dissemination of scientific and health-related information outside expert circles, especially before it has been confirmed as true, is outright dangerous, especially during a pandemic.[175]

NOTES

1. Ali Farazmand and Hasan Danaeefard, "Iranian Government's Responses to the Coronavirus Pandemic (COVID-19): An Empirical Analysis," *International Journal of Public Administration* 44, no. 11 (2021): 931–42. https://doi.org/10.1080/01900692.2021.1903926.

2. Laena Maunula, "The Pandemic Subject: Canadian Pandemic Plans and Communicating with the Public about an Influenza Pandemic," *Healthcare Policy* 9 (2013): 14–25. https://doi.org/10.12927/hcpol.2013.23587.

3. Adam Kamradt-Scott, *Managing Global Health Security: The World Health Organization and Disease Outbreak Control* (New York: Palgrave Macmillan, 2015); World Health Organization, *Coronavirus Disease: Infection Prevention and Control of Epidemic and Pandemic* (Geneva: World Health Organization, 2020).

4. Joseph P. Byrne and Jo N. Hays, *Epidemics and Pandemics: From Ancient Plagues to Modern-Day Threats* (Westport, CT: Greenwood, 2021); Jonathan D. Quick and Bronwyn Fryer, *The End of Epidemics: The Looming Threat to Humanity and How to Stop It* (New York: St. Martin's Press, 2018).

5. Kathleen Ambrose and Jonathan Matusitz, "Understanding Ebola in West Africa: Applying Human Ecology Theory," *Global Social Welfare* 5, no. 2 (2018): 109–16. https://doi.org/10.1007/s40609-017-0081-9.

6. Paul Siu Fai Yip, Bing Kwan So, Ichiro Kawachi, and Yi Zhang, "A Markov Chain Model for Studying Suicide Dynamics: An Illustration of the Rose Theorem," *BMC Public Health* 14 (2014): Article 625. https://doi.org/10.1186.

7. Meera Senthilingam, *Outbreaks and Epidemics: Battling Infection from Measles to Coronavirus* (London: Icon Books, 2020); Moyses Szklo and F. Javier Nieto, *Epidemiology: Beyond the Basics* (4th Ed.) (Burlington, MA: Jones & Bartlett, 2018).

8. Levent Akin and Mustafa Gökhan Gözel, "Understanding Dynamics of Pandemics," *Turkish Journal of Medical Sciences* 50 (2020): 515–9. https://doi.org/10.3906/sag-2004-133.

9. Emily P. Courtney, Jamie L. Goldenberg, and Patrick Boyd, "The Contagion of Mortality: A Terror Management Health Model for Pandemics," *British Journal of Social Psychology* 59, no. 3 (2020): 607–17. https://doi.org/10.1111/bjso.12392.

10. Yue Zhou, Jingwei Chi, Wenshan Lv, and Yangang Wang, "Obesity and Diabetes as High-Risk Factors for Severe Coronavirus Disease 2019 (Covid-19)," *Diabetes Metabolism Research and Reviews* 37, no. 2 (2021): e3377. https://doi.org/10.1002/dmrr.3377.

11. Daniel P. Oran and Eric J. Topol, "The Proportion of SARS-CoV-2 Infections That Are Asymptomatic: A Systematic Review," *Annals of Internal Medicine* (2021). https://doi.org/10.7326/M20-6976.

12. *Deutsche Welle*, "Peru Battles World's Highest Per Capita COVID Death Rate," *Deutsche Welle* (2021). Retrieved on October 31, 2021 from https://www.dw.com/en/peru-battles-worlds-highest-per-capita-covid-death-rate/av-58179128; available at https://www.statista.com/statistics/1104709/coronavirus-deaths-worldwide-per-million-inhabitants.

13. Rachel E. Menzies and Ross G. Menzies, "Death Anxiety in the Time of COVID-19: Theoretical Explanations and Clinical Implications," *The Cognitive Behaviour Therapist* 13, no. 19 (2020): 1–11. https://doi.org/10.1017/S1754470X20000215.

14. Tarun Bastiampillai, Stephen Allison, Jeffrey C. L. Looi, Julio Licinio, Ma-Li Wong, and Seth W. Perry, "The COVID-19 Pandemic and Epidemiologic Insights from Recession-Related Suicide Mortality," *Molecular Psychiatry* 25 (2020): 3445–7. https://doi.org/10.1038/s41380-020-00875-4.

15. International Monetary Fund, *World Economic Outlook, April 2020: The Great Lockdown* (Washington, DC: International Monetary Fund, 2020).

16. Dawn Gilbertson, "'Do Not Travel' List: The US State Department Is Raising the Alert Level for Most Countries Due to COVID," *USA Today* (April 20, 2021). Retrieved on April 20, 2021 from https://eu.usatoday.com/story/travel/news/2021/04/19/do-not-travel-list-covid-us-state-department-travel-warnings/7295408002.

17. Bastiampillai, Allison, Looi, Licinio, Wong, and Perry, "The COVID-19 Pandemic," 3445–7.

18. Cited in Debanjan Banerjee, Jagannatha Rao Kosagisharaf, and T. S. Sathyanarayana Rao, "'The Dual Pandemic' of Suicide and COVID-19: A Biopsychosocial Narrative of Risks and Prevention," *Psychiatry Research* 295 (2021). https://doi.org/10.1016/j.psychres.2020.113577.

19. Émile Durkheim, *Suicide: A Study in Sociology* (Milton Park, England: Routledge & Kegan Paul, 1897/1952).

20. Banerjee, Kosagisharaf, and Rao, "'The Dual Pandemic'".

21. Takanao Tanaka and Shohei Okamoto, "Increase in Suicide Following an Initial Decline during the COVID-19 Pandemic in Japan," *Nature Human Behaviour* 5 (2021): 229–38. https://doi.org/10.1038/s41562-020-01042-z.

22. William Wan, "For Months, He Helped His Son Keep Suicidal Thoughts at Bay. Then Came the Pandemic," *The Washington Post* (November 23, 2020): A1. Retrieved on April 8, 2021 from https://www.washingtonpost.com/health/2020/11/23/covid-pandemic-rise-suicides.

23. Available at https://www.publichealth.columbia.edu/public-health-now/news/study-shows-uptick-us-alcohol-beverage-sales-during-covid-19-pandemic.

24. Cited in Alison Knopf, "More Women with Children Drinking to Cope during Pandemic," *Journal of Child and Adolescent Psychopharmacology* 23, no. 10 (2021): 1–4. https://doi.org/10.1002/cpu.30613.

25. World Health Organization, *Risk Communication* (Geneva: World Health Organization, 2021).

26. Daniel Catalán-Matamoros, "The Role of Mass Media Communication in Public Health," in *Health Management: Different Approaches and Solutions*, ed. Krzysztof Smigorski (Rijeka, Croatia: InTech, 2011): 399–414.

27. E. M. Abdelwhab and H. M. Hafez, "An Overview of the Epidemic of Highly Pathogenic H5N1 Avian Influenza Virus in Egypt: Epidemiology and Control Challenges," *Epidemiology & Infection* 139, no. 5 (2011): 647–57. https://doi.org/10.1017/S0950268810003122.

28. Elaine Vaughan and Timothy Tinker, "Effective Health Risk Communication about Pandemic Influenza for Vulnerable Populations," *American Journal of Public Health* 99, no. 2 (2009): 324–32. https://doi.org/10.2105/AJPH.2009.162537.

29. Atefeh Vaezi and Shaghayegh Haghjooy Javanmard, "Infodemic and Risk Communication in the Era of CoV-19," *Advanced Biomedical Research* 9 (2020): 10–2. https://doi.org/10.4103/abr.abr_47_20.

30. Jonathan Matusitz, *Terrorism & Communication: A Critical Introduction* (Thousand Oaks, CA: Sage, 2013).

31. W. Timothy Coombs, *Ongoing Crisis Communication: Planning, Managing, and Responding* (Thousand Oaks, CA: Sage, 2007).

32. Matusitz, *Terrorism & Communication*, 407.

33. Carl Botan, "Ethics in Strategic Communication Campaigns: The Case for a New Approach to Public Relations," *The Journal of Business Communication* 34, no. 2 (1997): 188–202. https://doi.org/10.1177/002194369703400205.

34. Sara LaBelle and Jennifer H. Waldeck, *Strategic Communication for Organizations* (Berkeley, CA: University of California Press, 2020).

35. Botan, "Ethics in Strategic Communication Campaigns," 188–202.

36. J. M. Brown and E. A. Campbell, "Risk Communication: Some Underlying Principles," *Journal of Environmental Studies* 38, no. 4 (1991): 297–303. https://doi.org/10.1080/00207239108710674.

37. Ricardo J. Wray, Matthew W. Kreuter, Heather Jacobsen, Bruce Clements, and R. Gregory Evans, "Theoretical Perspectives on Public Communication Preparedness for Terrorist Attacks," *Family and Community Health* 27, no. 3 (2004): 232–41.

38. Matusitz, *Terrorism & Communication*, 407.

39. World Health Organization, *Infodemic* (Geneva: World Health Organization, 2021).

40. Ibid.

41. Helena Legido-Quigley, Nima Asgari, Yik Ying Teo, Gabriel M. Leung, Hitoshi Oshitani, Keiji Fukuda, Alex R. Cook, Li Yang Hsu, Kenji Shibuya, and David Heymann, "Are High-Performing Health Systems Resilient against the COVID-19 Epidemic?" *The Lancet* 395, no. 10227 (2020): 848–50. https://doi.org/10.1016/S0140-6736(20)30551-1.

42. Russell M. Viner, Simon J. Russell, Helen Croker, Jessica Packer, Joseph Ward, Claire Stansfield, Oliver Mytton, Chris Bonell, and Robert Booy, "School Closure and Management Practices during Coronavirus Outbreaks Including COVID-19: A Rapid Systematic Review," *The Lancet* 4, no. 5 (2020): 397–404. https://doi.org/10.1016/S2352-4642(20)30095-X.

43. Kiesha Prem, Yang Liu, Timothy W. Russell, Adam J. Kucharski, Rosalind M. Eggo, Nicholas Davies, Centre for the Mathematical Modelling of Infectious Diseases COVID-19 Working Group, Mark Jit, and Petra Klepac, "The Effect of Control Strategies to Reduce Social Mixing on Outcomes of the COVID-19 Epidemic in Wuhan, China: A Modelling Study," *The Lancet* 5, no. 5 (2020): E261-70. https://doi.org/10.1016/S2468-2667(20)30073-6.

44. Rebecca Webster, Sam Brooks, Louise Smith, Lisa Woodland, Simon Wessely, and G. James Rubin, "How to Improve Adherence with Quarantine: Rapid Review of the Evidence," *Public Health* 182 (2020): 163–9. https://doi.org/10.1016/j.puhe.2020.03.007.

45. See Nour Mheidly and Jawad Fares, "Leveraging Media and Health Communication Strategies to Overcome the COVID-19 Infodemic," *Journal of Public Health Policy* 41

(2020): 410–20. https://doi.org/10.1057/s41271-020-00247-w; John Zarocostas, "How to Fight an Infodemic," *The Lancet* 395, no. 10225 (2020): 676. https://doi.org/10.1016/S0140-6736(20)30461-X.

46. Daniel H. Solomon, Richard Bucala, Mariana J. Kaplan, and Peter A. Nigrovic, "The 'Infodemic' of COVID-19," *Arthritis & Rheumatology* 72, no. 11 (2020): 1806-8. https://doi.org/10.1002/art.41468.

47. Chris Bonell, Susan Michie, Stephen Reicher, Robert West, Laura Bear, Lucy Yardley, Val Curtis, Richard Amlôt, and G. James Rubin, "Harnessing Behavioural Science in Public Health Campaigns to Maintain 'Social Distancing' in Response to the COVID-19 Pandemic: Key Principles," *Journal of Epidemiology and Community Health* 74, no. 8 (2020): 617–9. https://doi.org/10.1136/jech-2020-214290.

48. Susan Michie, Maartje M. van Stralen, and Robert West, "The Behaviour Change Wheel: A New Method for Characterising and Designing Behaviour Change Interventions," *Implementation Science* 6 (2011): Article 42. https://doi.org/10.1186/1748-5908-6-42.

49. Bonell, Michie, Reicher, West, Bear, Yardley, Curtis, Amlôt, and Rubin, "Harnessing Behavioural Science," 617.

50. Rena Brar Prayaga and Ram S. Prayaga, "Mobile Fotonovelas within a Text Message Outreach: An Innovative Tool to Build Health Literacy and Influence Behaviors in Response to the COVID-19 Pandemic," *JMIR Mhealth Uhealth* 8, no. 8 (2020). https://doi.org/10.2196/19529.

51. Bonell, Michie, Reicher, West, Bear, Yardley, Curtis, Amlôt, and Rubin, "Harnessing Behavioural Science," 617.

52. Viktor Stojkoski, Zoran Utkovski, Petar Jolakoski, Dragan Tevdovski, and Ljupco Kocarev, "The Socio-Economic Determinants of the Coronavirus Disease (COVID-19) Pandemic," *medRxiv* (2020): 10–21. https://doi.org/10.1101/2020.04.15.20066068.

53. Joop van der Pligt, "Risk Perception and Self-Protective Behavior," *European Psychologist* 1, no. 1 (1996): 34–43. https://doi.org/10.1027/1016-9040.1.1.34.

54. Michael A. Hogg, "Influence and Leadership," in *Handbook of Social Psychology*, ed. Susan T. Fiske, Daniel T. Gilbert, and Gardner Lindzey (Hoboken, NJ: Wiley, 2010): 1166–207.

55. Matthew W. Kreuter and Stephanie M. McClure, "The Role of Culture in Health Communication," *Annual Review of Public Health* 25 (2004): 439–55. https://doi.org/101146/annurevpublhealth25101802123000.

56. Geoff Dench, Kate Gavron, and Michael Young, *The New East End: Kinship, Race and Conflict* (London: Profile Books, 2006).

57. Roy William Batterham, Melanie Hawkins, P. A. Collins, Rachelle Buchbinder, and Richard H. Osborne, "Health Literacy: Applying Current Concepts to Improve Health Services and Reduce Health Inequalities," *Public Health* 132 (2016): 3–12. https://doi.org/10.1016/j.puhe.2016.01.001.

58. Sarah-Jayne Blakemore, "Avoiding Social Risk in Adolescence," *Current Directions in Psychological Science* 27, no. 2 (2018): 116–22. https://doi.org/10.1177/0963721417738144.

59. Bonell, Michie, Reicher, West, Bear, Yardley, Curtis, Amlôt, and Rubin, "Harnessing Behavioural Science," 618.

60. Robert B. Cialdini, Linda J. Demaine, Brad J. Sagarin, Daniel W. Barrett, Kelton Rhoads, and Patricia L. Winter, "Managing Social Norms for Persuasive Impact," *Social Influence* 1, no. 1 (2006): 3–15. https://doi.org/10.1080/15534510500181459.

61. P. Wesley Schultz, Jessica M. Nolan, Robert B. Cialdini, Noah J. Goldstein, and Vladas Griskevicius, "The Constructive, Destructive, and Reconstructive Power of Social Norms," *Psychological Science* 18, no. 5 (2007): 429–34. https://doi.org/10.1111/j.1467-9280.2007.01917.x.

62. Matthew W. Seeger, "Best Practices in Crisis Communication: An Expert Panel Process," *Journal of Applied Communication Research* 34, no. 3 (2006): 232–44. https://doi.org/10.1080/00909880600769944.

63. Val Curtis, *Don't Look, Don't Touch, the Science behind Revulsion* (New York: Oxford University Press, 2013).

64. Jonathan Haidt, *The Righteous Mind: Why Good People Are Divided by Politics and Religion* (New York: Pantheon, 2012).

65. Seeger, "Best Practices in Crisis Communication," 235–9.

66. Magda Osman, "An Evaluation of Dual-Process Theories of Reasoning," *Psychonomic Bulletin & Review* 11 (2004): 988–1010. https://doi.org/10.3758/BF03196730.

67. Bonell, Michie, Reicher, West, Bear, Yardley, Curtis, Amlôt, and Rubin, "Harnessing Behavioural Science," 618.

68. Daniel Balliet, Laetitia B. Mulder, and Paul A. M. Van Lange, "Reward, Punishment, and Cooperation: A Meta-Analysis," *Psychological Bulletin* 137, no. 4 (2011): 594–615. https://doi.org/10.1037/a0023489.

69. Karen Glanz and Donald B. Bishop, "The Role of Behavioral Science Theory in Development and Implementation of Public Health Interventions," *Annual Review of Public Health* 31 (2010): 399–418. https://doi.org/10.1146/annurev.publhealth.012809.103604.

70. Michael Marmot, *The Marmot Review. Strategic Review of Health Inequalities in England Post-2010* (London: The Marmot Review, 2010).

71. Bonell, Michie, Reicher, West, Bear, Yardley, Curtis, Amlôt, and Rubin, "Harnessing Behavioural Science," 618.

72. Ibid, 618.

73. Chris Bonell, Farah Jamal, G. J. Melendez-Torres, and Steven Cummins, "'Dark Logic': Theorising the Harmful Consequences of Public Health Interventions," *Journal of Epidemiology and Community Health* 69, no. 1 (2015): 95–8. http://dx.doi.org/10.1136/jech-2014-204671.

74. John Drury, Holly Carter, Chris Cocking, Evangelos Ntontis, Selin Tekin Guven, and Richard Amlôt, "Facilitating Collective Psychosocial Resilience in the Public in Emergencies: Twelve Recommendations Based on the Social Identity Approach," *Frontiers in Pubic Health* 7 (2019): Article 141. https://doi.org/10.3389/fpubh.2019.00141.

75. Bonell, Michie, Reicher, West, Bear, Yardley, Curtis, Amlôt, and Rubin, "Harnessing Behavioural Science," 618.

76. Seeger, "Best Practices in Crisis Communication," 235–9.

77. Trang H. D. Nguyen and Dahn C. Vu, "Summary of the COVID–19 Outbreak in Vietnam—Lessons and Suggestions," *Travel Medicine and Infectious Disease* 37 (2020): 10–21. https://doi.org/10.1016/j.tmaid.2020.101651.

78. Le Van Tan, "COVID-19 Control in Vietnam," *Nature Immunology* 22 (2021): 261. https://doi.org/10.1038/s41590-021-00882-9.

79. Ibid, 261.

80. Nguyen and Vu, "Summary of the COVID-19 Outbreak in Vietnam," 10–2.

81. Toan Luu Duc Huynh, "The COVID-19 Containment in Vietnam: What Are We Doing?" *Journal of Global Health* 10, no. 1 (2020): 10–7. https://doi.org/10.7189/jogh.10.010338.

82. Thanh Ha Le and Thi Phuong Thao Tran, "Alert for COVID-19 Second Wave: A Lesson from Vietnam," *Journal of Global Health* 11 (2021). https://doi.org/10.7189/jogh.11.03012.

83. Available at https://www.youtube.com/watch?v=BtulL3oArQw.

84. Huynh, "The COVID-19 Containment in Vietnam," 10–7.

85. Sana Fazili, "Vietnam Is Dancing to the Tunes of Coronavirus Song to Spread Awareness about the Global Menace," *News18* (March 4, 2020). Retrieved on April 6, 2021 from https://www.news18.com/news/buzz/vietnam-is-dancing-to-the-tunes-of-corona virus-song-to-spread-awareness-about-the-global-menace-2525081.html.

86. Gautam Sunder, "Vietnamese Song 'Jealous Coronavirus' Created to Spread Awareness on COVID-19 Goes Viral," *The Hindu Times* (March 4, 2020): A1. Retrieved on April 6, 2021 from https://www.thehindu.com/entertainment/vietnamese-song-jealous-corona virus-created-to-spead-awareness-on-covid-19-goes-viral/article30981270.ece.

87. Ibid, A1.

88. Albert Bandura, *Social Foundations of Thought and Action: A Social Cognitive Theory* (Englewood Cliffs, NJ: Prentice Hall, 1986).

89. Albert Bandura, "Social Cognitive Theory of Mass Communication," in *Media Effects: Advances in Theory and Research*, ed. Jennings Bryant and Mary Beth Oliver (New York: Routledge, 2008): 94–124.

90. Albert Bandura, *Self-Efficacy: The Exercise of Control* (New York: W.H. Freeman, 1997).

91. Tahereh Shamizadeh, Leila Jahangiry, Parvin Sarbakhsh, and Koen Ponnet, "Social Cognitive Theory-Based Intervention to Promote Physical Activity among Prediabetic Rural People: A Cluster Randomized Controlled Trial," *Trials* 20, no. 98 (2019): 1–10. https://doi.org/10.1186/s13063-019-3220-z.

92. Albert Bandura, "Social Cognitive Theory of Self-Regulation," *Organizational Behavior and Human Decision Processes* 50, no. 2 (1991): 248–87. https://doi.org/10.1016/0749-5978(91)90022-L; Albert Bandura, "Health Promotion from the Perspective of Social Cognitive Theory," *Psychology & Health* 13, no. 4 (1998): 623–49. https://doi.org/10.1080/08870449808407422.

93. Chukwuemeka Vincent Okpara, Anibueze U. Anselm, Talabi Olajide Felix, Adelabu Omowale, and Verlumun Celestine Gever, "The Moderating Role of Colour in Modelling the Effectiveness of COVID-19 YouTube Animated Cartoons on the Health Behaviour of Social Media Users in Nigeria," *Health Promotion International* (2021). https://doi.org/10.1093/heapro/daab001.

94. Linus Abraham, "Effectiveness of Cartoons as a Uniquely Visual Medium for Orienting Social Issues," *Journalism & Communication Monographs* 11, no. 2 (2009): 118–65. https://doi.org/10.1177/152263790901100202.

95. Okpara, Anselm, Felix, Omowale, and Gever, "The Moderating Role of Colour".

96. Albert Bandura, "Social Cognitive Theory: An Agentic Perspective," *Annual Review of Psychology* 52 (2001): 1–26. https://doi.org/10.1146/annurev.psych.52.1.1.

97. Okpara, Anselm, Felix, Omowale, and Gever, "The Moderating Role of Colour".

98. Maurizin Trevisan, Linh Cu Le, and Anh Vu Le, "The COVID-19 Pandemic: A View from Vietnam," *American Journal of Public Health* 110, no. 8 (2020): 1153–3. 1 https://doi.org/10.2105/AJPH.2020.305751.

99. Bui Thi Thu Ha, La Ngoc Quang, Tolib Mirzoev, Nguyen Trong Tai, Pham Quang Thai, and Phung Cong Dinh, "Combating the COVID-19 Epidemic: Experiences from Vietnam," *International Journal of Environmental Research and Public Health* 17 (2020): 10–21. https://doi.org/10.3390/ijerph17093125.

100. *Channel News Asia*, "Vietnam's COVID-19 Pandemic Response Leader Sworn in as President," *Channel News Asia* (April 5, 2021). Retrieved on April 7, 2021 from https://www.channelnewsasia.com/news/asia/covid-19-vietnam-pandemic-response-leader-sworn-in-president-14559304.

101. Huynh, "The COVID-19 Containment in Vietnam," 10–7.

102. Tan, "COVID-19 Control in Vietnam," 261.

103. Vuong Minh Nong, Quyen Le Thi Nguyen, Tra Thu Doan, Thanh Van Do, Tuan Quang Nguyen, Co Xuan Dao, Trang Huyen Thi Nguyen, and Cuong Duy Do, "The Second Wave of COVID-19 in a Tourist Hotspot in Vietnam," *Journal of Travel Medicine* 28, no. 2 (2021). https://doi.org/10.1093/jtm/taaa174.

104. Ha, Quang, Mirzoev, Tai, Thai, and Dinh, "Combating the COVID-19 Epidemic: Experiences from Vietnam," 10–7.

105. Huynh, "The COVID-19 Containment in Vietnam," 10–7.

106. Giao Huynh, Thi Ngoc Han Nguyen, Van Khanh Tran, Kim Ngan Vo, Van Tam Vo, and Le An Pham, "Knowledge and Attitude toward COVID-19 among Healthcare Workers at District 2 Hospital, Ho Chi Minh City," *Asian Pacific Journal of Tropical Medicine* 13, no. 6 (2020): 260–5.

107. Ha, Quang, Mirzoev, Tai, Thai, and Dinh, "Combating the COVID-19 Epidemic: Experiences from Vietnam," 10–7.

108. Ibid, 10–7.

109. Quang Van Nguyen, Dung Anh Cao, and Son Hong Nghiem, "Spread of COVID-19 and Policy Responses in Vietnam: An Overview," *International Journal of Infectious Diseases* 103 (2021): 157–61. https://doi.org/10.1016/j.ijid.2020.11.154.

110. Michael T. Osterholm, Nicholas S. Kelley, Alfred Sommer, Edward A. Belongia, "Efficacy and Effectiveness of Influenza Vaccines: A Systematic Review and Meta-Analysis," *The Lancet* 12, no. 1 (2012): 36–44. https://doi.org/10.1016/S1473-3099(11)70295-X.

111. Kayvon Modjarrad and Wayne C. Koff, *Human Vaccines: Emerging Technologies in Design and Development* (Cambridge, MA: Academic Press, 2016).

112. Tish Davidson, *Vaccines* (Westport, CT: Greenwood Publishing, 2017).

113. Cited in Elinor Aspegren and John Bacon, "US to Begin Talks on Worldwide Vaccine Distribution; India Infections and Deaths Mounting: Live COVID-19 Updates," *USA Today* (May 5, 2021). Retrieved on May 5, 2021 from https://www.usatoday.com/story/news/health/2021/05/05/covid-vaccine-distribution-variants-mask-cdc-biden-india/4947182001.

114. Alison Shepherd, "Covid-19: Chile Joins Top Five Countries in World Vaccination League," *The British Medical Journal* 372, no. 718 (2021). https://doi.org/10.1136/bmj.n718.

115. John Bartlett, "Chile Imposes Lockdowns to Fight New Covid Wave despite Vaccination Success," *The Guardian* (March 28, 2021): A1. Retrieved on April 12, 2021 from https://www.theguardian.com/global-development/2021/mar/28/chile-coronavirus-lockdowns-vaccination-success.

116. Ehud Rinott, Ilan Youngster, and Yair E. Lewis, "Reduction in COVID-19 Patients Requiring Mechanical Ventilation Following Implementation of a National COVID-19 Vaccination Program—Israel, December 2020–February 2021," *Morbidity and Mortality Weekly Report* 70, no. 9 (2021): 326–8. https://doi.org/10.15585/mmwr.mm7009e3.

117. Katie Atwell, Jeremy K. Ward, and Sian Tomkinson, "Manufacturing Consent for Vaccine Mandates: A Comparative Case Study of Communication Campaigns in France and Australia," *Frontiers in Communication* 6 (2021): 1–17. https://doi.org/10.3389/fcomm.2021.598602.

118. *Reuters*, "Christ the Redeemer Lit Up with Vaccine Message," *Reuters* (May 16, 2021). Retrieved on May 16, 2021 from https://www.yahoo.com/news/christ-redeemer-lit-vaccine-message153643061.html.

119. Kin On Kwok, Kin-Kit Li, Wan In WEI, Arthur Tang, Samuel Yeung Shan Wong, and Shui Shan Lee, "Influenza Vaccine Uptake, COVID-19 Vaccination Intention and Vaccine Hesitancy among Nurses: A Survey," *International Journal of Nursing Studies* 114 (2021). https://doi.org/10.1016/j.ijnurstu.2020.103854.

120. Kin On Kwok, Gabriel M. Leung, Wai Yee Lam, and Steven Riley, "Using Models to Identify Routes of Nosocomial Infection: A Large Hospital Outbreak of SARS in Hong Kong," *Proceedings of the Royal Society B* 274 (2007): 611–8. https://doi.org/10.1098/rspb.2006.0026.

121. Edward S. Herman and Noam Chomsky, *Manufacturing Consent* (New York: Pantheon Books, 1988): 306.

122. Charles Allan McCoy, "Adapting Coercion: How Three Industrialized Nations Manufacture Vaccination Compliance," *Journal of Health Politics, Policy and Law* 44, no. 6 (2019): 823–54. https://doi.org/10.1215/03616878-7785775.

123. Dan M. Kahan, "CCP Risk Perception Studies Report No. 17," *Yale Law & Economics Research Paper* 491 (2014): 10–21. https://doi.org/10.2139/ssrn.2386034.

124. Sarah Schaffer DeRoo, Natalie J. Pudalov, and Linda Y. Fu, "Planning for a COVID-19 Vaccination Program," *Journal of the American Medical Association* 323, no. 24 (2020): 2458–9. http://doi.org/10.1001/jama.2020.8711.

125. Jerome Kim, Florian Marks, and John D. Clemens, "Looking beyond COVID-19 Vaccine Phase 3 Trials," *Nature Medicine* 27 (2021): 205–11. https://doi.org/10.1038/s41591-021-01230-y.

126. Nonie E. MacDonald and SAGE Working Group on Vaccine Hesitancy, "Vaccine Hesitancy: Definition, Scope and Determinants," *Vaccine* 33, no. 34 (2015): 4161–4. https://doi.org/10.1016/j.vaccine.2015.04.036.

127. Available at http://www.who.int/immunization/sage/sage_wg_vaccine_hesitancy_apr12/en.

128. Eve Dubé, Caroline Laberge, Maryse Guay, Paul Bramadat, Réal Roy, and Julie A. Bettinger, "Vaccine Hesitancy," *Human Vaccines & Immunotherapeutics* 9, no. 8 (2013): 1763–73. https://doi.org/10.4161/hv.24657.

129. World Health Organization, *SAGE Working Group Dealing with Vaccine Hesitancy* (Geneva: World Health Organization, 2015).

130. 13Helen Bedford, Katie Atwell, Margie Danchin, Helen Marshall, Paul Corben, and Julie Leask, "Vaccine Hesitancy, Refusal and Access Barriers: The Need for Clarity in Terminology," *Vaccine* 36, no. 44 (2018): 6556–8. https://doi.org/10.1016/j.vaccine.2017.08.004.

131. Cited in Atwell, Ward, and Tomkinson, "Manufacturing Consent for Vaccine Mandates," 1–17.

132. Kathryn Edwards and Jesse M. Hackell, "Committee on Infectious Diseases, the Committee on Practice and Ambulatory Medicine: Countering vaccine Hesitancy," *Pediatrics* 138, no. 3 (2016): 2016–46. https://doi.org/10.1542/peds.2016-2146.

133. Linda Y. Fu, Rachel Haimowitz, and Danielle Thompson, "Community Members Trusted by African American Parents for Vaccine Advice," *Human Vaccines & Immunotherapeutics* 15, no. 7 (2019): 1715–22. https://doi.org/10.1080/21645515.2019.1581553.

134. Rinott, Youngster, and Lewis, "Reduction in COVID-19 Patients," 326.

135. Smadar Shilo, Hagai Rossman, and Eran Segal, "Signals of Hope: Gauging the Impact of a Rapid National Vaccination Campaign," *Nature Reviews Immunology* 21 (2021): 198–9. https://doi.org/10.1038/s41577-021-00531-0.

136. Rinott, Youngster, and Lewis, "Reduction in COVID-19 Patients," 326.

137. Bruce Rosen, Sarah Dine, and Nadav Davidovitch, "Lessons In COVID-19 Vaccination from Israel," *Health Affairs* 41 (2021). https://doi.org/10.1377/hblog20210315.476220.

138. Bruce Rosen, Ruth Waitzberg, and Avi Israeli, "Israel's Rapid Rollout of Vaccinations for COVID-19," *Israel Journal of Health Policy Research* 10, no. 6 (2021): 1–14. https://doi.org/10.1186/s13584-021--00440-6.

139. Rosen, Dine, and Davidovitch, "Lessons In COVID-19 Vaccination from Israel".

140. Rosen, Waitzberg, and Israeli, "Israel's Rapid Rollout of Vaccinations for COVID-19," 1–14.

141. Nathan Jeffay, "Vaccines Shown to Protect even Those Who Don't Get Them—Israeli Study," *The Times of Israel* (April 5, 2021): A1. Retrieved on April 7, 2021 from https://www.timesofisrael.com/hope-for-herd-immunity-vaccines-shown-to-protect-israelis-who-dont-get-them.

142. Oren Milman, Idan Yelin, Noga Aharony, Rachel Katz, Esma Herzel, Amir Ben-Tov, Jacob Kuint, Sivan Gazit, Gabriel Chodick, Tal Patalon, and Roy Kishony, "SARS-CoV-2 Infection Risk among Unvaccinated Is Negatively Associated with Community-Level Vaccination Rates," *medRxiv* (March 31, 2021). https://doi.org/10.1101/2021.03.26.21254394.

143. Miriam Fauzia, "Fact Check: Israel Launching 'Green Pass' for Citizens Vaccinated against COVID-19," *USA Today* (March 2, 2021): A1. Retrieved on April 7, 2021 from https://www.usatoday.com/story/news/factcheck/2021/03/02/fact-check-israel-launching-green-pass-covid-19-vaccinated/6871965002.

144. Jon Sharman, "What Is Israel's Green Pass System and How Does It Work?" *The Independent* (April 5, 2021): A1. Retrieved on April 7, 2021 from https://www.independent.co.uk/news/world/middle-east/israel-green-pass-covid-passport-england-b1826771.html.

145. Oliver Holmes and Quique Kierszenbaum, "'We're in a Really Good Place': Is Israel Nearing the Covid Endgame?" *The Guardian* (April 2, 2021): A1. Retrieved on April 7, 2021 from https://www.theguardian.com/world/2021/apr/02/really-good-place-israel-nearing-covid-endgame.

146. Rüdiger Schmitt-Beck, "Bandwagon Effect," in *The International Encyclopedia of Political Communication*, ed. Gianpietro Mazzoleni (Hoboken, NJ: Wiley, 2015).

147. Kim Cheng Patrick Low, *Successfully Negotiating in Asia* (New York: Springer, 2020).

148. Amiluhur Soeroso and Dewi Turgarini, "Culinary versus Gastronomy: *Argumentum Ad Populum* Elimination," *E-Journal of Tourism* 7, no. 2 (2020): 193–204.

149. Rosen, Waitzberg, and Israeli, "Israel's Rapid Rollout of Vaccinations for COVID-19," 1–14.

150. Available at https://healthmanagement.org/c/hospital/news/why-is-israels-vaccination-programme-so-successful.

151. Maayan Lubell, "Israel's Ultra-Orthodox Jews Get COVID Vaccine but Still Face Resentment," *Reuters* (March 12, 2021). Retrieved on April 7, 2021 from https://www.reuters.com/article/health-coronavirus-israel-ultraorthodox/israels-ultra-orthodox-jews-get-covid-vaccine-but-still-face-resentment-idUSKBN2B42FK.

152. Ben Sales, "Will Orthodox Jews Listen to Their Leaders Regarding Vaccination?" *Sun Sentinel* (December 21, 2020): A1. Retrieved on April 7, 2021 from https://www.sun-sentinel.com/florida-jewish-journal/fl-jj-orthodox-jews-listen-leaders-vaccination-20201221-wadoumejczbtxfbzbs3edvxi7e-story.html.

153. Lubell, "Israel's Ultra-Orthodox Jews".

154. Steve Hendrix and Shira Rubin, "Anger Grows at Israel's Ultra-Orthodox Virus Scofflaws, Threatening Rupture with Secular Jews," *The Washington Post* (February 9, 2021): A1. Retrieved on April 7, 2021 from https://www.washingtonpost.com/world/middle_east/israel-ultra-orthodox-religious-coronavirus/2021/02/08/306e894a-6702-11eb-bab8-707f8769d785_story.html.

155. Lubell, "Israel's Ultra-Orthodox Jews".

156. *Al Jazeera*, "PM Netanyahu Denies Failing to Vaccinate Israel's Arabs," *Al Jazeera* (March 4, 2021). Retrieved on April 7, 2021 from https://www.aljazeera.com/news/2021/3/4/netanyahu-slams-criticisms-of-coronavirus-vaccination-campaign.

157. Joshua Zitser, "Israel, the Palestinians, and the COVID-19 Vaccination Rollout: The Legal and Moral Obligations," *Business Insider* (January 10, 2021). Retrieved on April 7, 2021 from https://www.businessinsider.com/israel-palestine-and-covid-19-vaccines-legal-and-moral-obligations-2021-1.

158. Ilan Ben Zion, "Israelis Gather for Passover, Celebrating Freedom from Virus," *ABC News* (March 27, 2021). Retrieved on April 7, 2021 from https://abcnews.go.com/International/wireStory/israelis-gather-passover-celebrating-freedom-virus-76719679.

159. Aaron Boxerman, "Arab Israelis Fret over Lagging Vaccination Rates as Ramadan Approaches," *The Times of Israel* (March 8, 2021): A1. Retrieved on April 7, 2021 from https://www.timesofisrael.com/arab-israelis-fret-over-lagging-vaccination-rates-as-ramadan-approaches.

160. *The Lancet Infectious Diseases*, "The COVID-19 Infodemic," *The Lancet Infectious Diseases* 20, no. 8 (2020): 875. https://doi.org/10.1016/S1473--3099(20)30565-X.

161. Ramona Boodoosingh, Lawal Olatunde Olayemi, and Filipina Amosa-Lei Sam, "COVID-19 Vaccines: Getting Anti-Vaxxers Involved in the Discussion," *World Development* 136 (2020). https://doi.org/10.1016/j.worlddev.2020.105177.

162. Cited in Justin Tallis, "Biden's Next Fight: Anti-Vaxxers Jeopardize Plans to Protect US against Covid," *CNBC* (February 10, 2021). Retrieved on May 17, 2021 from https://www.cnbc.com/2021/02/10/biden-covid-vaccine-anti-vaxxers-us.html.

163. Jennifer Agiesta, "CNN Poll: About a Quarter of Adults Say They Won't Try to Get a Covid-19 Vaccine," *CNN* (April 29, 2021). Retrieved on May 17, 2021 from https://www.cnn.com/2021/04/29/politics/cnn-poll-covid-vaccines/index.html.

164. Clyde W. Yancy, "COVID-19 and African Americans," *Journal of the American Medical Association* 323, no. 19 (2020): 1891–2. https://doi.org/10.1001/jama.2020.6548.

165. Available at https://www.dw.com/en/covid-19-vaccine-skepticism-spreads-in-bel gium/av-56583311.

166. Boodoosingh, Olayemi, and Sam, "COVID-19 Vaccines".

167. Alan Smith, Joanne Yarwood, and David M. Salisbury, "Tracking Mothers' Attitudes to MMR Immunisation 1996–2006," *Vaccine* 25 (2007): 3996–4002. http://dx.doi. org/10.1016/j.vaccine.2007.02.071.

168. Holly O. Witteman and Brian J. Zikmund-Fisher, "The Defining Characteristics of Web 2.0 and Their Potential Influence in the Online Vaccination Debate," *Vaccine* 30, no. 25 (2012): 3734–40. http://dx.doi.org/10.1016/j.vaccine.2011.12.039.

169. For example, see Anna Kata, "Anti-Vaccine Activists, Web 2.0, and the Post-Modern Paradigm: An Overview of Tactics and Tropes Used Online by the Anti-Vaccination Movement," *Vaccine* 30, no. 25 (2012): 3778–89. http://dx.doi.org/10.1016/j.vaccine. 2011.11.112.

170. Cornelia Betsch, Noel T. Brewer, Pauline Brocard, Patrick Davies, Wolfgang Gaissmaier, Niels Haase, Julie Leask, Frank Renkewitz, Britta Renner, Valerie F. Reyna, Constanze Rossmann, Katharina Sachse, Alexander Schachinger, Michael Siegrist, and Marybelle Stryk, "Opportunities and Challenges of Web 2.0 for Vaccination Decisions," *Vaccine* 30, no. 25 (2012): 3727–33. http://dx.doi.org/10.1016/j.vaccine.2012.02.025.

171. Ibid, 3727–33.

172. Jennifer Keelan, Vera Pavri, Ravin Balakrishnan, and Kumanan Wilson, "An Analysis of the Human Papilloma Virus Vaccine Debate on MySpace Blogs," *Vaccine* 28 (2010): 1535–40. http://dx.doi.org/10.1016/j.vac-cine.2009.11.060.

173. Vaezi and Javanmard, "Infodemic and Risk Communication".

174. Daniele Orso, Nicola Federici, Roberto Copetti, Luigi Vetrugno, and Tiziana Bovea, "Infodemic and the Spread of Fake News in the COVID-19-Era," *European Journal of Emergency Medicine* 27, no. 5 (2020): 327–8. https://doi.org/10.1097/MEJ.00000000 00000713.

175. *The Lancet Infectious Diseases*, "The COVID-19 Infodemic," 875.

CHAPTER 8

Entertainment–Education, Digital Games, and Celebrity Campaigns

Can stories, entertainment, games, or even celebrities' involvement succeed where traditional public health campaigns have failed? The task of this chapter is to address this important question. To begin, an extensive review of the literature indicates that Entertainment–Education programming can be an effective method for spreading prosocial and health content. It is believed that, under certain circumstances, such programming is even more productive than conventional media-based persuasive messages.[1] Also referred to as **edutainment**, **Entertainment–Education (EE)** is a communication strategy that aspires to ease a social problem or educate the public through a customized type of entertainment. It is defined by a series of approaches and methodologies that seek to apply different levels of mass media to instill social and behavior change.[2] EE works by leveraging entertainment content to contribute to "the process of directed social change, which can occur at the level of an individual, community, or society" by manipulating attitudes, social norms, and behaviors as the public gets exposed to nondidactic entertainment.[3]

Popular entertainment programs like soap operas are the most famous forms of EE to induce social change.[4] **Soap operas** portray real-life circumstances like friendships, love affairs, and family life. A soap opera is a radio or TV series that often addresses domestic situations and includes melodrama, ensemble actors, and sentimentality.[5] Entertainment in a media narrative format—e.g., dramas and sitcoms—as opposed to informational programs provided by the mass media—e.g., public service announcements (PSAs) on TV—constitutes a type of EE. Whereas the latter is defined as the deliberate use of mass media to

Fundamentals of Public Communication Campaigns, First Edition. Jonathan Matusitz.
© 2022 John Wiley & Sons Ltd. Published 2022 by John Wiley & Sons Ltd.

advocate development goals; EE also uses productions with prosocial messages that do not necessarily have commercial objectives.[6]

In television shows like soap operas, EE characters act as people whose behavior should be emulated by others to show how a desired behavior is performed in a particular health context. Social cognitive theory (SCT), described in Chapter 7, reminds us how people directly learn healthy behaviors by observing and imitating other people's behaviors. EE models are considered positive as they increase self-efficacy for adopting the proposed health behavior which, it is hoped, results in behavior change. The central causal process, here, is self-efficacy, which negotiates the link between EE messages and recommended behavior changes.[7]

Behavioral and Social Change

EE should not be confused with a theory of communication. Rather, it is an approach to diffuse ideas that generate behavioral and social change.[8] It originates in oral and performing arts traditions that were already observed several millennia ago—e.g., morality accounts, religious storytelling, and the spoken word.[9] Today, we see EE in both fiction and nonfiction programs that come in many formats: local street theater, music, puppetry, competitions, radio, TV, social media, and video games. A classic example of EE is *Sesame Street*, an American educational children's TV series broadcast in more than 120 countries. As a matter of fact, EE has been effectively planned, implemented, and assessed in many nations around the world for both children and adults.[10]

In addition to including health and other educational messages into popular entertainment platforms, EE has the mission of positively impacting awareness, knowledge, attitudes, and behaviors.[11] It is agreed that strictly persuasive approaches to designing health messages are generally less effective.[12] In fact, traditional health campaigns have a more difficult time reaching at-risk populations. Research[13] indicates that overweight and obese Americans are less prone to eating in a healthy way and exercising until entertainment magazines and EE programs focus on desirable behaviors. And health fairs and news conferences are insufficient to convince people not to smoke. As Huang, Friedman, Lin, and Thrasher (2018)[14] explain, this is ineffective "because smokers perceive it as having little personal relevance." It should come to no surprise, then, that the EE approach is growing in esteem and recognition. Research affirms the success of EE and the importance of integrating educational content in entertaining content. As such, it results in more positive attitudes about condom use,[15] in more knowledge about breast cancer,[16] in proper decisions to have mammograms,[17] or in signing up to be a cornea donor.[18]

To achieve this, EE uses TV, radio, theater, books, magazines, and other conduits to change attitudes and behaviors in desirable ways by embedding persuasive content with respect to both individual and public health.[19] Going back to Albert Bandura's (1986)[20] SCT, theoretical notions like modeling and social learning help design storylines that effectively disseminate health messages, knowledge, and correct habits. Storytelling, in particular, can alter the social contexts that impact health. A dramatic storyline about an unwanted pregnancy in a well-liked TV series can engender conversations about contraceptives, instilling the approval of norms that facilitate and endorse the use of contraceptives.[21] In a nutshell, SCT highlights the routes by which role models, overtly demonstrated behaviors, and portrayals of reinforcement increase the impact of mediated messages.[22]

Social Impact Entertainment (SIE)

Social impact entertainment (SIE) is an alternative to conventional entertainment, like movies and television, that intends to create huge entertainment value to have an impact on social attitudes. SIE programming has the same objectives as EE, but the processes are different. SIE programming has gained popularity in the United States since the twenty-first century, with media studios and companies now running social impact departments and academic institutions to examine the value of mass media projects for social change.[23] Professionals in this domain are mostly producers and directors who hope to add a social element to their entertainment, unlike the domain of EE, which works in the opposite direction; EE is often born out of a social change directive and the entertainment part is then formed around it.[24] Unlike many other characteristics of mainstream entertainment, SIE wants to be scientific in its decision-making approaches.[25] SIE has been used for multiplatform communication plans to reach publics dispersed across the media landscape. Producers and directors can imaginatively integrate elements of a story on various platforms, thereby creating many entry points across a whole spectrum of channels.[26]

Case Studies

The advent of modern-day EE is often traced back to an Australian radio program called *The Lawsons* in the 1940s,[27] which was built to diffuse farming messages to, indirectly, help the country win World War II battles in the Asia-Pacific region. In the early 1950s, *The Archers*, a British radio soap opera, was inspired by *The Lawsons* and also focused on agricultural messages, rural issues, and farming techniques.[28] Having broadcast about 20,000 episodes by late 2021, it is the longest-running drama in the world.[29] In the wake of the success of this program in Great Britain, a series of studies conducted in the 1950s and 1960s affirmed that this genre of "farm radio forums" contributed to the transferring of agricultural knowledge to farmers in remote regions like Ghana, India, Benin, and Thailand.[30]

Proof that EE can convey knowledge about agricultural techniques was manifest in more recent initiatives that taught Vietnamese farmers to distinguish between harmful and harmless insects and the appropriate times for using fertilizer.[31] EE studies from a range of disciplines widened the spectrum of programs under study to those with significant emphases beyond agriculture. The purpose was to demonstrate that educational media programs could support knowledge of mathematics and grammar,[32] health and nutrition,[33] and civics,[34] among other subjects. In the United States, the advancement of EE initiatives was fronted by PCI Media Impact and the Johns Hopkins Center for Communication Programs.[35] PCI Media Impact was inspired by the work of Sabido in Mexico and introduced the soap opera plan in India, Tanzania, and other remote countries. The Johns Hopkins Center for Communication Programs not only turned the plan into long-running stories; it also utilized EE as a key approach to their social and behavior change communication strategies.[36]

EE in the United States

In the United States, *ER* (1994–2009) and *Grey's Anatomy* (2005–present) remain the most famous TV series that draw on EE to teach about health matters. Although viewers may watch these two series for entertainment purposes, they also learn about a wide assortment of health-related issues that are strategically included in each program episode. For instance, *ER* addresses many contemporary health issues such as medical malpractice lawsuits, advanced care directives, and a plethora of up-to-date medical practices. Characters in *ER* are made to serve as role models for the manners by which people are expected to behave in healthcare contexts.[37] One study showed a 17% increase in the audience's familiarity with emergency contraception after *ER* featured a survivor of date rape being taken care of with a morning-after pill.[38] Even nonmedical television programs can function as EE in the United States. For example, in one of the episodes of *Beverly Hills 90210*, one of the characters, Steve, was raving about his flawless tan. His girlfriend detected a conspicuous mole on the back of his neck. Assuming it was skin cancer, he took a PA to the beach to extol the virtues of sunscreen. Viewers were probably not aware of what the scheme was, but the sunscreen reference was deliberately part of a public communication campaign organized by the Centers for Disease Control and Prevention (CDC). The CDC wanted to infuse *Beverly Hills 90210* with beneficial health messages. In fact, the federal agency has a department dedicated to instructing script writers and producers on how to insert health-related issues in their productions.[39]

More recently, to evaluate the positive effects of EE on its audiences, Hoffman et al. (2017)[40] randomly chose 89 African–American participants to watch (1) a "patient decision aid" video that had culturally adapted content about colorectal cancer screening options and theory-driven support in decision-making arranged in an EE format or (2) an "attention control" video on hypertension that included similarly detailed content. Participants consulted with their doctor and then filled out follow-up questionnaires that measured their knowledge, decisional conflict, self-advocacy, mindsets, perceived social norms, and life goals. After three months, completion of screening was evaluated through charts. Watching the culturally adapted decision aid greatly improved African–American patients' knowledge of colorectal cancer screening suggestions and options. It also considerably decreased their decisional conflict and enhanced their self-advocacy. No substantial differences were detected in the participants' attitudes, perceived social norms, or life goals. After three months, 23% of all participants had done a colonoscopy.

EE in the Latino World

A detailed description of the influence brought by Miguel Sabido—the pioneer of EE and originally a Mexican writer and producer—on Spanish-speaking EE is provided in the next section (i.e., narrative involvement). First, it would be interesting to look at a few case studies of EE in the Latino world. For instance, in a study conducted by Borrayo, Rosales, and Gonzalez (2017),[41] a cluster of 141 Spanish-speaking Latinas were randomly exposed to one of three materials: an EE story-based video, an educational video that was not story-based, and printed educational materials. Drawing on a repeated measures design, the impact of the EE story-based video on pretest to posttest measures was evaluated and balanced against the influence of the other two interventions. The EE story-based and nonstory-based interventions greatly widened Latinas' breast cancer knowledge, mammography self-efficacy, and social norms from pretest to posttest. However, the participants' pretest to posttest difference in mammography self-efficacy was much higher when contrasted with the difference of the other two interventions. The influence of the EE story-based intervention on self-efficacy and social norms was diminished by the participants' involvement in the story and connection with the story characters. EE story-based and nonstory-based interventions considerably educated and inspired Latinas to participate in mammography screening. The impact on mammography self-efficacy, a crucial antecedent to behavior change, can be better influenced by EE narratives.

East Los High is another example of an EE intervention using the storytelling approach.[42] This high-school teenage drama ran for four seasons, from 2013 to 2017, and was viewable in the United States on the video-on-demand platform Hulu. During its first season, the series addressed sexual and reproductive health among Latina/o Americans. In addition to running the episodes on television, digital media content offered entry points and more complexity to the stories. As such, a few characters posted blogs or video diaries, like Ceci—an important character who suddenly became pregnant and shared her experiences on her video blog—and Camila—who frequently discussed her struggles with mental health. These stories were typically accompanied by links to public health services and other trustworthy information sources, thereby forging relationships between the series and platforms with relevant content.[43]

Telenovelas are something to behold. Public health practitioners soon realized that Latin America's popular soap operas—known as **telenovelas**—are the perfect conduit to channel health and quality-of-life messages in the Americas and to prompt social change. An early sign of telenovelas' astronomical potential appeared in 1986 when a character on the Venezuelan-produced series *Cristal* revealed that she had breast cancer. This caused a high volume of women to request medical check-ups, both in Venezuela and Spain, where the show had a loyal following. In 2000, Camila, the heroine of the Brazilian telenovela *Lazos de Sangre* ("Blood Ties") revealed that she had leukemia. This led to a sharp rise in registered blood and bone marrow donors. From where do the power and influence of telenovelas come? Why do so many TV viewers identify with telenovela characters? These are burning questions, and many see their own daily situations being reproduced in those soap opera stories, an identification that keeps growing as time passes.[44]

EE in Africa

In Tanzania, *Twende na Wakati* ("Let's Go with the Times") was a radio soap opera broadcast for the first time in 1993. In the show, the main characters touted the virtues of family planning and HIV prevention. The influence of exposure to *Twende na Wakati* was unmistakable: Hundreds of thousands of sexually active adults decreased their numbers of sexual partners and used condoms on a more frequent basis.[45] Likewise, Shelus et al. (2018)[46] employed a mixed-methods approach to assess the impact of a serial radio drama in Rwanda, *Impano n'Impamba* ("A Gift for Today That Will Last a Long Time"), on fertility awareness and matters related to family planning. This study compared listeners with nonlisteners in a household survey administered nationwide ($n = 1,477$) and conducted in-depth interviews with 32 listeners. After exposure to *Impano n'Impamba*, listeners displayed higher fertility awareness than nonlisteners. They were also more likely to benefit from intermediate outcomes with respect to family planning—e.g., views on positive family planning norms, sentiments of self-efficacy, and heightened communication with others in regards to family planning.

In South Africa, the main purposes of soap operas are (1) to diffuse social cohesion messages for a post-Apartheid country, (2) to shock viewers by fostering personal emotional constructions, and (3) to stimulate dialogues and debates that tend to be brushed away by media outlets.[47] To this last point, interactions and meanings portrayed in soap operas have influenced how South Africans understand each other, their relationships, their identities, and their communities.[48] In a study conducted by Brown (2020),[49] also in South Africa, participants were chosen through convenient and purposive sampling. Results revealed that, although minority sexual identities remain an uncomfortable subject at home and are labeled as disgusting in everyday life, participants appreciated the visibility and realities of such minority sexual identities when depicted in soap operas. This is why the researcher recommended that soap operas be used more regularly as a pedagogical tool in the multitude of learning environments in South Africa.

EE in Asia

In China, *Don't Respond to Strangers* (*DRTS*) is the first and, to date, the only television drama there that was deliberately created to raise consciousness about the toxic aspect of domestic violence. Ultimately, the TV drama seeks to eradicate domestic violence and to guarantee protection of women's rights. At the onset, *DRTS* already proved to be effective in using fear appeals to make the public pay attention to domestic violence, encourage profound discussions on the issue, and get legislation passed.[50] *Tinka Sukh* is an EE radio soap opera in India. Literally meaning "Happiness Lies in Small Things," this EE approach has increasingly been used over the past few decades as a way to spur social change, at both the individual and social level, in that country.[51] In South Korea, various EE television programs illustrate the importance of the relationship between viewers and characters. These EE television programs have an indirect effect on motivation to sign up for organ donations through attitude and subjective norms.[52] Likewise, Hyuhn-Suhck Bae and Seok Kang (2008)[53] compared viewers and nonviewers of an EE series to determine the percentage of cornea donations. Viewers displayed a much higher level of participation and attitude towards cornea donation and were more inclined to sign up for it.

NARRATIVE INVOLVEMENT

On account of their narrative structure, EE messages stimulate participation in the storyline, or narrative involvement. **Narrative involvement** refers to the degree to which audiences follow events as they develop in a story.[54] A recurring notion across definitions is that of being predominantly engulfed within the storyline (instead of one's milieu) and displaying direct or indirect reactions to the narrative as it unfolds. Another term that is ordinarily employed is transportation.[55] **Transportation** is defined as "a convergent process, where all mental systems and capacities become focused on events occurring in the narrative."[56] This idea of being absorbed by the storyline is what makes EE message processing different from that of blatantly persuasive messages. EE programs that are framed by tremendously absorbing narratives foster conditions that are likely to increase positive influences on attitudes, intentions, and behaviors.[57] Owing to its narrative structure, EE enables the experience of transportation: a situation in which the viewer is absorbed into a story because his or her mental system and capacities are sharp-focused on the events happening in the narrative.[58] This feeling of being transported into a story world has the ability to influence audiences' real-world attitudes, intentions, and behaviors—a key process to support narrative persuasion.[59]

The Sabido Methodology

Besides transporting viewers into narratives themselves, EE also allows six forms of involvement with characters. In this section, involvement with characters serves to describe the all-encompassing category of concepts with respect to how audiences interact with characters.[60] This broad category is made up of (1) identification, (2) wishful identification, (3) perceived similarity, (4) parasocial interaction, (5) liking, and (6) markers. Social learning theory (SLT) hypothesizes that people select behaviors to attain desirable outcomes and that they learn about the consequences of such behaviors by observing others in their milieus, including behaviors depicted on television. Drawing upon the main tenets of this theory, academics and professionals elaborated an EE methodology: the **Sabido methodology**.[61] This is a methodology that pushes audiences to embrace desired behaviors by displaying role model characters who are rewarded for enacting those behaviors. The postulation is that viewers pair the TV characters with positive outcomes.

Mexican writer and producer **Miguel Sabido** took advantage of the insights of Albert Bandura to forge a genre of media that later became known as Entertainment–Education. Sabido quickly understood that entertainment media could be turned into written form and framed in a way that influences the knowledge, attitudes, and behaviors of viewers. This, in turn, can keep them involved thanks to its entertainment value—i.e., without giving them the appearance of teaching a lesson or instructing a course. Sabido himself used this communication approach profusely, starting with manifold successful telenovelas in Mexico in the 1970s. The approach, which would be dubbed the Sabido methodology, combines three types of characters: (1) A **positive character** who replicates desirable behaviors and is constantly recompensed for those behaviors; (2) a **negative character** who mimics undesirable behaviors and is unfailingly chastised for those behaviors; and (3) a **transitional character** who evolves from undesirable to desirable behavior as the program unfolds from episode to episode.[62]

Identification and Wishful Identification

Identification is an emotional and cognitive process whereby members of the audience assume the roles of characters in a storyline. Audiences forget about their own realities and momentarily put themselves in the shoes of the characters, espousing the characters' perspectives.[63] During identification, a viewer visualizes "being that character and replaces his or her personal identity and role as audience member with the identity and role of the character."[64] Identification is not to be confused with a related concept—wishful identification. **Wishful identification** is a phenomenon whereby a viewer aspires to be like the character, feels a dynamic yearning for emulating the figure,[65] and expresses undue respect for the character.[66]

Looking at the bigger picture, identification is different from wishful identification in the sense that the former reflects an emotional and cognitive process whereby the audience takes on the role of the character that they are following, rather than communicating the desire to metamorphose into the character.[67] Many believe that EE can shape behavior mainly through a direct influence of role modeling or observational learning. A person either watches or listens to a program and emulates an ideal character by copying his or her behavior on a daily basis or does not mimic the behavior displayed by negative role models. An illustration of this can be found in one of the first modern EE television programs, *Simplemente Maria*, aired in Peru in 1969. It enthused hundreds of female viewers to join for adult literacy and sewing classes after they noticed that the female lead character on television was doing the same.[68]

Perceived Similarity

Sometimes called **homophily**, **perceived similarity** denotes the degree to which a person perceives that he or she shares things in common with a character. Such commonalties include physical attributes, demographic characteristics, beliefs, personality traits, and/or values.[69] Similarity, here, is a cognitive assessment of what a person thinks he or she has in common with a figure, in contrast to identification—which is exemplified by empathy, common emotions, and lower self-awareness. From this vantage point, similarity functions by keeping one's own perspective while making evaluations about a character. On the other hand, identification necessitates assuming the position and experiencing events of a character.[70]

Parasocial Interaction

Parasocial interaction is defined as "the seeming face-to-face relationship between spectator and performer."[71] This alludes to the relationship between a viewer and a media figure, which reaches such a point that a pseudorelationship develops. These parasocial relationships bear similarities to traditional interpersonal relationships, with the exception that they are not returned by the media figure.[72] Past literature explains that both children and adults form parasocial bonds with news anchors, radio hosts, and fictional television characters. They seek advice from them and consider them as part of their social milieu, like friends and relatives.[73] The **absorption–addiction model** describes such parasocial interaction. The model confirms real instances of celebrity worship, whereby a coopted identity structure for some people enables psychological absorption with a celebrity in an effort to fashion an identity and a sense of self-actualization or gratification. The motivational factors driving this absorption might, in turn, concretize this process by adding the addictive component. In this case, celebrity worship becomes so extreme (and conceivably so delusional) that the person may not be sufficiently satisfied with the current status of the parasocial relationship.[74]

   Social learning theory (SLT), described earlier, is a major psychological theory underlying the efficacy of EE narratives. SLT rests on the premise that on-screen characters are potential role models and may improve viewers' self-efficacy for following new behaviors (or old behaviors that have never been adopted). As we have seen, new processes and social behaviors can be learned by observing and imitating those we see on the screen.[75] In this context, peer groups that enable the performance of violent crimes also nurture potential recruits into committing such behaviors by showing on-screen personas that perpetrate such types of crime. It is widely believed that youths are more predisposed to imitate others than their older counterparts.[76] Based on the core tenets of SLT, learning happens via three processes: interaction, imitation, and reinforcement. In the case of **learning through interaction**, learning is inspired by observation of, or connection to, others. It can be made possible through social interaction or social information (e.g., online). Learning through interaction can occur through social play or quarrelsome interactions. It contributes to the gradual learning of social skills. Learning through social information is associated with learning nonsocial skills, denoting a preference for solitary activities—although, on occasion, social information involves learning social skills too.[77]

In the case of **learning through imitation**, people learn by modeling themselves on others who are regarded as upright and worthy of admiration. Imitation, the essential component of SLT, has to do with watching what others do and mimicking that behavior. With respect to this element, the degree to which one emulates the action is contingent on what type of person is being observed, the kind of action being undertaken, and the outcomes emerging from the action.[78] Audiences gain knowledge about new forms of behaviors thanks to cognitive processing of information. In this manner, they are more inclined to learn the information that they watch on television. Viewers are also more predisposed to pay attention to programs when attractive characters addressing health-related issues are included. In the case of **learning through reinforcement**, audiences learn both through direct conditioning and replication of others' behaviors. Behavior can be strengthened by reward (positive reinforcement) or avoiding being punished (negative reinforcement). At the same time, it can be debilitated by resisting stimuli (positive punishment) or losing a reward (negative punishment). Learning through reinforcement depends on previous and current rewards or punishments for the action and the rewards and punishments paired with alternate actions.[79]

When parasocial interaction is done in groups, it can foster imagined communities. A concept developed by Anderson (1991),[80] **imagined communities** describe real or imagined relationships grounded in the "politics of identification." As Calhoun (1991)[81] corroborates it, "people without direct interpersonal relations with each other are led by the mediation of the world of political symbols to imagine themselves as members of communities defined by common ascriptive characteristics, personal tastes, habits, concerns." They are "imagined" because they do not pertain to direct or indirect relationships; instead, they inform "categorical identities."[82] On top of having direct interpersonal relationships (i.e., one-on-one interactions),[83] imagined communities can form in relation to television characters (even just one of them, although it is rarer).[84] By extension, new media technologies facilitate wider social reach when forging direct relationships (e.g., through digital communications, online video games, etc.). Conversely, they can also affect indirect relationships. For example, an activist can develop an indirect connection with a revered public figure who frequently appears on television or through speeches viewable on online social platforms like YouTube.[85]

Liking

Liking consists of positive appraisals of a character.[86] It can also be a social attraction and affinity that is measured through direct questionnaire items like "I would like to be friends with this person." Liking is analogous to parasocial interaction because it entails an assessment of a media figure and a certain level of desire for a friendship—if even hypothetical. This is a practical concept for understanding how audiences experience and identify with media figures to which they are exposed for the first time before a parasocial bond has had time to develop.[87] On this note, the **likeability heuristic** explains how audiences put more confidence in those whom they like—which also happens when these characters are fictional and played by popular actors.[88]

Markers

Markers are distinct identifiable components of messages like new words, phrases, or behaviors that ideally mimic new realities to disrupt the oppressive power structures within cultures.[89] The objective of markers is twofold: by trying to increase viewers' understanding, markers seek to accomplish EE interventions' goals, while also allowing strategists to examine conversations around the marker for monitoring or research purposes. The latter solves a chief issue: any marker-related occurrence can now be directly attributed to the EE program as a consequence of the marker's distinctiveness. For example, the Center for Media & Health cooperated with the Dutch television series *Good Times, Bad Times* to insert the markers *haperhoofd*—"stuttering head" in Dutch, alluding to cognitive malfunction after brain damage—and *cocakop*—"cocaine head" in Dutch, alluding to a person with a cocaine addiction—to track conversations around these markers by examining media sources and viewers' responses.[90] When markers are available on digital platforms, they do not automatically have to be words or phrases. There exist other forms and methods that can be easily replicated in photos and videos (e.g., symbols, signs, or dance moves). Markers can even be made up of digital stickers, animations, or enhanced versions of the real physical world. This can occur through Facebook Filters, Frames, or Snapchat Effects, attesting to the playfulness of viewers. Too, by incorporating stickers, Graphics Interchange Formats, and visual effects can help us understand particular scenes, characters, and events.[91]

DIGITAL GAMES AS HEALTH COMMUNICATION CAMPAIGNS

Digital games can serve as a gargantuan platform for health communication campaigns. They combine interest, recreation, enjoyment, thrill, experiment, and motivation. By and large, **digital games** are games played with the assistance of digital devices like computers and mobile phones.[92] Many people on this planet have played games. A **game** is, in and of itself, a rule-based type of play that involves a challenge to attain an objective and offers feedback on the player's progress towards that objective. Digital games consist of any form of digital media that operates on core principles of directions, challenges, and reactions to engage players in interactive play with the purpose of accomplishing a goal.[93] These games can be subdivided into sedentary and active video games. **Sedentary games** include a control scheme enabled by the game controller or keyboard and mouse (e.g., as we see in traditional PC games). **Active video games** work through the player's movements that are used to operate them (the games).[94]

In the broader sense, **gaming culture** refers to how digital and analog games function as intermediaries for diverse types of relationality.[95] On the subject of relationality, digital games include narrative features or expose players to a game world, both of which comprise elements of fantasy.[96] They often focus on **game fiction**, which is described as the incorporation of a fictional game universe or story.[97] Incorporation of game fiction is highly similar to the application of narrative anchors and has been established as helpful for learning as it positions and anchors learning within a specific framework.[98] It can additionally function as a cognitive tool for problem-solving.[99]

Gamification

Recent progress in **gamification**—gaming features available outside games[100]—has attracted a great deal of attention and interest in health communication campaigns. The alleged motivational power of gamification has turned it into a promising approach in communicative contexts. In a 2018 study about video gaming, 49% of the 2,001 US respondents said that they were video game players, with 10% assuming the persona of "gamer." The study also reported a multifaceted network of ideas on the subject of digital gaming, including attempts at developing teamwork and collaboration.[101] As one would expect, digital gameplay has benefited from rapid expansion in health communication campaigns. Though campaign planners are well aware that digital games are not a cure-all or a magic bullet, for the past decade, they have dabbed into the intrinsic complexities and benefits of digital gaming and the noteworthy opportunities that they offer for successful learning across disciplines.[102]

Well-crafted games can be meaningful milieus for learning and behavior change for the reason that they are experiential.[103] As Gray and Leonard (2018)[104] contend, gamification enables change agents (e.g., activists, etc.) to develop opportunities of experiential learning—to be "teachers of alternative narratives." Put another way, games themselves are not necessarily reactionary or forward-looking, but have the potential to be both. Gamification has already contributed a large amount to healthcare delivery. Since the early 2010s, it has served as the hands-on application of data and communication technologies in the provision of cost-effective care. Gamification enjoys even more popularity than the movie industry and is a passion and obsession across gender, age, and cultural boundaries.[105]

Games for Health Promotion Programs

In the context of health promotion programs, digital games can provide health-related information, feature characters with ideal health behaviors, and generate opportunities to observe unusual healthy lifestyles.[106] This can be achieved by modifying mediators (e.g., self-regulatory skill development) or by applying modification techniques (e.g., adapting and goal-setting).[107] Digital games may also produce continual effects by being inherently motivating for people to play more and more.[108] Under these circumstances, they have proved to be promising for advocating healthy lifestyles.[109] Healthy game-inspired lifestyles can avert a variety of diseases, like cancer, cardiovascular diseases, stroke, dementia, mental disorders, and diabetes.[110] Applying smart interventions to champion these lifestyles is, thus, of great public health significance. An examination of games for healthy lifestyle promotion indicated that they were able to modify (1) behavior (e.g., by walking more every day), (2) personal determinants of this behavior (e.g., knowledge, attitudes, behavioral norms, self-efficacy, abilities, and perceived environmental obstacles or facilitators), and (3) medical outcomes (e.g., body mass index). Even though the effects were not significant, they were consistent with the high volume of effects identified in related computer-delivered interventions. These effects were applicable across health behaviors (e.g., physical exercise, disease self-management, and social conduct).[111]

Game Features

Digital games possess many features that campaign planners can exploit to improve health-related learning and behavior change. Examples include interaction with socially complex game figures; collaboration with other players; interactivity based on physical exertion ("exergames" like the music video game *Dance Dance Revolution* and motion-detecting games on the *Kinect* or *Wii* game platforms); downloading of our personal health data into the game to make self-care the game mechanic or game-playing approach; and practice of decision-making skills that can aid players in averting relapse in their own situations—i.e., this is done by living realistic game scenes that spark, for instance, longings for tobacco, alcohol, or drugs. The availability of game features is wide-ranging and increasing as novel technologies can empower games to sense the environment, identify players' emotions during play, engage them in social media, gather data from many players, and custom-tailor the game experience to harmonize the player's interests and skills.[112]

GAMES FOR CHANGE (GFC), SERIOUS GAMES, AND PERSUASIVE GAMES

Games for Change (GfC) are digital or hybrid games used as a viable educational and persuasive platform thanks to their entertaining and motivating dispositions. Because such games are created for social and behavioral change, they are referred to as GfC, and they principally seek "to promote reflection and positive behavior changes in players in the physical world, through characteristics that persuade players to consider the social or political issue presented in the game."[113] Rather than using words, images, or moving picture, GfC apply a rule-structured approach and system of interactions to persuade players. GfC fall under a larger umbrella identified as Serious Games; they encompass all games that, in addition to entertainment, have been imbued with explicit objectives.[114]

Serious Games

Serious games provide an opportunity for investigating the premise that playing games paves the way for a form of learning that is meaningful, perpetual, and transferable to the real world. "Serious games" is defined in this context as any type of interactive digital game software for one or several players. Such games constitute "a genre that explicitly focuses on education. Thus, the genre has become associated with positively connoted features such as seriousness, education, or learning."[115] The concept of using games for purposes other than entertainment was first articulated in the book *Serious Games* by Clark C. Abt (1975).[116] When Abt brought up the subject in his book, he stated: "We are concerned with serious games in the sense that these games have an explicit and carefully thought-out educational purpose and are not intended to be played primarily for amusement."[117] The educational mission of serious games is not necessarily visible or explicit in the game's design, but can be incorporated into the game through the context for which it is used or in which it is embedded. From this perspective, for instance, a board game originally devised for amusement can be applied to military training to instill ideas of strategic thinking and core principles of tactical warfare. Whereas the learning process happens through a game, the anticipated effect may well be a real-world one.[118]

As one can see, serious games constitute entertaining platforms with an additional purpose of education. Players can nurture their knowledge and hone in their skills by overcoming a myriad of hindrances during gaming. Players' performances receive a score over the entire course of the gaming process.[119] In the event that players surmount an obstacle, they are bestowed awards like scores, progress into the game, and power. Educational components can be mixed with the gameplay, which are subconsciously absorbed by the players during the course of the gameplay, a phenomenon called **serious game assisted learning**.[120] One of the drivers for the efficiency of serious games in education is attributed to their effects on learners' temperaments. As an entertainment industry, gaming plays a crucial part in the development of temperaments such as desolation, joy, and anger. Successful serious games are those that have formed a positive mood to motivate players to keep advancing into the game, contributing to both heightened interest in gameplay and better academic performance. Motivated, thrilled, and returning players can unquestionably be engulfed in serious game assisted learning.[121] Because players can be fully immersed in digital games, the latter provide ample opportunities for campaign designers to promote healthy sexual behavior. The games' confidential aspect lends itself to addressing sensitive sexuality subjects and adapting messages to the individual player's needs that turn out to be intrinsically motivating.[122]

Serious games are believed to obtain their learning effects from no fewer than three sources: (1) By generating a state immersion or transportation, a condition in which the player gets fully immersed in the play without skepticism or incredulity, at the same time cultivating personally relevant experiences and profound liking towards the characters; (2) by creating flow, a state of elevated concentration in which the player feels the equilibrium between skills and challenge; and (3) by fulfilling the individual player's needs for power, independence, connectedness, arousal, entertainment, fantasy, or challenge.[123] Several reviews of the literature have ascertained the health-stimulating effects of serious games. These included health games pertaining to various behaviors and populations, such as games for cure, therapy, prevention, and professional education.[124] Literature reviews on healthy lifestyles predominantly centered on a single health behavior. For example, the study conducted by Guy, Ratzki-Leewing, and Gwadry-Sridha (2011)[125] focused on obesity prevention and the one by Guse et al. (2012)[126] on sexual behavior health among teens.

Persuasive Games

Persuasive games are video games that open new avenues for persuasion through their representational method of **procedurality** (rule-founded representations and interactions). They produce a new type of rhetoric by formulating processes of persuasion thanks to an abstraction of physical world mechanisms.[127] Bogost (2007)[128] calls it **procedural rhetoric**, a form of rhetoric that originates in the essential affordances of computers: running processes and operating rule-based symbolic manipulation. Video games can possess immense persuasive power that transcends other types of computational persuasion. This rhetoric has particular features in comparison with traditional rhetoric. As Bogost (2007)[129] continues, "I call this new form procedural rhetoric, the art of persuasion through rule–based representations and interactions rather than the spoken word, images, or moving pictures."

Not only can video games underlie and sustain current sociocultural positions, but they can also break away from these positions, causing hypothetically significant long-term sociocultural change. There are three domains in which video game persuasion has been evident and reveals great potential: politics, advertising, and learning.[130] Highly profitable games like *Mario Brothers* and *Grand Theft Auto* were initially designed for amusement and recreation but, in certain contexts, have been turned into serious games and persuasive games for purposes of learning and behavior change. They have also been used as a rationale for training in business, advertising, healthcare, and even administration by both nongovernmental organizations and educational institutions.[131]

SELF-DETERMINATION THEORY (SDT)

Developed by Ryan and Deci (2000),[132] **self-determination theory** (SDT) hypothesizes that people can be driven by intrinsic and/or extrinsic motivation and explains how basic psychological needs are indispensable for well-being. When we are intrinsically motivated, we perform activities because the activity itself is worthwhile, pleasurable, and consistent with our identities. On the other hand, when we are extrinsically motivated, we perform activities because they are essential in gaining rewards or avoiding punishments.[133] SDT has already been productively applied in the contexts of games[134] and gamification.[135] This application rests on psychological needs for skills, self-sufficiency, and social relatedness. Fulfillment of these needs is key to intrinsic motivation and, thereupon, to high-quality learning, with SDT accentuating the value of the environment in gratifying these psychological needs.[136] Augmenting learning environments with game design features alters these environments and conceivably influences learning outcomes. From a self-determination viewpoint, various types of feedback can act as fundamental learning processes sparked by game design elements. Constantly giving players–learners feedback is a cardinal feature of serious games.[137]

Intrinsic and Extrinsic Motivation

Intrinsic motivation "refers to doing something because it is inherently interesting or enjoyable."[138] **Extrinsic motivation** "refers to doing something because it leads to a separable outcome."[139] According to SDT, the reasons for people's choice to engage, wield efforts, and persevere in an activity can be placed along a continuum of self-determined regulation. The most common self-determined type of behavioral regulation is intrinsic motivation, which refers to the participation in an activity for the enjoyment and satisfaction coming from the activity itself. On the opposite side of the continuum stands amotivation, which denotes a lack of motivation or intention. Located in between is extrinsic motivation, which consists of behaviors that are performed to achieve goals separate from the activity itself.[140] Pleasure is a core notion in the spheres of media psychology and entertainment research. Intrinsically, media-based pleasure alludes to the penchant for and positive reaction to media exposure. Media scholars describe pleasure as an emotion,[141] an attitude,[142] or a *mélange* of cognition and affect.[143]

In the realm of video-game playing, enjoyment is primordial and refers to the satisfaction of intrinsic need based on SDT,[144] which is also activated by game mechanics. **Game mechanics** draw in a certain level of interaction with the game or the other players participating in the game activity. As a mechanism of interaction, "retroactivity" is a central component of the game mechanics that facilitates players' progress within the game.[145] To interact with a game implicates some measure of extrinsic motivation on the basis of its retroactions. This feature has been underlined by Dunwell, de Freitas and Jarvis (2011)[146] as a positive quality of games. A serious engagement of the player–learners within the game world can be construed as an indication that digital games can also boost the development of autonomous motivation.

Three fundamental psychological needs motivate people to assume certain behaviors and specify essential qualities for personal psychological health and well-being. These needs are the common and natural needs for autonomy, competence, and relatedness.[147] To have autonomy is to feel that we can act of our own volition and in harmony with our values and desires that are integrated into social norms and expectations. To have competence is to be able to conquer difficulties and bring a meaningful influence on one's milieu. To have relatedness is to interact, associate with, and care for others.

Autonomy

Autonomy is one of the core constituents of intrinsic motivation and can be regarded as the opposite of external control. Autonomy gives human beings a perception of freedom. It refers to the ability "to self-organize and regulate one's own behavior (and avoid heteronomous control), which includes the tendency to work towards inner coherence and integration among regulatory demands and goals."[148] In other words, it refers to "being the perceived origin or source of one's own behavior."[149] Perceived autonomy is high when people are given choices or when they participate in activities for their own interests and value. On the other hand, when the number of choices is limited, when there is too much control, or when the availabilities for methods of action are insufficient, perceived autonomy is compromised, which hinders intrinsic motivation. Put another way, when we have the liberty to follow an optimal outcome or undertake an activity without any external control, our perception of autonomy is high and, thereby, raises intrinsic motivation.[150]

When it comes to understanding video game playing, autonomy is measured by how much choice players are conferred within the game domain. Video game play that is external to the experimental environment is generally voluntary. Consequently, need satisfaction of autonomy for video game players is expected to be high. Need satisfaction of autonomy can also change based on autonomy-supportive attributes available in the video game design. Examples are game attributes that present flexibility over game strategies and character development, movement, and choice in regards to tasks and rewards. Players who benefit from greater levels of autonomy during game play come away with a happier experience than those who play games without a high level of autonomy within the game.[151]

Competence

Competence means "to engage optimal challenges and experience mastery or effectance in the physical and social worlds."[152] Klimmt and Hartmann (2006)[153] describe this concept as "the satisfaction of having imposed an effect on the environment." Within SDT, the idea of competence means that we experience pleasure when we feel that we are effective after participating in an activity. This craving for competence can lead us to "seek challenges that are optimal for their capacities and to persistently attempt to maintain and enhance those skills and capacities through activity."[154] Competence is a vital constituent of SDT and accentuates the need for challenge and the perception of effectiveness for developing intrinsic motivation.[155] Consequently, a proper equilibrium between the talent of the players and the challenge of the game is a prerogative in the design of current games.[156]

Competence in video games postulates a need for challenge and a belief in effectiveness at conquering those challenges posed by the video games. Need satisfaction of competence may be attained by enabling gamers to comfortably learn new skills, by presenting challenges with intensifying difficulty as the game unfolds, and by offering natural and efficient control of the hardware and software. Need satisfaction of competence is a key prominent predictor of a gratifying game experience as suggested by enjoyment motivation for prospective play in the future.[157] Cooperation and competition can be viewed as specifically valuable in this context. In the context of games, cooperation has the ability to influence the needs for both competence and relatedness.[158] Cooperation smooths the progress of teamwork and, therefore, the sense of being relevant to others. It also allows learners to overcome challenges that they could not normally overcome on their own, which can increase feelings of competence. Competition can lead to higher pressure which, in turn, motivates learners to participate and learn even more.[159]

Relatedness

Relatedness is another constituent that increases the likelihood of intrinsic motivation and helps understand one's willingness of being connected to others. These two aspects can lead game designers to make intrinsic motivation a special focus so as to create situations where players are provided with more significant choices during the game. This would improve the player's experience variation, along with the connection implemented with other players, paving the way for collaboration or competition.[160] Given this, it is easy to deduce that relatedness is a yearning for belonging and attachment to others as reflected in the following two definitions: (1) "To seek attachments and experience feelings of security, belongingness, and intimacy with others"[161] and (2) "Relatedness refers to feeling connected to others, to caring for and being cared for by those others, to having a sense of belongingness both with other individuals and with one's community."[162] In addition, that need for relatedness pertains to feelings of being with others and is not stimulated by the achievement of particular outcomes like acquiring higher social status.[163]

Within the video game domain, a laboratory study revealed that participating in video games with other players (instead of playing alone) was conducive to need satisfaction of relatedness, which was instrumental in enjoyment of game play.[164] A survey of massive interactive game players also revealed that need satisfaction of relatedness led to players' game enjoyment and motivation for potential play in the future.[165] Based on a review of the literature, for an interactive fitness game, attributes that facilitate players' competition or cooperation with others either (face-to-face or online) appear to be the most significant ones to encourage need satisfaction of relatedness.[166]

Dasein

SDT is established on a realization that we influence and are influenced by our environment.[167] In his *Being and Time* masterpiece, Martin Heidegger (2008),[168] a German philosopher in the twentieth century, laid stress on the human being as *Dasein* ("being there"). This concept is a solid pillar for historicizing and contextualizing SDT's description of human needs.[169] In German, *Dasein* is akin to existence. It is a being made up by its temporality; it clarifies and construes the meaning of being at a particular time.[170] Any game can, in theory, bestow players an experience of freedom and intuitive perception of its various constituents, and allow those players to interact with others. However, what distinguishes a relatively good game from an outstanding one is the design—i.e., the manner by which the game is made, what it means to its players. In-game action, then, is autonomously or intrinsically self-controlled.[171] A correspondent concept, **being-in-the-world** is the postulation that we can understand an unfamiliar phenomenon only if we put ourselves in the context of another person linked to that phenomenon (whether today or in the past).[172]

Dasein is framed as always-already being-in-the-world; to access a genuine experience, we need to immerse ourselves within a certain physiological, historical, sociocultural milieu that is meaningful. SDT offers a theoretical and empirical framework when considering design choices for video games to provide a genuine experience for the targeted users. Players are routinely forced to abide by in-game rules and stipulations, with countless in-game behaviors being externally motivated. For instance, players have to sacrifice their enjoyment so they can get a reward (e.g., a new weapon), acquire more experience points to progress to the next level, or amass items at the request of a character. The features of progression in the game, however, can be designed as more enjoyable so that the player will do things out of his or her own volition (instead of feeling that they are required do it in order to advance into the game).[173]

CELEBRITY HEALTH CAMPAIGNS

Celebrity health campaigns can be rewarding—for audiences in general, for third-party collaborators, and for the healthcare industry. They can be a teaching moment and increase the salience of issues for the greater social good. In late April 2021, the Biden administration launched a massive campaign for the greater social good: to convince more Americans to take the vaccine against COVID-19. The campaign, called "We Can Do This: Live," was directed at youths on social media and was composed of virtual events where superstars and athletes answered Americans' questions about the main vaccines available. Well-known people who volunteered for the campaign included actress Eva Longoria, Dallas Mavericks owner and billionaire entrepreneur Mark Cuban, and Kelly Ripa and Ryan Seacrest, the cohosts of "Live with Kelly and Ryan." Also lined up as volunteers were celebrities from NASCAR, the NBA, and the WNBA. The purpose, as per a detailed report of the campaign published by *NBC News*, was to exploit celebrities' charisma in order to reach US youths "directly in the places where they already consume content online, including social media, podcasts, YouTube, and more."[174] In mid-July 2021, Olivia Rodrigo, an American megastar with a No. 1 album (called *Sour*) on the Billboard 200 charts at that time, joined the campaign to motivate the unvaccinated youths to get their vaccines.[175]

Celebrity culture is ever-present in our everyday lives—especially today. It is interceded to audiences through the media. It leverages not only the production and intake of media content, but also the values (i.e., social, moral, etc.) fashioned in the world in which we live. In the context of health campaigns, **celebrity culture** is a practice whereby the media influences publics by determining how they can be affected by the advice given by prestigious people.[176] **Celebrities** are individuals who experience a large volume of media-related capital through their repeated presence in the public sphere.[177] Celebrity is "a genre of representation. It is a commodity traded by the promotions, publicity and media industries that produce these representations and their effects."[178] The term itself arguably originated in France in the 1850s[179] and its etymology is from the Latin *celebrem*, meaning both "fame" and "being thronged."[180] Contained within *celebrem* is the word *célèbre*, or "well-known in public" in the French language.[181]

Celebrities' Participation

Celebrities are routinely featured in modern public communication campaigns, notably in areas such as humanitarianism, social issues, and politics. Celebrity campaigns are conceived as a potentially convincing force in communications, with famous personalities regarded as more powerful than anonymous ones because they own "giant microphones" to promote causes or issues. Celebrity endorsement is a useful approach in the communicative process both with respect to attracting and keeping attention and in forging opportune associations that contribute to heightened knowledge of such causes or issues.[182] A multitude of nongovernmental organizations have come to the forefront of the media thanks to the use of celebrities as advocates for these organizations. In this manner, the celebrity becomes the conduit for the campaigns—an excellent means by which the campaign's message is diffused to audiences. Engaging in humanitarian work, celebrities perform a distinct form of activism. The power to draw audience attention to a cause is now the celebrities' strongest asset.[183] Ben Affleck launched the Eastern Congo Initiative, a campaign that he instituted in 2002. Halle Berry campaigns for cancer patients. Oprah Winfrey promotes education in South Africa. Salma Hayek campaigns for female victims of domestic violence. Sting is an environmentalist for the rainforest. Angelina Jolie and Brad Pitt campaign for the elimination of abject rural poverty. The list is never-ending.[184]

Celebrities' contributions to campaigns widen their reach to the world. This is due, in part, to their **charisma**, which Weber (1968)[185] defines as "a certain quality of an individual personality by virtue of which he is set apart from ordinary men and treated as endowed with supernatural, superhuman, or at least specifically exceptional quality." To take part in a public communication campaign, the celebrity takes advantage of the affective power oozed by the celebrity symbol. Affect can be easily channeled for humanitarian purposes. **Affect** refers to the energy invested in a particular situation or sphere. It is an investment made by a person to a cultural text and it depends on that person's **mattering map**—i.e., the person's appreciation or willingness to invest in a certain cultural text.[186] This degree of dedication exemplified by one's mattering map is what distinguishes the fan from other audience members. In contrast to others, the fan makes an active and enjoyable reconstruction of the cultural text. The cultural text created by the celebrity allows the public to actively take part in the fashioning of the celebrity by affirming meaning to their connection with the celebrity.[187]

Public Service Announcement (PSAs)

A celebrity endorsement is like a tribute. It can be used as a marketing ploy because a tribute is a written or spoken announcement on a noteworthy health issue or that sings the praises of a type of vaccine or medication. The most prevailing type of celebrity endorsement is the **public service announcement (PSA)**. A PSA is a free, nonpolemical, broadcast communiqué—e.g., to reduce alcohol-related birth defects, pregnant women should abstain from drinking alcohol.[188] PSAs have been a hallmark of health promotion tactics for a long time. However, the broadcasting of PSAs on a regular basis is no guarantee that the public will pay enough attention to change their attitudes or behaviors. For example, evidence to support the effectiveness of PSAs in decreasing problems like tobacco use is lacking.[189]

In both yesteryear and contemporary circumstances, a certain number of public health campaigns reliant on mass media have only benefited from limited financial resources. This is why they have been dependent on television and radio broadcasters to allocate time for PSAs. These campaigns are also limited in their success. A longitudinal study conducted by the Kaiser Family Foundation (KFF) revealed that reliance on PSAs can lead to campaign messages being shown during less popular time slots, causing lower message exposure to the target audience. Nongovernmental organizations like the American Cancer Society and the Red Cross are so intent on ensuring usage that they buy commercial airtime for their PSAs. The **Kaiser Family Foundation** (**KFF**) is a California-based philanthropic institution that specializes in healthcare issues facing the nation. KFF operates and supervises its own research and communications projects, ordinarily in alliance with external organizations.[190]

The release of a one-minute PSA with the title "The F-Word, Famine Is the Real Obscenity" took the world by storm in 2011. Celebrities recruited for this video included George Clooney, Idris Elba, Bono, Justin Long, Annie Lennox, Youssou N'Dour, Colin Farrell, Bill Nighy, K'Naan, and many others. It was sponsored by ONE, a global campaign against extreme poverty, and cofounded by Bono, the lead singer of U2. According to ONE's website, Bono, K'Naan, Annie Lennox, and George Clooney volunteered to be part of the PSA after the idea was presented to them. The campaign was set up by ONE's creative team under the management of Roxane Philson and Jeff Davidoff.[191] The concise video production was part of One's Hungry No More campaign, which wants governments to solve the problem of famine in Africa.[192] Owing to many East Africans embroiled in both conflict and famine, the ONE campaign directs our attention to Somalian refugees as well as the massive drought that has inflicted the entire Horn of Africa, which includes Kenya, Somalia, Ethiopia, Eritrea, and Djibouti. In the long run, these celebrities hope that Western humanitarianism brings a positive impact on agricultural security in East Africa. Thanks to wise investments made in parts of Ethiopia, farmers have displayed resiliency in the deeply ingrained crisis. Agricultural advancement is hailed as a long-term solution for East Africans, which can sustain the population when the food runs out.[193]

Case Study: Prince William's Mental Health Campaign

Sometimes called **mental illness**, **mental disorder**, or **psychiatric disorder**, a **mental health issue** is a behavioral or mental pattern that provokes considerable distress or harm of personal functioning.[194] In 2019, the most prevalent mental health issues around the globe included depression (impacting about 264 million people), bipolar disorder (about 45 million), dementia (about 50 million), and schizophrenia and other psychoses (about 20 million).[195] The causes of mental health issues are still unclear. It is important to understand what such issues are in order to measure their effects on ourselves and society at large. In the United States, 20.6% of adults experienced some forms of mental disorders in 2019. This was equivalent to 51.5 million people.[196] In the United Kingdom, mental health issues affect one in four people annually, bearing consequences on their physical health, close relationships, and financial stability.[197]

The Heads Up Campaign

In January 2019, at the World Economic Forum's Annual Meeting in Davos, Switzerland, the issue of mental health was emphasized by Prince William, Duke of Cambridge. However, it received scant attention.[198] A year later, in January 2020, a short video featuring British soccer stars—including Frank Lampard and Jesse Lingard—was broadcast at the beginning of 32 games over an entire weekend to motivate fans to reflect on their mental health and what measures they can take to improve it. The one-minute video, narrated by Prince William, was aired at stadiums, on the internet, and on television. The purpose was to reach millions of soccer fans across Great Britain. It was part of Public Health England's campaign.[199] The campaign heartened soccer fans and players alike to freely discuss their mental health strategies and experiences so they could help others who encountered such difficulties. Another intention of the Heads Up campaign was to eliminate the stigma that men face when revealing their feelings and help start a nationwide conversation. The initiative was immensely visible throughout the entire 2019–20 soccer season in Great Britain, which started in August 2019.[200] Ever since, the subject of mental health within professional soccer players has grown in popularity on account of additional publicity and promotion by Prince William on his "Royal Team Talk" television broadcast.

The Heads Together Campaign

In a video titled *Heads Together*, a cleverly scripted Prince William talked about mental health experiences with artist Lady Gaga before demanding the eradication of the stigma attached to mental illnesses. What the Duke of Cambridge did was engage in digital story-telling. **Digital storytelling**, whereby a person appears in a video or a social media platform to diffuse a message, has occasionally been used to motivate audiences to reexamine their attitudes towards mental health issues.[201] "Heads Together" is actually an initiative that he and his brother Prince Harry created in 2017—based on the fact that both have endured mental illnesses themselves. The royal princes' promptitude to converse about their own personal struggles with depression as a consequence of losing their mother in tragic circumstances—when they were still teenagers—is laudable, and has indubitably helped bring the issue to the forefront of the media.[202] The Heads Together campaign addresses stigmatization, raises awareness, and offers assistance to those with mental health challenges.[203] Today, the campaign is spearheaded by Prince William and Kate Middleton. Previously, it was by Prince Harry and Meghan Markle.[204] In July 2020, William and Kate donated $2.3 million to promote good mental health for frontline workers and others affected by the COVID-19 pandemic. The money was allocated to personal grief trauma counseling for personnel in ambulance, fire, police, and search and rescue services.[205] In May 2021, Prince Harry participated in a new series (for an Apple TV+ documentary) to discuss mental health issues with Oprah Winfrey. The series was created to destigmatize the topic.[206]

IMPACT OF CELEBRITY HEALTH DISCLOSURE

Health issues can receive substantive visibility when a celebrity dies, becomes ill, undergoes a medical procedure, or announces a health-related lifestyle change. In fact, health communication campaigns have developed plans and tactics to gain from media visibility of celebrity illnesses. This is simply called **opportunism**—taking advantage of an event to get something out of it.[207] The opportunism generated by the media coverage can significantly reduce the amount of money needed for advertising campaigns. A result of this is that celebrity health disclosure can contribute to heightened public awareness of an illness or condition. In March 2000, two years after the death of her husband Jay Monahan from colon cancer, *NBC News* journalist Katie Couric underwent an on-air colonoscopy on the *Today Show*. This segment was the mainspring of a weeklong series that discussed colon cancer awareness and promoted colorectal cancer screening. Her on-air colonoscopy sparked a monumental rise in colonoscopy screening rates during the nine months following her segment. The phenomenon was dubbed the "Katie Couric effect."[208]

Another famous example of celebrity health disclosure is that of Hollywood actress Angelina Jolie who, in May 2013, underwent a bilateral prophylactic mastectomy after being diagnosed with the BRCA-1 gene. The phenomenon was dubbed the "Angelina effect" because it generated an enormous surge in genetic clinic referrals across the world.[209] Now, the world knew what BRCA-1 was. BRCA-1 (BReast CAncer gene 1) and BRCA-2 (BReast CAncer gene 2) are genes that create proteins that repair damaged DNA. Every human being has two copies of each of these genes—one copy received from each parent. BRCA1 and BRCA2 are also referred to as tumor suppressor genes for the reason that, upon experiencing change, these genes can turn into harmful (or pathogenic) variants (or mutations), which gives rise to cancer.[210]

Enter Rock Hudson (1925–85), one of the first famous Hollywood actors to lose their life to AIDS-related complications. While undergoing treatment in Paris, Hudson told the press that he was about to lose his life to AIDS. In a subsequent press release, Hudson surmised that he may have contracted HIV through a blood transfusion from an infected donor during the many blood transfusions that he was injected in his heart bypass procedure. In the 1980s, blood was not tested for the then-unknown HIV/AIDS disease. Hudson spent his last days with dignity, enduring the devastation of his disease and the incursions of the tabloid press. Rock Hudson's tragic demise gave AIDS a face. It is believed that his long-time friend and then-President Ronald Reagan was so moved that he modified his position on efforts to campaign for AIDS awareness and testing.[211]

The Kylie Effect

Kylie Minogue is a good case study whereby more women have undergone cancer screenings regularly as a result of publicity surrounding celebrity health disclosure. Born in 1968, Kylie Minogue is an Australian singer, songwriter, and actress. She remains the highest-selling female Australian artist of all time. In May 2005, she was diagnosed with breast cancer. Her medical care and treatment in Melbourne, Australia, ignited a period of fierce media coverage. Soon after, she was transferred for surgery and subsequent chemotherapy treatment.[212] During her interview on *The Ellen DeGeneres Show* in 2008, Minogue admitted that her breast cancer had initially been misdiagnosed. As she commented, "Because someone is in a white coat and using big medical instruments doesn't necessarily mean they're right."[213]

To this day, Kylie Minogue is still recognized for the positive impression that she made by openly discussing her cancer diagnosis and treatment. In May 2008, the French Cultural Minister Christine Albanel said, "Doctors now even go as far as saying there is a 'Kylie effect' that encourages young women to have regular checks."[214] To verify this argument, Chapman, Holding, McLeod, and Wakefield (2005)[215] analyzed narratives on breast cancer in Australian television news programs that aired between May 17 and May 27, 2005. In each of these segments, the name of Kylie was clearly mentioned. The study concluded that news coverage of Kylie's breast cancer diagnosis ignited a skyrocketing rise in appointments for mammography in Australia alone. Likewise, Freedman, Mountain, Karina, and Schofield (2017)[216] note that, in the first six months after Kylie's public announcement, the number of breast screenings among women climbed in the English-speaking world, particularly in Australia.

The Selena Effect

Born in 1992, Selena Gomez is an American singer, actress, and producer. In 2015, she publicly announced her diagnosis with lupus and underwent a renal transplant for lupus nephritis. Lupus is an autoimmune disease in which the body's immune system wrongfully hurts healthy tissue in many areas of the body.[217] Selena Gomez first disclosed her diagnosis during her impassioned appearance on *The Ellen DeGeneres Show* on October 9, 2015. In another interview on August 30, 2016, with *People Magazine*, she revealed that she was taking a break from recording music and touring as a consequence of her lupus. A few months later, she posted an update with her followers on social media about her health status. On September 14, 2017, she shared another post on Instagram disclosing that she had just undergone a renal transplant. This post included a link to the lupusresearch.org website to motivate her followers to educate themselves on lupus.[218]

NOTES

1. Emily Moyer-Gusé, "Toward a Theory of Entertainment Persuasion: Explaining the Persuasive Effects of Entertainment–Education Messages," *Communication Theory* 18, no. 3 (2008): 407–25. https://doi.org/10.1111/j.1468-2885.2008.00328.x.
2. Arvind Singhal, Michael J. Cody, Everett M. Rogers, and Miguel Sabido, *Entertainment–Education and Social Change: History, Research, and Practice* (New York: Routledge, 2003).
3. Arvind Singhal and Everett M. Rogers, "The Status of Entertainment–Education Worldwide," in *Entertainment–Education and Social Change: History, Research, and Practice*, ed. Arvind Singhal, Michael J. Cody, Everett M. Rogers, and Miguel Sabido (New York: Routledge, 2003): 3–20.
4. Mohan J. Dutta-Bergman, "A Formative Approach to Strategic Message Targeting through Soap Operas: Using Selective Processing Theories," *Health Communication* 19, no. 1 (2006): 11–18. https://doi.org/10.1207/s15327027hc1901_2.
5. Ien Ang, *Watching Dallas: Soap Opera and the Melodramatic Imagination* (London: Methuen, 1985).
6. Arvind Singhal, and Everett M. Rogers, *Entertainment–Education: A Communication Strategy for Social Change* (Mahwah, NJ: Lawrence Erlbaum, 1999).
7. YoungJu Shin, Michelle Miller-Day, Michael L. Hecht, and Janice L. Krieger, "Entertainment–Education Videos as a Persuasive Tool in the Substance Use Prevention Intervention 'keepin' it REAL'," *Health Communication* 33, no. 7 (2018): 896–906. https://doi.org/10.1080/10410236.2017.1321163.
8. Arvind Singhal and Everett M. Rogers, "A Theoretical Agenda for Entertainment–Education," *Communication Theory* 12, no. 2 (2002): 117–35. https://doi.org/10.1111/j.1468-2885.2002.tb00262.x.
9. Douglas Storey and Suruchi Sood, "Increasing Equity, Affirming the Power of Narrative and Expanding Dialogue: The Evolution of Entertainment–Education over Two Decades," *Critical Arts* 27, no. 1 (2013): 9–35. https://doi.org/10.1080/02560046.2013.767015.

10. Suruchi Sood, Amy Henderson Riley, and Kristine Cecile Alarcon, "Entertainment–Education and Health and Risk Messaging," in *Oxford Research Encyclopedia of Communication*, ed. Jon Nussbaum (New York: Oxford University Press, 2017): 10–21.

11. Moyer-Gusé, "Toward a Theory of Entertainment Persuasion," 407.

12. Michelle Miller-Day and Michael L. Hecht, "Narrative Means to Preventative Ends: A Narrative Engagement Framework for Designing Prevention Interventions," *Health Communication* 28, no. 7 (2013): 657–70. https://doi.org/10.1080/10410236.2012.762861.

13. For example, see Amy Slater and Marika Tiggemann, "Media Matters for Boys Too! The Role of Specific Magazine Types and Television Programs in the Drive for Thinness and Muscularity in Adolescent Boys," *Eating Behaviors* 15, no. 4 (2014): 679–82. https://doi.org/10.1016/j.eatbeh.2014.10.002.

14. Li-Ling Huang, Daniela B. Friedman, Feng-Chang Lin, and James F. Thrasher, "Which Types of Anti-Smoking Television Advertisements Work Better in Taiwan?" *Health Promotion International* 33, no. 3 (2018): 545–55, 545. https://doi.org/10.1093/heapro/daw085.

15. Kristie M. Farrar, "Sexual Intercourse on Television: Do Safe Sex Messages Matter?" *Journal of Broadcasting & Electronic Media* 50, no. 4 (2006): 635–50. https://doi.org/10.1207/s15506878jobem5004_4.

16. Heather J. Hether, Grace C. Huang, Vicki Beck, Sheila T. Murphy, and Thomas W. Valente, "Entertainment–Education in a Media-Saturated Environment: Examining the Impact of Single and Multiple Exposures to Breast Cancer Storylines on Two Popular Medical Dramas," *Journal of Health Communication* 13, no. 8 (2008): 808–23. https://doi.org/10.1080/10810730802487471.

17. Holley A. Wilkin, Thomas W. Valente, Sheila Murphy, Michael J. Cody, and Grace Huang, Vicki Beck, "Does Entertainment–Education Work with Latinos in the United States? Identification and the Effects of a Telenovela Breast Cancer Storyline," *Journal of Health Communication* 12, no. 5 (2007): 455–69. https://doi.org/10.1080/10810730701438690.

18. Hyuhn-Suhck Bae, "Entertainment–Education and Recruitment of Cornea Donors: The Role of Emotion and Issue Involvement," *Journal of Health Communication* 13, no. 1 (2008): 20–36. https://doi.org/10.1080/10810730701806953.

19. Sohad Murrar and Markus Brauer, "Entertainment–Education Effectively Reduces Prejudice," *Group Processes & Intergroup Relations* 21, no. 7 (2018): 1053–77. https://doi.org/10.1177/1368430216682350.

20. Albert Bandura, *Social Foundations of Thought and Action: A Social Cognitive Theory* (Englewood Cliffs, NJ: Prentice Hall, 1986).

21. Roel O. Lutkenhaus, Jeroen Jansz, and Martine P. A. Bouman, "Tailoring in the Digital Era: Stimulating Dialogues on Health Topics in Collaboration with Social Media Influencers," *Digital Health* 5 (2019): 1–11.

22. Albert Bandura, "Health Promotion by Social Cognitive Means," *Health Education & Behavior* 31, no. 2 (2004): 143–64. https://doi.org/10.1177/1090198104263660.

23. Amy Henderson Riley and Caty Borum Chattoo, "Developing Multimedia Social Impact Entertainment Programming on Healthy Ageing for Hispanics in the United States," *The Journal of Development Communication* 30, no. 2 (2019): 16–29.

24. Kris Barker, Fatou Jah, and Scott Connolly, "A Radio Drama for Apes? An Entertainment–Education Approach to Supporting Ape Conservation through an Integrated Human Behaviour, Health, and Environment Serial Drama," *The Journal of Development Communication* 29, no. 1 (2018): 16–24.

25. Lewis D. Solomon, *Tech Billionaires: Reshaping Philanthropy in a Quest for a Better World* (Piscataway, NJ, Transaction Publishers, 2011).

26. Henry Jenkins, Sam Ford, and Joshua Green, *Spreadable Media: Creating Value and Meaning in a Networked Culture* (New York: New York University Press, 2013).

27. Singhal and Rogers, "The Status of Entertainment–Education Worldwide," 3–20.

28. David O. Poindexter, "A History of Entertainment–Education, 1958–2000," in *Entertainment–Education and Social Change: History, Research, and Practice*, ed. Arvind Singhal, Michael J. Cody, Everett M. Rogers, and Miguel Sabido (New York: Routledge, 2003): 21–37; John L. Sherry, "Prosocial Soap Operas for Development: A Review of Research and Theory," *Journal of International Communication* 4, no. 2 (1997): 75–101. https://doi.org/10.1080/13216597.1997.9751855.

29. Neil Midgley, "Archers 'No Longer Educates Farmers'," *The Daily Telegraph* (December 27, 2010): A1. Retrieved on May 24, 2021 from https://www.telegraph.co.uk/culture/tvandradio/8226200/Archers-no-longer-educates-farmers.html.

30. See H. C. Abell, "Assessment of the Project," in *An African Experiment in Radio Forums for Rural Development: Ghana, 1964/1965*, ed. H. C. Abell, W. F. Coleman, and A. A. Opoku (Paris: UNESCO, 1968); C. N. Anyanwu, *The Agricultural Radio Clubs in the Republic of Benin: A Case Study of Cultural Diffusion in West Africa* (Nigeria: University of Ibadan, 1978); Joseph E. Kivlin, Prodipto Roy, Frederick C. Fliegel, and Lalit K. Sen, *Communication in India: Experiments in Introducing Change* (Hyderabad: National Institute of Community Development, 1968).

31. N. H. Huan, H. V. Chien, P. V. Quynh, P. S. Tan, P. V. Du, M. M. Escalada, and K. L. Heong, "Motivating Rice Farmers in the Mekong Delta to Modify Pest Management and Related Practices through Mass Media," *International Journal of Pest Management* 54, no. 4 (2008): 339–46. https://doi.org/10.1080/09670870802403978.

32. Mark B. Ginsburg and Beatriz Arias-Goding, "Non-Formal Education and Social Reproduction/Transformation: Educational Radio in Mexico," *Comparative Education Review* 28, no. 1 (1984): 116–27.

33. Rasha A. Abdulla, "Entertainment–Education in the Middle East: Lessons from the Egyptian Oral Rehydration Therapy Campaign," in *Entertainment–Education and Social Change*, ed. Arvind Singhal, Michael J. Cody, Everett M. Rogers, and Miguel Sabido (New York: Routledge, 2003): 323–42.

34. M. Byram, C. Kaute, and K. Matenge, "Botswana Takes Participatory Approach to Mass Media Education Campaign," *Development Communication Report* 32 (1980): 10–21.

35. Jose G. Rimon and Suruchi Sood, "Institutionalizing Communication in International Health," *The Global Handbook of Health Communication*, ed. Rafael Obregon and Slivio Waisbord (Oxford: Wiley-Blackwell, 2012): 582–607.

36. Sood, Riley, and Alarcon, "Entertainment–Education and Health and Risk Messaging," 10–21.

37. Kevin B. Wright, Lisa Sparks, and Henry D. O'Hair, *Health Communication in the 21st Century* (Malden, MA: Blackwell, 2008).

38. Jane D. Brown and Kim Walsh-Childers, "Effects of Media on Personal and Public Health," in *Media Effects: Advances in Theory and Research* (2nd Ed.), ed. Jennings Bryant and Dolf Zillmann (Mahwah, NJ: Lawrence Erlbaum, 2002): 453–88.

39. Sheryl Gay Stolberg, "C.D.C. Plays Script Doctor to Spread Its Message," *The New York Times* (June 26, 2001): A1. Retrieved on May 24, 2021 from https://www.nytimes.com/2001/06/26/science/cdc-plays-script-doctor-to-spread-its-message.html.

40. Aubri S. Hoffman, Lisa M. Lowenstein, Geetanjali R. Kamath, Ashley J. Housten, Viola B. Leal, Suzanne K. Linder, Maria L. Jibaja-Weiss, Gottumukkala S. Raju, and Robert J. Volk, "An Entertainment-Education Colorectal Cancer Screening Decision Aid for African American Patients: A Randomized Controlled Trial," *Cancer* 123, no. 8 (2017): 1401–8. https://doi.org/10.1002/cncr.30489.

41. Evelinn A. Borrayo, Monica Rosales, and Patricia Gonzalez, "Entertainment–Education Narrative Versus Nonnarrative Interventions to Educate and Motivate Latinas to Engage in Mammography Screening," *Health Education & Behavior* 44, no. 3 (2017): 394–402. https://doi.org/10.1177/1090198116665624.

42. Hua Wang and Parvind Singhal, "*East Los High*: Transmedia Edutainment to Promote the Sexual and Reproductive Health of Young Latina/o Americans," *American Journal of Public Health* 106, no. 6 (2016): 1002–10. https://doi.org/10.2105/AJPH.2016.303072.

43. Roel O. Lutkenhaus, Jeroen Jansz, and Martine P. A. Bouman, "Toward Spreadable Entertainment–Education: Leveraging Social Influence in Online Networks," *Health Promotion International* 35, no. 5 (2020): 1241–50.

44. Arvind *Singhal*, Ketan Chitnis, and Ami Sengupta, "Cross-Border Mass-Mediated Health Narratives: Narrative Transparency, 'Safe Sex', and Indian Viewers," in *Narratives, Health, and Healing Communication Theory, Research, and Practice*, ed. Lynn M. Harter, Phyllis M. Japp, and Christina S. Beck (New York: Routledge, 2005): 169–88.

45. Everett M. Rogers, Petrer W. Vaughan, Ramadhan M.A. Swalehe, Nagesh Rao, Peer Svenkerud, and Suruchi Sood, "Effects of an Entertainment–Education Radio Soap Opera on Family Planning in Tanzania," *Studies in Family Planning* 30, no. 3 (1999): 193–211. https://doi.org/10.1111/j.1728-4465.1999.00193.x.

46. Victoria Shelus, Lauren VanEnk, Monica Giuffrida, Stefan Jansen, Scott Connolly, Marie Mukabatsinda, Fatou Jah, Vedasta Ndahindwa, and Dominick Shattuck, "Understanding Your Body Matters: Effects of an Entertainment–Education Serial Radio Drama on Fertility Awareness in Rwanda," *Journal of Health Communication* 23, no. 8 (2018): 761–72. https://doi.org/10.1080/10810730.2018.1527873.

47. Michele Tager, "The Black and the Beautiful: Perceptions of (a) New Generation (s)," *Critical Arts* 24, no. 1 (2010): 99–127. https://doi.org/10.1080/02560040903509226.

48. Suzanne de Castell and Mary Bryson, "Identity, Authority, Narrativity," in *Radical Interventions: Identity, Politics and Difference/s in Educational Praxis*, ed. Suzanne De Castell and Mary Bryson (Albany, NY: State University of New York Press, 1997): 1–14.

49. Anthony Brown, "Queering Family Dialogue through Entertainment Education: Narratives from Minority Sexual Identity Youth," *Journal of GLBT Family Studies* 16, no. 5 (2020): 475–87. https://doi.org/10.1080/1550428X.2019.1686720.

50. Zhiying Yue, Hua Wang, and Arvind Singhal, "Using Television Drama as Entertainment–Education to Tackle Domestic Violence in China," *Journal of Development Communication* 30, no. 1 (2019): 30–44.

51. Suruchi Sood, "Audience Involvement and Entertainment–Education," *Communication Theory* 12, no. 2 (2002): 153–72. https://doi.org/10.1111/j.1468-2885.2002.tb00264.x.

52. Hyeonju Jeong and Hyun Soon Park, "The Effect of Parasocial Interaction on Intention to Register as Organ Donors Through Entertainment–Education Programs in Korea," *Asia Pacific Journal of Public Health* 27, no. 2 (2015): 2040–8. https://doi.org/10.1177/1010539512472359.

53. Hyuhn-Suhck Bae and Seok Kang, "The Influence of Viewing an Entertainment–Education Program on Cornea Donation Intention: A Test of the Theory of Planned

Behavior," *Health Communication* 23, no. 1 (2008): 87–95. https://doi.org/10.1080/10410230701808038.

54. Bandura, "Health Promotion by Social Cognitive Means," 143–64.

55. Melanie C. Green and Timothy C. Brock, "The Role of Transportation in the Persuasiveness of Public Narratives," *Journal of Personality and Social Psychology* 79, no. 5 (2000): 701–21. https://doi.org/10.1037/0022-3514.79.5.701.

56. Ibid, 701.

57. Elsbeth D. Asbeek Brusse, Marieke L. Fransen, and Edith G. Smit, "Framing in Entertainment–Education: Effects on Processes of Narrative Persuasion," *Health Communication* 32, no. 12 (2017): 1501–9.

58. Green and Brock, "The Role of Transportation," 701–4.

59. Melanie C. Green, "Narratives and Cancer Communication," *Journal of Communication* 56, no. s1 (2006): S163–83. https://doi.org/10.1111/j.1460-2466.2006.00288.x.

60. For example, see Michael D. Slater and Donna Rouner, "Entertainment–Education and Elaboration Likelihood: Understanding the Processing of Narrative Persuasion," *Communication Theory* 12, no. 2 (2002): 173–91. https://doi.org/10.1111/j.1468-2885.2002.tb00265.x; Sood, "Audience Involvement and Entertainment," 153–72.

61. Arvind Singhal, Everett M. Rogers, and William J. Brown, "Harnessing the Potential of Entertainment–Education Telenovelas," *Gazette* 51, no. 1 (1993): 1–18.

62. Christopher Grady, Alice Iannantuoni, and Matthew W. Winters, "Influencing the Means but Not the Ends: The Role of Entertainment–Education Interventions in Development," *World Development* 138 (2021). https://doi.org/10.1016/j.worlddev.2020.105200.

63. Jonathan Cohen, "Defining Identification: A Theoretical Look at the Identification of Audiences with Media Characters," *Mass Communication and Society* 4, no. 3 (2001): 245–64. https://doi.org/10.1207/S15327825MCS0403_01.

64. Ibid, 251.

65. David C. Giles, "Parasocial Interaction: A Review of the Literature and a Model for Future Research," *Media Psychology* 4, no. 3 (2002): 279–305. https://doi.org/10.1207/S1532785XMEP0403_04.

66. Subhash C. Lonial and Stuart Van Auken, "Wishful Identification with Fictional Characters: An Assessment of the Implications of Gender in Message Dissemination to Children," *Journal of Advertising* 15, no. 5 (1986): 4–42. https://doi.org/10.1080/00913367.1986.10673032.

67. Moyer-Gusé, "Toward a Theory of Entertainment Persuasion," 410.

68. Arvind Singhal, Rafael Obregon, Everett M. Rogers, "Reconstructing the Story of *Simplemente Maria*, the Most Popular Telenovela in Latin America of All Time," *International Communication Gazette* 54 (1995): 1–15. https://doi.org/10.1177/001654929505400101.

69. Keren Eyal and Alan M. Rubin, "Viewer Aggression and Homophily, Identification, and Parasocial Relationships with Television Characters," *Journal of Broadcasting & Electronic Media* 47, no. 1 (2003): 77–98. https://doi.org/10.1207/s15506878jobem4701_5.

70. Cohen, "Defining Identification," 247–9.

71. Donald Horton and R. Richard Wohl, "Mass Communication and Para-Social Interaction: Observations on Intimacy at a Distance," *Psychiatry* 19, no. 3 (1956): 215–29, 215. https://doi.org/10.1080/00332747.1956.11023049.

72. Giles, "Parasocial Interaction," 280–7.

73. Cynthia Hoffner, "Children's Wishful Identification and Parasocial Interaction with Favorite Television Characters," *Journal of Broadcasting & Electronic Media* 40, no. 3 (1996): 389–402. https://doi.org/10.1080/08838159609364360.

74. Robert A. Reeves, Gary A. Baker, and Chris S. Truluck, "Celebrity Worship, Materialism, Compulsive Buying, and the Empty Self," *Psychology & Marketing* 29, no. 9 (2012): 674–9. https://doi.org/10.1002/mar.20553.

75. Albert Bandura, "Self-Efficacy: Toward a Unifying Theory of Behavioral Change," *Psychological Review* 84, no. 2 (1977): 191–215. https://doi.org/10.1037/0033-295X.84.2.191.

76. Jonathan Matusitz and Elena Berisha, *Female Terrorism in America: Past and Current Perspectives* (New York: Routledge, 2020).

77. Carel Van Schaik and Judith Burkart, "Social Learning and Evolution: The Cultural Intelligence Hypothesis," *Philosophical Transactions of the Royal Society* 366, no. 1567 (2011): 1008–16. https://doi.org/10.1098/rstb.2010.0304.

78. Tina Freiburger and Jeffrey Crane, "A Systematic Examination of Terrorist Use of the Internet," *International Journal of Cyber Criminology* 2, no. 1 (2008): 309–19.

79. Ronald L. Akers, Marvin D. Krohn, Lonn Lanza-Kaduce, and Marcia Radosevich, "Social Learning and Deviant Behavior: A Specific Test of a General Theory," *American Sociological Review* 44, no. 4 (1979): 636–55. https://doi.org/10.2307/2094592.

80. Benedict Anderson, *Imagined Communities: Reflections on the Origins and Spread of Nationalism* (London: Verso, 1991).

81. Craig Calhoun, "Indirect Relationships and Imagined Communities: Large Scale Social Integration and the Transformation of Everyday Life," in *Social Theory for a Changing Society*, ed. Pierre Bourdieu and James S. Coleman (Oxford: Westview Press, 1991): 95–121, 108.

82. Ibid, 108.

83. Jonathan Matusitz, "The Implications of the Internet for Human Communication," *The Journal of Information Technology Impact* 7, no. 1 (2007): 21–34.

84. Calhoun, "Indirect Relationships," 108–10.

85. Cristina Archetti, "Narrative Wars: Understanding Terrorism in the Era of Global Interconnectedness," in *Forging the World: Strategic Narratives and International Relations*, ed. Alister Miskimmon, Ben O'Loughlin, and Laura Roselle (Ann Arbor, MI: University of Michigan Press, 2017): 218–45.

86. Cynthia Hoffner and Joanne Cantor, "Perceiving and Responding to Mass Media Characters," in *Responding to the Screen: Reception and Reaction Processes*, ed. Jennings Bryant and Dolf Zillmann (Mahwah, NJ: Lawrence Erlbaum, 1991): 63–102.

87. Moyer-Gusé, "Toward a Theory of Entertainment Persuasion," 411.

88. Lutkenhaus, Jansz, and Bouman, "Toward Spreadable Entertainment–Education," 1243.

89. Hua Wang and Parvind Singhal, "Audience-Centered Discourses in Communication and Social Change: The 'Voicebook' of Main Kuch Bhi Kar Sakti Hoon, An Entertainment–Education Initiative in India," *Journal of Multicultural Discourses* 13, no. 2 (2018): 176–91. https://doi.org/10.1080/17447143.2018.1481857.

90. Martine P. A. Bouman, Constance H. C. Drossaert, Marcel E. Pieterse, "Mark My Words: The Design of an Innovative Methodology to Detect and Analyze Interpersonal Health Conversations in Web and Social Media," *Journal of Technology in Human Services* 30, n. 3 (2012): 312–26. https://doi.org/10.1080/15228835.2012.743394.

91. Lutkenhaus, Jansz, and Bouman, "Toward Spreadable Entertainment–Education," 1244–5.

92. Heidi Parisod, Anni Pakarinen, Lotta Kauhanen, Minna Aromaa, Ville Leppänen, Tapani N. Liukkonen, Jouni Smed, and Sanna Salanterä, "Promoting Children's Health with Digital Games: A Review of Reviews," *Games for Health Journal: Research, Development, and Clinical Applications* 3, no. 3 (2014): 145–58.

93. Debra A. Lieberman, "Designing Serious Games for Learning and Health in Informal and Formal Settings," in *Serious Games: Mechanisms and Effects*, ed. Ute Ritterfeld, Michael Cody, and Peter Vorderer (New York: Routledge, 2009): 117–30.

94. Parisod, Pakarinen, Kauhanen, Aromaa, Leppänen, Liukkonen, Smed, and Salanterä, "Promoting Children's Health with Digital Games," 145–58.

95. Bonnie Ruberg, "Permalife: Video Games and the Queerness of Living," *Journal of Gaming and Virtual Worlds* 9, no. 2 (2017): 159–73. https://doi.org/10.1386/jgvw.9.2.159_1.

96. Wendy L. Bedwell, Davin Pavlas, Kyle Heyne, Elizabeth H. Lazzara, and Eduardo Salas, "Toward a Taxonomy Linking Game Attributes to Learning: An Empirical Study," *Simulation & Gaming* 43, no. 6 (2002): 729–60. https://doi.org/10.1177/1046878112439444.

97. Michael B. Armstrong and Richard N. Landers, "An Evaluation of Gamified Training: Using Narrative to Improve Reactions and Learning," *Simulation & Gaming* 48, no. 4 (2017): 513–38. https://doi.org/10.1177/1046878117703749.

98. Douglas B. Clark, Emily E. Tanner-Smith, and Stephen S. Killingsworth, "Digital Games, Design, and Learning: A Systematic Review and Meta-Analysis," *Review of Educational Research* 86, no. 1 (2006): 79–122. https://doi.org/10.3102/0034654315582065.

99. Michelle D. Dickey, "Game Design Narrative for Learning: Appropriating Adventure Game Design Narrative Devices and Techniques for the Design of Interactive Learning Environments," *Educational Technology Research and Development* 54, no. 3 (2006): 245–63. https://doi.org/10.1007/s11423-006-8806-y.

100. Michael Sailer and Lisa Homner, "The Gamification of Learning: A Meta-Analysis," *Educational Psychology Review* 32 (2020): 77–112. https://doi.org/10.1007/s10648-019-09498-w.

101. Cited in Julie M. Sykes, "Digital Games and Language Teaching and Learning," *Foreign Language Annals* 51, no. 1 (2018): 219–24, 2020. https://doi.org/10.1111/flan.12325.

102. Jane McGonigal, *Reality Is Broken: Why Games Make Us Better and How They Can Change the World* (New York: Penguin, 2013); Kurt Squire, "Mobile Media Learning: Multiplicities of Place," *Horizon* 17, no. 1 (2009): 70–80. https://doi.org/10.1108/10748120910936162.

103. Margaret M. Hansen, "Versatile, Immersive, Creative and Dynamic Virtual 3-D Health Care Learning Environments: A Review of the Literature," *Journal of Medical Internet Research* 10, no. 3 (2008): e26.

104. Kishonna L. Gray and David J. Leonard, *Woke Gaming: Digital Challenges to Oppression and Social Injustice* (Seattle: University of Washington Press, 2018): 8.

105. Marjan Ghazisaeidi, Reza Safdari, Azadeh Goodini, Mahboobeh Mirzaiee, and Jebraeil Farzi, "Digital Games as an Effective Approach for Cancer Management: Opportunities and Challenges," *Journal of Education and Health Promotion* 6, no 1 (2017): 30–45. https://doi.org/10.4103/jehp.jehp_146_14.

106. Pamela M. Kato, "Video Games in Health Care: Closing the Gap," *Review of General Psychology* 14, no. 2 (2010): 113–21. https://doi.org/10.1037/a0019441.

107. Debbe Thompson, Riddhi Bhatt, Melanie Lazarus, Karen Cullen, Janice Baranowski, and Tom Baranowski, "A Serious Video Game to Increase Fruit and Vegetable Consumption Among Elementary Aged Youth (Squire's Quest! II): Rationale, Design, and Methods," *JMIR Research Protocols* 1, no. 2 (2012): e19. https://doi.org/10.2196/resprot.2348.

108. Pieter Wouters, Christof van Nimwegen, Herre van Oostendorp, and Erik D. van der Spek, "A Meta-Analysis of the Cognitive and Motivational Effects of Serious Games," *Journal of Educational Psychology* 105, no. 2 (2013): 249–65. https://doi.org/10.1037/a0031311.

109. Ann DeSmet, Ross Shegog, Dimitri Van Ryckeghem, Geert Crombez, and Ilse De Bourdeaudhuij, "A Systematic Review and Meta-Analysis of Interventions for Sexual Health Promotion Involving Serious Digital Games," *Games for Health Journal* 4, no. 2 (2015): 78–90. http://doi.org/10.1089/g4h.2014.0110.

110. See Nancye M. Peel, Roderick J. McClure, and Helen P. Bartlett, "Behavioral Determinants of Healthy Aging," *American Journal of Preventive Medicine* 28, no. 3 (2005): 298–304. https://doi.org/10.1016/j.amepre.2004.12.002.

111. See Paul Krebs, James O. Prochaska, and Joseph S. Rossi, "A Meta-Analysis of Computer-Tailored Interventions for Health Behavior Change," *Preventive Medicine* 51, no. 3 (2010): 214–21. https://doi.org/10.1016/j.ypmed.2010.06.004.

112. Debra A. Lieberman, "Designing Digital Games, Social Media, and Mobile Technologies to Motivate and Support Health Behavior Change," in *Public Communication Campaigns* (4th Ed.), ed. Ronald E. Rice and Charles K. Atkin (Thousand Oaks, CA: Sage, 2012): 273–87.

113. Igor Revoredo Hosse and Rachel Zuanon, "Games for Change: The Strategic Design of Interactive Persuasive Systems," in *Universal Access in Human-Computer Interaction. Access to Learning, Health and Well-Being*, ed. Margherita Antona and Constantine Stephanidis (New York: Springer, 2015): 442–53, 443.

114. Ibid, 443.

115. Ute Ritterfeld, Michael Cody, and Peter Vorderer, *Serious Games: Mechanisms and Effects* (New York: Routledge, 2009): 11.

116. Clark Abt, *Serious Games* (New York: Viking Compass, 1975).

117. Ibid, 9.

118. Ibid, 9–12.

119. Mohamad Nazry, Nor Nazrina, and Daniela M. Romano, "Mood and Learning in Navigation-Based Serious Games," *Computers in Human Behavior* 73 (2017): 596–604. https://doi.org/10.1016/j.chb.2017.03.040.

120. Yu Zhonggen, "A Meta-Analysis of Use of Serious Games in Education over a Decade," *International Journal of Computer Games Technology* 2 (2019): 1–8. https://doi.org/10.1155/2019/4797032.

121. Ibid, 1–8.

122. DeSmet, Shegog, Van Ryckeghem, Crombez, and De Bourdeaudhuij, "A Systematic Review," 78–90.

123. Elizabeth A. Boyle, Thomas M. Connolly, Thomas Hainey, and James M. Boyle, "Engagement in Digital Entertainment Games: A Systematic Review," *Computers in Human Behavior* 28, no. 3 (2012): 771–80. https://doi.org/10.1016/j.chb.2011.11.020; Karl M. Kapp, *The Gamification of Learning and Instruction: Game-Based Methods and Strategies for Training and Education* (Hoboken, NJ: Wiley, 2012).

124. Esmaeel Rahmani and Suzanne Austin Boren, "Videogames and Health Improvement: A Literature Review of Randomized Controlled Trials," *Games for Health Journal* 1, no. 5 (2012): 331–41. http://doi.org/10.1089/g4h.2012.0031.

125. Stacey Guy, Alexandria Ratzki-Leewing, and Femida Gwadry-Sridhar, "Moving Beyond the Stigma: Systematic Review of Video Games and Their Potential to Combat Obesity," *International Journal of Hypertension* 5 (2011). https://doi.org/10.4061/2011/179124.

126. Kylene Guse, Deb Lev, Summer Martins, Andrea Lira, Jenna Gaarde, Whitney Westmorland, and Melissa Gilliam, "Interventions Using New Digital Media to Improve Adolescent Sexual Health: A Systematic Review," *Journal of Adolescent Health* 51, no. 6 (2012): 535–43. https://doi.org/10.1016/j.jadohealth.2012.03.014.

127. Ian Bogost, *Persuasive Games: The Expressive Power of Videogames* (Cambridge, MA: MIT Press, 2007).

128. Ibid, ix.

129. Ibid, ix.

130. Available at http://bogost.com/books/persuasive_games.

131. Cited in Thomas M. Connolly, Elizabeth A. Boyle, Ewan MacArthur, Thomas Haineya, and James M. Boyle, "A Systematic Literature Review of Empirical Evidence on Computer Games and Serious Games," *Computers & Education* 59, no. 2 (2012): 661–86. https://doi.org/10.1016/j.compedu.2012.03.004.

132. Richard M. Ryan and Edward L. Deci, "Intrinsic and Extrinsic Motivations: Classic Definitions and New Directions," *Contemporary Educational Psychology* 25, no. 1 (2000): 54–67. https://doi.org/10.1006/ceps.1999.1020.

133. Edward L. Deci, "Effects of Externally Mediated Rewards on Intrinsic Motivation," *Journal of Personality and Social Psychology* 18 (1971): 105–15. https://doi.org/10.1037/h0030644.

134. See Scott Rigby and Richard M. Ryan, *Glued to Games: How Video Games Draw Us in and Hold Us Spellbound: How Video Games Draw Us in and Hold Us Spellbound* (Santa Barbara, CA: Praeger, 2011).

135. For example, see Elisa D. Mekler, Florian Brühlmann, Alexandre N. Tuch, and Klaus Opwis, "Towards Understanding the Effects of Individual Gamification Elements on Intrinsic Motivation and Performance," *Computers in Human Behavior* 71 (2017): 525–34. https://doi.org/10.1016/j.chb.2015.08.048; Michael Sailer, Jan Ulrich, Hense, Sarah Katharina Mayr, and Heinz Mandl, "How Gamification Motivates: An Experimental Study of the Effects of Specific Game Design Elements on Psychological Need Satisfaction," *Computers in Human Behavior* 69 (2017): 371–80. https://doi.org/10.1016/j.chb.2016.12.033.

136. Richard M. Ryan and Edward L. Deci, "Overview of Self-Determination Theory: An Organismic Dialectical Perspective," in *Handbook of Self-Determination Research*, ed. Richard M. Ryan and Edward L. Deci (Rochester, NY: University of Rochester Press, 2002): 3–33.

137. Wouters, van Nimwegen, van Oostendorp, and van der Spek, "A Meta-Analysis," 249–65.

138. Ryan and Deci, "Intrinsic and Extrinsic Motivations," 55.

139. Ibid, 55.

140. Wei Peng, Jih-Hsuan Lin, Karin A. Pfeiffer, and Brian Winn, "Need Satisfaction Supportive Game Features as Motivational Determinants: An Experimental Study of a

Self-Determination Theory Guided Exergame," *Media Psychology* 15, no. 2 (2012): 175–96. https://doi.org/10.1080/15213269.2012.673850.

141. Peter Vorderer, Christoph Klimmt, and Ute Ritterfield, "Enjoyment: At the Heart of Media Entertainment," *Communication Theory* 14, no. 4 (2004): 388–408. https://doi.org/10.1093/ct/14.4.388.

142. Robin L. Nabi and Marina Krcmar, "Conceptualizing Media Enjoyment as Attitude: Implications for Media Effects Research," *Media Psychology* 14 (2004): 288–310. https://doi.org/10.1111/j.1468–2885.2004.tb00316.x.

143. Arthur Raney and J. Bryant, "Moral Judgment in Crime Drama: An Integrated Theory of Enjoyment," *Journal of Communication* 52 (2002): 402–15. https://doi.org/10.1093/joc/52.2.402.

144. Ron Tamborini, Nicholas David Bowman, Allison Eden, Matthew Grizzard, and Ashley Organ, "Defining Media Enjoyment as the Satisfaction of Intrinsic Needs," *Journal of Communication* 60, no. 4 (2010): 758–77. https://doi.org/10.1111/j.1460-2466.2010.01513.x.

145. Ralph Koster, *Theory of Fun for Game Design* (2nd Ed.) (Sebastopol, CA: O'Reilly Media, 2013).

146. Ian Dunwell, Sara De Freitas, and Steve Jarvis, "Four-Dimensional Consideration of Feedback in Serious Games," in *Digital Games and Learning*, ed. S. De Freitas and P. Maharg (New York: Continuum Publishing, 2011): 42–62.

147. Ryan and Deci, "Intrinsic and Extrinsic Motivations," 54–67.

148. Edward L. Deci and Richard M. Ryan, "The 'What' and 'Why' of Goal Pursuits: Human Needs and the Self-Determination of Behavior," *Psychological Inquiry* 11, no. 4 (2000): 227–68, 252. https://doi.org/10.1207/S15327965PLI1104_01.

149. Ryan and Deci, "Overview of Self-Determination Theory," 8.

150. Edward L. Deci, Richard Koestner, and Richard M. Ryan, "A Meta-Analytic Review of Experiments Examining the Effects of Extrinsic Rewards on Intrinsic Motivation," *Psychological Bulletin* 125, no. 6 (1999): 627–68. https://doi.org/10.1037/0033-2909.125.6.627.

151. Richard M. Ryan, C. Scott Rigby, and Andrew Przybylski, "The Motivational Pull of Video Games: A Self-Determination Theory Approach," *Motivation and Emotion* 30 (2006): 344–60. https://doi.org/10.1007/s11031-006-9051-8.

152. Deci and Ryan, "The 'What' and 'Why' of Goal Pursuits," 252.

153. Christoph Klimmt and Tilo Hartmann, "Effectance, Self-Efficacy, and the Motivation to Play Video Games," in *Playing Video Games: Motives, Responses, and Consequences*, ed. Peter Vorderer and Jennings Bryant (Mahwah, NJ: Lawrence Erlbaum, 2006): 133–45, 137.

154. Ryan and Deci, "Overview of Self-Determination Theory," 7.

155. Ryan, Rigby, and Przybylski, "The Motivational Pull of Video Games," 9051–8.

156. Andrew Przybylski, C. Scott Rigby, and Richard M. Ryan, "A Motivational Model of Video Game Engagement," *Review of General Psychology* 14, no. 2 (2010): 154–66. https://doi.org/10.1037/a0019440.

157. Andrew Przybylski, Richard M. Ryan, and C. Scott Rigby, "The Motivating Role of Violence in Video Games," *Personality and Social Psychology Bulletin* 35, no. 2 (2009): 243–59. https://doi.org/10.1177/014616720832726.

158. Rigby and Ryan, *Glued to Games*.

159. Juan C. Burguillo, "Using Game Theory and Competition-Based Learning to Stimulate Student Motivation and Performance," *Computers & Education* 55, no. 2 (2010): 566–75. https://doi.org/10.1016/j.compedu.2010.02.018.
160. Hosse and Zuanon, "Games for Change," 444–6.
161. Deci and Ryan, "The 'What' and 'Why' of Goal Pursuits," 252.
162. Ryan and Deci, "Overview of Self-Determination Theory," 7.
163. Edward L. Deci and Richard M. Ryan, *Intrinsic Motivation and Self-Determination in Human Behaviour* (New York: Plenum, 1985).
164. Tamborini, Bowman, Eden, Grizzard, and Organ, "Defining Media Enjoyment," 758–77.
165. Ryan, Rigby, and Przybylski, "The Motivational Pull of Video Games," 9051–8.
166. Peng, Lin, Pfeiffer, and Winn, "Need Satisfaction Supportive Game Features," 175–96. https://doi.org/10.1080/15213269.2012.673850.
167. Richard M. Ryan, "Psychological Needs and the Facilitation of Integrative Processes," *Journal of Personality* 63, no. 3 (1995): 397–427. https://doi.org/10.1111/j.1467-6494.1995.tb00501.x.
168. Martin Heidegger, *Being and Time* (New York: Harper Perennial Modern Thought, 2008).
169. Steven Conway and Bradley Elphinstone, "Da-Sein Design: Linking Phenomenology with Self-Determination Theory for Game Design," *Journal of Gaming & Virtual Worlds* 9, no. 1 (2017): 55–69. https://doi.org/10.1386/jgvw.9.1.55_1.
170. Jerry Willis, *Foundations of Qualitative Research: Interpretive and Critical Approaches* (Thousand Oaks, CA: Sage, 2007).
171. Conway and Elphinstone, "Da-Sein Design," 58.
172. Willis, *Foundations of Qualitative Research*, 106.
173. Conway and Elphinstone, "Da-Sein Design," 58.
174. Cited in Lovelace Jr., Berkeley, "Biden Administration to Use Celebrities, Athletes in Campaign to Combat COVID Vaccine Hesitancy," *CNBC* (April 22, 2021). Retrieved on May 6, 2021 from https://www.cnbc.com/2021/04/22/white-house-to-use-celebrities-athletes-in-ad-campaign-to-combat-covid-vaccine-hesitancy.html.
175. Katie Rogers, "At the White House, Olivia Rodrigo Says Vaccines Are 'Good 4U'," *The New York Times* (July 14, 2021): A1. Retrieved on July 14, 2021 from https://www.nytimes.com/2021/07/14/us/politics/olivia-rodrigo-biden-vaccines.html.
176. Su Holmes and Sean Redmond, *Framing Celebrity: New Directions in Celebrity Culture* (New York: Routledge, 2006).
177. Nick Couldry, *Media, Society, World: Social Theory and Digital Media Practice* (Cambridge: Polity, 2012).
178. Graeme Turner, *Understanding Celebrity* (Thousand Oaks, CA: Sage, 2004): 9.
179. Prosper Poitevin, *Nouveau dictionnaire universel de la langue française* (Vol. I) (Paris: F. Charerot, 1856).
180. Chris Rojek, *Celebrity* (London: Reaktion Books, 2001): 9.
181. Ibid, 9.
182. Angela Carroll, "Brand Communications in Fashion Categories Using Celebrity Endorsement," *Journal of Brand Management* 17 (2009): 146–58. https://doi.org/10.1057/bm.2008.42.

183. David S. Meyer, "The Challenge of Cultural Elites: Celebrities and Social Movements," *Sociological Inquiry* 65, no. 2 (1995): 181–206. https://doi.org/10.1111/j.1475-682X.1995.tb00412.x.

184. *Look to the Stars*, "Charitable & Philanthropic Celebrities," *Look to the Stars* (2013). Retrieved on May 6, 2021 from http://www.looktothestars.org/celebrity.

185. Max Weber, *On Charisma and Institution Building* (Chicago, IL: The University of Chicago Press, 1968): 48.

186. Lawrence Grossberg, *We Gotta Get Out of This Place. Popular Conservatism and Postmodern Culture* (New York: Routledge, 1992).

187. John Fiske, "The Cultural Economy of Fandom," in *The Adoring Audience: Fan Culture and Popular Media*, ed. Lisa A. Lewis (London: Routledge, 1992): 30–49.

188. Myleea Hill and Marceline Thompson-Hayes, *From Awareness to Commitment in Public Health Campaigns: The Awareness Myth* (Lanham, MD: Lexington Books, 2020).

189. Siti Faidul Maisarah Abdullah, Ilya Yasnorizar Ilyas, and Noor Ashmalia Mohd Ashraff, "Barriers Towards the Effectiveness of an Anti-Smoking Campaign Program in Malacca," *Journal of Education and Social Sciences* 3 (2016): 99–105.

190. Matt James, Tina Hoff, Julia Davis, and Robert Graham, "Leveraging the Power of the Media to Combat HIV/AIDS," *Health Affairs* 24, no. 3 (2005): 854–7. https://doi.org/10.1377/hlthaff.24.3.854.

191. Adrian Lovett, "The F-Word: Why We Did It," (2011). Retrieved on May 6, 2021 from http://www.one.org/international/blog/the-f-word-why-we-did-it.

192. *BBC News*, "Bono One Campaign Advert Faces TV Ban," *BBC News* (October 7, 2011). Retrieved on May 6, 2021 from https://www.bbc.com/news/entertainment-arts-15215682.

193. Felicity Morse, "Famine Is Real F-Word: Celebs Speak Out in ONE Campaign Drought Video," *The Huffington Post* (October 3, 2011): A1. Retrieved on May 6, 2021 from https://www.huffingtonpost.co.uk/2011/10/03/famine-is-real-f-word-cel_n_991822.html.

194. American Psychiatric Association, *Understanding Mental Disorders: Your Guide to DSM-5* (Washington, D.C.: American Psychiatric Association, 2015).

195. World Health Organization, *Mental Disorders* (Geneva: World Health Organization, 2020).

196. National Alliance on Mental Illness, *Mental Health by the Numbers* (Arlington, VA: National Alliance on Mental Illness, 2021).

197. Cited in Paul Avis, "Present and Correct?" *Occupational Health & Wellbeing* 71, no. 2 (2019): 22–3.

198. Paul Illingworth, "How Do We Engage Global Communities in the De-Stigmatisation of Mental Illness?" *British Journal of Nursing* 30, no. 3 (2021). https://doi.org/10.12968/bjon.2021.30.3.184.

199. Elisabeth Mahase, "Star Studded Mental Health Film to Be Shown at 32 Football Games over Weekend," *The British Medical Journal* 368 (2020). https://doi.org/10.1136/bmj.m6.

200. Guy Davies, "Prince William Launches New Mental Health Campaign to Tackle Men's Well-Being in Grassroots Soccer," *ABC News* (May 15, 2019). Retrieved on May 25, 2021 from https://abcnews.go.com/International/prince-william-launches-mental-health-campaign-tackle-mens/story?id=63049251.

201. Michael Nycyk and Craig Mack, "Using Digital Storytelling to Reduce the Stigma Surrounding Mental Illness: Real, Bold and Defined Social Marketing Strategies," *Journal of Digital & Social Media Marketing* 7, no. 2 (2019): 121–7.

202. Laurence Baldwin and Gemma Robbins, "School Nursing and Primary Care: The New Frontline?" in *Nursing Skills for Children and Young People's Mental Health*, ed. Laurence Baldwin (New York: Springer, 2020): 83–96.

203. M. Thakkar and K. L. Lortie, "Effects of Idols in Youths," *INOSR Arts and Management* 6, no. 1 (2020): 44–8.

204. Laura Clancy, "'This Is a Tale of Friendship, a Story of Togetherness': The British Monarchy, Grenfell Tower, and Inequalities in the Royal Borough of Kensington and Chelsea," *Cultural Studies* (2020). https://doi.org/10.1080/09502386.2020.1863997.

205. *The Associated Press*, "Prince William, Kate Donate for Pandemic Mental Health Work," *The Associated Press* (July 23, 2020). Retrieved on May 25, 2021 from https://apnews.com/article/virus-outbreak-mental-health-health-prince-harry-queen-elizabeth-ii-95e102dddcf10da6eb89531f5c8941cf.

206. Amy Woodyatt, "Prince Harry and Oprah Winfrey Discuss Mental Health in New Series Trailer," *CNN* (May 18, 2021). Retrieved on July 19, 2021 from https://www.cnn.com/2021/05/18/entertainment/harry-oprah-show-intl-scli/index.html.

207. Bart Nooteboom, "Trust, Opportunism and Governance: A Process and Control Model," *Organization Studies* 17, no. 6 (1996): 985–1010. https://doi.org/10.1177/017084069601700605.

208. Peter Cram, A. Mark Fendrick, John Inadomi, Mark E. Cowen, Daniel Carpenter, and Sandeep Vijan, "The Impact of a Celebrity Promotional Campaign on the Use of Colon Cancer Screening the Katie Couric Effect," *Journal of the American Medical Association* 163, no. 13 (2003): 1601–5. https://doi.org/10.1001/archinte.163.13.1601.

209. G. Rahmani, "Selena Gomez, Lupus and the Impact of Celebrity Health Disclosure on Public Awareness," *Lupus* 27, no. 6 (2018). https://doi.org/10.1177/0961203317742714.

210. Available at https://www.cancer.gov/about-cancer/causes-prevention/genetics/brca-fact–sheet#what-are-brca1-and-brca2.

211. Jennifer Brier, "Reagan and AIDS," in *A Companion to Ronald Reagan*," ed. Andrew L. Johns (Hoboken, NJ: Wiley, 2015): 221–37; Richard Horton, "Offline: A President, Undone by Prejudice," *The Lancet* 389, no. 10068 (2017): P489. https://doi.org/10.1016/S0140-6736(17)30268-4.

212. Kirsten Aiken, "Media Coverage of Kylie Minogue: Circulation or Compassion?" *ABC Radio* (May 22, 2005). Retrieved on May 24, 2021 from https://www.abc.net.au/correspondents/content/2004/s1373909.htm.

213. *BBC News*, "Kylie Says 'I Was Misdiagnosed'," *BBC News* (April 8, 2008). Retrieved on May 24, 2021 from http://news.bbc.co.uk/2/hi/entertainment/7336164.stm.

214. *ABC News*, "Kylie Receives Top French Honour," *ABC News* (May 5, 2008). Retrieved on May 24, 2021 from https://www.abc.net.au/news/2008-05-06/kylie-receives-top-french-honour/2426438.

215. Simon Chapman, Simon Holding, Kim McLeod, and Melanie Wakefield, "Impact of News of Celebrity Illness on Breast Cancer Screening: Kylie Minogue's Breast Cancer Diagnosis," *The Medical Journal of Australia* 183, no. 5 (2005): 247–50. https://doi.org/10.5694/j.1326-5377.2005.tb07029.x.

216. Rebecca Freedman, Helen Mountain, Dian Karina, and Lyn Schofield, "A Retrospective Exploration of the Impact of the 'Angelina Jolie Effect' on the Single State-Wide Familial Cancer Program in Perth, Western Australia," *Journal of Genetic Counseling* 26 (2017): 52–62. https://doi.org/10.1007/s10897-016-9982-5.

217. Donald E. Thomas, Jr., *The Lupus Encyclopedia: A Comprehensive Guide for Patients and Families* (Baltimore, MD: The Johns Hopkins University Press, 2014).

218. Rahmani, "Selena Gomez".

COMMUNICATION CAMPAIGNS FOR SOCIAL JUSTICE AND SOCIAL CHANGE

CHAPTER 9

Social Justice and Social Change

The third major part of this book focuses on public communication campaigns for social justice and social change. The next three chapters (i.e., 10, 11, and 12), in particular, focus exclusively on the #MeToo campaign, campaigns for LGBTQ+ rights, and Black Lives Matter campaigns. All three are paradigms of campaigns for social justice and social activism. They seek to engender profound, long-lasting changes within society and even the world at large. It is a fight for equality and justice in support of minority or disenfranchised groups. The two brief case studies provided in this chapter are the campaigns against female genital mutilation (FGM) in Africa and against honor killing in Pakistan. These types of struggles to improve society—and, in this case, the living conditions of women—are often struggles to change the status quo, or cultural politics. **Cultural politics** refers to the way that culture—including citizens' attitudes, opinions, beliefs, and perspectives, as represented in civic life, the media, and the arts—shapes society and political opinion, and forms the basis of social, economic, and legal realities. Cultural politics is also defined as the collection of cultural backgrounds, social practices, and political processes through which citizens' daily lives are distinctively produced within a particular milieu or civilization.[1] The second part of this chapter focuses on campaigning for environmental policies and what nongovernmental organizations are.

What Is Social Justice?

By and large, **social justice** is the relation of balance between people and society that is determined by comparing distribution of disparities, from individual freedoms to possibilities for equal privilege.[2] The National Association of Social Workers (2021)[3] defines it as

Fundamentals of Public Communication Campaigns, First Edition. Jonathan Matusitz.
© 2022 John Wiley & Sons Ltd. Published 2022 by John Wiley & Sons Ltd.

"the view that everyone deserves equal economic, political and social rights and opportunities. Social workers aim to open the doors of access and opportunity for everyone, particularly those in greatest need." Although official definitions for social justice differ, they share things in common: equal rights, equal opportunities, and equal treatment.[4] Rawls's (1971)[5] take on social justice rests on two principles: First, all citizens should enjoy basic freedoms (e.g., freedom of speech, liberty of conscience, and political participation) and, second, differences in the distribution of basic goods should only be allowed if they, at a minimum, benefit the least advantaged groups. Ultimately, the objective of a social justice campaign is to build solidarity among and from the people. **Solidarity** is the state of sharing interests, goals, principles, and sympathies to develop a sociopsychological sense of unity of groups or classes. It is established through the connections in society that bind individuals together as one. Explained differently, it is social cohesion constructed from dependence that people have on each other in both developing and developed societies.[6] Solidarity among people—who have most likely never met each other, whether face-to-face or online—is particularly salient when social movements develop.

Social Movements

Social movements are peaceful or bellicose performances, displays, or campaigns by which common citizens make collective claims on certain issues or groups. They are a sustained, organized public endeavor to take collective actions.[7] Tarrow (1994)[8] defines a social movement as "collective challenges [to elites, authorities, other groups or cultural codes] by people with common purposes and solidarity in sustained interactions with elites, opponents and authorities." He makes a clear distinction between social movements and political parties and advocacy groups. Social movements are often the by-product of the disintegration or breakdown of previously consolidative social structures. Collective action, then, is born out of a social imbalance spawned by the malfunctioning of social institutions.[9]

Social movement theory (**SMT**) describes the social production and propagation of meaningful ideas from united groups and how they act and communicate as a collective. According to SMT, people get together based on common values and beliefs. They have similar interpretations of the world, outlooks on how things ought to be, and means of causation. The most flourishing movements that attract supporters and that can survive under tyrannical circumstances over a long period of time are those that produce and disseminate powerful ideas—i.e., which resonate within a particular sociocultural context. Thanks to the internet, campaigns like those led by Black Lives Matter can travel the world with just a few mouse clicks. **Traveling theory** describes how people and ideas travel from one area to another.[10]

The capacity of an individual to launch a social movement, whether for getting legislation passed or by publicly calling ideas and social norms into question, depends on the quality of the message that he or she articulates, the meanings entrenched, and his or her likelihood to identify with the audience or society at large. Tarrow (2005)[11] argues that peace activists who successfully spearhead social movements are able to (1) electrify followers of social movements, (2) present new maneuvers into their catalogs of protests, (3) influence the methods of other peace activists; (4) forge urban and international networks to heighten opportunities for others to collaborate inside and outside their milieus; and (5) convince younger activists to make waves at both the national and international level.

Peace activism is "more like a series of waves that lap on an international beach, retreating repeatedly into domestic seas but leaving incremental changes on the shore."[12] Social movements specializing in international human rights may foreshadow the dawn of a global civic society.[13]

Social Justice Warriors (SJWs)?

Social justice warrior (SJW) is a pejorative term for an activist who vouches for socially progressive ideas—like feminism, equality, and multiculturalism. The charge that an individual is an SJW implies that he or she is seeking self-gratification rather than deep-seated conviction, and gets bogged down in unveracious arguments.[14] Also referred to as **slacktivist** or **clicktivist**, SJW has become associated with a distasteful philosophy of progressive or liberal activism symbolized by adoption of computer-mediated organizational processes—e.g., being active in online awareness movements and hashtag activism—and propensity for confrontational discursive approaches when interacting with opponents.[15] Rather, the term "social activist" or "social justice seeker" would be more appropriate and more accurate. **Social justice seekers** are committed to a particular cause because they genuinely want to see transformation in certain aspects of culture, like the elimination of homelessness and poverty, feeding the poor, fighting against gentrification, and alleviating racial tensions and racist mindsets.[16]

In his *Quest for Cosmic Justice*, Thomas Sowell (2001)[17] adds that social justice campaigns strive to erase needless disadvantages. This term is known as **Cosmic Justice**, which refers to the existential *raison d'être* of social justice. This ethos is shared by every person who has the goal of achieving a social balance on a large scale and extirpating the attitudes, beliefs, behaviors, or even the apparatuses that are thought to be problematic and afflicting certain groups. More often than not, the SJW meme is displayed by antagonists to frame social activists as possessing nonnormative, weird-looking bodies, distinct brains (e.g., ones governed by emotion instead of logic), and monstrous personalities. Such rhetoric is arguably dangerous.[18] Social activists continuously have to face and vanquish such political demonology. **Political demonology** is the "inflation, stigmatization, and dehumanization of political foes."[19] However, by designing and organizing compelling communication campaigns, social activists can manage to exhibit an aura of power, legitimacy, and authenticity to their constituents.

THE ULTIMATE OBJECTIVE OF SOCIAL JUSTICE CAMPAIGNS: SOCIAL CHANGE

Public communication campaigns try to occasion social change by influencing audiences' behaviors and, thereby, assist nonprofit organizations in carrying through their missions. One recurring challenge that exists for any movement aiming for social change is that of conceiving and upholding a public communication campaign that forms a major aspect of its practical base. Such campaigns comprise more than the overall rational choice to marshal resources and follow interests that are unambiguous to society at large. They also necessitate discursive development of interests and identities in a continuing process of communication with the campaign's base.

What Is Social Change?

Social justice campaigns are generally undertaken by noninstitutional actors, strive for profound systemic transformation, and aspire to change conditions at the macro level (like policy decisions or projects).[20] A concept that captures the essence of this statement is social change. **Social change** consists of reshaping the social order of society. It may involve altering social institutions, social behaviors, or social relations.[21] Social change can vary based on the pace of change, the type of horizon, and external forces. Social change is also defined as "the significant alteration of social structures (that is patterns of social action and integration), including consequences and manifestations of such structures embodied in norms (rules of conduct), values, and cultural products and symbols."[22] Social change is unmethodically pervasive and global—limited to neither developing nor developed regions. It can be seen at any moment and across a multiplicity of contexts as a result of political and economic *bouleversements*, frantic mass migration, or natural or human-made disasters.[23]

An important distinction needs to be made between incremental social change and dramatic social change. **Incremental social change** is a situation in which a slow event evolves into an incremental but deep societal transformation, which gradually reshapes the social and/or normative apparatus. It can also reshape or jeopardize the cultural identity of certain groups. On the other hand, **dramatic social change** is a situation in which a rapid event evolves into a deep societal transformation and provokes a breakdown in the stability of the socionormative structures and also jeopardizes the cultural identity of certain groups.[24] To be judged dramatic, a social change has to be fast and include a "break with the past."[25] An oft-cited example in the literature is the fall of the Communist system in Eastern Europe and the Soviet Union.[26] As one can see, social change is connected to change of social structure. **Social structure** embodies an apparatus of socioeconomic stratification, social institutions, establishments, national policies, and legislation that help crystallize the rules, roles, behaviors, and values of societal members.[27] From this vantage point, social structure speaks for institutions or, more specifically, "collective rules and resources that structure behavior."[28]

Manifestations of Social Change

Social change occurs over time and has far-reaching outcomes for society. Noteworthy illustrations of such change have sprung from social movements in civil rights, women's rights, and LBGTQ+ rights, to name a few. Social relations, institutions, and cultural norms can be forever altered as a consequence of these social change movements. In essence, social change is a framework by which human interactions and relationships remold sociocultural institutions over time, leaving a profound mark on groups.[29] The multiple manifestations of social change include:

- **Continuous change**: also called **open-ended change**, it is a category of social change that is cultivated mainly for the sake of change.
- **Fabian change**: progressive and reformist incremental advancement in society according to the method of the **Fabian Society**. The Fabian society is a British institution that has the mission to promote the golden rules of democratic socialism through gradualist and reformist endeavor in democracies, instead of revolutionary overthrow.[30]

- **Radical change**: deep-rooted change of features and parameters of certain aspects of society, usually in the style of political radicalism. **Political radicalism** indicates the aspiration to reshape or replace the fundamental principles of a culture or political system.[31]
- **Revolutionary change**: rampant, radical, and far-reaching change, with inclusion of violence and longing for starting afresh.[32]
- **Transformational change**: a New-age perspective on social change, with fewer negative connotations or ramifications. It is a process of causing substantial change in the culture and work (or functioning) mechanisms of a society. These changes experience immense transformations in processes, people, and, ordinarily, technology.[33]
- **Top-down change**: change that comes from leadership. A top-down approach to change existing conditions seeks an imposed change because the initiative emanates from the top. Top-down change is more apposite when the change is strategically essential and involves massive departures from existing forms and functions. It does not take the masses into account during the decision-making process.[34]
- **Bottom-up change**: change that comes from the grassroots. Also called **grass-roots activism**, bottom-up change is a method that people use when pursuing social change from the ground up; it is the most basic level of activity that galvanizes the huddled masses to make decisions that favor change. Bottom-up change does not have to go along with a political party line. It is a self-determining collective of people who care for solving specific problems and revamping the state of affairs.[35]

The next section is a case study on a type of campaign that advocates specifically for bottom-up change: the campaign against female genital mutilation (FGM) in Africa. Violence against women domestically and globally needs to be unashamedly recognized as a practice that not only chips away at a country's cultural stability; it is also an inconspicuous form of barbarous act. A myriad of seeds of terrorism are sown against women's rights.[36]

Case Study 1:   Campaign against Female Genital Mutilation (FGM) in Africa

Female genital mutilation (FGM) is an example of both overt and covert savagery. FGM is a technique of severing the partial or total external female genitalia for nonmedical aims.[37] Another common rationale for using this procedure is to regulate women's sexuality. In a certain number of cultures, one form of FGM is **infibulation**, which requires the surgical removal of the clitoris and labia of a female and sewing together the contours of the vulva to guarantee that no sexual intercourse occurs.[38] By shrinking or eradicating sexual desire, infibulation is thought to avert premarital sex and adultery—and, by the same token, to make women more faithful to their husbands.[39] To the extent that FGM allows men to govern their women's sexual functions, it perpetuates the presumption that wives are their husbands' property.[40]

Statistics

More than 125 million women (both adults and underage) have endured FGM, and roughly three million of them are subjected to it annually.[41] The World Health Organization brings the estimate up to at least 200 million.[42] For girls aged 4–12, the practice assumes a rite of passage to womanhood. In some cultures, FGM is performed even a few days after birth, the moment that precedes marriage, or after delivering the first child. Girls may have to withstand the procedure alone or in the presence of peers from their tribe. Under these conditions, FGM is undertaken by a respected practitioner—like a senior woman—who grew up in a family of respected practitioners. Nevertheless, in more recent times, it has also been conducted by trained healthcare professionals, like doctors, nurses, and midwives.[43]

In Africa, conventional procedures of FGM vary according to ethnic regions. Whereas some implement the procedures on girls between the ages of six and eight, others prefer to put it into operation at birth or a few days before marriage.[44] The severance process is done alone or in a collective of approximately 40 women or more using the same instruments during the entire course of the procedure.[45] The practice is frequently performed in a ceremonial fashion, in the midst of food, music, and gifts. The circumcisers are normally religious leaders devoid of proper training, midwives, or birth attendants. These circumcisers tend to employ jagged or razor-edged devices like knives, scissors, clippers, or hot things.[46] In the majority of cases, the site for the "surgery" is not sterile and medical anesthetics are absent. It is incredible to observe that the ensuing wound is sewed with rudimentary items such as thorns. When it comes to infibulation, the two sides of the labia majora are usually held together with spikes or stitches while the legs are tied together for a few weeks (sometimes up to 40 days). Restoring the wound can be done by applying ointments, herbal medleys, or animal feces, which is believed to help accelerate the healing process.[47]

The End FGM/C Social Change Campaign

Created in the United Kingdom in 2014, the five-year End FGM/C Social Change Campaign was created to muster people for momentum, a momentum that creates opportunities to curtail the practice of FGM on the African continent. The campaign tried to achieve this by being active at global, regional, and grassroots levels to raise awareness, change attitudes, and influence behaviors. Important strategies included strategic communication, media-based activism, coalition building, and the incorporation of evidence and success stories to prompt sociopolitical commitment and financial incentives to embrace change. The program was led by Equality Now and FORWARD, in concert with a confederation of partners, and supported by the Department for International Development (DFID) in the United Kingdom.[48]

The core message of the communication campaign revolved around three foundational values: (1) Do not cause harm (which can be the by-product of senseless and poorly executed initiatives); (2) obtain the support from African leaders and land owners (who tend to have a lot of clouts in their regions; hence, they can easily be used as change agents); and (3) get FGM to be officially recognized as savagery against women and girls. In order to sculpture a unifying movement, the campaign developed a system of national coalitions and grassroots activist organizations in 10 key countries in Africa. Within these countries, the campaign sought to furnish key players with resources like communication expertise, services, and products to ensure social norms change and accountability. Activities consisted of organizing mass media campaigns, establishing and allocating communications resources for frontline staff and community groups, and collaborating with reporters and civic groups to support accountability and encourage governments to live up to their human rights promises to shield women and girls from FGM.[49]

Communicating Facts to the Public

What this case study has demonstrated, so far, is that social change is transformation of interactions and relationships within society, those that can remold cultural and social structures, with the ambition of transforming unwholesome practices and institutions into ones that are better, bolder, healthier, and fairer.[50] An important intent of the End FGM/C Social Change Campaign was to communicate facts to the public about FGM. Efua Dorkenoo was a Ghanaian–British campaigner and program director for the End FGM/C Social Change Campaign in the United Kingdom. In the summer of 2014, she made the following statement: "The act itself [FGM] is at the core of the control of female sexuality—and it's because of the control dimension, there's always going to be resistance." As she continued, "That resistance means, she believes, that only a whole-system approach to prevention driven by government agencies will work." In her own words again: "These girls need special pathways. They need to be followed and monitored until they are out of risk. We need early identification, and to get social care to the table, because they are not at the table."[51] As the Royal College of Nursing (2016)[52] avers, communication, even when interpreters are not necessary, has to remain clear and transparent, based on forthright and unguarded language and symbols. Relevant photos or diagrams can be useful. It is imperative to not only avoid information underload or overload but, also, to make sure that the public understands the whole FGM-related predicament of African women. Some of the women without any direct exposure to FGM may have never seen nonmutilated female genitalia.

ADVOCATING FOR HUMAN RIGHTS

Human rights are moral codes or norms for fundamental principles of human behavior and are expected to be protected in domestic and international law.[53] Basic human rights are prerequisites for meeting the obligations inherent to human relationships. Slavery, torture, and fear of unreasonable arrest, in addition to substandard healthcare, deficient education, and insufficient economic means, erode human beings' potential to enjoy decent living and human relationships. As a provider of fundamental obligations, an individual can affirm both that others ought to assure them protection from slavery, torture, and fear of unreasonable arrest, and that those others are indebted to that individual with the obligations to guarantee such assurance.[54] Human rights are assumed to guard us from abuse and harm. They constitute the yardstick of measure by which we protect our humanity. Thus, one would hope that human rights would be recognized and inviolable in any situation.[55] Our capacity to make effective decisions and to turn them into desired outcomes is referred to as agency. **Agency** is a method by which we employ our unique resources and talents, and exploit relevant opportunities, to attain our desired outcomes.[56] Agency is a primordial concern for emancipatory politics, in antiracist, feminist, and anticolonialist initiatives. For example, giving attention to and decrying women's lack of agency has been politically cardinal for feminism, with early liberal feminist intellectuals like Mary Wollstonecraft who campaigned for women's rights.[57]

Absolute Rights and Natural Rights

Absolute rights are rights that enjoy the highest protection and cannot be denigrated in any shape or form.[58] **Natural rights** are the prepolitical rights that we have when official political authority is lacking; that is, it is natural for us to benefit from such rights.[59] **Natural rights theory** hypothesizes that we have certain rights—e.g., rights to life, freedom, and property—on grounds of their human nature instead of established laws or conventions.[60] As English philosopher Thomas Hobbes (1651/1958)[61] put it:

> The Right of Nature, which writers commonly call *jus naturale*, is the liberty each man has to use his own power, as he will himself, for the preservation of his own nature—that is to say, of his own life—and consequently of doing anything which, in his own judgement and reason, he shall conceive to be the aptest means thereunto.

Natural rights theory in regards to property gained prominence with the writings of John Locke (1690/1980) in his *Two Treatises of Government*. The centerpiece of his political philosophy was to protect individual rights against authoritarianism. So, he deemed it essential to prove such rights (i.e., property rights) as being endowed with legitimacy regardless of, and antecedent to, any form of government. This take on natural rights theory has inspired contemporary legal proceedings in a common law sense.[62] Natural rights theory sees us as key to the survival of social and interpersonal relations, irrespective of any culture or tradition.[63]

Conscientization

Rooted in post-Marxist critical theory, and sometimes called **critical consciousness**, **conscientization** (from *conscientização* in Portuguese) is a social concept advanced by Brazilian educator, philosopher, and theorist Paulo Freire (1970).[64] The goal of conscientization is to impart an in-depth understanding of the world by exposing social and political contradictions and inequalities, and by describing how common citizens feel about them. Conscientization also requires tackling the oppressive dimensions in our lives by improving not only people's conditions, but also the frame from which they see and experience their environments. This can only be done by raising concerns about the aforementioned contradictions and inequalities, even if it means causing public shame about these injustices, and by providing the incentive to join forces for social change.[65] Conscientization is a type of critical social analysis. Also known as **critical reflection**, **critical social analysis** is an academic discipline that identifies both manifest and hidden social inequalities and that constructs a framework for explaining the unfair exercise of sociopolitical power that engenders them.[66] Hopper's (1999)[67] definition contains its major components:

> Learning to think critically about accepted ways of thinking and feeling, discerning the hidden interests in underlying assumptions and framing notions (whether these be class-, gender-, race/ethnicity- or sect-based). It means learning to see, in the mundane particulars of ordinary lives, how history works, how received ways of thinking and feeling serve to perpetuate existing structures of inequality.

The purpose is to increase the audience's awareness of existing sociopolitical conditions, like becoming aware of injustice and discrimination; investigating direct relations between marginalization and sociopolitical predicaments; experiencing membership in a disenfranchised group; and enabling debate of critical moments that raise consciousness of power differentials.[68] Ultimately, an advocacy campaign wants to attain **collective identification**, which entails sentiments of solidarity, collective efficacy, and common culture.[69] It consists of many classes—e.g., sex, race, immigration status, sexual orientation, and other characteristics. The approach of collective identification is a redefinition of one's class-based identity—an approach that is collectively liberating and enfranchising. Making these changes happen offers a notion of positive estimation *vis-à-vis* one's social group and one's affiliation with it.[70] This feeling of collectivity is expected to infuse action or change for both oneself and the collective.[71]

Critical Questioning

Public advocacy campaigns that champion human rights typically engage in critical questioning. **Critical questioning** is a technique of coaching and "problematization" used by social theorists to expose the dominant social narratives that uphold oppression. Because they constitute a large part of the daily life of oppressed people, they generally go unquestioned. Through critical social analysis, these narratives are uncovered and reframed as a problem that marginalized groups must resist. The campaign designer constructs the message to challenge the "assumed normal."[72] Part of developing critical social analysis entails helping facilitators highlight concrete examples, particularly on local and personally relevant concerns.[73] Critical questioning guides audiences towards understanding how certain groups are marginalized and how society keeps such marginalization alive.[74] Critical questioning can enhance political self-efficacy. **Political self-efficacy** helps individuals develop a sense of confidence to take steps to improve their plight. Feeling empowered for concrete individual and community action is key to social change.[75] Though this construct is not brought up as often, it is tacit. It can elucidate the ways by which people can engage in activism with some expectations of success. Naturally, there exist other motives, like hope, which may not hinge on a belief that success will only come through political activism.[76]

Citizen Participation

Citizen participation refers to citizen action for increased public decision-making. The bases of citizen participation rest on communicating messages, cultivating relationships, developing the ability to act, and maintaining or altering conditions. Arguments in favor of citizen participation stress the benefits to people, communities, and institutions, including enhanced knowledge, authority, power, and problem-solving skills.[77] Citizen participation paves the way for the betterment of education, neighborhood living, the environment, transparency in politics and institutions, and services responsible for citizens and their families.[78] For this reason, citizen participation is "a process in which individuals take part in decision-making in the institutions, programs, and environments that affect them."[79] Public communication campaigns can contribute to citizen participation through cognitive mobilization. **Cognitive mobilization** states that, in developed societies, the way citizens' political participation is materialized is influenced by the fact that citizens tend to be more educated and enjoy wider access to information.[80] Access to education is essential because it translates into more autonomy for subjects with respect to bureaucratized forms and traditional hierarchies linked to politics (i.e., the political party), a penchant for new (unorthodox) types of participation and, in brief, a resemblance to the method of direct (top-down) democracy.[81]

Case Study 2:   Campaign against Honor Killing in Pakistan

Also called **shame killing, honor killing** is the killing of a family member because the executor thinks that (1) the victim caused shame to the family and/or (2) the victim dishonored the moral values of a community or religion.[82] More precisely, honor killing is described as an act of violence based on the perception of family dishonor. For example, the female victim is said to have violated her chastity through fornication or adultery, thereby breaching a chastity code. By bringing shame to her collectivity, the latter is severely damaged and the only way to regain its honor is by killing the woman.[83] Justifications for honor killing include divorce or separation from one's spouse, rejection of an arranged marriage, involvement in an inappropriate relationship (according to the family or community), sexual relations outside marriage, becoming a rape victim, inappropriate style of dress, homosexual relations, or rejection of one's faith.[84]

Beyond Individual Family Matters and across Cultures

Honor killings are not necessarily committed by individual family members. Occasionally, the task is assumed by extended family or community members; contextual pressures require that dishonorable female actions be addressed through this cruel method. Female gossip contributes a great deal to these murders.[85] Honor killing is generally framed as a particular method of execution in "traditional" cultures.[86] The slaying of female victims is observed across cultures and religions, especially patriarchal environments that have age-old interpretations of honor and shame. In fact, some patriarchal environments report much higher rates of honor crimes. In this context, the meaning of honor is different than reputation or prestige. An individual's honor is conceived as having sacred value and something more treasurable to him or her than even his or her own life. It is a fundamental part of life. Losing one's honor is tantamount to losing one's life; and a model human being lives for his or her honor. Accordingly, an individual will make extreme decisions to protect this sacred honor by committing the ultimate sin: killing. This practice is customary not only in Muslim and Arab cultures, but also in Mediterranean cultures in Spain, Greece, and Italy.[87]

Humanity Healing International's Campaign

Since the mid-2010s, Humanity Healing International—a Pennsylvania-based humanitarian, nonprofit organization advocating spiritual activism—has conducted a communication campaign against the practice of honor killings. It specializes in organizing and furnishing women with the knowledge and skills necessary for empowerment. Five hundred women dispersed equally across 10 targeted regions of Pakistan are handpicked and trained to be Women Community Agents (WCAs) to build up a community-focused women empowerment system and activists' network to combat brutality against women through active and bold participation.[88] The WCA women serve as change agents to catalyze bottom-up social change. Once the 10 WCA groups receive adequate training, these 500 women start working in their areas to inform other women about their rights and opportunities through a public advocacy campaign composed of media conferences, public rallies, and a petition campaign directed at the Pakistan National Assembly's Standing Committee Members and lawmakers. In the long run, Humanity Healing International hopes that the practice of honor killing will end and Pakistani society will move towards gender equality.[89]

In this context, a campaign against honor killing can help audiences develop not only a critical consciousness of the importance of women's basic human rights, but also Freire's (1973)[90] conscientization. In this process, change agents can help local Pakistani locales fathom out women's considerable lack of status in relation to men, and, in doing so, introduce the concept of self-agency. A central mission of Humanity Healing International's campaign is to open the public's eyes about the epidemic of honor killing, which can only be achieved by changing the mindset of Pakistani society and raising consciousness of what makes this type of ritual atrocious. Honor killing is to be distinguished from pure and psychopathic homicide, serial murder, a crime committed in the heat of passion, revenge killing, and domestic violence. Honor killing is deeply entrenched in codes of morality and behavior that have crystallized certain cultures.[91] This is why the introduction of this chapter began with the argument that a campaign for social justice is often a struggle to change the status quo or cultural politics.

Citizen Participation

Citizen participation in the decisions that affect Pakistani lives is an imperative of Pakistani society. Pakistani citizens should not depend on public officials or community leaders to make decisions regarding their lives simply because they have been raised with long-established cultural norms. A concrete metamorphosis ought to take place in the name of greater direct citizen involvement. This ethos is expected to develop as Pakistani mindsets towards women become more respectful as well as decentralized and linked to other advocacy issues. Broadly speaking, the philosophy of citizen participation should become a fundamental component of civic life and democratic credo in Pakistan, a country of over 230 million inhabitants. Humanity Healing International's campaign is a perfect example of community improvement activated through civic action and volunteer effort. When various community resources and skills are deployed for a definite campaign goal, the larger society can be enlivened for action, using all institutional domains (e.g., media, schools, workplaces, government agencies, corporations, and civic groups). This type of collaboration facilitates the inclusion of campaign goals across key realms of daily community life.[92] As a nonprofit organization, Humanity Healing International operates as a vehicle through which citizens can combine their interests, express their preferences, and practice the power required to initiate sustained change. Altogether, the organization fulfills the role of watchdog, activist, mobilizer, pedagogue, researcher, infomediary, and policy consultant.[93]

CAMPAIGNING FOR ENVIRONMENTAL POLICIES

It should also be recognized that campaigning for social change is not only about basic human rights. Public communication and mass media campaigns can induce observance of environmental policies. Lawmakers get environmental policies passed to encourage this type of social change. At the national level, agencies articulate more specific policies applicable across different societal levels. At the micro level, such policies, for instance, can eventually lower people's energy consumption—e.g., by supporting investments in solar panels and home insulation. At the meso level, lawmakers might inspire manufacturers to produce energy-efficient appliances and motivate industries to rely on fossil fuels more effectively. At the macro level, nations might adopt a more balanced energy program underscoring the value of renewable or nonfossil sources like water, biomass, wind, and sun.[94]

The benefit of public communication as a vehicle for social change across large audiences is contested. Recent studies on sustainable behavior among homeowners reveal that, even when they have sufficient knowledge on environmental issues and are predisposed to act sustainably, they may still not modify their behaviors because of potential inconveniences or psychological barriers to modifying their behavior.[95] Some studies even suggest that environmental public communications produce more disappointing results because they rely on so-called linear or rational choice models.[96] These models postulate a direct causation between diffusing facts and information and behavior change, without considering the sociopsychological mechanisms that shape actual displays of environmental behavior. It is not unreasonable to say that public campaigners ignore sociopsychological processes when planning their public communication initiatives because they can be intricate and less well understood. Public communicators are generally well-versed in the application of two linear models in particular: the knowledge–attitude–behavior model[97] and the Shannon–Weaver model of communication.[98]

One approach for campaign designers to raise consciousness about environmental issues is to have a well-defined call for action that explains how each issue can be addressed. An examination of research on self-efficacy and at-work performance demonstrated that calls for action are most effective when supplemented by authentic information and clear-cut guidelines.[99] In the context of environmental public communication, it translates into a call for people to "reduce their car use" than to "reduce their carbon footprint." The chances of instilling action and adherence to environmental policies can also be increased when audiences understand the message and believe the issue is relevant to them.[100] Adapting messages to personally relevant values will boost the impact of environmental communication. The literature suggests that stressing the importance of saving money, well-being, and recycling can motivate us to act sustainably, given that such values are more personally relevant than public communication that uses abstract language regarding environmental care.[101]

Corporate Social Responsibility (CSR)

Corporate social responsibility (**CSR**) is the notion that organizations, particularly (but not only) corporations, have a moral duty to care for the interests of consumers, staff, shareholders, communities, and the environment at large in all parts of their activities. It is important to differentiate CSR from charitable donations and "good works" (e.g., Habitat for Humanity or Ronald McDonald House). CSR transcends mere charity and operates on the principle that a responsible organization should seriously consider its impact on the environment (and its people) when making decisions. This requires the organization to balance the needs of all with its dream of generating profits and reward its constituents adequately. The idea of CSR can be traced back to the writings of Andrew Carnegie and others. Carnegie, an American industrialist and founder of US Steel, conveyed the charity principle as he saw it as necessary for capitalism to function properly. The **charity principle** is the philosophy that more resourceful members of society help their less resourceful counterparts, including the jobless, the disabled, the diseased, and the elderly. These could receive assistance, either directly or indirectly, from institutions like churches, settlement houses, and other civic organizations. Carnegie criticized the "captains of industry"—or "robber barons"—for flouting broader social concerns in their quest for wealth and power. In the nineteenth century, **robber barons** were businesspeople who used exploitative maneuvers to become rich.[102]

Public communication campaigns that focus on CSR follow the assumption that "corporations have obligations to society that extend beyond mere profit-making activities"[103] and that social responsibility should seek to reduce societal harm to a minimum and implement strategic functions.[104] When applied judiciously, CSR can become a determinant of titanic social progress, as the corporation uses its vast resources, skills, and insights to decisions that benefit society.[105] Campaigns name moral obligation as an important motivation for undertaking radical social change. They stress that a better reputation and consumer loyalty are also great motivations for ideal social behavior because they would ensure higher sustainability, reputation, and liberty to operate. When CSR campaigns derive from an organization's central business objectives, they convert into investments that make the operating environment of the organization better. For example, when communities are more educated or healthier, they produce better and more productive workers. When they have excellent school systems, then corporations can attract higher-qualified people because the highly educated ones want their sons and daughters to attend high-performing schools. CSR campaigns that tackle these issues are a worthy investment because they produce returns that facilitate the organizations' dreams of achieving core business goals.[106]

Ecological Responsibility

Ecological responsibility is the philosophy that organizations devoted to environmentally responsible causes—e.g., recycling, conserving energy, consumer boycotting, and so forth—have higher accountability for the ecological footprint that they carry on their environment, its citizens, and the organizations' own stakeholders.[107] An illustration of this is ethical investing. Also called **socially responsible investing**, **ethical investing** denotes an investment strategy determined to create both financial return and social good to the fullest. Ethical investing began with the Religious Society of Friends (Quakers). In 1758, the Quaker Philadelphia Yearly Meeting made it clear that is members were not permitted to undertake unethical investments. One of the pioneers of ethical investing was John Wesley (1703–91), a key founder of the Methodist Church. A sermon of his, titled "The Use of Money," details his two basic creeds of social investing—i.e., do no harm to your neighbor through your corporate activities and stay away from industries like tanning and chemical production that contaminate rivers and streams.[108]

Modern ethical investing campaigns began during the Vietnam War. Many people living during that era recall the photo from June 1972 of a nine-year-old girl who was running naked towards a photographer. Her back was burning from the napalm discharged on her settlement. That picture triggered furor against Dow Chemical (the second largest chemical company in the world), also the producer of napalm, and sparked nationwide rallies and boycotts against Dow Chemical and other corporations profiteering from the Vietnam War.[109] Later during that decade, ethical investing campaigns directed their attention towards nuclear power and car emissions control. These issues established the groundwork for the type of campaigns that we see today.[110]

Green Campaigns for Young Green Audiences

Green campaigns comprise all activities responsible for creating and facilitating any exchanges meant to fulfill individual and social needs—in order to make the satisfaction of these needs occur—with the lowest adverse impact possible on the natural environment. Green campaigns include a wide assortment of advocacy messages, such as (1) product modification, (2) modifications to the production process, (3) new packaging, and (4) new advertising. The outcome, for example, is that, in this new era, resorts have begun advertising themselves as ecotourist facilities that offer unique experiences with nature or that operate in a way that sharply reduces their environmental impact.[111] **Green audiences** are composed of people who predicate their behavior on environmentally sound conditions and products and who are ready to make more effort or pay more money for bettering the environment.

It should not be surprising that many green campaigns target Millennials and Generation Z youths. In a March 2021 scientific poll titled "Sustainability & Consumerism: US Consumer Behaviors and Preferences," conducted by Compose[d], a digital creative services and strategy agency, and MaCher, a promotional product and design organization, revealed that 53% of Millennials and Generation Z youths have changed their mindsets for "environmental reasons." Also known informally as **zoomers**, **Generation Z** is the age bracket that includes people born between the mid- to late 1990s and the early 2010s. They are twice more likely than any other age group to be willing to change their behavior out of "environmentally friendly" motives. This growing consumer bracket, together with **Millennials**—those generally born between 1981 to 1996—are twice to thrice more likely than older generations to be green audiences.[112] Munerah, Koay, and Thambiah (2021)[113] found that, for these two generations, CSR campaigns occasion a long-term impact on individual norms. With respect to green beauty products in particular, the mere fact of being aware of positive consequences, efficiency, social norms, individual norms, and CSR campaigns in general, causes young audiences to develop more positive attitudes towards such products.

NONGOVERNMENTAL ORGANIZATIONS

The vast majority of public communication campaigns that advocate for social justice and social change are run by nongovernmental organizations. This is in contrast to other types of campaigns, like those centered on public health or antiterrorist behavior, which have included more governmental or state-run initiatives. Commonly referred to as **NGOs**, **nongovernmental organizations** are nonprofit, self-governing local, domestic, or international organizations—which could nevertheless be funded by governments—that charge themselves with solving charitable, philanthropic, human rights, social, educational, healthcare, public policy, environmental, or other issues, usually to create long-lasting changes in accordance with their objectives.[114] They are sometimes founded by citizens, celebrities, or politicians themselves. They could take the form of clubs or associations that offer services, benefits, and space to members. On occasion, the term is employed as a synonym for "civil society organization" to allude to any association established by citizens. However, this is not how the term is expected to be used in the media or daily parlance, as mentioned in major dictionaries.[115]

The Types of Nongovernmental Organizations

The term was first coined in 1945 by the United Nations.[116] Nongovernmental organizations have been private agencies that promote global development or indigenous or religious groups established nationally or regionally—to name just a few categories. Multifarious charitable and religious organizations that round up private finances and spend them on the development of society also fall under that umbrella.[117] Here is a selective list of different types of nongovernmental organizations:

- **Community-based organizations** emerge from people's own initiatives. They can be responsible for raising awareness of disadvantaged collectives, assisting them in understanding their rights in accessing basic services, and offering such services.[118]
- **Citywide organizations** consist of organizations like chambers of commerce, partisanships between business and educational groups, and leagues of community organizations.[119]
- **Faith-based organizations** are organizations driven by their faiths and beliefs to make society a better place by, for instance, converting locals into their religions and improving the overall well-being of the underprivileged.[120]
- **International nongovernmental organizations** can be secular agencies like Save the Children, SOS Children's Villages, OXFAM, the Ford Foundation, Global March against Child Labor, and the Rockefeller Foundation. They are generally responsible for financing local organizations, institutions, and projects.[121]

Each of these four types of nongovernmental organizations has, as their *raison d'être*, a mission that is not based on financial profit. On the contrary, they have a multitude of reasons for existence that guide their enterprises and activities. For example, these enterprises and activities entail putting pressure on particular environmental concerns or human rights violations, promoting educational charities, setting up shelters for victims of domestic violence, sponsoring cultural initiatives, creating new forms of religious gatherings, supporting legal foundations, and funding humanitarian assistance programs. The list is endless. Such nongovernmental organizations are well-known for their colossal international endeavors that employ or recruit hundreds or even thousands of satellite organizations in all corners of the world.[122]

For a large part, nongovernmental organizations strive to uphold the dignity of citizens when the latter have been threatened by the authoritarianism or tyranny of the state. Those organizations play a pivotal role in (1) combating violations of human rights either directly or by endorsing certain "test cases" through the court system; (2) providing direct assistance to individuals whose rights have been gravely infringed; (3) pleading in favor of changes to local, national, or international laws; (4) aiding in the development of the substance of these laws; and (5) diffusing knowledge and honor of human rights among populations.[123]

The Four Orientations

The orientation of nongovernmental organizations is important not only in regards to the outcomes produced—and, consequently, for the optimism that audiences may express about the progress of human rights across the world—but also because the orientation can function as a tool to be used by individuals and groups across all walks of life.[124] Upon examining the works by multiple scholars,[125] four types of orientations have been identified:

1. **Charitable orientation** works through a top-down structure with only a modicum of participation or input by beneficiaries. In this case, nongovernmental organizations perform activities that serve to meet the needs of disadvantaged groups. This is a throwback to the top-down type of social change mentioned earlier.
2. **Service orientation** occurs when nongovernmental organizations perform activities like providing health, family planning, or education services for which the core project is developed by the nongovernmental organization. Staff or volunteers are

counted on to make sure that people benefit from services to the fullest. Service orientation incorporates direct assistance to those in need.

3. **Participatory orientation** is epitomized by initiatives involving local people in the execution of a project by donating money, utensils, appliances, land, materials, labor, and so forth. In traditional community development projects, participation begins a definition of tasks to perform and continues into the planning and implementation steps. Participatory orientation also involves individual engagement in broader international efforts to catalyze change even in the farthest places. For example, letter-writing campaigns are a productive tactic used by Amnesty International and similar entities. People flood leaders and public servants with letters from thousands of its members across the globe to petition the release of political prisoners. Street actions or protest, with the wide coverage that these commonly attract, also constitute another example.[126]

4. **Empowering orientation** strives to assist disadvantaged or disenfranchised groups in the formulation of a better understanding of the social, political, and economic problems overwhelming them, and to raise awareness of their own adeptness at controlling their lives. In this type of orientation, participation of the beneficiaries with nongovernmental organizations—here, they are merely facilitators—is at the highest level. A great many human rights campaigns adopt the empowering approach and work hard at guaranteeing protection of civil and political rights. Without a doubt, civil and political rights are only one category of the manifold human rights classified by the international community. To this day, new rights are still added to the list. Upon considering all this and all the activities that nongovernmental organizations have conducted to combat poverty, urban conflicts, racism, healthcare issues, homelessness, and environmental problems, to name just a few, the probable volume of nongovernmental organizations involved in human rights activism, in any shape or form, could easily be in the hundreds of thousands on this planet. Those organizations may try to support protection of basic rights at different stages or levels, and the approaches they adopt will fluctuate based on the category of objectives. Are they specific or general? Are they long-term or short-term? Do they have local, regional, national, or international scope?[127]

Each orientation is shepherded by volunteers or private people. Most of their strength derives from members of the community providing voluntary backing to their cause. This type of collaboration is significant to those individuals who may not otherwise contribute to the development of human rights worldwide. Nongovernmental organizations survive by sustaining a widespread network—formal or informal—of supporters who can be marshaled for events that may both attract media attention and affect policy changes. This goes to show that they rely on healthy relations with audiences to meet their objectives. Foundations and charities set up elaborate communication campaigns to gather financial contributions and apply standard or novel lobbying strategies with governments.[128]

NOTES

1. Barbara Cruikshank, *Cultural Politics: Political Theory and the Foundations of Democratic Order* (Ithaca, NY: Cornell University Press, 2000); bell hooks, *Yearning: Race, Gender, and Cultural Politics* (2nd Ed.) (New York: Routledge, 2014).

2. Ayelet Banai, Miriam Ronzoni, and Christian, Schemmel, *Social Justice, Global Dynamics: Theoretical and Empirical Perspectives* (New York: Taylor and Francis, 2011).

3. National Association of Social Workers, *Social Workers Are Essential* (Washington, D.C.: National Association of Social Workers, 2021).

4. The San Diego Foundation, *What Is Social Justice?* (San Diego, CA: The San Diego Foundation, 2016).

5. John Rawls, *A Theory of Justice* (Cambridge, MA: Harvard University Press, 1971).

6. Kurt Bayertz, *Solidarity* (Dordrecht, The Netherlands: Kluwer Academic Publishers, 1999).

7. Charles Tilly, *Social Movements, 1768–2004* (Boulder, CO: Paradigm Publishers, 2004).

8. Sydney Tarrow, *Power in Movement: Collective Action, Social Movements and Politics* (Cambridge: Cambridge University Press, 1994): 3–4.

9. Charles Tilly, Louise A. Tilly, and Richard Tilly, *The Rebellious Century: 1830–1930* (Cambridge, MA: Harvard University Press, 1975).

10. Jonathan Matusitz, *Terrorism & Communication: A Critical Introduction* (Thousand Oaks, CA: Sage, 2013).

11. Sidney Tarrow, *The New Transnational Activism* (Cambridge: Cambridge University Press, 2005).

12. Ibid, 219.

13. Ronnie Lipschutz, *Global Civic Society and Global Environmental Governance* (Albany, NY: SUNY Press, 1996); James Rosenau, *Turbulance in World Politics: A Theory of Change and Continuity* (Princeton, NJ: Princeton University Press, 1990).

14. James Hasson, *Stand Down: How Social Justice Warriors Are Sabotaging America's Military* (Washington, D.C.: Regnery, 2019); Mark T. Mitchell, *Power and Purity: The Unholy Marriage That Spawned America's Social Justice Warriors* (Washington, D.C.: Regnery, 2020).

15. Matthew Foy, "Erecting and Impaling the Monstrous Social Justice Warrior in The Green Inferno," *The Popular Culture Studies Journal* 6, no. 2 (2018): 369–98.

16. William K. Carroll and Robert S. Ratner, "Sustaining Oppositional Cultures in 'Post-Socialist' Times: A Comparative Study of Three Social Movement Organisations," *Sociology* 35, no. 3 (2001): 605–62. https://doi.org/10.1177/S0038038501000311.

17. Thomas Sowell, *The Quest for Cosmic Justice* (New York: Simon & Schuster, 2001).

18. Adrienne L. Massanari and Shira Chess, "Attack of the 50-Foot Social Justice Warrior: The Discursive Construction of SJW Memes as the Monstrous Feminine," *Feminist Media Studies* 18, no. 4 (2018): 525–42. https://doi.org/10.1080/14680777.2018.1447333.

19. Michael Paul Rogin, *Ronald Reagan, the Movie* (Berkeley, CA: University of California Press, 1987): xiii.

20. J. Robert Cox, *Environmental Communication and the Public Sphere* (Thousand Oaks, CA: Sage, 2012).

21. Steven Vago, *Social Change* (4th Ed.) (Upper Saddle River, NJ: Prentice Hall, 1999).

22. Wilber E. Moore, *Social Change* (Englewood Cliffs, NJ: Prentice-Hall, 1963): 34.

23. See Francis Fukuyama, *The Great Disruption: Human Nature and the Reconstitution of Social Order* (New York: Free Press, 1999).

24. Roxane de la Sablonnière, "Toward a Psychology of Social Change: A Typology of Social Change," *Frontiers in Psychology* 8 (2017): Article 397. https://doi.org/10.3389/fpsyg.2017.00397.

25. Achilles A. Armenakis, M. Ronald Buckley, and Arthur G. Bedeian, "Survey Research Measurement Issues in Evaluating Change: A Laboratory Investigation," *Applied Psychological Measurement* 10, no. 2 (1986): 147–57. https://doi.org/10.1177/014662168601000204.

26. Vladimir Kollontai, "Social Transformations in Russia," *International Social Science Journal* 51, no. 159 (1999): 103–21. https://doi.org/10.1111/1468–2451.00180.

27. Cited in de la Sablonnière, "Toward a Psychology of Social Change," Article 397.

28. Douglas V. Porpora, "Four Concepts of Social Structure," *Journal for the Theory of Social Behaviour* 19, no. 2 (1989): 195–211, 195. https://doi.org/10.1111/j.1468–5914.1989.tb00144.x.

29. Philip N. Cohen, *The Family: Diversity, Inequality, and Social Change* (3rd Ed.) (New York: W. W. Norton & Company, 2020).

30. A.M. McBriar, *Fabian Socialism and English Politics, 1884–1918* (Cambridge: Cambridge University Press, 1962).

31. Jonathan Smucker, *Hegemony How-To: A Roadmap for Radicals* (Stirling, England: AK Press, 2017).

32. Henry Louis Gates, Jr., *Stony the Road: Reconstruction, White Supremacy, and the Rise of Jim Crow* (New York: Penguin, 2020).

33. Valerie A. Brown and John A. Harris, *The Human Capacity for Transformational Change: Harnessing the Collective Mind* (New York: Routledge, 2014).

34. James M. Kouzes and Barry Z. Posner, *The Truth about Leadership: The No-fads, Heart-of-the-Matter Facts You Need to Know* (San Francisco, CA: Jossey-Bass, 2010).

35. Skaidrė Žičkienė, "Grassroots Activism and Sustainable Development," in *Encyclopedia of Sustainability in Higher Education*, ed. Leal Filho (New York: Springer, 2019): 1–10.

36. Amy Caiazza, *Why Gender Matters in Understanding September 11: Women, Militarism, and Violence* (Washington, D.C.: Institute for Women's Policy Research, 2001).

37. Jasmine Abdulcadir, Maria Rodriguez, and Lale Say, "Research Gaps in the Care of Women with Female Genital Mutilation: An Analysis," *BJOG: An International Journal of Obstetrics & Gynaecology* 122, no. 3 (2015): 294–303. https://doi.org/10.1111/1471-0528.13217.

38. Newman Wadesango, Symphorosa Rembe, and Owence Chabaya, "Violation of Women's Rights by Harmful Traditional Practices," *The Anthropologist* 13, no. 2 (2011): 121–9. https://doi.org/10.1080/09720073.2011.11891187.

39. Efua Dorkenoo, *Cutting the Rose-Female Genital Mutilation: The Practice and its Prevention* (London: Minority Rights Publication, 1994); Asma El Dareer, *Woman, Why Do You Weep?* (London: Zed Press, 1982); Helen Kijo-Bishimba, Sharon Lee, and John Wallace, *Report on the Findings of Research into the Practice of Female Genital Mutilation in Tanzania* (Dar Es Salaam, Tanzania: Konrad Adeneur Foundation/Legal and Human Rights Center, 1999).

40. Elizabeth Heger Boyle, Fortunata Songora, and Gail Foss, "International Discourse and Local Politics: Anti-Female-Genital-Cutting Laws in Egypt, Tanzania, and the United States," *Social Problems* 48, no. 4 (2001): 524–44. https://doi.org/10.1525/sp.2001.48.4.524.

41. Abdulcadir, Rodriguez, and Say, "Research Gaps in the Care of Women," 294.

42. Retrieved on June 23, 2019 from https://www.who.int/reproductivehealth/topics/fgm/prevalence/en.

43. Anika Rahman and Nahid Toubia, *Female Genital Mutilation: A Practical Guide to Worldwide Laws & Policies* (New York: Zed Books, 2001).

44. Linda A. Morison, Ahmed Dirir, Sada Elmi, Jama Warsame, and Shamis Dirir, "How Experiences and Attitudes Relating to Female Circumcision Vary According to Age on Arrival in Britain: A Study among Young Somalis in London," *Ethnicity & Health* 9, no. 1 (2004): 75–100. https://doi.org/10.1080/1355785042000202763.

45. Akin-Tunde A. Odukogbe, Bosede B. Afolabi, Oluwasomidoyin O. Bello, and Ayodeji S. Adeyanju, "Female Genital Mutilation/Cutting in Africa," *Translational Andrology and Urology* 6, no. 2 (2017): 138–48. https://doi.org/10.21037/tau.2016.12.01.

46. Nawal M. Nour, "Female Genital Cutting: Impact on Women's Health," *Seminars in Reproductive Medicine* 33, no. 1 (2015): 41–6. https://doi.org/10.1055/s-0034-1395278.

47. Cited in Ganiyu O. Shakirat, Muhammad A. Alshibshoubi, Eldia Delia, Anam Hamayon, and Ian H. Rutkofsky, "An Overview of Female Genital Mutilation in Africa: Are the Women Beneficiaries or Victims?" *Cureus* 12, no. 9 (2020). https://doi.org/10.7759/cureus.10250.

48. Department for International Development, *End FGM/C Social Change Campaign* (London: Department for International Development, 2014).

49. Ibid.

50. Nell Edgington, *Reinventing Social Change: Embrace Abundance to Create a Healthier and More Equitable World* (Vancouver: Page Two, 2021).

51. Louise Tickle, "Calling for an End to Female Genital Mutilation," *The Guardian* (July 2, 2014): A1. Retrieved on May 27, 2021 from https://www.theguardian.com/global-development-professionals-network/2014/jul/02/end-female-genital-mutilation-roundtable.

52. Royal College of Nursing, *Female Genital Mutilation* (London: Royal College of Nursing, 2016).

53. Rhona Smith, *International Human Rights Law* (9th Ed.) (New York: Oxford University press, 2020).

54. Joshua Cohen, "Minimalism about Human Rights: The Most We Can Hope for?" *The Journal of Political Philosophy* 12, no. 2 (2004): 190–213. https://doi.org/10.1111/j.1467-9760.2004.00197.x.

55. David A. Frenkel and Yotam Lurie, "Human Rights in Industrial Relations: The Israeli Approach," *Business Ethics: A European Review* 12, no. 1 (2003): 33–40. https://doi.org/10.1111/1467-8608.00303.

56. Nahid Afrose Kabir, *Young British Muslims: Identity, Culture, Politics and the Media* (Edinburgh: Edinburgh University Press, 2010).

57. Susan Hekman, "Subjects and Agents: The Question for Feminism," in *Provoking Agents: Gender and Agency in Theory and Practice*, ed. Judith K. Gardiner (Urbana Champaign, IL: University of Illinois Press, 1995): 194–207.

58. David Scott, "The Politics of Prisoner Legal Rights," *The Howard Journal of Crime and Justice* 52, no. 3 (2013): 233–50. https://doi.org/10.1111/hojo.12017.

59. John Hasnas, "Toward a Theory of Empirical Natural Rights," *Social Philosophy and Policy* 22, no. 1 (2005): 111–47. https://doi.org/10.1017/S0265052505041051.

60 Ellen Frankel Paul, Fred D. Miller, and Jeffrey Paul, *Natural Rights Liberalism from Locke to Nozick* (Cambridge: Cambridge University Press, 2005).

61. Thomas Hobbes, *Leviathan*, ed. Herbert Schneider (Indianapolis, IN: Bobbs-Merrill, 1651/1958): 109.

62. Barbro Björkman and Sven Ove Hansson, "Bodily Rights and Property Rights," *Journal of Medical Ethics* 32, no. 4 (2006): 209–14. https://doi.org/10.1136/jme.2004.011270.

63. Ralph McInerny, "Natural Law and Human Rights," *The American Journal of Jurisprudence* 36, no. 1 (1991): 1–14. https://doi.org/10.1093/ajj/36.1.1.

64. Paulo Freire, *Pedagogy of the Oppressed* (New York: Continuum, 1970).

65. Andrea Cornwall, "Women's Empowerment: What Works?" *Journal of International Development* 28, no. 3 (2016): 342–59. https://doi.org/10.1002/jid.3210.

66. Carlos P. Hipolito-Delgado and Courtland C. Lee, "Empowerment Theory for the Professional School Counselor: A Manifesto for What Really Matters," *Professional School Counseling* 10, no. 4 (2007): 327–32. https://doi.org/10.1177/2156759X0701000401.

67. Kim Hopper, "John Berger and Eric Holtzman," *Social Policy* 30, no. 2 (1999): 13–21, 13.

68. Roderick J. Watts and Carlos P. Hipolito-Delgado, "Thinking Ourselves to Liberation? Advancing Sociopolitical Action in Critical Consciousness," *The Urban Review* 47, no. 5 (2015): 847–67. https://doi.org/10.1007/s11256-015-0341-x.

69. Lorraine M. Gutierrez, "Understanding the Empowerment Process: Does Consciousness Make a Difference?" *Social Work Research* 19, no. 4 (1995) 229–37. https://doi.org/10.1093/swr/19.4.229.

70. Julio Cammarota, "From Hopelessness to Hope: Social Justice Pedagogy in Urban Education and Youth Development," *Urban Education* 46, no. 4 (2011): 828–44. https://doi.org/10.1177/0042085911399931.

71. E. Summerson Carr, "Rethinking Empowerment Theory Using a Feminist Lens: The Importance of Process," *Affilia* 18, no. 1 (2003): 8–20. https://doi.org/10.1177/0886109902239092.

72. Maritza Montero, "Methods for Liberation: Critical Consciousness in Action," in *Psychology of Liberation*, in Maritza Montero and Christopher C. Sonn (New York: Springer, 2009): 73–91.

73. A. A. Akom, Julio Cammarota, and Shawn Ginwright, "Youthtopias: Towards a New Paradigm of Critical Youth Studies," *Youth Media Reporter: The Profession Journal of the Youth Media Field* 2, no. 4 (2008): 1–30; Shawn Ginwright and Julio Cammarota, "Youth Activism in the Urban Community: Learning Critical Civic Praxis within Community Organizations," *International Journal of Qualitative Studies in Education* 20, no. 6 (2007): 693–710. https://doi.org/10.1080/09518390701630833.

74. Danielle Kohfeldt and Regina Day Langhout, "The Five Whys Method: A Tool for Developing Problem Definitions in Collaboration with Children," *Journal of Community & Applied Social Psychology* 22, no. 4 (2012): 316–29. https://doi.org/10.1002/casp.1114.

75. Matthew A. Diemer and David L. Blustein, "Critical Consciousness and Career Development among Urban Youth," *Journal of Vocational Behavior* 68, no. 2 (2006): 220–32. https://doi.org/10.1016/j.jvb.2005.07.001.

76. Watts and Hipolito-Delgado, "Thinking Ourselves to Liberation?" 849.

77. Howell S. Baum, "Citizen Participation," in *International Encyclopedia of the Social & Behavioral Sciences* (2nd Ed.), ed. James D. Wright (Amsterdam: Elsevier, 2015).

78. Abraham Wandersman and Paul Florin, "Citizen Participation and Community Organizations," in *Handbook of Community Psychology*, ed. Julian Rappaport and Edward Seidman (Boston: Springer, 2000): 247–72.

79. Kenneth Heller, Richard H. Price, Shulamit Reinharz, Stephanie Riger, and Abraham Wandersman, *Psychology and Community Change: Challenges of the Future* (Homewood, IL: Dorsey, 1984): 339.

80. Ronald Inglehart, *The Silent Revolution: Changing Values and Political Styles among Western Publics* (Princeton, NJ: Princeton University Press, 1977).

81. Antonio Alaminos and Clemente Penalva, "The Cognitive Mobilization Index: Crises and Political Generations," *SAGE Open* 2, no. 1 (2012). https://doi.org/10.1177/2158244012440437.

82. Karen Tintori, *Unto the Daughters: The Legacy of an Honor Killing in a Sicilian–American Family* (New York: St. Martin's Press, 2007).

83. Eva Reimers, "Representations of an Honor Killing," *Feminist Media Studies* 7, no. 3 (2007): 239–55. https://doi.org/10.1080/14680770701477867.

84. Robert Paul Churchill, *Women in the Crossfire: Understanding and Ending Honor Killing* (New York: Oxford University Press, 2008); Gökçe Yurdakul and Anna C. Korteweg, "Gender Equality and Immigrant Integration: Honor Killing and Forced Marriage Debates in the Netherlands, Germany, and Britain," *Women's Studies International Forum* 41, no. 3 (2013): 204–14. https://doi.org/10.1016/j.wsif.2013.07.011.

85. Max Gluckman, "Papers in Honor of Melville J. Herskovits: Gossip and Scandal," *Current Anthropology* 4, no. 3 (1963): 307–16. https://doi.org/10.1086/200378; Alexander Rysman, "How the 'Gossip' Became a Woman," *Journal of Communication* 27, no. 1 (1977): 176–80. https://doi.org/10.1111/j.1460-2466.1977.tb01814.x.

86. Yotam Feldner, "'Honor' Murders: Why the Perps Get Off Easy," *Middle East Quarterly* 7, no. 4 (2000): 41–50; Dicle Kogacioglu, "The Tradition Effect: Framing Honor Crimes in Turkey," *Journal of Cultural Feminist Studies* 5, no. 2 (2004): 118–51. https://doi.org/10.1215/10407391-15-2-118.

87. Recep Doğan, "Is Honor Killing a 'Muslim Phenomenon'? Textual Interpretations and Cultural Representations," *Journal of Muslim Minority Affairs* 31, no. 3 (2011): 423–40. https://doi.org/10.1080/13602004.2011.599547.

88. Humanity Healing International, *Advocacy Against Honor Killings* (Oil City, PA: Humanity Healing International, 2021).

89. Ibid.

90. Paulo Freire, *Education for Critical Consciousness* (New York: Seabury Press, 1973).

91. Phyllis Chesler, "Worldwide Trends in Honor Killings," *Middle East Quarterly* 17, no. 2 (2010): 3–11.

92. Neil Bracht and Ronald E. Rice, "Community Partnership Strategies in Health Campaigns," in *Public Communication Campaigns* (4th Ed.), ed. Ronald E. Rice and Charles K. Atkin (Thousand Oaks, CA: Sage, 2012): 289–304.

93. National Democratic Institute, *Citizen Participation* (Washington, D.C.: National Democratic Institute, 2021).

94. Gerdien de Vries, "Public Communication as a Tool to Implement Environmental Policies," *Social Issues and Policy Review* 14, no. 1 (2020): 244–72. https://doi.org/10.1111/sipr.12061.

95. For example, see Gerdien de Vries, M. Rietkerk, and R. Kooger, "The Hassle Factor as a Psychological Barrier to a Green Home," *Journal of Consumer Policy* 43 (2020): 345–52. https://doi.org/10.1007/s10603-019-09410-7.

96. For example, see Matthew J. Hornsey and Kelly S. Fielding, "Understanding (and Reducing) Inaction on Climate Change," *Social Issues and Policy Review* 14, no. 1 (2020): 3–35. https://doi.org/10.1111/sipr.12058.

97. Steven H. Chaffee and Connie Roser, "Involvement and the Consistency of Knowledge, Attitudes, and Behaviors," *Communication Research* 13, no. 3 (1986): 373–99. https://doi.org/10.1177/009365086013003006.

98. Claude Shannon and Warren Weaver, *A Mathematical Model of Communication* (Urbana Champaign, IL: University of Illinois Press, 1949).

99. Alexander D. Stajkovic and Fred Luthans, "Self-Efficacy and Work-Related Performance: A Meta-Analysis," *Psychological Bulletin* 124, no. 2 (1998): 240–61. https://doi.org/10.1037/0033-2909.124.2.240.

100. de Vries, "Public Communication as a Tool," 252.

101. Ecologic Institute, *Influences on Consumer Behavior: Policy Implications beyond Nudging. Policy Brief for the European Commission, Environment DG* (Berlin: Ecologic Institute, 2014).

102. George Cheney, Lars Thoger Christensen, Theodore E. Zorn, and Shiv Ganesh, *Organizational Communication in an Age of Globalization: Issues, Reflections, Practices* (Long Grove, IL: Waveland Press, 2010).

103. Paul Godfrey and Nile W. Hatch, "Researching Corporate Social Responsibility: An Agenda for the 21st Century," *Journal of Business Ethics* 70, no. 1 (2007): 87–98, 87. https://doi.org/10.1007/s10551-006-9080-y.

104. Michael E. Porter and Mark R. Kramer, "Strategy & Society: The Link between Competitive Advantage and Corporate Social Responsibility," *Harvard Business Review* 84, no. 12 (986): 78–92.

105. Ibid, 80.

106. Maureen Taylor, "Corporate Social Responsibility Campaigns: What Do They Tell Us About Organization–Public Relationships?" in *Public Communication Campaigns* (4th Ed.), ed. Ronald E. Rice and Charles K. Atkin (Thousand Oaks, CA: Sage, 2012): 259–72.

107. Richard J. Borden, "Psychology and Ecology: Beliefs in Technology and the Diffusion of Ecological Responsibility," *The Journal of Environmental Education* 16, no. 2 (1984):14–9. https://doi.org/10.1080/00958964.1985.10801948.

108. Mark Anthony Camilleri, "The Market for Socially Responsible Investing: A Review of the Developments," *Social Responsibility Journal* 17, no. 3 (2021): 412–28. https://doi.org/10.1108/SRJ-06-2019-0194.

109. Maria O'Brien Hylton, "'Socially Responsible' Investing: Doing Good versus Doing Well in an Inefficient Market," *The American University Law Review* 42, no. 1 (1992): 1–52.

110. R. Bruce Hutton, Louis D'Antonio, and Tommi Johnsen, "Socially Responsible Investing: Growing Issues and New Opportunities," *Business & Society* 37, no. 3 (1998): 281–305. https://doi.org/10.1177/000765039803700303.

111. For example, see Pravin Ransure, "'Green Marketing" Its Impact on Society: Emerging Challenges & Opportunities," *International Research Journal of Multidisciplinary Studies* 3, no. 9 (2017): 1–6. Aswin Sangpikul, "Ecotourism Mix, Good Practice, and Green Marketing: An Approach Towards the Quality Tourism Business," *Naresuan University Journals* 10, no. 1 (2017): 10–21.

112. Jason Parkin, "94% of Adult Consumers Say a More Sustainable Lifestyle is Important Finds Study from Compose[d] x MaCher," *Compose[d]* (May 6, 2021). Retrieved on May 28, 2021 from https://composedcreative.com/blog.

113. Siti Munerah, Kian Yeik Koay, and Seethaletchumy Thambiah, "Factors Influencing Non-Green Consumers' Purchase Intention: A Partial Least Squares Structural Equation Modelling (PLS-SEM) Approach," *Journal of Cleaner Production* 280, no. 1 (2021). https://doi.org/10.1016/j.jclepro.2020.124192.

114. Thomas Davies, *NGOs: A New History of Transnational Civil Society* (New York: Oxford University Press, 2014); David Lewis and Nazneen Kanji, *Non-Governmental Organizations and Development* (New York: Routledge, 2009).

115. Mary Kaldor, "Civil Society and Accountability," *Journal of Human Development* 4, no. 1 (2003): 5–27. https://doi.org/10.1080/1464988032000051469; Jan Aart Scholte, Civil Society and Democratically Accountable Global Governance," *Government and Opposition* 39, no. 2 (2004): 211–33. https://doi.org/10.1111/j.1477-7053.2004.00121.x.

116. Stanley Meisler, *United Nations: A History* (New York: Grove Press, 2011).

117. Brijesh Nalinakumari and Richard MacLean, "NGOs: A Primer on the Evolution of the Organizations that Are Setting the Next Generation of 'Regulations'," *Environmental Quality Management* 14, no. 4 (2005): 1–21. https://doi.org/10.1002/tqem.20054.

118. Kelly Leroux, "Nonprofits as Civic Intermediaries: The Role of Community-Based Organizations in Promoting Political Participation," *Urban Affairs Review* 42, no. 3 (2007): 410–22. https://doi.org/10.1177/1078087406292257.

119. Asma Lailee Moh and Noor Hisham Nawi, "Faith-Based Organisations (FBO): A Review of Literature on their Nature and Contrasting Identities with NGO in Community Development Intervention," *European Journal of Economics and Business Studies* 2, no. 1 (2016): 14–28.

120. Ibid, 14–7.

121. For example, see Irini Ibrahim and Norazlina Abdul Aziz, "The Roles of International NGOs in the Conservation of Bio-Diversity of Wetlands," *Procedia—Social and Behavioral Sciences* 42 (2012): 242–7. https://doi.org/10.1016/j.sbspro.2012.04.187; G. Bharathi Kamath, "Training Need and Gap Analysis with Regard to NGOs in Mangalore," *IUP Journal of Organizational Behavior* 10, no. 2 (2011): 55–65; Segun Oshewolo, "Limited Policy Engagement of Non-Governmental Organizations: A Guilt Trip on the Nigerian State," *Journal of Sustainable Development in Africa* 13, no. 1 (2011): 142–52.

122. Jens Steffek and Kristina Hahn, *Evaluating Transnational NGOs: Legitimacy, Accountability, Representation* (New York: Palgrave Macmillan, 2010).

123. James Ron, Ramos, Howard, & Rodgers, Kathleen, "Transnational Information Politics: NGO Human Rights Reporting, 1986–2000," *International Studies Quarterly* 49, no. 3 (2005): 557–87. https://doi.org/10.1111/j.1468-2478.2005.00377.x; Kathryn Sikkink, "Human Rights, Principled Issue–Networks, and Sovereignty in Latin America," *International Organization* 47, no. 3 (1993): 411–41. https://doi.org/10.1017/S0020818300028010.

124. Michael Freeman, *Human Rights* (New York: Polity, 2017).

125. Nalinakumari and Richard MacLean, "NGO," 1–21; David Baride Ngeh, "Non-Governmental Organizations (NGOS) and Rural Development in Nigeria," *Mediterranean Journal of Social Sciences* 4, no. 5 (2013): 107–12. https://doi.org/10.5901/mjss.2013.v4n5p107; Cousins Williams, *Non-Governmental Initiatives in ADB: The Urban Poor and Basic Infrastructure Services in Asia and the Pacific* (Manila: Asian Development Bank, 1991).

126. Stephen Hopgood, *Keepers of the Flame: Understanding Amnesty International* (Ithaca, NY: Cornell University Press, 2006).

127. Council of Europe, *Compass: Manual for Human Rights Education with Young People* (Strasbourg, France: Council of Europe, 2017).

128. Niveen Labib Eid and Anton Robert Sabella, "A Fresh Approach to Corporate Social Responsibility (CSR): Partnerships between Businesses and Non-Profit Sectors," *Corporate Governance* 14, no. 3 (2014): 352–62. https://doi.org/10.1108/CG-01-2013-0011.

CHAPTER 10

The #MeToo Campaign

Campaigning for policy change may be considered unnecessary or precipitate by a public that does not consider the problem a serious one. In the case of sexual misconduct, activists may have concluded that the audience ought to be persuaded that the issue goes beyond a mere victim–perpetrator understanding. Only then could activists galvanize the audience to put enough pressure for causing institutional, social, or legal change. This is partly how the #MeToo campaign was born. An important principle is that an all-inclusive and collegial space or work atmosphere contributes to better quality of life for all. On the other hand, an atmosphere that facilitates unprofessionalism, wrongdoing, harassment, bullying, and discrimination can have negative consequences on a person's health and reduce his or her ability to be productive and advance in his or her career path.[1] #MeToo is different from other online- or media-driven campaigns in the sense that celebrities have played a much larger role, not just for the simple fact that it is a campaign, but also because of how the campaign has unfolded—first, as victims; then, as vocal activists.[2] Before discussing the #MeToo campaign around the world, the author deems it important to outline key concepts, definitions, statistics, and facts of sexual misconduct today.

SEXUAL MISCONDUCT: KEY TERMS AND DEFINITIONS

Sexual misconduct is an overarching term for misconduct of a sexual nature that is based, to some level, on personal power or authority—which renders the occurrence inappropriate or even criminal. A recurrent theme, and the rationale for the term "misconduct," is that these violations take place at work or in circumstances of power imbalance. It shapes the situation as an offense that violates an individual's body or boundary in the domain of sexuality or intimate relationships.[3] Two of the most common types of sexual misconduct discussed in the mainstream mass media are sexual harassment and rape culture (described next). What comes after that is an explanation of intimate partner violence (IPV).

Sexual Harassment and Rape Culture

Sexual harassment is a category of harassment that contains some form of explicit or implicit sexual overtones, such as the uninvited or improper assurance of rewards in exchange for sexual favors—a phenomenon called **quid pro quo**. Sexual harassment can range from verbal indiscretions to sexual abuse or assault. Harassment allegations on the basis of sex, not only sexual conduct or language, are on the rise. They can happen at any social setting like the place of employment, the house, school, and even church. Both victims and perpetrators can be of any gender.[4] When the employer is the harasser, he or she can engage in unlawful employment discrimination.[5] Sexual harassment is also regarded as a category of gender-based violence that could be an organizational, criminal, or ethical matter.[6]

The notion of rape culture emerged in the 1970s during the second-wave feminism era.[7] Scholars have described **rape culture** as "a pervasive ideology that effectively supports or excuses sexual assault."[8] Research has identified five areas that facilitate and keep rape culture alive: (1) Uncompromising adherence to firm, traditional gender roles, (2) sexist attitudes and behaviors, (3) unsympathetic sexual beliefs (i.e., considering women's participation in casual sex as inappropriate, while it could be less problematic for men to do it), (4) antagonism and suspicion towards women, and (5) deeming violence a convenient and often necessary reaction.[9] Most of these areas fall under the umbrella concept of **toxic masculinity**, which advocates cultural norms like patriarchy and male social dominance. In the long term, toxic masculinity can be unwholesome to both women and men in society.[10]

Intimate Partner Violence (IPV)

Intimate partner violence (**IPV**) is mistreatment or assault that takes place in close relationships. "Intimate partners" could be both current or previous spouses and dating partners. IPV can escalate on the basis of the manner by which it happens and how extreme it is. It can vary from one instance of violence that could nevertheless have durable impact to multiple grave instances over several years. IPV is often suffered by women and girls, and is the number one reason for homicide death for adult women. It is also experienced by about 30% of men (but with a lower gravity). Individuals who have undergone IPV are at higher risk of serious mental health disorders—i.e., mood, anxiety, and eating disorders, as well as posttraumatic stress disorder and substance or alcohol abuse—and grave physical health problems—i.e., cardiovascular diseases, chronic pain, sleep disorders, gastrointestinal issues, sexually transmitted diseases, and brain trauma.[11]

IPV includes six categories of behavioral violence. **Physical violence** occurs when someone harms or attempts to harm a partner by assaulting, kicking, or employing another form of physical force. **Sexual violence** occurs when someone forces or tries to force a partner to participate in a sexual activity, including penetration and touching, or a nonphysical sexual activity (e.g., sexting)—all of which happens without the partner's consent. **Stalking** refers to a pattern of constant, undesired attention and contact by a partner that triggers fear or concern for his or her own safety or the safety of a third party (that is either close to the victim or the perpetrator, or both). **Psychological aggression** occurs when someone uses verbal and nonverbal communication in order to hurt a partner mentally or emotionally and/or to exert domination over that partner.[12] **Domestic violence** encompasses a spectrum of violations that occur within a domestic situation. It is a comprehensive term that includes various forms of abuse perpetrated by a current or ex-partner.[13] **Family violence** is one committed within families—whether in the household or even after separation—and often consists of violence between husband and wife in the presence of other family members. This is why it can also lead to child abuse. Family violence can be physical, sexual, psychological, or financial.[14]

SEXUAL MISCONDUCT: STATISTICS AND FACTS

The number of women who are victims of sexual misconduct is staggering. For instance, according to UN Women, as of early 2021, around the world, approximately 730 million women—virtually one in three—have experienced IPV on at least one occasion in their lifetime (30% of women aged 15 and up). This statistic does not take sexual harassment into account. Contacts with helplines have increased fivefold in some nations as rates of IPV have skyrocketed because of the negative corollaries of the COVID-19 pandemic.[15] The World Health Organization, too, affirms that one in three women experiences IPV around the world. It is the most prevalent—and, at the same time, the least reported—human rights violation. Though it is highly common in times of peace and political/economic growth, it escalates when a crisis afflicts a nation. Indeed, studies indicate that IPV in humanitarian difficulties is generally devastating. A 2018 survey in South Sudan revealed that more than 50% of women with a current or ex-intimate partner had suffered from IPV, while almost 30% of women experienced sexual violence by a nonpartner. In times of conflict, women's bodies themselves become battlefields, with the body becoming a weapon of humiliation and oppression. Risks are magnified because women can be expelled from their houses and abandoned by their support networks, whereas the legal protection apparatus is eroded or eliminated.[16]

There are a great many negative health consequences attributed to IPV. These include a scope of conditions that have adverse effects on the heart, the digestive system, the reproductive system, muscles, and bones, many of which are chronic. Survivors can suffer from depression and nervous breakdowns. They run a more significant risk for embarking on a lifestyle that is risky to their health, such as smoking, binge drinking, and unprotected casual sex. Under these conditions, IPV is a serious public health issue that carries many individual and social implications.[17]

Situation in the United States

According to the Centers for Disease Control and Prevention, in the United States, as of 2019, approximately 25% of women and almost 10% of men have experienced physical sexual violence, inappropriate touch, and/or stalking at least once and reported some form of sexual misconduct. Over 43 million women and 38 million men have experienced psychological violence by a close partner or an acquaintance in their lifetime. This type of misconduct begins early and can reemerge over the course of the lifespan. When IPV occurs in adolescence, it is called **teen dating violence** (TDV). TDV affects millions of US adolescents annually. Over 10 million women and 5 million men who reportedly experienced physical sexual violence, inappropriate touch, and/or stalking by an intimate partner in their lifetime admitted that they first encountered these forms of misconduct when they were minors.[18]

Men and women tend to differ in their levels of sexual misconduct victimhood. For example, women are much more likely than men to experience rape. Twenty percent of women, but only 1 in 71 men, will be raped at least once.[19] By extension, sexual misconduct is influenced by a set of laws that, generally speaking, make certain settings more vulnerable. Sexual misconduct is not addressed as often as it should be through official channels. Notwithstanding who is selected as the gatekeeper—e.g., a police officer, a human resources representative, or campus authority—sexual misconduct survivors, by far, decide not to file a formal report. Many reasons explain this, but most are related to the theme of systemic failure.[20]

Situation on US College Campuses

During the period 1995–2013, American women aged 18 to 24 had the highest proportion of rape and sexual assault victimizations in relation to women in all other age brackets. College-age male victims represented 17% of rape and sexual assault cases against students and 4% against nonstudents. As a general rule, perpetrators known to the victim (e.g., a friend, acquaintance, or intimate partner) are responsible for most of campus sexual assaults. In fact, college-age women knew their perpetrator in roughly 80% of rape and sexual assault cases, irrespective of their enrollment status. Underreporting is a plague on US college campuses. As per the Bureau of Justice Statistics' National Crime Victimization Survey, for that same period of 1995–2013, only 20% of undergraduate women who were raped or assaulted told the police.[21] US female adolescents and young adults are particularly vulnerable to severe sexual misconduct. For this age group, although nonstudent females experience even higher proportions of victimization than students in their situations, the prevalence of sexual assault on campus is disturbing.[22]

Situation in the US Workplace

Workplace sexual misconduct is frequent. A nationwide survey of 1,000 men and 1,000 women enquired about harassment and assault in various situations. About 38% of the female respondents claimed to have been sexually harassed at work. The result for men was only 13%. The study included verbal harassment and cyber-harassment as forms of sexual harassment. Also on the list was sexual harassment of a physically aggressive type.[23] Qualitative accounts, especially those surfacing in the aftermath of #MeToo, reveal that women with careers in predominantly male industries or with a disproportionately high male presence have to withstand sexual harassment at much higher rates.[24]

In the present day, the most comprehensive compilation of workplace harassment cases was published by the US Equal Employment Opportunity Commission's Select Task Force on the Study of Harassment in the Workplace. As stated by the Task Force, the reported occurrence of workplace sexual harassment of women ranges from 25% to 85%, which tends to hinge on the types of questions asked and the sampling method. When investigators asked randomly selected female participants whether they had endured one or more "specific sexually based behaviors, such as unwanted sexual attention or coercion," the rate of reported harassment stood at 40%.[25] The Task Force proved to be cautious when it insisted that workplace harassment is intersectional, meaning that individuals can "experience harassment on the basis of more than one identity group."[26] While data in this area still needs to be more robust, one study on intersectional dynamics suggested that minority females are more likely to experience a higher incidence of harassment than their nonminority counterparts.[27]

THE #METOO CAMPAIGN: GENERAL PERSPECTIVES

The #MeToo campaign rose from the conception that victims of sexual misconduct should not be alone; other people endure similar trauma. On October 5, 2017, *The New York Times* published the Harvey Weinstein scandal. Hollywood actresses like Ashley Judd and Rose McGowan accused Weinstein of making sexual advances to and assaulting them when they were trying to pursue acting roles. Up to that point, Weinstein fancied his high position of power and eminence as a Hollywood mogul, having produced smash hits like *Pulp Fiction*, *Good Will Hunting*, and *Shakespeare in Love*. The Weinstein scandal dramatically worsened as additional stars shared similar accounts. Weinstein was removed from his own corporation on October 8, 2017, which later filed for bankruptcy.[28] Under arrest on rape charges in 2018 and having to appear in court for two years, he was found guilty of two of five felonies in February 2020, was sentenced to 23 years in jail, and is serving his prison term at Wende Correctional Facility.[29]

The #MeToo Movement

The **#MeToo** (or **Me Too**) campaign, with many versions of it around the world, is a social movement that exposes sexual harassment and sexual violence after victims make allegations of sexual misconduct public.[30] On October 15, 2017, Hollywood actress Alyssa Milano posted a request on Twitter to respond with the hashtag #metoo if any of her followers had faced harassment or assault. Her tweet spread like wildfire. The online campaign quickly became a global phenomenon, which generally received widespread support. Within one day of Milano's request online, 85 million users had already shared the hashtag in an attempt to lay bare the pervasiveness of sexual harassment and assault.[31] Notwithstanding the fact that Milano's tweet attracted global attention to the #MeToo campaign, it originated from Tarana Burke, an American activist from The Bronx, NY. Burke launched the movement in 2007 and employed the phrase "metoo" to show solidarity with girls and women who endured sexual violence.[32]

The #MeToo movement's potential to expose and take abusive leaders out of their influence is a success because it speaks to the dangers of gender-based power differentials. The movement wants to redraw the parameters for holding power, fame, and wealth in society. The Weinstein scandal erupted one year after the US presidential election, in which Donald Trump had boasted on video that fame allowed him to grope women without obtaining their consent.[33] Consent is a centerpiece of the #MeToo-inspired argument, exemplified by accounts like the one published in January 2018 on Babe.net. It was a story by an anonymous 23-year-old girl who claimed to have been forced into a sexual encounter with American comedian Aziz Ansari.[34] Two takeaways are essential to the significance of the #MeToo campaign. First, sexual misconduct is universal. Second, until the Harvey Weinstein scandal exploded, traditional legal channels had failed to rectify this problem.[35]

Hashtag Activism and User Generated Content

As we will see, there have been many #MeToo campaigns around the world. The main channel of communication has been online social media, starting with a strategy called hashtag activism. **Hashtag activism** is a phrase that sprung up from several media outlets to denote the use of Twitter's hashtags for online activism. The phrase is also applied to the act of expressing support for a cause through a "like" or "share" on any online platform or social networking site, such as Facebook or Twitter.[36] The far-reaching potentiality of hashtag activism became apparent in 2011, when #IranElection operated as an energizing tool for Iranians to protest a questionable election. It provided international audiences with a front-row seat to a burgeoning revolution. Since then, activists have created and disseminated a wide assortment of hashtags, including #ArabSpring, #Kony2012, #JusticeForTrayvon, #BlackLivesMatter, #PrayforParis, #WomensMarch, #MarchforOurLives, #GeorgeFloyd, and #ICantBreathe. Jackson, Bailey, and Foucault Welles (2020)[37] investigated how and why Twitter is such a popular platform for long-established disenfranchised populations, including African Americans, women, and transgender communities. The researchers explained how disadvantaged groups, with lower access to élite media spaces, can now benefit from hashtag activism to increase the visibility of counternarratives, to reject fake news and conspiracy theories, and to develop diverse networks of advocacy.

Hashtag activism has become an avenue for victimized communities to join forces, send a "common denominator" message, and relay their personal accounts on social media platforms. As a reaction to then-presidential candidate Donald Trump boasting about grabbing women by their genitals and giving them kisses without their consent, millions of users disseminated the #NotOkay hashtag as an opportunity to disclose their own experiences of sexual misconduct and add comments about the consequences of minimizing sexual misconduct by high-profile figures. An analysis of Twitter users' hashtags revealed that the top two priorities, for most users, were (1) to identify and condemn rape culture and (2) to teach boys and men how to stop violence against women.[38] Another key feature of online platforms is the creation of content and interaction. To this note, **User Generated Content** is a term that most people use to designate any type of content created by users in digital networks. It is publicly available for other users' examination and access.[39] Therefore, social networking sites like Twitter are structured platforms that not only represent a quality source of social identity, but that also enable such User Generated Content.[40] Participants in the #MeToo campaigns can access all this information from their smartphones so they can share their daily activities, ideas, or individual experiences. These connected devices can produce vast amounts of data.[41]

THE #METOO CAMPAIGN: POSITIVE IMPACT IN THE UNITED STATES

Not only have the #MeToo endeavors been productive to a certain extent, but they have also opened the floodgates in multiple areas. #MeToo continues to be in headlines and public debates and has outwardly produced many tangible outcomes towards decreasing sexual misconduct. By 2018, Facebook group Pantsuit Nation had already three million members. The group had posted hundreds of thousands of personal accounts of misogyny, at a time when an extraordinary number of women ran for office in the United States.[42] Comparable to other social justice and empowerment campaigns that seek to break silence, the mission of #MeToo, as originally laid out by Tarana Burke and subsequent activists who did not hesitate to embrace it, is to empower women—particularly young and vulnerable ones—through understanding, unanimity, and teamwork. This can be done by strength in numbers and by unequivocally showing how many survivors of sexual assault and harassment are vocal in the public sphere.[43]

Removing Perpetrators from Positions of Power

The #MeToo campaign has set off a chain reaction, in the legal process, for removing high-profile harassers from positions of power. The 2021 sexual scandal revolving around allegations against New York Governor Andrew Cuomo attests to this.[44] Under a reformed legal system, reporters would first publicize sexual misconduct claims and, subsequently, non-state actors, like employers, voters, audiences, online users, or corporations, would determine whether the claims justify removal of the accused. This process is part of an evolving social norm: that sexual misconduct makes any individual ineligible to hold office or a position of power.[45] In the year preceding the Weinstein public disgrace, fewer than 30 famous people were removed from their positions as a result of public allegations of sexual misconduct. In the year after the scandal, more than 200 were.[46] Owing to (1) a high number of widely publicized posts and reactions from famous American personalities (particularly in Hollywood), (2) the aforementioned start of the campaign in October 2017, and (3) massive media coverage and public debates on sexual misconduct, the proportion of high-profile dismissals were unprecedented—and, as we will see, so were the criticism and backlash.[47]

High-profile dismissals in the United States included Charlie Rose, Matt Lauer, Kevin Spacey, Mario Batali, and Al Franken. The #MeToo campaign also exposed the manners by which the legal process can be cleverly perverted to facilitate and conceal misconduct. Weinstein was able to cover his tracks for almost four decades through the manipulation of contracts, threats, and his powerful network. Weinstein entered into numerous settlement agreements that enclosed nondisclosure and nondisparagement clauses. In many cases, these agreements not only forbade victims from discussing their Weinstein case with anyone, but they also forced them to talk about the movie mogul in a positive manner.[48]

Impact on US Employer Disciplinary Practices

The #MeToo campaign has also brought flaws in employers' disciplinary practice procedures to light. These internal compliance procedures would often cause judges and juries to be more lenient towards arguments that the employer's actions were not so unreasonable.[49] Today, however, the #MeToo campaign has caused employer disciplinary practices to be reshaped in some form. Employers feel obligated to assume a more punitive line of action to documented sexual misconduct. A more punitive approach includes a wider range of coherent forms of discipline, like termination, demotion, promotion denials, or pay cuts. Employers are also more prone to modifying executive employment contracts and privacy policies to allow themselves more leeway when disciplining employees for documented misconduct, and to release reports if need be.[50] The #MeToo campaign is gradually fostering a climate of forced transparency in employment practices. Employees who have encountered sexual harassment or discrimination are now speaking publicly more than before, compelling employers to take actions. To this point, proposed legislation in many US states intends to restrict employers' abilities to include provisions in contracts that prohibit employees from speaking publicly.[51]

Impact on US College Campuses

By paralyzing offenders, #MeToo has managed to "warn" or prevent would-be perpetrators from abusing their positions of power to sexually harass subordinate colleagues or students. The likelihood of public disgrace has certainly been a deterrent, to those who pursue careers in academic or administrative leadership, from engaging in misconduct.[52] In 2018–9, the University of California (UC) system made national headlines after severe allegations of sexual misconducted surfaced. Hundreds of reports had been filed at all nine UC campuses, notably UC Berkeley, Davis, Irvine, Los Angeles, and San Diego, but few of them had been taken seriously. Things changed quickly.[53] To tackle the problem of sexual misconduct within scientific settings, BethAnn McLaughlin launched the #MeTooSTEM movement and hashtag. She demanded that the National Institutes of Health stop funding anyone guilty of misconduct charges.[54] In addition, many allegations from 2016 reemerged in the gymnastic world against former US Gymnastics doctor Larry Nassar of Michigan State University. Thanks to #MeToo, Nassar became infamous again for sexually assaulting gymnasts as young as six years old when they were receiving treatment.[55] Despite the fact that no action was taken after the initial allegations arose in 2016, and the fact that more than 150 women came forward, Nassar was tried and sentenced to life imprisonment. The president of Michigan State University, Lou Anna Simon, left her position in the aftermath of the scandal.[56]

Impact on US Legal Reforms

The impact of #MeToo on legal reforms and judicial interpretations is something to behold. The campaign has swayed the way by which courts apply the "severe or pervasive" requirement in harassment law. Drawing on their book, *Unequal: How America's Courts Undermine Discrimination Law*, which details common trends for courts to subvert discrimination law, Sperino and Thomas (2017)[57] describe many cases of offensive conduct that the courts did not see as sufficiently severe or pervasive for trial. Confidential agreements and mandatory arbitration put survivors in a corner and devalue or obscure legal claims, compromising the law's ability to instigate social change.[58] On another note, official job descriptions, in addition to standardized and objective hiring procedures, are key to all recruitment, including medical leadership openings. As a consequence of #MeToo, job descriptions are obligated to avoid gender-specific terms, and fair searches should be conducted to identify and embolden all eligible candidates to apply. Assessment criteria for hiring and promotion should also be listed and stipulated clearly and applied across the board to avert discrimination and inequities.[59]

US federal law contains several restrictions that are often mirrored in similar state statutes. For instance, Title VII and most state statutes do not shield many low-wage workers, including independent contractors—e.g., home healthcare and domestic workers—and bottom-floor employees in workplaces (especially those with fewer than 15 workers). In general, neither federal nor state harassment law favors lawsuits against individual offenders. Only employers are accountable, which allows abusers whom managers like to avoid personal accountability. Title VII also applies comparatively low damage caps, based on the stature and volume of the organization, which considerably lowers incentives for victims to sue, for attorneys to take such cases, and for management to avoid and rectify harassment. Immigrants encounter additional barriers when seeking affordable legal representation because legal agencies funded by the federal government are often barred from helping undocumented people. They may also not possess the required English proficiency or financial resources to handle lawsuits or find a private lawyer.[60]

THE #METOO CAMPAIGN: POSITIVE IMPACT AROUND THE WORLD

In December 2017, *Time Magazine* declared the #MeToo movement its Person of the Year. The campaign carries on today and has wielded a positive impact worldwide, including countries like Australia, South Korea, France, Sweden, and the UK—among countless others. In fact, by 2019, the attention-grabbing #MeToo hashtag campaign was a regular staple in over 85 nations. Similar local campaigns can be found in dozens more. Women who had experienced mistreatment, harassment, and discrimination can now voice their concerns *en masse*, joining forces across borders to demand change.[61]

Australia

As the #MeToo campaign rose in popularity, Australian reporter and screenwriter Benjamin Law launched the hashtag #HowIWillChange to inspire men to willingly and openly prompt actionable change against climates of sexual misconduct. "Guys, it's our turn," said Law on Twitter. As he continued, "After yesterday's endless #MeToo stories of women being abused, assaulted, and harassed, today we say #HowIWillChange."[62] #HowIWillChange is meant to transform men by involving them in discussions about sexual misconduct and by demanding that they reflect on their potential contributions (direct or indirect) to rape culture.[63]

It is certainly not easy for people to understand how their beliefs, behaviors, and attitudes feed rape culture based on covert or unconscious dynamics that have determined how people socialize with one another.[64] It can also be challenging to visualize why some of these dynamics are troublesome when, on the face of it, they seem irrelevant to occurrences of overt sexual violence. Examples of such problematic dynamics could include deep-rooted assumptions that only men should head the household, men should be the ones to be assertive (and women passive), and women should not enjoy the same sexual rights.[65]

This transformation of thinking has been facilitated by feminist theory, which postulates that (1) men are the main culprits of violence, (2) socially constructed notions of masculinity tend to promote or perpetuate violence, and (3) nonperpetrating men should provide efforts in changing troublesome gender dynamics.[66] This shift is also substantiated by research proving that men exert a high degree of influence over other men's behaviors. Hence, men can assume a more important role in prevention endeavors.[67] Including men as allies to encourage prosocial behaviors can reduce resistance of other men by redefining their involvement as instrumental—which is a better approach than putting them in a position of blame.[68]

South Korea

In South Korea, #MeToo has enthused many women to make their cases public with allegations of sexual misconduct. Their highly publicized allegations have jumpstarted the mobilization of mass protests and requests for legal reform. In South Korea, the movement's effect is manifested through policy proposals and the revamping of laws on sexual misconduct and IPV. This stands in sharp contrast to Japan, where the #MeToo campaign has made much slower strides. Fewer women spoke out publicly, and if they did, many chose to stay anonymous. The campaign is still restricted to a small number of cases that led to the creation of a support network for female journalists. The disparities in outcomes in these two nations can be attributed to the power of women's participation in civil society and the type of the media coverage in each situation. Nevertheless, even in South Korea, women are still facing a huge backlash like victim-blaming and social and professional sanctions for voicing their concerns.[69]

In that country, the flourishing #MeToo campaign began with a TV interview of Seo Ji-hyun, an attorney who had the unparalleled courage to publicly accuse Ahn Tae-geun, her former supervisor (who also happened to be a senior prosecutor), of sexual misconduct. Her move encouraged hundreds of women to come forward, causing the unforeseen resignation of key Korean sports figures, academic élites, and politicians. In January 2019, both Ahn Tae-geun and Lee Myung-haeng—one of the first actors blamed for sexual harassment in South Korea's entertainment industry—were sent to prison for two years and eight months, respectively. In another successful case in February 2019, ex-presidential candidate Ahn Hee-jung—initially acquitted on charges of sexual violence—was sentenced to jail for three and a half years.[70]

France, Sweden, and the UK

In France, Marlène Schiappa, France's gender equality minister, motivated by the formidable reaction to the hashtag #BalanceTonPorc ("Expose Your Pig")—the French hashtag pushing victims to expose their harassers—crafted an exhaustive bill on sexual harassment. It was approved by the French Senate in August 2018. It extends the statute of limitations for sex crimes, includes punishment for cyberstalking, cat-calling, and "upskirting"—taking nonconsensual pictures underneath a woman's skirt—and imposes financial penalties for street harassment. The law was applied for the first time a month later, when a man was found guilty and had to pay 300 euros (about $350) for obscene and derogatory comments.[71]

In Sweden, the #MeToo movement was sparked by the highly publicized case of photographer Jean-Claude Arnault in 2018, which led to the abrogation of the Nobel Prize in literature that year. After the first allegation of sexual misconduct against Arnault, 18 women stepped forward with similar allegations that had occurred over a period of 20 years. In October 2018, he was found guilty of rape and sentenced to two years of imprisonment. When he appealed the verdict two months later, the appeals court increased his sentence to two-and-a-half years. And in the United Kingdom, within months of the advent of the #MeToo campaign, the Parliament passed new legislation for its members.[72]

THEORIES: SPIRAL OF SILENCE

Developed by Noelle-Neumann (1974),[73] the **spiral of silence** theory posits that societal institutions like the government, the media, or the academic world impose opinions onto mainstream life. For this reason, people tend to avoid voicing their true opinions out of fear of being ostracized. The spiral of silence theory highlights the risks of feeling such pressure, which causes us to self-censor (especially when we are in the minority). This may be exacerbated by the possibility of retaliation by those who disagree.[74] A climate of silence is characterized by the refusal, by a group of people, to utter any disagreement on certain subjects.

From this perspective, it is the phenomenon whereby we engage in unspoken agreements out of fear of possible reprisals. Though it has been established, by now, that not all women choose to remain silent, the majority of them do because they are afraid or uncomfortable vis-à-vis the subject of sexual misconduct (or their personal experiences with it) when that subject is raised. Other reasons exist for silence on the part of victims. For some, experiencing rape more than once will shut their mind for a very long time. Other victims not only feel used for sex, but they also fear that they will not be taken seriously or they will be subject to public shaming.[75]

A Platform for Women

The #MeToo campaign has conceived a platform for women to shatter a glass ceiling of silence. Silence is a conspicuous sign of the impact of violence. If #MeToo can empower individuals to break the walls of silence and expose decades of pain in the quest for justice, then this can be highly positive.[76] Therefore, women of the #MeToo campaign should justly be acclaimed for conquering long-established silence about sexual misconduct. As explained in the next major section, the overall campaign has also been criticized for both ignoring the role that a minority woman played in creating the movement 10 years earlier and in failing to acknowledge the distinct types of harassment (and the higher vulnerability to it) that minority women regularly face on a daily basis.[77]

Indeed, just like #MeToo has been disparaged for its excessive focus on White Western women's experiences, key non-White personalities have fronted the overall campaign and increased its visibility. Such women include, for instance, Oprah Winfrey whose inspirational Golden Globes presentation in January 2018 (i.e., "a new day on the horizon") drew massive attention, and Mexican Hollywood actress Salma Hayek. Many regard #MeToo as a promising platform for developing feminist solidarity along the lines of class, race, and gender. Rapper Cardi B has been a powerful voice about #MeToo's focus on this novel form of femininity that is framed as admirable.[78]

Battling Long-Established Traditions

Silence can be both overt and subtle. For a long time, this issue remained obscure for a mixture of sociocultural, religious, professional, legal, and even service-related reasons. For example, lack of services and proper legal channels offered no help to victims, which prevented sexual misconduct from being adequately tackled. Put simply, victims may consider it unproductive to step forward if the state is reluctant to taking measures to punish perpetrators adequately. In like fashion, sociocultural traditions could be inhibiting too—sometimes long-held beliefs that society would pour disdain on the victims. Some religious traditions, including those suggesting that women's behaviors invite sexual misconduct, hinder enlightenment of the issue. Young women and girls fear that exposing their experiences with sexual violence will lower their chances of marriage.[79]

Organizational factors that are conducive to sexual misconduct at work include poor management, power differentials, and a spiral of silence.[80] The value of the spiral of silence theory is obvious here because it echoes a situation where a "mob" subjugates—directly or indirectly—female employees who are reduced to silence as a consequence of male dominance. This is perpetuated across various structures of society.[81] To put it succinctly, the spiral of silence theory helps readers understand why silence on the part of survivors persists. To the victim, to avoid ostracization matters more than presenting facts and, in the process, improving society. From this angle, it is not unreasonable to say that they also choose to remain silent to avoid further physical harm. On the other hand, it is fair to argue that a certain number of societies contribute tremendously to such conspiracy of silence. One reason lies in the social expectations for members of the community to uphold long-established traditions of the group at large.[82]

THEORIES: MUTED GROUP THEORY

Developed by Ardener (1975),[83] **muted group theory** hypothesizes that, within many cultures, the dominant group contributes the most to the language system (e.g., speech norms, acceptable vs. nonacceptable words, and grammar), while subordinate groups feel obligated to employ the dominant language system to be heard or taken seriously by mainstream society. Moreover, the dominant group may dismiss the voice of subordinate groups for the simple reason that they represent the lower power. As the dominant group formulates and articulates the language system, actors within the subordinate group have to embrace the dominant-driven language to express or assert themselves. The problem, however, is that this communicative approach may lead to loss and distortion of information as the subordinate groups cannot frame their thoughts clearly. This is why, in due course, these subordinate groups can feel or will be muted. Still today, a certain portion of the media establishment will empower dominant public opinion to mute minority beliefs or cultural issues.

Marginalized or Muted Groups

People victimized by sexual violence can feel as members of marginalized or muted groups, as they are rendered into silence and subjugation after being assaulted by member of dominant groups (e.g., powerful White men) because they may not possess the skills to describe their abuse. For this reason, muted group theory is analogous to a feminist and cross-cultural theory because the latter illustrates systems of communication and social representation of nondominant groups like women and cultural minorities. It acknowledges that many traditions, norms, and attitudes favor men over women.[84] Traditions, norms, and attitudes "in all societies, tend to be to the advantage of the men and to the disadvantage of the women and other subordinate groups."[85] Mutedness derives from lack of power, and those with lower power are more hesitant to voice their opinions. When they do, they are directly or indirectly muffled or made invisible.[86]

The language of most cultures does not treat all its speakers equally. According to the theory, men can more easily push their privileged worldview or do it more thoroughly in the public sphere. Muted group theorists often remind us that women are not the sole muted group, though they account for half of the global population and are still the most marginalized (and muted) group in the world.[87] Women and other subordinate groups do not enjoy the same level of freedom as men when expressing what they want, when and where they want it, because the language and its norms have been shaped and framed by the dominant group. So, women's perceptions diverge from men's because women's subordination means that they do not experience and view life in the same way. At the same time, the language and its norms for speaking are not always custom-made for describing women's experiences from their point of view. Therefore, women are "muted."[88]

Case Study: China

China's #MeToo campaign has been ascribed the nickname #MiTu (米兔) by its advocates—a straightforward phonetic translation of "me too," which also means "rice bunny" in Mandarin. For this reason, pictures of bunnies are now the symbol of China's version of the #MeToo campaign. Starting in early 2018, Chinese women joined the global #MeToo campaign to expose and fight sexual misconduct.[89] By September 2018, more than 50 public allegations had been published on social media against élite men in various industries, including academia, the media establishment, and nongovernmental organizations.[90] Most of the accused were demoted or removed from their positions. China's #MiTu was first visible on college campuses, where many famous professors were accused of sexual misconduct by current and former students.[91]

On January 1, 2018, Luo Xixi—a former graduate student at Beihang University in Beijing—posted an accusation on Chinese social media against Professor Chen Xiaowu, then her supervisor.[92] As stated in Luo's post, Chen harassed Luo on a frequent basis while she was pursuing her doctoral studies. Luo's post quickly attracted millions of views. Beihang University's administrators soon responded to Luo's allegation by terminating Chen. Motivated by the successful outcome of Luo's allegations, more Chinese women stepped forward and shared their own experiences of sexual misconduct committed by university professors. Only two weeks after Luo's public allegation, students and alumni from more than 50 universities circulated online petitions, requesting that their schools develop systems to prevent and handle sexual harassment on college campuses.[93] To express solidarity, 56 professors from the best universities in China joined one of the petitions to call for institutions of higher education in the country to set up reporting channels for sexual misconduct claims.[94]

However, as opposed to their Western counterparts, many women's efforts to apply the noble principles of the #MiTu campaign to their own predicaments have encountered major obstacles in China. Chinese authorities continue to apply various methods of censorship to suppress the growth of human rights activism by muting groups associated with that. #MiTu supporters have to constantly adapt their behaviors and approaches to sidestep censorship and keep the campaign up and running. Besides government censorship, the #MiTu campaign also faces social hurdles. For example, large populations, notably the working classes and other marginalized segments, still have a hard time voicing their opinions. On the other hand, deep-seated power structures allow men in higher ranks of society to stay "untouchable."[95]

THEORIES: INTIMATE PUBLICITY, EPISTEMIC INJUSTICE, AND CRITICAL RACE FEMINISM

A theoretical concept developed by Berlant (1998),[96] **intimate publicity** traces how various audiences unite around common affective intensities and do so intimately. Examining the formation and circulation of intimate publics helps understand the development of shared concerns, attention, and detachment (or attachment). Intimacy denotes the powerful and affective linkages between entities that unite to form a "common denominator" public. As Berlant explains, "To intimate is to communicate with the sparest of signs and gestures, and at its root intimacy has the quality of eloquence and brevity."[97]

The formation of intimate publicity is shaped by the expectation that members "share a worldview and emotional knowledge that they have derived from a broadly common historical experience."[98] Many intimate publics develop through common experiences of injustices and work hard to make life better and more tolerable for marginalized groups.[99] Berlant (2008)[100] maintains that intimate publics composed of oppressed and exploited communities act "as a porous, affective scene of identification among strangers that promises a certain experience of belonging and provides a complex of consolation, confirmation, discipline, and discussion about how to live as an x."

Through intimacy, a large community cultivates a deeply felt notion of what it means to be a member of one of those groups and, in many cases, to suffer as a result of this. Such emotionally laden histories and experiences entail that even the most successful intimate publics have to respect a certain boundary, while also representing and comprising a large body of people who have common qualities or experiences. Fundamental to the formation of belonging and felt notion of intimacy is the development of affective investments. Affective investments are the "inarticulable affective commitments that are mobilized through discourse and social conditions."[101]

Epistemic Injustice

Epistemic injustice is another theoretical concept in regards to marginalized groups. In this case, it explains how their fight against injustice stems from their lack of representation in the realm of knowledge. It emphasizes the unfair exclusion and silencing of their accomplishments; perversion or misrepresentation of their meanings or contributions; discrediting of their status or reputation in communicative practices; unjust differences in authority; and unjustified distrust.[102] On occasion, we refuse to believe speakers because of unwarranted prejudices—implicit or explicit.[103] One corollary is that marginalized groups' abilities to make arguments and provide testimony can be impaired.[104]

The #MeToo campaign has brought epistemic injustice to the forefront of the media. Activists have shifted the audience's sympathy in support of survivors by transforming the default response into belief, instead of suspicion. The hashtag has demonstrated how widespread sexual misconduct is.[105] Survivors without visibility and wealth are less likely to find reporters willing to publish their stories. The media favors White female victims for a long time, despite the fact that minority women face higher rates of sexual violence.[106] Fricker (2013)[107] specializes in studies of epistemic injustice, particularly cases of racial and sexual stereotyping and bias. An example would be a case where a speaker's testimony is conferred lower credibility because of their being Black or female, which would be less likely if hearing the testimonies of a White male. Fricker adds that the negative consequences of epistemic injustice affect a person's livelihood, and it is especially true if he or she has experienced other forms of social injustice in the past. This is why epistemic injustice is highly correlated to social injustice.

Enter the story of Khadija Siddiqi, a student at a Pakistani law school who, in 2016, was stabbed 23 times by a fellow classmate after rejecting his sexual advances. She survived the assault. Part of an élite circle, her aggressor was later found innocent by a court system that systematically defends perpetrators of crimes against women. However, Khadija came out of her silence—and over two million supporters used the hashtag #JusticeforKhadija to publicize her case on social media, which eventually helped her win her appeal. "Today is a day of victory for all women," she proudly told journalists on the steps of Pakistan's Supreme Court in January 2019, after over two years of court hearings. As she continued, "A precedent has been set that if you raise your voice for truth, you will taste victory."[108] Women in similar situations around the world are challenging critics of the #MeToo campaign. Equipped with only social media platforms and strong determination, they want many more victims to jump on the bandwagon of justice. Like the Khadija Siddiqi case, they are increasingly winning their cases.[109]

Critical Race Feminism

Critical race feminism provides an in-depth examination of the legal status and rights of women of color across the world. Under that conceptual approach, important questions would be, "What is the *de jure* and *de facto* legal status of women of color?" "Are there certain groups of minority women in the United States, Europe, or other nations of the developing world that enjoy more privileges that other groups of minority women?"[110] Critical race feminism is a theoretical framework that "combats racial and gender oppression from multiple standpoints."[111] It employs a multidisciplinary approach to improving the rights of women of color by mixing, for example disciplines in the social sciences and humanities, including education. The law is a first step—but not a sufficient one—to end discrimination and achieve success.[112]

Critical race feminism adds fresh insights when investigating the question as to whether #MeToo is a White women's campaign. The answer is not simple; it is yes and no. On the one hand, sexual violence and harassment are what many women experience— not just White women. Such misconduct has been frequent for women of color in the workplace. It is the case for both enslaved women and a certain number of women in low-wage service professions. The global popularity of the hashtag—e.g., sparking legal changes in Sweden and upsetting the applecart for élite academia in India—is evidence that sexual misconduct is not just a US White women's issue. On the other hand, upon examining US media coverage of the campaign and most of the spokespeople and victims in recent scandals, the problem is framed as White women's pain, which explains why most media coverage centers on these women's pain.[113]

Presently, antidiscrimination law in the United States uses what courts believe should be an objective victim standard to investigate sexual misconduct allegations. From this perspective, the law neglects the intricateness inherent to gender and racial subordination. The harasser's stereotype and prejudice can make a minority victim more vulnerable to harassment. The value of her testimony may not be taken as seriously as it should, and others might even question whether she was hurt by the harasser's undesired conduct. Antidiscrimination law also ignores how a victim's own understanding of others' perceptions about the minority group to which she belongs can affect her own reaction to the harassment that she experienced.[114]

By following a new standard based on a clear stipulation that the victim's multidimensional identity and background should be taken into account, courts would recognize how the existing standard, though seemingly objective, was framed from the lens of White men, notably because case law in the United States tends to be developed by White male judges.[115] Critical race feminism can help unravel both male biases in support of those alleged to be the harassers (during sexual harassment cases) and replace these biases with the use of intersection of gender, race, socioeconomic status, gender identity, disability, national origins, and other relevant classes in the court system.[116]

THEORIES: SOCIAL IDENTITY THEORY

Social identity theory (SIT) rests on the premise that identification with a group shapes individual and group behaviors, attitudes, and norms.[117] A key concern of SIT is the group's influence of one's perceptions of the self and others with whom one identifies (i.e., in-group) and one's perceptions of others with whom one does not identify (i.e., out-group). According to SIT, we look at ourselves and others as group members with a shared social identity, which is mostly due to group membership.[118] Above all, the more we identify with other members of our group, the higher the influence of perceptions of the group norms exerts on us. Of equal relevance is the fact that information that seems inconsistent between a person and his or her group causes cognitive dissonance.[119]

In-Groups vs. Out-Groups

SIT hypothesizes that the groups—e.g., social class, family, or even gender-based groups—to which we belong increase our pride and self-esteem. They offer a notion of social identity: a feeling of belonging to some aspects of society. Under the umbrella of social identity falls social identification because we embrace the identity of the group on which we count or rely.[120] After classifying ourselves as part of a group and identifying with that group, we like to evaluate that group as compared to groups. In order to keep a high level of self-esteem, our group needs to fare well in comparison with other groups.[121]

We also like to compare ourselves with members of our own in-group; that is, members with whom we connect. We adjust our behavior to how we believe these peers are behaving. In regards to public communication campaigns, we might compare ourselves with our neighbors. If we connect with people in our neighborhood based on social status, we may be influenced by their new behaviors or attitudes as a result of a campaign message. Social identity is a component of a person's self-concept that is based on his or her awareness of his or her membership of a group. The value and emotional relevance linked to that membership are meaningful.[122] Social identity describes how identification functions as a social process: at the personal, social, and institutional levels.[123] Put another way, social identity is the perception of the self-concept that matters to particular aspects of social behavior.[124]

Male vs. Female Perceptions of #MeToo

A certain number of men and women differ in their outlooks on the social issues that are at the core of the #MeToo campaign. Principally, men tend to exhibit more tolerance of sexual harassment, are less negative towards sexual assault, and are more likely to fault rape victims for their experiences of assault.[125] These gender differences are attributed, in part, to dissimilarities in group-based gender identity. When men oppose the #MeToo campaign, this may be due to group-level processes. We know, for example, that men and women have an inclination to regard social interactions between the sexes through intrinsically different angles.[126] Encounters deemed as sexual harassment by women may be deemed as harmless flirtation by men. Even if both evaluate the same encounter similarly, men may be motivated to resist the #MeToo campaign on account of in-group favoritism and unwillingness to support other men.[127] Therefore, these arguments for gender differences in response to #MeToo lay emphasis on intergroup variations and intragroup consistency.

Suarez and Gadalla (2010)[128] stress emphatically that men and women do not advocate the same philosophies with respect to sexual misconduct. Men are more willing to embrace rape myths than women. Rape myths encompass multiple beliefs, including criticizing rape victims for not handling their assault properly, exonerating the perpetrator, and minimizing the far-reaching consequences of rape for the victim.[129] The more people support rape myths, the more they see rape and interpersonal violence as normal behavior, thereby showing a higher disposition to commit sexual aggression and coercion.[130] For the reason that men support rape myths more than women do, the former might be more likely to ridicule people posting the hashtag #MeToo and point the finger at victims themselves. Glick and Fiske (1996)[131] described an additional category of sexism, termed **benevolent sexism**, which consists of taking a seemingly positive, yet patronizing, attitude towards women—i.e., that women ought to be beloved and shielded from harm. In many cases, this stance evokes a patriarchal protection of traditional women (e.g., housewives), but resentment towards non-traditional women (e.g., female leaders or promiscuous women).[132]

THE #METOO CAMPAIGN: NEGATIVE IMPACT

The massive influence of the #MeToo campaign is indisputable: Women are making unprecedented steps towards equality and justice in hopes of fashioning a new horizon across the world. Whereas the campaign has achieved milestones, a chorus of disapproval has also emerged. Defamation lawsuits, continued harassment, and even arrests have been part of serious attempts at deprecating and silencing women (sometimes with dire consequences). There is still a long way. More time and energy are needed to achieve substantive change in certain domains. It will be a challenging path to chip away at the male privilege enshrined into laws and sociocultural practices.[133] In January 2018, French actress Catherine Deneuve was among 100 women who signed an open letter condemning the #MeToo campaign and women's decisions to publicly dishonor alleged perpetrators of sexual misconduct. Deneuve argued that it was a witch hunt against the right to make sexual advances. As written in the letter, "Men have been punished summarily, forced out of their jobs when all they did was touch someone's knee or try to steal a kiss." When sitting down with the *Agence France Presse* news agency, Monty Python star Terry Gilliam said that #MeToo was analogous to a "mob rule" that produced a "world of victims." His comments made it evident that the parameters for appropriate sexual conduct are a matter of opinion. They nonetheless triggered a backlash from other celebrities.[134]

Egypt and China

In Egypt, at least two women have been jailed for sharing their accounts of sexual harassment on social media. Owing to its deep suppression of dissent, the government has framed the #MeToo campaign as a form of illicit rebellion: May El Shamy, an Egyptian woman who filed a police report against her boss, has been subject to a smear campaign falsely accused her of being a member of the Muslim Brotherhood (considered a terrorist organization in that country and other Muslim nations). In September 2018, after openly blaming the government for not shielding women from harassment, activist Amal Fathy was found guilty of **sedition** (i.e., rebellion against the state) and imprisonment for two years, on the grounds that she was sabotaging the country's image. A few months earlier, a Lebanese tourist who shared a video on social media to criticize sexual harassment in Egypt was apprehended at the Cairo airport for disseminating conspiracies. Although these women were released from jail and had their sentences commuted, others did not benefit from such luck.[135]

In China, despite serious efforts of the #MiTu campaign activists described earlier, female activists are under constant surveillance or arrested for their advocacy. Within minutes, the government erases any #MeToo comments from the Chinese social media platform Weibo. Students at Peking University who were active with the #MeToo movement faced serious adverse actions after requesting that the university release information about an old case of sexual assault that caused a student to commit suicide. The alleged perpetrator was a professor. Yue Xin, a female student and a 2019 Foreign Policy Global Thinker, was one of the students, but was almost expelled, which provoked widespread outrage. At some point, police raided a condo where Yue and other activists were staying. She has disappeared ever since.[136]

The Danger of Passive Empathy

Organizing a campaign on the basis of empathy is both an encouraging and risky undertaking. It is risky because advocates may bring together what Boler (1997)[137] calls "passive empathy." **Passive empathy** is grounded in an "irreducible difference—a recognition that I am not you," Boler argues, and "empathy is possible only by virtue of this distinction."[138] Such empathy is "passive" because it allows perpetrators, and even victims, to display sentiments of common ground, understanding, as well as fear and remorse, instead of making the effort of being self-reflexive. Passive empathy is the act of putting oneself in another person's shoes without the risk of doing so in reality. As Ahmed (2014)[139] contends, "empathy sustains the very difference that it may seek to overcome."

Passive empathy, particularly the type that we see the most in the public sphere, may facilitate a "consumption of the other,"[140] analogous to the process of "eating the other" that bell hooks (1992)[141] has conceptualized. "Eating the other" is predicated on the notion that marginalized groups are considered exotic others to be consumed by gazing perpetrators. As Hemmings (2012)[142] continues, "empathy may lead to sentimental attachment to the other, rather than a genuine engagement with her concerns, then; or worse, it may signal a cannibalization of the other masquerading as care." Accordingly, passive empathy hinders the progress of social justice campaigns because "passive empathy produces no action towards justice but situates the powerful Western eye/I as the judging subject, never called upon to cast her gaze at her own reflection."[143]

The type of empathy that #MeToo promotes is "transformative," not "passive."[144] **Transformative empathy** recommends listening instead of distancing or looking at an individual as the Other. It necessitates self-reflexivity and change of one's own attitudes and beliefs. The empathy that Tarana Burke proposes allows anger and rage that survivors of sexual violence naturally feel. Burke started the #MeToo campaign in 2006 to attain "empowerment through empathy" for sexual violence victims. Burke had been encouraged to raise awareness and create networks of connections between survivors through MeToo. This decision was made after coming to terms with her own experience of rape and after expressing regrets about having abruptly ending a conversation initiated by a 13-year-old girl who was sexually molested. The girl's story was shared at a Just Be youth camp, a project that Burke developed and where she served as a counselor. Just Be specialized in the health, well-being, and wholeness of female minority youths.[145]

Lastly, the blatant neglect of disabled women from the #MeToo campaign is another sign of the hypocrisy of passive empathy.[146] Hemmings (2018)[147] avers that #MeToo promotes an awareness of sexual misconduct as principally experienced through a lived process between men and women, thus ignoring broader circles of people who encountered harassment too. These broader circles include cis-women, trans-men and -women, and gender nonconforming individuals and queer individuals of color.

NOTES

1. Jayna M. Holroyd-Leduc and Sharon E. Straus, "#MeToo and the Medical Profession," *Canadian Medical Association Journal* 190 (2018): E972–3. https://doi.org/10.1503/cmaj.181037.
2. Abby Ohlheiser, "How# MeToo Really Was Different, According to Data," *The Washington Post* (January 22, 2018): A1. Retrieved on March 23, 2021 from https://www.washingtonpost.com/news/the-intersect/wp/2018/01/22/how-metoo-really-was-different-according-to-data.
3. See Jennifer S. Hirsch and Shamus Khan, *Sexual Citizens* (New York: W. W. Norton & Company, 2021); Mary Schuster, *The Victim's Voice in the Sexual Misconduct Crisis: Identity, Credibility, and Proof* (Lanham, MD: Lexington Books, 2021).
4. Roxella T. Cavazos and Sandra R. McCandless, *Sexual Harassment and Retaliation: A Practical Guide for Plaintiff and Defense* (Chicago, IL American Bar Association, 2020).
5. William E. Foote and Jane Goodman-Delahunty, *Understanding Sexual Harassment: Evidence-Based Forensic Practice* (2nd Ed.) (Washington, DC: American Psychological Association, 2021).
6. Adrienne O'Neil, Victor Sojo, Bianca Fileborn, Anna J. Scovelle, and Allison Milner, "The #MeToo Movement: An Opportunity in Public Health?" *The Lancet* 391, no. 10140 (2018): P2587–9. https://doi.org/10.1016/S0140-6736(18)30991-7.
7. Morgan E. PettyJohn, Finneran K. Muzzey, Megan K. Maas, and Heather L. McCauley, "#HowIWillChange: Engaging Men and Boys in the #MeToo Movement," *Psychology of Men & Masculinities* 20, no. 4 (2019): 612–22. https://doi.org/10.1037/men0000186.
8. See Martha R. Burt, "Cultural Myths and Supports for Rape," *Journal of Personality and Social Psychology* 38, no. 2 (1980): 217–30, 218. https://doi.org/10.1037/0022-3514.38.2.217.
9. Nicole L. Johnson and Dawn M. Johnson, "An Empirical Exploration into the Measurement of Rape Culture," *Journal of Interpersonal Violence* 36, no. 1 (2021): NP70–95. https://doi.org/10.1177/0886260517732347.
10. Jared Yates Sexton, *The Man They Wanted Me to Be: Toxic Masculinity and a Crisis of Our Own Making* (Berkeley, CA: Counterpoint, 2019).
11. Marianna Mazza, Giuseppe Marano, Carlo Lai, Luigi Janiri, and Gabriele Sania, "Danger in Danger: Interpersonal Violence during COVID-19 Quarantine," *Psychiatry Research* 289 (2020): 10–21. https://doi.org/10.1016/j.psychres.2020.113046.
12. Kathleen C. Basile and Jeffrey E. Hall, "Intimate Partner Violence Perpetration by Court-Ordered Men: Distinctions and Intersections among Physical Violence, Sexual Violence, Psychological Abuse, and Stalking," *Journal of Interpersonal Violence* 26, no. 2 (2011): 230–53. https://doi.org/10.1177/0886260510362896.
13. Caroline Bradbury-Jones and Louise Isham, "The Pandemic Paradox: The Consequences of COVID-19 on Domestic Violence," *Journal of Clinical Nursing* 29, no. 13 (2020): 2047–9. https://doi.org/10.1111/jocn.15296.

14. Nicole van Gelder, Amber Peterman, Alina Potts, Megan O'Donnell, Kelly Thompson, Niyati Shah, and Sabine Oertelt-Prigione, "COVID-19: Reducing the Risk of Infection Might Increase the Risk of Intimate Partner Violence," *EClinicalMedicine* 21, no. 1 (2020): 1–3. https://doi.org/10.1016/j.eclinm.2020.100348.

15. Available at https://www.unwomen.org/en/what-we-do/ending-violence-against-women/facts-and-figures#notes.

16. Available at https://www.who.int/news-room/feature-stories/detail/violence-against-women.

17. Available at https://www.cdc.gov/violenceprevention/intimatepartnerviolence/fastfact.html.

18. Ibid.

19. National Sexual Violence Resource Center, *Statistics about Sexual Violence* (Harrisburg, PA: National Sexual Violence Resource Center, 2015).

20. Deborah Tuerkheimer, "Beyond #MeToo," *New York University Law Review* 94 (2019): 1146–1208.

21. Sofi Sinozich and Lynn Langton, *Rape and Sexual Assault Victimization among College-Age Females, 1995–2013* (Washington, DC: US Department of Justice, 2014).

22. David Cantor, Bonnie Fisher, Susan Chibnall, Reanne Townsend, Hyunshik Lee, Carol Bruce, and Gail Thomas, *Report on the AAU Campus Climate Survey on Sexual Assault and Sexual Misconduct* (Rockville, MD: Westat, 2015).

23. Cited in Tuerkheimer, "Beyond #MeToo," 1159–60.

24. Stefanie K. Johnson, Jessica F. Kirk, and Ksenia Keplinger, "Why We Fail to Report Sexual Harassment," *Harvard Law Review* 129, no. 1 (2016): 10–21.

25. Chai R. Feldblum and Victoria A. Lipnic, *Select Task Force on the Study of Harassment in the Workplace* (Washington, DC: US Equal Employment Opportunity Commission, 2016).

26. Ibid, 13.

27. Ibid, 14.

28. Elizabeth C. Tippett, "The Legal Implications of the MeToo Movement," *Minnesota Law Review* 57 (2018): 229–302.

29. *The Irish Times*, "Harvey Weinstein Moved to Maximum Security Prison to Serve 23-Year Sentence," *The Irish Times* (March 19, 2020): A1. Retrieved on March 19, 2021 from https://www.irishtimes.com/news/world/us/harvey-weinstein-moved-to-maximum-security-prison-to-serve-23-year-sentence-1.4207025.

30. Halley Bondy, *#MeToo and You: Everything You Need to Know about Consent, Boundaries, and More* (San Francisco, CA: Zest Books, 2021).

31. *CBS News*, "More than 12M 'Me Too' Facebook Posts, Comments, Reactions in 24 Hours," *CBS News* (October 17, 2017). Retrieved on March 23, 2021 from https://www.cbsnews.com/news/metoo-more-than-12-million-facebook-posts-comments-reactions-24-hours.

32. Cited in Tippett, "The Legal Implications of the MeToo Movement," 231.

33. Jessica A. Clarke, "The Rules of #MeToo," *University of Chicago Legal Forum* 2019 (2019): 37–84.

34. Rosalind Gill and Shani Orgad, "The Shifting Terrain of Sex and Power: From the 'Sexualization of Culture' to #MeToo," *Sexualities* 21, no. 8 (2018): 1313–24. https://doi.org/10.1177/1363460718794647.

35. Clarke, "The Rules of #MeToo," 37.

36. Mae Elise Cannon, *Beyond Hashtag Activism: Comprehensive Justice in a Complicated Age* (Downers Grove, IL: InterVarsity Press, 2020).

37. Sarah J. Jackson, Moya Bailey, and Brooke Foucault Welles, *#HashtagActivism: Networks of Race and Gender Justice* (Cambridge, MA: MIT Press, 2020).

38. Megan K. Maas, Heather L. McCauley, Amy E. Bonomi, and S. Gisela Leija, "'I Was Grabbed by My Pussy and Its #NotOkay': A Twitter Backlash against Donald Trump's Degrading Commentary," *Violence against Women* 24, no. 14 (2018): 1739–50. https://doi.org/10.1177/1077801217743340.

39. José Ramón Saura and Dag Bennett, "A Three-Stage Methodological Process of Data Text Mining: A UGC Business Intelligence Analysis," *Symmetry-Basel* (2021). https://doi.org/10.13140/RG.2.2.11093.06880.

40. Momoka Fujita, Paul Harrigan, and Geoffrey N. Soutar, "Capturing and Co-Creating Student Experiences in Social Media: A Social Identity Theory Perspective," *Journal of Marketing Theory and Practice* 26, no. 1 (2018): 55–71. https://doi.org/10.1080/10696679.2017.1389245.

41. Ana Reyes-Menendez, José Ramón Saura, and Stephen B. Thomas, "Exploring Key Indicators of Social Identity in the #MeToo Era: Using Discourse Analysis in UGC," *International Journal of Information Management* 54 (2020): 102–29. https://doi.org/10.1016/j.ijinfomgt.2020.102129.

42. Ashwini Tambe, "Reckoning with the Silences of #MeToo," *Feminist Studies* 44, no. 1 (2018): 197–203. https://doi.org/10.15767.

43. Christie D'Zurilla, "In Saying #MeToo, Alyssa Milano Pushes Awareness Campaign about Sexual Assault and Harassment," *Los Angeles Times* (October 16, 2017): A1. Retrieved on March 19, 2021 from https://www.latimes.com/entertainment/la-et-entertainment-news-updates-october-2017-htmlstory.html#in-saying-metoo-alyssa-milano-pushes-awareness-campaign-about-sexual-assault-and-harassment.

44. Jesse McKinley, "Cuomo Faces New Claims of Sexual Harassment from Current Aide," *The New York Times* (March 19, 2021): A1. Retrieved on July 3, 2021 from https://www.nytimes.com/2021/03/19/nyregion/alyssa-mcgrath-cuomo-harassment.html.

45. Cited in Clarke, "The Rules of #MeToo," 41–2.

46. Audrey Carlsen, Maya Salam, Claire Cain Miller, Denise Lu, Ash Ngu, Jugal K. Patel, and Zach Wichter, "#MeToo Brought Down 201 Powerful Men. Nearly Half of Their Replacements Are Women," *The New York Times* (October 23, 2018): A1. Retrieved on March 20, 2021 from https://www.nytimes.com/interactive/2018/10/23/us/metoo-replacements.

47. Dubravka Zarkov and Kathy Davis, "Ambiguities and Dilemmas around #MeToo: #ForHow Long and #WhereTo?" *European Journal of Women's Studies* 25, no. 1 (2018): 3–9. https://doi.org/10.1177/1350506817749436.

48. Cited in Tippett, "The Legal Implications of the MeToo Movement," 234–6.

49. Ibid, 234–6.

50. Ibid, 236.

51. Ibid, 258.

52. Clarke, "The Rules of #MeToo," 46.

53. *CBS News*, "More than 12M 'Me Too' Facebook Posts".

54. Nicole Infarinato and Marie Anne O'Donnell, "BethAnn McLaughlin: Protecting Neurons and Women in Science," *Journal of Cell Biology* 217, no. 11 (2018): 3769–71. https://doi.org/10.1083/jcb.201810065.

55. Brian A. Eiler, Rosemary Al-Kire, Patrick C. Doyle, and Heidi A. Wayment, "Power and Trust Dynamics of Sexual Violence: A Textual Analysis of Nassar Victim Impact Statements and #MeToo Disclosures on Twitter," *Journal of Clinical Sport Psychology* 13, no. 2 (2019): 290–310. https://doi.org/10.1123/jcsp.2018-0056.

56. Leslie A. Fischer and Allison Daniel Anders, "Engaging with Cultural Sport Psychology to Explore Systemic Sexual Exploitation in USA Gymnastics: A Call to Commitments," *Journal of Applied Sport Psychology* 32, no. 2 (2020): 129–45. https://doi.org/10.1080/10413200.2018.1564944.

57. Sandra F. Sperino and Sujaa A. Thomas, *Unequal: How America's Courts Undermine Discrimination Law* (New York: Oxford University Press, 2017).

58. Cited in Clarke, "The Rules of #MeToo," 38.

59. Holroyd-Leduc and Straus, "#MeToo and the Medical Profession," E972.

60. Deborah L. Rhode, "#MeToo: Why Now? What Next?" *Duke Law Journal* 69 (2019): 377–428.

61. Meighan Stone and Rachel Vogelstein, "Celebrating #MeToo's Global Impact," *Foreign Policy* (March 7, 2019). Retrieved on March 23, 2021 from https://foreignpolicy.com/2019/03/07/metooglobalimpactinternationalwomens-day.

62. Alanna Vagianos, "In Response To #MeToo, Men Are Tweeting #HowIWillChange," *The Huffington Post* (October 18, 2017): A1. Retrieved on March 20, 2021 from https://www.huffpost.com/entry/in-response-to-metoo-men-are-tweeting-howiwillchange_n_59e79bd3e4b00905bdae455d.

63. PettyJohn, Muzzey, Maas, and McCauley, "#HowIWillChange," 612.

64. Johnson and Johnson, "An Empirical Exploration," NP70–1.

65. Michael S. Kimmel and Matthew Mahler, "Adolescent Masculinity, Homophobia, and Violence: Random School Shootings, 1982–2001," *American Behavioral Scientist* 46, no. 10 (2003): 1439–58. https://doi.org/10.1177/0002764203046010010.

66. Michael Flood, "Involving Men in Efforts to End Violence against Women," *Journal of Men and Masculinities* 14, no. 3 (2011): 358–77. https://doi.org/10.1177/1097184X10363995.

67. Patricia M. Fabiano, H. Wesley Perkins, Alan Berkowitz, Jeff Linkenbach, and Christopher Stark, "Engaging Men as Social Justice Allies in Ending Violence against Women: Evidence for a Social Norms Approach," *Journal of American College Health* 52, no. 3 (2003): 105–12. https://doi.org/10.1080/07448480309595732.

68. Victoria L. Banyard, Elizabeth G. Plante, and Mary M. Moynihan, "Bystander Education: Bringing a Broader Community Perspective to Sexual Violence Prevention," *Journal of Community Psychology* 32, no. 1 (2004): 61–79. https://doi.org/10.1002/jcop.10078.

69. Linda Hasunuma and Ki-young Shin, "#MeToo in Japan and South Korea: #WeToo, #WithYou," *Journal of Women, Politics & Policy* 40, no. 1 (2019): 97–111. https://doi.org/10.1080/1554477X.2019.1563416.

70. Stone and Vogelstein, "Celebrating #MeToo's Global Impact".

71. Henry Samuel, "Film of Woman 'Punched' for Confronting Wolf-Whistler Shocks France as Fines Set to Be Introduced," *The Telegraph* (July 30, 2018): A1. Retrieved on March 23, 2021 from https://www.telegraph.co.uk/news/2018/07/30/film-woman-punched-confronting-wolf-whistler-shocks-france-fines.

72. Stone and Vogelstein, "Celebrating #MeToo's Global Impact".

73. Elisabeth Noelle-Neumann, "The Spiral of Silence: A Theory of Public Opinion," *Journal of Communication* 24, no. 2 (1974): 43–51. https://doi.org/10.1111/j.1460-2466.1974.tb00367.x.

74. J. David Kennamer, "Self-Serving Biases in Perceiving the Opinions of Others: Implications for the Spiral of Silence," *Communication Research* 17, no. 3 (1990): 393–404. https://doi.org/10.1177/009365090017003006; Xudong Liu and Shahira Fahmy, "Exploring the Spiral of Silence in the Virtual World: Individuals Willingness to Express Personal Opinions in Online versus Offline Settings," *Journal of Media and Communication Studies* 3, no. 2 (2011): 45–57.

75. Mofoluke I. Akoja and Abimifoluwa Glory Anjorin, "Social Media and Women's Culture of Silence on Sexual Violence: Perception of Babcock University's Female Undergraduates," *Communication Cultures in Africa* 2, no. 1 (2020): 50–76.

76. Stavroula Pipyrou, "#MeToo Is Little More than Mob Rule // vs //#MeToo Is a Legitimate Form of Social Justice," *HAU: Journal of Ethnographic Theory* 8, no. 3 (2018): 415–9. http://dx.doi.org/10.1086/701007.

77. Angela Onwuachi-Willig, "What about #UsToo? The Invisibility of Race in the #MeToo Movement," *Yale Law Journal Forum* 128 (2018): 105–20.

78. Gill and Orgad, "The Shifting Terrain of Sex and Power," 1318–21.

79. Ibid, 57.

80. Reena Pattani, Shiphra Ginsburg, Alekhya Mascarenhas Johnson, Julia E Moore, Sabrina Jassemi, and Sharon E Straus, "Organizational Factors Contributing to Incivility at an Academic Medical Center and Systems-Based Solutions: A Qualitative Study," *Academic Medicine* 93, no. 11 (2018): 1569–75. https://doi.org/10.1097/ACM.0000000000002310.

81. Godswill Okiyi, Chinwe Odionye, and Adenike Okeya, "Socio-Cultural Variables and Media Coverage of Girl Child Marriages," *Journal of Communication and Media Studies* 1, no. 2 (2020): 10–21.

82. Khaya Gqibitole, "The Quiet Violence of Rape: Unnamed Survivors, Unnameable Scars," *Open Journal of Social Sciences* 8, no. 8 (2020): 86–104. https://doi.org/10.4236/jss.2020.88007.

83. Shirley Ardener, *Perceiving Women* (London: Malaby Press, 1975).

84. Ezekiel S. Asemah, Angela Nwammuo, and Adeline O. A. Nkwam-Uwaoma, *Theories and Models of Communication* (Jos, Nigeria: Jos University Press, 2017).

85. Ibid, 253.

86. Okiyi, Odionye, and Okeya, "Socio-Cultural Variables," 5.

87. Cheris Kramarae, *Women and Men Speaking: Frameworks for Analysis* (Rowley, MA: Newbury House Publishers, 1981).

88. Ibid: 1.

89. Jing Zeng, "You Say #MeToo, I Say #MiTu: China's Online Campaigns against Sexual Abuse," in *#MeToo and the Politics of Social Change*, ed. Bianca Fileborn and Rachel Loney-Howes (New York: Palgrave Macmillan, 2019): 71–83.

90. Mandy Zuo, "China's #MeToo Revival: Famed Activists, TV Host and Writer Named," *South China Morning Post* (July 27, 2018). Retrieved on March 23, 2021 from https://www.scmp.com/news/china/society/article/2157204/well-known-activists-among-accused-metoo-campaign-gathers-pace.

91. Jing Zeng, "From #MeToo to #RiceBunny: How Social Media Users Are Campaigning in China," *The Conversation* (February 6, 2018). Retrieved on March 23, 2021 from https://theconversation.com/from-metoo-to-ricebunny-how-social-media-users-are-campaigning-in-china-90860.

92. Simon Denyer and Amber Ziye Wang, "Chinese Women Reveal Sexual Harassment, but #Metoo Movement Struggles for Air," *The Washington Post* (January 9, 2018): A1. Retrieved on March 23, 2021 from https://www.washingtonpost.com/world/asia_pacific/chinese-women-reveal-sexual-harassment-but-metoo-movement-struggles-for-air/2018/01/08/ac591c26-cc0d-4d5a-b2ca-d14a7f763fe0_story.html.

93. Viola Zhou and Sarah Zheng, "Chinese Students Use #Metoo to Take Fight against Sexual Harassment to Elite Universities," *South China Morning Post* (January 16, 2018): A1. Retrieved on March 23, 2021 from https://www.scmp.com/news/china/society/article/2128341/chinese-students-use-metoo-take-fight-against-sexual-harassment.

94. Zeng, "You Say #MeToo," 72.

95. Ibid, 72.

96. Lauren Berlant, "Intimacy: A Special Issue," *Critical Inquiry* 24, no. 2 (1998): 281–8. https://doi.org/10.1086/448875.

97. Ibid, 281.

98. Lauren Berlant, *The Female Complaint: The Unfinished Business of Sentimentality in American Culture* (Durham, NC: Duke University Press, 2008): viii.

99. For example, see Neetu Khanna, "Poetics of Progressive Feeling: The Visceral Aesthetics of Mulk Raj Anand," *Journal of Postcolonial Writing* 51, no. 4 (2015): 449–61. https://doi.org/10.1080/17449855.2015.1050123; Jennifer C. Nash, "Practicing Love: Black Feminism, Love Politics, and Post-Intersectionality," *Meridians* 11, no. 2 (2011): 1–24. https://doi.org/10.2979/meridians.11.2.1.

100. Berlant, *The Female Complaint*, viii.

101. Ashley Noel Mack and Bryan J. McCann, "'Strictly an Act of Street Violence': Intimate Publicity and Affective Divestment in the New Orleans Mother's Day Shooting," *Communication and Critical/Cultural Studies* 14, no. 4 (2017): 334–50, 337. https://doi.org/10.1080/14791420.2017.1366661.

102. Miranda Fricker, *Epistemic Injustice: Power and the Ethics of Knowing* (New York: Oxford University Press, 2007).

103. Rachel McKinnon, "Epistemic Injustice," *Philosophy Compass* 11, no. 8 (2016): 437–46. https://doi.org/10.1111/phc3.12336.

104. Christopher Hookway, "Some Varieties of Epistemic Injustice: Reflections on Fricker," *Episteme* 7, no. 2 (2010): 151–63. https://doi.org/10.3366/E1742360010000882.

105. Tambe, "Reckoning with the Silences of #MeToo," 198.

106. Tarana Burke, "#MeToo Was Started for Black and Brown Women and Girls. They're Still Being Ignored," *The Washington Post* (November 9, 2017): A1. Retrieved on March 20, 2021 from https://www.washingtonpost.com/news/post-nation/wp/2017/11/09/the-waitress-who-works-in-the-diner-needs-to-know-that-the-issue-of-sexual-harassment-is-about-her-too.

107. Miranda Fricker, "Epistemic Justice as a Condition of Political Freedom," *Synthese* 190, no. 7 (2013): 1317–32. https://doi.org/10.1007/s11229-012-0227-3.

108. Salman Masood, "Woman Stabbed 23 Times in Pakistan Wins Appeal against Assailant's Acquittal," *The New York Times* (January 23, 2019): A1. Retrieved on March 23, 2021 from https://www.nytimes.com/2019/01/23/world/asia/pakistan-stabbing-khadija-siddiqi.html.

109. Stone and Vogelstein, "Celebrating #MeToo's Global Impact".

110. Richard Delgado and Jean Stefancic, *Critical Race Theory: An Introduction* (3rd Ed.) (New York: New York University Press, 2017); Also, see Audrey Pafford and Jonathan Matusitz, "ABC's *Quantico*: A Critical Discourse Analysis of Female Superiority and Racial Stereotypes," *Critical Studies in Television* 12, no. 3 (2017): 273–88. https://doi.org/10.1177/1749602017717167.

111. Venus E. Evans-Winters and Jennifer Esposito, "Other People's Daughters: Critical Race Feminism and Black Girls' Education," *Educational Foundations* 24, no. 1 (2010): 11–24, 19.

112. Cherese D. Childers-McKee and Kathy Hytten, "Critical Race Feminism and the Complex Challenges of Educational Reform," *The Urban Review* 47 (2015): 393–412. https://doi.org/10.1007/s11256-015-0323-z.

113. Tambe, "Reckoning with the Silences of #MeToo," 199.

114. Angela Onwuachi-Willig, "Meritor Savings Bank v. Vinson, 477 US 57 (1986)," in *Feminist Judgments: Rewritten Opinions of the United States Supreme Court*, ed. Kathryn M. Stanchi, Linda L. Berger, and Bridget J. Crawford (Cambridge: Cambridge University Press, 2016): 297–321.

115. Sperino and Thomas, *Unequal*, 20–1.

116. Cited in Onwuachi-Willig, "What about #UsToo?" 110.

117. Henri Tajfel, "Social Identity and Intergroup Behaviour," *Social Science Information* 13, no. 2 (1974): 65–93. https://doi.org/10.1177/053901847401300204.

118. Dominic Abrams and Michael A. Hogg, *Social Identity and Social Cognition* (Malden, MA: Blackwell, 1999).

119. Demis E. Glasford, Felicia Pratto, and John F. Dovidio, "Intragroup Dissonance: Responses to Ingroup Violation of Personal Values," *Journal of Experimental Social Psychology* 44, no. 1 (2008): 1057–64. https://doi.org/10.1016/j.jesp.2007.10.004.

120. Henri Tajfel and John C. Turner, "The Social Identity Theory of Inter-Group Behavior," in *Psychology of Intergroup Relations*, ed. Stephen Worchel and William G. Austin (Chicago, IL: Nelson-Hall, 1986): 7–24.

121. Michael A. Hogg and Dominic Abrams, *Social Identifications: A Social Psychology of Intergroup Relations and Group Processes* (London: Routledge, 1988).

122. Henri Tajfel, "Individuals and Groups in Social Psychology," *British Journal of Social and Clinical Psychology* 18, no. 2 (1979): 183–90. https://doi.org/10.1111/j.2044-8260.1979.tb00324.x.

123. Richard Jenkins, *Social Identity* (2nd Ed.) (London: Routledge, 2004).

124. Henri Tajfel, *Human Groups and Social Categories: Studies in Social Psychology* (Cambridge: Cambridge University Press, 1981).

125. Nuray Sakallı-Uğurlu, Zenep S. Yalçın, and Peter Glick, "Ambivalent Sexism, Belief in a Just World, and Empathy as Predictors of Turkish Students' Attitudes toward Rape Victims," *Sex Roles* 57, no. 11 (2007): 889–95. https://doi.org/10.1007/s11199-007-9313-2; Madeleine van der Bruggen and Amy Grubb, "A Review of the Literature Relating to Rape Victim Blaming: An Analysis of the Impact of Observer and Victim Characteristics on Attribution of Blame in Rape Cases," *Aggression and Violent Behavior* 19, no. 5 (2014): 523–31. https://doi.org/10.1016/j.avb.2014.07.008.

126. David C. Geary, *Male, Female: The Evolution of Human Sex Differences* (Washington, DC: American Psychological Association, 1998); Deborah Tannen, *You Just Don't Understand* (New York: Ballantine Books, 1990).

127. Henri Tajfel, *Social Identity and Intergroup Relations* (Cambridge: Cambridge University Press, 1982).

128. Eliana Suarez and Tahany M. Gadalla, "Stop Blaming the Victim: A Meta-Analysis on Rape Myths," *Journal of Interpersonal Violence* 25, no. 11 (2010): 2010–35. https://doi.org/10.1177/0886260509354503.

129. Diana L. Payne, Kimberly A. Lonsway, and Louise E. Fitzgerald, "Rape Myth Acceptance: Exploration of Its Structure and Its Measurement Using the Illinois Rape Myth Acceptance Scale," *Journal of Research in Personality* 33, no. 1 (1999): 27–68. https://doi.org/10.1006/jrpe.1998.2238.

130. Suarez and Gadalla, "Stop Blaming the Victim," 2010–35.

131. Peter Glick and Susan T. Fiske, "The Ambivalent Sexism Inventory: Differentiating Hostile and Benevolent Sexism," *Journal of Personality and Social Psychology* 70, no. 3 (1996): 491–512. https://doi.org/10.1037/0022-3514.70.3.491.

132. Nuray Sakallı-Uğurlu, "Ambivalent Sexism, Gender, and Major as Predictors of Turkish College Students' Attitudes toward Women and Men's Atypical Educational Choices," *Sex Roles* 62, no. 7 (2010): 427–37. https://doi.org/10.1007/s11199-009-9673-x.

133. Stone and Vogelstein, "Celebrating #MeToo's Global Impact".

134. Pipyrou, "#Me Too Is Little More than Mob Rule," 415.

135. Sudarsan Raghavan and Heba Farouk Mahfouz, "In Egypt, a #MeToo Complaint Can Land a Woman in Jail," *The Washington Post* (October 25, 2018): A1. Retrieved on May 10, 2021 from https://www.washingtonpost.com/world/in-egypt-a-metoo-complaint-can-land-a-woman-in-jail/2018/10/24/3a2fe5a0-d6db-11e8-a10f-b51546b10756_story.html.

136. Stone and Vogelstein, "Celebrating #MeToo's Global Impact".

137. Megan Boler, "The Risks of Empathy: Interrogating Multiculturalism's Gaze," *Cultural Studies* 11, no. 2 (1997): 253–73, 256. https://doi.org/10.1080/09502389700490141.

138. Ibid, 256.

139. Sara Ahmed, *The Cultural Politics of Emotion* (2nd Ed.) (New York: Routledge, 2014): 30.

140. Boler, "The Risks of Empathy," 258.

141. Bell hooks, *Black Looks: Race and Representation* (New York: Routledge, 1992).

142. Clare Hemmings, "Affective Solidarity: Feminist Reflexivity and Political Transformation," *Feminist Theory* 13, no. 2 (2012): 147–61, 152. https://doi.org/10.1177/1464700112442643.

143. Boler, "The Risks of Empathy," 259.

144. Ibid, 259.

145. Michelle Rodino-Colocino, "Me Too, #Metoo: Countering Cruelty with Empathy," *Communication and Critical/Cultural Studies* 15, no. 1 (2018): 96–100. https://doi.org/10.1080/14791420.2018.1435083.

146. Emily Flores, "The #MeToo Movement Hasn't Been Inclusive of the Disability Community," *TeenVogue* (April 24, 2018). Retrieved on March 23, 2021 from https://www.teenvogue.com/story/the-metoo-movement-hasnt-been-inclusive-of-the-disability-community.

147. Clare Hemmings, "Resisting Popular Feminism: Gender, Sexuality, and the Lure of the Modern," *Gender, Place & Culture* 25, no. 7 (2018): 963–77. https://doi.org/10.1080/0966369X.2018.1433639.

CHAPTER 11

Public Communication Campaigns for LGBTQ+ Communities

The issue of fundamental rights for LGBTQ+ individuals has been addressed through a myriad of public communication campaigns across the world. Campaigns emphasize that sexual rights form an essential component of human rights and should be the intrinsic rights of all human beings. **LGBTQ+** is an acronym that stands for lesbian, gay, bisexual, transgender, queer, and others. Developed in the 1990s, the term is a variation of the acronym LGB, which gradually replaced the term "gay" when alluding to the broader LGBT community in the mid- to late 1980s. The acronym, in addition to its common variants, operates as an umbrella concept for sexuality and gender identity.[1] People generally employ LGBTQ+ to refer to all the communities contained within "LGBTTTQQIAA" (lesbian, gay, bisexual, transgender, transsexual, two-spirited, queer, questioning, intersex, asexual, and ally). LGBTQ+ is the more frequently employed term in the community, arguably because it comes across as more user-friendly.[2]

In February 2021, a Gallup poll on lesbian, gay, bisexual, or transgender identification revealed that 5.6% of American adults identified as LGBTQ+. This represented an increase from the previous 4.5% in Gallup's poll conducted in 2017. Almost 87% of Americans claimed to be heterosexual or straight, and 7.6% chose not to answer the question about their sexual orientation. Over 50% of LGBTQ+ adults (54.6%) said that they were bisexual. Approximately 25% identified as gay, in contrast to 11.7% lesbians and 11.3% transgenders.

Fundamentals of Public Communication Campaigns, First Edition. Jonathan Matusitz.
© 2022 John Wiley & Sons Ltd. Published 2022 by John Wiley & Sons Ltd.

An important reason for the rise in LGBTQ+ identification over time is attributed to the fact that younger generations are far more inclined to see themselves as something other than heterosexual. In the February 2021 Gallup poll, over 15% of adult members of Generation Z (those aged 18 to 25 in 2022) considered themselves in those terms. On the other hand, LGBTQ+ identification is less and less present as generations get older, including 2% or less of people born before 1965—i.e., aged 58 and older in 2022—in the United States.[3]

LGBTQ+: KEY TERMS AND DEFINITIONS

Before discussing public communication campaigns in detail, fundamental terms and definitions relating to the LGBTQ+ community ought to be provided to readers. To begin, **sexual orientation** encompasses the four constructs of sexual attraction, identity, conduct, and relationships with other people. As a general rule, it is surmised that individuals are likely to be heterosexual (attraction to people of a different gender), homosexual (gay or lesbian, meaning attraction to people of the same gender), and bisexual (attraction to both genders). Sexual orientation is a continuing pattern of romantic or sexual attraction (or a mixture of both) to people of the opposite gender, the same gender, or to both genders (or more than one gender).[4] In like fashion, **sexual attractiveness** or **sex appeal** is a person's ability to magnetize the sexual or erotic interests of others, and it is a driver for sexual selection or mate choice. The attraction can be based on an individual's physical or other attributes, or to such attributes in the context where they emerge. The attraction may be to an individual's body language, gait, voice, or even smell.[5]

Gender Expression and Gender Identity

Upon looking at phrases like "gender expression" and "gender identity," the word "gender" seems to be of significance. **Gender** refers to how women, men, and nonbinary people conduct themselves based on feminine, masculine, or fluid features of men and women. Gender is always in flux and is rooted in the norms that cultures ascribe to "being a man," meaning masculinity, or "being a woman," meaning femininity.[6] Thus, gender is founded on circumstances of a culture because the meanings of what masculine and feminine are differ across cultures and evolve over time.[7] As Nelson and Nelson (2010)[8] explain, gender is "conceptualized as the socially defined roles, attitudes and values which society ascribes as appropriate for one sex or the other." **Gender expression** refers to an individual's behavioral signs towards masculine, feminine, or other variant clothing, appearance, voice, and body properties. Gender expression is gender presentation because people's behaviors, mannerisms, curiosities, and appearances tend to reflect who they are. It is linked to gender in both personal and sociocultural contexts.[9]

Gender identity is a conception of oneself as male, female, or other gender-related construct. We can change gender identity in our lives. We could wish, at some point, to receive gender reassignment treatment (i.e., to become transgender) or simply resist the idea of being either a man or a woman. Hence, gender identity is the personal conception of one's own gender. It can correspond to someone's assigned sex at birth or can diverge from it.[10] As such, the aforementioned **transgender** describes any person whose gender identity differs from the gender that a person was assigned at birth. Likewise, people whose gender identity and assigned-at-birth gender remain the same are called **cisgender**. When we assume that all, or virtually all, humans are cisgender, we believe in **cisnormativity**.[11]

In the same way that **queer** entails an opposition to fixed identity categories,[12] those who want to be called **genderqueer** resist the idea that each human being falls in one of two fixed categories—male or female. This phenomenon is also called **nonbinary**. To further explain the gender spectrum, academics and practitioners alike have employed generic pronouns such as "they." "They" is also an oft-used singular pronoun for a generic or hypothetical individual in English. With this said, to circumvent the use of the pronoun "they," a certain number of members of the LGBTQ+ community (and their allies) are now using neopronouns. **Neopronouns** are words created to replace long-established pronouns like "he" or "she" that serve as pronouns without showing any sign of gender.[13] Examples include "ze" and "zir" in English[14] and "elle" in Spanish (instead of "el" and "ella").[15] Finally, the term **sexual minority** refers to people whose sexual orientation stands apart from the heterosexual majority in society.[16]

Opposition and Homophobia

Since it was coined in the 1970s in the United States, the term **homophobia** is educed to denote biased attitudes and actions against nonheterosexual orientation.[17] Like most of the terms mentioned earlier, "homophobia" is fluid and contextual. For example, the acronym LGBTQ+ includes concepts on gender and sexuality to which not every member of that community agrees. Because such detractors, who can also be allies and members of nonheterosexual communities, resist the LGBTQ+ designation (or some aspects of it), they have been accused of homophobia themselves. A recurring argument is that transgender and transsexual causes should not be mixed with those of lesbian, gay, and bisexual (LGB) people because the lifestyles and motives can be different. This line of reasoning accentuates that being transgender or transsexual pertains more to gender identity than other constructs.[18] In addition, some of the same-sex individuals vehemently criticize what they see as same-sex propaganda. Hence, these critics, too, are labeled as homophobes. They resent the idea of political and social solidarity, of even campaigning for LGBTQ+ rights (e.g., gay pride and marches). Others believe that creating labels based on grouping together people with nonheterosexual orientations aggravates the situation because it reinforces the myth that being a member of the LGBTQ+ community makes that member deficiently different from the mainstream heterosexual society.[19]

In a more extreme case, in India, LGBTQ+ communities face many problems that their non-LGBTQ+ counterparts do not face. They are frowned down upon by the mainstream classes. Sexual intercourse between two individuals of the same sex is considered unlawful and punishable. According to Section 377 of the Indian Penal Code, same-sex intercourse was a crime. Non-LGBTQ+ people could adopt boys and girls, live freely in society, and follow a career of their own choosing. On the other hand, LGBTQ+ folks encountered difficulties in adoption because they were charged with violating Indian mores—e.g., the belief was that homosexuals could inculcate dangerous ideas in their adopted children. LGBTQ+ people were scorned in social settings and publicly dishonored for their choice of partners. They had a more difficult time pursuing a career of their choice because a certain number of non-LGBTQ+ people said that they did not want to have anything to do with them. Mainstream society considered LGBTQ+ folks to be mentally ill and refused to believe that they were born that way.[20] Section 377 was repealed in 2018.[21]

AN INTRODUCTION TO LGBTQ+ CAMPAIGNS

In 1973, the American Psychiatric Association (APA) withdrew homosexuality from its handbook on mental disorders. It was a first in the history of the United States: it was recognized that a disease should not exist for the simple reason that it has been proclaimed to be a disease. In the case of smallpox or cholera, these were diseases that truly existed and became extinct through the elimination of incidences of these diseases. The depathologization of homosexuality is attributable to the sociocultural context of the 1960s and early 1970s, an era symbolized by large-scale campaigns seeking expanded freedom for all kinds of expressions of sexuality.[22]

Today, public communication campaigns for LGBTQ+ communities are principally movements that comprise a group of activities that develop relationships to inspire audiences in supporting LGBTQ+ rights. There is no doubt that LGBTQ+ individuals have enjoyed heightened focus, both domestically and globally, as an at-risk group for certain health conditions. Systemic and cultural determinants—including racial, religious, political, and individual factors—can exacerbate problems of health discrepancies and access to care within the LGBTQ+ community. For instance, it has been ascertained that sexual minority status continues to have a negative impact on access to healthcare, which is even worse if the person belongs to multiple marginalized groups.[23] Research across several countries also affirms that LGBTQ+ individuals experience poorer mental health than their heterosexual counterparts.[24]

Civil Society Organizations (CSOs) and Institutional Actors

Many public communication campaigns for LGBTQ+ rights are designed and conducted by civil society organizations (CSOs) and institutional actors. Composed of community-based organizations and nongovernmental organizations, a **civil society organization (CSO)** refers to a nonprofit, voluntary citizens' group with many interests and ties and arranged on a local, national, or international platform. Task-focused and run by leaders with a common interest, CSOs perform a range of activities and humanitarian functions, deliver citizens' requests to governments, keep an eye on policies, and inspire political participation—especially at the local level.[25] Social capital is central to the success of such campaigns, both with respect to building a sense of personal identity and connecting within the community, as well as building bridges with society at large. Maximizing WUNC—worthiness, unity, numbers, and commitment—is a useful tool of communication for such campaigns.[26]

Pro-LGBTQ+ CSOs can display their strength, their visibility and pride, and their indefatigable pleas for equality. The approaches that CSOs take may differ by country and the political climate in which they operate, but the ultimate mission is the same: fighting for social acceptance, new legislation that guarantees equality and nondiscrimination, punishment for hate crimes, and state-sanctioned same-sex partnerships (or the same rights and privileges for marriage). Broad public expressions of LGBTQ+ advocacy are merely part of the strategies adopted by such CSOs. The latter have sprung up around the world as the institutional symbol of a broader social movement.[27]

Though CSOs have gained visibility and raised public awareness, institutional actors are generally more productive when it comes to making decisions for policy outcomes.[28] Like CSOs, they nevertheless provide much effort to reach out to society for social acceptance and approval from governments.[29] The types of institutions and political opportunities have an effect on the probability for success.[30] Researchers investigating the state-by-state enactment of the Equal Rights Amendment in the United States insist that movements have a bearing on policy and attitude change. More precisely, they indicate a link between CSOs (and institutional actors), attitude change, and political party support of causes like LGBTQ+ rights.[31]

Signaling and Human Rights Language

A predominant tactic used in pro-LGBTQ+ campaigns is signaling. **Signaling** is the practice by advocacy groups to convince audiences to publicly support lawmakers.[32] Instead of relying mostly on direct persuasion, campaigners may create more impact by devoting their energy and resources to campaign components that impact indirect or secondary audiences who can (1) wield interpersonal influence on focal people or (2) help change conditions that influence behavior. Advocacy campaigns have great potential for motivating change agents with close connections to focal individuals and for creating an impact on institutions and government agencies at the local and national levels.[33]

A campaign may try to modify the environment indirectly by diffusing messages to focal individuals who will act as intermediaries between the campaign and lawmakers. After all, the latter are the ones responsible for opening up or blocking opportunities based on the legislation that they get passed. Focal individuals' decisions depend on the constraints and opportunities in their social milieus. Examples are financial expenses, local policies, industry practices, commercial messages, social factors, and community services. Lawmakers in sectors like government, business, education, and healthcare can set interventions in motion that change the environment.[34]

Social media is a favorite platform for signaling because public communication campaigns get mass audiences to anonymously denounce anti-LGBTQ+ people or policies. Hence, signaling produces a great many new affective connections and solidarities—on a global scale. One technique of pro-LGBTQ+ and similar types of advocacy campaigns is the use of human rights language to "signal" a common denominator among all humans. Human rights language enables campaign communicators to become stronger actors in international relations and to promote their cause in their own countries and arenas.[35] Human rights frames are useful for groups that want to direct our attention to a certain category of wrong (i.e., withholding of freedoms, lack of access to healthcare, or unwarranted discrimination). In many instances, reference to human rights facilitates the audience's identification with a category of victims and the rights and privileges that should be granted to them. Invoking human rights language can help claim the moral high ground and hone in ties with others around the world. Many anonymous supporters join pro-LGBTQ+ movements online to call out human wrongs and champion human dignity. Human rights frames expand horizons and opportunities for advocates to join forces with institutions with shared interests in human dignity. Such frames boost advocates' abilities to exert influence on norm-violating governments.[36]

Case Study 1:   The GLAAD Campaigns

Founded in 1985 by activists and authors Arnie Kantrowitz, Darrell Yates Rist, and Vito Russo, **GLAAD** stands for Gay and Lesbian Alliance Against Defamation and is an advocacy organization that specializes in disseminating accurate media depictions of the LGBTQ+ community—whom GLAAD used to call "queer" community—and monitoring the media establishment. The organization actually started as a protest against defamatory coverage of queer people. Its mission has since extended to the entertainment world and its representations of the LGBTQ+ community.[37] GLAAD also promotes its goals by running public education campaigns with favorable lesbian, gay, bisexual, and transgender images.[38] The first action that GLAAD took was criticize the manner by which *The New York Times* was reporting on the AIDS epidemic and the gay community. The first reported negotiation between the newspaper and GLAAD "took place in February 1987. A variety of long-standing problems were discussed, including AIDS coverage and some improvement followed."[39]

Soon after, GLAAD circulated a media reference manual on transgender issues of which the purpose was to list and describe troublesome and/or defamatory terms and practices. These terms and practices were divided into four categories: wrongful terminology, outdated terminology, defamatory terminology, and problematic practices.[40] On the whole, GLAAD's manual created a glossary and style guide designed to promote the use of "fairer," neutral, and nondiscriminatory language. Such an approach became familiar in media activism. Future guides on other controversial issues like racism and mental illness began to proliferate.[41] GLAAD successfully employed various approaches with news editors around the nation to encourage the obliteration of stereotypes and more inclusion of gays and lesbians in daily news coverage. GLAAD also persuaded reporters to refuse writing news stories that might paint homosexuals with a negative brush. Now, more journalists were convinced that any written or verbal attack on homosexuality is "hate speech," which will inevitably cause "hate crimes."[42]

In the early 2000s, GLAAD launched its **AM/FM Activism** initiative, an online platform that enables local activists to use published resources needed for responding to defamatory claims within their own communities. This digital organizing tool has motivated members of the LGBTQ+ community to rebut defamatory comments by media outlets through images, words, and their personal accounts.[43] GLAAD's influence flourished over the years as the LGBTQ+ community became more active in the public sphere. In early 2013, GLAAD announced that it had officially dropped the "Gay & Lesbian Alliance Against Defamation" from its name and would, from that point forward, be known only as the initialism GLAAD to convey its mission more accurately. The name change was a pledge to absorb bisexual and transgender people in their endeavors to protect the community in its entirety.[44] GLAAD redefined itself as the media relations branch of the LGBTQ+ community through its collaboration with news, entertainment, sports, and social networking sites with the quintessential agenda to change society.[45]

The "Be an Ally and a Friend" Campaign

Launched in 2007, "Be an Ally and a Friend" was a public service announcement (PSA) campaign that asked viewers to take actions about the discrimination and prejudice encountered by LGBTQ+ folks and to check their GLAAD.org website, filled with valuable resources for parents, youths, relatives, and friends. As stated on the GLAAD website: "LGBT people are our mothers, fathers, sons, daughters, sisters, brothers, aunts, uncles and cousins. This is a fact and it isn't going away. You have the opportunity to be an ally and a friend at home, school, church and work." As the PSA continues, "A straight ally can merely be someone who is supportive and accepts the LGBT person, or a straight ally can be someone who personally advocates for equal rights and fair treatment."[46]

The 25 PSAs—released periodically throughout 2007—featured 22 A-rated celebrities from the world of television, film, and sports. Each PSA channels viewers towards web-based resources that "give them the tools to be straight allies and combat homophobia."[47] Under the heading "Ten Ways to Be an Ally and a Friend," GLAAD recommended that heterosexual Americans "listen, be open-minded, and be willing to talk. Be inclusive and invite LGBT friends to hang out with your friends and family." Also included in the online segment was the following statement: "Don't assume that all your friends and coworkers are straight. Someone close to you could be looking for support in their 'coming out' process. Not making assumptions will give them the space they need."[48] The guide denounced homophobic comments and jokes, urging concerned citizens to "let your friends, family and coworkers know that you find them offensive." In addition to the 10 tips on tolerance, the GLAAD online guide listed many other headings, including "Things You Can Do for Transgender Equality," "When Your Mom or Dad Is Gay," "Straight Spouses," and "Equal Rights, Not Special Rights."[49]

The "Be an Ally and a Friend" campaign featured two other focal points: the need to accept our LGBTQ+ friends or relatives and the awareness that homophobic words can be as harmful as weapons. These focal points pushed the public to "be an ally and a friend," directing viewers to online resources to acquire the tools to be straight allies and condemn homophobia. There were several 20- and 30-second versions of the campaign, even versions in Spanish and the American Sign Language.[50] In 2010, for example, Sofia Vergara, a Colombian–American television personality, participated in the PSA to encourage Latinos and Latinas to be allies and friends to the LGBTQ+ community. The PSA was meant to show support for such communities in Latin America.[51]

Cabosky (2014)[52] examined over 200 media releases by GLAAD (during the 2011–2 period) to determine how the releases framed the organization's image and the varying degrees of power that they sought to confer to the LGBTQ+ community. Overall, GLAAD's releases signaled the importance placed on issues of violence against LGBTQ+ individuals and the involvement of famous LGBTQ+ personalities and allies at media events. Particularly exposed was the media's lack of focus on advocating or covering less controversial issues based on principles of equality or because, in most cases, LGBTQ+ individuals in question were not famous. Indeed, the releases indicated a general lack of power for nonélite people within the movement. Nevertheless, the use of social networking sites and online petitions created by nonélite advocates demonstrated new forms of public communication models that departed from two-way symmetrical or asymmetrical models. Rather, they moved closer to fluid and dynamic models, bestowing ordinary activists more power within the LGBTQ+ movement.

The "Talking to the Middle" Campaign

In January 2008, GLAAD ran a campaign titled *Talking to the Moveable Middle about Marriage* (i.e., *Talking to the Middle*). *Talking to the Middle* was actually a "written" campaign disseminated through a published 40-page booklet for advocates. The purpose was to strengthen the need to replace rights claims by emotionally coated arguments (i.e., see the pathos side of persuasion in Chapter 3). The campaign also strove to exploit voter psychology. Congruent with a study that attracted a great deal of attention within the advocacy community, in which 57% of participants believed that homosexuals "did not share their basic values," *Talking to the Middle* diffused the all-embracing belief among moderate audiences that "gay people aren't like me."[53] Describing these audiences as more resistant to change than actually biased against LGBTQ+ people, *Talking to the Middle* asserted the following:

> If gay people weren't seen as outsiders, including gay people in marriage would be less problematic. To address this outsider status, we need to help Americans think about gay people as part of the community. Communications [should] emphasize common ground. In terms of marriage, this means talking about marriage in a way that echoes how straight Americans talk—and think—about marriage.[54]

LGBTQ+ people seemed to face a dichotomous situation. On the one hand, arguments in favor of equal rights made them appear to be self-centered, as epitomized in the following: "If we only talk about rights and protections, we risk reinforcing the misperception that gay people don't enter marriage in the same spirit as straight people." On the other hand, overly discussing social legitimacy and validation of their relationships intimidated voters afraid that marriage as an institution could go further downhill. Consequently, they would oppose what they perceived as the increased devaluation that would occur by the inclusion of LGBTQ+ people. *Talking to the Middle* recommended to find a happy medium between the dichotomies, like a prudent selection of which concrete harms to stress. It could be as simple as choosing between the right to visit one's partner at the hospital or the right to take a leave of absence to care for one's sick partner. Under this new paradigm, it could be winningly argued that not respecting these rights would thwart "the ability of committed couples to take care of and be responsible for each other."[55]

GLAAD's Campaign through Televised Productions

GLADD tirelessly works to guarantee equitable and accurate representations of LGBTQ+ people in the entertainment media as well.[56] In 1997, the CSO ran a campaign called "Let Ellen out" to shine a light on media's neglect of lesbian and gay representations on prime-time television. The campaign focused on the comedy series *Ellen*, starring Ellen DeGeneres. At that time, the series had the only nonheterosexual lead character on US television before *Will & Grace* came along. *Ellen* widened viewers' perspectives about sexual minorities being on TV and launched a trend for LGBTQ+-focused programming.[57] A few weeks before *Will & Grace* premiered, GLAAD lauded the depictions of Will and his flamboyant buddy, Jack, as "different types of gay men—both of which are valued within the community." Owing to the negative stereotypes of gay men that were the hallmark of prime-time television since its infancy, the two gay characters on *Will & Grace* were now seen as progressive.[58] GLAAD's endeavors flew in the face of **queerbaiting**, a marketing ploy in which entertainment producers only "hint" at LGBTQ+ romance or representation—rather than giving a genuine depiction of it—in television series.[59]

Using another example of GLAAD's campaigning for more inclusive prime-time television shows, in 2007–8, the *Grey's Anatomy* producers, writers, and cast, aggressively pushed for authentic portrayals of LGBTQ+ people by working on new storylines based on first-hand experiences at all levels of production. Enter Sara Ramirez and Sam Smith, two key actors in *Grey's Anatomy*. Their membership of the LGBTQ+ community and their connection with GLAAD contributed to better on-screen performances, making these representations more realistic and resonating with audiences. Representations become genuine to audiences when they identify with the characters on the screen.[60] Actresses of *Grey's Anatomy* agreed to embody lesbian and bisexual identities. The production team was afraid of creating stereotypes, so they asked GLAAD for additional help. The more important piece of season 4, Callie and Erica's first kiss, grew into the only lesbian and bisexual relationship with major characters on prime-time television at that time. The success of season 4 is credited to the detailed, thought-out, and authentic storyline that *Grey's Anatomy* developed. The TV series constructed a sequence of characters and situations with which a specific audience was able to identify.[61]

In 2012, GLAAD's president Herndon Griddick maintained that messages conveyed through on-screen depictions can mirror a minority group's proximity to real-life admiration and acceptance in mainstream society. As he explained through a press release:

> This year's increase of LGBT characters on television reflects a cultural change in the way gay and lesbian people are seen in our society. More and more Americans have come to accept their LGBT family members, friends, coworkers, and peers, and as audiences tune into their favorite programs, they expect to see the same diversity of people they encounter in their daily lives.[62]

This statement reflects GLAAD's aspiration to raise pro-LGBTQ+ awareness inside households through network television series—both in the United States and around the world. It is GLAAD's hope that audiences understand LGBTQ+ issues and become inspired by fictional characters on the screen.

APPLYING AGENDA-SETTING THEORY TO GLAAD'S CAMPAIGNS

Developed by McCombs and Shaw (1972),[63] **agenda-setting theory** predicates that the media can influence or maneuver public awareness and concern of salient issues. More precisely, by manipulating viewers and creating a pecking order of news prevalence, the media tells audiences what to think about.[64] Because news organizations expose certain issues to the detriment of others, they also transform the standards by which we evaluate phenomena, people, or objects. For instance, the higher attention paid to the subject of campaign finance reform (in an election) by the media, the more likely that subject will be used to evaluate the candidates by the audience. Agenda-setting theory rests on the premise that people do not have extensive knowledge on many subjects and do not consider all of what they do know when making decisions. Instead, they make superficial decisions based on the things they see, read, or hear in the media.[65]

Implications for Campaigns

The fundamental theory of change that guides most public communication campaigns designed for policy change is agenda-setting theory, which includes media, audiences, and policy agenda setting, in that order.[66] The concept of topical salience pertains to campaign impact on the perceived significance of social problems and policy issues. Advocates produce news media coverage to energize the public in order to influence lawmakers so they can pass legislation that addresses particular problems. Achieving constant visibility in the news media is crucial for creating an agenda-setting effect, which is a frequent advocacy strategy directed at opinion leaders and lawmakers in society. Thanks to agenda setting, news coverage can shape the policy agenda on various programs, rules, and laws. A key element consists of reinforcing the public's beliefs about the effectiveness of policies and interventions that are proposed, which contributes to favorable public opinion (and direct pressure) that can help persuade institutions to open up or block opportunities.[67] Taken as a whole, campaign planners must be fully cognizant of the fact that the policy agenda is influenced by what audiences think, deem important, and do. The audiences' thoughts and actions, in turn, are shaped (at least, partially) by the media. So, public communication campaigns can trigger a chain reaction in the agenda-setting process. They achieve this mainly on two fronts: by attempting to influence issues on the media's agenda (and how they get reported through media advocacy) and by communicating to audiences directly.[68]

Making LGBTQ+ a Salient Issue

Because agenda building takes place when efforts "increase the salience of certain topics over others in news media content,"[69] public communication campaigns are able to successfully set the LGBTQ+ agenda. GLAAD has advanced LGBTQ+ issues by giving them more prominence in the mass media. From the beginning, the objective was to mold the audience's perceptions regarding the dangers of "defamatory coverage" of LGBTQ+ people. Thanks to GLAAD's campaigns, which started in the 1980s, audiences became more familiar with concepts of which they did not have a full grasp before (e.g., queer, transgender, etc.). Condemnation of the Boy Scouts of America's anti-LGBTQ+ positions dominated GLAAD's releases—with the mission of ending the Boy Scouts' restrictions imposed on gay scouts and leaders. Between 2012 and 2014, about 20 releases were made on the subject, making it a salient issue in the media during that two-year span. GLAAD also made at least 15 releases advocating Spirit Day, a yearly event created to "memorialize those who lost their lives to bullying." To assist in awareness advocacy, the CSO collaborated with corporations, government agencies, and well-known personalities. During the Obama administration, the White House participated in GLAAD's campaigns with superstars, companies, and millions of Americans by "going purple" to endorse LGBTQ+ youths on Spirit Day.[70]

GLAAD's efforts bore their fruits. In 2016, the CSO managed to make Spirit Day the world's most important antibullying campaign in the mass media. The campaign also brought antibullying resources into classrooms around the globe by encouraging educators to take a stand against bullying by organizing events and rallies. The campaign also made a Spirit Day kit for use in classrooms in several languages.[71] According to GLAAD et al. (2011),[72] "not every person who is the target of anti-LGBT bullying is LGBT. Many who are bullied are targeted because of their perceived sexual orientation or because they do not conform to someone's expectations about gender." When public communication campaign designers act as information subsidies, they convey tailored information to both media organizations and general audiences to inform about what issues to bring up and how to cover them. This is particularly true in an era where most pieces of information are available with just a few mouse clicks.

Queer Theory

Queer theory attempts to unsettle a power structure that has established heteronormativity as the norm.[73] It uncovers the problems associated with sociocultural actions and discourses that produce rigid sexual categories and identities. These categories and identities place people into unnecessarily restrictive labels, at the same time perpetuating heteronormative power dynamics.[74] Espousing the philosophy that humans are made up of too many features to be compartmentalized into a handful of categories, queer theory works to oppose, for instance, the idea of defining and essentializing two lesbians into the same broad category as they could easily be very different in their ways, lifestyles, and backgrounds.[75]

An investigation of pro-LGBTQ+ organizations reported that they felt compelled to employ "equality" as a strategic frame to connect with majority audiences. This underlines the challenge that minority organizations face when trying to disrupt the power structure and communicate to audiences outside the LGBTQ+ activist base. As public advocacy organizations like GLAAD navigate political and communication contexts, queer theory can be used to critique the objectives, actions, and rhetoric used by those organizations for making LGBTQ+ issues more prominent in the media.[76] Those with organizational power can not only develop and frame the organization's mission, but also wisely choose the movement's members through strategic representations—aided, in part, by the organization's public relations materials. Also available are public relations approaches that may confer lower-level individual stakeholders more power in an effort to "counter or resist a dominance model," including a technique of "build(ing) alliances with other(s)."[77]

Case Study 2:   Campaign against Homophobia in Poland

After the fall of Communism, tolerance of new minority groups became a hot topic in all nations of Central and Eastern Europe. It is necessary to see which values are salient throughout the region to contextualize the debate and to start by focusing on the 1980s and 1990s as these were "winds of change" for lifestyles, attitudes, and laws. In the present day, the most prevalent attitudes in the West and in international organizations in support of gays and lesbians are a byproduct of the sexual revolution of the 1970s. No serious debate occurred behind the Iron Curtain until 1989. The **Iron Curtain** was a political barrier dividing Europe between the Western and Eastern areas. In the 1990s, the Eastern European region, including Poland, created opportunities for reconciliation with minority groups that had been ignored or discriminated during the Communist era.[78]

Gay and Lesbian Organizations in Poland

Gay and lesbian organizations have been active in Poland—a nation of 37 million inhabitants—since the mid-1980s and have experienced sociopolitical and institutional change. Collective action assumed by Polish gays and lesbians had a slow start even after the fall of the Berlin Wall in 1989. At the dawn of the twenty-first century, same-sex issues were still being stymied by strong opposition from Polish society and were a frequent subject of nation-wide public debates.[79] Transgender matters and other sexual orientations were now part of the wider LGBTQ+ movement in that country. Marches for the tolerance and equality of LGBTQ+ people were prohibited or beleaguered by far-right counterprotestors in numerous Polish cities.[80] For over half a century, Poles experienced decades of misinformation and radical codes of beliefs during the Communist era. State dogma in the People's Republic of Poland—the official name of the country until 1989—instructed that "homosexuality was a symptom of 'Western depravity' and did not fit socialist morality."[81]

According to its tenets on sexual morals, the Church rejects the precept that same-sex couples are equal to heterosexual couples. Church teachings on sex and marriage remain exact, clear, and strict. Sexual relations should be between a man and a woman and only happen after marriage and for procreation purposes. Still to this day, in-vitro fertilization and going to a sperm bank are both deemed highly immoral.[82] Although more than 80% of Poles were still opposing LGBTQ+ rights at the end of the twentieth century, the circumstances have somewhat changed in recent years. Based on a 2019 CBOS opinion survey conducted in Poland, 66% of respondents said that gays and lesbians should not be allowed to marry, 67% said that they should not engage in PDA or make open declarations about their sexuality in public, and 84% believed that they should not be permitted to adopt children.[83]

Campaign against Homophobia

In 2001, the CSO **Campaign against Homophobia** (or *Kampania Przeciw Homofobii* [KPH] in Polish) was founded as both an advocacy and political organization. It has led many actions, notably handing out flyers that champion acceptance and tolerance of homo-sexuals in society.[84] The CSO has also conducted massive information campaigns with the slogan "I'm gay, I'm lesbian" at universities and a photo-based campaign "Let them see us" in the streets of Polish main cities.[85] Today, Campaign against Homophobia remains an important LGBTQ+ organization in Poland, striving to reach out to both the LGBTQ+ community and the wider public, and petitioning the government for equal rights. Advocates feel as though they are waging a "morality politics" battle because of the fierce resistance from the conservative government and Catholic religious entities in the country. While one of the past governmental administrations formed by the party "Law and Justice" was unam-biguously homophobic, the government led by Donald Tusk, Prime Minister of Poland from 2014 to 2019, was driven by the party Civic Platform. The party was considered liberal on economic issues, but overly conservative on social issues.[86]

In regards to the photo-based campaign "Let them see us" in 2003, Campaign against Homophobia ran a photo exhibit and billboard initiative that displayed photographs of 30 pairs of lesbians and gay men holding hands. They looked young and urban. The title "Let them see us" served as a reminder that LGBTQ+ folks were not willing to remain invisible. The campaign was open to visitors in five galleries around the country and was followed by that billboard initiative. Each picture was accompanied by the words "Let them see us." The campaign was financed by the office of the Government Plenipotentiary for Equal Status of Men and Women and by the Dutch Embassy.[87]

In the spring of 2004, precisely when Poland joined the European Union, Campaign against Homophobia ran a public awareness campaign titled "Culture for tolerance" in Kraków, the second-largest city in Poland. The purpose was to legitimize the LGBTQ+ community in the public sphere and allow them to operate freely outside gay clubs and private homes. The pinnacle of the campaign was a march for tolerance.[88] Some representatives of Campaign against Homophobia jointly released an open letter in which they stated that the Poles' opposition to LGBTQ+ rights did not make sense because they had just voted in favor of membership of the European Union, where democracy is the rule. As written in the open letter: "When our festival will be held, Poland will already have become part of that family of nations for whom democracy is a superior value and the public sphere is not reserved for the advocates of one ideology."[89]

The name of the CSO itself, Campaign against Homophobia, was a way to position the organization as the main player against "homophobia." At the time, the term was rarely used in the Polish public sphere. The diffusion of an early flyer underlined that fact. Even the software used for the flyer did not recognize the term. All the early leaflets of the CSO included a detailed description of homophobia, usually citing American psychologist George Weinberg. The concept was not chosen for its local resonance (which was nonexistent), but for the legitimacy it conferred through its originality and foreign—i.e., Western—origin. The application of both "homophobia" and "discrimination" frames echoed an external dimension. It related the LGBTQ+ movement to the global successes that these concepts granted the movement in the United States and Western European nations. Therefore, it helped integrate Polish advocacy groups into the wider LGBTQ+ network across the world. Particularly, Lambda-Warszawa (beginning in 2000) and Campaign against Homophobia (beginning in 2002) developed deep ties with ILGA-Europe. ILGA stands for International Lesbian, Gay, Bisexual, Trans, and Intersex Association. In the case of Campaign against Homophobia, the collaboration became stronger over the years, with several activists from the CSO becoming involved in politics.[90]

Challenging Ignorance

A key feature of the campaign's framing was its peaceful orientation. Campaign against Homophobia strategically elected not to frame messages in a rhetoric of political conflict and avoided mentioning their opponents. Evident during marches organized by the Kraków-based satellite of the organization in 2004 and 2005, the peaceful discursive strategy prohibited slogans that underlined "against" and applauded those campaigning "for" the universal principles of tolerance, equality, democracy, and love. The overarching frame was a campaign that challenged ignorance about LGBTQ+ individuals. When Campaign against Homophobia pushed for social change, no groups or institutions notorious for discrimination were identified. In the five publications and four websites that the CSO created between 2001 and 2004, the only perpetrator of homophobia expressly mentioned was "ignorance."[91] As exemplified in an excerpt from a 2001 brochure: "Ignorance surrounding homosexuality leads to myths and stereotypes that perpetuate homophobia. To change this, education is essential. As we know, the unknown awakens fear."[92]

Another crucial campaign took place in Polish universities called "I am a gay. I am a lesbian. Get to know us!" It invited "students (and others) [to] speak with gays, lesbians, as well as experts in the fields of human rights, psychology, and sexology."[93] Consistent with the main tenets of agenda-setting theory, through that campaign, the CSO attempted to challenge the Polish public's ignorance by diffusing new categories and adding their definition to the public debate. The chief aim of the "Let them see us" and "Get to know us!" campaigns was to convey the sentiment of who "we are"—to raise awareness of LGBTQ+ existence—and the feeling of empathy/identification within audiences. In essence, the framing of such campaigns derived from identity politics, in which representations of LGBTQ+ issues are quintessential.[94]

Through a creative method of diversification, campaigns can challenge ignorance without compromising their message or departing from the frames associated with previous discursive opportunities. **Diversification** refers to the use of a wider and more diverse spectrum of frames within a movement—one that can include both rigid and flexible frames. Taking diversification into account is helpful because it eliminates the misconception that countermovement emergence corresponds with the revocation of previous alignment frames. Rather, we witness a coexistence between various frames, some of which are long-established and others are more creative. As one can imagine, diversification can give rise to frame disputes that can fracture a movement or invite new LGBTQ+ players. In this sense, diversification fosters multiple opportunities for movement maturity—thanks to an assorted repertoire that can help movements navigate through varying social environments.[95]

The Situation Today

The symbolic representations of initiatives like Campaign against Homophobia in Poland have produced what Bernstein (1997)[96] coins **identities for critique**, stressing the importance of difference, as opposed to **identities for education**, insisting on similarity with the dominant society and on heteronormativity. Campaign against Homophobia illustrates how these processes of identity framing are linked to the desire for gender and sexual transparency and the aspiration to freely circulate knowledge about LGBTQ+ issues.[97] Today, the campaign maintains a website (http://www.mojeprawa.info) that lists and describes multiple legal issues that they are still facing, like problems with registering same-sex partnerships.[98]

Campaign against Homophobia continues to partner with other public awareness campaigns. It created a clever billboard campaign titled "You're not alone," which displayed pictures of men and women dressed as professionals, like doctors and teachers, among others. The purpose was to kindly remind the audience that LGBTQ+ folks are part of Polish society and right next door. The campaign began in Warsaw and other large cities, then moved into smaller towns and remote regions. By the same token, Campaign against Homophobia has reached out to women's groups with a coalition approach in mind—i.e., to develop a broader base so that audiences in general reshape their own perceptions of LGBTQ+ rights.[99] Thanks to these initiatives, the status of LGBTQ+ individuals in Poland has been on the political agenda and a topic of discussion within the Polish public sphere.[100]

Case Study 3:   LGBTQ+ Campaigns in Brazil

The LGBTQ+ movement in Brazil has been hailed as one of the oldest and largest movements in Latin America and among the most politically visible on the continent.[101] In fact, according to the Guinness World Records, the São Paulo Gay Pride Parade remains the world's largest gay pride celebration, with four million people in attendance in 2009.[102] On June 7, 2015, Viviany Beleboni, a Brazilian transgender actress and activist, caused a stir at the 19th gay pride parade in São Paulo when she appeared in Jesus form—i.e., nailed on the cross and covered in blood—under a slogan that read "Enough of homophobia!" Her intense symbolic gesture drew an unmistakable parallel between Jesus's suffering on the cross and the dangers of religiously inspired violence and discrimination against LGBTQ+ individuals. Yet, just like the São Paulo parade, the act of protest instantly became a global news item.[103]

LGBTQ+ rights in Brazil, a nation of over 220 million people, are among the most advanced in Latin America and the non-Western world. In 2011, the Brazilian Federal Supreme Court legalized same-sex marriage and bestowed it with the same rights as those conferred to traditional marriages and stable unions. In 2013, the National Justice Council passed legislation that required all notaries to certify same-sex marriages.[104] Early activists used vivid antiauthoritarian language so as to fashion a strong homosexual identity. They were greatly inspired by Marxist and anarchist philosophies.[105] They began campaigning for democracy in the 1970s and their struggle for homosexual emancipation was predicated on a bigger fight for sociocultural change.[106] Early campaigners worked closely with young activists, students, and Leftist organizations, which all called for the removal of the boundaries imposed by the political public sphere at that time.[107]

The Situation Today

Today, the dynamic and diverse LGBTQ+ movement is active in many areas, making significant headway in society and the culture at large, as well as in government. Common among those many areas is the fight for visibility, already obvious through the expansion of a "pink market" within urban centers in the country. Visibility is also manifest through the astronomical boom of gay pride parades, the increasingly fair and balanced coverage of LGBTQ+ issues in the mainstream media, and the growing presence of gays and lesbians in the entertainment industry. The large LGBTQ+ movement in Brazil consists of a decentralized and varied constellation of over 300 organizations from all parts of the country. These 300+ organizations spearhead political struggles, awareness campaigns for social reform, and the provision of resources and services to LGBTQ+ individuals.[108]

With this said, however, significant obstacles remain standing. According to a 2007 *BBC News* article,[109] activists calculated that, between 1980 and 2006, close to 2,700 LGBTQ+ folks were murdered in Brazil (most of whom, it is believed, were killed because of their sexuality). According to the Grupo Gay da Bahia, Brazil's oldest-continuing LGBTQ+ organization, almost 200 of such folks were brutally murdered in 2008 as a result of homophobia, which is in sharp contrast to the 35 LGBTQ+ individuals in Mexico, 25 in the United States, 15 in Peru, four in Argentina, and none in Chile. As same-sex issues become more visible and politically powerful on the agenda, the country continues to square off against crimes targeting sexual deviance.[110] Violence against "sexual deviants" has always been a problem in Brazil, the nation with the highest percentage of deadly crimes against LGBTQ+ individuals in the world.[111] About 45% of all LGBTQ+ in Brazil have filed reports on their experience of violence.[112]

Despite the fact that progress has been noted, it is easy to witness the difficulties encountered by LGBTQ+ people when trying to access healthcare as a consequence of prejudicial and discriminatory behavior, often adopted by healthcare practitioners themselves.[113] Gender and sexuality are also a primary focus of evangelical groups. A question about transgenderism on a high-school standardized examination attracted massive criticism from Brazil's growing evangelical right, which believes that gender-based education is pushing the envelope. In 2017, the government sided with religious groups by removing any mention of gender identity from curriculums. A significant minority of right-wing politicians in state and city administrations are attempting to pass a legal ban on any debate regarding gender diversity and sexual orientation in classrooms.[114]

The Brazil without Homophobia Campaign

In 2004, the Brazilian government launched the **Brazil without Homophobia** campaign (or *Programa Brasil sem Homofobia* in Portuguese). It became a hallmark for public policies in favor of the LGBTQ+ population.[115] The initiative developed messages formulated through the lens of "full citizenship" rights for sexual minority groups.[116] It was a way for LGBTQ+ individuals to be socially acknowledged not just as men or women, but as people deserving the same rights and not be subjected to ambiguous circumstances.[117] The campaign was a clapback at the rising levels of violence experienced by the LGBTQ+ population. According to a survey administered in Rio de Janeiro, over 56% of respondents claimed that they had already "gone through experiences such as name calling, verbal abuse, and threats related to homosexuality."[118] The mission was to grant full citizenship to all.[119]

One of the most concrete outcomes of the Brazil without Homophobia campaign was the first National Conference of Gays, Lesbians, Bisexuals, Travesties, and Transsexuals, held in the capital city in June 2008 and attended by Lula, then the President of Brazil. At the conclusion of the conference, the Inter-Ministerial Technical Commission established the National Plan for the Promotion of LGBT Citizenship and Human Rights, with positive measures to be taken by various offices. The plan's main goal was "fighting stigma and discrimination on grounds of sexual orientation and gender identity."[120] Addressing homophobia and its sociocultural impact has been highlighted by many scholars as a key policy strategy. The plan has been glorified as a potential driver for the reduction of discrimination and exclusion towards LGBTQ+ people, particularly in terms of access to healthcare and other basic necessities.[121]

The Free & Equal Campaign

The **Free & Equal Campaign** is an international public awareness campaign led by the United Nations Human Rights Office. The campaign advocates equal rights and treatment for LGBTQ+ individuals around the globe, and is concretized through collaborations with United Nations offices, CSOs, and national and civil experts.[122] Since 2014, the United Nations System in Brazil has implemented the Free & Equal Campaign there, raising consciousness of homophobic and transphobic crime and prejudice, and promoting honor of the rights of the LGBTQ+ population. *Trans-Formaçao*, a pilot project, was specifically designed to encourage participation of transpeople in decision-making processes, improve their social inclusion, and tackle the pervasive violence and negative stereotypes towards them. In this context, Brazil acknowledges the contributions that local participants can bring when halting hostile public behavior and discrimination. Local volunteers can voice their disagreements with the practice of terminating LGBTQ+ individuals from their jobs, bullying students or expelling them from schools, and denying them healthcare. By the spring of 2019, 24 leaders had already been trained to serve as United Nations community volunteers in the *Trans-Formaçao* project in Salvador (north of Rio de Janeiro), creating opportunities for empowerment on a local scale. The 24 community volunteers acquired knowledge on gender, inequalities, public policies for transpeople, social inclusion, and job availabilities, among others.[123]

The ultimate purpose of the Free & Equal Campaign is to consolidate LGBTQ+ networks in Brazil and empower current and future leaders in the advocacy of human rights through mentoring programs.[124] One of the campaign's techniques is to disseminate messages on equality from the United Nations and identify and challenge dangerous generalizations of the LGBTQ+ population. This is done in both traditional and digital networking. Based on the tenets of the Diffusion of Innovations theory described in Chapter 1, the campaign relies on volunteers who act as change agents to alter the attitudes of local populations there. Campaigning on LGBTQ+ issues is not merely about ensuring legislative change. It should also be about changing people's hearts and minds. This is especially needed in milieus where hate crime is still high. One solution would be to denounce the routines that have reoriented discourses of dissent. It is necessary to reclaim the dominant space as one that is challenged. The Free & Equal Campaign wants citizens to become involved with challenging the patterns and practices that consider public places and spaces commercial opportunities that, in the end, tend to nullify protests through routine.[125]

The Diversity in School Campaign

Diversity in School is a campaign that raises consciousness, understanding, and honor of sociocultural differences by offering traditional and online courses on ethnic relations and LGBTQ+ rights for students, teachers, and school administrators in the Brazilian public school system. These courses are designed to make personnel and students in schools aware of their full potential for fostering a climate of inclusion. This campaign is the product of a collaboration between the Brazilian government (Secretariat for Policies on Women's Affairs, Secretariat for the Promotion of Policies on Racial Equality, and the Ministry of Education), the British Council, and the Latin American Center on Sexuality and Human Rights (CLAM) from the State University of Rio de Janeiro. CLAM was charged with devising the curriculum and methodology. Since 2008, over 40,000 teachers have been trained all over the nation.[126]

This campaign also seeks to get schools and teachers to honor the moral convictions of students and families of all walks of life, thereby opening opportunities for debates on sexual, moral, and religious matters in the classroom.[127] Endeavors to increase diversity in education can be seen across the civil society and federal spheres—what is called "Union, States and Municipalities" in Brazil. It has been mostly inspired by the phrase "Cultura Viva," which denotes an inclusion approach to all cultures (without exception). This was already put on the table after the 2001 Universal Declaration of Cultural Diversity specializing on cultural pluralism and human rights.[128]

NOTES

1. Jeannie Gainsburg, *The Savvy Ally: A Guide for Becoming a Skilled LGBTQ+ Advocate* (Lanham, MD: Rowman & Littlefield, 2020).
2. Mercan Efe Güney and İrem Ayhan Selçuk, "LGBTTs of Turkey between the East and the West: The City and the World through Their Eyes in the Case of Izmir," *Gender, Place & Culture* 23, no. 10 (2016): 1392–403. https://doi.org/10.1080/0966369X.2016.1160870.

3. Jeffrey M. Jones, *LGBT Identification Rises to 5.6% in Latest US Estimate* (Washington, DC: Gallup, 2021).
4. Ruth Colker, *Sexual Orientation, Gender Identity, and the Law in a Nutshell* (Saint Paul, MN: West Academic Publishing, 2016).
5. Mark Cook and Robert McHenry, *Sexual Attraction* (Oxford: Pergamon Press, 2013).
6. Jonathan Matusitz and Elena Berisha, *Female Terrorism in America: Past and Current Perspectives* (New York: Routledge, 2020).
7. Michael S. Kimmel, *The Gender Society* (London: Oxford University Press, 2010).
8. Ediomo-Ubong Nelson and Inima E. Nelson, "Violence against Women in Nigeria: The Factors and the Dynamics," *The Constitution* 10, no. 2 (2010): 80.
9. Deana Morrow and Lori Messinger, *Sexual Orientation and Gender Expression in Social Work Practice: Working with Gay, Lesbian, Bisexual, and Transgender People* (New York: Columbia University Press, 2006).
10. Alex Stitt, *ACT for Gender Identity* (London: Jessica Kingsley Publishers, 2020).
11. Jake Pyne, "Trans People and Cisnormativity in Shelter Services," *Canadian Social Work Review* 28, no. 1 (2011): 129–37.
12. Jack Halberstam, *The Queer Art of Failure* (Durham, NC: Duke University Press, 2011).
13. Evan D. Bradley, "The Influence of Linguistic and Social Attitudes on Grammaticality Judgments of Singular 'They'," Language Sciences 78 (2020). https://doi.org/10.1016/j.langsci.2020.101272.
14. Ibid.
15. Sakshi Venkatraman, "A Gender Neutral Spanish Pronoun? For Some, 'Elle' Is the Word," NBC News (October 14, 2020). Retrieved on July 5, 2021 from https://www.nbcnews.com/news/latino/gender-neutral-spanish-pronoun-some-elle-word-n1242797.
16. Jenna M. Calton, Lauren Bennett Cattaneo, and Kris T. Gebhard, "Barriers to Help Seeking for Lesbian, Gay, Bisexual, Transgender, and Queer Survivors of Intimate Partner Violence," *Trauma Violence Abuse* 17, no. 5 (2016): 585–600. https://doi.org/10.1177/1524838015585318.
17. Angelo Brandelli Costa, Rodrigo Oliva Peroni, Denise Ruschel Bandeira, and Henrique Caetano Nardi, "Homophobia or Sexism? A Systematic Review of Prejudice against Nonheterosexual Orientation in Brazil," *International Journal of Psychology* 48, no. 5 (2012): 900–9. https://doi.org/10.1080/00207594.2012.729839.
18. Jonathan Alexander and Karen Yescavage, *Bisexuality and Transgenderism: InterSEXions of The Others* (Philadelphia, PA: Haworth Press, 2004); Melissa M. Wilcox, *Coming Out in Christianity: Religion, Identity, and Community* (Bloomington, IN: Indiana University Press, 2003).
19. Matt Bernstein Sycamore, *That's Revolting! Queer Strategies for Resisting Assimilation* (New York: Soft Skull Press, 2005).
20. Gajendra Singh Chauhan and Tanu Shukla, "Social Media Advertising and Public Awareness: Touching the LGBT Chord!" *Journal of International Women's Studies* 18, no. 1 (2016): 145–55.
21. Joe Sommerlad, "Section 377: How India Brought an End to the Criminalisation of Its LGBT+ Community," *The Independent* (September 6, 2018): A1. Retrieved on October 25, 2021 from https://www.independent.co.uk/news/world/asia/section-377-india-gay-sex-crime-lgbt-supreme-court-dipak-misra-a8525116.html.
22. Costa, Peroni, Bandeira, and Nardi, "Homophobia or Sexism?" 901.

23. Lara M. Stepleman, Jiby Yohannan, Samantha M. Scott, Lauren L. Titus, Joan Walker, Eliot J. Lopez, Lauren Wooten Smith, Alexis L. Rossi, Thomas M. Toomey, and Elizabeth D. Eldridge, "Health Needs and Experiences of a LGBT Population in Georgia and South Carolina," *Journal of Homosexuality* 66, no. 7 (2019): 989–1013. https://doi.org/10.1080/00918369.2018.1490573.

24. Jeffery Adams, Pauline Dickinson, and Lanuola Asiasiga, "Mental Health Issues for Lesbian, Gay, Bisexual, and Transgender People: A Qualitative Study," *International Journal of Mental Health Promotion* 15, no. 2 (2013): 105–20. https://doi.org/10.1080/14623730.2013.799821.

25. Kelly LeRoux and Mary K. Feeney, *Nonprofit Organizations and Civil Society in the United States* (New York: Routledge, 2014).

26. Charles Tilly, *Identities, Boundaries & Social Ties* (Boulder, CO: Paradigm Publishers, 2005).

27. Ronald Holzhacker, "National and Transnational Strategies of LGBT Civil Society Organizations in Different Political Environments: Modes of Interaction in Western and Eastern Europe for Equality," *Comparative European Politics* 10 (2012): 23–42. https://doi.org/10.1057/cep.2010.21.

28. See Justin Greenwood, *Interest Representation in the European Union* (Basingstoke, England: Palgrave Macmillan, 2003).

29. See David Lowery, "Why Do Organized Interests Lobby? A Multi-Goal, Multi-Context Theory of Lobbying," *Polity* 39, no. 1 (2007): 29–54. https://doi.org/10.1057/palgrave.polity.2300077.

30. Sydney Tarrow, *The New Transnational Activism* (Cambridge: Cambridge University Press, 2005).

31. Sarah A. Soule and Susan Olzak, "When Do Movements Matter? The Politics of Contingency and the Equal Rights Amendment," *American Sociological Review* 69, no. 4 (2004): 473–97. https://doi.org/10.1177/000312240406900401.

32. Holzhacker, "National and Transnational Strategies," 28.

33. Charles K. Atkin and Charles T. Salmon, "Communication Campaigns," in *Handbook of Communication Science* (2nd Ed.), ed. Charles Berger, Michael Roloff, and David R. Roskos-Ewoldsen (Thousand Oaks, CA: Sage, 2010): 419–35.

34. Charles K. Atkin and Ronald E. Rice, "Theory and Principles of Public Communication Campaigns," in *Public Communication Campaigns* (4th Ed.), ed. Ronald E. Rice and Charles K. Atkin (Thousand Oaks, CA: Sage, 2012): 3–20, 7.

35. Kerstin Martens, "Professionalized Representation of Human Rights NGOs to the United Nations," *The International Journal of Human Rights* 10, no. 1 (2006): 19–30.

36. Julie Mertus, "The Rejection of Human Rights Framings: The Case of LGBT Advocacy in the US," *Human Rights Quarterly* 29 (2007): 1036–64. https://doi.org/10.1353/hrq.2007.0045.

37. Michael Schiavi, *Celluloid Activist: The Life and Times of Vito Russo* (Madison: University of Wisconsin Press, 2011).

38. Laurel Lampela, "Lesbian and Gay Artists in the Curriculum: A Survey of Art Teachers' Knowledge and Attitudes," *Studies in Art Education* 42, no. 2 (2001): 146–62.

39. Committees, Media Committee Press Releases and Information: Gay and Lesbian Alliance against Defamation (GLAAD), 1988–1989, ACT UP: The AIDS Coalition to Unleash Power: Series VII, Committees, MS Box 32, Folder 2, New York Public Library, *Archives of Sexuality and Gender.*

40. Anna Hornell, "'I Wasn't Born a Boy—I Was Born a Baby': Best Practices Versus Accepted Practices in News Coverage of the Transgender Community," *Bachelor's Thesis, California Polytechnic State University, San Luis Obispo* (December 2014).

41. Marcus O'Donnell, "Gay-Hate, Journalism and Compassionate Questioning: Journalism's Response to the Matthew Shepard Case," *Asia Pacific Media Educator* 19 (2009): 112–25.

42. Louis P. Sheldon, "Homosexual Propaganda Campaign Based on Hitler's 'Big Lie' Technique," *Traditional Values* 18, no. 10 (2018): 1–8.

43. Kristen Schilt, "'AM/FM Activism': Taking National Media Tools to a Local Level," *Journal of Gay & Lesbian Social Services* 16, no. 3 (2004): 181–92. https://doi.org/10.1300/J041v16n03_12.

44. Jase Peeples, "GLAAD Affirms Commitment to Trans and Bi People, Alters Name," *The Advocate* (March 24, 2013). Retrieved on April 2, 2021 from https://www.advocate.com/politics/2013/03/24/glaad-affirms-commitment-trans-and-bi-people-alters-name.

45. Joseph M. Cabosky, "Framing an LGBT Organization and a Movement: A Critical Qualitative Analysis of GLAAD's Media Releases," *Public Relations Inquiry* 3, no. 1 (2014): 69–89. https://doi.org/10.1177/2046147X13519638.

46. Available at https://www.glaad.org/resources/ally.

47. Ibid.

48. Cited in Susan Jones, "Homosexual Advocacy Group Offers Tolerance Tips to 'Straight' Allies," *CNS News* (July 7, 2008). Retrieved on April 3, 2021 from https://cnsnews.com/news/article/homosexual-advocacy-group-offers-tolerance-tips-straight-allies.

49. Ibid.

50. *Pink News*, "Straight People Encouraged to Come Out for Gay Rights," *Pink News* (September 5, 2007). Retrieved on April 3, 2021 from https://www.pinknews.co.uk/2007/09/05/straight-people-encouraged-to-come-out-for-gay-rights.

51. Brandon Voss, "Sofía Vergara: Sofia's Choice," *The Advocate* (September 14, 2011). Retrieved on April 3, 2021 from https://www.advocate.com/arts-entertainment/television/2011/09/14/sofias-choice-sofia-vergara.

52. Cabosky, "Framing an LGBT Organization," 69–70.

53. Cited in Nan D. Hunter, "Varieties of Constitutional Experience: Democracy and the Marriage Equality Campaign," *UCLA Law Review* 64 (2017): 1662–726, 1692.

54. Ibid.

55. Ibid, 1693.

56. Valerie Palmer-Mehta and Kellie Hay, "A Superhero for Gays? Gay Masculinity and *Green Lantern*," *The Journal of American Culture* 28, no. 4 (2005): 390–404. https://doi.org/10.1111/j.1542-734X.2005.00242.x.

57. Cited in Ron Becker, "Gay-Themed Television and the Slumpy Class: The Affordable, Multicultural Politics of the Gay Nineties," *Television & New Media* 7, no. 2 (2006): 184–215. https://doi.org/10.1177/1527476403255830.

58. Kathleen Battles and Wendy Hilton-Morrow, "Gay Characters in Conventional Spaces: *Will and Grace* and the Situation Comedy Genre," *Critical Studies in Media Communication* 19, no. 1 (2002): 87–105. https://doi.org/10.1080/07393180216553.

59. Elizabeth Bridges, "A Genealogy of Queerbaiting: Legal Codes, Production Codes, 'Bury Your Gays' and 'The 100 Mess'," *The Journal of Fandom Studies* 6, no. 2 (2018): 115–32. https://doi.org/10.1386/jfs.6.2.115_1.

60. Tanya D. Zuk, "Coming Out on *Grey's Anatomy*: Industry Scandal, Constructing a Lesbian Story Line, and Fan Action," in *Queer Female Fandom*, ed. Julie Levin Russo and Eve Ng, special issue of *Transformative Works and Cultures* 24 (2017): 10–21. https://doi.org/10.3983/twc.2017.01168.

61. Ibid, 14–5.

62. Cited in Matt Kane, "GLAAD Study Records Highest Percentage Ever of LGBT Series Regulars on Broadcast Television, Cable LGBT Character Count Also Rises," *GLAAD* (October 5, 2012). Retrieved on April 3, 2021 from www.glaad.org/releases/glaad-study-records-highest-percentage-ever-lgbt-series-regulars-broadcast-television-cable.

63. Maxwell Mccombs and Donald L. Shaw, "The Agenda-Setting Function of Mass Media," *Public Opinion Quarterly* 36, no. 2 (1972): 176–87. https://doi.org/10.1086/267990.

64. Maxwell Mccombs, "A Look at Agenda-Setting: Past, Present and Future," *Journalism Studies* 6, no. 4 (2005): 543–57. https://doi.org/10.1080/14616700500250438.

65. Shanto Iyengar and Donald R. Kinder, *News that Matters: Television and American Opinion* (Chicago, IL: The University of Chicago Press, 1987).

66. Marielle Bohan-Baker, "Pitching Policy Change," *The Evaluation Exchange* 7, no. 1 (2001): 3–4.

67. Atkin and Rice, "Theory and Principles of Public Communication Campaigns," 3–20.

68. Julia Coffman, *Public Communication Campaign Evaluation: An Environmental Scan of Challenges, Criticisms, Practice, and Opportunities* (Cambridge, MA: Harvard Family Research Project, 2002).

69. Spiro Kiousis and Xu Wu, "International Agenda-Building and Agenda-Setting: Exploring the Influence of Public Relations Counsel on US News Media and Public Perceptions of Foreign Nations," *International Communication Gazette* 70, no. 1 (2008): 58–75, 58. https://doi.org/10.1177/1748048507084578.

70. Cited in Cabosky, "Framing an LGBT Organization," 76.

71. Ibid, 76–7.

72. Available at https://issuu.com/trevorproject/docs/talking_about_suicide_and_lgbt_populations/2.

73. Ruth Goldman, "Who Is that Queer Queer? Exploring Norms around Sexuality, Race, and Class in Queer Theory," in *Queer Studies: A Lesbian, Gay, Bisexual, and Transgender Anthology*, ed. Genny Beemyn and Michele Eliason (New York: New York University Press, 1996): 169–82.

74. Judith Butler, *Gender Trouble: Feminism and the Subversion of Identity* (New York: Routledge, 1990).

75. Natalie T. J. Tindall and Richard D. Waters, "Coming Out to Tell Our Stories: Using Queer Theory to Understand the Career Experiences of Gay Men in Public Relations," *Journal of Public Relations Research* 24, no. 5 (2012): 451–75. https://doi.org/10.1080/1062726X.2012.723279.

76. Cabosky, "Framing an LGBT Organization," 72.

77. Bruce K. Berger, "Power Over, Power With, and Power to Relations: Critical Reflections on Public Relations, the Dominant Coalition, and Activism," *Journal of Public Relations Research* 17, no. 1 (2005): 5–28, 18. https://doi.org/10.1207/s1532754xjprr1701_3.

78. Marta Selinger, "Intolerance toward Gays and Lesbians in Poland," *Human Rights Review* 9 (2008): 15–27. https://doi.org/10.1007/s12142-007-0026-2.

79. Agnès Chetaille, "Poland: Sovereignty and Sexuality in Post-Socialist Times," in *The Lesbian and Gay Movement and the State: Comparative Insights into a Transformed Relationship*, ed. Carol Johnson, David Paternotte, and Manon Tremblay (Farnham, England: Ashgate, 2011): 119–33.

80. Jon Binnie and Christian Klesse, "'Like a Bomb in the Gasoline Station': EastWest Migration and Transnational Activism around Lesbian, Gay, Bisexual, Transgender and Queer Politics in Poland," *Journal of Ethnic and Migration Studies* 39, no. 7 (2013): 1107–24. https://doi.org/10.1080/1369183X.2013.778030.

81. Krzysztof Kliszyński, "A Child of a Young Democracy: The Polish Gay Movement, 1989–1999," in *Pink, Purple, Green: Women's, Religious, Environmental and Gay/Lesbian Movements in Central Europe Today*, ed. Helena Flam (New York: Columbia University Press, 2001): 161–8, 161.

82. Selinger, "Intolerance toward Gays and Lesbians in Poland," 20–2.

83. Adam Easton, "LGBT Rights: New Threat for Poland's 'Rainbow Families'," *BBC News* (March 17, 2021). Retrieved on March 24, 2021 from https://www.bbc.com/news/world-europe-56412782.

84. Conor O'Dwyer, "Does the EU Help or Hinder Gay-Rights Movements in Postcommunist Europe? The Case of Poland," *East European Politics* 28, no. 4 (2012): 332–52.

85. Magdalena Mikulak, "Godly Homonormativity: Christian LGBT Organizing in Contemporary Poland," *Journal of Homosexuality* 66, no. 4 (2019): 487–509. https://doi.org/10.1080/00918369.2017.1414501.

86. Holzhacker, "National and Transnational Strategies," 32.

87. Agnieszka Graff, "We Are (Not All) Homophobes: A Report from Poland," *Feminist Studies* 32, no. 2 (2006): 434–49. https://doi.org/10.2307/20459096.

88. Human Rights House Foundation, *A Tolerant Krakow?* (Oslo: Human Rights House Foundation, 2004).

89. Available at https://ntnuopen.ntnu.no/ntnu-xmlui/bitstream/handle/11250/2711480/Nr%2023_B5.pdf?sequence=1 (p. 28).

90. Phillip M. Ayoub and Agnès Chetaille, "Movement/Countermovement Interaction and Instrumental Framing in a Multi-Level World: Rooting Polish Lesbian and Gay Activism," *Social Movement Studies* 19, no. 1 (2020): 21–37. https://doi.org/10.1080/14742837.2017.1338941.

91. Ibid, 29.

92. KPH leaflet, *O równe prawa wszystkich!!!*, Warsaw, 2001.

93. KPH leaflet, *Kalendarz 2012, 10 lat KPH*, Warsaw, 2011.

94. Ayoub and Chetaille, "Movement/Countermovement Interaction," 30.

95. Ibid, 26.

96. Mary Bernstein, "Celebration and Suppression: The Strategic Uses of Identity by the Lesbian and Gay Movement," *American Journal of Sociology* 103, no. 3 (1997): 531–65. https://doi.org/10.1086/231250.

97. Ayoub and Chetaille, "Movement/Countermovement Interaction," 30.

98. Gregory E. Czarnecki, "Analogies of Pre-War Anti-Semitism and Present-Day Homophobia in Poland," in *Beyond the Pink Curtain: Everyday Life of LGBT People in Eastern Europe*, ed. Roman Kuhar and Judit Takács (Ljubljana, Slovenia: Mirovni Institut, 2007): 327–44.

99. Holzhacker, "National and Transnational Strategies," 33–5.

100. Łukasz Szulc, "Queer in Poland: Under Construction," in *Queer in Europe: Contemporary Case Studies*, ed. Robert Gillett (New York: Routledge, 2016): 159–72.

101. Javier Corrales, "Understanding the Uneven Spread of LGBT Rights in Latin America and the Caribbean, 1999–2013," *Journal of Research in Gender Studies* 7, no. 1 (2017): 52–82.

102. http://saopaulo.gaypridebrazil.org.

103. Daniella Corcioli Azevedo Rocha, "Identity, Representations and Performativity: Words, Actions, and Crucifixion in the Gay Pride Parade in São Paulo," *Revista Brasileira de Linguística Aplicada* 19, no. 4 (2019): 849–70. http://dx.doi.org/10.1590/1984–6398201914837.

104. Elaine Reis Brandão and Cristiane da Silva Cabral, "Sexual and Reproductive Rights under Attack: The Advance of Political and Moral Conservatism in Brazil," *Sexual and Reproductive Health Matters* 27, no. 2 (2019): 76–86. https://doi.org/10.1080/26410397.2019.1669338.

105. Edward Macrae, "Homosexual Identities in Transitional Brazilian Politics," in *The Making of Social Movements in Latin America—Identity, Strategy and Democracy*, ed. Arturo Escobar and Sonia E. Alvarez (San Francisco, CA: Westview Press, 2012): 185–203.

106. Marcelo Daniliauskas, *Relações de gênero, diversidade sexual e políticas públicas de educação: uma análise do Programa Brasil sem Homofobia* (São Paulo: Universidade de São Paulo, 2011).

107. Rafael de la Dehesa, *Queering the Public Sphere in Mexico and Brazil: Sexual Rights Movements in Emerging Democracies* (Durham, NC: Duke University Press, 2010).

108. Cited in Shawn R. Schulenberg, "Policy Stability without Policy: The Battle over Same-Sex Partnership Recognition in Brazil (2009)," *APSA 2009 Toronto Annual Meeting Paper*. http://dx.doi.org/10.2139/ssrn.1451907.

109. *BBC News*, "Sao Paulo Holds Gay Pride Parade," *BBC News* (June 11, 2007). Retrieved on April 2, 2021 from http://news.bbc.co.uk/2/hi/americas/6738905.stm.

110. Cited in Schulenberg, "Policy Stability without Policy".

111. Wallace Góes Mendes and Cosme Marcelo Furtado Passos da Silva, "Homicide of Lesbians, Gays, Bisexuals, Travestis, Transexuals, and Transgender people (LGBT) in Brazil: A Spatial Analysis," *Ciência & Saúde Coletiva* 25, no. 5 (2020): 10–21. https://doi.org/10.1590/1413-81232020255.33672019.

112. Grupo Gay da Bahia, *Assassinato De Homossuais (LGBT) No Brasil: Relatório 2014* (Salvador, Bahia: Grupo Gay da Bahia, 2015).

113. Ibid.

114. Anthony Faiola and Marina Lopes, "LGBT Rights Threatened in Brazil under New Far-Right President," *The Washington Post* (February 18, 2019): A1. Retrieved on April 2, 2021 from https://www.washingtonpost.com/world/the_americas/lgbt-rights-under-attack-in-brazil-under-new-far-right-president/2019/02/17/b24e1dcc-1b28-11e9-b8e6-567190c2fd08_story.html.

115. Costa, Peroni, Bandeira, and Nardi, "Homophobia or Sexism?" 902.

116. Kyja Noack-Lundberg, "Queer Counterpublics in Australia, Mexico and Brazil," *Cultural Studies Review* 17. no. 2 (2011): 367–75.

117. Grazielle Tagliamento and Vera Paiva, "Trans-Specific Health Care: Challenges in the Context of New Policies for Transgender People," *Journal of Homosexuality* 63, no. 11 (2016): 1556–72. https://doi.org/10.1080/00918369.2016.1223359.

118. https://vcongresso.estudosculturais.com/wp-content/uploads/sites/6/2016/09/school-and-homophobia-violence-justified-as-jokes.pdf.

119. Tagliamento and Paiva, "Trans-Specific Health Care," 1157.

120. Sergio Carrara, "Discrimination, Policies, and Sexual Rights in Brazil," *Cadernos de Saúde Pública* 28, no. 1 (2012): 184–9. https://doi.org/10.1590/S0102-311X2012000100020.

121. Ilana Mountian, *A Critical Analysis of Public Policies on Education and LGBT Rights in Brazil* (Falmer, England: Institute of Development Studies).

122. Alex Redcay, Elisabeth Counselman Carpenter, Sheila McMahon, Wade Luquet, Karen Rice, and Roseanna Lance, "The Arc of Justice: Examining Policies and Laws to Advance the Human Rights of Transgender and Gender Expansive Children," *Journal of Human Rights and Social Work* 4 (2019): 156–63. https://doi.org/10.1007/s41134-019-00102-3.

123. Lua Da Mota Stabile, "Local Volunteers in Brazil Promote the Rights of LGTBI and Work to Prevent Hostile Public Attitudes and Discrimination" *UN Volunteers* (May 17, 2019). Retrieved on April 2, 2021 from https://www.unv.org/Success-stories/Local-volunteers-Brazil-promote-rights-LGTBI-and-work-prevent-hostile-public.

124. Ibid.

125. I. R. Lamond, "The Challenge of Articulating Human Rights at an LGBT 'Mega-Event': A Personal Reflection on Sao Paulo Pride 2017," *Leisure Studies* 37, no. 1 (2018): 36–48. https://doi.org/10.1080/02614367.2017.1419370.

126. Sergio Carrara, Marcos Nascimento, Aline Duque, and Lucas Tramontano, "Diversity in School: A Brazilian Educational Policy against Homophobia," *Journal of LGBT Youth* 13, no. 1 (2016): 161–72. https://doi.org/10.1080/19361653.2016.1160269.

127. Barbara M. Arisi, Arianna Sala, and Simone Ávila, "Teaching Sexual Diversity in Brazilian Schools: An Education Experience in Foz do Iguaçu," *Teaching Anthropology* 8, no. 1 (2018): 33–42.

128. https://en.unesco.org/creativity/monitoring-reporting/periodic-reports/brazil-2016-report.

CHAPTER 12

Black Lives Matter Campaigns

The United States of America is at a turning point in history, one that we have witnessed before. We are experiencing unprecedented times that resonate with events lived in the last century. Examining the situation of African Americans can generate sensitivity to their experiences and an understanding of how their past and present mirror each other.[1] When Africans first arrived as slaves in 1619, a structure based on racial differences was established in the United States. White supremacy, rooted in the myths of White superiority and Black inferiority, has eclipsed deep problems associated with racial inequality and injustice, often leading to assigning blame to the victims.[2] Sometimes called the Movement for Black Lives, **Black Lives Matter** (**BLM**) is a US decentralized sociopolitical movement denouncing such White supremacy, particularly long-established police brutality and racially motivated violence against African Americans. The movement is composed of a wide range of individuals and groups.[3] As an overarching organization, its individuals and groups also campaign against systemic racism, racial injustice, and hurdles to policy changes that would create more fairness and accountability for African Americans and other minority communities.[4]

A certain number of detractors criticize BLM for launching campaigns that are too broad or unrealistic. If attention is paid only to what the movement's leaders claim or write, then the criticism has merit. Yet, it would be useful to unveil the various outcomes that could be achieved by BLM, suggesting that its public communication campaigns have had considerable cultural, political, economic impacts.[5] In regards to economic impact, for example, the Target Corporation, one of the biggest retailers in the United States, pledged to spend over $2 billion with Black-owned businesses by 2025. It will do so by purchasing their brands, recruiting Black-owned construction or advertising companies, and developing a new platform for start-ups. George Floyd lost his life in Target's hometown of Minneapolis, also the place of the trial for the police officer who fatally kneeled on Floyd's neck. One

Fundamentals of Public Communication Campaigns, First Edition. Jonathan Matusitz.
© 2022 John Wiley & Sons Ltd. Published 2022 by John Wiley & Sons Ltd.

Target store, near the site of the tragedy, had to be totally rebuilt and some other stores were destroyed during the riots in the summer of 2020. In 2020–1, major corporations like Nike, Walmart, and Ulta Beauty made public racial-equity promises, like featuring more Black individuals in their advertisements and decreasing the amount of police or security personnel in stores. Generation Z—those adolescents and 20-somethings who tend to develop relationships with brands—are more concerned about social justice than previous generations.[6]

GROWTH OF A MOVEMENT

BLM was founded by Patrisse Cullors, Alicia Garza, and Opal Tometi.[7] In July 2013, the movement was ignited by the propagation of the hashtag #BlackLivesMatter (created by Cullors herself) on social networking sites after George Zimmerman was acquitted in the fatal shooting of African–American teenager Trayvon Martin. The shooting occurred 17 months earlier in Sanford, FL.[8] According to a poll by the Pew Research Center in June 2020, BLM was highly popular in the United States. Two-thirds of American adults said that they agreed with BLM, with 38% strongly supporting the organization. This attitude is much stronger among African Americans, although most of Caucasian (60%), Hispanic (77%), and Asian (75%) Americans show a significant percentage of support.[9]

BLM embodies a symbol of encouragement for racial equality and justice, which also entails addressing disparities in healthcare access, unwarranted imprisonment of certain minority groups, trauma, healing, and getting citizens to be involved in active antiracist campaigns. In 2014, BLM became a household name during its street protests as a result of the deaths of two African Americans, that of Michael Brown—which took place in Ferguson, MO, a city close to St. Louis—and Eric Garner in New York City.[10] Breonna Taylor, Ahmaud Arbery, Rayshard Brooks, and Jacob Blake are more recent names of African Americans whose tragic deaths stood out from the innumerable Black lives that have been lost. For BLM, they only represent the tip of the iceberg of racial trauma experienced by African Americans.[11] The philosophy is, first and foremost, picking up courage to combat race-based violence and prejudicial policing. At the macro level, it is a public stand against White privilege and supremacism; its supreme aspiration is to upset the status quo by forcing the United States to steadfastly investigate the manners by which state-sponsored actors treat African Americans as, at best, second-class citizens. At the same time, BLM underscores the dauntlessness of Black Love and community.[12]

Roots in the Civil Rights Movement

Although the BLM movement is relatively new, African Americans have challenged systemic racism and oppression in the United States for a long time.[13] However, there has not been the type of sustained attention and activism exhibited by African Americans and their allies since the Civil Rights Movement, all of which is partly attributable to BLM's endeavors on the streets and on social media.[14] To this very last point, social networking sites have helped BLM diffuse narratives around its mission to change the status quo and the powers that be, although the movement does not depend uniquely on social media for its success.[15] For advocates during the Civil Rights Movement of the 1950s and 1960s who are still alive today, the BLM movement brings new hope. Late US Representative John Lewis, who passed away in July 2020, inspired by demonstrators and supportive of the BLM campaigns stated, "We must use our time and our space on this little planet that we call Earth to make a lasting contribution, to leave it a little better than we found it, and now that need is greater than ever before."[16]

George Floyd's Death

The movement made even bigger national headlines and attracted global attention during the massive George Floyd protests in 2020 following the killing of the man by Minneapolis police officer Derek Chauvin. On May 25, 2020, George Floyd was apprehended for attempting to use a counterfeit $20 bill to buy cigarettes. During the arrest, one of the officers on duty, Derek Chauvin, who was Caucasian, restrained George Floyd by pinning him down on the ground and placing his knee on his neck. Despite George Floyd's pleas that Derek Chauvin stop the torture because he was unable to breathe, the officer continued to force him in that position for 8 minutes and 46 seconds, during which he became unconscious and died. News of George Floyd's death triggered immediate protest of police brutality, with the first protest occurring in Minneapolis on the next day, May 26, 2020.[17]

Approximately 15 to 26 million people took part in the 2020 BLM protests in the United States, making it one of the biggest movements in the nation's history. Although the movement consists of many views and a wide array of demands, it mostly focuses on criminal justice reform.[18] With 4.5 million followers on Instagram, and one million on Twitter (as of July 2021), BLM is also connected with millions of followers around the world—and probably more because of multiple demographic and usage tracking patterns across social networking sites. On April 20, 2021, after a long-standing trial, Derek Chauvin was found guilty of second-degree unintentional murder, third-degree murder, and second-degree manslaughter.[19]

Black Lives Matter UK

BLM is a global organization. Created in the United States, it has spread to countries like the United Kingdom and Canada, where the initialism "BLM" can be seen in various forms on social media platforms and accounts (e.g., BLM Denmark).[20] Black Lives Matter UK (or BLMUK), for instance, was officially matriculated as a community benefit organization in September 2020 under the name Black Liberation Movement UK, which it felt compelled to do in order to receive donations. The British group was registered by Adam Elliott Cooper, an academic, Alexandra Wanjiku Kelbert, a doctoral student, and Lisa Robinson, the head of a Nottingham-based social initiative. BLMUK collected £1.2m in donations through a GoFundMe campaign, after the George Floyd protests in summer 2020. In the United Kingdom, over 260 towns and cities organized protests in June and July—from Monmouth in Wales to Shetland in Scotland. British historians have referred to these protests as the largest antiracism rallies since the slavery epoch. BLMUK planned a massive-scale antiracism campaign across rural communities.[21]

At some point in 2020, BLMUK openly supported Palestinian rights to autonomy and sovereignty by meeting with pro-Palestinian groups and activists and showing solidarity with them.[22] In February 2021, BLMUK announced that it intended to donate £600,000 to grassroots organizations across the country. The funds were awarded in two phases. The first round consisted of a £170,000 donation divided in small grants to 14 organizations that want to "improve Black people's lives in a racist society" and with which BLMUK had collaborated over the past five years. The second round took place in late 2021, where groups were kindly asked to apply for the remaining funds that were initially reserved for other organizations.[23]

BLM CAMPAIGNS: AN INTRODUCTION

To begin, BLM's campaigns have been a clear departure from the leadership model of the singular, charismatic leader. BLM's campaigns have invigorated a multiplicity of grassroots activist groups in all sorts of communities. Only a handful are full-time organizers. Like most staff and volunteers in the movement, most BLM activists engage in an unsophisticated, democratic, and vigorous crusade, bent on remaining independent from both the US political establishment and long-standing African–American leaders, like Jesse Jackson and Al Sharpton. The latter are regarded as more interested in punditry than in popular struggle.[24] BLM's campaign style marks a shifting political perspective within historically disenfranchised communities and is consistent with present-day conceptions of power and politics within public communication campaigns.

BLM's attributes of spontaneity and self-organization mirror the styles of genuine campaigns rather than a calculated airing of grievances. Although far from being perfect, its campaigns devote ample time and energy to groups closer to the margins—African Americans, women, LGBTQ+ folks, and various nonélites—through the creation of blogs, reports, open letters, and even songs that call the names of unknown victims of police violence ("Say Her Name," as one of these campaigns is dubbed). These approaches symbolize inclusiveness and a dream of being able to legally do a radical redistribution of power relations. By setting up vigils, sit-ins, marches, and other events in the name of slain African Americans, campaigns such as "Say Her Name" are fighting the obliteration or alienation of such individuals who, for a long time, encountered higher rates of police brutality and incarceration than their White counterparts.[25]

BLM's campaign planners want audiences to acknowledge and turn their attention the various needs and experiences of citizens during the course of community research processes. It is important to better understand how to make progress over simply recognizing and attending to diversity by understanding how phenomena like group marginalization can be aggravated by power and systemic oppression. BLM seeks to place these realities within historical and sociopolitical contexts and assist audiences in understanding how to reach these objectives—i.e., by fighting against dominant powers at different levels and in their relationships with communities. From this vantage point, BLM is framing a new visual rhetoric.

Framing a New Visual Rhetoric

One solution for BLM's campaigns to gain more traction was to create a new visual rhetoric for Black protests. Whereas the Civil Rights Movement in the 1950s and 1960s depended a great deal on the courage and outstanding speaking skills of charismatic Black male leaders (and only a few Black women),[26] the twenty-first century BLM movement has put African–American women at the face of its campaigns, with many men only fulfilling a supporting role. These women wear colorful braids, have nose rings and provocative T-shirts, and take control of traditional media platforms or revolutionize new ones. This unprecedented approach of antitraditionalism was done on purpose.[27] As was the case for the Civil Rights Movement, the present movement fighting for racial equality poses an unmistakable threat to status quo race relations.

Worldwide, strategists for BLM campaigns apply the main tenets of framing theory, namely how public communication initiatives should be designed to achieve definite political goals (see Chapter 4). Framing is an effort to accomplish core tasks: steering attention towards a specific problem, ascribing blame for such problem, formulating a realistic solution, and encouraging action.[28] To encourage action, BLM stresses the gravity and urgency of the problem and what noble moral priorities should be undertaken. To this end, BLM spearheading activists believe that it is essential to frame the ills caused by the problem as systemic injustice rather than accident or misfortune. Emphasizing the disproportionate rate of African Americans killed by police and all those instances whereby excessive force was used against unarmed Blacks are both approaches to highlight injustice and inspire participation in the movement. Consequently, BLM has managed to make racial inequalities—especially those pertaining to policing practices—a core issue in today's society, framing injustice as a rationale to be up in arms.[29]

Symbolic Representation

Part of the framing strategy embedded within BLM campaigns is symbolic representation. By displaying photos of protest pictures alongside photos of Black victims, BLM frames protestors and the general public as potential victims of police brutality and fashions a massive form of collective identity. Slogans like "Hands up, don't shoot" and "We can't breathe" reference the slayings of Michael Brown and Eric Garner, respectively. Symbolic representations of victimhood are designed to motivate the public to become associated with a larger collective. An illustration of this is the act of protestors to lie dead on the streets—i.e., "die-ins"—to personify, through this performance, real victims. The Campaign Zero website (discussed in detail later), which posts many images of this kind, includes one of these pictures to promote their vision or cause. "We the Protesters" offers an activist blueprint with a collection of protest signs pictures. Most of them display names and photos of victims. Other signs turn protestors directly into victims with glaring lines like "You are killing us," "We all are Michael Brown," or "Our daughters will be next."[30]

Another form of symbolic representation is the clever application of colors to the "look and feel" of the campaign websites. The use of design elements like color is contextual and hardly possible to evaluate with certainty with respect to its meaning. Nevertheless, there is a captivating feature of color use in this type of campaign material. In particular, BLM's black and bright yellow colors are also employed by groups against police brutality in Canada and the United Kingdom, among other places. This goes to show that the internationalization of the movement has extended their political mourning to other places. Victims of police brutality in America, then, could be related to victims of police brutality around the world.[31]

CAMPAIGN AGAINST POLICE BRUTALITY

Racialized police brutality is not only a common topic in the mass media; it has also been reshaped by BLM within the public discourse.[32] Police brutality in the United States is the unjustified, exaggerated, and/or unlawful use of force against civilians by US police officers. Examples of police brutality include, but are not limited to, assault, battery, muddle, torture, and homicide. Other types of police brutality encompass harassment, unreasonable arrest, intimidation, and verbal insults, among others.[33] To put it concisely, police brutality is the baseless use of physical force and actions by police in order to bully, harass, or dehumanize.[34]

According to the Statista Research Department, the direction of deadly police shootings in the United States is on the increase, with no fewer than 132 civilians fatally shot (16 of whom were Black) during the first two months of 2021 alone. In 2020, 1,004 fatal police shootings occurred, a little more than the 999 that happened in 2019. The proportion of deadly police shootings among African Americans was much higher than that of any other racial group; there were 35 fatal shootings per million people as of February 2021.[35] By extension, police brutality is a social determinant of health that exceedingly impacts the health of racial minorities. Studies have shown a significant relationship between police violence and health, mainly with respect to physical and mental health outcomes of those who suffer from police violence.[36]

Three Types of Victimhood

BLM campaigns unite against police brutality both pre- and postmortem. The identification of the dead as victims of structural violence is key to counteracting the impact of the postmortem violence that takes personhood away from the dead.[37] This cognitive tactic facilitated the criminalization of George Floyd when far-right activists tried to direct our attention to his past criminal record and imprisonment, rather than making us focus on the fact that he should have been treated by Derek Chauvin as a person. The content of BLM-related websites and social networking pages provides a threefold victimhood for those unfairly slain by police. It is an effort to resist criminalization discourses through visual choices, instead of explicit argumentation. First, **objective victimhood** is developed through indexical symbolization of the dead. Police brutality presents itself as a real social problem that has killed those shown in graphics and statistics. Second, **exemplary victimhood** appears when a handful of those victims become known figures that embody the entire collective of the dead. In the BLM movement, this representation does not serve to portray the dead as martyrs, but to depict them as persons who live like most of us do. Finally, most symbolic representations relate to the construction of what should be termed **collective victimhood** based on symbolic representation. BLM and its websites emblematically associate the dead to advocates, demonstrators, and the movement through images of protest or photos of victims that speak to the values and objectives of the movement.[38]

Campaign Zero

Campaign Zero is a campaign for American police reform launched in the summer of 2015 when BLM was denounced for demonizing police and having no plan to concretely end police brutality. The summer of 2015 was the acme of the first BLM protests, which took place in the aftermath of the killing of Michael Brown in Ferguson, MO, in 2014. Campaign Zero is often called a BLM initiative in the mainstream media.[39] The plan is composed of a 10-point policy manifesto that details institutional policing reforms to vanquish police brutality towards African Americans.[40] The campaign's planning cadre includes BLM leaders like Brittany Packnett, Samuel Sinyangwe, DeRay Mckesson, and Johnetta Elzie.[41] Campaign Zero also cooperates with Mapping Police Violence.[42]

Campaign Zero is unambiguous about proposing and carrying out institutional police reforms to quell unwarranted police brutality against racial minorities. The platform advances reasonable, concrete, and nonthreatening policies that would not only help moderate brutality against such communities, but also challenge the broader social plague of anti-Black racism that the police sometimes mirror.[43] Campaign Zero's "Police Use of Force Project" calls for reevaluating the current application of force policies of large police departments across the nation. The purpose is to find out what rules the police must obey and whether these policies can avert police violence. BLM campaign framers also want to determine how many police departments truly adhere to policies on use of force.[44] As per its website titled www.joincampaignzero.org, Campaign Zero has gathered and advanced policy solutions for police reform in 10 areas:

1. **End of Broken Windows Policing**: This proposed policy serves to decriminalize offenses that do not jeopardize public safety, do away with profiling and unnecessary "stop and frisk" policies, and develop new approaches to mental health crises. Broken Windows policing is rooted in the works of Edward Banfield, a conservative urban thinker in the 1960s who claimed that racial inequalities were not caused by structural causes or political and economic inequality as most present-day theorists posit.[45] **Broken Windows** was applied to clampdowns on petty crimes like graffiti, public urination, and prowling, under the assumption that neighborhood disorder led to such offenses and attracted (would-be) felons who would eventually perpetrate more dangerous offenses in these neighborhoods.[46]

2. **Community Oversight**: This policy would put strong civilian oversight structures in place and remove obstacles to report police misconduct. BLM thinks that this measure is necessary because community oversight is the public's duty as well.[47]

3. **Limited Use of Force**: This policy would create standards and motivate police to refrain from using excessive force. This can be done by revamping policies about use of force by local police, ending traffic-based police shootings and high-speed chases, and improving accountability for use of excessive force in any context (even one that would justify it). Unjustified anti-Black violence committed by the police, even if is "race-neutral," could be considered a type of social cleansing.[48]

4. **Independent Investigations and Prosecutions**: This policy would lower the standard of proof in legal proceedings against police, benefit from federal funds for independent investigations and prosecutions, create a State Special Prosecutor's Office for actionable cases, and require independent investigations for any instance of deadly shooting. The "blue code of silence" dissuades police from reporting fellow officers who could be found guilty of misconduct.[49] BLM has scored a few concrete victories. Sporadic cases of police officers being prosecuted and disciplined for misconduct point to the fact that public backlash can move the needle even within the most rigid police systems.[50]

5. **Community Representation**: This policy would recruit police officers who embody the demographic features of their communities and employ community feedback to inform evaluators. As Ringaux and Cunningham (2021)[51] put it, modifications of leadership practices within police departments could improve hiring and retention of minority police officers within North American policing forces.

6. **Filming the Police**: This policy would require body cameras on police and legalize the right to record them. This type of accountability is crucial because, in many cases, the sole witnesses to police violence are fellow officers, or the very victims who are framed as noncredible sources in court.[52]

7. **Training**: This policy would devote a great deal of time and energy in strict and sustained training. Training police is indispensable to teach officers how to

de-escalate and use nonlethal force. This prerequisite would include the officer's "tactical conduct and decisions" before (or in lieu of) using deadly force.[53] Training police also consists of establishing statewide standardized tests with, *inter alia*, questions centered on "unconscious" or "implicit" racial bias. Performance evaluations should be tied to such training and testing. Brandl and Stroshine (2012)[54] substantiate the notion that training "has long been considered essential in controlling the use-of-force by the police."

8. **End Policing for Profit**: This policy would stop police department quotas, decrease fines and costs for low-income citizens, prohibit property seizure, and force police budgets to cover misconduct fines. For-profit policing and exploiting the disadvantaged for financial extraction (which goes to the state or local government) is evocative of early slave neighborhood watches that codified the power for patrols to extract money from Black slaves, specifically "fowls or provisions found in the hands of any negro who is away from home without a ticket."[55]

9. **Demilitarization**: This policy would put a stop to politicians' and law enforcement officials' dream of militarizing local law enforcement on the premise that it would ensure public and officer safety, with early studies ostensibly supporting those claims.[56] BLM calls for ending the federal government's 1033 Program that would provide local police departments with military-style weapons. Since the 1990s, this Department of Defense's initiative has poured billions of dollars' worth of high-performance military weapons into local agencies. Although a valuable resource, and given the overall lack of data on militarized policing, this practice has significant deficiencies that could skew inferences if neglected.[57] For these reasons, BLM advances local restrictions on the provision of military weapons to police.

10. **Fair Police Contracts**: This policy would lift obstructions to misconduct investigations and civilian oversight, make police disciplinary history available to police departments and to the public, and guarantee financial accountability for officers and police departments that slay unarmed citizens. Put another way, BLM wants to avoid any recruitment of officers who are unfit to serve.[58] In fact, a *Boston Globe* (2020)[59] editorial argued that policymakers should clear policies regarding police discipline and accountability from the collective bargaining process.

Campaign Zero is arranged into three categories: interventions, interactions, and accountability. The three categories range from large policing initiatives to preventive measures for influencing individual interactions involving police officers. Also included are processes to hold officers accountable in the event of police brutality. Campaign Zero tackles the problem of police brutality from these three different angles. **Interventions** take a large approach, at the macro level, to abolish the amalgamation of Blackness with criminality by altering policies that target minority groups. Interventions adopt a critical approach of the relationship between the hyper-criminalization of Black communities and the unfettered capitalist orientation to profit from targeting these communities. Patrols, police officers, prison administrators, and other officials surveilling people of color have been the ones to receive part of the profits.[60] Interventions seek to confront this problematic relationship which not only overstates the correlation between race and crime (i.e., a staple of systemic racism), but which also stereotypes the victims who are already caught within the web of systemic racism.[61]

Interactions view police officers' actual behaviors on a micro level and seek to change them from a preventive or front-end approach. By altering police attitudes in a preventive fashion, the goal is to influence and reform police behavior during their interactions with citizens. This could be accomplished through strict and fair training of officers and better representation of police forces.[62] The final component of the three-part model includes those items within accountability. **Accountability** intends to institute checks on police power and behavior, which has been predominantly absent.[63] Examples include more thorough reporting of instances of police violence (in an attempt to classify and evaluate the patterns of such violence) and develop built-in mechanisms for police accountability by equipping police with body cameras.[64] Notwithstanding the fact that numerous proposals for tackling police brutality have been put on the table, current discussions tend to avoid a key driver of police violence and obstacle to accountability: use of force policies. These policies would codify the laws that regulate the degree and type of force that police are allowed to use against citizens, including deadly force.[65]

CAMPAIGN AGAINST SYSTEMIC RACISM

Racism refers to any action, deliberate or unintended, based on race or skin pigmentation that subjugates a group or individual based on their race or skin pigmentation.[66] A particular form of racism is systemic racism. Also known as **structural racism** or **institutional racism**, **systemic racism** is a category of racism that is established as common practice within society, a cultural group, or an organization. It can give rise to issues such as discrimination in legal proceedings, employment, housing, healthcare, politics, and schooling, just to name a few.[67] It is institutional inequality on the basis of race. Other examples include school segregation and **redlining** (i.e., denying someone adequate services because he or she resides in a racially associated area).[68]

Because the effectiveness of systemic racism rests on some type of action (e.g., policy implementation) based on a belief system (e.g., stereotypes), it can be interpreted as one of many outcomes born out of implicit bias. To this point, according to the American Civil Liberties Union (ACLU), both implicit and explicit bias can stem from racial disparities witnessed within the criminal justice system. The ACLU notes that African Americans are 10 times more likely to be imprisoned for drug charges than Caucasians, and three times more likely to be arrested for cannabis possession than their White counterparts.[69]

Campaign against the Unfair Justice System

BLM has been synonymous with protests against systemic racism in the court system. For the organization, the deceptive aspect of justice demonstrates society's refusal to care for Black lives. This is why many attempts have been made to bereave White supremacism of the oxygen it needs to uphold these long-standing attitudes and the state violence that they occasion. The organization unveils—in an easier and faster manner than ever before (thanks to the universality of social media)—how these attitudes have engendered hyper-segregation, the school-to-prison conduit, over-unemployment, and housing discrimination. By highlighting the pervasive violence, as well as the delusions, falsehoods, hypocrisies, and double standards that so characterize the justice system, BLM impugns the very pillars upon which Americans believe their democracy rests: that all human beings are made equal and that all are entitled to life, liberty, and the pursuit of happiness.[70]

Through public service announcements (PSAs), media communiqués, Twitter and Instagram posts, and infographics, BLM conveys the idea that African Americans in residentially segregated districts across the nation encounter a multiplicity of socioeconomic, environmental, and political obstacles that negatively impact their lives and neighborhoods.[71] One of BLM's PSAs in 2020 started with the following statement: "The battle to end racial discrimination and prejudice is an important mission we must all undertake together." As stated a few sentences later, "We need to acknowledge the social inequalities that exist and where they stem from. It is important that we take the time to listen, appreciate and embody the essence of antidiscrimination and antiracist activities."[72] As BLM points out, as a consequence of discrimination and racism in the legal system, determinants of quality of life indicate lower educational achievement, adverse health outcomes, fewer options for employment, and hampered political involvement for low-income African Americans. On the whole, residentially segregated communities illustrate how systemic racism and inequality constrain community development.[73]

Systemic racism also entails "tacit" expectations about race that favor institutions and the status quo by creating a type of "Us vs. Them" frame.[74] As the earlier-referenced PSA explains, "We cannot be silent in the face of racism, discrimination and prejudice that are both overt and subtle." Systemic racism is structural disparity; it is a state of massive-scale inequalities whereby African Americans are ascribed a lower status than the privileged. As the mechanisms of systemic racism are continuously shaped across history and contemporary times, it is not hard to see how state policies, institutional practices, symbolic representations, and other norms contribute to strengthening ways to perpetuate racial group inequalities.[75] Bureaucracies are entrenched within structural practices that certainly accentuate neutral or color-blind policies.[76] On the face of it, they seemingly consider all groups equal but, in practice, signal racially disproportionate outcomes.[77] Gooden (2014)[78] describes this situation as a model of abundant racial inequalities that identifies systemic racism as a key driver for perpetuating disparities across various domains in life—health, schooling, criminal justice, financial well-being, housing, and environment.

Combating the Four Domains of Power

One approach for describing BLM's campaign efforts is by identifying four domains of power from the organization's myriad of PSAs, media communiqués, Twitter and Instagram posts, and infographics. The four domains of power are structural, disciplinary, cultural, and interpersonal. The **structural domain of power** consists of public policies that develop and control the social institution. Social hierarchy emerges within social institutions like banks, insurance companies, police forces, the real estate profession, educational institutions, supermarkets, restaurants, hospitals, and government offices. When citizens apply rules, regulations, and public policies daily to sustain social hierarchy or resist it, their agency and actions form the **disciplinary domain of power**. Increasingly reliant on strategies of surveillance, citizens keep one another accountable and even self-censor by integrating disciplinary practices into their own actions. The **cultural domain of power** denotes social institutions and practices that generate the hegemonic ideas for preserving social inequalities or counterhegemonic ideas to denounce inequitable social relations. Through traditional media, social networking sites, journalism, and educational curricula, the cultural domain creates representations, ideas, and philosophies about social inequality. The **interpersonal domain of power** embraces the manifold experiences that citizens live within outright distressing interactions with people of authority.[79] For example, from May and July 2020, after George Floyd was brutally killed, BLM diffused many messages against the White oppressive interpersonal domain of power. It occurred at a time when the entire world witnessed the brutality committed by Derek Chauvin against Floyd. The police officer's knee on

Floyd's neck for 8 minutes and 46 seconds—a fatal encounter during which the African American became unconscious and stopped breathing—was one of the numerous quintessential emblems of systemic racism against which BLM was campaigning.

Denouncing Respectability Politics

BLM remains unimpressed with **respectability politics**, the philosophy that oppressed groups can gain support for their cause by following simple standards of decency or etiquette. It is a type of moralistic discourse used by high-profile "minority group" figures like Reverend Al Sharpton. When these people display respectability politics, it could as well be an attempt to control some of their fellow group members. Adherents of respectability politics often project their personal values as being harmonious with dominant values. They may opt not to rally against the mainstream for its refusal to embrace the marginalized group into the mainstream. They proclaim that diversity can also be seen within the dominant group.[80] As BLM advocates are keenly aware, rituals of decorum will not honor dark skin that a certain number of the dominant society abhor. BLM refuses to engage in indirect victim blaming. In fact, for BLM leaders, respectability politics contributes, in part, to systemic racism. As they maintain, empty narratives stress Black-on-Black crime or recommend cultural rehabilitation while avoiding truthful dissent. These perspectives perpetuate the dangerous premise that Black pathology—not merely White supremacism—is to blame for the state's systematic targeting of African Americans.[81]

A NOTE ON BLM'S SOCIAL MEDIA USAGE

Many of today's campaigns use social media to influence, organize, and take to the streets. Social media creates space for digital social networks that enable activists to develop connections and social capital. After interviewing many protest participants in Taiwan, Nien (2017)[82] explained how social media produces "weak ties" that bind protesters with disparate identities. They join forces against a common enemy. Hwang and Kim (2015)[83] employed a social capital framework to explain how online networks create both weak and strong ties. Both have a positive impact on willingness to take part in movements. The researchers stressed the essence of shared narratives, philosophies, and/or collective identity as a foundation for bringing groups together. They indicated that the ability to unite various interests around a cause is crucial.[84]

Forming Coalitions with Like-Minded Activists

For BLM leaders, social networking sites are key to their organizing efforts in three respects: (1) For mustering internal and external resources, (2) for forming coalitions with similar organizations and other social movements, and (3) for regulating the core message of the movement.[85] BLM touts its outspoken rejection of hierarchy and centralized leadership—in so doing, it brands itself as "leader-ful," with a flat structure, and with an intersectional strategy that dignifies groups like queer women of color. Social media opens doors for exposing the causes of like-minded activists. This can be done by diffusing information about other subjects of focus and by using social networking sites to "comment on" and getting involved in those areas during the course of information transmission. Explained differently, social media opens doors for creating interactive relationships with like-minded activists thanks to novel forms of coalition-focused organizing. Too, digital networking options such as "likes" or "followers" can enhance the profile and status of an organization with only a few mouse clicks.[86]

On top of forming connections with similar others within the BLM movement, group administrators can take advantage of the social media to garner resources from outside supporters and lay participants. For instance, for the reason that social media pages can be accessed without having to sign up or attend in-person gatherings, BLM factions online can easily establish a large base of followers to expedite strategic action. Attracting followers can be achieved by keeping an online presence. This type of coalition building often emerges out of the development of alliances between groups, as opposed to the development of relationships among individual leaders that eventually take the form of internal connection building.[87]

Slacktivism

Slacktivism is the practice of endorsing a political or social cause through communiqués on social networking sites or online petitions. As a general rule, relatively little effort or commitment is needed. This approach may bring about little impact, as in a situation where participants feel satisfied that they have done it. These free or comparatively cheap efforts can still be effective.[88] Nummi, Jennings, and Feagin (2019)[89] ascertain that a great volume of the support and awareness generated by the BLM movement is made possible through social media. In a similar vein, studies demonstrate that the slacktivist attribute of this movement has been correlated with a positive impact on further involvement in the cause. Given that participants are able to contribute from their technological devices heightens awareness and involvement from other audiences. Not all online participation is worthless. The interviewees of Mundt, Ross, and Burnett's research (2018)[90] explain how grassroots activism driven by social media is impactful and powerful for contributing to BLM campaigns. As stated by a BLM group administrator in the Southwestern United States: "We hit social heavily, and we travel so we can talk with people on other side of the country. We are firm believers in the organizing capability of social media to make people come together."

INTERSECTIONALITY: AN INTRODUCTION

There is no standard definition of intersectionality. However, the majority of scholars would associate several of the following tenets with intersectionality: Racism, sexism, class exploitation, and comparable philosophies of oppression intersect and mutually shape one another.[91] By and large, **intersectionality** is an analytic frame of reference that seeks to identify how interlocking mechanisms of power affect communities who are most disenfranchised in society. Developed by Kimberlé Crenshaw (1989),[92] intersectionality reckons that diverse types of social stratification—i.e., social status, race, sexual orientation, age, disability, and sex—do not operate independently from one other but are interconnected.[93] Pheonix (2006)[94] states further that intersectionality is a practical term to describe "the complex political struggles and arguments that seek to make visible the multiple positioning that constitutes everyday life and the power relations that are central to it."

Intersectionality is a critical approach for examining the effects of oppression on people and the sociopolitical apparatuses of power and privilege that downgrade people and their communities. Power is a construct that is fundamental to human experience and that is routinely addressed in both intersectionality and modern-day society.[95] Michel Foucault (1997),[96] the late French philosopher, viewed power as ubiquitous in all instances of communication and relationships, irrespective of social status. Power relations are not rigid; they evolve over time and function both invisibly and overtly. For BLM, intersectionality is important because it raises consciousness as to the necessity of resisting the inherent power of the majority in US society, one that upholds a White, male, heterosexual, and patriarchal ethos.

Rooted in Historical Marginalization

The origins of the construct of intersectionality can be traced back to the history of the United States. The shared histories of the American women's rights campaigns and American race relations, in concert with multiple theoretical strands—e.g., the critical analysis of the modern subject, poststructuralism, critical feminist theory, and critical legal studies—have spawned and operationalized the construct of intersectionality in American studies.[97] Therefore, intersectionality is grounded in US historical marginalization and facilitates in-depth examination of individuals' lived experiences of such marginalizations. It investigates how oppressions and positionalities are intertwined to engender unique situations. It is a method of deepening research by concentrating on how multiple positionalities intersect with one another. Intersectionality symbolizes fluid, constantly evolving theoretical notions. As more scholars understand and apply it, new forms of intersectionality emerge. The example of masculinities is indicative of the way intersectionality transcends the traditional race/gender/class framework and assumes many additional positionalities that are often ignored—e.g., masculinity, disability, age, sexual orientation, and transnationality, to name a few.

A meaningful application of intersectionality is in the domain of massive-scale, historically rooted and hierarchical power systems.[98] From this vantage point, intersectionality denotes the interaction of what has been portrayed as "systems of hostility and depreciation,"[99] "interlocking systems of domination,"[100] or the organizing foundations of society,[101] all of which contribute to the development of the self in society. Put another way, this application of intersectionality views identity constructs like gender, race, and sexuality through the lens of systemic forces that have built society since its early oppressive roots (instead of attributes featured by individuals).[102] Overall, intersectionality is a conceptualization of the way hierarchy works in relation to historically oppressed groups, particularly minorities.

Embedded in Neo-Marxist and Feminist Scholarship

Intersectionality is a popular term among neo-Marxist scholars. Falling under the umbrella concept of the "New Left," **neo-Marxism** is a school of thought that seeks to identify and tackle sociocultural and political problems within modern society, with particular attention paid to class warfare and male-dominated hierarchy.[103] Neo-Marxism integrates Max Weber's general conception of social inequality, like status and power, within Marxist philosophy. Neo-Marxism reached its first apogee during the New Left movements that occurred in the 1960s and 1970s in the Western world.[104] The **New Left** is a broad spectrum of left-wing intellectual currents that advocates for social justice issues like civil rights, political rights, legal reform, feminism, gay and lesbian rights, abortion rights, gender emancipation, and pro-drug attitudes. The New Left contributed to university campus mass protests (including the Free Speech Movement) and neo-Marxist movements in that era. The latter diverged from earlier Leftist movements that were more focused on labor activism and, instead, specialized in social activism. Neo-Marxist scholars generally work from a post-modernist perspective.[105] Within the context of this chapter, **postmodernism** is a comprehensive theoretical paradigm that denounces knowledge claims and value systems as socially conditioned and historically steeped, conceptualizing them as the fruits of political, historical, and sociocultural discourses and structures—and which transmit these discourses and hierarchies to future generations.[106]

What African–American, queer, and neo-Marxist feminists do is grapple with the most essential theoretical and normative matter within feminist scholarship; that is, the recognition of differences among groups, especially women. It pertains to the most critical problem that present-day feminism faces: the deep-rooted and tedious legacy of its exclusions. This legacy of exclusion has been thoroughly described by neo-Marxist thinkers who indicate that feminist theory is still predominantly White. Hence, its promise to integrate nonprivileged women has yet to be fulfilled.[107] Put another way, intersectionality mixes the constructs of sex and gender with race and ethnicity.[108] As demonstrated by intersectionality efforts since its origins, social hierarchy shapes the experiences that generate the categories that intersect. White males still dominate by a large measure. Domination-and-subordination is the interplay that invigorates this structure. It is this comprehensive dynamic that neo-Marxist and feminist scholars are critical of, exposing the "uncritical and disturbing acceptance of dominant ways of thinking about discrimination."[109]

Allyship

A related term is allyship. **Allyship** is the process of supporting disenfranchised groups by promoting social justice, inclusion, and human rights by members of privileged groups. Behaviors that fall under allyship consist of activism, using inclusive language, and fighting against various types of discrimination like racism, sexism, homophobia, transphobia, xenophobia, and ableism, among others.[110] Allies tend to be members of communities with comparatively higher power, status, and/or other resources.[111] A key illustration of successful activism is the ability of disenfranchised groups to harness the support of such allies.[112] This is why allyship is also called **ally activism**—i.e., collective action in support of, or in concert with, a disadvantaged group.[113]

INTERSECTIONALITY AND BLM

BLM's framers, as well as leaders of similar movements, are resolute about incorporating discourses of intersectionality in their campaigns. Their discourses attach great importance to Black lives, including, among others, Black women, feminists, and members of the LGBTQ+ community.[114] This is a radical departure from the approach of traditional Black freedom campaigns, which placed cisgender Black men at the center of their fight for social justice and racial equality, thereby deliberately sidelining cisgender Black women and the LGBTQ+ population who might be considered undeserving of rights within the confines of capitalist heteropatriarchy.[115] It is important to keep in mind that some of the originators of BLM—i.e., Patrisse Cullors, Alicia Garza, and Opal Tometi—are women. Garza and Cullors are LGBTQ+ and Tometi is the child of immigrants. Before their involvement with BLM affairs, their activism consisted of assisting domestic workers and immigrants, pushing for legal reform, supporting victims of domestic violence, and making pleas for healthcare rights—particularly for Black, Indigenous, people of color (BIPOC). Therefore, BLM's framers not only live their intersectionality today, but they have also promoted it for many years. For Cullors, Garza, and Tometi, the personal and political naturally mix, and the political is incontestably intersectional.[116]

Case Study 1:   Alicia Garza's Herstory Campaign

Alicia Garza's (2014)[117] **Herstory** seeks to expand the discourse of social justice and racial equity by including Black lives and accentuating BLM's vehement commitment to intersectionality. Though BLM makes race the focus of its campaigns, the CSO acknowledges that race intersects with gender, sexuality, socioeconomic status, religion, disability, and other categories. As such, BLM works to confront more than just systemic racism; it wants to challenge all forms of structural sexism, homophobia, transphobia, and classism because those mechanisms of tyranny have a long-term combined effect with racism in the lives of BIPOC. And because systems of oppression intersect, no human being can truly enjoy freedom until everyone does.[118] Garza's Herstory campaign exemplifies years of BLM efforts, from social media platforms, to diffuse a racially liberatory message for African Americans and other minority groups. For instance, Garza articulates how the accomplishments by African–American queer women have been stolen or neglected.[119] Herstory becomes a campaign that places intersectional Blackness in the present-day struggle for freedom. It informs strategies to raise BLM's participants' intersectional critical consciousness. Such a campaign positively affects society at large because its core message underlines actions that can ensure Black liberation for women and LGBTQ+ folks.[120]

In a nutshell, the Herstory campaign hypothesizes that authentic social change can only happen by solving structural social problems. Campaigns directed at Black feminist politic fulfill two essential functions of modern discourse: recognize the experiences and needs of an oppressed group and draw the attention of mainstream politicians to listen and respond.[121] LGBTQ+ activists have used a similar frame to combat oppression, even as they work hard on all fronts of their campaigns. LGBTQ+ participants implemented a successful initiative during the Movement for Black Lives National Convening in Cleveland in the summer of 2015. They graced the stage during one session to denounce what they perceived as symbols of transphobia and heterosexism within the broader movement. Honesty in addressing patriarchal and heteronormative structures could be an important test of BLM's long-term viability.[122] Herstory focuses on social identities that are routinely regarded as marginal or invisible because they are essentialized as subsets of larger, and "more important," collectives. This illustrates how intersectionality exposes the intricate nature of power, weakening all reductive models of oppression.[123] This approach also helps intersectionality scholars and strategists resist the **oppression Olympics**—the aspiration to have one identity (not necessarily our own) or one type of subordination seen as more important or essential than others.[124]

Case Study 2:   The BLMTO Campaign

At Toronto Pride 2016, members of Black Lives Matter Toronto (BLMTO) organized a sit-in during the Pride parade to expose the marginalization of racial groups and make their demands for equity and inclusion clear, particularly for future Pride celebrations.[125] BLMTO also confronted White supremacist and heteropatriarchal authority by pledging to engage in more activism and magnify the voices of the unfairly treated LGBTQ+ population of color. BLMTO specializes in intersectionality through action, one that extends beyond the "colorblind" intersectionality that White individuals have coopted in order to remove race from LGBTQ+ issues.[126] At that Toronto Pride event, BLMTO was able to catalyze change thanks to their intersectional political action, so much so that the Toronto Pride Board of Directors agreed to adopt BLMTO's requests for more funding for and representation of BIPOC at Toronto Pride.[127]

More specifically, BLMTO's campaign focuses on more diversity in staffing, a commitment to hiring more Black American Sign Language interpreters, more funding and freedom for community spaces like Black Queer Youth, and most contentiously, the exclusion of police forces from future parades.[128] This intervention created a ricochet among other BLM chapters, which soon interrupted local Pride marches to make similar demands. Such interventions exemplify opposition to physical and epistemic violence wreaked on Black women and LGBTQ+.[129] This BLMTO campaign drew the attention of Toronto Pride and its organizers in a way that upsets the normalization of state presence and participation in Pride, Toronto Pride's own anti-BIPOC history, and the deception about the multiculturalism of Canada's society and leadership. BLMTO's assistance by BLM's global network, its own constituents' diaspora positionalities, and its organization of protests within a homo-nationalist milieu all strengthen Black queer diaspora and global condemnation of homonormativity and anti-Blackness—all of which, again, have been perpetuated by mainstream gay events, like Toronto Pride, and long-established colonial states, like Canada.[130]

Harper and Schneider (2003)[131] discuss the advancement of LGBTQ+ affairs in today's society. As they remark, "community development, prevention, and intervention with LGBTQ+ communities cannot be separated from social activism." Making efforts at disrupting White superiority within the LGBTQ+ community is a political struggle in that most White queer and transpeople cannot fathom the enormous racial privilege that they enjoy. Activist organizations like BLMTO deem it primordial to engage in political action in order to make White LGBTQ+ folks, and even their non-LGBTQ+ counterparts, seriously think about their Whiteness and how it is instrumental in oppressing others.[132]

STANDPOINT THEORY, CRITICAL RACE THEORY, AND CRITICAL SOCIAL JUSTICE

Three theories can be used to explain the messages and actions of BLM's campaigns. To begin, **standpoint theory** is predicated upon the idea that our knowledge creates some degree of authority and the power from such authority molds our opinions in everyday life.

The core concept is that our own perspectives are influenced by our experiences in social locations and social groups.[133] A **standpoint** is a mental position or angle regarding certain issues, principles, or objects, often emerging from our circumstances or beliefs. A standpoint is a place from which we interpret the world. It determines how those adopting it socially construct the universe. It is a position according to which those issues, principles, or objects are compared and evaluated. Unfair treatment experienced by various social groups engender differences in their standpoints.[134]

Standpoint feminism, for example, postulates that feminist social science should be applied from the standpoint of women or specific groups of women because they are more qualified or experienced to understand certain characteristics or dimensions of the world.[135] An assumption of Garza's Herstory campaign is that historically disenfranchised groups like African–American women share experiences based on their social locations and social groups within a hierarchical structure. Hence, they will face comparable constraints and opportunities. Deeply rooted institutional power relations that hegemonize or dominate these groups will produce knowledge born out of shared experiences.[136] Although it is important to recognize that White supremacism suppresses many people, in the United States, subjugation of Black slaves and subsequent intentional efforts to perpetuate Black subordination make anti-Blackness distinct from the types of racism that affect others.[137]

Critical Race Theory

Critical race theory is another theoretical framework for understanding systemic racism. Its precepts shine a light on the immersion of racism within US society and the mechanisms through which presumably race-neutral establishments, systems, policies, and practices uphold White supremacism.[138] The precepts of critical race theory are that (1) racism is commonplace and omnipresent, rather than an abnormality; (2) racism is difficult to redress because claims of objectivity and meritocracy disguise and shield the power and privilege of White people; (3) race is socially constructed and maneuvered; (4) the standpoint of Black people regarding racism is legitimate and appropriate; and (5) critical race theorists must strive for social justice.[139] An important concept that capture the essence of some of these principles is implicit bias. **Implicit bias** is an unconscious attribution of negative qualities or characteristics to all members of particular groups—i.e., usually members of long-established disenfranchised groups.[140] By extension, implicit bias can include microaggressions. **Microaggressions** are subtle, indirect, or unintentional discriminatory or derogatory actions towards marginalized groups. They can be verbal or behavioral, are usually brief and commonplace, and occur on a frequent basis.[141]

Critical race theorists believe that African–American children receive excessively higher suspension rates than White boys and girls, even for similar offenses, because of their experienced history of unfair treatment.[142] In addition, African–American children endure or witness unnerving rates of violence in their districts and schools, which bear a detrimental effect on their development, both separately and together.[143] Mistry, Vandewater, Huston, and Mcloyd (2002)[144] analyzed an ethnically diverse sample of primarily African–American families. They discovered that the parents' economic difficulties indirectly affected their children's adaptation because of the impact of such difficulties on parental well-being. This, in turn, negatively affected their relationships with their children and the children's adaptation in school. Some mental health practitioners notice these types of impacts.

BLM advocates that critical race theory be taught in schools so that all can learn about social justice and racial equity. Ultimately, this material would pave the way for changes in the structures and mechanisms that perpetuate both systemic and individual racism. BLM remarks that race-based policing in the United States evolved from brutal Southern slave patrols that arbitrarily arrested slaves, to the supremacist abomination of lynching and Jim Crow laws, and to contemporary police violence *à la* Derek Chauvin. It is also manifested through (1) the "stop and frisk" technique used on African Americans who may be less likely to possess a weapon than their White counterparts and (2) the slayings of unarmed African Americans by the police and the constant criminalization of these victims (e.g., George Floyd) by law enforcement and media outlets. Police killings are framed as modern-day lynching[145] with legal policies akin to Jim Crow laws; all are contemporary embodiments of racism.[146]

Disagreement with Critical Race Theory

It is important to mention that critical race theory has been criticized by activists and scholars alike. For example, Christopher Rufo (2021),[147] a Georgetown University graduate and a documentary filmmaker for *PBS*, believes that critical race theory is a smokescreen for neo-Marxist identity politics championed by the New Left in Western academia and the mainstream media. **Identity politics** denotes a political approach by which individuals of a particular race, gender, religion, social status, or other category develop political agendas based on core characteristics of such categories.[148] Furthermore, just like intersectionality, identity politics interlocks systems of oppression that may impact the lives of members of any of those groups and promotes political agendas based on the shared experiences of oppression of members of those groups against the White dominant identity—which, today, still accounts for the largest racial group in the West.[149]

Wilfred Reilly (2020),[150] Associate Professor of Political Science at Kentucky State University, thinks that critical race theory and identity politics are dividing people more than anything else. Gitlin (1995)[151] corroborates this argument when he writes that "what began as an assertion of dignity, a recovery from exclusion and denigration, and a demand for representation, has also developed a hardening of its boundaries." Ayaan Hirsi Ali (2021),[152] a Somali-born activist and best-selling author, calls identity politics a type of "tribalism" that is "dividing our nation." Rufo (2021)[153] adds that critical race theorists disseminate tropes that are filled with identity politics—e.g., "equity," "social justice," "diversity," "inclusion," and "culturally responsive teaching"—to avoid employing "neo-Marxism" in their campaigns because it would be less persuasive ("equity" can be considered code for Marxism). In the end, Rufo continues, critical race theorists want to plant and breed division within society. Rufo goes as far as saying that they "reject equality" because equality is tantamount to "mere nondiscrimination" and is camouflage for White supremacism, patriarchy, and authoritarianism.[154]

Some commentators on critical race theory came up with the term "wokeism." In an attempt to put an end to racism and social injustice,[155] **wokeism** (or **wokeness**) is the "ideology that views reality as socially constructed and defined by power, oppression, and group identity."[156] In his book titled *Woke Racism: How a New Religion Has Betrayed Black America*, John McWhorter (2021),[157] Associate Professor of Linguistics at Columbia University, and a self-identified Black Democrat, criticizes wokeism as being pejorative and an exaggeration of victimhood on the part of critical race theorists and activists. McWhorter goes as far as saying that present-day antiracist campaigns in the United States actually harm the African–American community because they infantilize Black people or treat them as simpletons. More importantly, antiracist campaigns, he continues, are so noxious that they contain a racial essentialism that bears close resemblance to White supremacist arguments of the past.

Fundamentally, today's antiracism of today is a form of racism. This is why he believes that aggressive efforts should not be made to decenter Whiteness.

Critical Social Justice

A similar theoretical concept, **critical social justice** approaches the phenomenon of social justice by describing inequality as deeply entrenched within the fabric of society. However, it places more emphasis on groups rather than individuals and on how social injustice leads to unfair access to resources between those groups.[158] Critical social justice prioritizes the aforementioned equity over equality; favors collectivism over individualism; considers healthcare as a right for all; confronts neoliberal policies; and associates racialization, cultural degradation, and discrimination with the key drivers for social injustice.[159] A critical social justice frame elicits profoundly moral questions. For instance, why do particular groups disproportionately suffer from illnesses? Or what are the social contributors to differences in healthcare and social status?[160]

Just like critical race theory and identity politics, critical social justice points the finger at social privilege and Whiteness. **Social privilege** denotes special treatment or favoritism in society. It clearly benefits certain groups to the detriment of others.[161] A certain number of academics, like Peggy McIntosh (2019),[162] demonstrate a pattern where those who benefit from social privilege refuse to admit it. Such a denial, then, creates even more instances of injustice against those who do not enjoy the same social privilege. Social privilege is a meaningful ethical approach from which to explain differential treatment of BIPOC by police forces.

Whiteness denotes the societal privilege that benefits White people over non-White people in certain areas, particularly White people who find themselves in similar social, political, or financial situations.[163] Grounded in European colonialism and imperialism, and the Atlantic slave trade, Whiteness has spawned an innumerable amount of policies and situations, in the West, that have managed to protect White racial privileges, national citizenships, and other categories of rights and benefits.[164] Critical social justice theorists claim that institutions of higher education sustain inequality through supremacy, patriarchy, class-based differentials, and White normativity.[165] Peggy McIntosh (1989)[166] wrote that White normativity emerges when privileging White attitudes and forms of knowledge becomes neutral and commonplace.

NOTES

1. Henrika McCoy, "Black Lives Matter, and Yes, You Are Racist: The Parallelism of the Twentieth and Twenty-First Centuries," *Child and Adolescent Social Work Journal* 37 (2020): 463–75. https://doi.org/10.1007/s10560-020-00690-4.
2. Marlene F. Watson, William L. Turner, and Paulette Moore Hines, "Black Lives Matter: We Are in the Same Storm But We Are Not in the Same Boat," *Family Process* 59, no. 4 (2020): 1362–73. https://doi.org/10.1111/famp.12613.
3. Fabio Rojas, "Moving Beyond the Rhetoric: A Comment on Szetela's Critique of the Black Lives Matter Movement," *Ethnic and Racial Studies* 43, no. 8 (2020): 1407–13. https://doi.org/10.1080/01419870.2020.1718725.
4. Olga M. Segura, *Birth of a Movement: Black Lives Matter and the Catholic Church* (Ossining, NY: Orbis Books, 2021).

5. Rojas, "Moving beyond the Rhetoric," 1407.

6. Melissa Repko, "Target Says It Will Spend More Than $2 Billion with Black-Owned Businesses by 2025," *CNBC* (April 7, 2021). Retrieved on April 8, 2021 from https://www.cnbc.com/2021/04/07/target-to-spend-2-billion-with-black-owned-businesses-by-2025.html.

7. Adam Szetela, "Black Lives Matter at Five: Limits and Possibilities," *Ethnic and Racial Studies* 43, no. 8 (2020): 1358–83. https://doi.org/10.1080/01419870.2019.1638955.

8. Jelani Ince, Fabio Rojas, and Clayton A. Davis, "The Social Media Response to Black Lives Matter: How Twitter Users Interact with Black Lives Matter through Hashtag Use," *Ethnic and Racial Studies* 40, no. 11 (2017): 1814–30. https://doi.org/10.1080/0141 9870.2017.1334931.

9. Kim Parker, Juliana Menasce Horowitz, and Monica Anderson, *Amid Protests, Majorities Across Racial and Ethnic Groups Express Support for the Black Lives Matter Movement* (Washington, D.C.: Pew Research Center, 2020).

10. Nikita Carney, "All Lives Matter, but So Does Race: Black Lives Matter and the Evolving Role of Social Media," *Humanity & Society* 40, no. 2 (2016): 180–99. https://doi.org/10.1177/0160597616643868.

11. Shalonda Kelly, Gihane Jérémie-Brink, Anthony L. Chambers, and Mia A. Smith-Bynum, "The Black Lives Matter Movement: A Call to Action for Couple and Family Therapists," *Family Process* 59, no. 4 (2020): 1374–88. https://doi.org/10.1111/famp.12614.

12. Julius Bailey and David J. Leonard, "Black Lives Matter: Post-Nihilistic Freedom Dreams," *Journal of Contemporary Rhetoric* 5, no. 3 (2015): 67–77.

13. Myrtle P. Bell, Daphne Berry, Joy Leopold, and Stella Nkomo, "Making Black Lives Matter in Academia: A Black Feminist Call for Collective Action Against Anti-Blackness in the Academy," *Gender, Work, & Organization* 28, no. S1 (2021): 39–57. https://doi.org/10.1111/gwao.12555.

14. Watson, Turner, and Hines "Black Lives Matter," 1362–5.

15. Joy Leopold and Myrtle P. Bell, "News Media and the Racialization of Protest: An Analysis of Black Lives Matter Articles," *Equality, Diversity and Inclusion* 36, no. 8 (2017): 720–35. https://doi.org/10.1108/EDI-01-2017-0010.

16. Cited in Jonathan Capehart, "John Lewis to Black Lives Matter Protesters: 'Give Until You Cannot Give Any More'," *The Washington Post* (June 10, 2020): A1. Retrieved on March 12, 2021 from https://www.washingtonpost.com/opinions/2020/06/10/john-lewis-black-lives-matter-protesters-give-until-you-cannot-give-any-more.

17. Matt Furber, Audra D. S. Burch, and Frances Robles, "What Happened in the Chaotic Moments Before George Floyd Died," *The New York Times* (May 29, 2020). Retrieved on March 12, 2021 from https://www.nytimes.com/2020/05/29/us/derek-chauvin-george-floyd-worked-together.html; Evan Hill, Ainara Tiefenthäler, Christiaan Triebert, Drew Jordan, Haley Willis, and Robin Stein, "8 Minutes and 46 Seconds: How George Floyd Was Killed in Police Custody," *The New York Times* (May 31, 2020): A1. Retrieved on March 12, 2021 from https://www.nytimes.com/2020/05/31/us/george-floyd-investigation.html.

18. Larry Buchanan, Quoctrung Bui, and Jugal K. Patel, "Black Lives Matter May Be the Largest Movement in US History," *The New York Times* (July 3, 2020): A1. Retrieved on March 12, 2021 from https://www.nytimes.com/interactive/2020/07/03/us/george-floyd-protests-crowd-size.html.

19. Holly Bailey, "Derek Chauvin Guilty of Murder and Manslaughter in the Death of George Floyd," *The Washington Post* (April 20, 2021): A1. Retrieved on May 11, 2021 from https://www.washingtonpost.com/nation/2021/04/20/guilty-verdict-chauvin-trial.

20. Bell, Berry, Leopold, and Nkomo, "Making Black Lives Matter in Academia," 42.

21. Aamna Mohdin, "Black Lives Matter UK to Start Funding Groups from £1.2m Donations" *The Guardian* (February 18, 2021): A1. Retrieved on March 12, 2021 from https://www.theguardian.com/world/2021/jan/11/black-lives-matter-uk-to-start-funding-groups-from-12m-donations.

22. Juman Simaan, "Occupational Apartheid in Palestine, Global Racism, and Transnational Solidarity: Update on Simaan (2017)," *Journal of Occupational Science.* https://doi.org/10.1080/14427591.2021.1880265.

23. Aamna Mohdin, "Black Lives Matter UK to Give £600,000 in Funding to Campaign Groups," *The Guardian* (January 11, 2021): A1. Retrieved on March 12, 2021 from https://www.theguardian.com/world/2021/feb/18/black-lives-matter-uk-to-give-600000-in-funding-to-campaign-groups.

24. Russell Rickford, "Black Lives Matter: Toward a Modern Practice of Mass Struggle," *New Labor Forum* 25, no. 1 (2016): 34–42. https://doi.org/10.1177/1095796015620171.

25. Ibid, 37–9.

26. Georgina, Hickey, "The Respectability Trap: Gender Conventions in 20th Century Movements for Social Change," *Journal of Interdisciplinary Feminist Thought* 7, no. 1 (2013): Article 2.

27. Allissa V. Richardson, "Dismantling Respectability: The Rise of New Womanist Communication Models in the Era of Black Lives Matter," *Journal of Communication* 69, no. 2 (2019): 193–213. https://doi.org/10.1093/joc/jqz005.

28. Robert D. Benford and David A. Snow, "Framing Processes and Social Movements: An Overview and Assessment," *Annual Review of Sociology* 26, no. 1 (2000): 611–39. https://doi.org/10.1146/annurev.soc.26.1.611; Erving Goffman, *Frame Analysis: An Essay on the Organization of Experience* (Cambridge, MA: Harvard University Press, 1974).

29. Kevin Drakulich, Kevin H. Wozniak, John Hagan, and Devon Johnson, "Race and Policing in the 2016 Presidential Election: Black Lives Matter, the Police, and Dog Whistle Politics," *Criminology* 58 (2020): 370–402. https://doi.org/10.1111/1745-9125.12239.

30. María Florencia Langa and Philip Creswell, "Aligned with the Dead: Representations of Victimhood and the Dead in Anti-Police Violence Activism Online," in *Death Matters: Cultural Sociology of Mortal Life*, ed. Tora Holmberg, Annika Jonsson, and Fredrik Palm (New York: Palgrave Macmillan, 2019): 199–220, 212–3.

31. Ibid, 213.

32. Osagie K. Obasogie and Zachary Newman, "Police Violence, Use of Force Policies, and Public Health," *American Journal of Law & Medicine* 43 (2017): 279–95. https://doi.org/10.1177/0098858817723665.

33. Leonard N. Moore, *Black Rage in New Orleans: Police Brutality and African American Activism from World War II to Hurricane Katrina* (Baton Rouge, LA: Louisiana State University Press, 2010).

34. Hannah L. F. Cooper and Mindy Fullilove, "Editorial: Excessive Police Violence as a Public Health Issue," *Journal of Urban Health* 93, no. 1 (2016): S1–7. https://doi.org/10.1007/s11524-016-0040-2.

35. Available at https://www.statista.com/statistics/585152/people-shot-to-death-by-us-police-by-race.

36. Cited in Sirry Alang, Donna McAlpine, Ellen McCreedy, and Rachel Hardeman, "Police Brutality and Black Health: Setting the Agenda for Public Health Scholars," *American Journal of Public Health* 107, no. 5 (2017): 662–5. https://doi.org/10.2105/AJPH.2017.303691.

37. Langa and Creswell, "Aligned with the Dead," 215.

38. Ibid, 215.

39. Krithika, Varagur, "How Black Lives Matter Activists Plan to 'Check the Police'," *The Huffington Post* (January 15, 2017). Retrieved on March 13, 2021 from https://www.huffingtonpost.com/entry/police-union-contract-project_us_565f4193e4b08e945fedb444.

40. Vanessa Lopez-Littleton, Brandi Blessett, and Julie Burr, "Advancing Social Justice and Racial Equity in the Public Sector," *Journal of Public Affairs Education* 24, no. 4 (2018): 449–68. https://doi.org/10.1080/15236803.2018.1490546.

41. Harold Pollack, "A Crime and Policing Expert Critiques Black Lives Matter's Police-Reform Plan," *New York Magazine* (August 24, 2015). Retrieved on March 13, 2021 from https://www.thecut.com/2015/08/expert-critiques-black-lives-matters-plan.html.

42. Conor Friedersdorf, "Will Black Lives Matter Be a Movement That Persuades?" *The Atlantic* (September 24, 2015). Retrieved on March 13, 2021 from https://www.theatlantic.com/politics/archive/2015/09/will-black-lives-matter-be-a-movement-that-per-suades/407017.

43. Langa and Creswell, "Aligned with the Dead," 215–22.

44. Cited in Obasogie and Newman, "Police Violence, Use of Force Policies," 281.

45. Charles W. Mills, "White Supremacy as Sociopolitical System: A Philosophical Perspective," in *White Out: The Continuing Significance of Racism*, ed. Ashley W. Doane and Eduardo Bonilla-Silva (New York: Routledge, 2003): 35–48.

46. J. Phillip Thompson, "Broken Policing: The Origins of the 'Broken Windows' Policy," *New Labor Forum* 24, no. 2 (2015): 42–7. https://doi.org/10.1177/1095796015579993.

47. Alecia McGregor, "Politics, Police Accountability, and Public Health: Civilian Review in Newark, New Jersey," *Journal of Urban Health* 93, no. 1 (2016): 141–53. https://doi.org/10.1007/s11524-015-9998-4.

48. Orisanmi Burton, "To Protect and Serve Whiteness," *North American Dialogue* 18, no. 2 (2015): 38–50.

49. Ronald Weitzer and Rod K. Brunson, "Strategic Responses to the Police among Inner-City Youth," *The Sociological Quarterly* 50, no. 2 (2009): 235–56. https://doi.org/10.1111/j.1533-8525.2009.01139.x.

50. Rickford, "Black Lives Matter," 36.

51. Catherine Ringaux and J. Barton Cunningham, "Enhancing Recruitment and Retention of Visible Minority Police Officers in Canadian Policing Agencies," *Policing and Society* 31, no. 4 (2021): 454–82. https://doi.org/10.1080/10439463.2020.1750611.

52. Ben Brucato, "Policing Made Visible: Mobile Technologies and the Importance of Point of View," *Surveillance & Society* 13, no. 3 (2015): 455–73. https://doi.org/10.24908/ss.v13i3/4.5421.

53. See www.joincampaignzero.org.

54. Steven G. Brandl and Meghan S. Stroshine, "The Role of Officer Attributes, Job Characteristics, and Arrest Activity in Explaining Police Use-of-Force," *Criminal Justice Policy Review* 24, no. 5 (2012): 551–72, 564. https://doi.org/10.1177/0887403412452424.

55. Cited in Burton, "To Protect and Serve Whiteness," 43.

56. Jonathan Mummolo, "Re-Evaluating Police Militarization," *Nature Human Behaviour* 5 (2021): 181–2.

57. Ibid, 81–2.

58. See www.joincampaignzero.org.

59. *Boston Globe*, "Don't Let Labor Agreements Thwart Police Accountability," *Boston Globe* (2020, June 4): A1. Retrieved on March 13, 2021 from https://www.bostonglobe.com/2020/06/04/opinion/dont-let-labor-agreements-thwart-police-accountability/?event=event25.

60. Michelle Fine and Jessica Ruglis, "Circuits and Consequences of Dispossession: The Racialized Realignment of the Public Sphere for US Youth," *Transforming Anthropology* 17, no. 1 (2009): 20–33. https://doi.org/10.1111/j.1548-7466.2009.01037.x; Chris Hayes, *A Colony in a Nation* (New York: W. W. Norton & Company, 2017).

61. Ashley W. Doane, "Rethinking Whiteness Studies," in *White Out: The Continuing Significance of Racism*, ed. Ashley W. Doane and Eduardo Bonilla-Silva (New York: Routledge, 2003): 3–18.

62. Available at http://digital.auraria.edu/content/AA/00/00/68/08/00001/AA00006808_00001.pdf.

63. Robert Bernasconi, "When Police Violence Is More Than Violent Policing," *The New Centennial Review* 14, no. 2 (2014): 145–52. https://doi.org/10.14321; Steve Martinot, "On the Epidemic of Police Killings," *Social Justice* 39, no. 4 (2014): 52–75.

64. See www.joincampaignzero.org.

65. Obasogie and Newman, "Police Violence, Use of Force Policies," 280.

66. Derald Wing Sue, "A Model for Cultural Diversity Training," *Journal of Counseling & Development* 70, no. 1 (1991): 99–105. https://doi.org/10.1002/j.1556-6676.1991.tb01568.x.

67. Ibram X. Kendi, *How to Be an Antiracist* (New York: One World, 2019).

68. Diane C. Emling, *Institutional Racism and Restorative Justice: Oppression and Privilege in America* (New York: Routledge, 2019).

69. Cited in Reshawna L. Chapple, George A. Jacinto, Tameca N. Harris-Jackson, and Michelle Vance, "Do #BlackLivesMatter? Implicit Bias, Institutional Racism and Fear of the Black Body," *Ralph Bunche Journal of Public Affairs* 6, no. 1 (2017): Article 2.

70. Bailey and Leonard, "Black Lives Matter," 68–9.

71. For example, see Candice LaShara Edrington and Nicole Lee, "Tweeting a Social Movement: Black Lives Matter and its use of Twitter to Share Information, Build Community, and Promote Action," *Journal of Public Interest Communications* 2, no. 2 (2018): 10–21. https://doi.org/10.32473/jpic.v2.i2.p289; Charles Athanasopoulos Sugino, "Smashing the Icon of *Black Lives Matter*: Afropessimism & Religious Iconolatry," *Prose Studies* 40, no. 1 (2018): 71–91. https://doi.org/10.1080/01440357.2019.1656400.

72. Available at https://www.saisia.ca/black_lives_matter__psa.

73. Brandi Blessett and Vanessa Littleton, "Examining the Impact of Institutional Racism in Black Residentially Segregated Communities," *Ralph Bunche Journal of Public Affairs* 6, no. 1 (2017): Article 3.

74. Anne Warfield Rawls and Waverly Duck, "'Fractured Reflections' of High-Status Black Male Presentations of Self: Nonrecognition of Identity as a 'Tacit' Form of Institutional Racism," *Sociological Focus* 50, no. 1 (2017): 36–51. https://doi.org/10.1080/00380237.2016.1218215.

75. Kiara C. Wesley, "Disparities in Mental Health Care and Homeownership for African Americans and Latinos in the United States," in *Diversity in Couple and Family Therapy: Ethnicities, Sexualities, and Socioeconomics*, ed. Shalonda Kelly (Santa Barbara, CA: Praeger, 2017): 393–419.

76. Terrance Ruth, Jonathan Matusitz, and Demi Simi, "Ethics of Disenfranchisement and Voting Rights in the US: Convicted Felons, the Homeless, and Immigrants," *American Journal of Criminal Justice* 42, no. 1 (2017): 56–68. https://doi.org/10.1007/s12103-016-9346-6.

77. Blessett and Littleton, "Examining the Impact of Institutional Racism," Article 3.

78. Susan T. Gooden, *Race and Social Equity: A Nervous Area of Government* (New York: M. E. Sharpe, 2014).

79. Patricia Hill Collins, "The Difference That Power Makes: Intersectionality and Participatory Democracy," in *The Palgrave Handbook of Intersectionality in Public Policy: The Politics of Intersectionality*," ed. Olena Hankivsky and Julia S. Jordan-Zachery (New York: Palgrave Macmillan, 2019): 167–92.

80. E. Frances White, *Dark Continent of Our Bodies: Black Feminism and the Politics of Respectability* (Philadelphia, PA: Temple University Press, 2001).

81. Rickford, "Black Lives Matter," 36.

82. Wei Ling Nien, "What Is the Role of Social Media in Establishing a Chain of Equivalence between Activists Participating in Protest Movements?" *Online Journal of Communication and Media Technologies* 7, no. 3 (2017): 182–215. https://doi.org/10.29333/ojcmt/2606.

83. Hyesun Hwang and Kee-Ok Kim, "Social Media as a Tool for Social Movements: The Effect of Social Media Use and Social Capital on Intention to Participate in Social Movements," *International Journal of Consumer Studies* 39, no. 5 (2015): 478–88. https://doi.org/10.1111/ijcs.12221.

84. Jill M. Bystydzienski and Steven P. Schacht, *Forging Radical Alliances across Difference: Coalition Politics for the New Millennium* (Lanham, MD: Rowman & Littlefield, 2001); R. Chávez Karma, "Counter-Public Enclaves and Understanding the Function of Rhetoric in Social Movement Coalition-Building," *Communication Quarterly* 59, no. 1 (2011): 1–18. https://doi.org/10.1080/01463373.2010.541333.

85. Marcia Mundt, Karen Ross, and Charla M. Burnett, "Scaling Social Movements through Social Media: The Case of Black Lives Matter," *Social Media + Society* (2018). https://doi.org/10.1177/2056305118807911.

86. Ruth Milkman, "A New Political Generation: Millennials and the Post-2008 Wave of Protest," *American Sociological Review* 82, no. 1 (2017): 1–31. https://doi.org/10.1177/0003122416681031.

87. Mundt, Ross, and Burnett, "Scaling Social Movements through Social Media".

88. James Dennis, *Beyond Slacktivism: Political Participation on Social Media* (New York: Palgrave Macmillan, 2018).

89. Jozie Nummi, Carly Jennings, and Joe Feagin, "#BlackLivesMatter: Innovative Black Resistance," *Sociological Forum* 34, no. 1 (2019): 1042–64. https://doi.org/10.1111/socf.12540.

90. Mundt, Ross, and Burnett, "Scaling Social Movements through Social Media" (no page number available).

91. Patricia Hill Collins and Sirma Bilge, *Intersectionality* (Cambridge: Polity, 2016).

92. Kimberlé Crenshaw, "Demarginalizing the Intersection of Race and Sex: A Black Feminist Critique of Antidiscrimination Doctrine, Feminist Theory and Antiracist Politics," *University of Chicago Legal Forum* 4 (1989): 139–67.

93. Ange-Marie Hancock, *Intersectionality: An Intellectual History* (New York: Oxford University Press, 2016): 187.

94. Ann Pheonix, "Editorial: Intersectionality," *European Journal of Women's Studies* 13 (2006): 187–92.

95. Ellis Furman, Amandeep Kaur Singh, Natasha A. Darko, and Ciann Larose Wilson, "Activism, Intersectionality, and Community Psychology: The Way in Which Black Lives Matter Toronto Helps Us to Examine White Supremacy in Canada's LGBTQ Community," *Community Psychology in Global Perspective* 4, no. 2 (2018): 34–54.

96. Michel Foucault, "The Ethics of the Concern of the Self as a Practice of Freedom," in *Michel Foucault: Ethics, Subjectivity and Truth*, ed. Paul Rabinow (New York: The New Press, 1997): 281–301.

97. Brooke Ackerly and Rose McDermott, "Recent Developments in Intersectionality Research: Expanding beyond Race and Gender," *Politics & Gender* 8, no. 3 (2011): 367–70. https://doi.org/10.1017/S1743923X12000359; Rita Kaur Dhamoon, "Considerations on Mainstreaming Intersectionality," *Political Research Quarterly* 64, no. 1 (2011): 230–43. https://doi.org/10.1177/1065912910379227.

98. Anastasia Vakulenko, "'Islamic Headscarves' and the European Convention on Human Rights: An Intersectional Perspective," *Social & Legal Studies* 16, no. 2 (2007): 183–99. https://doi.org/10.1177/0964663907076527.

99. Ladelle McWhorter, "Sex, Race, and Biopower: A Foucauldian Genealogy," *Hypatia* 19, no. 3 (2004): 38–62, 55.

100. Sherene Razack, "Speaking for Ourselves: Feminist Jurisprudence and Minority Women," *Canadian Journal of Women and the Law* 4 (1991): 400–58, 454.

101. Davina Cooper, "'And You Can't Find Me Nowhere': Relocating Identity and Structure within Equality Jurisprudence," *Journal of Law and Society* 27, no. 2 (2000): 249–72. https://doi.org/10.1111/1467–6478.00153.

102. Vakulenko, "'Islamic Headscarves'," 185.

103. Andrew Arato, *From Neo-Marxism to Democratic Theory: Essays on the Critical Theory of Soviet-Type Societies* (New York: Routledge, 2016).

104. Raymond Murphy, "The Concept of Class in Closure Theory: Learning from Rather than Falling into the Problems Encountered by Neo-Marxism," *Sociology* 20, no. 2 (1986): 247–64. https://doi.org/10.1177/0038038586020002006.

105. K. L. Julka, "Herbert Marcuse's Messianic Humanism: Politics of the New Left," *Social Scientist* 7, no. 12 (1979): 13–23. https://doi.org/10.2307/3516740.

106. Alex Callinicos, *Against Postmodernism: A Marxist Critique* (Cambridge: Polity, 1999); Perry Anderson, *The Origins of Postmodernity* (London: Verso, 1998).

107. Kimberlé Crenshaw, "Demarginalising the Intersection of Race and Sex: A Black Feminist Critique of Antidiscrimination Doctrine, Feminist Theory and Antiracist Politics," in *Framing Intersectionality: Debates on a Multi-Faceted Concept in Gender Studies*, ed. by Helma Lutz, Maria Teresa Herrera Vivar, and Linda Supik (Farnham, England; Ashgate, 2011): 21–33.

108. Catharine A. MacKinnon, "Intersectionality as Method: A Note," *Signs* 38, no. 4 (2013): 1019–30.

109. Crenshaw, "Demarginalizing the Intersection of Race and Sex," 150.

110. Jenifer Becker, "Active Allyship," *Public Services Quarterly* 13, no. 1 (2017): 27–31. https://doi.org/10.1080/15228959.2016.1261638.

111. Lisa Droogendyk, Stephen C. Wright, Micah Lubensky, and Winnifred R. Louis, "Acting in Solidarity: Cross-Group Contact between Disadvantaged Group Members and Advantaged Group Allies," *Journal of Social Issues* 72, no. 2 (2016): 315–34. https://doi.org/10.1111/josi.12168.

112. Emina Subašić, Katehrine J. Reynolds, and John C. Turner, "The Political Solidarity Model of Social Change: Dynamics of Self-Categorization in Intergroup Power Relations," *Personality and Social Psychology Review* 12, no. 4 (2008): 330–52. https://doi.org/10.1177/1088868308323223.

113. Samantha A. Montgomery and Abigail J. Stewart, "Privileged Allies in Lesbian and Gay Rights Activism: Gender, Generation, and Resistance to Heteronormativity," *Journal of Social Issues* 68, no. 1 (2012): 162–77. http://dx.doi.org/10.1111/j.1540-4560.2012.01742.x.

114. Sarah J. Jackson, "(Re)Imagining Intersectional Democracy from Black Feminism to Hashtag Activism," *Women's Studies in Communication* 39, no. 4 (2016): 375–9. http://dx.doi.org/10.1080/07491409.2016.1226654.

115. Andrea Smith, "Heteropatriarchy and the Three Pillars of White Supremacy: Rethinking Women of Color Organizing," in Color of Violence: The Incite! Anthology, ed. *Incite! Women of Color Against Violence* (Cambridge, MA: South End Press, 2006): 66–73.

116. Jackson, "(Re)Imagining Intersectional Democracy," 375–6.

117. Alicia Garza, "A Herstory of the #BlackLivesMatter Movement by Alicia Garza," *The Feminist Wire* (October 7, 2014): A1. Retrieved on March 15, 2021 from https://www.thefeministwire.com/2014/10/blacklivesmatter–2.

118. Blair Imani, *Modern HERstory* (Berleley, CA: Ten Speed Press, 2018).

119. Available at https://thefeministwire.com/2014/10/blacklivesmatter–2.

120. Milagros Castillo-Montoya, Joshua Abreu, and Abdul Abad, "Racially Liberatory Pedagogy: A Black Lives Matter Approach to Education," *International Journal of Qualitative Studies in Education* 32, no. 9 (2019): 1125–45. https://doi.org/10.1080/0951 8398.2019.1645904.

121. Jackson, "(Re)Imagining Intersectional Democracy," 376.

122. Rickford, "Black Lives Matter," 39.

123. Angela Harris and Zeus Leonardo, "Intersectionality, Race-Gender Subordination, and Education," *Review of Research in Education* 42, no. 1 (2018): 1–27. https://doi.org/10.3102/0091732X18759071.

124. Smith, "Heteropatriarchy and the Three Pillars of White Supremacy," 66–73.

125. Sarah-Joyce Battersby, "Black Lives Matter Protest Scores Victory after Putting Pride Parade on Pause," *Toronto Star* (July 3, 2016): A1. Retrieved on March 15, 2021 from https://www.thestar.com/news/gta/2016/07/03/black-lives-matter-protest-scores-victory-after-putting-pride-parade-on-pause.html.

126. Anna Carastathis, "Identity Categories as Potential Coalitions," *Signs: Journal of Women in Culture and Society* 38, no. 4 (2013): 941–65. https://doi.org/10.1086/669573.

127. Taylor Simmons, "'Enough Is Enough': Pride Toronto Board Member Explains Decision to Ban Police from Parade," *CBC News Toronto* (January 23, 2017). Retrieved on March 15, 2021 from http://www.cbc.ca/news/canada/toronto/pride-board-member-response-1.3947820.

128. Ali Greey, "Queer Inclusion Precludes (Black) Queer Disruption: Media Analysis of the Black Lives Matter Toronto Sit-In during Toronto Pride 2016," *Leisure Studies* 37, no. 6 (2018): 662–76. https://doi.org/10.1080/02614367.2018.1468475.

129. Dominique Thomas and Allana Zuckerman, "Black Lives Matter in Community Psychology," *Community Psychology in Global Perspective* 4, no. 2 (2018): 1–8.

130. Khyree D. Davis, "Transnational Blackness at Toronto Pride: Queer Disruption as Theory and Method," *Gender, Place & Culture* (2021). https://doi.org/10.1080/0966369X.2020.1819208.

131. Gary W. Harper and Margaret Schneider, "Oppression and Discrimination among Lesbian, Gay, Bisexual, and Transgendered People and Communities: A Challenge for Community Psychology," *American Journal of Community Psychology* 31, no. 3 (2003): 243–52, 251. https://doi.org/10.1023/a:1023906620085.

132. Furman, Singh, Darko, and Wilson, "Activism, Intersectionality, and Community Psychology," 45.

133. Gaile Pohlhaus, "Knowing Communities: An Investigation of Harding's Standpoint Epistemology," *Social Epistemology* 16, no. 3 (2002): 283–98. https://doi.org/10.1080/0269172022000025633.

134. Sandra Harding, *The Feminist Standpoint Theory Reader: Intellectual and Political Controversies* (New York: Routledge, 2003).

135. Maheshvari Naidu, "Wrestling with Standpoint Theory … Some Thoughts on Standpoint and African Feminism," *Agenda* 24, no. 83 (2010): 24–35.

136. Patricia Hill Collins, "Comment on Hekman's 'Truth and Method: Feminist Standpoint Theory Revisited': Where's the Power?" *Signs: Journal of Women in Culture and Society* 22, no. 2 (1997): 375–81. https://doi.org/10.1086/495162.

137. Bell, Berry, Leopold, and Nkomo, "Making Black Lives Matter in Academia," 43.

138. Kimberlé Crenshaw, Neil Gotanda, Gary Peller, and Kendall Thomas, *Critical Race Theory: The Key Writings That Formed the Movement* (New York: New Press, 1995).

139. Tony N. Brown, "Critical Race Theory Speaks to the Sociology of Mental Health: Mental Health Problems Produced by Racial Stratification," *Journal of Health and Social Behavior* 44, no. 3 (2003): 292–301. https://doi.org/10.2307/1519780.

140. Christine Jollst and Cass R. Sunstein, "The Law of Implicit Bias," *California Law Review* 94 (2006): 969–96.

141. Derald Wing Sue, *Microaggressions and Marginality: Manifestation, Dynamics, and Impact* (Hoboken, NJ: Wiley, 2010).

142. Anne Gregory and Rhona S. Weinstein, "The Discipline Gap and African Americans: Defiance or Cooperation in the High School Classroom," *Journal of School Psychology* 46, no. 4 (2008): 455–75. https://doi.org/10.1016/j.jsp.2007.09.001.

143. Linda A. Cedeno, Maurice J. Elias, Shalonda Kelly, and Brian C. Chu, "School Violence, Adjustment, and the Influence of Hope on Low-Income, African American Youth," *American Journal of Orthopsychiatry* 80, no. 2 (2010): 213–26. https://doi.org/10.1111/j.1939-0025.2010.01025.x.

144. Rashmita S. Mistry, Elizabeth A. Vandewater, Aletha C. Huston, and Vonnie C. McLoyd, "Economic Well-Being and Children's Social Adjustment: The Role of Family Process in an Ethnically Diverse Low-Income Sample," *Child Development* 73, no. 3 (2002): 935–51. https://doi.org/10.1111/1467-8624.00448.

145. David G. Embrick, "Two Nations, Revisited: The Lynching of Black and Brown Bodies, Police Brutality, and Police Control in 'Post-Racial' Amerikkka," *Critical Sociology* 41, no. 6 (2015): 835–43. https://doi.org/10.1177/0896920515591950.

146. Raygine Diaquoi, "Symbols in the Strange Fruit Seeds: What 'the Talk' Black Parents Have with Their Sons Tells Us about Racism," *Harvard Educational Review* 87, no. 4 (2017): 512–37. https://doi.org/10.17763.

147. Christopher F. Rufo, "What Critical Race Theory Is Really About," *The New York Post* (May 6, 2021): A1. Retrieved on May 12, 2021 from https://nypost.com/2021/05/06/what-critical-race-theory-is-really-about.

148. Mary Bernstein, "Identity Politics," *Annual Review of Sociology* 31 (2005): 47–74. https://doi.org/10.1146/annurev.soc.29.010202.100054; Todd McGowan, *Universality and Identity Politics* (New York: Columbia University Press, 2020).

149. Ashley Jardina, *White Identity Politics* (Cambridge: Cambridge University Press, 2019).

150. Wilfred Reilly, *Taboo: 10 Facts You Can't Talk About* (Washington, D.C.: Regnery Publishing, 2020).

151. Todd Gitlin, "The Rise of 'Identity Politics': An Examination and a Critique," in *Higher Education Under Fire: Politics, Economics, and the Crisis of the Humanities*, ed. Michael Berube and Cary Nelson (New York: Routledge, 2019): 308–25, 308.

152. Ayaan Hirsi Ali, "I Saw Tribalism Rip a Country Apart—and Now It's Happening in America," *The New York Post* (May 11, 2021): A1. Retrieved on May 12, 2021 from https://nypost.com/2021/05/11/i-saw-tribalism-rip-a-country-apart-and-now-its-happening-here/amp/?__twitter_impression=true.

153. Rufo, "What Critical Race Theory Is Really About," A1.

154. Ibid, A1.

155. Joseph Ching Velasco, "You Are *Cancelled*: Virtual Collective Consciousness and the Emergence of Cancel Culture as Ideological Purging," *Rupkatha Journal on Interdisciplinary Studies in Humanities* 12, no. 5 (2020): 1–7. https://dx.doi.org/10.21659/rupkatha.v12n5.rioc1s21n2.

156. Alexander Weiner, "Sleeping Woke: Cancel Culture and Simulated Religion," *Medium* (July 17, 2020). Retrieved on May 31, 2021 from https://medium.com/rebel-wisdom/sleeping-woke-cancel-culture-and-simulated-religion-5f96af2cc107.

157. John McWhorter, *Woke Racism: How a New Religion Has Betrayed Black America* (London: Portfolio, 2021).

158. Özlem Sensoy and Robin J. DiAngelo, *Is Everyone Really Equal? An Introduction to Key Concepts in Social Justice Education* (2nd Ed.) (New York: Teachers College Press, 2017).

159. Sheryl Reimer Kirkham and Annette J. Browne, "Toward a Critical Theoretical Interpretation of Social Justice Discourses in Nursing," *Advances in Nursing Science* 29, no. 4 (2006): 324–39. https://doi.org/10.1097/00012272-200610000-00006.

160. Annette J. Browne and Denise S. Tarlier, "Examining the Potential of Nurse Practitioners from a Critical Social Justice Perspective," *Nursing Inquiry* 15, no. 2 (2008): 83–93. https://doi.org/10.1111/j.1440-1800.2008.00411.x.

161. Jan Pakulski, *Globalising Inequalities: New Patterns of Social Privilege & Disadvantage* (Crows Nest, Australia: Allen & Unwin, 2005).

162. Peggy McIntosh, *On Privilege, Fraudulence, and Teaching as Learning: Selected Essays 1981–2019* (New York: Routledge, 2019).

163. Adria McCardy and Jonathan Matusitz, "Power in *Hidden Figures*: A Critical Discourse Analysis," *International Journal of Media & Cultural Politics* 17, no. 1 (2021): 3–17. https://doi.org/10.1386/macp_00035_1.
164. Helen Morgan, *The Work of Whiteness: A Psychoanalytic Perspective* (New York: Routledge, 2021).
165. bell hooks, *Teaching Community: A Pedagogy of Hope* (New York: Routledge, 2003).
166. McIntosh, *On Privilege, Fraudulence, and Teaching as Learning,*" 1–5.

PART IV

TERRORIST, EXTREMIST, AND ANTI–TERRORIST COMMUNICATION CAMPAIGNS

CHAPTER 13

Terrorist Communication Campaigns

Two Major Case Studies

This chapter defines fundamental terms related to terrorism, extremism, radicalization, indoctrination, and the weaponization of language as a whole. Two large-scale case studies, the FARC in Colombia and the Rwanda Genocide in 1994, thoroughly demonstrate how public communication campaigns can be used to turn hatred and extreme violence into an addiction or a way of life. As Lenin famously said, "the purpose of terror is to terrorize."[1] Such malevolent killing violates the most fundamental conceptions of morality that buttress most social institutions (religious and secular alike). **Terrorism** can be defined as an intentional and insensible form of violence, making it uncontrollable and, in the eyes of many, transcending the mere concept of warfare.[2] Indeed, unlike warfare, terrorism is symbolized by the political or ideological motivation of violence, the noncombatant nature of its perpetrators, and by their covert or clandestine *modus operandi*. Although terrorism causes fewer casualties than warfare (and other specific forms of violence) annually, it seems to attract as much attention from the audience.[3]

Title 22 of the United States Code defines terrorism as politically motivated violence committed in a stealthy and surreptitious manner against noncombatants. Scholars with expert knowledge in that field incorporate an additional aspect in the definition: the act is perpetrated to produce a fearful state of mind within an indirect audience—i.e., an audience that is different and usually distant from the victims. To consider an act "terrorism" or not is also contingent on whether a legal, moral, or behavioral approach is adopted to interpret the act. When a legal or moral approach is taken, the interpreter's values matter more than the act itself.[4] For Garrison (2004),[5] terrorism is "the use of terror as a tool to achieve desired goals." It is seen as psychologically more harmful than other types of catastrophes. As opposed to sociotechnical catastrophes, fury and indignation in the aftermath of a terrorist attack are an intended consequence. Indeed, the amount of casualties and suffering as a result of terrorism is attributed to intentional human actions, and its aim to cause fear within the large population is psychological warfare.[6] Given all these circumstances, terrorism is akin to "a new species of trouble" because it involves a relatively low number of people wreaking immense havoc in a very short period.[7]

VIOLENT EXTREMISM, RADICALIZATION, AND INDOCTRINATION

Violent extremism consists of many types of dangerous actions, including those who "support or commit ideologically motivated violence to further political goals."[8] In most cases, the common reasons for violent extremism are attributed to social marginalization, governmental totalitarianism, ethnic fragmentation, and poorly administered areas, where citizens suffer from an identity crisis, unfettered corruption, and violations of their basic human rights. Underdeveloped countries, in particular, experience toxic violence and violent extremism.[9] A certain number of groups, which see themselves as persecuted and marginalized (sometimes for centuries), resort to violence as a method to alleviate their unfair treatment and obtain freedom and dignity. At the same time that these groups get supported by both internal and external sources, they launch large-scale public communication campaigns for propagandistic, fundraising, and recruitment purposes.[10]

Terrorism and extremism are interlaced in many ways. It is not easy to address terrorism without tackling the danger of extremism. This is why counterterrorism practitioners deem it important to neutralize extremist propaganda to prevent additional recruitment and actions by terrorist movements.[11] Ideology is a core constituent of both terrorism and extremism. Violent extremism, in particular, has been placed at the forefront of policy-making decisions across both Western and non-Western governments, despite the difficulty in reaching an agreement on a universal definition of either terrorism or violent extremism.[12] Striegher (2015)[13] distinguishes the latter term from terrorism by arguing that extremism does not meet the threshold of terrorism because it is merely an ideology or viewpoint. On the other hand, terrorism entails intimidation, coercion, and physical violence.

Radicalization

Radicalization refers to a gradual path towards attitude and behavior change through a process of persuasion and socialization into extreme beliefs. Eventually, these extreme beliefs can translate into violent actions.[14] The concept of radicalization can have various meanings. A person can have radical ideas without actually resorting to—or even thinking about resorting to—violence to put those ideas into practice. However, in the context of this chapter, radicalization should be viewed as the proclivity to use violence (i.e., terrorist acts) in order to generate lasting changes in society. Put simply, radicalization is the path towards becoming a terrorist.[15] Radicalization is more likely when socioeconomic inequality and political outrage are the norm. Radicalized individuals often experience feelings of despair and humiliation over injustice and believe that there are no alternatives to bring about change peacefully. Radicalization can also happen for people who feel empathy for the oppressed and desire to show more than symbolic support.[16]

Because radicalization is the process by which people eventually adopt radical or extremist views,[17] there is a direct connection between extremism and violence, which tends to exacerbate the stigmatization of nonviolent communities. Radicalism is not a problem in all cases.[18] Although radical ideologies have instigated some of the worst atrocities in the history of humankind, they can also be positive drivers of social and attitudinal change (e.g., the abrogation of slavery in the United States).[19] When radicalization is designed for evil purposes, it could be best understood as the cognitive element of the path towards violence. It is the process by which we "are introduced to an overtly ideological message and belief system that encourages movement from moderate, mainstream beliefs towards extreme views."[20]

Indoctrination

Unlike radicalization, **indoctrination** is more than a process; it is an operation. More precisely, it is the operation of inculcating ideas, attitudes, beliefs, or cognitive approaches within the mind of a person. Indoctrination is more of a technique. For example, through social conditioning and emotional dependency, indoctrination precludes an individual from believing that he or she is about to become an evil terrorist, or even allowed to think.[21] Many terms can refer to this process, including brainwashing, thought reform, forceful influence, behavioral manipulation, and exploitative persuasion.[22] Indoctrination is a premeditated operation whereby the manipulator makes sure that the subjects benefit from reeducation.[23] The subjects will gradually embrace views that espouse, encourage, and legitimize terrorism as the main avenue for action. With indoctrination, radical ideas develop into "a willingness to directly support or engage in violent acts."[24] It is important to remark that radicalization is not confined to the performance of violence. Terrorist and extremist groups rely on campaigns of indoctrination that will churn out indoctrinated supporters, some of whom may never wantonly kill people *per se*, but who are still inclined to endorse the use of violence for advancing their group's agenda.[25]

TERRORIST COMMUNICATIONS

Scholars[26] have debated the scope of public communication campaigns of terrorism since the mid-twentieth century. They tend to locate the multiplicity of constraints and structures of terrorism—concentrating on how it permeates technology, public forums, academia, and even the legal system. Understanding the systems and mechanisms that trivialize acts of extreme violence and make terrorism "meaningful" is essential. An examination of authoritarian, propagandistic communication campaigns can inform us on where terrorist movements want to take us and how they want to do it.[27] As French Renaissance philosopher Montaigne reminds us, falsehood can be made truthful. Unconstrained by logic and ethics, terrorist communicators bent on weaponizing language have boundless possibilities.[28]

Terrorist vs. Traditional Communication Campaigns

Many purposes of terrorist communication campaigns are analogous to their traditional nonterrorist or nonextremist counterparts. Both terrorist and traditional versions specify what their campaigns are designed for: (1) To accomplish desired outcomes, (2) in a certain way, (3) which can only happen through a change of beliefs, attitudes, and behaviors, and (4) within a period of time. What the campaigns advocate and the expectations from the audiences are clear. As is the case with health communication campaigns, for example, terrorist groups with low visibility will have a hard time gaining visibility, as well as financial support, social support, and recruitment of volunteers. This means that they will be less likely to trigger changes in beliefs, attitudes, and behaviors within target audiences.[29] As outlined in the 10 steps of Chapter 2, campaigners, whether terrorists or health communicators, develop their strategies based on painstaking audience analysis and adapt their messages and conveyance methods accordingly.

With this said, in contrast to traditional communication campaigns, when terrorist groups integrate public relations into their message delivery strategies, they weaponize language. This is not done merely as a symbolic system, but also as a way to lay the foundations of physical violence as effectively as possible. Terrorist organizations weaponize language to intensify social anger, to aggravate the image of enemies and scapegoats, and to legitimize terror. Terrorist communication campaigns are, in and of themselves, a form of violence—according to the United States Code and that of virtually all countries in the world—not only because they incite extreme violence, but also because they produce long-term effects that go beyond the victim population. The danger of terrorism lies both in the violence itself and the communication campaigns conducted through various forms of media and channels that seek to influence and coerce the public. Among those forms of communication, terrorist narratives—that use traditional media like the radio or contemporary ones like the internet and social networking sites—are still attracting a great deal of attention. The contribution of propaganda to the process of radicalization and indoctrination is of utmost importance.[30]

Terrorist Communications until and after the Twenty-First Century

Terrorists' communication strategies cannot be separated from their political strategies, as their actions and rhetoric work in tandem towards a desired outcome and end state. Their communication goals are crafted according to such desired end state. Their main long-term communication goal is a strategic one: the spreading of their movement through global means of information to diverse audiences (i.e., the direct targeted audience, the media establishment, and even the world at large). Primarily, communication strategies serve to reshape the thought process and identity of their direct targeted audiences. Radicalization is at work here. Until the dawn of the twenty-first century, terrorists diffused their campaigns to audiences through traditional methods like televised propaganda, radio messages, one-on-one indoctrination, recorded speeches on cassette tapes, fax, and even press conferences. Then came a transformation of their strategic communications thanks to technological advances and the growing popularity of the internet. For instance, the Al-Jazeera news channel (based in Qatar) became a conduit for diffusing Osama bin Laden's jihad campaign. Al-Jazeera, in turn, provided the recorded speeches to CNN and other global news networks.[31]

Today, the internet is a public sphere for people to be recruited and radicalized for violence.[32] The deep and revolutionizing effects that online and networked technologies have on campaigning seem self-evident at this point and have already been discussed in detail in the literature.[33] As a communication means and agent of influence, the internet is a powerful conduit of propaganda. In many respects, terrorists conduct their web-based campaigns in the same manner that contemporary political campaigns use the web. Both seek to attract users, to rope them in by engaging them in a life-changing experience, to influence their needs, to recommend ways to fulfill a goal, and to inspire and guide audiences by offering them a choice and a higher-level motivation. Campaigning via social networking sites fosters opportunities for social bonding and induces the need for personal contact. These elements, highly visible on terrorist websites, can be co-opted in counterterrorist campaigns too. However, before counterterrorist campaigns are designed, campaign planners should know the profiles of would-be terrorists susceptible to recruitment, and secondly, the messages that will affect them the most. Planners also need to have a full grasp of how these people are influenced: what communication channels they favor, to whom they pay attention, the impact of peer networks, and how to reach them in the most optimal way.[34] Chapter 16 deals exclusively with this topic.

Case Study 1:   The FARC in Colombia

Also known as Fuerzas Armadas Revolucionarias de Colombia (i.e., The Revolutionary Armed Forces of Colombia), the **FARC** are a Colombian Marxist–Leninist terrorist organization that have targeted the Colombian government and innocent civilians since the 1960s. The FARC consider themselves an army and profess to defend the poor against the exploitative capitalist élite of Colombia.[35] They are the longest-continuing guerrilla group in the Western Hemisphere and one of the oldest on the planet.[36] The origins of the FARC stem from a lengthy civil war—a period of unusually cruel, protracted land battles—between the Conservatives and Liberals in that South American nation. During that phase, known as *La Violencia* (1948–58), approximately 200,000 lives were lost.[37]

Colombians on both sides of the civil war were financed and equipped by their respective parties. One of the rebel leaders was Manuel Marulanda, who would become the founder of the FARC. A peasant farmer with no official education, he led a guerilla group in 1948 that included 14 of his cousins. Talented at waging guerilla warfare against the Conservative government, Marulanda began his vocation as an insurgent.[38] In 1964, he persuaded 350 peasants to form a mobile guerilla unit, and the FARC were born. The Colombian leader was resolved on radically transforming society. For him, Colombia's democracy was exploitative and elitist. More precisely, the population was not equally divided in the arable portions of the Western part of the country. It was an economy powered by capitalist agricultural production and primary extraction industries, which had caused significant disparities within the population.[39] Soon after the birth of the FARC in 1964, the organization was able to generate funds through terrorism, narcotics trafficking, and abducting people.[40]

The FARC's Ideology

The FARC's ideology is excessively nationalist and anticapitalist, with its discourses grounded in early progressive ideology. The FARC cleverly avoid articulating their opposition rhetoric in Marxist terms even if their penchant for revolution is purely Marxist.[41] The FARC lament the chaotic effects of South-American–style democracy, perceiving Colombia's political régime as a tyrannical liberal–conservative scheme.[42] The mission of protecting the basic human rights of excluded and marginalized peasants would engender a state where real social justice would see the light of day. In the "new Colombia," the State would be "the major owner of strategic resources like oil, natural gas, carbon, gold, diamonds and nickel."[43] The FARC lay emphasis on what they regard as a continuous and structurally ingrained economic struggle, strikingly characterized by very high jobless rates, insufficient social security, profound deficiencies in healthcare and education, lack of adequate housing, and unfair access to electricity and running water. The FARC also stress the lack of affordable bank loans and infrastructure like asphalted roads linking the cities with the countryside. Underlying the massive poverty is the inequitable land reforms which remain at the core of conflict in Colombia: the fight for land.[44]

The FARC's leaders believe that they must replace the Colombian establishment, still the main target of their struggle today.[45] The leaders have used the concept of "Colombian establishment" since the end of the twentieth century, when FARC commander Alfonso Cano mentioned the "responsibility for the management of the country by what has been labeled the establishment."[46] One of the reasons for the FARC's success is attributable to the steady following among Colombia's disadvantaged, especially the peasant farmers and indigenous groups who reside in remote rural areas.[47] Some detractors advance the idea of looking at the FARC as a guerrilla organization that uses terrorist tactics to advance its objectives.[48] However, because of the high volume of civilian deaths, the FARC are considered a terrorist organization by Colombia and many foreign governments, including that of the United States. The terrorist group has amassed immense resources through the narcotic trade (e.g., coca, opium, and cannabis)—through both cultivation or security for drug traffickers.[49]

The FARC's Structure

The FARC are composed of a political wing and radical militant wing in its structure. The political arm of the FARC is concerned with the educational component of the organization. Members have to be present at cultural meetings in which they debate current political affairs.[50] They are also required to study Marxist and revolutionary propaganda. It is part of what was described as indoctrination earlier.[51] Political training is a condition for a rebel to be promoted to the level of commander, and all rank-and-file members and foot soldiers are forced to join small units of the guerrilla-endorsed Clandestine Communist Party of Colombia (PCCC).[52]

In the late 1990s, the FARC represented the largest, wealthiest, and best-equipped guerrilla organization in Latin America. Scattered among 60 war fronts, the organization counted 12,000 to 15,000 members within its ranks—up from a few thousand in the early 1980s and only a couple of hundred in the 1960s.[53] In 2002, the FARC intensified their terrorist activities against the government. They allegedly had about 170,000 members.[54] In 2003, the FARC's generated profits from blackmail, racketeering, abduction, and the narcotic trade were equivalent to 2% of Colombia's GDP.[55] During that time, the Colombian government could not wield much power in the country, and the FARC controlled 40% of territory.[56] Today, the FARC still have a considerably deep and extensive network of illegal activities.[57]

THE FARC'S COMMUNICATIONS

To launch their public communication campaigns for recruitment against the fraudulent capitalist élite of Colombia, the FARC have applied a mixture of digital communication media. They have created several Twitter feeds, a multitude of websites (each with a blog), and YouTube videos that frame their core message. Many of these online communication media are made in both Spanish and English, highlighting efforts provided by the FARC to reach out to wider audiences for their strategic communications. These modern methods of communication have complemented, instead of replacing, the traditional methods used by the FARC to diffuse messages to key audiences—e.g., press communiqués, printed materials, and radio programs.[58]

Four Types of Audiences

FARC's strategic communications are aimed at four core audiences: (1) The FARC's rank-and-file members; (2) the masses in the FARC's controlled areas; (3) Colombia's élites; and (4) the global community. The methods, messages, and goals behind the FARC's communications are adapted to each audience to a certain degree. The FARC leaders' ability and effectiveness to get their messages across to each audience are quite diverse. For the first key audience, the rank-and-file members, representatives of the terrorist group used to meet in Havana to organize press conferences and individual media interviews with both the Colombian and international media establishment to get their message out. Notwithstanding the rapid evolution of their communications and their notoriety for committing killings and wrongdoings, a great part of the FARC's message is still grounded in mid-twentieth-century ideological rhetoric.[59]

The FARC's second key audience is the Colombian populace that resides in areas where the FARC exert some degree of control. The proportion of the Colombian populace living under their control has greatly decreased since the dawn of the twenty-first century. However, even an approximation of how many people live there is hard to determine because so many illicit guerrillas that control these territories are associated with the FARC. Nor has the Colombian government managed to wield steady control over war zones. The methods employed by the FARC to extend their strategic communications to that population overlap considerably with those used for rank-and-file members. The reason is that some of the latter are located in the same areas and may not have access to digital communication media.[60]

The FARC's third key audience are the Colombian élite. Naturally, a core constituent of the élite is the government of Colombia and its negotiating personnel in Havana. The FARC's strategic communications extend beyond the government to other important political and economic players. Nevertheless, for this last group, the FARC's communication initiatives have been a profound failure because their past and current violence overshadows their tweets, online communiqués, and YouTube videos. The fourth and final key audience is the global community, including the United States. The best indication of this global messaging effort is the FARC's frequent publication of their views on multiple digital platforms in both Spanish and English. The intent of doing it English is to inform the small FARC audience in the United States, in hopes that the latter exerts influence on the US government's position *vis-à-vis* the terrorist organization and the protracted conflict in Colombia.[61]

La Voz de la Resistencia

During a public communication campaign, radio includes no visuals, but stimulates our imagination. An important radio station used by the FARC is **La Voz de la Resistencia** (*The Voice of the Resistance*). Described as a guerrilla radio program by the Colombian government, *La Voz de la Resistencia* is the most prominent station of the terrorist organization's Bolivarian Radio Network. It allows them to communicate with their audiences in the areas that they control (in Eastern and Central Colombia). The communications often deal with the FARC's "propaganda, recruitment messages, and popular local music."[62] In fact, the *Voice of the Resistance* program functions thanks to six mobile transmitters.[63] It is these mobile transmitters that enable the FARC to promise the Colombian populace that they will find a long-term solution to the "people's grievances."[64]

Though *La Voz de la Resistencia* was temporarily shut down by the Colombian military in the early 2010s,[65] the FARC's radio station can now be heard along the Colombian–Ecuadorian border. The FARC's hymn plays at 9:00 a.m., followed by popular songs, known as *vallenatos farianos*, until midday. *Vallenatos farianos* are traditional Latin American musical compositions. Core messages are delivered intermittently until 5:00 p.m. Throughout the day, the radio announcers criticize the Colombian government, which they accuse of "giving itself to the American empire," and bring up revolutionary principles like those of Simón Bolívar. FARC members or supporters send kind regards to one another. *La Voz de la Resistencia* is a venue for FARC's talents like Julian Conrado. Conrado plays the guitar and sings about love that blooms in the trenches, and trenches, resembling a bird's nest are built for savoring love. It is unmistakable that the radio-based campaign is designed to lure youths to join their ranks, to make it seem like the FARC are cool because they play music and dance segments, and comradery with one another is a staple of the organization. There is a great deal of propaganda "transmitted from the corner of resistance..." of reported military victories that will "reach the liberty of the people..." "from this war that bleeds our country." "Attention! Yanquis out of South America!"[66]

APPLYING SPEECH ACT THEORY TO THE FARC'S PUBLIC COMMUNICATION CAMPAIGNS

Developed by John L. Austin (1962)[67] and John Searle (1969),[68] **speech act theory** predicates that communicators speak to accomplish intended actions and, in that process, the public concludes or interprets intended meaning based on what those communicators uttered.[69] Speech act theory originates in Ludwig Wittgenstein's theories. An Austrian–British philosopher, Wittgenstein advanced that meaning is rooted in pragmatic tradition, illustrating the importance of using language to attain objectives within particular situations.[70] By adhering to rules to achieve a goal, communication becomes analogous to a language game. Consequently, a speech act is more than merely a meaning; words can be crafted to get things done.[71]

Locutionary, Illocutionary, and Perlocutionary Acts

Austin (1962)[72] proposes three types of speech acts: locutionary, illocutionary, and perlocutionary speech acts. **Locutionary acts** are the referential attributes of utterances; each declaration has to be meaningful, grammatically and communicatively, in a speech. Put simply, the simple utterance of words is a locutionary act. **Illocutionary acts** are acts designed to say something—which implies doing something as well. Therefore, when people speak, they promise, command, threaten, convince, and so forth. The illocutionary act "performs its deed at the moment of the utterance."[73] This also means that locutionary and illocutionary acts involve conventions. Lastly, **perlocutionary acts** are, in Austin's (1978)[74] terms, "what we bring about or achieve by saying something" and bring about certain outcomes. The differences between illocutionary and perlocutionary values of speech acts lie in the effects and consequences that they generate, as well as the reciprocity aspect of communication. Explained differently, although simultaneous effect is important for illocutionary speech acts, irrespective of the intention of the communicator, intended or unintended outcomes of communication are what matters for perlocutionary speech acts.[75]

Speech is used to describe the universe and phenomena, and to fulfill other functions and actions. In the domains of terrorism and national security, the communicator does not necessarily act in harmony with the truth, but to frame audiences in a way that will motivate them to take actions in support of the communicator's wishes—actions that are inspired by the act. In a sense, a speech act is a type of frame because the public does not know the intentions of the communicator, but the display of the speech act itself. Therefore, the truth of the issue at hand is not always relevant to the communicator except for the outcome produced.[76] From this perspective, terrorist discourse involves both illocutionary and perlocutionary speech acts. Words can lead the public to perpetrate terrorist attacks or harm others.[77] The formulations of words "suggest that linguistic injury acts like physical injury."[78]

The Bolivarian Populist Campaign

Understanding the FARC's strategic communications methods and objectives requires an analysis not only of the how, what, to whom, and why of the organization's speech acts, but also of the context in which they are made. Contemporary guerrilla warfare is mostly about winning people's "hearts and minds" and the resultant propaganda is a significant part of it. The FARC's most famous campaign was conducted under the banner of Bolivarian populism.[79] Also known as **Bolivarian Revolution**, **Bolivarian populism** is a left-leaning social movement in South America. It is named after Simón Bolívar, a nineteenth-century Latin American revolutionary leader born in Venezuela. According to the late Venezuelan president Hugo Chávez, Bolivarian populism has the mission to assemble a mass movement to apply the principles of **Bolivarianism**—popular democracy, economic autonomy, fair redistribution of revenues, and an end to political corruption—in Venezuela. He applied Bolívar's ideas from an authoritarian perspective.[80]

Bolivarian populism encompasses not only political discourses of protest (e.g., against Western-style capitalist policies), but also strategies of fighting hegemonic formations within society with the assistance of peasants and the development of Bolivarian circles.[81] By the late 1990s, the FARC had gathered roughly 17,000 troops dispersed over 60 fronts. It gained Bolivarian support from *cocaleros* (coca growers), poverty-stricken peasants, and radical students active at Colombian universities.[82] In an effort to distance themselves from what some audiences regarded as out-of-style Marxist philosophy, the FARC began employing Bolivarian rhetoric throughout the 1990s, to be in ideological harmony with President Hugo Chávez's revolutionary approach in neighboring Venezuela. On top of local and regional support, the FARC even managed to draw support from European nongovernmental organizations and governments, and invited in its jungle-filled region the director of the New York Stock Exchange.[83]

Bolivarian populism purports to attend to the needs of the population. As the FARC launched their campaign in Central and Eastern Colombia, they conveyed the message that the Colombian government is tyrannical, does not attend to the needs of peasants, and is depraved and crooked. These messages have raised the suspicion of a certain number of peasants in these areas. The FARC's proposals for the establishment of a "people-oriented" government are based on narrow ideological criteria that conflict with the political inclinations of those peasants.[84] On the other hand, the organization's messages have also changed the minds of some of these people against the State.[85]

The FARC have given the semblance of metamorphosis from an ideologically driven political and military activism to an approach that presents itself as a seemingly more peaceful alternative (hoping that it would resonate with a significant minority of Colombians). The correlation between speech and action represents the essence of the intention to harm. The FARC's campaign strategists want to ensure that words translate into actions. Speech act theory tells us that "to speak is to act in the world, and to act with the purpose of influencing, preserving, or changing it in certain ways."[86] The FARC's campaigns have borne their fruits. Although today they present an outwardly softer version of the Marxist–Leninist philosophy, they still manage to rope in new recruits to train for attacks against the Colombian government—i.e., the supreme enemy of the modern Bolivarian Revolution. In a Human Rights Watch article published in late 2020, the FARC continue to threaten or kill citizens who oppose them and support the government.[87]

The basic semantic intention of the FARC's campaigns is to rally people so they align with the terrorist group's demands, which function more than just recruitment. They also serve as tools for real-world actions that new recruits will be emboldened to do. This readiness to perpetrate terrorist attacks, as a result of powerful rhetoric, reflects the concept of perlocutionary act. As a matter of fact, in late March 2021, the new recruits acted on the Bolivarian rhetoric that they had been fed for months by detonating a car bomb that injured a great many people in a small town in Western Colombia.[88]

Using Human Rights Language

Although the FARC retain the language of class struggle in their campaigns, the organization's political discourse has relatively diverged from Marxist–Leninist rhetoric.[89] To make their political message more appealing, the FARC have used human rights language. By displaying a semblance of human rights values in areas from which they seek to attract support, the FARC attempt to fortify the political landscape that made them successful in the past. As an illustration, the FARC have been questioned by their local populace (including reporters) about their inclusion of children in their guerrilla tactics. One FARC leader offered the rationale for the relentless use of youths that the organization complies with Article 38 of the United Nations Convention on the Rights of the Child.[90] By referencing international legal standards, the FARC ooze an image of an organization that has a penchant for human rights, which lends them a legitimizing image that may be sufficiently persuasive to local populations.

Today, part of the FARC's strategy of human rights language is the avoidance of threats *vis-à-vis* their audiences. On the contrary, the FARC make a myriad of promises for a better world—a world devoid of capitalist exploitation of the poor. This is an embodiment of illocutionary act. One of the criteria for a speech act to count as a promise is that the promise must work in favor of the "promise." The distinction between a promise and a threat is that "a promise is a pledge to do something for you, not to you. A threat is a pledge to do something to you, not for you."[91] It is crucial to investigate the details of the locution, because the choice of words of any speech act also influences its meaning. This is markedly true when persuasive intents are at stake. In this case, the FARC encourage Colombian youths to join their ranks, learn how to fight, and resist elitist oppression through physical force. Semantically speaking, the order in which the message is presented is important when it comes to understanding the purpose of the speech act.[92]

By using human rights language, the FARC have been able to establish relational satisfaction with their audience. As Huang (2001)[93] explains it, this is evident when we can witness "the extent to which one party feels favorably towards the other because positive expectations about the relationship are reinforced" and "the extent to which one party believes and feels that the relationship is worth spending energy." To demonstrate that the FARC encourage new recruits to commit terrorism, it is important to show how the campaign strategists published communications for that purpose. In the case of the FARC, their campaigns indicate that, through recruitment of newbies, they aspire to advance their terrorist agenda and their objectives of fighting the White ruling élite in Colombia.

THE FARC'S PROPAGANDA

Terrorism is also a propagandistic deed. A terrorist attack, in and of itself, conveys the message that change can occur. The propagandistic impact is in the process of drawing the public's attention and diffusing the message through the violence.[94] Three Italian anarchists (Errico Malatesta, Carlo Cafiero, and Emilio Covelli) advanced the notion of Propaganda by Deed through multiple letters sent to each other between July and October 1876.[95] **Propaganda** refers to intentionally deceptive communication. It is public communication directed at a large collective of people and conceived to shape attitudes and behavior in times of crisis. Propaganda employs a set of rhetorical strategies and cognitive heuristics to make particular statements and to derive broader assumptions from those statements, without providing sufficient evidence or data. Propaganda rests on a utilitarian approach to truth and information. Truth is subjected to the purpose of expediency. In a certain number of communication campaigns, truth forfeits its value and "belief" and "credibility" become prioritized.[96]

The ethos of propaganda is that it is created to be opinion forming, and the core of its method is that it is manipulative. Propaganda operates through simplification, appealing images, deception, and cognitive techniques that erode or circumvent rationality.[97] In his book titled *What Is to Be Done*, Vladimir Lenin advanced the approach of propaganda and agitation, which required followers of the Communist Party to employ (1) propaganda to radicalize the educated and intelligent populace and (2) agitation—through slogans, narratives, and half-truths—to take advantage of the grievances of the uneducated and ignorant populace. Every unit in the Communist Party was to organize Agit-Prop events for propaganda and agitation.[98] As Lenin further taught, deception through propaganda is legitimate because the end justifies the means. As he continued, "To tell the truth is a petty bourgeois habit, whereas for us to lie is justified by our objectives."[99]

Although propaganda seeks to manipulate the masses, it does not automatically or inevitably prevail. In many cases, it fails to sway the target audience in its first attempt. The propagandist must persist or find other ways to change people's attitudes or behaviors, and must be cognizant that those people may wake up to the fact that manipulation is at work. Propaganda relies on communication diffused mostly through language with its deep, cultural meanings. Symbolic words like freedom, justice, and equality are common in radical or extremist campaigns. In essence, symbols are propagandists' tools, cleverly appropriated to mold people.[100]

Institutional Theory and Organizational Legitimacy

In Colombian Spanish, the word propaganda can mean both advertising and the manipulation of media by armed actors. The Colombian population is not always aware of the latter definition. The work of the FARC's propaganda framers is never located in a vacuum. It is part of an overarching process of misinformation and false claims designed to abuse the ideological weakness of Colombians' conceptions of the world.[101] This brings two concepts to mind, concepts from organizational communication: institutional theory and organizational legitimacy. **Institutional theory** suggests that the survival of an organization depends not only on physical resources and technical knowledge, but also on the organization's legitimacy in the eyes of the public. Legitimacy is often defined as "a generalized perception or assumption that the actions of an entity are desirable, proper, or appropriate within some socially constructed system of norms, values, beliefs and definitions."[102] **Organizational legitimacy** reflects consistency between systemic norms and social values related to or implied by an organization's activities. Organizations can develop legitimacy in two ways: follow current social norms or manipulate social norms to the organization's own advantage.[103] The FARC naturally follow the second option.

To uphold their organizational legitimacy, the FARC posture themselves as "an expression of the people," a political and military organization of which the aim is the "solution of the problems that affect the more than thirty million Colombians who live in poverty."[104] Labeling themselves as *marxistas*, *comunistas*, and *bolivarianos*, with a nice coat of Bolivarian rhetoric, representatives of the FARC propagandize their struggle for emancipation from the "White ruling élite" whose unfair treatment of the peasants and whose political and economic interests "are not the interests of the working people nor of the revolutionaries."[105] This is how an organization enhances its image in order to strengthen or frame relationships with its publics.[106] At the same time, the FARC organize numerous terrorist attacks and premeditated killings—an old guerrilla tactic to chip away at governmental control and legitimacy and to weaken popular support for the government. The FARC's frequent assassination targets are mayors, police forces, paramilitaries, and retired or off-duty military officers.[107]

The FARC's organizational legitimacy is effective when their revolutionary discourse helps them camouflage practices that are in no way revolutionary, such as guerrilla vigilantism and security services subsidized through racketeering profits collected by the organization. Upon closer examination, the civil war that they have waged since 1964 is infused by sporadic compromises and agreements. Enemies fight each other in one area of the country, whereas in another they cut deals, as is the case with the FARC and narcotraffickers.[108] Not all Colombians realize that the FARC's optimistic-looking campaigns are actually subjecting them to their guerrilla-inspired administration, totalitarianism, sectarianism, weapons, and numerous acts of brutality. Their propaganda efforts are contradicted by their actions. For example, the FARC are involved in a colossal export of illegal commodities like cocaine (whose profits increase in proportion to the illegal status of the drug).[109] Here, there is a wide gap between discourse and reality, in spite of the FARC's self-declared mission to radically transform Colombian society to the benefit of the people. It should come to no surprise that the organization's progress into a "political movement" will also involve militant factions into the country's political landscape that will have access to key institutions.[110]

The Deception of the Marquetalia Campaign

The Marquetalia campaign was arguably the FARC's first major public communication campaign. The **Marquetalia Republic** is a term used to informally refer to one of the territories in rural Colombia which Communist peasant militants controlled in the wake of *La Violencia* (1948–58). After the government assault on Marquetalia on May 27, 1964, a founding document was crafted: "The Agrarian Program." This document, as attested by Commander Simón Trinidad, includes a summary report of what happened to this community of peasants and a description of their objectives: a political remedy to prevent such attacks from occurring in the future.[111] The FARC launched their Marquetalia campaign based on that document and raised their legitimacy on it. An interesting element of the campaign was the facility with which they persuaded locals to raise taxes for new landlords, threaten retaliation if they did not want to pay, abduct the landlords' friends or relatives for ransom, and even suggest that help one another by redistributing some of the profits to the disadvantaged.[112]

The FARC's Marquetalia campaign propagated the provably false narrative that a tiny collective of 48 peasants were attacked by as many as 16,000 government soldiers in the largest military operation at that time. These soldiers were trained or advised by the United States. The reality is that many more peasants were present, but only 48 of them were armed. Nevertheless, the propaganda that the FARC disseminated bore close resemblance to that of David and Goliath. It also propagated a myth about the first people who joined the militant groups and a myth related to the territory from which they came (Tolima and its periphery) and their ancestors (the Pijaos). Ultimately, the FARC's provably false narrative was used as foundation for joining them against Goliath because it was the responsibility of peasant farmers to regain their dignity—together as blood brothers—by fighting and resisting the oppressor.[113]

Whereas it is normal for organizations to respond to their contexts, it is also normal for them to influence their contexts by shaping public opinion. This is why the FARC customarily manipulate their relationships with their audiences to reach their agenda in the most optimal manner. Taken as a whole, the tragedy of the government assault on Marquetalia was the foundation on which the FARC developed their first communication campaign and fashioned an image of heroic struggle.[114] Thus, the event of the attack has spawned a somewhat misleading discourse founded on the immortality and heroism of what became the first members of the organization, and on the justifiable nature of the organization's actions from that point forward. Indeed, it gave the FARC a "just cause" to launch a terrorist movement in the transition towards an ideal postcapitalist country based on so-called Bolivarian principles.[115]

Case Study 2:   The Rwanda Genocide

Definitions

Genocide refers to an organized practice of exterminating a group, or a certain percentage of people from that group, within a specific time frame. The victim group is considered to have different ethnic, racial, or otherwise organic attributes.[116] Sometimes equated with ethnic, racial, or even gender-based terrorism,[117] depending on the intent for the mass killing, genocide can also be defined as "a form of one-sided mass killing in which the state or other authority intends to destroy a group, as that group and membership in it are identified by the perpetrator."[118] According to the United Nations, genocide is a massive effort to eliminate—directly by massacring them or indirectly by occasioning conditions (e.g., mass famine) that contribute to their death—an entire group of people. The United Nations Genocide Convention, which defines genocide as "acts committed with the intent to destroy in part or in whole a national, ethnic, racial, or religious group as such," does not include the slaying of members of a political group.[119]

There are two key drivers of genocide: precarious life conditions in society and group conflict. When both drivers are combined, group-based violence is more likely. A third driver—which, in concert with the other two reasons, can lead to group-based violence—is self-interest. This can cause what Smith (1999)[120] has termed **utilitarian genocide** (i.e., self-serving mass killing). In particular, self-interest gives rise to one of two forms of violence: (1) Violence by a dominant group against a subordinate group requesting that the latter leave (or cease to exist), and (2) violence against indigenous groups motivated by an interest to take the area that they have inhabited for a long time.[121]

Why the Rwanda Genocide?

The **Rwanda Genocide** in 1994 was noteworthy for its quick time frame, (virtually) nonmediatized violence, and widespread participation.[122] Statistics about the number of people who lost their lives during the 1994 genocide vary between 700,000 (predominantly the minority Tutsi population, in addition to 50,000 politically moderate Hutus)[123] and 1,000,000 people.[124] All those people were slaughtered in a record time of three months. Between April and July 1994, Rwanda was the scene of an immense genocide and ethnically and politically driven mass killings in that region.[125] The Hutus were a large majority comprising 85% of the population, whereas the Tutsis were a minority of only 14%. The ethnic disparity became a breeding ground for the targeting of ethnicity, as the Other or the Enemy who was easy to differentiate.[126] The majority of weapons used were machetes and clubs, instead of machine guns and grenades.[127] Other corollaries of the Rwanda Genocide included the displacement of two million refugees in neighboring Zaire (now the Democratic Republic of the Congo), Tanzania, and Burundi, and jails replete with more than 100,000 suspects in the genocide.[128]

Because of the lack of media coverage, the world barely witnessed the tragedy and was only shocked by the scope of the atrocities after the fact. After learning of the Rwanda Genocide, most viewers had a hard time understanding it at first.[129] The genocide ended when the Rwandan Patriotic Front (RPF) seized Kigali, the country's capital city, and deposed the genocidal leadership.[130] Many efforts have been provided to understand this historical event. First, some have underlined the unwavering decline of the economic conditions and the growing disparities from the mid-80s onwards.[131] Second, others have pointed the finger at the unsustainable demographic pressure and the lack of availability of land.[132] Third, others have tried to explain from where the anti-Tutsi frustrations originated and why the Hutus created a socially and culturally oppressive climate.[133] Fourth, an additional group of detractors have highlighted the inherent genocidal aspect of the ideology that emerged after the Rwandan revolution of 1959–61.[134] Finally, the plane that was carrying President Habyarimana, a Hutu himself, was struck down on April 6, 1994, an incident believed to have reawakened deep-seated ethnic tensions, thereby prompting the genocide of the Tutsis.[135]

AN INTRODUCTION TO RADIO CAMPAIGNS

The power of radio to overcome barriers of space and time was long recognized before the internet.[136] In fact, before the introduction of the internet, it was the fastest mass media diffuser.[137] For a large part of the twentieth century, radio broadcasting was the most valuable channel for airing information nationally and internationally.[138] Such technological device was regularly used for conducting public communication campaigns. The level of audience reach could be astronomical. The high correlation between radio broadcasting and the success of terrorist movements should be of particular significance to academics and professionals alike.

Radio campaigns were used extensively to familiarize large populations with messages that were not always accessible through other traditional media like television and newspapers. Exposure to radio messages was often passive, unlike campaigns today that use new technologies (e.g., the internet, social media, and mobile phones), where message recipients not only have access to much more information but, also, they can actively choose to seek information and ignore other materials. This can be achieved through a simple mouse click on a web link. Radio campaigns were of short or long duration. They stood alone or were complemented by other forms of media or organized components, like institutional outreach.[139] Lastly, radio campaigns were operated through direct or indirect approaches that sought to change the behaviors and attitudes of entire groups of people. In the final analysis, the purpose was to influence the decision-making process at either the individual or group level.[140]

Spreading Propaganda and Lies

Radio can become a major platform for spreading propaganda and lies about a certain group. Message reach is a yardstick of measure in any mobilization effort. Success is a function of receiver accessibility, reasonable transmission signal, and regular listening habit. In past extremist campaigns, radio was a primary medium for connecting people. The firmest attempts to place radio broadcasting under state control were the policies carried out by totalitarian régimes.[141] Bosnian radio broadcasts instigated ethnic war when they began diffusing the ideology of nationalism. The gradual impact of one-sided messages inflamed hatred over a long period of time.[142] Taylor and Kent (2000)[143] also stress the instrumental role of nationalist radio in the Bosnian War as an enabler of genocide.

Joseph Goebbels, Hitler's chief propagandist, called radio "the most important instrument of mass influence that exists anywhere."[144] Élites in charge of totalitarian states routinely use mass media—often under their direct supervision—in order to catalyze popular support of and participation in attacks against certain groups.[145] Evidence from multiple countries shows that, when oppression of particular groups in society becomes officially part of the élite's ideology, the chances of a conflict transitioning into genocide are significantly higher.[146] Goebbels orchestrated a highly effective scheme of mass persuasion, principally resorting to propaganda messages through motion pictures and radio broadcasts. Fully cognizant of the power of the media, Goebbels regulated the press school for journalists and exercised a monopoly over radio broadcasting.[147] He convinced the industry to manufacture affordable radio sets, had loudspeakers installed in public spaces, and dispatched radio agents to spy on the use of those radios.[148] Between 1933 and 1942, the radio audience jumped from 4.5 to 16 million in Germany alone.[149]

Radio as "Truth-Teller" in Rwanda

The popularity of radio in Africa grew quickly thanks to colonial and postcolonial development. Before these developments, communication was mostly oral. A village pundit or respected philosopher—or anyone with a designated role—was charged with interpreting the "repository of a culture's myth and wisdom."[150] All over sub-Saharan Africa, radio became the most popular vehicle for public communication. Radio sets and batteries were abundant and relatively low-cost. On the other hand, print media had lower circulation outside large cities and were mostly accessed by urban and educated élites. Television was only accessible to the same privileged classes[151] because it was expensive and, depending on the elevation of terrains or hills, it was sometimes impossible to receive a clear signal. Radio, however, could reach almost 90% of a country like Rwanda. The manufacture of radios was financed by foreign investors and the National Republican Movement for Democracy and Development (MRND) régime, the leading political party of Rwanda from 1975 to 1994 that was presided by Juvénal Habyarimana.[152]

Radio was also popularized by UNESCO and other global humanitarian organizations as a development tool. Rwandan political leaders quickly coopted its potential to secure their nation-state. In 1970, there was one radio receptor for every 120 people in Rwanda. In 1990, it was one radio for 13 people.[153] Radio was a highly trusted tool in that country, with multiple polls in the 1980s confirming that the vast majority of the population perceived radio as a truth-teller.[154] The role of broadcasting morphed from an instrument for development to "a kind of political megaphone."[155] Although oral tradition was still strong and illiteracy was prevalent, radio had a greater impact. According to Hachten (1974),[156] "listeners tend to conceive it as literally the government itself speaking." African leaders had long understood this impact.[157] Furthermore, a certain number of African nations had long traditions of hierarchy and dictatorship. They could consolidate blind obedience to the orders of officials thanks to radio broadcasts. The rate of rote obedience was exceptionally high in Rwanda.[158] As a Tutsi businessman whose family was murdered during the genocide explained, "The popular masses in Rwanda are poorly educated. Every time the powers that be say something, it's an order. They believe someone in political authority. Whatever this person demands, it's as if God is demanding it."[159]

RADIO MACHETE

Thanks to the power of radio, the Rwandan government could easily propagandize an interpretation of the world for its people. In other words, the government used radio as the main agenda-setting and framing tool. Given the population's low rate of literacy and limited foreign language skills, and given the lack of alternative media sources, many Rwandans became increasingly reliant on radio for information about government and the country. Radio broadcasts became a breeding factory for terroristic violence used as a preemptive self-defense mechanism to fight Tutsi political supremacy. The level of animosity in the anti-Tutsi campaign was so high that the communication campaign itself was nicknamed Radio Machete. **Radio Machete** was also the moniker of the Radio Télévision Libre des Mille Collines (RTLM), a radio station established by Hutu extremists in the Rwandan government in 1993 in reaction to sweeping changes that had allowed Tutsis and moderate Hutus to take leadership roles in the administration.[160] Radio Machete is a classic example of the risks inherent to media liberalization. The campaign framed public choice and reinforced radical ideas to which many people had already been exposed during face-to-face rallies.[161]

Kill-or-Be-Killed Frame

The crux of the Radio Machete campaign was the application of the kill-or-be-killed frame. The frame consisted of narratives that relayed the importance of eliminating the Tutsi people and that provided instructions on how to do it. Propaganda scholars explain that the intense words of propagandists can shape attitudes. **Language intensity** includes **tropes** (i.e., figures of speech), strong and vivid language, and emotionally charged phrases. It is the scope of political discourse, social advocacy, hate speech, and eloquent public speaking.[162] As Radio Machete was the unique source of news for most Rwandans, it should come to no surprise that radio broadcasts were highly persuasive in triggering kill-or-be-killed behaviors in villages where the Hutu populace was quite uneducated and illiterate and where Tutsis were the small minority there.[163] Melvern (2000)[164] writes that Radio Machete was "a propaganda weapon unlike any other." As she continues, "the influence of hate radio must never be underestimated."[165] On December 2, 1993, the radio station broadcast the following message:

> Tutsi are nomads and invaders who came to Rwanda in search of pasture, but because they are so cunning and malicious, the Tutsi managed to stay and rule. If you allow the Tutsi–Hamites to come back, they will not only rule you in Rwanda, but will also extend their power throughout the Great Lakes Region.[166]

Campaign communicators aver that preemptive violence against the Tutsis was the best solution because it was "self-defense."[167] In her content analysis of recorded Radio Machete broadcasts, Kimani (2007)[168] explains that the most frequent incendiary declarations were provably false reports of Tutsi RPF rebel atrocities, accusations that Tutsis in the region were preparing a major military coup, and rumors that the RPF sought total domination over the Hutus. Key elected officials, including Prime Minister Jean Kambanda, spew such lies on air. The phrasing employed in broadcasts was dehumanizing.[169]

Another observer, a reporter, argued that "when the radio said it was time to kill the people opposed to the government, the masses slid off a dark edge into insanity."[170] A United Nations investigator also concluded that the toxicity of radio propaganda was "all the more effective because, it is said, the Rwandan peasant has a radio culture of holding a transistor up to his ear in one hand and holding a machete in the other, waiting for orders emitted by RTLM."[171] In a major court ruling in 2003, the United Nations International Criminal Tribunal for Rwanda (ICTR) found two Radio Machete announcers and a print journalist guilty of provoking genocide, the first international court to reach such a verdict since the

Nuremberg conviction of Julius Streicher in 1946. Streicher was the publisher of the vitrioli-cally antisemitic newspaper *Der Stürmer*.[172] The contributors to genocidal journalism and hate radio were guilty of weaponizing speech and committing indirect genocide as if they had personally done so.[173] In brief, radio became the embodiment of the Rwanda Genocide. Still today, Rwanda is the archetypical case of hate radio precipitating genocide.[174]

Valérie Bemeriki: Charismatic Broadcaster

Valérie Bemeriki is a Rwandan woman convicted of war crimes in the Rwanda Genocide. She has served her sentence in the Kigali Central Prison since 1999. It is widely believed that Bemeriki's virulent anti-Tutsi campaign on the RTLM earned the radio station the sobriquet "Radio Machete."[175] During the genocide, Bemeriki regularly disclosed the names and addresses of Tutsis falsely accused of being accomplices, which led to their massacre by Hutu paramilitaries like the Impuzamugambi and Interahamwe. Bemeriki became noto-rious for framing genocidal language in a vernacular form of tongue-in-cheek humor.[176] Bemeriki was a proponent of machetes as standard weaponry and instructed listeners to "not kill those cockroaches with a bullet—cut them to pieces with a machete."[177] The perva-sive and pernicious role that Bemeriki played in the public communication campaign of genocide attests to her charismatic power coming from a single radio station.

Charisma refers to a communicator's ability to command and captivate the public.[178] There are three basic charismatic attributes: authority, credibility, and social attractiveness. Authorities, credible persuaders, and attractive communicators induce attitude change through various methods.[179] Authorities can influence audiences through **compliance**. People embrace a particular behavior not necessarily based on the content of the message, but because they expect "to gain specific rewards or approval and avoid specific punish-ments or disapproval by conforming."[180] In other terms, listeners or viewers are now on the same wavelength as an authority figure because they expect to gain rewards or avoid punish-ment. Credible communicators, on the other hand, shape attitudes through **internaliza-tion**. We adopt suggestions made by credible communicators because they correspond to our values or attitudes. Attractive communicators—thanks to their personalities or appear-ance—can wield influence through affective or emotional processes like **identification**. People identify with attractive speakers because of what they project themselves to be, or they want to develop a parasocial interaction with these communicators (see Chapter 8).[181] **Credibility** is defined as "the attitude toward a source of communication held at a given time by a receiver."[182] It is the public's perceptions of the communicator's qualities.

Media System Dependency Theory

Developed by Rokeach and Defleur (1976),[183] **media system dependency theory** rests on the premise that the more we rely on the media to fulfill our needs, the more important the media becomes in our lives, and therefore the more impactful the media will be on us. Put simply, mass media are most effective when the media establishment either controls information resources not available to the public elsewhere or when alternative media are difficult to be found. This form of hegemonic power gives the media ammunition for control over information.[184] One technical fact is that RTLM could only receive FM, thereby pre-cluding many listeners from accessing international news that used short waves. This fact alone demonstrates how dependent most Rwandans were on only one medium for information.[185] In environments with little diversity and a modicum of alternatives, the media is authoritative and users' dependency is high. By contrast, a low degree of media dependency illustrates a (much) higher degree of media diversity, with various sources available. In pluralistic environments, trust in the mainstream media is less common, and media effects are less significant.[186] When the media commands a lot of power, the effects of broadcasts on morale and feelings of alienation are visible. Constantly negative mass media portrayals of social groups can push people to commit some of the worst atrocities that humankind has ever witnessed.[187]

Media dependency can be viewed as both a potential for long-term media effects and a sign of the magnitude of the mass media in a social context.[188] Affective media effects—i.e., the power of pathos is rhetoric (see Chapter 3)—are more obvious in times of increased dependency. A profound effect is **desensitization**, which happens when lengthy exposure to violent messages can have a deadening or suppressing effect on the audience's compassion towards other groups, thereby creating insensitivity or the lack of desire to feel sorry for enemies.[189] McQuail (1994)[190] hypothesized that such pathos-induced effects tend to be greater in times of instability, and there are several reasons, all congruent with media dependency theory. During major crises, people may become more dependent on the media for information, instruction, and/or leadership. They may be aware of crucial events only through the media and the latter are so influential in situations outside the domain of personal experience. The Radio Machete campaign inculcated information in Hutu listeners that caused them to spurn, dehumanize, and dread the Tutsis. Radio framed, eased, and legitimized violence and became a vehicle for the materialization of genocide. In Rwanda, radio was analogous to the voice of God. When radio cried out for violence, many Rwandans behaved accordingly, thinking that they were being credited for perpetrating these atrocities.[191] Kellow and Steeves (1998)[192] assert that radio indoctrinated the audience by "instilling a pronounced fear and hatred that previously had not been part of the everyday culture."

Many of the radio's announcers came from the mainstream media establishment. This was part of a larger campaign to diminish the role of the mainstream media and boost Rwandans' reliance on state radio. Some publications shut down as a consequence of Radio Machete's massive recruitment campaign. Soldiers at every checkpoint had a radio set so they could amplify the sounds of broadcasts to be heard by entire communities. Messages were articulated as legitimate anti-Tutsi acts. In this way, the radio station sanctioned the most extreme sadisms against the minority group. For example, in May 20, 1994, a communiqué depicted Tutsis in an untrue situation where they rounded up guns and used them to kill Hutu families. They were also accused of setting their houses on fire and hiding in a church to plan another attack. This was justification for Hutus to destroy the church.[193] To sum it all up, Radio Machete was a voice of authority that issued commands and directions on how to kill, which Hutus obeyed. In their groundbreaking study titled *Les Médias du Génocide*, Chrétien, Dupaquier, Kambanda, and Ngarambe (1995)[194] put forward the idea that the Hutus had two main tools: "The radio and the machete, the first to give and receive orders, the second to execute them."

EUPHEMISMS IN THE RADIO MACHETE CAMPAIGN

Euphemistic language can be used by communicators when they want to make wrongful behavior look respectable and to fashion a rhetoric of nonresponsibility. Euphemisms function as moral rationalization. Typically, human beings do not engage in harmful conduct unless they have rationalized it to themselves, lifting up the morality of their behaviors.

In this process, destructive conduct now looks personally and socially acceptable because it has been euphemized as fulfilling worthy or moral purposes. From this vantage point, human beings can move forward with their genocidal plan based on a fictitious moral imperative while, at the same time, preserving their positive conception of themselves as agents acting on moral grounds.[195]

Euphemisms: A Description

A **euphemism** is a substitution of a good-natured or less unpleasant phrase for one that expresses something distasteful to the audience.[196] "Euphemism" stems from Greek and signifies "good speech." A euphemistic phrase is used to cloak issues through intentional deception or to convey judicious language.[197] Euphemism is **lexical ambiguity**, a linguistic technique that allows two or more possible meanings.[198] It is **Aesopian language** because it can contain a seemingly innocuous meaning while, in reality, there is a deeper meaning lurking inside the phrase. Only educated audiences with a special agenda may readily understand that deeper meaning. Aesopian language is a reference to Aesop, an Ancient Greek storyteller who used language and characters that were hard to decipher at first glance.[199] Aesopian language was mentioned by Herbert Marcuse (1964)[200] in his book *One-Dimensional Man* where it was compared to Orwellian language. In simple terms, it is the notion that certain forms of communication serve to "suppress certain concepts or keep them out of the general discourse within society."

In *Euphemism, Spin, and the Crisis in Organizational Life*, Stein (1998)[201] argued that euphemism does not represent a social construction of reality, but a deliberate attack on meaning because it deflects our attention away from reality. This happens through vague and ambiguous language, like small phenomena that are too arcane, profound, or intellectual. Part of the reason is that (1) only intended listeners may understand it or (2) they evoke feelings and emotionality instead of facts. Euphemisms are "economical with the truth;" they are deceptive, whether by purposefully communicating false information or omitting important facts.[202]

Euphemisms in Terrorism

Language plays an indisputable role in influencing our perception of our actions. Dangerous conduct can be obfuscated by euphemistic language, and depending on how it is framed, it can make the conduct look honorable. As we have seen, euphemistic language can reduce feelings of personal responsibility for crimes against humanity. As such, Al-Qaeda calls the September 11, 2001 terrorist attacks as legitimate revenge against symbols of American domination, greed, and consumerism. Yet, they never mention the innocence of the 3,000 people who perished. Euphemizing is a maleficent weapon; people express less guilt when their inhumanity is given an immaculate label.[203] Euphemisms exemplify the sanitizing of language. By obscuring atrocious activities in innocuous-sounding phrasing, the activities lose much of their animosity. For example, enemies are "disposed of" people (instead of "killed"). The terrorists do not see themselves as "terrorists," but as "freedom fighters," "soldiers," or "heroes."[204]

After warfare, genocide was the second leading cause of preventable violent deaths in the twentieth century. The term **ethnic cleansing** has been used by both perpetrators and scholars alike. Yet, it is still a euphemism for genocide (despite being devoid of any legal status). "Ethnic cleansing" was, indeed, the euphemism, first used by the offenders, and later by witnessing communities, before being used by a certain amount of scholars to refer to mass killings, unjustifiable extrajudicial executions, collective rape, famine, and demolition of homes and religious institutions.[205] Euphemistic language refuses to acknowledge reality and allows users to distance themselves from terrorist acts and their victims. It also leads to "the denial of obvious reality, though it consumes much psychological energy, and allows perpetrators [and bystanders] to avoid feelings of responsibility and guilt."[206]

Euphemisms in the Rwanda Genocide

The discourse of the Radio Machete campaign, with its coded words to rationalize violence, was interpreted by the audience as a call to genocide. The targets soon became at the center of the genocide for three months.[207] Language shapes the way we think, the patterns on which actions rest. Activities can take many forms, depending on how they are framed by language. During the Rwanda Genocide, euphemistic language was conducive to unmatched killings in that nation's history. Hutu radio journalists were experts at euphemistic expressions that managed to both diffuse and disguise their true intentions. It was coded rhetoric that appeared upright on the surface and that alleviated self-responsibility on the part of the genociders (an adaptation of the French *génocidaires*). Camouflage was a key constituent of genocidal propaganda; it was able "to lay asleep opposition; to surprise; to reserve to a man's self a fair retreat."[208]

The clever use of euphemisms served a definite purpose: to go out of the cities and remove the real enemies from the land—i.e., those "hiding" in remote areas. Indeed, dislocated into rural areas, towns, and villages, the victim populations were completely vulnerable. Devoid of weapons and of official United Nations protection, their physical isolation made them an easy prey for disposal.[209] Euphemisms to kill innocent villagers played down the gravity and the callousness of their crimes. It became a common and efficient tool for the suppression of meaning because what happened to those villagers was not spelled out explicitly. Euphemisms simply facilitated the pretense that, with hindsight, perpetrators could not really know whether or not the minority victims were innocent. According to Clapham (1998),[210] "groups who sought a genocidal solution" exploited opportunities for "negotiation" to actually prepare for likely trials and convictions for their actions, and had no intention of agreeing with the fact that they knew exactly what they were doing.

Euphemisms for Killing

After Hutu President Habyarimana's private plane was brought down by a surface-to-air missile on April 6, 1994, RTLM joined the chorus of allegations against the Tutsi population and began calling for a "final war" to "cleanse" them. The coded phrase was "cut down the tall trees," an allusion to the physically taller foe (i.e., the Tutsis).[211] The killers' machetes, the weaponry during the genocide, were called "tools."[212] Hutu radio broadcasters diffused their anti-Tutsi campaign calling for their destruction by telling the listeners that they needed to "go to work" on them.[213] The verb "work" was an incentivizing euphemism because the act of killing was not only their everyday duty (just like work), but it also demanded physical labor (like something that was rewarding at the end of the day). The verb "work" was reminiscent of "the communal work parties of the 1970s and 1980s," which had arguably boosted the self-esteem of the genociders involved (even if the campaign provided little financial compensation to the killers).[214]

Indeed, Radio Machete's appeal to "work" was inspired by contemporary discourses of communal development, thereby reframing communal labor as a duty for ethnic survival (sometimes called "civil defense") at a moment of national upheaval. "Mobilize yourselves," said Radio Machete's announcer Georges Ruggiu to listeners during the genocide. As he continued, "Work you the youth, everywhere in the country, come to work with your army. Come to work with your government to defend your country."[215] As a Christian missionary from a Western country, who spoke Kinyarwanda (the main official language of Rwanda), explained: "Every morning, RTLM was in the habit of asking listeners, 'Hello, good day, have you started to work yet?'"[216]

In another example, "clearing the bush" was originally used to refer to clearing land for cultivation; it was soon coopted for clearing the Tutsis from the land.[217] Prunier (1995)[218] echoes that argument by describing how chopping up men was "bush clearing" and murdering women and children was "pulling out the roots of the bad weeds." Not surprisingly, Hutu genociders had an easy time with their abominable actions because campaign strategists sugarcoated language.[219] The same type of powerful metaphorical and euphemistic language was already employed during the Rwandan Revolution (1959–61), when Hutus were sporadically slaughtered in neighboring Burundi. Multiple references to agricultural labor were used for inciting people to kill the innocent. These tropes presented the advantage of being open to double entendres. On the one hand, coded messages were used to conceal the gruesomeness of what was happening; on the other hand, the audiences exposed to these messages were reminded of their responsibility to obediently contribute to this "special shared work."[220] This is why another coded phrase calling for the elimination of the Tutsi population was to "finish off the 1959 revolution."[221]

Euphemisms in Kinyarwanda

Spoken by almost 10 million people, Kinyarwanda is the most important ethnic language in Rwanda. Ambiguous Kinyarwanda phrases were spread profusely during the preparation for the "ethnic cleansing," and even during its execution. Aside for Christian missionaries and translators who spoke the language, outsiders who were not fluent in it could not understand the euphemisms used during the campaign. Yet, they were direct and unambiguous to both Hutu natives who turned out to be killers and the Tutsi victims.[222] The number of Kinyarwanda words and expressions to essentialize, demonize, and dehumanize the minority population were plentiful: *umwanzi* (opponent), *inyenzi* (cockroaches), and *Inyeshyamba* (forest dwellers or maquisards). On a similar note, a variety of terms were employed to justify the task of killing Tutsis: *kwihora* or *kwitura* (retribution), *gukora hejuru* (take up arms), and *kwiva inyuma* (all means possible).[223]

The genocide was called a "big job," *akazi gakomeye*, or "special work," *umuganda*. Killing was often referred to as "tree felling."[224] Likewise, in regards to "communal work" mentioned earlier, the word *interahamwe*, which more precisely means communal work parties, had a historical resonance because the same verbiage was used in previous revolutions and evolved into a "youth party organization." This was actually code for "death squad" during the Rwanda Genocide.[225] During the weeks following April 6, 1994, Radio Machete constantly ordered the extermination of all Tutsis, calling them *inkotanyi* (a derogatory allusion to the RPF).[226] Because *interahamwe* connotes a positive approach to solidarity ("communal work"), it spawned the concept of *Abashyirahamwe* during the radio campaigns. It meant to be united in to reach a collaborative group goal, like peasants and farmers in agricultural projects. Members of the Union Nationale Rwandaise, a political party favoring the return of the Kingdom of Rwanda (abolished in 1961), were also called *Abashyirahamwe*. Other anti-Tutsi militia groups enjoyed being labeled similarly euphemistic names like *Impuzamugambi* (a group with a common purpose) and *Abakombozi* (saviors or liberators).[227]

Proponents of the Rwanda Genocide went as far as taking verses or characters from the Bible, referring to President Habyarimana as Christ, and claiming that the Virgin Mary would agree with revenge for his assassination.[228] During Habyarimana's presidency itself, Rwandans' motivations for discipline were inspired by weekly *umuganda* (collective) sessions (a reference to the Twelve Apostles), involving moments of "animation," including respectful gestures and thanks towards his régime (a reference to prayer), and much collective chanting and clapping (a reference to rejoice and praise). These rituals were performed as a form of indoctrination to prepare ordinary individuals for the job of killing. Eventual obedience was acquired from many of those who first opposed the killings after reading propaganda pamphlets. Those who were set to kill the Tutsis were even guaranteed rewards, ranging from alcohol to booty (e.g., the land and home of each family killed).[229]

Euphemisms to Hurt Women

The fact that Tutsi women were murdered *en masse* during the Rwanda Genocide attests to the fact that they were perceived as dangerous to the Hutu majority. For one thing, in the Gikongoro Province (a former province in the southwest of the country with a significant minority of Tutsis), women had six children on average,[230] which explains the genociders' willingness to produce a high death toll among females (to prevent the existence of future generations). The Hutu terrorists sought to regain the lost ground of patriarchy and their dominance. Tutsi women were considered a huge obstacle, in the terrorists' minds, to the return of patriarchy and dominance because, in many respects, they were well positioned between the two groups. The Rwandan Genocide was not only a roadmap towards political supremacy; it was also a massive program to reconfigure gender.[231]

Decisions to hurt women were taken at "the little house," the actual name of the small group of Hutus who plotted the genocide of Tutsi females. "The little house" included two of Rwanda's most (in)famous women: Agathe Habyalimana (the president's widow) and Pauline Nyiramasuhuko (the Minister for Family Welfare and the Advancement of Women). The small group also worked to guarantee immunity for genociders (but it eventually did not work).[232] Hutu extremists raped Tutsi women during the mass roundups. They also raped Hutus opposed to the régime, as well as women of either ethnicity for the simple reasons that they were prominent in the country and disliked by the leaders. After each mass rape, the women were "given" to soldiers or militia. On many occasions, the women became the "wives" of those who killed their relatives. Rwandans referred to the victims as "wives of soldiers."[233]

Hundreds of thousands of Tutsi women, and a few thousand Hutu women linked to Tutsis or married into their families, were genocided in 1994. The many other survivors suffered from profound trauma. The mass rapes occurred in every part of the country.[234] Hurting women was a key element of the "final solution" to the "problem" of the Tutsi population. Many Tutsi women experienced breast-related issues or were raped before being murdered.[235] Others had spears planted inside their bodies (from vagina to mouth). Pregnant women had their fetuses removed from their bodies. And others were forced to have sex with their own family members before being exterminated.[236]

Today, every April, the official month of observance and commemoration, there are haunting reminders that unrepentant genociders are still present among the survivors. In

April 2008, a former perpetrator threw a grenade at one of those genocide memorials, killing one person.[237] The previous April, an individual who participated in a radio show expressed the need to "finish the job."[238] At the same time, genocide deniers have claimed that the killing was legitimate because it was "war," a false claim that is still propagated by former Rwanda genociders across the border in the Eastern Congo, by those in prison after being tried at the ICTR, and by certain exile groups in Europe. The Rwandan government and survivors have a legitimate fear that deniers—or "assassins of memory" (in Pierre Vidal-Naquet's words)—are paving the way for future anti-Tutsi violence.[239]

NOTES

1. Cited in Arthur H. Garrison, "Defining Terrorism: Philosophy of the Bomb, Propaganda by Deed and Change through Fear and Violence," *Criminal Justice Studies* 17, no. (2004): 259–79, 276. https://doi.org/10.1080/1478601042000281105.

2. Martha Crenshaw, "The Psychology of Terrorism: An Agenda for the 21st Century," *Political Psychology* 21, no. 2 (2000): 405–20. https://doi.org/10.1111/0162-895X.00195; Jonathan Matusitz and Demi Simi, "US Government Deception in the Luis Posada Scandal: Information Manipulation Theory," *Latin American Policy* 12, no. 1 (2021): 57–68. https://doi.org/10.1111/lamp.12210.

3. Jonathan Matusitz, *Communication in Global Jihad* (New York: Routledge, 2021).

4. Charles L. Ruby, "The Definition of Terrorism," *Analyses of Social Issues and Public Policy* 2, no. 1 (2002): 9–14. https://doi.org/10.1111/j.1530-2415.2002.00021.x.

5. Garrison, "Defining Terrorism," 263.

6. Thomas F. Ditzler, "Malevolent Minds: The Teleology of Terrorism," in *Understanding Terrorism: Psychological Roots, Consequences, and Interventions*, ed. Fathali M. Moghaddam and Anthony J. Marsella (Washington, DC: American Psychological Association, 2004): 187–206.

7. Paul Slovic, "Terrorism as Hazard: A New Species of Trouble," *Risk Analysis* 22, no. 3 (2002): 425–6. https://doi.org/10.1111/0272-4332.00053.

8. The White House, Office of the Press Secretary, *Strategic Implementation Plan for Empowering Local Partners to Prevent Violent Extremism in the United States* (2011). Retrieved on March 26, 2021 from https://www.whitehouse.gov/sites/default/files/sip-final.pdf.

9. Jonathan Matusitz, "Symbolism in Female Terrorism: Five Overarching Themes," *Sexuality & Culture* 23, no. 3 (2019): 1332–44. https://doi.org/10.1007/s12119-019-09624-4.

10. Rizwan Naseer, Musarat Amin, and Zaib Maroof, "Countering Violent Extremism in Pakistan: Methods, Challenges and Theoretical Underpinnings," *NDU Journal* 12 (2019): 100–16.

11. Ibid, 106.

12. Joshua M. Roose, "Male Supremacism," in *The New Demagogues*, ed. Joshua M. Roose (New York: Routledge, 2021): 80–108.

13. Jason-Leigh Striegher, "Violent Extremism: An Examination of a Definitional Dilemma," in *The Proceedings of [the] 8th Australian Security and Intelligence Conference*, Perth, Western Australia (November 30–December 2, 2015): 75–86.

14. Mark Sedgwick, "The Concept of Radicalization as a Source of Confusion," *Terrorism and Political Violence* 22, no. 4 (2010): 479–94. https://doi.org/10.1080/09546553.2010.491009.

15. Andrew Silke, "Holy Warriors: Exploring the Psychological Processes of Jihadi Radicalization," *European Journal of Criminology* 5, no. 1 (2008): 99–123. https://doi.org/10.1177/1477370807084226.

16. Maeghin Alarid, "Recruitment and Radicalization: The Role of Social Media and New Technology," in *Impunity: Countering Illicit Power in War and Transition*, ed. Michelle Hughes and Michael Miklaucic (Washington, DC: National Defense University, 2016), 313–29.

17. Alaina Rahaim and Jonathan Matusitz, "Patty Hearst and the Symbionese Liberation Army (SLA): An Examination through Differential Association Theory," *Journal of Applied Security Research* 15, no. 3 (2020): 408–22. https://doi.org/10.1080/19361610.2019.1710094.

18. Lene Kühle and Lasse Lindekilde, *Radicalization among Young Muslims in Aarhus* (Aarhus, Denmark: The Centre for Studies in Islamism and Radicalisation & Department of Political Science, 2010).

19. Owen Frazer and Christian Nünlist, *The Concept of Countering Violent Extremism* (Zurich: ETH Zürich, 2015).

20. Garth Davies, Christine Neudecker, Marie Ouellet, Martin Bouchard, and Benjamin Ducol, "Toward a Framework Understanding of Online Programs for Countering Violent Extremism," *Journal for Deradicalization* 6 (2016): 51–86, 52.

21. Denise Winn, *The Manipulated Mind: Brainwashing, Conditioning and Indoctrination* (Los Altos, CA: Malor Books, 2017).

22. Samuel Leistedt, "Behavioural Aspects of Terrorism," *Forensic Science International* 228, no. 1 (2013): 21–27. https://doi.org/10.1016/j.forsciint.2013.02.004.

23. Kathleen Taylor, *Brainwashing: The Science of Thought Control* (Oxford: Oxford University Press, 2004).

24. Anja Dalgaard-Nielsen, "Violent Radicalization in Europe: What We Know and What We Do Not Know," *Studies in Conflict & Terrorism* 33, no. 9 (2010): 797–814, 798. https://doi.org/10.1080/1057610X.2010.501423.

25. Davies, Neudecker, Ouellet, Bouchard, and Ducol, "Toward a Framework Understanding," 53.

26. For example, see Pierpaolo Antonello, *Imagining Terrorism: The Rhetoric and Representation of Political Violence in Italy 1969–2009* (New York: Routledge, 2017); Adam Banks, *Race, Rhetoric, and Technology* (New York: Routledge, 2005); Mark Lawrence McPhail, *The Rhetoric of Racism Revisited* (New York: Rowan & Littlefield, 2001).

27. Celine-Marie Pascale, "The Weaponization of Language: Discourses of Rising Right-Wing Authoritarianism," *Current Sociology Review* 67, no. 6 (2019): 898–917. https://doi.org/10.1177/0011392119869963.

28. Ibid, 911.

29. Jodi Vittori, "All Struggles Must End: The Longevity of Terrorist Groups," *Contemporary Security Policy* 30, no. 3 (2009): 444–66. https://doi.org/10.1080/13523260903326602.

30. Anne Aly, Dana Weimann-Saks, and Gabriel Weimann, "Making 'Noise' Online: An Analysis of the Say No to Terror Online Campaign," *Perspectives on Terrorism* 8 (2014): 33–46.

31. Magdalena Wojcieszak, "Al Jazeera: A Challenge to the Traditional Framing Research," *International Communication Gazette* 69, no. 2 (2007): 115–28. https://doi.org/10.1177/1748048507074925.

32. Michael S. Waltman, "Teaching Hate: The Role of Visual Imagery in the Radicalization of White Ethno-Terrorists in the United States," in *Visual Propaganda and Extremism in the Online Environment*, ed. Carol K. Winkler and Cori E. Dauber (Carlisle Barracks, PA: Strategic Studies Institute, 2014): 83–103.

33. Richard Perloff, *The Dynamics of Political Communication: Media and Politics in a Digital Age* (2nd Ed.) (New York: Routledge, 2018).

34. Aly, Weimann-Saks, and Weimann, "Making 'Noise' Online," 35.

35. Steven Dudley, *Walking Ghosts: Murder and Guerrilla Politics in Colombia* (New York: Routledge, 2004).

36. Mark Peceny and Michael Durnan, "The FARC's Best Friend: US Antidrug Policies and the Deepening of Colombia's Civil War in the 1990s," *Latin American Politics and Society* 48, no. 2 (2006): 95–116. https://doi.org/10.1111/j.1548-2456.2006.tb00348.x.

37. Michael Shifter, "Colombia on the Brink: There Goes the Neighborhood," *Foreign Affairs* 78, no. 4 (1999): 4–20.

38. Alexander Grenoble and William Rose, "David Galula's Counterinsurgency: Occam's Razor and Colombia," *Civil Wars* 13, no. 3 (2011): 280–311. https://doi.org/10.1080/13698249.2011.600003.

39. Andres Cala, "The Enigmatic Guerrilla: FARC's Manuel Marulanda," *Current History* 99, no. 634 (2000): 56–9.

40. Michael Chertoff, "Tools against Terror: All of the above," *Harvard Journal of Law & Public Policy* 32, no. 1 (2009): 219–29.

41. Susan L. Macek and Howard J. Wiarda, "Democratization and Political Terrorism in Latin America," in *Democratic Development and Political Terrorism: The Global Perspective*, ed. William Crotty (Holliston, MA: Northeastern Publishing, 2005): 455–72.

42. Diana Sofia Giraldo, Ismael Roldan, and Miguel Angel Florez, *Periodistas, Guerra y Terrorismo* (Santa Fe de Bogota: Universidad Sergio).

43. Ibid.

44. Nora-Christine Braun, "Displacing, Returning, and Pilgrimaging: The Construction of Social Orders of Violence and Non-violence in Colombia," *Civil Wars* 11, no. 4 (2009): 455–76. https://doi.org/10.1080/13698240903403832; Nazih Richani, "The Political Economy of Colombia's Protracted Civil War and the Crisis of the War System," *Journal of Conflict Studies* 21, no. 2 (2001): 50–77.

45. Eduardo Posada Carbó, "Language and Politics: On the Colombian 'Establishment'," *Latin American Research Review* 42, no. 2 (2007): 111–35. https://doi.org/10.1353/lar.2007.0026.

46. Cited in Jacobo Arenas, *Cese al fuego. Una historia política de las FARC* (Bogotá: Editorial Oveja Negra, 1985).

47. Frank Stafford and Marco Palacios, *Colombia: Fragmented Land, Divided Society* (New York: Oxford University Press, 2002).

48. Gérard Chaliand, *Guerrilla Strategies: A Historical Anthology from the Long March to Afghanistan* (Berkeley, CA: University of California Press, 1983).

49. Rachel Ehrenfeld, *Narco-Terrorism* (New York: Basic Books, 1992).

50. Francisco Gutiérrez-Sanín, "Criminal Rebels? A Discussion of Civil War and Criminality from the Colombian Experience," *Politics and Society* 32, no. 2 (2004): 257–80. https://doi.org/10.1177/0032329204263074.

51. Paul S. Nader, "Former Members' Perspectives Are Key to Impacting the FARC," *Journal of Strategic Security* 6, no. 1 (2013): 73–83. http://dx.doi.org/10.5038/1944-0472.6.1.7.

52. Juan E. Ugarriza and Mathew Craig, "The Relevance of Ideology to Contemporary Armed Conflicts: A Quantitative Analysis of Former Combatants in Colombia," *Journal of Conflict Resolution* 57, no. 3 (2012): 445–77. https://doi.org/10.1177/0022002712446131.

53. Ibid, 445–77.

54. Jennifer S. Holmes, Sheila Amin Gutierrez de Pineres, and Kevin M. Curtin, "A Subnational Study of Insurgency: FARC Violence in the 1990s," *Studies in Conflict & Terrorism* 30, no. 3 (2007): 249–65. https://doi.org/10.1080/10576100601148456.

55. Ugarriza and Craig, "The Relevance of Ideology to Contemporary Armed Conflicts," 445–77.

56. Vinay Jawahar and Michael Shifter, "State Building in Colombia: Getting Priorities Straight," *Journal of International Affairs* 58, no. 2 (2004): 143–54.

57. Francisco Gutiérrez-Sanín, "Telling the Difference: Guerrillas and Paramilitaries in the Colombian War," *Politics & Society* 36, no. 1 (2008): 3–34. https://doi.org/10.1177/0032329207312181.

58. Dan Restrepo, "FARC Strategic Communications & The Colombian Peace Process," *Florida International University* (2015). Retrieved on May 1, 2021 from http://lacc.fiu.edu/research/publications/policy-roundtable-paper-restrepodoc.pdf.

59. Ibid.

60. Ibid.

61. Ibid.

62. R. Kim Cragin and Sara A. Daly, *The Dynamic Terrorist Threat: An Assessment of Group Motivations and Capabilities in a Changing World* (Santa Monica, CA: RAND, 2004): 38.

63. Seden Akcinaroglu and Efe Todkemir, "To Instill Fear or Love: Terrorist Groups and the Strategy of Building Reputation," *Conflict Management and Peace Science* 35, no. 4 (2018): 355–77. https://doi.org/10.1177/0738894216634292.

64. Gutiérrez-Sanín, "Telling the Difference," 5–15.

65. *BBC News*, "Colombia Farc Rebel Radio Station 'Shut Down' by Army," *BBC News* (November 19, 2011). Retrieved on May 1, 2021 from https://www.bbc.com/news/world-latin-america-15807096.

66. Cited in Paula Delgado-Kling, "Talking about Colombia." Retrieved on May 1, 2021 from https://talkingaboutcolombia.com/2011/02/08/farc-radio-station.

67. John L. Austin, *How to Do Things with Words* (Cambridge, MA: Harvard University Press, 1962).

68. John R. Searle, *Speech Acts: An Essay in the Philosophy of Language* (Cambridge: Cambridge University Press, 1969).

69. Sophia Brown and Jonathan Matusitz, "US Church Leaders' Responses to the Charleston Church Shooting: An Examination Based on Speech Act Theory," *Journal of Media and Religion* 18, no. 1 (2019): 27–37. https://doi.org/10.1080/15348423.2019.1642008.

70. Cited in A. C. Grayling, *Wittgenstein: A Very Short Introduction* (New York: Oxford University Press, 2001).

71. Stephen Littlejohn, "Speech Act Theory," in *Encyclopedia of Communication Theory*, ed. Stephen Littlejohn and Karen Foss (Thousand Oaks, CA: Sage, 2009): 919–21.

72. Austin, *How to Do Things with Words*, 100–10.

73. Judith Butler, *Excitable Speech: A Politics of the Performative* (New York: Routledge, 1997): 3.

74. John L. Austin, *Logic and Language* (Oxford: Blackwell, 1978): 109.

75. Butler, *Excitable Speech*, 3–5.

76. Matt McDonald, "Securitization and the Construction of Security," *European Journal of International Relations* 14, no. 4 (2008): 563–87. https://doi.org/10.1177/1354066108097553.

77. Mari J. Matsuda, Charles R. Lawrence, III, Richard Delgado, and Kimberle Williams Crenshaw, *Words that Wound: Critical Race Theory, Assaultive Speech, and the First Amendment* (New York: Routledge, 1993); Catherine Mackinnon, *Only Words* (Cambridge, MA: Harvard University Press, 1996).

78. Butler, *Excitable Speech*, 4.

79. John A. Gentry and David E. Spencer, "Colombia's FARC: A Portrait of Insurgent Intelligence," *Intelligence and National Security* 25, no. 4 (2010): 453–78. https://doi.org/10.1080/02684527.2010.537024.

80. Thomas A. Marks, "Colombian Military Support for 'Democratic Security,'" *Small Wars & Insurgencies* 17, no. 2 (2006): 197–220. https://doi.org/10.1080/09592310600563108; Kurt Weyland, "The Threat from the Populist Left," *Journal of Democracy* 24, no. 3 (2013): 18–32. https://doi.org/10.1353/jod.2013.0045.

81. Oliver Marchart, "Elements of Protest," *Cultural Studies* 26, no. 2 (2012): 223–41. https://doi.org/10.1080/09502386.2011.636194.

82. Guri Waalen Borch and Kirsti Stuvøy, "Practices of Self-Legitimation in Armed Groups: Money and Mystique of the FARC in Colombia," *Distinktion: Scandinavian Journal of Social Theory* 9, no. 2 (2008): 97–120. https://doi.org/10.1080/1600910X.2008.9672966.

83. Jim Rochlin, "Plan Colombia and the Revolution in Military Affairs: The Demise of the FARC," *Review of International Studies* 37, no. 2 (2011): 715–40. http://dx.doi.org/10.1017/S0260210510000914.

84. Román D. Ortiz, "Insurgent Strategies in the Post-Cold War: The Case of the Revolutionary Armed Forces of Colombia," *Studies in Conflict & Terrorism* 25, no. 2 (2002): 127–43. https://doi.org/10.1080/105761002753502484.

85. Nader, "Former Members' Perspectives," 73–83.

86. Cited in Odin Lysaker and Henrik Syse, "The Dignity in Free Speech: Civility Norms in Post-Terror Societies," *Nordic Journal of Human Rights* 34, no. 2 (2016): 104–23. http://dx.doi.org/10.1080/18918131.2016.1212691.

87. Available at https://www.hrw.org/world-report/2021/country-chapters/colombia.

88. Manuel Rueda, "Car Bomb Wounds 19 in Town in Western Colombia," *The Star* (March 26, 2021): A11. Retrieved on May 12, 2021 from https://www.thestar.com/news/world/americas/2021/03/26/car-bomb-wounds-19-in-town-in-western-colombia.html.

89. Thomas A. Marks, "Counterinsurgency in the Age of Globalism," *The Journal of Conflict Studies* 27, no. 1 (2007): 10–21.

90. Garry Leech, *Beyond Bogota: Diary of a Drug War Journalist in Colombia* (Chicago, IL: Beacon Press, 2009).

91. Cited in Jacob Mey, *Pragmatics: An Introduction* (2nd Ed.) (Malden, MA: Blackwell, 2001): 50–60.

92. Daniel Marcu, "Perlocutions: The Achilles' Heel of Speech Act Theory," *Journal of Pragmatics* 32, no. 12 (2000): 1719–41. https://doi.org/10.1016/S0378-2166(99)00121-6.

93. Yi-Hui Huang, "Values of Public Relations: Effects on Organization–Public Relationships Mediating Conflict Resolution," *Journal of Public Relations Research* 13, no. 4 (2001): 265–301, 267. https://doi.org/10.1207/S1532754XJPRR1304_01.

94. Garrison, "Defining Terrorism," 259–79.

95. Ulrich Linse, "'Propaganda by Deed' and 'Direct Action': Two Concepts of Anarchist Violence," in *Social Protest, Violence and Terror in Nineteenth and Twentieth Century Europe*, ed. Wolfgang J. Mommsen and Gerhard Hirschfeld (London: Berg Publishers, 1982): 201–29.

96. David Miller and Piers Robinson, "Propaganda, Politics and Deception," in *The Palgrave Handbook of Deceptive Communication*, ed. Tony Docan-Morgan (New York: Palgrave Macmillan, 2019): 969–88.

97. Douglas Walton, "What Is Propaganda, and What Exactly Is Wrong with It," *Public Affairs Quarterly* 11, no. 4 (1997): 383–413.

98. Jean-Numa Ducange and Serge Wolikow, "The Century of Leninism," *Actuel Marx* 62, no. 2 (2017): 11–25.

99. Arnaud de Borchgrave, "Disseminating Disinformation," *Society* 19 (1982): 79–81. https://doi.org/10.1007/BF02698976.

100. Richard M. Perloff, *The Dynamics of Persuasion: Communication and Attitudes in the 21st Century* (2nd Ed.) (Mahwah, NJ: Lawrence Erlbaum, 2003).

101. Alex Fattal, "Hostile Remixes on YouTube: A New Constraint on pro-FARC Counterpublics in Colombia," *American Ethnologist* 41, no. 2 (2014): 320–35. https://doi.org/10.1111/amet.12078.

102. Mark C. Suchman, "Managing Legitimacy: Strategic and Institutional Approaches," *Academy of Management Review* 20, no. 3 (1995): 571–610, 574. https://doi.org/10.5465/AMR.1995.9508080331.

103. John Dowling and Jeffrey Pfeffer, "Organizational Legitimacy: Social Values and Organizational Behavior," *Pacific Sociological Review* 18, no. 1 (1975): 122–36. https://doi.org/10.2307/1388226.

104. Cited in Gentry and Spencer, "Colombia's FARC," 453–78.

105. Ibid, 453–78.

106. James L. Everett, "Public Relations and the Ecology of Organizational Change," in *Handbook of Public Relations*, ed. Robert L. Heath (Thousand Oaks, CA: Sage, 2001): 311–20.

107. Cited in Gentry and Spencer, "Colombia's FARC," 453–78.

108. Ramiro Ceballos Melguizo and Francine Cronshaw, "The Evolution of Armed Conflict in Medellín: An Analysis of the Major Actors," *Latin American Perspectives* 28, no. 1 (2001): 110–31. https://doi.org/10.1177/0094582X0102800107.

109. Paul Collier, Anke Hoeffler, and Dominic Rohner, "Beyond Greed and Grievance: Feasibility and Civil War," *Oxford Economic Papers* 61, no. 1 (2009): 1–27. https://doi.org/10.1093/oep/gpn029.

110. Luis Alberto Matta, *Poder capitalista y violencia política en Colombia: terrorismo de estado y genocidio de la Unión Patriótica* (Bogotá: Ideas y Soluciones Gráficas, 2002).

111. Juan Guillermo Ferro Medina and Graciela Uribe Ramón, *El orden de la Guerra* (Las FARC-EP: Entre la organización y la política, Bogotá: Centro Editorial Javeriano, 2002).

112. Guy Gugliotta, "The Colombian Cartels and How to Stop Them," in *Drug Policy in the Americas*, ed. Peter Smith (Boulder, CO: Westview Press, 1992): 1–28.

113. Medina and Ramón, *El orden de la Guerra*.

114. Daniel Pécaut, "Guerra, proceso de paz y polarización política," in *Violencias y estrategias colectivas en la región andina*, ed. Gonzalo Sánchez and Eric Lair (Bogotá: Grupo Editorial Norma, 2004), 73–102.

115. Borch and Stuvøy, "Practices of Self–Legitimation in Armed Groups," 105–12.

116. Scott Straus, "Contested Meanings and Conflicting Imperatives: A Conceptual Analysis of Genocide," *Journal of Genocide Research* 3, no. 3 (2001): 349–75. https://doi.org/10.1080/14623520120097189.

117. See Jonathan Matusitz, "Gender Communal Terrorism or War Rape: Ten Symbolic Reasons," *Sexuality & Culture* 21, no. 3 (2017): 830–44. https://doi.org/10.1007/s12119-017-9424-z; Demi Simi and Jonathan Matusitz, "War Rape Survivors of the Second Congo War: A Perspective from Symbolic Convergence Theory," *Africa Review* 6, no. 2 (2014): 81–93. https://doi.org/10.1080/09744053.2014.914636; Victoria Terhune and Jonathan Matusitz, "The Uighurs Versus the Chinese Government: An Application of Realistic Conflict Theory," *Journal of Applied Security Research* 11, no. 2 (2016): 139–48. https://doi.org/10.1080/19361610.2016.1137174.

118. Damir Mirković, "Ethnic Conflict and Genocide: Reflections on Ethnic Cleansing in the Former Yugoslavia," *Annals AAPSS* 548 (1996): 191–99, 197.

119. Ervin Staub, "Genocide and Mass Killing: Origins, Prevention, Healing and Reconciliation," *Political Psychology* 21, no. 2 (2000): 367–82. https://doi.org/10.1111/0162-895X.00193.

120. Roger W. Smith, "State Power and Genocidal Intent: On the Uses of Genocide in the Twentieth Century," in *Studies in Comparative Genocide*, ed. Levon Chorbajian and George Shirinian (New York: St. Martin's, 1999): 3–14.

121. Robert K. Hitchcock and Tara M. Twedt, "Physical and Cultural Genocide of Various Indigenous Peoples," in *Century of Genocide: Eyewitness Accounts and Critical Views*, ed. Samuel Totten, William S. Parsons, and Israel W. Charny (New York: Garland, 1997): 372–407.

122. Alison Des Forges, *Leave None to Tell the Story: Genocide in Rwanda* (New York: Human Rights Watch, 1999).

123. Ervin Staub, Laurie Anne Pearlman, Alexandra Gubin, and Athanase Hagengiman, "Healing, Reconciliation, Forgiving and the Prevention of Violence after Genocide or Mass Killing: An Intervention and Its Experimental Evaluation in Rwanda," *Journal of Social and Clinical Psychology* 24, no. 3 (2005): 297–334. https://doi.org/10.1521/jscp.24.3.297.65617.

124. Christine L. Kellow and H. Leslie Steeves, "The Role of Radio in the Rwandan Genocide," *Journal of Communication* 48, no. 3 (1998): 107–28. https://doi.org/10.1111/j.1460–2466.1998.tb02762.x.

125. Lars Waldorf, "Revisiting *Hotel Rwanda*: Genocide Ideology, Reconciliation, and Rescuers," *Journal of Genocide Research* 11, no. 1 (2009): 101–25. https://doi.org/10.1080/14623520802703673.

126. Filip Reyntjens, "Rwanda: Genocide and Beyond," *Journal of Refugee Studies* 9, no. 3 (1996): 240–51. https://doi.org/10.1093/jrs/9.3.240.

127. Reyntjens, "Rwanda: Genocide and Beyond," 240–51.

128. Kellow and Steeves, "The Role of Radio in the Rwandan Genocide," 107–28.

129. Mette Kaalby Vestergaard, *The Challenges of Forecasting Intelligence: Reassessing Warnings of the 1994 Rwandan Genocide from a Theoretical Perspective* (Odense: University of Southern Denmark, 2019).

130. Philip Gourevitch, *We Wish to Inform You that Tomorrow We Will be Killed with Our Families: Stories from Rwanda* (New York: Picador, 1998).

131. Stefaan Marysse, Tom De Herdt, and Élie Ndayambaje, "Rwanda. Appauvrissement et ajustement structurel," *Cahiers Africains* 12 (2000): 10–21.

132. Luc Bonneux, "Rwanda: A Case of Demographic Entrapment," *Lancet* 344, no. 8938 (1994): 1689–90. http://dx.doi.org/10.1016/S0140-6736(94)90464-2.

133. Jean-Claude Willame, "Aux sources de l'hecatombe rwandaise," *Cahiers Africains* 14 (1995): 10–21.

134. Colette Braeckman, *Rwanda: Histoire d'un genocide* (Paris: Fayard, 1994).

135. Waldorf, "Revisiting *Hotel Rwanda*, 101–25.

136. Marshall McLuhan, *Understanding Media: The Extensions of Man* (Boston, MA: McGraw-Hill, 1964).

137. Catherine A. Luther and Douglas A. Boyd, "American Occupation Control over Broadcasting in Japan, 1945–1952," *Journal of Communication* 47, no. 2 (1997): 39–59. https://doi.org/10.1111/j.1460-2466.1997.tb02705.x.

138. Alexander Russo, "Defensive Transcriptions: Radio Networks, Sound-on-Disc Recording, and the Meaning of Live Broadcasting," *The Velvet Light Trap* 54 (2004): 4–17. https://doi.org/10.1353/vlt.2004.0018.

139. Palwinder Singh Bhatia, "Use of Radio for Health Promotion and Behavior Change: An Analysis," *International Journal of Physical Education, Sports and Health* 4, no. 4 (2017): 103–5.

140. Ibid, 104.

141. Silvio R. Waisbord, "Leviathan Dreams: State and Broadcasting in South America," *The Communication Review* 1, no. 2 (1995): 201–26. https://doi.org/10.1080/10714429509388259.

142. James J. Sadkovich, *The US Media and Yugoslavia, 1991–1995* (Westport, CT: Praeger, 1998); Mark Thompson, *Forging War: The Media in Serbia, Croatia and Bosnia-Hercegovina* (Luton: University of Luton Press, 1999).

143. Maureen Taylor and Michael L. Kent, "Media in Transition in Bosnia: From Propagandistic Past to Uncertain Future," *Gazette* 62, no. 5 (2000): 355–78.

144. David Welch, *The Third Reich: Politics and Propaganda* (London: Routledge, 2002): 184.

145. Harold D. Lasswell, *Propaganda Technique in World War I* (Cambridge: MIT Press, 1971); Alfred McClung Lee, "The Analysis of Propaganda: A Clinical Summary," *American Journal of Sociology* 51, no. 2 (1945): 126–35. https://doi.org/10.1086/219744.

146. Barbara Harff, "No Lessons Learned from the Holocaust? Assessing Risks of Genocide and Political Mass Murder since 1955," *American Political Science Review* 97 (2003): 57–73. http://dx.doi.org/10.1017/S0003055403000522.

147. Vladimir Bratić, "Examining Peace-Oriented Media in Areas of Violent Conflict," *The International Communication Gazette* 70, no. 6 (2008): 487–503. https://doi.org/10.1177/1748048508096397.

148. Garth S. Jowett and Victoria O'Donnell, *Propaganda and Persuasion* (Thousand Oaks, CA: Sage, 1999).

149. Oliver Thomson, *Mass Persuasion in History* (New York: Crane, Russak and Company, 1977).

150. Clifford G. Christians, Kim B. Rotzoll, and Mark Fackler, *Media Ethics: Cases and Moral Reasoning* (White Plains, NY: Longman, 1991): 338.

151. Graham Mytton, "From Saucepan to Dish," in *African Broadcast Cultures: Radio in Transition*, ed. Richard Fardon and Graham Furniss (Oxford: James Currey, 2000): 21–41.

152. Allan Thompson, *The Media and the Rwandan Genocide* (London: Pluto Press, 2007).

153. Jean-Pierre Chrétien, Jean-François Dupaquier, Marcel Kambanda, and Joseph Ngarambe, *Rwanda: les médias du génocide* (Paris: Karthala, 1995).

154. Tharcisse Gatwa, *The Churches and Ethnic Ideology in the Rwandan Crisis (1900–1994)* (Milton Keynes, England: Regnum Books International, 2005).

155. Louise M. Bourgault, *Mass Media and Sub-Saharan Africa* (Bloomington, IN: Indiana University Press, 1995): 80.

156. William A. Hachten, "Broadcasting and Political Crisis," in *Broadcasting in Africa: A Continental Survey of Radio and Television*, ed. Sydney Head (Philadelphia, PA: Temple University Press, 1974): 395–8, 396.

157. Graham Mytton, *Mass Communication in Africa* (London: Edward Arnold, 1983).

158. Alan Zarembo, "Judgment Day," *Harpers* 294, no. 1763 (1997): 68–80.

159. Cited in Bill Berkeley, "Sounds of Violence: Rwanda's Killer Radio," *New Republic* 21, no. 8 (1994): 18–9, 19.

160. Jamie Frederic Metzl, "Rwandan Genocide and the International Law of Radio Jamming," *The American Journal of International Law* 91, no. 4 (1997): 628–51. https://doi.org/10.2307/2998097.

161. Scott Straus, "What Is the Relationship between Hate Radio and Violence? Rethinking Rwanda's 'Radio Machete'," *Politics & Society* 35, no. 4 (2007): 609–37. https://doi.org/10.1177/0032329207308181.

162. Perloff, *The Dynamics of Persuasion*, 202.

163. David Yanagizawa-Drott, "Propaganda and Conflict: Evidence from the Rwandan Genocide," *The Quarterly Journal of Economics* 129, no. 4 (2014): 1947–94. https://doi.org/10.1093/qje/qju020.

164. Linda Melvern, *A People Betrayed: The Role of the West in Rwanda's Genocide* (London: Zed Books, 2000): 71.

165. Ibid, 25.

166. Cited in Linda Melvern, *Intent to Deceive: Denying the Genocide of the Tutsi* (London: Verso, 2020): 169.

167. Mark Frohardt and Jonathan Temin, "The Use and Abuse of Media in Vulnerable Societies," in *The Media and the Rwanda Genocide*, ed. Allan Thompson (London: Pluto Press, 2007): 389–403.

168. Mary Kimani, "RTLM: The Medium that Became a Tool for Mass Murder," in *The Media and the Rwanda Genocide*, ed. Allan Thompson (London: Pluto Press, 2007): 110–24.

169. Yanagizawa-Drott, "Propaganda and Conflict," 1947–64.

170. Quoted in Kellow and Steeves, "The Role of Radio in the Rwandan Genocide," 124.

171. Quoted in Chrétien, Dupaquier, Kambanda, and Ngarambe, *Rwanda*, 7.

172. International Criminal Tribunal for Rwanda, *The Prosecutor v. Ferdinand Nahimana, Jean-Bosco Barayagwiza, and Hassan Ngeze, ICTR Case No. 99-52-T* (The Hague: International Criminal Tribunal for Rwanda, December 3, 2003).

173. Catharine A. MacKinnon, "Prosecutor v. Nahimana, Barayagwiza, & Ngeze. Case No. ICTR 99-52-T," *The American Journal of International Law* 98, no. 2 (2004): 325–30. https://doi.org/10.2307/3176734.

174. Mark Levene, *Genocide in the Age of Nation State* (London: I. B. Tauris, 2005).

175. Cited in Thompson, *The Media and the Rwandan Genocide.*

176. Cassandra Cotton, "'Where Radio is King': Rwanda's Hate Radio and the Lessons Learned," *Atlantic International Studies Journal* 4 (2007): 4–11.

177. Cited in Jean-Pierre Bucyensenge, "At a Time When Rwanda Sunk into Darkness with the Slaughter of over a Million People within Just 100 Days, There Are Certain Individuals Who Stood Out as Key Masterminds," *The New York Times* (April 7, 2014): A1. Retrieved on April 21, 2021 from https://www.newtimes.co.rw/section/read/74417.

178. Perloff, *The Dynamics of Persuasion*, 151.

179. Herbert C. Kelman, "Compliance, Identification, and Internalization: Three Processes of Attitude Change," *Journal of Conflict Resolution* 2, no. 1 (1958): 51–60. https://doi.org/10.1177/002200275800200106.

180. Ibid, 53.

181. Ibid, 53–4.

182. James C. McCroskey, *An Introduction to Rhetorical Communication* (7th Ed.) (Boston, MA: Allyn & Bacon, 1997): 87.

183. Sandra J. Ball-Rokeach and Melvin L. DeFleur, "A Dependency Model of Mass-Media Effects," *Communication Research* 3, no. 1 (1976): 3–21. https://doi.org/10.1177/009365027600300101.

184. Yariv Tsfati and Yoram Peri, "Mainstream Media Skepticism and Exposure to Sectorial and Extranational News Media: The Case of Israel," *Mass Communication & Society* 9, no. 2 (2006): 165–87. https://doi.org/10.1207/s15327825mcs0902_3.

185. Dina Temple-Raston, "Journalism and Genocide," *Columbia Journalism Review* 41, no. 3 (2002): 18–9.

186. Nikolaus Georg Edmund Jackob, "No Alternatives? The Relationship between Perceived Media Dependency, Use of Alternative Information," *International Journal of Communication* 4 (2010): 589–606.

187. William K. Carroll and R. S. Ratner, "Media Strategies and Political Projects: A Comparative Study of Social Movements," *The Canadian Journal of Sociology* 24, no. 1 (1999): 1–34. https://doi.org/10.2307/3341476.

188. Sandra J. Ball-Rokeach, "A Theory of Media Power and a Theory of Media Use: Different Stories, Questions, and Ways of Thinking," *Mass Communication and Society* 1, no. 1 (1998): 5–40. https://doi.org/10.1080/15205436.1998.9676398.

189. Sandra J. Ball-Rokeach, "The Origins of Individual Media-System Dependency: A Sociological Framework," *Communication Research* 12, no. 4 (1985): 485–570. https://doi.org/10.1177/009365085012004003.

190. Denis McQuail, *Mass Communication Theory: An Introduction* (London: Sage, 1994).

191. Roméo Dallaire and Brent Beardsley, *Shake Hands with the Devil: The Failure of Humanity in Rwanda* (Toronto: Random House, 2003).

192. Kellow and Steeves, "The Role of Radio in the Rwandan Genocide," 124.

193. Chrétien, Dupaquier, Kambanda, and Ngarambe, *Rwanda*, 185–95.

194. Ibid, 191.

195. Albert Bandura, *Social Foundations of Thought and Action: A Social Cognitive Theory* (Englewood Cliffs, NJ: Prentice-Hall, 1986).

196. Jonathan Matusitz, "Euphemisms for Terrorism: How Dangerous Are They?" *Empedocles: European Journal for the Philosophy of Communication* 7, no. 2 (2016): 225–37. https://doi.org/10.1386/ejpc.7.2.225_1.

197. Philip Howard, *Euphemisms: The State of the Language* (London: Penguin, 1986).

198. James Pustejovsky, *The Generative Lexicon* (Cambridge: MIT Press, 1995).

199. Alan Filreis, "'Words with "All the Effects of Force:' Cold-War Interpretation," *American Quarterly* 39, no. 2 (1987): 306–12.

200. Herbert Marcuse, *One-Dimensional Man* (Boston, MA: Beacon Press, 1964): 96.

201. Howard F. Stein, *Euphemism, Spin and the Crisis in Organizational Life* (Westport, CT: Quorum Books, 1998).

202. W. Peter Robinson, "Lying in the Public Domain," *American Behavioral Scientist* 36, no. 3 (1993): 359–82. https://doi.org/10.1177/0002764293036003007.

203. Gabriel Weimann, "The Psychology of Mass-Mediated Terrorism," *American Behavioral Scientist* 52, no. 1 (2008): 69–86. https://doi.org/10.1177/0002764208321342.

204. Jonathan Matusitz, *Terrorism & Communication: A Critical Introduction* (Thousand Oaks, CA: Sage, 2013).

205. Rony Blum, Gregory H. Stanton, Shira Sagi, and Elihu D. Richter, "'Ethnic Cleansing' Bleaches the Atrocities of Genocide," *European Journal of Public Health* 18, no. 2 (2007): 204–9. https://doi.org/10.1093/eurpub/ckm011.

206. Ervin Staub, *The Roots of Evil: The Origins of Genocide and Other Group Violence* (New York: Cambridge University Press, 1989): 29.

207. Gregory S. Gordon, "Music and Genocide: Harmonizing Coherence, Freedom and Nonviolence in Incitement Law," *Santa Clara Law Review* 50 (2010): 607–46.

208. Perez Zagorin, *Ways of Lying: Dissimulation, Persecution and Conformity in Early Modern Europe* (Cambridge, MA: Harvard University Press, 1990): 256.

209. Vahakn N. Dadrian, "Patterns of Twentieth Century Genocides: The Armenian, Jewish, and Rwandan Cases," *Journal of Genocide Research* 6, no. 4 (2004): 487–522. https://doi.org/10.1080/1462352042000320583.

210. Christopher Clapham, "Rwanda: The Perils of Peacemaking," *Journal of Peace Research* 35, no. 2 (1998): 193–210, 209. https://doi.org/10.1177/0022343398035002003.

211. Nir Kalron, "The Great Lakes of Confusion," *African Security Review* 19, no. 2 (2010): 25–37. https://doi.org/10.1080/10246029.2010.503056.

212. Cited in Li, "Echoes of Violence," 15.

213. Darryl Li, "Echoes of Violence: Considerations on Radio and Genocide in Rwanda," *Journal of Genocide Research* 6, no. 1 (2004): 9–27. https://doi.org/10.1080/1462352042000194683.

214. Adam Jones, "Gender and Genocide in Rwanda," *Journal of Genocide Research* 4, no. 1 (2002): 65–94. https://doi.org/10.1080/14623520120113900.

215. Li, "Echoes of Violence," 14–8.

216. Ibid, 14–8.

217. Jones, "Gender and Genocide in Rwanda," 65–94.

218. Gerard Prunier, *The Rwanda Crisis 1959–1994: History of a Genocide* (London: Hurst, 1995): 138, 142.

219. Edward Diener, John Dineen, Karen Endresen, Arthur L. Beaman, and Scott C. Fraser, "Effects of Altered Responsibility, Cognitive Set, and Modeling on Physical Aggression and Deindividuation," *Journal of Personality and Social Psychology* 31, no. 2 (1975): 328–37. http://dx.doi.org/10.1037/h0076279.

220. René Lemarchand, *Burundi: Ethnic Conflict and Genocide* (Cambridge: Cambridge University Press, 1996): 125.

221. Gordon, "Music and Genocide," 607–46.

222. Charles Mironko, "Igitero: Means and Motive in the Rwandan Genocide," *Journal of Genocide Research* 6, no. 1 (2004): 47–60. https://doi.org/10.1080/1462352042000194700.

223. Ibid.

224. Mahmood Mamdani, *When Victims Become Killers: Colonialism, Nativism, and the Genocide in Rwanda* (Princeton, NJ: Princeton University Press, 2014).

225. Jean-Pierre Chrétien, Jean-François Dupaquier, Marcel Kambanda, and Joseph Ngarambe, *Rwanda: les médias du génocide* (Paris: Karthala, 1995): 305.

226. Kellow and Steeves, "The Role of Radio in the Rwandan Genocide," 107–28.

227. Mironko, "Igitero," 47–60.

228. Chrétien, Dupaquier, Kambanda, and Ngarambe, *Rwanda*, 360.

229. African Rights, *Rwanda: Death, Despair and Defiance* (London: African Rights, 1995); Gerard Prunier, *The Rwanda Crisis 1959–1994: History of a Genocide* (London: Hurst, 1995).

230. Cited in Marijke Verpoorten, "The Death Toll of the Rwandan Genocide: A Detailed Analysis for Gikongoro Province," *Population* 60, no. 4 (2005): 331–67. https://doi.org/10.3917/popu.504.0401.

231. Christopher Taylor, "A Gendered Genocide: Tutsi Women and Hutu Extremists in the 1994 Rwanda Genocide," *PoLAR: Political and Legal Anthropology Review* 22, no. 1 (1999): 42–54. https://doi.org/10.1525/pol.1999.22.1.42.

232. René Lemarchand, "The Rwanda Genocide," in *Century of Genocide: Eyewitness Accounts and Critical Views*, ed. Samuel Totten, William S. Parsons, and Israel W. Charny (New York: Garland Publishing): 408–17.

233. Catherine Bonnet, "Le viol des femmes survivantes du génocide au Rwanda," in *Rwanda, un génocide du XXe siècle*, ed. Raymond Verdier, Emmanuel Decaux, and Jean-Pierre Chrétien (Paris: Editions L'Harmattan, 1995): 17–29.

234. Ibid, 18–24.

235. Adam Jones, "Gender and Genocide in Rwanda," *Journal of Genocide Research* 4, no. 1 (2002): 65–94, https://doi.org/10.1080/14623520120113900.

236. Christopher Taylor, "A Gendered Genocide: Tutsi Women and Hutu Extremists in the 1994 Rwanda Genocide," *PoLAR: Political and Legal Anthropology Review* 22, no. 1 (1999): 42–54. https://doi.org/10.1525/pol.1999.22.1.42.

237. Waldorf, "Revisiting *Hotel Rwanda*," 101–25.

238. International Crisis Group, *The Congo: Solving the FDLR Problem Once and For All* (Brussels: International Crisis Group, 2005).

239. Pierre Vidal-Naquet, *Les assassins de la mémoire* (Paris: La Découverte, 1987).

CHAPTER 14

Public Communication Campaigns of White Supremacism

White supremacism is an ideology advancing that the White race is superior to other races and, as such, should dominate or exterminate them.[1] White supremacism is rooted in the widely debunked theory of scientific racism and its pseudoscientific assertions. Along the lines of similar movements like neo-Nazism, White supremacists target people of other races, immigrants, and Jews.[2] **White supremacist terrorism** is a class of terrorism carried out by nonstate actors whose objectives include, but are not limited to, (1) racial dominance; (2) hostility towards government authority; and (3) virulent disapproval of abortion.[3] Contemporary right-wing terrorism is often made synonymous with White supremacist terrorism and became popular in the West in the 1970s.[4] It is "violence perpetrated by organized groups against racial [and other] minorities in the pursuit of White and Aryan supremacist agendas."[5]

Notwithstanding the election of the first African–American president in the United States, the danger posed by White supremacist violence is unrelenting. It is imperative that academics and policymakers alike understand the massive motivators of White supremacist campaigns. With the aid of the internet and social media, their public communication campaigns are no longer in the periphery and promote a transnational identity principally based on racial and nationalistic dogmas. The campaigns have also managed to manipulate debates on immigration and globalization into the present mainstream political discourse. This has led to the regularization of White supremacist language and lexicons, thereby turning far-right beliefs—until recently, long dismissed as abhorrent by most Americans—into potential options on matters related to immigration and social culture. White supremacist campaigns can carry an unfavorable impact on society, empowering people who espouse such extremist views, while desensitizing audiences to hate speech and the violent acts associated with it. "Lone-wolf" incidents of White supremacist terrorism are far from unlikely, as witnessed by the shooting rampages in places like Oak Creek in Wisconsin, Charleston, Pittsburgh, San Diego, and El Paso.[6]

A Violent Ideology

The unprecedented influence of White supremacist organizations goes beyond their influence on social media. By advocating racial hatred and violence, they can radically transform society in many ways. The two case studies detailed in this chapter—i.e., the "It's Okay to Be White" and the 2020 voter fraud campaigns—ascertain White supremacist violence based on, *inter alia*, hate speech (still, to this day, the most noticeable harmful aspect on social media). Although not all White supremacists refer to themselves as members of the Ku Klux Klan, they still espouse an ideology of White supremacism, which attests to the rhetorical capabilities of that doctrine. Organizational and doctrinal disparities are obvious across these organizations, but they all share the common denominator of believing in the imminent cataclysm of "White racial genocide" and the belief that a multicultural society is anathema to European American values.[7] They are adamant about maintaining White racial power in reaction to changing demographics that they cannot fathom. The US Census Bureau estimates that Caucasians will no longer be the majority by 2044, which has anchored fear and odium into the minds of White supremacists.[8]

While the White supremacist philosophy is not entirely violent, much of their ethos can directly or indirectly cause violence. Being associated with a White supremacist organization is inherently associated with a penchant for enacting or supporting violence in the name of the ideology. Again, just like organizational and doctrinal differences exist between those groups, the degree of violence that is promoted varies across the White supremacist spectrum. For radicals allied with vigilantism, "splinter cells," and "lone actors," their penchant for violence translates into planned attacks like terrorism, bombings, and mass shootings.[9] Such approaches fall under the umbrella concept of "leaderless resistance," which is a strategy of opposition that facilitates and encourages people or small groups to perform acts of political violence; they perform these independently of any organization, leadership-based structure, or network of support.[10] These extremists see themselves as more efficient when working alone than operating within the confines of a group because they have more mobility, can work in full anonymity, and do not seem to worry about infiltration from law enforcement. In addition to those White supremacists who amass high-powered assault rifles and plan terror plots, some of these people are also involved in street violence with less sophisticated weapons. Their techniques of combat include traditional physical assaults and hate crimes.[11]

Statistics on Right-Wing Terrorism

As mentioned in the previous section, not all White supremacists are terrorists, but those who are have been called right-wing extremists. To this point, however, Simi (2010)[12] argues that there is no meaningful distinction between the two "versions" of White supremacists. The destructiveness of events like the 1995 Oklahoma City Bombing and the 2017 "Unite the Right" rally in Charlottesville, Virginia, corroborates this idea. The "Unite the Right" rally, marked by the presence of loud White men with tiki torches, was the embodiment of the White Power Movement as it materialized from the online sphere that it had been festering in for the previous two decades. This rally, replete with far-right messages, and the fierce clashes with counterprotestors, was a shocker around the world.[13] The event culminated with the killing of Heather Heyer and defined the moment of the White Power Movement. In spite of the earth-shattering effects of the "Unite the Right" rally in the United States in mid-August 2017, for those who have done a close examination of the far right, this incident was a more visible face to a movement that was simply out of the radar for a while.[14]

Right-wing terrorism is on the rise in the United States and across Europe. In mid-March 2021, only one year after COVID-19 became the official pandemic in the world, there were close to 4,000 anti-Asian hate crime incidents—mostly against women—in the United States alone.[15] Right-wing extremists were already responsible for about 50 killings in 2018, a 26% increase over 2017. According to an Anti-Defamation League's report (2019),[16] 2018 was the fourth-worst year for murders inspired by domestic extremism since 1970; of those attacks, right-wing extremists carried out 78% of them. On July 23, 2019, Christopher A. Wray, the 8th Director of the Federal Bureau of Investigation (FBI), spoke at a Senate Judiciary Committee hearing to announce that the FBI apprehended about 100 domestic terrorists between October 2018 and July 2019. Most of them had White supremacist affiliations. Wray said that the agency was "aggressively pursuing [domestic terrorism] using both counterterrorism resources and criminal investigative resources and partnering closely with our state and local partners," but it was also worried about the violence itself (not merely its ideology). During that time frame, a similar proportion of arrests took place around the world. Prior to that hearing on July 23, 2019, Wray had already warned that White supremacism was becoming more dangerous in the United States.[17]

Based on statistics from the Center for Strategic and International Studies on terrorist events published in June 2020, the most serious threat presumably comes from White supremacism. Between 1994 and 2020, almost 900 terrorist attacks and attempts took place in the United States. White supremacist terrorists were responsible for most—57%—of those attacks and attempts, unlike 25% conducted by left-wing terrorists, 15% by religious terrorists, 3% by separatist terrorists, and 0.7% by other types of terrorists. In the 1990s, the majority of White supremacist attacks targeted abortion clinics. Since 2014, such attacks have often been directed at citizens and institutions because of religious, racial, or ethnic motives. State agencies, governmental buildings, and law enforcement forces were also frequent White supremacist targets between 1994 and 2020, particularly attacks by militias and national sovereignty organizations.[18]

Key Terms on White Supremacism

The point was made that White supremacism is an extremist ideology. By definition, **ideology** is a one-sided perspective or worldview limited by preconceived notions of the world, mental representations, convictions, attitudes, and evaluations. Ideologies are common for members of particular social groups. They are instrumental in establishing and upholding unfair power differentials through rhetoric: for instance, by nurturing "superior identity" narratives, by coopting discourses, or by monopolizing public spheres ("gatekeeping").[19] In many cases, ideologies are subtle or camouflaged within messages, disguised within coded language.[20] In the vein of most extremist ideologies, White supremacist campaigns stress the importance of preserving their long-established identities. In the context of this chapter, **identity** is a construct whereby people negotiate their own (and others') category memberships across a multiplicity of situations, via rhetorical and other social practices.[21] Identity can be both a "label" ascribed by people to themselves and a label given to them by others.[22]

White supremacist groups espouse nativism as an ideology for their campaigns. **Nativism** combines nationalism with xenophobia to request that states favor members of the native group (i.e., European Americans) and treat nonnative elements disparagingly because they are perceived as a fundamental threat to the monolithic nation-state.[23] Nonnative elements are essentialized on the basis of race, ethnicity, or religion, and can include subgroups within the native racial group, like LGBTQ+ folks and sections of the international community.[24] In their more recent communication campaigns, most White supremacist organizations have seemingly promoted an ethnopluralist genre of nativism that is more acceptable to voters.[25] **Ethnopluralism** sees cultures as equal but distinct and, thus, not reconcilable. Supporters of ethnopluralism purport to acknowledge cultural differences, but claim that these differences must be shielded from phenomena like mass migration, cultural domination, and one-worldism. The cultural *mélange* that takes place in multicultural societies is interpreted as a form of national suicide.[26] This is why White supremacists promote the concept of **ethnocracy**, an ethnic democracy where primacy will be placed on protecting one's own people. Through ethnopluralism, they picture a culturally diverse sphere made up of monocultural nation-states.[27]

When prominence is placed on protecting one's own kind, the concepts of nativism and ethnopluralism can quickly morph into exclusionary populism. Unlike **inclusionary populism**, which makes requests that physical benefits and political rights be granted to historically disenfranchised groups, **exclusionary populism** describes "the people" in a much narrower sense, centering on a specific sociocultural group and disregarding minority groups. Accordingly, exclusionary populism strives to rule out certain groups from "the people" and restrict their access to equal benefits and entitlements.[28] The political tendencies listed in this section have often been designated by scholars as Fascist. **Fascism** is a philosophy that combines extremism, nativism, and exclusionary populism. It promotes a national rebirth and the violent overthrow of the liberal democratic régime, which is regarded as depraved, corrupt, and against the common **denizen** (i.e., citizen). The purpose of a national rebirth is to create "a new type of political system, a new élite, a new type of human being."[29]

Lastly, White supremacism is a form of hegemonic ideology. A type of unreasonable dominance and power of one group over other groups, **hegemony** denotes the obstinate effort of an ideological movement to preserve its power through alliance-creating strategies. The concept originated in the works of Antonio Gramsci (1971),[30] an Italian philosopher who condemned class identities as embedded within rigid economic and social relations. In the case of White supremacism, class identities have shifted from the economic to the cultural realm. Social identities, then, become crystallized by culture, which determines social distinctions and rationalizes social problems as phenomena caused by the incommensurable aspect of different cultures.[31] The next several sections point to the male hegemony that White supremacists display towards what they perceive as "dangerous" feminist, anti-conservative White male attitudes.

WHITE SUPREMACIST CAMPAIGNING THROUGH THE MANOSPHERE

The **manosphere** is a network of groups and websites that espouse male supremacy and subjugation of women. Marwick and Caplan (2018)[32] define it as "a loose collection of interlinked sites ... steeped in misogyny (and in some cases racism)." Promoting traditional gender roles is a frequent expression within the manosphere. The manosphere takes the **red**

pill, a phrase used to describe an awakening to the importance of fighting to maintain such traditional gender roles. It is associated with men who open their eyes to the reality of their brothers being subjugated by women. It also implies an awakening to the reality of "immigrant invasion" because the latter is perceived as posing a threat to White masculine values in the Western world—a view promulgated by renown White nationalist Pat Buchanan. As a viable remedy to being perceived as effeminate, White supremacists uphold their red-pilled state by aggressively exhibiting masculine attitudes towards women.[33]

The MGTOW Campaign

The manosphere consists of three web-based groups—Men's Rights Activists (MRAs), Pick-Up Artists (PUAs), and Men Going Their Own Way (MGTOWs)—that have been erroneously considered individual groups with different practices and philosophies.[34] We can focus, for example, on **Men Going Their Own Way**. MGTOW is a supremacist manosphere-based group that has launched a campaign based on principles from the Men's Liberation Movement. More specifically, the campaign promotes individualistic, self-emboldening masculine actions (e.g., competition, virile activities, and so forth). The ideology and rhetoric of MGTOW turn misogynistic beliefs into mainstream ideas that even make online harassment seem normal.[35] Jones, Trott, and Wright (2020)[36] ran a multiphased thematic analysis of over 10,000 campaign tweets from three key MGTOW leaders. The findings report a correlation between MGTOW's ideology and toxic masculinity, demonstrating that their appetite for online harassment is profoundly misogynistic and imposes strict boundaries that protect heterosexual, hegemonic masculinity. The thematic analysis also shows that, although the misogyny and aggressiveness engendered by MGTOW is not extreme in and of itself, their rationalization of misogynistic beliefs makes it normalized. The study provides fresh insights on the overheterogeneous and overmasculine attributes of the manosphere.

Ferber (2000)[37] compared the rhetoric of such a movement with that of hate groups. Both generate language that frame men as attacked by powerful entities that seek to emasculate men to the benefit of other genders and identities. Both groups interpret feminism as a dangerous belief that threatens the quintessence of both men and women. It redefines women in ways never seen before, increasingly in positions of power over men. Ferber contended that both groups redefine men in a shameful fashion (because of their emasculation). The discourses concoct a solution to this issue: for men—White men especially—to go back to their core masculine selves in order to reclaim supremacy over women (as well as immigrants and other racial groups). To this day, scholarly literature about the manosphere is limited.

Global Participation

This informal network of websites is united in its opposition to feminism and advancement of misogyny. Locally, each website contributes greatly to creating space for an iteration of masculinity to grow. Globally, the manosphere constructs a large infrastructure for masculinities to mobilize in a process of construction and sunder.[38] The White supremacist men's rights movement has attracted widespread media attention from all corners of the globe. The abundance of "rights" groups, media platforms, and concerns is evident and requires consideration to the subtleties among different White supremacists' goals and grievances.

Nevertheless, the overarching interests and strategies of male domination remain clear. More importantly, the growing popularity of this phenomenon provides a starting point to consider when observing non-White groups actually supporting White supremacists. While the latter are predominantly Western, the movement is growing in a non-Western direction as well—particularly in India.[39]

The Alt-Right

An abbreviation of alternative right, **Alt-Right** is a comprehensive term to describe groups that surmise that European ancestry and White identity and principles (e.g., Judeo-Christian values and traditional gender roles) are under threat by political correctness, social justice reforms, and massive immigration. The Alt-Right has a wide online following in gaming communities and in the adoption of memes. The term was invented by Richard Spencer, an American neo-Nazi and White supremacist, as part of his supreme mission to sway the public into believing that the aforementioned hateful ideologies are reasonable options in the political spectrum.[40] Richard Spencer was editing *The American Conservative* and *Taki's Magazine* before creating AlternativeRight. and *Radix Journal*. The Alt-Right started as an online project centered on anonymous websites like 4chan, 8chan, and Reddit's r/TheRedPill as well as far-right online forums like American Renaissance, VD ARE, Breitbart, and Counter-Currents.com. These diverse groups had the common denominator of standing up against establishment conservatives, which the Alt-Right calls **cuckservatives**, a portmanteau of cuckold—the husband of an unfaithful wife—and conservative. Cuckservatives are accused of having been disloyal to conservativism by cowardly embracing hegemonic liberal philosophies like equality and multiculturalism.[41]

The Alt-Right takes an antagonistic stance towards US culture and government. Spencer and his followers are inspired by the antimodernist, revolutionary, and Fascist right. Capitalizing on social media platforms like 4chan and 8chan, Reddit, YouTube and Twitter, the Alt-Right campaigns with derision, impudence, and humor to transform far-right politics into a trendy, hip movement. By challenging long-standing political norms and making ex-President Donald Trump an ally, the Alt-Right has turned large swaths of the political landscape in the United States into mainstreaming far-right phenomena.[42] The Alt-Right today projects itself as a large sociopolitical collective of youths who are tech-savvy, leaderless, digitally connected, and well-versed in internet jargon to normalize and reshape White supremacist beliefs through the promotion of Western chauvinism or White identity politics.[43]

Gender is as essential to the Alt-Right ethos as race. The sociopolitical movement formulates a traditionalist gender doctrine that envisions a return to patriarchy and heterosexual masculinity, believed to be under constant attack. Because it consists mostly of men united by misogyny and male victimhood, the Alt-Right bears close resemblance to the manosphere. Both subscribe to the conviction that "not all men are created equal."[44] Indeed, the Alt-Right believes that human inequality is acceptable. It is a fact of life that is reflected in the differences between races, nations, culture, genders, and sexual orientations. Heterosexual White Western men are at the top of the food chain.[45] Not surprisingly, then, hatred towards feminism is widespread in Alt-Right rhetoric. Masculinity has become a political identity by nature. It is mixed with major populist messages aimed at supporters. It is particularly the case for working-class men, and more and more for middle-class and white-collar men. Having a full grasp of this aspect of populism allows us to get the full picture to determine what has led to the popularity of populism in the world at this particular point. At the same time that populism is rising, hardline, fundamentalist religious groups and hatred and hostility towards feminism are rising too.[46]

Leaderless Resistance

Campaigning through the manosphere has also been facilitated by leaderless resistance. **Leaderless resistance** is a social resistance approach in which small, autonomous groups of people go up against an established institution.[47] Using the model of leaderless resistance developed by Louis Beam (1992),[48] an American White supremacist himself, online communications like message bulletin boards are useful to disseminate Alt-Right-sounding or manosphere-like messages, to maintain communication between participants and supporters, and rope in new members with minimal difficulties.[49] The internet has been pivotal in facilitating its popularity and expansion.[50] The universality of online communications and social networking platforms has been a driver for White supremacism, which continues to experience noteworthy changes.[51] In simple terms, leaderless resistance advocates the separation from large White supremacist groups (e.g., Aryan Nations, National Alliance, Hammerskins, etc.) in support of smaller independent units that can campaign more easily for their supreme ideologies. During the course of this change, groups can redefine their images or rebrand themselves as wardens of traditional Judeo-Christian principles within Western civilization. Again, popularity and expansion of far-reaching White supremacist ideologies are made possible by the co-option of the internet and all it can offer.[52] The two case studies described in this chapter—"It's Okay to Be White" and the 2020 voter fraud campaign—will demonstrate the devastating impact of online campaigns on real-world behavior.

Case Study: "It's Okay to Be White"

"It's Okay to Be White" is a campaign initiated by the website 4chan, more specifically its forum /pol/, in 2017. Giant flyers and stickers with the sentence "It's Okay to Be White" have been made visible on the streets and university campuses in the United States, Canada, Australia, and the United Kingdom.[53] The campaign has been endorsed by White supremacists including neo-Nazis, former Ku Klux Klan Grand Wizard David Duke, and *The Daily Stormer*.[54] A report by the Anti-Defamation League explains how the expression itself has been employed by the White supremacist movement since 2001 when it was seen in the title of a song by a White Power rock band called Aggressive Force. In 2005, it was also spotted on flyers and slogans voiced by the United Klans of America.[55] Lyrics of *It's Okay to Be White* by Aggressive Force read the following: "It's okay to be White, Strength through pride, You have inside, It's okay to be White, It's okay to be White, Loyalty within you, Have with your kin."[56] The anthem's lyrics send a direct message to those with personal guilt about being White. The song reminds listeners that they are "taught to feel guilty of the whole White race" and, then, concludes with a catchy chorus: "It's okay to be proud and it's okay to be bold and it's okay to be White."

Social Media Platforms

The **"Politically Incorrect"** (**/pol/**) was introduced in 2011 as a sphere for repugnant views that, by that year, had begun to monopolize most of the boards on 4chan. /pol/ touts itself as an ideal space for far-right users—i.e., Anons3—to debate politics or views considered politically incorrect. Nevertheless, its posture as a true beacon of free speech offers a safe haven for 4chan's most vehemently bigoted participants. Although not all comments on /pol/ should necessarily be labeled far-right or even neo-Nazi, its pages are inundated by symbols of the swastika, racial slurs, antisemitic and Islamophobic posts, and misogynistic sentiment.[57] The /pol/ board's advantage of remaining anonymous, in addition to its subcultural elements immersed in memetics, inside jokes, and hard-to-decipher language, explains why countless users are still donating their money to that online platform. One user encouraged his or her peers to take advantage of the AirDrop feature on iPhones, an app which enables Apple users to effortlessly send files to other Apple devices in the proximity. "Targets will see the image preview for the 'It's Okay to Be White' poster regardless if they choose to accept and save it," that user asserts.[58]

Posts with texts like "It's Okay to Be White" have mushroomed on other social media sites as well, as it is now acceptable to express feelings of White nationalism in public spheres.[59] More precisely, the campaign has somewhat shifted from 4chan to other social media platforms where the message's merits are continuously debated within the colloquial racial communications taking place online.[60] In a qualitative analysis of YouTube videos, where the video bloggers expressly endorsed the feeling that "it's okay to be White," Brooks (2020)[61] discovered that the video bloggers used strategic engagement with certain perspectives of colorblindness while staying away from others. As Brooks continued, the planners of the "It's Okay to Be White" campaign were able to adapt their message on YouTube. This technique was so successful that other video bloggers who provided alternative, conservative angles on news, media, and entertainment applied the same strategies of colorblind race discourse as did those who self-identify as White supremacists and members of the Alt-Right.

Different Locations

Various locations have been subject to hatred as a result of the "It's Okay to Be White" campaign. For example, in Tennessee, in an act of vandalism, such White supremacist flyers were placed on Borchuck Plaza (at East Tennessee State University) "over the memorial plaques of those five pioneering individuals who desegregated our institution during the 1950s," ETSU President Noland said in November 2019. "It is clear that the posting and placement of these flyers was an attempt to create division in our community and I am disgusted by this act," he continued.[62] Across the Pond, in England, a number of posters with the phrase "It's Okay to Be White" appeared around Bristol's city center. The posters, which featured this exclusive type of messaging, were condemned on social media and by residents. Students from the University of Bristol unleashed their anger on Twitter. As one commentator wrote, "These posters have been put up on campus. My university, ladies and gentlemen."[63] In Scotland, a multiplicity of stickers reading "It's Okay to Be White" in block capitals turned up on street lights and drain pipes around the city center of Perth. Perth City Center's councilor Peter Barrett said: "This is despicable hate speech. It is covert racism disguising white supremacist views. People should be in no doubt this is no innocuous joke."[64]

White Male Victimization Narratives

The "It's Okay to Be White" campaign also features online participants dressed up in Halloween costumes that wear A4 sheets of paper and stickers with the phrase, "It's Okay to Be White," all the while walking through their local neighborhoods. The centerpiece of this ritual is the advancement of White supremacist ideals in mainstream spaces; this is achieved by using language that claims Whiteness should also be part of multiculturalism. Not only does this rhetorical approach render the campaign more acceptable to audiences predisposed to dislike overt displays of racism; it also produces opportunities to generate what is now being called **salt**, an angry Leftist reaction on social media or sensational news segments in the mass media. Because the statement "It's Okay to Be White" can be interpreted as relatively harmless, angry reactions can be co-opted by the Alt-Right as a master-narrative of White male victimization, further reinforcing the alleged threatened lives of people within this group.[65] Nevertheless, what they call an innocuous phrase could spark a media backlash and, possibly, violence.[66]

If truth be told, the expression "It's Okay to Be White" is evocative of some of the core attributes of red pills, for which White supremacist rhetors try to offer justifications of the Left's erosion of White Western identity.[67] Upon looking at online posts and threads about the campaign, the red pill rhetoric often emerges when users allude to the fictitious accusation of White guilt that has disheartened the White nation. A core constituent of the White supremacist ideology hypothesizes that young White men are being indoctrinated into believing in their own culpability for race-based violence of the past, like slavery and colonization.[68] As Ferber (2000)[69] points out, such discourse positions antiracist efforts—often attacked as being merely "reverse racism"—as part of a permeating conspiracy to infuse a deep-seated "guilt complex" in White people. In this case, White supremacist rhetors insist that guilt and shame are weaponized in order to paralyze heterosexual White men. The phrase "It's Okay to Be White," then, exists as a tacit allusion that some invisible subversive forces claim that the opposite is true.

Just as the unseen meaning of the phrase is loaded with White victimization depictions, effective red pill campaigns are those inspired by the active conditioning of potential supporters. Alt-Right trolls display little concern for the way their enemies perceive them, but they do not hesitate exploiting the assumed "useful idiocy" of normies (i.e., people with no specific position on that subject). Although Alt-Righters do not pay attention to their opponents, they motivate each other to befriend normies or try to convince them.[70] As one informative post on trolling, published in The Right Stuff 36 (a far-right blog), explains,

> You should assume that you will never manage to convince your ideological enemies of the merit of your position. Rather, the purpose of trolling is to convince people reading your comments of the merit of your position. On many different web forums, lurkers outnumber posters by 10 to one. The purpose of trolling raids is to convince these anonymous people, not the person you disagree with. As such, you can win hearts and minds even when met with universal opposition.[71]

By airing their grievances concerning accusations of White guilt, avid followers—like /pol/ users—project themselves as militants in the passive resistance ready to push back against the oppressive forces of White genocide. In this context, the phrase, "It's Okay to Be White," is conceived as an affirmative statement, claiming little more than Whites' natural right to express pride in their own kind.[72] Whiteness as "heritage" is something to behold. It is the embodiment of the rhetorical versatility of a massive-scale campaign that has emerged in the way White supremacists construct the term "heritage." Their use of the word "heritage" originates from a nationwide debate concerning the importance of Confederate memorials in the United States. White supremacists invoke the notion of "heritage" in conversations on Confederate history, a history that glorifies White, Confederate combatants and generals as heroes. Though a certain number of educated and uneducated citizens believe that the statues should remain, a significant group of antiracist activists and academics link these memorials to racist agendas and legacies,[73] suggesting that focus on "history" is actually focus on White heritage. The concept of "heritage" becomes the hallmark of a massive bigoted campaign that shows strong allegiance to White supremacism. The "It's Okay to Be White" campaign sounds like "immigrants are taking away our heritage"—a heritage of White dominance.

THE PROUD BOYS

Founded by Gavin McInnes, a Canadian political commentator and writer, the **Proud Boys** are a White supremacist and neo-Fascist group of men that encourages and enacts political violence in North America.[74] They are an Alt-Right subsidiary movement advertised to young men as a fraternity-like collective that honors "Western ideals." They operate on the principle of both symbolic and physical violence, and the group is expanding.[75] The Proud Boys became a household name in August 2017 when multiple members notoriously attended the "Unite the Right" rally in Charlottesville, Virginia. After one woman was murdered and 19 others were seriously wounded in a vehicle-ramming attack, McInnes "disavowed" the Proud Boys who were present.[76] The next year, in 2018, the organization was temporarily designated as an extremist organization by the FBI.[77] In February 2021, the Canadian government added the Proud Boys to its list of terrorist organizations. They became one of 13 groups labeled as terrorist organizations. Canada is the first country to do so. This designation as a terrorist organization would allow the government to freeze the group's assets and impose terrorism-related penalties. Funding the organization or buying Proud Boys artifacts would also be considered a federal offense.[78]

The Proud Boys' Ideology

Just like the "It's Okay to Be White" campaign, the Proud Boys believe that men are victimized by feminist, progressive, and anti-White ideals. On September 15, 2016, Gavin McInnes presented the Proud Boys to the world. In his announcement, he declared that "being Proud of Western culture today" was akin to "being a crippled, Black, lesbian Communist in 1953."[79] The Proud Boys compare modern feminism to a crusade against White males, particularly the conservative ones. Rather than pointing the finger at neoliberal policies, which excessively affect working-class males, the Proud Boys attribute their predicament to women who are flying in the face of the natural order of things. This aspiration to regain the natural order of things and wield domination is termed, by members, **radical traditionalism**. In the academic sphere, radical traditionalism is a category of fundamentalism that considers traditional gender roles as ones that should be enforced.[80] Under this philosophical model, gender equality is vanquished by antifeminist rhetoric and coded words—e.g., Western chauvinism as code for White, multiculturalism as code for White genocide, etc.—are no longer in use. On the other hand, acrimonious labels are ascribed to feminists and civil rights activists to pigeonhole them as opponents.[81]

As McInnes stated on his *Gavin McInnes Show*, "Maybe the reason I'm sexist is because women are dumb. No, I'm just kidding, ladies. But you do tend to not thrive in certain areas—like writing."[82] To further prove that the Alt-Right, ultranationalist groups, and the manosphere share some much in common, one can simply look at what McInnes stated in a 2015 interview. As such, "women earn less in America because they choose to," they are "less ambitious," and the gender pay gap is "sort of God's way—this is nature's way—of saying women should be at home with the kids."[83] Unlike certain White supremacist derivations like the manosphere, the Proud Boys expressly champion political violence against their opponents, particularly those on the Left. After one of those happened (a huge fight in New York), McInnes commented, "I want violence, I want punching in the face. I'm disappointed in Trump supporters for not punching enough."[84] In one 2017 segment of the *Gavin McInnes Show*, he said, "We will kill you. That's the Proud Boys in a nutshell. We will kill you. We look nice, we seem soft, we have boys in our name ... we will assassinate you."[85]

The Proud Boys' Campaign Tactics

Deliberate provocation is a staple of the Proud Boys' campaign tactics for recruitment. Their choice of words and symbolic representation of violence are molded to elicit strong reactions in others. Members enjoy sporting attire with pugnacious slogans like "Female Tears" or "Leftists get the Chopper." The latter is a reference to the extreme tactic used by Chilean dictator Augusto Pinochet, whose régime killed political opponents by throwing them from choppers (i.e., helicopters).[86] Speaking of deliberate provocation, on January 29, 2018—which marked the one-year anniversary of the Quebec mosque massacre where six people lost their lives and another 19 were injured in a White supremacist attack—the Proud Boys and other groups overtly opposed a memorial at both Mel Lastman Square and Nathan Phillips Square in Toronto. The purpose was to "debunk the myth of systematic Islamophobia." Their decision to protest during the commemoration of the mosque massacre was an attempt to provoke a reaction from—and aggravate the suffering of—Muslims traumatized by this tragedy.[87]

Another campaign tactic is **cultural hijacking**, the practice whereby the symbols and discourse of civil rights advocates are reframed to further far-right narratives. The purpose is not to appropriate civil rights symbolism, but to minimize the communicative impact of groups from which the symbols stemmed. By absorbing civil rights jargon into their White Western male philosophy, the Proud Boys hijack discourses of marginalization and shape new narratives that put their so-called situations of precarity on a pedestal. After hijacking these terms, they impute new designations to the groups from which they have hijacked. Civil rights leaders become SJWs, snowflakes, or the dogmatic Left. Among the culturally hijacked concepts, the one that seems to be the most recurrent is *Uhuru*—Swahili for African solidarity. The Proud Boys have "stolen" *Uhuru* to make it a rallying cry, in a manner analogous to the military use of "Oohrah" in the US Navy since the second part of the twentieth century.[88]

A third campaign tactic is manipulating communication. A few years prior to the formation of the Proud Boys, McInnes mentioned a strategy during his account of his work overseas. In his memoir titled *The Death of Cool*, McInnes (2013)[89] wrote: "Being White in Taiwan is like being famous ... Actually, they get mad if you say White because that is politically incorrect. The term is Western." Western now surfaces in the Proud Boys first degree, a stage during which members must produce a video declaring that they are "Proud Western Chauvinists." Both "Western" and "chauvinists" are a form of manipulative communication because they camouflage the Proud Boys' misogyny and White nationalist beliefs. For many years, McInnes has cleverly crafted plausible deniability by obscuring his links to White supremacism and White nationalism. By 2016, he became even more steeped in hate communication and was better equipped to promote his brand of extremism. Before he attempted to disown the Proud Boys to avoid deportation to Canada, he trivialized the degree and impact of the violence that he had initially inspired.[90]

Another example of manipulation of communication is the Proud Boys' accent placed on "self-love." The rise in popularity of Alt-Right and White supremacist groups has often been equated as a rise in mainstream "hatred." The conjecture of this designation lies in the fact that these groups are regarded primarily through the lens of their shared hatred for a great many non-White people and groups. However, in recent years, the rhetoric of groups like the Proud Boys is not articulated through hatred, but in terms of "self-love." That is, they do not hate others, but they are concerned about protecting themselves. Even if we believe these words and the claims that they are only interested in sustaining and defending their White values, the type of "self-love" they express is morally and politically dangerous for the precise reason that it is ingrainedly linked to a fundamental disdain for non–Whites.[91]

Case Study: The "2020 Voter Fraud" Campaign

After the November 2020 US presidential election, then-President Donald Trump conducted a 77-day campaign to overturn the election results. Notwithstanding the fact that Trump's lawyers determined within 10 days after the election that legal recourse had no merit because it was not grounded in factual evidence, the "2020 voter fraud" campaign was supported by a significant minority of Trump supporters. On December 18, four days after the Electoral College voted in favor of President-elect Joe Biden, Trump requested that his supporters attend a large gathering before the January 6, 2021 Congressional vote count. The purpose was to bolster up his objection to the validity of the election results in key states. As Trump commented in his tweet, "Big protest in D.C. on January 6. Be there, will be wild!"[92] On January 1, 2021, Women for America First secured a permit with an approximate attendance of 5,000 for a freedom rally called "March for Trump."[93] In late 2020 and early 2021, Amy Kremer (chair of Women for America First) delivered speeches at multiple events across the nation as part of her bus tour to boost attendance at the January 6 rally and back Trump's efforts to subvert the election result.[94]

Massive endorsement of conspiracy theories, even by those in political power, can agitate the population at large (and the institutions that they cherish or hate), thereby lending more legitimacy and credibility to conspiracy theories. Conspiracy theorists are obsessed with hard-to-verify ideas that are ingrained and influential in mainstream culture. Although conspiracy-thinking and radical ideologies are different types of extreme thoughts and behavior, they can still share common ground.[95] Their common ground can raise serious safety concerns when the conspiracy claims that "(1) one group is superior to another, (2) one group is under attack by another group, or (3) the threat is apocalyptic (existential threat) in nature."[96]

More importantly, the "2020 voter fraud" campaign had White supremacist undercurrents because the campaign mirrored then-President Donald Trump's antiimmigration campaign as a deliberate attempt at destabilizing American exceptionalism and the pillars of American democracy as a whole. This is especially true when the "2020 voter fraud" conspiracists constantly evoked the notion that Democrats and Leftists are duplicitous with their push for massive immigration to America. In January 2018, Donald Trump exposed his antiimmigration stance towards Haitians and African immigrants during negotiations for producing a bipartisan immigration deal. According to the Associated Press, Trump stated, "Haiti? Why do we want people from Haiti here?" And in regards to Africa, "Why do we want these people from all these shit-hole countries here? We should have more people from places like Norway."[97] Trump was accused of displaying favoritism towards White immigrants to the detriment of people of color. Both the "2020 voter fraud campaign" and the former president's antiimmigration campaign co-opted the concept of "patriotism" as a pretense to "take back our country" from the power-greedy élite or the powers that be. Both campaigns professed to combat what they have called the New World Order.

Opponents to the November 2020 Election Results

Opponents to the November 2020 election results purportedly campaigned in the name of the American people to change attitudes towards the voting process as a whole. The problem is that the 2020 voter fraud campaign was not necessarily grounded in facts. Support for fact-checking is predicated on the presumption that mistakes occur sporadically in an otherwise functioning information order. This understanding just does not concur with the assembly-line production of conspiracy theories that define a great volume of the international political landscape. The spread of disinformation narratives is not merely a craze; it is also a feature, as exemplified by Facebook's insufficient measures to rectify deliberate lies in political ads. In this context, to depend on fact-checking and media literacy campaigns seems quite vain, and probably appeals principally to people who do not need them.[98]

The "2020 voter fraud campaign" had already attempted to prevent the counting of Electoral College ballots for a few weeks before the event, and called for aggressive actions against Congress, Vice-President Mike Pence, and security forces.[99] Plans were made on "al-tech" platforms with little connection to more important social media platforms like Reddit or Twitter, which had bans in place to remove violent language and images. Websites such as TheDonald.win (affiliated with the Reddit forum r/The_Donald), Parler (a social networking site), Telegram (a free and open source), Gab (a social network for free speech), and others, served as discussions for prior previous Trump rallies and plans for storming the Capitol.[100]

There were some calls for committing violence on January 6 on major social media platforms, such as Twitter and TikTok, although most comments on these platforms did not explicitly mention any fighting.[101] Many of the commentators pleaded for violence a few weeks before the event, with some users discussing how to evade police on the streets, which devices to bring to forcibly open doors, and how to illegally bring weapons into the US Congress.[102] There were also conversations on their perceived need to tackle law enforcement. After clashes with Washington D.C. forces during demonstrations on December 12, 2020, the Proud Boys and other far-right organizations expressively opposed the support of law enforcement.[103] At least one organization, Stop the Steal, published on December 23,

2020 its plans to storm the Capitol with guarantees to "escalate" if met with resistance from law enforcement.[104] In due course, the campaign that called for violence led to the 2021 Capitol insurrection.

The 2021 US Capitol Riots

Also called the **2021 storming of the United States Capitol** or the **2021 Capitol insurrection**, the **US Capitol riots** were a forceful attack against the US Congress in Washington, D.C. on January 6, 2021. A large group of supporters of President Donald Trump attempted to undo his defeat in the 2020 presidential election by obstructing the joint session of Congress that was meeting there. The purpose of the meeting was to count electoral votes to officialize Joe Biden's victory. The Capitol premises were locked down and legislators and personnel were forced to leave while insurgents occupied and defaced the building for several hours. Over 140 people were wounded in the storming. Five people lost their lives either right before, during, or shortly after the incident.[105] On that day, the crowd that stormed the US Capitol was estimated at approximately 800. Although it was widely believed that this violent move was done in support of President Donald Trump, observers made other assumptions with respect to who the insurgents were. For the reason that a number of them overtly displayed symbols of right-wing militias, detractors asked for a crackdown on such groups.[106]

The unprecedented havoc in the nation's Capitol began around noon on January 6, 2021 at a "Save America" gathering at the Ellipse, a park not far from the White House. At that rally, Trump called for his supporters to physically go to Capitol Hill, where Congress was meeting to formalize Joe Biden as the 46th President of the United States.[107] That rally, however, was held on the false assumption that he had actually won the election and it was unfairly taken away from him. During the rally, he was quoted as uttering the following,

> Republicans are constantly fighting like a boxer with his hands tied behind his back. It's like a boxer. And we want to be so nice. We want to be so respectful of everybody, including bad people. And we're going to have to fight much harder. We're going to walk down to the Capitol, and we're going to cheer on our brave senators and congressmen and women, and we're probably not going to be cheering so much for some of them, because you'll never take back our country with weakness. You have to show strength, and you have to be strong.[108]

After his speech, a group of demonstrators marched to the Capitol and entered. Members of the giant squad went door-to-door brandishing Confederate flags, pillaging the offices of senators and congress people, and spewing the false narrative repeated by President Trump since November—that he was the authentic winner of the election.[109] Images disseminated in the mass media showed several men in Speaker Pelosi's office, while other photos depicted a man walking off with a podium and individuals on the House Floor. The Capitol Police even discovered pipe bombs on the Capitol Hill campus and learned about dangerous schemes where some of the "mobsters" had anticipated to abduct and kill members of Congress. Ex-Capitol Police Chief Sund thinks that the storming of the Capitol was part of a broader "planned and coordinated attack."[110] After the insurrection, the Associated Press examined public and online records of over 120 rioters and reported that most of them disseminated conspiracy theories about the 2020 presidential election on social media and were also fans of other QAnon and Deep State conspiracy theories. Furthermore, a few of those records indicate that users had threatened Democratic and Republican politicians before the insurrection.[111] The event can be described as "Extremely Online," with rioters acting as "pro-Trump internet personalities" streaming live footage and taking selfies at the same time.[112]

To be **Extremely Online** refers to being an active participant in internet culture. Those who are Extremely Online tend to believe that online posts matter a lot. It is a facetious term to allude to individuals who spend a great amount of time on social media platforms like Twitter. "Extremely Online" was used in a tweet for the first time in 2014.[113] Donald Trump's supporters have expressed great pride in being Extremely Online and do not hesitate to describe those bureaucrats and the departments and agencies they represent as an example of a Deep State designed to preserve and exert power behind the scenes.[114] A **Deep State** is a form of governance that consists of potentially secret and illicit networks of power that act separately from a state's political leadership. They have an agenda and objectives of their own.[115]

QAnon

The mob that stormed the US Capitol on January 6, 2021 included members of the Proud Boys, neo-Nazis, White supremacists, and QAnon supporters, some of whom brandished Confederate and Trump banners.[116] **QAnon** is a US far-right conspiracy theory according to which a dark league of Satan-worshipping, cannibalistic pedophiles was operating an international child sex-trafficking network and planned to knock down President Donald Trump while in office.[117] The QAnon conspiracy surfaced on October 28, 2017, on 4chan's /pol/ (i.e., the politically incorrect page) in a series of posts called "Calm Before the Storm." To this point, an anonymous user with the signature "Q" claimed that "Hillary Clinton will be arrested between 7:45 AM–8:30 AM. EST on Monday—the morning on Oct 30, 2017."[118] As stated on the QAnon Alerts Website, the mission of QAnon is to run "a massive information dissemination program meant to (a) expose massive global corruption and conspiracy to the people and (b) cause the people to research further to aid further in their 'great awakening'."[119]

The popularity of QAnon turned out to be one of the most widespread and dangerous conspiracy theories in contemporary US history. In 2020 in particular, the conspiracy theory gained enormous visibility, thereby diffusing even more disinformation of that kind all over the internet. In fact, it is no longer a simple conspiracy theory that unites a small clique of individuals based on false beliefs. Rather, it is now a deep cult-like campaign that does not merely operate in an online space. Not only has QAnon acquired global traction (e.g., in countries like Germany), but its followers have now joined forces in the physical world to perpetrate acts of violence. QAnon and its supporters represent some of the fiercest purveyors of disinformation online, exacerbating an already divided American public.[120]

In addition to gaining traction in the Alt-Right, White nationalist, and broader American conservative circles, the QAnon social movement has spawned various conjectures and sub-theories that have been quoted and supported by prominent legislators and media personalities.[121] Evidence shows that terrorists and would-be terrorists on the far right have been inspired by the movement's doctrines, particularly the Deep State, anti-Democratic Party, "Jewish World Order," and anti-Muslim/antiimmigrant narratives.[122] Although QAnon was first seen on **4chan**, an online message board composed of threads and related comments, the movement migrated to 8chan in November 2017 after facing a barrage of censorship and limitations in its abilities to post comments. 8chan has been associated with multiple terrorist attacks after the perpetrators posted their manifestos on the platform. As a consequence,

8chan was shut down, compelling the platform to reinvent itself.[123] Known as **8kun** today, it is an online image board made up of user-created message boards. Each board is moderated by an owner, allowing a modicum of interaction from site administration.[124]

The exponential growth of QAnon has evolved from simple disinformation mostly disseminated online to real-world acts of political violence. A great deal of the propaganda observed on alternative websites and social media platforms regarding QAnon is intentional sharing of disinformation. Nevertheless, the internet engenders a very easy environment for both misinformation and disinformation to be shared to mass audiences in a fast manner.[125] A 2018 analysis by the Massachusetts Institute of Technology reported that "falsehood diffused significantly farther, faster, deeper and more broadly" than truth on Twitter, particularly when it comes to political news.[126] In addition, social media has become a major platform for users to get their news in real time. The modern media ecosystem can also magnify the scope of conspiracy theories and disinformation because they have higher reach than verified information.[127]

QAnon followers have promoted certain fronts in the meme wars by running campaigns in reaction to current events. For instance, after Trump's impeachment, one follower proclaimed a counterattack. "Must declare a memewar on the Democrats in districts Trump won" as written in the post. "This is part of the 2020 memewar anons." Labeling Democratic senators as traitors, QAnon followers mention the names of vulnerable politicians in swing districts for a specific purpose: "Part of the 2020 memewar NEEDS to be strategically targeting these now VERY VULNERABLE democrats with memes so that not only are they voted out of office but democrats lose the House."[128] The dangerous outcome is obvious here: in 2020–1, the QAnon movement became a worldwide phenomenon thanks to internet-based campaigns like the "2020 voter fraud" one. Many local and national affiliates of the social movement such as QAnon France, QAnon UK, and QAnon Germany have jumped on the bandwagon. The antivaccine protests in Germany and the Save the Children rallies campaign in the United Kingdom are examples of real QAnon crusades.[129]

Group Polarization and Groupthink

The incident on Capitol Hill, starting with the declarations made by the former President of the United States, unmistakably had the attributes of a *coup d'état* and the ensuing incident that was duly called insurrection.[130] After the January 6, 2021 riots at the US Capitol, tech giants felt compelled to take drastic measures against social media users who were inciting violence or propagating election fraud conspiracy theories. Donald Trump, whose tweets were blamed for inciting the Capitol riots, was quickly removed from a number of social media platforms, just like some of his public allies.[131] Upon looking at the big picture, what the "2020 voter fraud" campaign and the subsequent 2021 US Capitol insurrection have shown, and what QAnon and internet-based conspiracy breeding factories have produced, is a highly concerning phenomenon of group polarization and groupthink.

Understanding critical psychological characteristics that provide reasons as to why conspiracy theories emerge and spread is essential when attempting to rewire extreme believers, especially those of the far right. Group polarization and groupthink are two manifestations of psychological behavior that can contribute to the spiraling of conspiracy theories, violent extremism, and terrorism. **Group polarization** refers to the proclivity of a group of individuals to make decisions on the basis of what they believe or see other people doing.[132] Group polarization often gives rise to the reinforcement of ideologies after being immersed in a milieu of like-minded people.[133]

Groupthink is a phenomenon whereby group members make decisions that are more extreme than their individual inclinations, generally due to the desire to belong and adapt to group norms. Groupthink causes group members to lose their ability to welcome alternative viewpoints and approaches, including counternarratives and all evidence that opposes their beliefs.[134] This is a frequent occurrence within extremist communities, as people will likely follow the herd and abandon their sense of autonomy. This circumstance is referred to as **herd behavior**. Protests, riots, and civil disorder are personifications of herd behavior.[135] Group polarization can emerge naturally when people—correctly or erroneously—assume they have common opinions on a multiplicity of topics. This can be observed in QAnon supporters' behaviors, overflowing with disdain and distrust towards political élites.[136]

NOTES

1. Jonathan Matusitz and Elena Berisha, *Female Terrorism in America: Past and Current Perspectives* (New York: Routledge, 2020).
2. Colin Flint, *Spaces of Hate: Geographies of Discrimination and Intolerance in the USA* (New York: Routledge, 2004); George Fredrickson, *White Supremacy* (Oxford: Oxford University Press, 1981).
3. Seth G. Jones, Catrina Doxsee, and Nicholas Harrington, *The Escalating Terrorism Problem in the United States* (Washington, DC: Center for Strategic & International Studies, 2020).
4. Assaf Moghadam and William Lee Eubank, *The Roots of Terrorism* (New York: Infobase Publishing, 2006).
5. Kathleen M. Blee, "Women and Organized Racial Terrorism in the United States," in *Terrorism in Perspective*, ed. Sue Mahan and Pamala L. Griset (Thousand Oaks, CA: Sage, 2013): 262–90, 262.
6. Steven Windisch, Pete Simi, Kathleen Blee, and Matthew DeMichele, "On the Permissibility of Homicidal Violence: Perspectives from Former US White Supremacists," *Perspectives on Terrorism* 14, no. 6 (2020): 65–76.
7. Leonard Zeskind, *Blood and Politics: The History of the White Nationalist Movement from the Margins to the Mainstream* (New York: Farrar, Straus and Giroux, 2009).
8. Heidi Beirich, *White Supremacy Flourishes amid Fears of Immigration and Nation's Shifting Demographics* (Montgomery, AL: Southern Poverty Law Center, February 20, 2019).
9. Windisch, Simi, Blee, and DeMichele, "On the Permissibility of Homicidal Violence," 65–76.
10. Betty Dobratz and Lisa Waldner, "Repertoires of Contention: White Separatist Views on the Use of Violence and Leaderless Resistance," *Mobilization: An International Quarterly* 17, no. 1 (2012): 49–66.
11. Pete Simi and Robert Futrell, *American Swastika: Inside the White Power Movement's Hidden Spaces of Hate* (2nd Ed.) (Lanham, MD: Rowman & Littlefield, 2015).
12. Pete Simi, "Why Study White Supremacist Terror? A Research Note," *Deviant Behavior* 31, no. 3 (2010): 251–73. https://doi.org/10.1080/01639620903004572.
13. Shannon E. Reid, Matthew Valasik, and Arunkumar Bagavathi, "Examining the Physical Manifestation of Alt-Right Gangs: From Online Trolling to Street Fighting," in *Gangs in the Era of Internet and Social Media*, ed. Chris Melde and Frank Weerman (New York: Springer, 2020): 105–34.

14. Kathleen Belew, *Bring the War Home: The White Power Movement and Paramilitary America* (Cambridge: Harvard University Press, 2018); Lane Crothers, *Rage on the Right: The American Militia Movement from Ruby Ridge to the Trump Presidency* (Lanham, MD: Rowman & Littlefield, 2019); Jessie Daniels, "The Algorithmic Rise of the 'Alt-Right'," *Contexts* 17, no. 1 (2018): 60–5. https://doi.org/10.1177/1536504218766547.

15. Kimmy Yam, "There Were 3,800 Anti-Asian Racist Incidents, Mostly against Women, in Past Year," *NBC News* (March 16, 2021). Retrieved on May 26, 2021 from https://www.nbcnews.com/news/asian-america/there-were-3-800-anti-asian-racist-incidents-mostly-against-n1261257.

16. Anti-Defamation League, *Murder and Extremism in the United States in 2018 Center on Extremism* (New York: Anti-Defamation League, January 10, 2019).

17. Morgan Chalfant, "FBI's Wray Says Most Domestic Terrorism Arrests This Year Involve White Supremacy," *The Hill* (July 23, 2019): A1. Retrieved on March 30, 2021 from https://thehill.com/homenews/administration/454338-fbis-wray-says-majority-of-domestic-terrorism-arrests-this-year.

18. Seth G. Jones, Catrina Doxsee, and Nicholas Harrington, *The Escalating Terrorism Problem in the United States* (Washington, DC: Center for Strategic & International Studies, 2020).

19. Ruth Wodak, *The Politics of Fear: What Right-Wing Populist Discourses Mean* (London: Sage, 2015).

20. Kurt Sengul, "Critical Discourse Analysis in Political Communication Research: A Case Study of Right-Wing Populist Discourse in Australia," *Communication Research and Practice* 5, no. 4 (2019): 376–92. https://doi.org/10.1080/22041451.2019.1695082.

21. Anna Triandafyllidou and Ruth Wodak, "Conceptual and Methodological Questions in the Study of Collective Identities: An Introduction," *Journal of Language and Politics* 2, no. 2 (2003): 205–23. https://doi.org/10.1075/jlp.2.2.02tri.

22. Margaret Wetherell, *Identities, Groups and Social Issues* (London: Sage, 1996).

23. Cas Mudde, *The Far Right in America* (London: Routledge, 2017).

24. Matt Golder, "Far Right Parties in Europe," *Annual Review of Political Science* 19 (2016): 477–97. https://doi.org/10.1146/annurev-polisci-042814-012441.

25. Jens Rydgren, "Is Extreme Right-Wing Populism Contagious? Explaining the Emergence of a New Party Family," *European Journal of Political Research* 44, no. 3 (2005): 413–37. https://doi.org/10.1111/j.1475-6765.2005.00233.x.

26. Roger Griffin, "Interregnum or Endgame? The Radical Right in the 'Post-Fascist' Era," *Journal of Political Ideologies* 5, no. 2 (2000): 163–78. https://doi.org/10.1080/713682938.

27. Golder, "Far Right Parties in Europe," 480.

28. Ibid, 479.

29. Griffin, "Interregnum or Endgame?" 165.

30. Antonio Gramsci, *Selections from Prison Notebooks* (London: Lawrence and Wishart, 1971).

31. Ferruh Yilmaz, "Right-Wing Hegemony and Immigration: How the Populist Far-Right Achieved Hegemony through the Immigration Debate in Europe," *Current Sociology* 60, no. 3 (2012): 368–81. https://doi.org/10.1177/0011392111426192.

32. Alice E. Marwick and Robyn Caplan, "Drinking Male Tears: Language, The Manosphere, and Networked Harassment," *Feminist Media Studies* 18, no. 4 (2018): 543–59, 543. https://doi.org/10.1080/14680777.2018.1450568.

33. John Bryden and Eric Silverman, "Underlying Socio-Political Processes Behind the 2016 US Election," *PLoS ONE* 14, no. 4 (2019): e0214854. https://doi.org/10.1371/journal.pone.0214854; Pierce Alexander Dignam and Deana A. Rohlinger, "Misogynistic Men Online: How the Red Pill Helped Elect Trump," *Signs* 44, no. 3 (2019): 589–612. https://doi.org/10.1086/701155.

34. See Scott Wright, Verity Trott, and Callum Jones, "'The Pussy Ain't Worth It, Bro': Assessing the Discourse and Structure of MGTOW," *Information, Communication & Society* 23, no. 6 (2020): 908–25. https://doi.org/10.1080/1369118X.2020.1751867; Donna Zuckerberg, *Not All Dead White Men: Classics and Misogyny in the Digital Age* (Cambridge, MA: Harvard University Press, 2018).

35. Callum Jones, Verity Trott, and Scott Wright, "Sluts and Soyboys: MGTOW and the Production of Misogynistic Online Harassment," *New Media & Society* 22, no. 10 (2020): 1903–21. https://doi.org/10.1177/1461444819887141.

36. Ibid, 1903–4.

37. Abby L. Ferber, "Racial Warriors and Weekend Warriors," *Men and Masculinities* 3, no. 1 (2000): 30–56. https://doi.org/10.1177/1097184X00003001002.

38. Lise Gotell and Emily Dutton, "Sexual Violence in the 'Manosphere': Antifeminist Men's Rights Discourses on Rape," *International Journal for Crime, Justice and Social Democracy* 5, no. 2 (2016): 65–80. https://doi.org/10.5204/ijcjsd.v5i2.310.

39. Alexis de Coning, "Men's Rights Movement/Activism," in *The International Encyclopedia of Gender, Media, and Communication*, ed. Ingrid Bachmann, Valentina Cardo, Sujata Moorti, and Cosimo Marco Scarcelli (Hoboken, NJ: Wiley, 2020).

40. Daniel Rueda, "Neoecofascism: The Example of the United States," *Journal for the Study of Radicalism* 14, no. 2 (2020): 95–126. https://doi.org/10.14321/jstudradi.14.2.0095.

41. Blair Taylor, *Alt-Right Ecology: Ecofascism and Far-Right Environmentalism in the United States* (New York: Routledge, 2019): 15.

42. Ibid, 16.

43. Rory McVeigh and Kevin Estep, *The Politics of Losing: Trump, the Klan, and the Mainstreaming of Resentment* (New York: Columbia University Press, 2019).

44. Richard B. Spencer, "The Metapolitics of America," (July 4, 2020). Retrieved on January 27, 2021 from https://radixjournal.com/2020/07/2014-7-4-the-metapolitics-of-america.

45. Taylor, *Alt-Right Ecology*, 15.

46. Joshua M. Roose, "Male Supremacism," in *The New Demagogues*, ed. Joshua M. Roose (New York: Routledge, 2021): 80–108.

47. Paul Joosse, "Leaderless Resistance and Ideological Inclusion: The Case of the Earth Liberation Front," *Terrorism and Political Violence* 19, no. 3 (2007): 351–68. https://doi.org/10.1080/09546550701424042.

48. Louis Beam, *Leaderless Resistance* 12 (1992): 12–3.

49. See Mattias Gardell, "Urban Terror: The Case of Lone Wolf Peter Mangs," *Terrorism and Political Violence* 30, no. 5 (2018): 793–811. https://doi.org/10.1080/09546553.2018.1444796; Paul Joosse, "Leaderless Resistance and the Loneliness of Lone Wolves: Exploring the Rhetorical Dynamics of Lone Actor Violence," *Terrorism and Political Violence* 29, no. 1 (2017): 52–78. https://doi.org/10.1080/09546553.2014.987866.

50. John E. Finn, *Fracturing the Founding: How the Alt-Right Corrupts the Constitution* (Lanham, MD: Rowman & Littlefield, 2019).

51. See Ben Makuch and Mack Lamoureux, "Neo-Nazis Are Organizing Secretive Paramilitary Training across America," *VICE* (November 20, 2018). Retrieved on January 27, 2021 from https://www.vice.com/en_us/article/a3mexp/neo-nazis-are-organizing-secretive-paramilitary-training-across-america; Ben Makuch and Mack Lamoureux, "New Paramilitary Training Video Emerges of Neo-Nazi Terror Group," *VICE* (August 20, 2019). Retrieved on January 27, 2021 from https://www.vice.com/en_ca/article/wjw5d4/new-paramilitary-training-video-emerges-of-neo-nazi-terror-group.

52. Shannon E. Reid and Matthew Valasik, *Alt-Right Gangs: A Hazy Shade of White* (Berkeley, CA: University of California Press, 2020).

53. Anti-Defamation League, *From 4Chan, Another Trolling Campaign Emerges* (New York: Anti-Defamation League, November 6, 2017).

54. Michael Edison Hayden, "The 'It's Okay to Be White' Meme Was Backed by Neo-Nazis and David Duke," *Newsweek* (November 19, 2017). Retrieved on April 13, 2021 from https://www.newsweek.com/neo-nazi-david-duke-backed-meme-was-reported-tucker-carlson-without-context-714655.

55. Anti-Defamation League, *From 4Chan*.

56. Cited in Robert Futrell, Pete Simi, and Simon Gottschalk, "Understanding Music in Movements: The White Power Music Scene," *The Sociological Quarterly* 47, no. 2 (2006): 275–304, 299. https://doi.org/10.1111/j.15338525.2006.00046.x.

57. George Hawley, *The Alt-Right: What Everyone Needs to Know* (New York: Oxford University Press, 2019).

58. Daniel Craig Botha, "Bridging White Supremacist Discourse: An Ethnography of the Online World of the 'Alt-Right'," *Unpublished Master's Thesis* (2021), Victoria University of Wellington.

59. Andrea M. Hawkman, "'Let's Try and Grapple All of This': A Snapshot of Racial Identity Development and Racial Pedagogical Decision Making in an Elective Social Studies Course," *The Journal of Social Studies Research* 43, no. 3 (2019): 215–28. https://doi.org/10.1016/j.jssr.2018.02.005.

60. Marcus A. Brooks, "It's Okay to Be White: Laundering White Supremacy through a Colorblind Victimized White Race-Consciousness Raising Campaign," *Sociological Spectrum* 40, no. 6 (2020): 400–16. https://doi.org/10.1080/02732173.2020.1812456.

61. Ibid, 400.

62. Janelle Griffith, "'It's Okay to Be White' Signs At a Tennessee University Prompt Probe," *NBC News* (November 5, 2019). Retrieved on April 14, 2021 from https://www.nbcnews.com/news/us-news/it-s-okay-be-white-signs-posted-tennessee-university-campus-n1076596.

63. Sophie Gallagher, "'It's Okay to Be White' Posters Put Up in Bristol City Centre," *The Independent* (January 30, 2020): A1. Retrieved on April 14, 2021 from https://www.independent.co.uk/life-style/bristol-its-ok-be-white-posters-university-racism-park-street-a9309746.html.

64. Ross Gardiner, "Disgust as Perth City Centre Peppered with 'It's Okay to Be White' Neo-Nazi Stickers," *The Courier* (December 17, 2019): A1. Retrieved on April 14, 2021 from https://www.thecourier.co.uk/fp/news/local/perth-kinross/1042887/disgust-as-perth-city-centre-peppered-with-its-okay-to-be-white-neo-nazi-stickers.

65. Botha, "Bridging White Supremacist Discourse".

66. Jason Wilson, "It's OK to Be White' Is Not a Joke, It's Careless Politicians Helping the Far Right," *The Guardian* (October 16, 2018): A1. Retrieved on April 13, 2021 from https://www.theguardian.com/commentisfree/2018/oct/16/its-ok-to-be-white-is-not-a-joke-its-careless-politicians-helping-the-far-right.

67. Bharath Ganesh, "Weaponizing White Thymos: Flows of Rage in the Online Audiences of the Alt Right," *Cultural Studies* 34, no. 6 (2020): 892–924. https://doi.org/10.1080/09502386.2020.1714687.

68. Joseph A. Schafer, Christopher Mullins, and Stephanie Box, "Awakenings: The Emergence of White Supremacist Ideologies," *Deviant Behaviour* 35, no. 3 (2014): 173–96. https://doi.org/10.1080/01639625.2013.834755.

69. Ferber, "Racial Warriors and Weekend Warriors," 30–56. https://doi.org/10.1177/1097184X00003001002.

70. George Hawley, *Making Sense of the Alt-Right* (New York: Columbia University Press, 2017): 70–5.

71. Ibid, 72.

72. Botha, "Bridging White Supremacist Discourse".

73. For example, see Phillip Kennicott, "Sorry, Mr. President, You Are the Reason Confederate Memorials Must Come Down," *The Washington Post* (August 16, 2017). Retrieved on January 16, 2021 from https://www.washingtonpost.com/entertainment/museums/statues-make-definitive-state-ments-thats-why-confederate-memorials-must-come-down/2017/08/16/75755368-8293-11e7-b359-15a3617c767b_story.html?utm_term=.55e194df9f52; James Chase Sanchez, "Confederate Memorials Symbolize Racism, and They Belong in History Museums," *Dallas Morning News* (July 27, 2017). Retrieved on January 16, 2021 from https://www.dal-lasnews.com/opinion/commentary/2017/07/27/confederate-memorials-symbolize-racismand-belong-history-muse-ums.

74. Alexandra Minna Stern, *Proud Boys and the White Ethnostate: How the Alt-Right Is Warping the American Imagination* (Boston, MA: Beacon Press, 2020).

75. Julia R. DeCook, "Memes and Symbolic Violence: #Proudboys and the Use of Memes for Propaganda and the Construction of Collective Identity," *Learning, Media and Technology* 43, no. 4 (2018): 485–504. https://doi.org/10.1080/17439884.2018.1544149.

76. Selena Couture and Heather Davis-Fisch, "The Relentless Struggle for Commemoration," *Canadian Theatre Review* 174 (2018): 5–8. https://doi.org/10.3138/ctr.174.001; Adam Klein, "From Twitter to Charlottesville: Analyzing the Fighting Words between the Alt-Right and Antifa," *International Journal of Communication* 13 (2019): 297–318.

77. Eli Rosenberg, "FBI Considers Proud Boys Extremists with White-Nationalist Ties, Law Enforcement Officials Say," *The Washington Post* (November 19, 2018): A1. Retrieved on January 24, 2021 from https://www.washingtonpost.com/nation/2018/11/20/fbi-says-proud-boys-have-white-nationalist-ties-law-enforcement-officials-say.

78. N'dea Yancey-Bragg, "Canada Becomes First Nation to Declare the Proud Boys a Terrorist Organization," *USA Today* (February 3, 2021): A1. Retrieved on February 3, 2021 from https://www.usatoday.com/story/news/world/2021/02/03/canada-declares-proud-boys-terrorist-organization/4372307001.

79. Cited in Derek Hawkins, Cleve R. Wootson, Jr., and Craig Timberg, "Trump's 'Stand By' Remark Puts the Proud Boys in the Spotlight," *The Washington Post* (September 30, 2020): A1. Retrieved on January 24, 2021 from https://www.washingtonpost.com/nation/2020/09/30/proudboys1001.

80. Reid and Valasik, *Alt-Right Gangs*.

81. John Grant and Fiona MacDonald, "The 'Alt' Right, Toxic Masculinity, and Violence," in *Turbulent Times, Transformational Possibilities? Gender and Politics Today and Tomorrow*, ed. Fiona MacDonald and Alexandra Dobrowolsky (Toronto: University of Toronto Press, 2020): 368–88.

82. Gavin McInnes, "We Are Not Alt-Right," *Proud Boy Magazine* (2017). Retrieved on January 24, 2021 from https://officialproudboys.com/proud-boys/we-are-not-alt-right.

83. Ed Mazza, "Gavin McInnes, Fox News Guest, Says Women Are 'Less Ambitious' and 'Happier at Home'," *The Huffington Post* (May 15, 2015): A1. Retrieved on January 29, 2021 from https://www.huffpost.com/entry/gavin-mcinnes-women-happier-at-home_n_7289048.

84. Daily News Editorial Board, "Profile in Rage: Too Late, New York Republicans Distance Themselves from Gavin McInnes," *New York Daily News* (October 16, 2018). Retrieved on January 29, 2021 from https://www.nydailynews.com/opinion/ny-edit-mcinnis-20181015-story.html.

85. McInnes, "We Are Not Alt-Right".

86. Carlos Huneeus and Lake Sagaris, *The Pinochet Regime* (Boulder, CO: Lynne Rienner Publishers, 2010).

87. Samantha Kutner, *Swiping Right: The Allure of Hyper Masculinity and Cryptofascism for Men Who Join the Proud Boys* (The Hague: International Centre for Counter-Terrorism, 2020).

88. Ibid.

89. Gavin McInnes, *The Death of Cool* (New York: Charles Scribner's Sons, 2013): 70.

90. Cited in Kutner, *Swiping Right*.

91. Michael J. Monahan, "Racism and 'Self-Love': The Case of White Nationalism," *Critical Philosophy of Race* 9, no. 1 (2021): 1–15. https://doi.org/10.5325/critphilrace.9.1.0001.

92. Will Carless, "Nation's Capital Braces for Violence as Extremist Groups Converge to Protest Trump's Election Loss," *USA Today* (January 4, 2021): A1. Retrieved on April 19, 2021 from https://eu.usatoday.com/story/news/nation/2021/01/04/january-6-dc-protests-against-election-certification-could-violent/4132441001.

93. Andrew Beaujon, "Here's What We Know about the Pro-Trump Rallies that Have Permits," *Washingtonian* (January 5, 2021). Retrieved on April 19, 2021 from https://www.washingtonian.com/2021/01/05/heres-what-we-know-about-the-pro-trump-rallies-that-have-permits.

94. Joseph Tanfani, Michael Berens, and Ned Parker, "How Trump's Pied Pipers Rallied a Faithful Mob to the Capitol," *Reuters* (January 11, 2021). Retrieved on April 19, 2021 from https://www.reuters.com/article/us-usa-trump-protest-organizers-insight/how-trumps-pied-pipers-rallied-a-faithful-mob-to-the-capitol-idUSKBN29G2UP.

95. Ross Frennet and S. Joost, *The Impact of Conspiracy Narratives on Violent RWE and LWE Narratives* (Brussels: Brussels Radicalisation Awareness Network, 2021).

96. Ibid, 3.

97. Alan Fram and Jonathan Lemire, "Trump: Why Allow Immigrants from 'Shithole Countries'? *Associated Press* (January 12, 2018). Retrieved on January 16, 2021 from https://www.apnews.com/fdda2ff0b877416c8ae1c1a77a3cc425.

98. W. Lance Bennett and Steven Livingston, "A Brief History of the Disinformation Age Information Wars and the Decline of Institutional Authority," in *The Disinformation Age: Politics, Technology, and Disruptive Communication in the United States*, ed. W. Lance Bennett and Steven Livingston (Cambridge: Cambridge University Press, 2021): 3–40.

99. Garrett M. Graff, "Behind the Strategic Failure of the Capitol Police," *Politico* (January 8, 2021). Retrieved on April 19, 2021 from https://www.politico.com/news/magazine/2021/01/08/capitol-police-failure-456237.

100. Sheera Frenkel, "The Storming of Capitol Hill Was Organized on Social Media," *The New York Times* (January 6, 2021): A1. Retrieved on April 19, 2021 from https://www.nytimes.com/2021/01/06/us/politics/protesters-storm-capitol-hill-building.html.

101. Jane Lytvyenko and Molly Hensley-Clancy, "The Rioters Who Took over the Capitol Have Been Planning Online in the Open for Weeks" *BuzzFeed News* (January 6, 2021). Retrieved on April 19, 2021 from https://www.buzzfeednews.com/article/janelytvynenko/trump-rioters-planned-online.

102. Frenkel, "The Storming of Capitol Hill," A1.

103. Jordan Green, "'We're gonna Kill Congress': Trump's Far-Right Supporters Promise Violence at Today's DC Protests," *The Raw Story* (January 6, 2021). Retrieved on April 19, 2021 from https://www.rawstory.com/proud-boys-rally.

104. Jemima McEvoy, "Capitol Attack Was Planned Openly Online for Weeks—Police Still Weren't Ready," *Forbes* (January 7, 2021). Retrieved on April 19, 2021 from https://www.forbes.com/sites/jemimamcevoy/2021/01/07/capitol-attack-was-planned-openly-online-for-weeks-police-still-werent-ready/?sh=35bc71de76e2.

105. *BBC News*, "Capitol Riots: Who Has the FBI Arrested So Far?" *BBC News* (March 5, 2021). Retrieved on April 14, 2021 from https://www.bbc.com/news/world-us-canada-55626148; Lauren Leatherby, Arielle Ray, Anjali Singhvi, Christiaan Triebert, Derek Watkins, and Haley Willis, "How a Presidential Rally Turned into a Capitol Rampage," *The New York Times* (January 12, 2021): A1. Retrieved on April 14, 2021 from https://www.nytimes.com/interactive/2021/01/12/us/capitol-mob-timeline.html.

106. Robert A. Pape and Keven Ruby, "The Capitol Rioters Aren't Like Other Extremists," *The Atlantic* (February 2, 2021): A1.

107. Julia Jacobo, "A Visual Timeline on How the Attack on Capitol Hill Unfolded," *ABC News* (January 10, 2021). Retrieved on April 15, 2021 from https://abcnews.go.com/US/visual-timeline-attack-capitol-hill-unfolded/story?id=75112066.

108. Cited in Charlie Savage, "Incitement to Riot? What Trump Told Supporters Before Mob Stormed Capitol," *The New York Times* (January 12, 2021): A1. Retrieved on April 14, 2021 from https://www.nytimes.com/2021/01/10/us/trump-speech-riot.html.

109. Jacobo, "A Visual Timeline".

110. Cited in Allison G. Knox, "Extended Commentary: The Capitol Insurrection, Emergency Management and Mutual Aid Agreements: What Questions Need to be Answered?" *International Social Science Review* 97, no. 1 (2021): Article 19.

111. Michael Biesecker, Michael Kunzelman, Gillian Flaccus, and Jim Mustian, "Records Show Fervent Trump Fans Fueled US Capitol Takeover," *The Associated Press* (January 10, 2021). Retrieved on April 19, 2021 from https://apnews.com/article/us-capitol-trump-supporters-1806ea8dc15a2c04f2a68acd6b55cace.

112. Nick Penzenstadler, "Internet Detectives Swarmed the Effort to ID Capitol Riot Mob, with Mixed Results," USA Today (January 14, 2021): A1. Retrieved on April 19, 2021 from https://eu.usatoday.com/story/news/2021/01/14/internet-detectives-swarm-effort-id-capitol-riot-mob/6643515002.

113. Jay Hathaway, "What Does It Mean to Be Extremely Online?" *The Daily Dot* (May 29, 2018). Retrieved on April 19, 2021 from https://www.dailydot.com/unclick/what-does-it-mean-to-be-extremely-online.

114. Tyler Johnson, "Depth Charges: Does 'Deep State' Propagandizing Undermine Bureaucratic Reputations?" *Journal of Applied Social Theory* 1, no. 3 (2021): 62–93.

115. Mike Lofgren, *The Deep State: The Fall of the Constitution and the Rise of a Shadow Government* (New York: Penguin, 2016).

116. Dan Barry and Sheera Frenkel, "'Be There. Will Be Wild!': Trump All but Circled the Date," *The New York Times* (January 6, 2021): A1. Retrieved on April 19, 2021 from https://www.nytimes.com/2021/01/06/us/politics/capitol-mob-trump-supporters.html.

117. Kevin Roose, "What Is QAnon, the Viral Pro-Trump Conspiracy Theory?" *The New York Times* (August 28, 2020): A1. Retrieved on April 19, 2021 from https://www.nytimes.com/article/what-is-qanon.html.

118. Cited in Amarnath Amarasingam and Marc-André Argentino, "The QAnon Conspiracy Theory: A Security Threat in the Making?" *CTC Sentinel* 13, no. 7 (2020): 37–43, 37.

119. Cited in Amanda Garry, Samantha Walther, Rukaya Mohamed, and Ayan Mohammed, "QAnon Conspiracy Theory: Examining its Evolution and Mechanisms of Radicalization," *Journal for Deradicalization* 26 (2021): 152–216, 160.

120. Ibid, 152–3.

121. Jane Coaston, "#QAnon, the Scarily Popular Pro-Trump Conspiracy Theory, Explained," *Vox* (August 21, 2020). Retrieved on April 19, 2021 from https://www.vox.com/policy-and-politics/2018/8/1/17253444/qanon-trump-conspiracy-theory-reddit.

122. Brendan Joel Kelley and Hatewatch Staff, "QAnon Conspiracy Increasingly Popular with Antigovernment Extremists," Southern Poverty Law Center (April 23, 2019). Retrieved on April 19, 2021 from https://www.splcenter.org/hatewatch/2019/04/23/qanon-conspiracy-increasingly-popular-antigovernment-extremists.

123. Brandy Zadrozny and Ben Collins, "QAnon Explained: The Antisemitic Conspiracy Theory Gaining Traction around the World," *NBC News* (August 14, 2018). Retrieved on April 19, 2021 from https://www.nbcnews.com/tech/tech-news/how-three-conspiracy-theorists-took-q-sparked-qanon-n900531.

124. Stephane J. Baele, Lewys Brace, and Travis G. Coan, "The 'Tarrant Effect': What Impact Did Far-Right Attacks Have on the 8chan Forum?" *Behavioral Sciences of Terrorism and Political Aggression* (2021). https://doi.org/10.1080/19434472.2020.1862274.

125. Garry, Walther, Mohamed, and Mohammed, "QAnon Conspiracy Theory," 162.

126. Soroush Vosoughi, Deb Roy, and Sinan Aral, "The Spread of True and False News Online," *Science* 359, no. 6380 (2018): 1146–51. https://doi.org/10.1126/science.aap9559.

127. Martin Innes, "Techniques of Disinformation: Constructing and Communicating 'Soft Facts' after Terrorism," *The British Journal of Sociology* 71, no. 2 (2020): 284–99. https://doi.org/10.1111/1468-4446.12735.

128. Available at https://8kun.top/qresearch/res/7556525.html#7556525.

129. Julien Bellaiche, "Qanon: A Rising Threat to Democracy?" *The Journal of Intelligence, Conflict, and Warfare* 2 (2020): 165–9.

130. Knox, "Extended Commentary," Article 19.

131. Allegra Hobbs, "Trump's Expulsion from Social Media: When Is It Time to Ban an Account?" *SAGE Business Cases Originals Express Case* (2021). http://dx.doi.org/10.4135/9781529775181.

132. David G. Myers and Helmut Lamm, "The Group Polarization Phenomenon," *Psychological Bulletin* 83, no. 4 (1976): 602–27. https://doi.org/10.1037/0033-2909.83.4.602.

133. Clark McCauley and Sophia Moskalenko, "Mechanisms of Political Radicalization: Pathways toward Terrorism," *Terrorism and Political Violence* 20, no. 3 (2008): 415–33. https://www.tandfonline.com/doi/pdf/10.1080/09546550802073367.

134. Irving L. Janis, *Victims of Groupthink: A Psychological Study of Foreign-Policy Decisions and Fiascoes* (Boston, MA: Houghton Mifflin, 1972).

135. Dan Braha, "Global Civil Unrest: Contagion, Self-Organization, and Prediction," *PLoS ONE* 7, no. 10 (2012): e48596. https://doi.org/10.1371/journal.pone.0048596.

136. Garry, Walther, Mohamed, and Mohammed, "QAnon Conspiracy Theory," 155.

CHAPTER 15

Public Communication Campaigns of Islamophobia and Antisemitism

Islamophobia and antisemitism have pervaded societies for centuries, with antisemitism having roots even before the Common Era. This chapter examines the dividing lines that populist campaigns have created against Muslims and Jews in two specific countries: India and Hungary, respectively. Public communication campaigns rooted in populism frame certain groups as posing a major threat to democracy because of their religions, traditions, and/or collective identities. Hence, populist leaders believe that they should change people's attitudes and behaviors by making them aware of such "threats." One corollary is that prejudicial attitudes towards certain groups—especially when amped during crisis situations—can inflame social disorder, stereotyping, agitation, mutual blame, anxiety, and, more importantly, violence and death—all of which, in turn, cause psychological stress and trauma (besides social rejection). Social justice and welfare may also be hampered because of these characteristics.[1]

Populism is paramount to such prejudicial attitudes and the substance of many far-right parties.[2] **Populism** considers society as distributed between two homogeneous and incompatible groups: "the pure people" and "the corrupt élite." This philosophy advances that policies should express the general will of the people.[3] It is, thus, opposed to pluralism and elitism.[4] In contrast to the latter, populism views the people as the morally superior group, whereas pluralism is regarded as "polluting" society. **Pluralism** considers society as a large entity made up of multiple communities whose dissimilar interests must be bridged through

---

Fundamentals of Public Communication Campaigns, First Edition. Jonathan Matusitz.
© 2022 John Wiley & Sons Ltd. Published 2022 by John Wiley & Sons Ltd.

a process of bargaining. On the other hand, populism dislikes the notion that there should be dissimilar interests within "the people" and, on that basis, only favors "the pure people" so that no division exists and no subsequent compromise is needed. A consequence is that populism has a tendency to simplify political issues, classifying them into black and white and pushing for yes or no answers.[5]

ISLAMOPHOBIA: AN INTRODUCTION

Highly mediatized Islamist terrorist incidents like the September 11, 2001 terrorist attacks, the 2002 Bali bombings, the July 7, 2005 London bombings, the 2008 Mumbai attacks, the November 13, 2015 Paris attacks, the March 22, 2016 Brussels attacks, and the Orlando Pulse nightclub shooting (in 2016 as well) have brought the constructs of Islam and Islamophobia to the limelight. An important outcome is that a vastly growing focus has been laid on Muslim identity.[6] Images of jihadist attacks, the Islamization of the world, Muslim women wearing the veil or headscarf, and Middle Eastern men with long beards have all played a part in the growing fear and hatred of Muslims.[7]

Former US President Donald Trump has been accused of kindling fear and contempt towards Muslims. Media and political critics have denounced him for raising such suspicions about Muslims, for implementing more widespread surveillance of their mosques and activities, and for preserving the policy of unfair registration of Muslims in government databases.[8] Within a week of assuming his role as President, he finalized his campaign promise by imposing a "Muslim ban." In so doing, he signed an executive order temporarily forbidding refugees and immigrants from seven Muslim-majority countries from setting foot in the United States and putting a stop to the Syrian refugee program. Two federal courts blocked his order, claiming that the ban on Muslims entering the country was unconstitutional.[9] Taken as a whole, the growing focus placed on Muslims in the media, in concert with communication and actions taken by powerful state actors like Donald Trump, has stoked the flames of Islamophobia within multiple audiences.

Origins of the Word

Centuries ago, European intellectuals were already publishing works about the dangers of the Prophet Muhammad's teachings and the doctrine of Islam as a whole. Examples of such scholars were Humphrey Prideaux (an Anglican theologian) in 1697, Voltaire (the French philosopher) in 1742, Charles Godfrey Leland (an American journalist) in 1874, and Paul Casanova in 1911.[10] Etymologically speaking, the actual word "Islamophobia" can be traced back to the French language. *Islamophobie* was first used in early twentieth-century France where it described the hostility or mistrust of Islam.[11] In its French version, *islamophobie* was introduced by two Muslims immediately after WWI.[12] More precisely, the term *islamophobie* was introduced in 1922 by Nasreddine Dinet (born as Alphonse-Étienne Dinet), a French painter who admired the "oriental" or "Eastern" world and who converted to Islam. Dinet argued that anti-Islamic views were becoming prominent in the Western world and that an irrational fear of Muslims was rising.[13]

Current Definitions

According to the *Merriam-Webster* (2016)[14] dictionary, a **phobia** is an exaggerated, inexplicable, or illogical fear of a specific object, class of objects, concept, or event. When amalgamating "Islam" and "phobia," we have Islamophobia, or that exaggerated, inexplicable, or illogical fear of Islam and/or Muslims. **Islamophobia** is the stereotypical oversimplification of Islam and/or Muslims that can lead to the discrimination or harassment of Muslims.[15] Ali et al. (2011)[16] have a similar definition: an exaggerated fear, hatred, and hostility towards Islam and Muslims as a result of negative stereotypes of the latter. This further causes bias, discrimination, marginalization, and exclusion of Muslims from social, political, and civic circles.

In the eyes of Hollar and Naureckas (2008),[17] Islamophobia refers to hostility *vis-à-vis* Islam and Muslims that tends to demonize an entire faith, portraying it as essentially inferior, and assigning it an inherent, fundamental host of deplorable characteristics such as irrationality, narrowness, and violence. In like fashion, Islamophobia is "an irrational fear of or prejudice towards Muslim people or people who may appear to be Muslim."[18] Gardell (2010)[19] frames Islamophobia as a socially reproduced prejudice and dislike of Islam and Muslims. From this perspective, actions and practices that target, exclude, or victimize people by sheer virtue of being Muslims and being associated with Islam constitute Islamophobia. A recurrent theme within Islamophobic discourse is "the question of civilization, the notion that Islam engenders a worldview that is fundamentally incompatible with and inferior to Western culture."[20] In many Western nations, public discourse is illuminated by the theory that Muslim communities are the ones that willingly "self-segregate" in dominant societies.[21]

Satirical Cartoons

Islamophobia can be supplemented with satirical commentary and symbolism. Enter the *Jyllands-Posten* Muhammad cartoons scandal. Occasionally referred to as the Muhammad cartoons crisis, the scandal began after the Danish daily broadsheet newspaper *Jyllands-Posten* included 12 editorial cartoons on September 30, 2005, most of which mocked the Prophet Muhammad through portrayals and drawings of the supreme figure of Islam in all sorts of situations. The newspaper declared that the intent was to add fresh insights to the conversation about criticism of Islam and self-censorship. Muslim groups in Denmark decried that decision and the satirical cartoons led to violent demonstrations around the globe, including Muslim countries, a few months later. In another (more tragic) example, *Charlie Hebdo*, a French satirical weekly magazine, has practiced the same type of derisive journalism for several decades, which culminated with the *Charlie Hebdo* shooting on January 7, 2015. Al-Qaeda terrorists managed to enter the offices of *Charlie Hebdo* in the center of Paris and killed 12 people (mostly journalists). The rationale for satirical Muhammad cartoons draws on a global campaign to fight free speech restrictions. However, in the vast majority of Muslim traditions, it is deemed highly blasphemous to draw or represent the Prophet. This, coupled with the notion that the cartoons from the two newspapers insulted Muhammad and Islam, can outrage many Muslims and instigate death threats.[22]

Case Study 1:   Islamophobia in India

Hinduism and Islam are the two most predominant religions in India. Both religious groups have coexisted peacefully as often as not, mutually showing consideration for each other's sacraments and traditions. The proportion of members of both groups living in harmony considerably exceeds their more terrorizing counterparts.[23] Nevertheless, Hindus and Muslims have also had a tumultuous coexistence in that country, sometimes reflected by intense conflicts, like Kashmir violence in 1989 (up to 100,000 people may have lost their lives), the Gujarat religious riots in 2002 (about 1,000 deaths), and the Muzaffarnagar riots in 2013 (62 deaths).[24] More importantly, as a result of the Partition of India in 1947, when Pakistan was created as an autonomous Muslim nation, up to two million people died in the ensuing conflict.[25] The rupture of Hindu–Muslim relations was reignited in the 1960s and 1970s, but a climax was reached in 1992, when a far-right Hindu crowd of thousands, which included several representatives of the powerful Hindu nationalist Bharatiya Janata Party (BJP), destroyed the Babri mosque in Ayodhya.[26] As of 2019, the BJP is India's biggest political party with respect to representation in the national parliament.[27]

Ashutosh Varshney (2003),[28] professor at Brown University and author of the widely acclaimed *Ethnic Conflict and Civic Life: Hindus and Muslims in India*, thinks that the early March 2020 riots in Delhi bear some resemblance to organized pogroms. India has witnessed such atrocities before. The above-referenced Gujarat religious riots of 2002 occurred when Narendra Modi—the 14th and current Prime Minister of India—was the state's chief minister. Most of the 1,000 casualties were Muslims. In 1984, in Delhi, close to 3,000 Sikhs lost their lives after Hindu nationalists targeted them as a result of Prime Minister Indira Gandhi' assassination by her Sikh bodyguards. In both tragedies, riots were very likely organized with some collusion from the state police.[29]

Hindutva or Hindu Nationalism

Vinayak Damodar Savarkar was an idealist who was imprisoned by the British on many occasions. In 1923, while incarcerated as a political prisoner in a notorious cellular jail, Savarkar penned an immensely influential pamphlet called *Who Is a Hindu?* which defined what "Hinduness" was and detailed a political future for India. The pamphlet's most substantial (and controversial) contribution was its description of a "Hindu" as any individual who adopted India as both his or her homeland and holy land, which inherently excluded Muslims and Christians who looked at geopolitical places outside India as their holy lands.[30] Sometimes referred to as the **Hindu right** or **Hindu nationalism**, **Hindutva** (which means "Hinduness" in English) is the most prevalent form of Hindu nationalism in India.[31] As a political doctrine, Hindutva is supported by the Hindu far-right, paramilitary organization Rashtriya Swayamsevak Sangh (RSS), the right-wing organization Vishva Hindu Parishad (VHP), the aforementioned BJP, and other groups, collectively called the Sangh Parivar.[32] The Hindutva movement has been depicted as a derivative of right-wing extremism and as quasi-Fascist because of its obsession with having a homogenized Hindu majority and cultural hegemony.[33]

As we will see in the next sections, Hindutva public communication campaigns have applied an array of communicative techniques and strategies to ameliorate Hindu lives and make India a stronger Hindu majority. By squelching Muslims, Hindutva thinks it can make India a better place. For example, the Hindutva campaign against what nationalists perceive as "love jihad" is an effort to protect Hindu women from Muslim men, as the latter are perceived as converting Hindu women to Islam—through deceit and marriage—in order to gradually Islamize the country.[34] It goes without saying that these claims have been called unsubstantiated and part of the Islamophobia campaign of the Hindu far right.[35] This type of campaign operates like a public will campaign; it tries to marshal the public for policy change and to legitimize the alleged reality of the growing Muslim threat (in the public eye) as an incentive for policy change.

The Persistence of Islamophobia

As India's largest minority group, Muslims consists of about 200 million individuals in that part of the world.[36] Despite being the largest minority group, Muslims sometimes find themselves omitted from the mainstream political power spheres in India. The historical clash between Muslims and Hindus has been co-opted and magnified by Hindutva activists to portray Indian Muslims as dangerous outsiders with inauspicious plans to subjugate the Hindu majority. The excuses for violence against Muslims cannot be separated from the broader geopolitical and historical occurrences in India. The Islamophobic propaganda used to vilify them has materialized through incidents of mob violence against Muslims who have been accused of massacring cows. Ultranationalist Hindu groups consider the act of murdering Muslims for slaughtering cows as *the* Hindu duty on multiple occasions. This problem is complicated by the political silence of the nation's leadership on these acts.[37]

In the eyes of ultranationalist Hindus, Pakistan is equated with the cursed land. It is the land of those who stabbed India in the back by calling for a separate nation. In fact, it is a grave insult to ask a Hindu to go to Pakistan because the request is filled with implication that one is not Indian. The group to be blamed for the creation of Pakistan—and the subsequent betrayal of India—are the Muslims in India. To this effect, when a person is doomed to being sent to Pakistan, he or she will never be forgiven for going to the land of Muslims, who remain (in the minds of ultranationalist Hindus) traitors. Hence, the concept of "Muslim" is equated not only with humiliation, but also with antinationalism.[38]

In a similar vein, despite the fact that the Indian Constitution bans discrimination on the basis of caste, the Brahminical caste system still determines most present-day political, legal, social, cultural, and economic affairs in India—including riots and violence against particular groups. Caste-based violence is integral to Hindutva and is fused with other matrices of oppression. Hindu nationalism purports to be the best alternative to secular nationalist discourses because they are said to have failed to honor the Hindutva agenda. Kashmir is a perfect example of a situation where an entire region (with a population of 14 million people) is considered as the unwanted or the Other by ultranationalists. As for the ongoing occupation of Kashmir, Muslim militants over there are not terrorists, as the Indian government portrays them; rather, it is the revival of Kashmiri movement for sovereignty and freedom from the Indian occupation.[39]

Sociocultural alienation has instigated frequent processes and conditions that contribute to religion-based inequality and marginality. It is sometimes the case that Islamophobic attitudes in India are harbored by people who have had little interaction with this religious community in the first place. Culturally disparate principles and religious ideas might create discomfort and resultant hostility. It is obvious that these circumstances give rise to prejudice towards a major out-group. This has far-reaching implications for both policy and practice.[40] The byproduct of Islamophobia can be devastating. Between 2015 and 2017, more than 50 Muslim men were arbitrarily hanged across the country on suspicions of eating beef—the cow is the most sacred animal for Hindus. The killings were not perpetrated in the name of religion, but under the pretense of nationalism. Therefore, the combined acts of eating beef and of being Muslim become antinational and, in turn, anti-Indian. Within the dangerous growing popularity of jingoistic Hindu nationalism, the predicament for Muslims in India is that of being Indian as Muslims.[41]

ISLAMOPHOBIA DURING THE COVID-19 PANDEMIC IN INDIA: GENERAL INFORMATION

By October 2021, the COVID-19 pandemic in India had already caused 35 million positive cases (with a daily rate of 10,000 to 20,000 cases) and 450,000 deaths.[42] The pandemic could not have appeared at a better time for the BJP government, a time that was already shaken by massive-scale protests that had exploded after the passing of the Citizenship Amendment Act (CAA) in December 2019. The Act allows non-Muslim religious minorities from Pakistan, Bangladesh, and Afghanistan to be granted citizenship status in an expeditious manner, but Muslim applicants do not have that privilege. This is the first legal instance of religious profiling, though forbidden by the Indian Constitution, that is forthrightly used to refuse to give Indian citizenship to Muslim applicants. In summer 2019, Home Minister Amit Shah declared in the Indian Parliament that the National Register of Citizens (NRC) would be extended to the entire nation of India. The NRC is a painstaking bureaucratic formality adopted in the Northeastern state of Assam that threatens almost two million Muslims with statelessness. Reasonable fears that the CAA and the NRC would be used in combination with each other provoked nationwide protests. The NRC will declare Indian Muslims who do not have essential documents as foreigners, whereas the CAA will make sure that they are not allowed to apply for citizenship.[43]

Fears of Islamic Revivalism

During the first stages of the pandemic in March 2020, the Republic of India traced multiple cases of COVID-19 to a Muslim missionary group that held its yearly conference in Delhi. Healthcare practitioners were anxious to find anyone who had contact with the participants. COVID-19 fears and religious hostilities were already creating divisiveness in India, and the two forces soon intermingled. Videos fallaciously declaring to show members of the missionary group spitting on law enforcement and regular citizens went viral on social media, worsening an already dangerous climate for Muslims.[44] The name of the Muslim missionary group is **Tablighi Jamaat**, of which the mission is to beseech Muslims and fellow members to return to traditional Islam in regards to ritual, dress, and personal behavior. The organization is believed to have between 12 million to 80 million members around the world,[45] with most of them living in South Asia,[46] and a presence in virtually every nation. Tablighi Jamaat remains one of the most influential Islamic movements since the twentieth century. Islamic revivalism is a social movement in Islam that calls for stronger commitment to the fundamental tenets of Islam.[47] It has caused Hindu nationalists to be afraid.

The March 2020 incident that centered on Tablighi Jamaat arrived only a few weeks after religious **pogroms** (organized massacres of a targeted religious group) were orchestrated by

Hindutva radicals that took the lives of many Muslims in Delhi. A spike in hateful tweets confirmed their anxieties over COVID-19 that intermixed with long-running phobia against Islamic revivalism in India. Those pogroms represented India's deadliest organized violence in Delhi for almost a decade. The first pogroms occurred in late February 2020—right before US President Donald Trump landed in India to meet with Prime Minister Narendra Modi—and soon escalated into mass riots, with radical Hindu crowds targeting Muslim residence in the city's northeast. At least 45 people were murdered—mostly Muslims.[18]

Hindu extremists capitalized on the fear and enmity towards the country's 200 million Muslims. Those sentiments were inflamed by the improper decision of a small Muslim group—i.e., the ill-advised annual conference organized by Tablighi Jamaat during the COVID-19 outbreak.[49] The violence ravaged the Northeastern part of Delhi for four days as mosques were burned to the ground, Muslims were immolated within their own homes, and other Muslims were dragged out into the streets and arbitrarily hanged. Their businesses and properties were also burned. In streets where Hindus and Muslims had coexisted peacefully for many years, corpses could be found amid discarded and burned-out vehicles, bicycles, broken glass, and enflaming shopfronts. The police were accused of facilitating or even joining Hindu mobs. Hindu mobs were apprehending men in the streets to check their ID cards.[50]

From Unfounded Anxieties to Othering

Though it is important to mention that there was violence on both sides, it was the Muslim group of Delhi that was disproportionately targeted by Hindu mobs (arguably composed of tens of thousands of assailants). In Chand Bagh, one of the most affected areas, only Islamic businesses—e.g., hair salons, ice-cream parlors, and butchers—were destroyed. On one street corner, the carbonized cases of hundreds of oranges, bananas, and watermelons were scattered in front of a Muslim fruit stall, with a putrid odor of burnt fruit that could be smelled from afar.[51] These were the outcomes of unfounded anxieties over the COVID-19 outbreak and long-established Islamophobia in India. Infectious diseases are notorious for triggering irrational fear. History demonstrates that such fear can be used as leverage for discriminating and committing violence against the Other. Indeed, blaming the Other is an age-old approach to rationalize hatred based on mysterious, misunderstood, uncontrollable, and distressing diseases.[52]

Othering is a philosophical concept that denotes the practice of producing an "Us vs. Them" dichotomy, thus making efforts to antagonize certain "others" from one's in-group and, in broader terms, the entirety of the society.[53] It has eventually come to be interpreted as a concept in the social sciences that encapsulates multiple manifestations of prejudice based on out-group identity. Examples of this are plentiful. Othering and resultant prejudice were a frequent occurrence against farmers in the classical Black Death (i.e., the bubonic plague) of the fourteenth century and the Indians during the 1826–37 cholera pandemic (at the heart of the British rule).[54]

PUBLIC COMMUNICATION CAMPAIGN OF ISLAMOPHOBIC HASHTAGS

The smartphone market in India has benefited from a massive burgeoning since 2013. This growth has been facilitated with the introduction of Jio mobiles that use market-capturing techniques such as the introduction of highly affordable data plans.[55] Among the manifold smartphone applications widely available in the country, WhatsApp is exceptionally popular. With over 400 million users, India is WhatsApp's largest market.[56] Most users are part of any of the several major WhatsApp groups. The type of messages that are shared in these groups can vary from "hello" messages to medical evaluations. Because using that application is an essential part of daily routine for a sizeable percentage of smartphone users, it has been co-opted as a platform for communication by political parties. To this point, the 2019 Indian election was called by the news media the "WhatsApp election."[57]

#CoronaJihad

In late March 2020, Islamophobic hashtags were propagated immediately after the news that COVID-19 allegedly originated from that Muslim missionary group (i.e., Tablighi Jamaat). Within a few days, a public communication campaign to heighten animosity towards Muslims was facilitated by numerous tweets with the hashtag **#CoronaJihad**. In just five days, #CoronaJihad turned up on more than 300,000 Twitter accounts and various websites and was seen by a whopping 165 million people on Twitter, according to statistics shared with the *Time* magazine by Equality Labs, a digital human rights group. Equality Labs activists believed that many of the tweets clearly violated Twitter's rules on hate speech, but only a handful of them were taken down. "We are committed to protect and serve the public conversation as we navigate this unprecedented global public healthcare crisis," read a statement that the tech giant provided to *Time*. "We continue to remain vigilant."[58]

The #CoronaJihad campaign accused the Muslim population in India to intentionally spread COVID-19. The campaign enjoyed immense popularity across major communication networks of India's right-wing majoritarian groups, which perpetuated both the myth of the Muslim-inspired outbreak and other Islamophobic topics. WhatsApp continues to be an important application in the communication networks of such groups.[59] Yet, both mainstream Indian media and social media also contributed to the popularity of this campaign of baseless accusations. When dangerous myths flourish and percolate to regions, cities, families, and other WhatsApp groups, they become normalized like a daily household name.[60]

The variety of messages in the WhatsApp groups that fueled the #CoronaJihad campaign can be classified in the following four categories: (1) Online comments about the Tablighi Jamaat incident and similar messages that blame the Muslims for the spread COVID-19; (2) videos that show security forces beating Muslim men who allegedly dishonored social distancing norms, followed by online comments that applauded such actions; (3) messages about the alleged bloodsucking or ingratiating behavior of Muslims and the need to reject them; and (4) online comments about how Muslims regularly attack police forces and healthcare workers.[61]

#TablighiJamatVirus

A similar hashtag campaign was called **#TablighiJamatVirus**, which was an allusion to #CoronaJihad. Hate activists wanted to launch a parallel campaign to increase visibility and Islamophobic impact. Attached to what soon developed into a viral tweet was a bogus video that was actually recorded in Thailand, not India. The authors of the video provided no evidence that the "perpetrator" of the violence was a member of the Delhi branch of Tablighi Jamaat. Nevertheless, the video was watched by many people. Another video associated with #TablighiJamatVirus was circulated on both Facebook and Twitter and claimed to show Muslims deliberately sneezing on each other. It was quickly rebutted by the fact-checking organization AltNews. Another tweet, which produced 2,000 retweets before it was taken down by Twitter for violation of the rules, included a satirical cartoon of a Muslim man wanting to push a Hindu off a cliff. Although that specific tweet was removed, other cartoons blaming Muslims for COVID-19, and shared by the same account with over 15,000 followers, were still accessible on the internet in late spring 2020.[62]

Disastrous Consequences

The way the Hindutva WhatsApp groups launched their public hate campaign illustrates how the platform can be turned into a steady interface to intensify the degree and reach of physical violence. While the WhatsApp platform, in and of itself, should not be held responsible for the production of dangerous content like #CoronaJihad and #TablighiJamatVirus, or acts of physical violence *per se*, the manner in which the platform shapes such acts of extremism can be understood within the framework of Gillespie's (2018)[63] argument that platforms play a role in guiding and framing the shape of public discourse. The two hashtags encouraged alleged BJP workers to take cricket bats to hammer a group of Muslim social activists who were giving out free dry food to slum dwellers in Northeast Bangalore, requesting that they do "not feed Hindus." The attack came at a time when Hindutva campaign leaders recommended that Muslims be shot for diffusing a potentially deadly virus, while disregarding Chief Minister B.S. Yediyurappa's warning against denigrating Muslims over the outbreak.[64]

It is important to note that Muhammad Saad Khandalvi, the leader of the Delhi branch of Tablighi Jamaat, did not respect the two notices sent by the authorities to stay home during the lockdown. Khandalvi still held the religious conference and was subsequently charged with manslaughter after the meeting was said to have caused 1,023 new infections.[65] However, spreading COVID-19 was not his intention and, more importantly, it is the Islamophobic campaigns and ensuing physical violence towards Muslim communities at large that should be of concern to scholars, practitioners, and authorities alike. These new occurrences of Islamophobia in India could have long-term political, social, and health implications. The excessive alienation of the Muslim community could augment the frequency of infections and mortality, not to mention the higher number of infected Muslims who would be too fearful to reveal their diseases out of concern of being attacked.[66] It could further lead to ostracization of Muslims into separate communities, where they would feel better about living in overcrowded places with "their own," but could not practice social distancing properly.[67]

AN APPLICATION OF TERROR MANAGEMENT THEORY (TMT)

Developed by Solomon, Greenberg, and Pyszczynski (1991),[68] **Terror Management Theory (TMT)** predicates that all human motives fundamentally come from a biologically based need for survival or self-preservation. Relative contentment when navigating harsh existential realities is made easier through the creation and preserving of culture, which serves to better handle the terror by providing a shared symbolic context—a context that impregnates the universe with structure, meaning, predictability, and more realistic expectations. Put another way, TMT postulates that our awareness of adversities (including the ineluctability of death) wields great influence on various aspects of our thinking processes, emotions, motivations, and behaviors. Human beings manage possible moments of anxiety (as a result of this awareness) by (1) remaining firm in believing that their cultural worldviews are valid and (2) preserving their cultural self-esteem by meeting the standards of value inherent to these worldviews.[69]

Cultural Survival through Prejudice

TMT focuses on both the conscious and unconscious reasons to believe that one's own cultural worldviews reflect the real world as it is, and that one's attitudes and beliefs (as well as the group's) make a reasonable contribution to that reality. These motives guide behaviors across a wide spectrum of situations.[70] Over time, people in every society cherish cultural worldviews that interpret the universe or society as possessing rationality, stability, and permanence. Growing up into these cultural worldviews causes people to believe in protection against fear of harm or destruction, because it allows them to produce standards of value for a meaningful life as well as ways of coping with death. Through socialization, people live up to the standards valued by the culture and acquire higher cultural self-esteem. This is why they believe in a higher chance of cultural survival.[71]

Culture can be mentally visualized as collection of options with values attached to them.[72] Values are formed through experience and socialization and contribute to the reproduction of cultures. From this vantage point, culture is both creative and dependent as it develops through various processes while shaping outcomes.[73] This is a throwback to Anthony Giddens's duality of structure described in Chapter 6. Looking at culture as a set of values, developed both through material and socialization phenomena, liberates one from the constraints of a monolithic culture or an identitarian one where culture becomes extremely bound to factors such as race, religion, gender, class, or nationality. Naturally, negative values like prejudice towards the Other are often associated with a culture, in which case prejudicial values facilitate motivations for cultural survival. This is why it is crucial to understand the origins of cultural prejudice and how such negative values are constructed over time.[74]

TMT explains how such cultural socialization generates the fiction that an in-group is protected from the symbolic threat of an out-group and how the "good ones" can manage that threat.[75] Cultural worldviews create social constructions of the world, including supporting one's cultural values (e.g., the belief in the inherent superiority of one's group) and rejecting the Other's identity and belief system. Espousing these cultural worldviews can provide a sense of cultural survival by giving in-group members notions of permanence and meaning in the face of threats. Self-esteem, obtained by measuring up with expectations of one's cultural worldview, is said to mitigate external threats. This can be done by making us feel like valuable members of our culture, and we may even be remembered after death.[76]

TMT and Islamophobia

TMT is a useful model to investigate psychological factors that promote or discourage support for violent extremism and counterterrorist policies. According to TMT, domination, disgrace, and perceived injustice menace the self-esteem and cultural worldviews that protect the in-group from death-related anxiety. Problems surface when one interacts with others who hold significantly different worldviews or who view each other with contempt. This contradicts the validity of one's own worldview and self-esteem, thereby eroding one's ability to cope with anxiety. People control such threats to psychological contentment by denigrating the "threatening" out-groups, attempting to make them adopt our worldviews, or, if the threat is too important, simply annihilating them altogether.[77]

In India, the result has been hostility and violence towards the "threatening" Muslim out-group as a way of containing this threat. Hindutva extremists have rigid, totalitarian worldviews. They yearn for structure, construct their 4,500-year-old nation in terms of absolute good and evil, and believe that only *they* hold the truth—a staple of religious fundamentalists. This is why their campaigns are steeped in Islamophobia and activists are prone to reacting to the "Muslim threat" with hostility towards their alleged opposing worldviews. Radical political conservatism seems like an effective way of rationalizing violence, conceivably because of the key role that morality plays in ensuring self-esteem and death transcendence.[78] In their mission to make India a better place, Hindutva activists make Hindu nationalism the sacred and Muslim presence in the nation the profane. If truth be told, such a nativist attitude deems *all* "non-natives" outsiders or strangers who, if not properly immersed into Hindu culture, need to be ousted.

A dangerously false narrative during the #CoronaJihad hashtag campaign included the fabricated footage of a Muslim man from the Delhi branch of Tablighi Jamaat knowingly coughing on others. The content called Muslims "vile minded people."[79] As readers know by now, attacks on Indian Muslims, inflamed by the sacred-profane dichotomy, were aggravated by the public hate campaign, which rapidly grew into a crusade against the so-called Muslim-originated COVID-19 evil. Disease-avoidance mechanisms are directed at groups that are not legitimate sources of a disease.[80] Individuals believe that they can preserve their cultures by launching public campaigns against them and keeping them at bay—"them" as carriers of the disease. This psychological defense makes the in-group feel safer and more assured at the experience of a crisis, by placing the onus of the problem on the Other.[81] TMT supports this hypothesization as fear of death gives rise to disproportionate stigmatization. In this case, Hindu extremists ran a campaign to ascribe an external locus of control to an unprecedented pandemic in modern times which, ultimately, increased a misperceived sense of assurance. In light of the fact that Muslims in the present context were portrayed as the pathogen threat, the feelings of revulsion and incentives to avoid them become a natural consequence, in a nation with a long history of Islamophobia. As Hindus become more nationalistic, they might take more prejudicial actions against their long-standing enemy.[82]

ANTISEMITISM: AN INTRODUCTION

It has become conventional to observe that antisemitism can abound even in countries that have little or no actual Jewish presence. **Antisemitism** is intolerance of, hatred of, or discrimination against Jews for motives linked to their Jewish heritage. An individual who holds such attitudes is called an "anti-Semite."[83] Thus, antisemitism is the hatred or disdain of Jews for being Jewish. The concept was invented in the 1870s by Wilhelm Marr, a German anarchist who wanted to express his anti-Jewish positions in a more modern academic verbiage and also to differentiate it from Christian anti-Judaism.[84] It was simply a more scientific term for *Judenhass* ("Jew-hatred").[85]

Antisemitic Ideology and Prejudice

Antisemitic ideology encompasses a wide domain of irrational thought processes that can be examined effectively from a cognitive angle.[86] It is challenging to find a comprehensive definition of antisemitism beyond the fact that it invariably entails many elements of negative attitudes or assumptions about Jews. Fein (1987)[87] defines it as an enduring system of beliefs—explicit or latent—about Jews as a whole. On an individual scale, it reveals itself through negative feelings; on a cultural scale, as falsehoods, ideology, and popular traditions; and on a practical scale, as social or legal discrimination, political rallying against Jews, and collective or even state-run violence against them so as to chase them out (or even massacre them) for being Jews.

From a more general perspective, antisemitism is a form of prejudice. The same theoretical models that explain group-based prejudice help us understand why particular people or groups of people entertain such attitudes.[88] Examples of antisemitic prejudice include the pogroms that took place right before the First Crusade in 1096, the banishment from England in 1290, the mass killings of Spanish Jews in 1391, the torment during the Spanish Inquisition, the expulsion from Spain in 1492, the Cossack bloodbath in Ukraine (seventeenth century), the multiple pogroms in Russia, the Dreyfus affair, the Holocaust, the official Soviet anti-Jewish laws, and the Jewish exodus from Arab and Muslim nations.[89] More recently, during the military conflict between Israel and Gaza in May 2021, Jewish groups raised concerns about the drastic spike in antisemitic hate crimes in the United States. This should come to no surprise as the Anti-Defamation League located more than 17,000 tweets that included variations of the phrase "Hitler was right" between May 7 and May 14, 2021 alone.[90]

Scapegoating and False Accusations

It is a well-established fact that, throughout history and still to this day, Jews have been victims of scapegoating. **Scapegoating** is the practice of victimizing an exclusive person or group for undeserved blame and resultant antagonistic treatment.[91] It is easy to witness a deluge of deeply felt public anger directed against a scapegoat. This is coupled with insane ideology, propagation of dehumanizing messages by leaders, cultural norms that inspire cruelty against an out-group, the formation of special terror units prepared to execute violent acts, and the absence of solid constitutionally based principles of tolerance and checks and balances.[92] Scapegoating often occurs through false allegations against Jews. Examples include Jewish deicide, antisemitic canards, and charges of well poisoning in the Middle Ages.

Jewish deicide is the wrongful attribution of responsibility for the death of Jesus to the Jewish people as a collective. This "deicide" claim is articulated through the ethnoreligious epithet Christ-killer.[93] During the Second Vatican Council (1962–5), the Roman Catholic Church led by Pope Paul VI issued an official statement that rejected the accusation that Jews were responsible for the crucifixion of Jesus.[94] An **antisemitic canard** is an anti-Jewish falsehood. It conjures up a French-derived English phrase for "hoax." Despite being widely debunked, antisemitic canards are part of broader anti-Jewish conspiracies. For instance, **blood libel** (or **blood accusation**) is the myth that Jews abducted and killed the children of Christians so they could use their blood for religious rituals during Jewish celebrations. Likewise, **host desecration** was the myth that, in the Middle Ages, Jews stole hallowed or sacred hosts (i.e., communion wafers or sacramental bread) and desecrated them to reconstruct the crucifixion of Jesus by piercing or setting the host on fire. The accusations were based only on the accounts provided by the accusers.[95]

During the Plague of 1347–51, **well poisoning** was a conspiracy against "Jewish poisoners" that became standard antisemitic language. Any unexpected or uncontrollable deterioration of health was often attributed to poisoning. Europe was hit by three waves of the bubonic plague throughout the late Middle Ages. Crowded cities were the most affected by the disease, with as much as 50% of the population dying from it. Survivors could not find a logical or scientific explanation. Jews living in those crowded cities, particularly in clearly segregated ghettos, aroused suspicion. The ravaging bubonic plague, thus, became the trigger for antisemitic persecutions, with countless Jews burned at the stake, or forcefully put in synagogues and private residences that would soon be set on fire.[96] "Well poisoning" was a frequent accusation in 1953 during Stalin's last days, when hundreds of Jewish doctors in the Soviet Union were arrested or executed based on the false accusation of having killed famous Communist leaders.[97] Similar allegations were made in the 1980s and 1990s in Arab and Muslim indoctrination communiqués that created the myth that Jews were spreading AIDS and other contagious diseases.[98]

Holocaust Denial

Also known as the **Shoah**, the **Holocaust** was the genocide of Jews during World War II in Europe. Six million Jews were annihilated in a manner that is hard to imagine except in the minds of the perpetrators: the Nazis who implemented the Final Solution—the Nazi plan for the genocide of Jews, which they almost achieved to the fullest extent. Aside from Jews, another five million innocent people were slaughtered, and this statistic does not account for deaths during the battles of World War II. **Holocaust denial** is the act of denying, minimizing, or ignoring the Holocaust.[99] The main premises of Holocaust denial are that the Third Reich (i.e., the Nazi government) did not have a Final Solution or the intention of genociding the Jews. Other false claims are that Nazi authorities did not design death camps and gas chambers to kill the Jews *en masse*, or that the actual number of murdered Jews was considerably lower than the historically established figure of 6,000,000. Most statements of Holocaust denial insinuate or unambiguously advance that the Holocaust is a hoax created by Jewish conspiracy to further the interest of Jews to the detriment of other peoples. Reparations claims for other groups' historical persecutions derive their moral authority and approaches from official decisions made in support of Holocaust victims. Such **Holocaust parallelism** has been applied by otherwise victimized groups to obtain support and sympathy from the West.[100]

Case Study 2:   Antisemitism in Hungary

Hatred is the sentiment that accompanies defensive impulses, especially during their most intense stages. If an actor is perceived as a threat, the subject will react with a hostile response that will be accompanied by the defensive impulses mentioned: hateful feelings. This is a standard mechanism that accounts for mass violence and antisemitism even in the absence of a reasonable threat or attack.[101] Antisemitism in present-day Hungary remains a controversial issue. In 1990, after the shift from Communism to democracy, and the call for free speech and freedom of the press, antisemitism in Hungary surfaced as well and continued to intensify. This phenomenon has led to heated discussions as to whether socioeconomic changes were the reason for the sharp increase in antisemitism (and the rapid proliferation of antisemitic views) or whether resentment towards Jews became visible again as a result of post-Communist civil liberties.[102]

Past Perspectives

Until the 2010s, global media had devoted little attention to Hungarian politics. Today, however, a multitude of news reports and analyses have raised concerns about rampant antisemitism in this nation of fewer than 10,000,000 people. A general perception in the international press is that the country's democracy is failing. Detractors contend that economic difficulties contribute greatly to the rise of extremism. Nevertheless, increasing evidence points to the fact that economic indicators are only part of the problem in Hungary. The unwillingness to cope appropriately with the history of World War II is mirrored in the educational system, leading to an atmosphere of intolerance. The rise of extremism is usually the result of a complex set of factors. If we have gleaned anything from history—both the recent events of 9/11 and the more distant past of Nazism—it is that we must not ignore warning signs and we must not dismiss preposterous distortions of the truth as mere rantings of madmen.[103]

Contemporary Perspectives

Since the late twentieth century, antisemitism in Hungary has formed an institutional apparatus, while verbal and physical violence against Jews has skyrocketed, causing a huge gap between its earlier manifestations in the 1990s and more recent incidents.[104] One of the major reasons for institutionalized antisemitism is the widely supported Hungarian party Jobbik, which obtained 17% of the vote in the April 2010 national election. Far-right circles, which range from nationalist shopping markets to ultraradical and neo-Nazi festivals and events, have also played an important part in the establishment of Hungarian antisemitism in the twenty-first century. Jobbik, the "Movement for a Better Hungary," spearheads the new trend of far-right politics. In many respects, it resembles far-right organizations in Europe, although it has distinct characteristics. For example, in contrast to the vast majority of radical right-wing parties in Europe, Jobbik has passed Muslim-friendly policies.[105]

Support for anti-jewish views, 1994–2011

	Year	Fully Agree (%)	Agree (%)
Jewish intellectuals control the press and cultural sphere	1994	12	18
	2002	13	21
	2006	12	19
	2011	14	21
There exists a secret Jewish network determining political and economic affairs	1994	9	14
	2002	8	14
	2006	10	17
	2011	14	20
It would be best if Jews left the country	1994	11	12
	1995	5	
	2002	3	6
	2006	5	7
	2011	8	12

(Continued)

(Continued)

In certain areas of employment, the number of Jews should be limited	1994	8	9
	2002	3	9
	2006	5	10
	2011	7	12
The crucifixion of Jesus is the unforgivable sin of the Jews	1994	15	11
	1995	23	
	2002	8	9
	2006	8	12
	2011	9	12
The suffering of the Jewish people was God's punishment	1994	12	12
	1995	17	
	2002	7	10
	2006	7	7
	2011	5	9
Jews are more willing than others to use shady practices to get what they want	2006	8	13
	2011	9	17
The Jews of this country are more loyal to Israel than to Hungary	2006	8	15
	2011	12	15

Kovács, András, "Antisemitic Prejudice and Political Antisemitism in Present-Day Hungary," *Journal for the Study of Antisemitism* 4, no. 2 (2012): 443–69, 447.

The table on the previous page provides a detailed progression of antisemitism in Hungary within the adult population. As one can see, between 1994 and 2006, 10 to 15% of the Hungarian adult population were vehemently antisemitic. Anti-Jewish attitudes were a reaction to political campaigns because they became more prominent in election years and then went down to its previous level. This trend changed again after 2006, and the surveys show a rise in prejudice since 2009.[106]

THE "CHRISTIAN-NATIONAL" CAMPAIGN IN HUNGARY

In April 2010, **Viktor Orbán**, leader of the center-right Fidesz party, won Hungary's parliamentary elections by a wide margin, running on a nationalist-populist ticket. He became Prime Minister.[107] Under Orbán's "Christian-national" campaign, with deep antisemitic undertones, Christianity was attached to the nativist cause, mobilizing popular beliefs against refugees, the Roma, and the "lazy" poor.[108] Hungary was once the epitome of classic transition to democracy. Today, it is the textbook example of populism and nationalism.[109] Orbán and his party not only control most of the operations of the legislative and executive branches, but they also regulate or influence many spheres of social life, including business, education, the arts, religious activities, and sports.[110] The Christian-national climate in Hungary has inspired the legitimization of national identity politics (rooted in the past) in a certain number of Western nations. In this case, it reflects a desire to return to pre-World War II Hungary, when it was steeped in Christianity. The widespread opposition to political correctness and gender politics has led Hungarian populists to believe that the growing impact of progressive-liberal values is more harmful than good.[111]

A Reminiscence of Hungarian Complicity in the Holocaust

Prime Minister Orbán has employed antisemitic tropes to share his picture of Hungarian nationalism and has been accused of minimizing Hungarian collusion with Nazism in the Holocaust—even though he has financially supported Jewish institutions and causes. More precisely, Viktor Orbán has sought to make World War II Hungary look innocent and has worked hard to embellish the image of Admiral Miklos Horthy's interwar government, which kept Hungary mostly detached from foreign influence but passed some of the most flagrant anti-Jewish policies outside Nazi Germany. Horthy was the ruler of Hungary from 1920 to 1944. Under Orbán, antisemitic writers from the Horthy era were added to the national curriculum, and the Constitution was changed to inform that the Horthy administration was not liable for its actions during the final 14 months of World War II, when most Hungarian Jews were deported and murdered in the Nazi death camps.[112]

At Szabadság tér (i.e., "Liberty Square") in Budapest, one can look at a stone memorial whose symbols tacitly minimize Hungarian complicity in the Holocaust. It depicts an eagle—a symbol of Nazism—assailing a submissive angel representing Hungary, a juxtaposition meaning that Hungarian leaders were victims of Nazi aggression (rather than collaborators).[113] Szilard Demeter, Director of Budapest's Petofi Museum of Literature, and a fervent supporter of Viktor Orbán, likened the Hungarian-born Jewish billionaire Soros to a "liberal Führer" and Europe as "his gas chamber." He also called Poland and Hungary "the new Jews." "Poison gas flows from the capsule of a multicultural open society, which is deadly to the European way of life," he stated in writing. After a huge backlash in both Hungary and other countries, Demeter apologized half-heartedly and removed his article from Origo, a Hungarian social media outlet.[114]

Hate Communication Campaigns

The Hungarian government's overt information campaigns have shaped the country's communication environment. In 2017 alone, about a quarter of a billion dollars went to cover costs for billboards, brochures, television advertisements, and mass mailings—thanks to which Orbán attacked Hungary's opponents like Brussels (i.e., the headquarters of the European Parliament) and George Soros. In fact, Hungarians today are less concerned about Russia than Brussels and George Soros. The government went so far as organizing a public communication campaign to "stop the Soros package" because it was accused of restricting civil society. Many critics compare the anti-Soros campaign with antisemitism. Without a doubt, the image of a Jewish entrepreneur and liberal philanthropist leading a global conspiracy is a typical antisemitic trope. Portraying Soros as a dangerous and distrusted personality is an embodiment of Othering. The situation here represents an "Us vs. Them" dichotomy—with Soros being the epitome of "Them." The campaign planners were fully cognizant of the popular reactions that would be generated by billboards across the nation saying, "We shall not let Soros have the last laugh."[115]

Soros has become Hungary's victim of twenty-first-century antisemitism. Soros's Hungarian background has made him a particularly useful bogeyman. His face can be seen across the country through images that could have been extracted from nineteenth-century antisemitic campaigns, all reminiscent of the old antisemitic lie of a wealthy, powerful socialite Jew using his fortune in a questionable way to destroy the fabric of society. Orbán even exploited the antisemitic lie that Jews—here, exemplified by Soros—are responsible for unnatural race *mélange*, in this case with Islamic migrants.[116] A big plus for the campaign against Soros is not only that he is a Jew, but also that he can be framed as an "umbrella enemy"—the Jewish puppet master who tries to use his clouts to influence the Hungarian government's foes, including liberal nongovernmental organizations, the opposition parties, and the European Union.[117]

A key principle of that hate communication campaign is that a loss of the Fidesz party would signal the demise of White, Christian Hungary. Notwithstanding income disparities among Hungarians, Orbán is still popular among the poor thanks to his exploitation of identity-based fears.[118] The Fidesz party's rhetoric could be seen all around the nation during the elections of spring 2018. Billboards were loaded with government-sponsored ads with a core antiimmigration message: "Stop." Because these billboards conveyed an overarching nationalist message—the preservation of Christian Europe—during the election of spring 2018, these attacks on George Soros and the Hungarian government's foes are easy to interpret as indirectly antisemitic.[119]

Intertextuality

Introduced by Julia Kristeva (1980),[120] a Bulgarian–French philosopher and literary critic, the term **intertextuality** refers to the practice of taking separate texts in order to find shared meanings. Intertextuality entails a relationship between juxtaposed texts. The texts, then, can be examined via relational processes as if they were conversing with each other.[121] According to Kristeva (1980), "any text is the absorption and transformation of another."[122] New texts build on content from the previous, producing a new text that shares commonalties with old texts. Consequently, readers can locate the meaning of a text by comparing it to another one as language tends to refer back to itself.[123] Fundamental concepts of the intertextual strategy are "influence" and "inspiration." On the one hand, influence privileges an older text over a more recent text for which it functions as a source. On the other hand, inspiration considers the more recent one as an improvement over the previous one.[124]

Within the context of this chapter, like Goldstein in Orwell's *1984*, Soros's conspicuous face on billboards and in public communication campaigns was designed to illustrate Hungary's enemy Number One. Like Goldstein, Soros is a Jew. Many of his most vocal adversaries in and outside Hungary saw him as running an international plot that included other Jewish figures like the Rothschilds, as well as the Freemasons and Illuminati.[125] As a more elaborate example of intertextuality, Viktor Orbán's address at the 170th anniversary of the Hungarian Civic Revolution and War of Independence of 1848–9 was jaw-dropping in its antisemitic imagery:

> We must fight against an opponent which is different from us. Their faces are not visible but are hidden from view; they do not fight directly, but by stealth; they are not honorable, but unprincipled; they are not national, but international; they do not believe in work, but speculate with money; they have no homeland, but feel that the whole world is theirs. They are not generous, but vengeful, and always attack the heart—especially if it is red, white, and green [Hungarian national colors].[126]

Although Orbán did not mention the word "Jew," observers could hardly decipher a more classic example of antisemitism, based primarily on fear of domination by a global Jewish cabal.[127] Drawing on the principles of intertextuality, the Prime Minister's address was heavily inspired by Győző Istóczy's address to the Hungarian legislature in 1878: "Jewish interests, Jewish politics, Jewish statesmen, Jewish journalists, Jewish financiers direct the destiny of all the great states." In both addresses, Jews are leaders who want to dominate the world (e.g., "feeling that the whole world is theirs"). As Győző Istóczy's speech continues, "[Jews] influence all governments. Jews are the international agitators who incite Europe's Christians against one another, so as to destroy them through war, insofar as they have not already destroyed them through corruption." Upon comparing both texts, one can easily notice the similarity between "destroy them" and "attack the heart."[128]

The Protocols of the Elders of Zion

Lastly, Viktor Orbán alleged that there was a "Soros Plan" to force Hungary to accept immigrants at its own costs. In this campaign, he portrayed Soros as the veiled master of all liberal nongovernmental organizations and the forces in the European Union that seek to shove the agenda of multiculturalism and LGBTQ+ issues down Hungarians' throats, an agenda that Orbán's campaign framed as an attack on Judeo-Christian values. The mass migration of Muslims in Europe and Hungary was perceived by Orbán and other right-wing leaders as part of same plot to chip away at those values. In theory, the "Soros Plan" has been likened to the notorious *Protocols of the Elders of Zion*.[129]

The Protocols of the Elders of Zion was a widespread and seemingly believable Russian fake text published in 1903. It contained a litany of antisemitic accusations, mostly centered around a fictitious group of influential Jewish seniors who planned a domination of the world by covertly supporting political and economic movements: both capitalism and Communism. As an illustration of intertextuality, the symbol of financial conspirators supporting the anticapitalist Left is replicated in the anti-Soros campaign, but there are more concrete associations as well. The leaders of the manipulators in the *Protocols* were members of the Rothschild family,[130] and a great deal of the anti-Soros campaign, as seen on social media as well, linked Soros to the present Rothschild banking monopoly. Moreover, both the *Protocols* and the anti-Soros discourse associated the Freemasons and their Illuminati acolytes with the global domination conspiracy.[131]

After it was first printed in Russia in 1903, *The Protocols of the Elders of Zion* was translated into many languages and circulated across all continents in the twentieth century. Henry Ford financed the printing of 500,000 copies that were released throughout the United States in the 1920s. Henry Ford (1948)[132] penned a series of antisemitic pieces in a compilation titled "The International Jew: The World's Foremost Problem," in *The Dearborn Independent*, a newspaper that he owned. The Third Reich publicized the *Protocols* as if it were an authentic document, although it had already been debunked as spurious. After the Nazi Party ascended to power in 1933, it forced all German classrooms to use the text as required course material. Hitler used it as a major justification for devising the Holocaust.[133] In 1993, the Russian court in Moscow finally admitted that *The Protocols of the Elders of Zion* was a forgery.[134]

NOTES

1. Kanika K. Ahuja, Debanjan Banerjee, Kritika Chaudhary, and Chehak Gidwani, "Fear, Xenophobia and Collectivism as Predictors of Well-Being during Coronavirus Disease 2019: An Empirical Study from India," *International Journal of Social Psychiatry* (2020). https://doi.org/10.1177/0020764020936323.

2. Hans-Georg Betz, *Radical Right-Wing Populism in Western Europe* (New York: St. Martin's, 1994); Hans-Georg Betz and Stefan Immerfall, *The New Politics of the Right: Neo-Populist Parties and Movements in Established Democracies* (New York: St. Martin's, 1998).

3. Cas Mudde, "The Populist Zeitgeist," *Government and Opposition* 39, no. 4 (2004): 541–63. https://doi.org/10.1111/j.1477-7053.2004.00135.x.

4. Cas Mudde and Rovira Kaltwasser, "Exclusionary versus Inclusionary Populism: Comparing Contemporary Europe and Latin America," *Government and Opposition* 48, no. 2 (2013): 147–74. https://doi.org/10.1017/gov.2012.11.

5. Roger Eatwell, "The New Extreme Right Challenge," in *Western Democracies and the New Extreme Right Challenge*, ed. Roger Eatwell and Cas Mudde (London: Routledge, 2004): 1–16.

6. Jonathan Matusitz, *Global Jihad in Muslim and Non-Muslim Contexts* (New York: Palgrave Macmillan, 2020).

7. Shirin Housee, "What's the Point? Anti-Racism and Students' Voices against Islamophobia," *Race Ethnicity and Education* 15, no. 1 (2012): 101–20. https://doi.org/10.1080/13613324.2012.638867.

8. Maggie Haberman, "Donald Trump Calls for Surveillance of 'Certain Mosques' and a Syrian Refugee Database," *The New York Times* (November 21, 2015): A24. Retrieved on March 31, 2021 from https://www.nytimes.com/2015/11/22/us/politics/donald-trump-syrian-muslims-surveillance.html.

9. Washington v. Trump, No. 17–35105, slip op. at 5, 24–26 (9th Circuit, February 9, 2017) (*per curiam*).

10. Fernando Bravo López, "Towards a Definition of Islamophobia: Approximations of the Early Twentieth Century," *Ethnic and Racial Studies* 34, no. 4 (2011): 556–73. https://doi.org/10.1080/01419870.2010.528440.

11. Chris Allen, *Islamophobia* (Farnham, England: Ashgate Publishing, 2010).

12. S. Sayyid and AbdoolKarim Vakil, *Thinking through Islamophobia* (Cambridge: Cambridge University Press, 2010).

13. Erik Bleich, "What Is Islamophobia and How Much Is There? Theorizing and Measuring an Emerging Comparative Concept," *American Behavioral Scientist* 55, no. 12 (2011): 1581–1600. https://doi.org/10.1177/0002764211409387; François Pouillon, *Les deux vies d'Étienne Dinet, peintre en Islam: L'Algerie et l'heritage colonial* (Paris: Editions Balland, 1997).

14. Merriam-Webster, *The Merriam-Webster Dictionary* (Springfield, MA: Merriam-Webster, 2016).

15. Leon Moosavi, "The Racialization of Muslim Converts in Britain and Their Experiences of Islamophobia," *Critical Sociology* 41, no. 1 (2015): 41–56. https://doi.org/10.1177/0896920513504601.

16. Wajahat Ali, Eli Clifton, Matthew Duss, Lee Fang, Scott Keyes, and Faiz Shakir, *Fear, Inc.: The Roots of the Islamophobia Network in America* (Washington, D.C.: Center for American Progress, 2011).

17. Julie Hollar and Jim Naureckas, *Smearcasting: How Islamophobes Spread Fear, Bigotry and Misinformation* (New York: Fairness and Accuracy in Reporting, 2008).

18. Dhaya Ramarajan and Marcella Runell, "Confronting Islamophobia in Education," *Intercultural Education* 18, no. 2 (2007): 87–97, 87. https://doi.org/10.1080/14675980701327197.

19. Mattias Gardell, *Islamophobia* (Stockholm: Leopard, 2010).

20. Matti Bunzl, "Between Anti-Semitism and Islamophobia: Some Thoughts on the New Europe," *American Ethnologist* 33, no. 4 (2005): 499–508. https://doi.org/10.1525/ae.2005.32.4.499.

21. Jonas R. Kunst, Talieh Sadeghi, Hajra Tahir, David Lackland Sam, and Lotte Thomsen, "The Vicious Circle of Religious Prejudice: Islamophobia Makes the Acculturation Attitudes of Majority and Minority Members Clash," *European Journal of Social Psychology* 46, no. 2 (2016): 249–59. https://doi.org/10.1002/ejsp.2174.

22. Dustin J. Byrd, *Unfashionable Objections to Islamophobic Cartoons: L'Affaire Charlie Hebdo* (Cambridge: Cambridge Scholars Publishing, 2017).

23. Mohammed Sinan Siyech and Akanksha Narain, "Beef-Related Violence in India: An Expression of Islamophobia," *Islamophobia Studies Journal* 4, no 2 (2018): 181–94.

24. Debanjan Banerjee, Jagannatha Rao Kosagisharaf, and T.S. Sathyanarayana Rao, "'The Dual Pandemic' of Suicide and COVID-19: A Biopsychosocial Narrative of Risks and Prevention," *Psychiatry Research* 295 (2021). https://doi.org/10.1016/j.psychres.2020.113577.

25. Howard Spodek, "Pogrom in Gujarat, 2002: Neighborhood Perspectives," *The Journal of Asian Studies* 72, no. 2 (2013): 417–21. https://doi.org/10.1017/S0021911813000053.

26. Bruce Matthews, "Christian Evangelical Conversions and the Politics of Sri Lanka," *Pacific Affairs* 80, no. 33 (2007): 455–72.

27. *India Today*, "BJP Inducts 7 Crore New Members, Creates Membership Drive Record," *India Today* (August 29, 2019): A1. Retrieved on July 15, 2021 from https://www.indiatoday.in/india/story/bjp-inducts-7-crore-new-members-creates-membership-drive-record-1593164-2019-08-29.

28. Ashutosh Varshney, *Ethnic Conflict and Civic Life: Hindus and Muslims in India* (New Haven, CT: Yale University Press, 2003).

29. Veena Das, *Life and Words: Violence and the Descent into the Ordinary* (Berkeley, CA: University of California Press, 2007).

30. Cited in Siyech and Narain, "Beef-Related Violence in India," 183.

31. Jyotirmaya Sharma, *Hindutva: Exploring the Idea of Hindu Nationalism* (New York: HarperCollins, 2016).

32. Ram Puniyani, *Contours of Hindu Rashtra: Hindutva, Sangh Parivar, and Contemporary Politics* (Delhi: Palkaz Publications, 2006).

33. Prabhat Patnaik, "Fascism of Our Times," *Social Scientist* 21, no. 3 (1993): 69–77. https://doi.org/10.2307/3517631.

34. Charu Gupta, "Allegories of 'Love Jihad' and Ghar Wapasi: Interlocking the Socio-Religious with the Political," in *Rise of Saffron Power: Reflections on Indian Politics*, ed. Mujibur Rehman (New Delhi: Routledge, 2018): 84–110.

35. Nishant Upadhyay, "Hindu Nation and Its Queers: Caste, Islamophobia, and De/coloniality in India," *Interventions* 22, no. 4 (2020): 464–80. https://doi.org/10.1080/1369801X.2020.1749709.

36. Foyaz Mughal, "'Jews and Apostate Muslims Deserve Punishment': How Jihadists Justify Coronavirus to Hustle for Recruits," *Haaretz* (April 12, 2020): A1. Retrieved on April 25, 2020 from https://www.haaretz.com/world-news/.premium-jews-and-apostate-muslims-deserve-punishment-jihadists-coronavirus-hustle-1.8759662.

37. Siyech and Narain, "Beef-Related Violence in India," 181–2.

38. Zehra Mehdi, "'Phobia of Religion: Religion as Islam': A Political Argument and a Psychoanalytic Inquiry of Islamophobia in India," *International Journal of Applied Psychoanalytic Studies* 14, no. 3 (2017): 222–44. https://doi.org/10.1002/aps.1535.

39. Upadhyay, "Hindu Nation and Its Queers," 466–9.

40. Kanika K. Ahuja and Debanjan Banerjee, "The 'Labeled' Side of COVID-19 in India: Psychosocial Perspectives on Islamophobia during the Pandemic," *Frontiers in Psychiatry* (2021). https://doi.org/10.3389/fpsyt.2020.604949.

41. Mehdi, "'Phobia of Religion," 222–44.

42. The data is available at https://covid19.who.int/table.

43. Chandana Mathur, "COVID–19 and India's Trail of Tears," *Dialectical Anthropology* 44 (2020): 239–42. https://doi.org/10.1007/s10624-020-09611-4.

44. Billy Perrigo, "It Was Already Dangerous to Be Muslim in India. Then Came the Coronavirus," *Time* (April 3, 2020). Retrieved on April 24, 2020 from https://time.com/5815264/coronavirus-india-islamophobia-coronajihad.

45. Zacharias P. Pieri, *Tablighi Jamaat and the Quest for the London Mega Mosque: Continuity and Change* (New York: Palgrave Macmillan, 2015).

46. Ateeq A. Rauf and Ajnesh Prasad, "Temporal Spaces of Egalitarianism: The Ethical Negation of Economic Inequality in an Ephemeral Religious Organization," *Journal of Business Ethics* 162 (2020): 699–718. https://doi.org/10.1007/s10551-018-4006-z.

47. Jan Ali, "Islamic Revivalism: The Case of the Tablighi Jamaat," *Journal of Muslim Minority Affairs* 23, no. 1 (2003): 173–81. https://doi.org/10.1080/13602000305935.

48. Ravi Agrawal, "Why India's Muslims Are in Grave Danger," *Foreign Policy* (March 2, 2020). Retrieved on April 24, 2020 from https://foreignpolicy.com/2020/03/02/india-muslims-delhi-riots-danger.

49. Mughal, "'Jews and Apostate Muslims Deserve Punishment,'" A1.

50. Hannah Ellis-Petersen, "Inside Delhi: Beaten, Lynched and Burnt Alive," *The Guardian* (March 1, 2020): A1. Retrieved on April 24, 2020 from https://www.theguardian.com/world/2020/mar/01/india-delhi-after-hindu-mob-riot-religious-hatred-nationalists.

51. Ibid.

52. Dorothy Nelkin and Sander L. Gilman, "Placing Blame for Devastating Disease," *Social Research* 55, no. 3 (1988): 361–78.

53. Fred Dervin, "Cultural Identity, Representation and Othering," in *The Routledge Handbook of Language and Intercultural Communication*, ed. Jane Jackson (New York: Routledge, 2012): Chapter 11.

54. Jo N. Hays, *Epidemics and Pandemics: Their Impacts on Human History* (Santa Barbara, CA: Abc–clio, 2005).

55. Shakuntala Banaji, Ram Bhat, Anushi Agarwal, Nihal Passanha, and Mukti Sadhana Pravin, "Whatsapp Vigilantes: An Exploration of Citizen Reception and Circulation of

WhatsApp Misinformation Linked to Mob Violence in India," *London School of Economics* (2019). Retrieved on April 12, 2021 from https://eprints.lse.ac.uk/104316/1/Banaji_whatsapp_vigilantes_exploration_of_citizen_reception_published.pdf.

56. Elyse Samuels, "How Misinformation on WhatsApp Led to a Mob Killing in India," *The Washington Post* (February 21, 2020): A1. Retrieved on April 12, 2021 from https://www.washingtonpost.com/politics/2020/02/21/how-misinformation-whatsapp-led-deathly-mob-lynching-india.

57. Madhumita Murgia, Stephanie Findlay, and Andres Schipani, "India: The Whatsapp Election," *The Financial Times* (May 5, 2019): A1. Retrieved on April 12, 2021 from https://www.ft.com/content/9fe88fba-6c0d-11e9-a9a5-351eeaef6d84.

58. Perrigo, "It Was Already Dangerous to Be Muslim in India".

59. Fathima Nizaruddin, "Role of Public WhatsApp Groups within the Hindutva Ecosystem of Hate and Narratives of 'CoronaJihad'," *International Journal of Communication* 15 (2021): 1102–19.

60. Ibid, 1105–8.

61. Ibid, 1108.

62. Perrigo, "It Was Already Dangerous to Be Muslim in India".

63. Tarleton Gillespie, *Custodians of the Internet: Platforms, Content Moderation, and the Hidden Decisions That Shape Social Media* (New Haven, CT: Yale University Press, 2018).

64. K. M. Rakesh, "Assault and Warning 'Not to Feed Hindus' in Bangalore," *The Telegraph* (April 10, 2020): A1. Retrieved on April 24, 2020 from https://www.telegraphindia.com/india/coronavirus-lockdown-assault-and-warning-not-to-feed-hindus-in-bangalore/cid/1763658?ref=topic-stories.

65. *BBC News*, "India Coronavirus: Tablighi Jamaat Leader on Manslaughter Charge over Covid-19," *BBC News* (April 16, 2020). Retrieved on April 25, 2020 from https://www.bbc.com/news/world-asia-india-52306879.

66. Aniruddha Ghosal, Sheikh Saaliq, and Emily Schmall, "Indian Muslims Face Stigma, Blame for Surge in Infections," *ABC News* (April 25, 2020). Retrieved on March 19, 2021 from https://abcnews.go.com/Health/wireStory/islamophobia-large-cluster-affects-indias-virus-fight-70344026.

67. Ahuja and Banerjee, "The 'Labeled' Side of COVID-19 in India".

68. Sheldon Solomon, Jeff Greenberg, and Tom Pyszczynski, "A Terror Management Theory of Social Behavior: The Psychological Functions of Self-Esteem and Cultural Worldviews," *Advances in Experimental Social Psychology* 24 (1991): 93–159. https://doi.org/10.1016/S0065-2601(08)60328-7.

69. Tom Pyszczynski, Sheldon Solomon, and Jeff Greenberg, "Chapter One—Thirty Years of Terror Management Theory: From Genesis to Revelation," *Advances in Experimental Social Psychology* 52 (2015): 1–70. https://doi.org/10.1016/bs.aesp.2015.03.001.

70. Tom Pyszczynski, Zachary Rothschild, Matt Motyl, and Abdolhossein Abdollahi, "The Cycle of Righteous Destruction: A Terror Management Theory Perspective on Terrorist and Counter-Terrorist Violence," in *Terrorism and Torture: An Interdisciplinary Perspective*, ed. Werner G. K. Stritzke, Stephan Lewandowsky, David Denemark, Joseph Clare, and Frank Morgan (Cambridge: Cambridge University Press, 2009): 154–78.

71. Victor G. Cicirelli, "Fear of Death in Older Adults: Predictions from Terror Management Theory," *The Journals of Gerontology: Series B* 57, no. 4 (2002): 358–66. https://doi.org/10.1093/geronb/57.4.P358.

72. Will Kymlicka, *Multicultural Citizenship: A Liberal Theory of Minority Rights* (Oxford: Clarendon Press, 1995).

73. Jacqueline Best and Matthew Paterson, *Cultural Political Economy* (New York: Routledge, 2010).

74. J. P. Singh, "Race, Culture, and Economics: An Example from North–South Trade Relations," *Review of International Political Economy* (2020). https://doi.org/10.1080/09 692290.2020.1771612.

75. Jeff Greenberg and Jamie Arndt, "Terror Management Theory," in *Handbook of Theories of Social Psychology: Collection: Volumes 1 & 2*, ed. Paul A. M. Van Lange, Arie W. Kruglanski, and E. Tory Higgins (Thousand Oaks, CA: Sage, 2011): 398–415.

76. Jeff Greenberg "Terror Management Theory: From Genesis to Revelations," in *Meaning, Mortality, and Choice: The Social Psychology of Existential Concerns*, ed. Phillip Shaver and Mario Mikulincer (Washington D.C.: American Psychological Association, 2012): 17–35.

77. Tom Pyszczynski, Zachary Rothschild, and Abdolhossein Abdollahi, "Terrorism, Violence, and Hope for Peace: A Terror Management Perspective," *Current Directions in Psychological Science* 17, no. 5 (2008): 318–22. https://doi.org/10.1111/j.1467-8721.2008.00598.x.

78. John T. Jost, Jack Glaser, Arie W. Kruglanski, and Frank J. Sulloway, "Political Conservatism as Motivated Social Cognition," *Psychological Bulletin* 129, no. 3 (2003): 339–75. https://doi.org/10.1037/0033-2909.129.3.339; John T. Jost and Orsolya Hunyady, "Antecedents and Consequences of System-Justifying Ideologies," *Current Directions in Psychological Science* 14, no. 5 (2005): 260–5. https://doi.org/10.1111/j.0963-7214.2005.00377.x.

79. Perrigo, "It Was Already Dangerous to Be Muslim in India".

80. Robert Kurzban and Mark R. Leary, "Evolutionary Origins of Stigmatization: The Functions of Social Exclusion," *Psychology Bulletin* 127, no. 2 (2001): 187–208. https://doi.org/10.1037/0033-2909.127.2.187.

81. Patrick W. Corrigan, "Mental Health Stigma as Social Attribution: Implications for Research Methods and Attitude Change," *Clinical Psychology* 7, no. 1 (2000): 48–67. https://doi.org/10.1093/clipsy.7.1.48.

82. Ahuja and Banerjee, "The 'Labeled' Side of COVID-19 in India".

83. Deborah E. Lipstadt, *Antisemitism: Here and Now* (New York: Schocken, 2019).

84. Moshe Zimmermann, *Wilhelm Marr: The Patriarch of Antisemitism* (New York: Oxford University Press, 1986).

85. Sanford Ragins, *Jewish Responses to Anti-Semitism in Germany, 1870–1914: A Study in the History of Ideas* (Cincinnati, OH: Hebrew Union College Press, 1980).

86. Aaron Beck, *Prisoners of Hate* (New York: HarperCollins, 1999).

87. Helen Fein, "Dimensions of Antisemitism: Attitudes, Collective Accusations, and Actions," in *The Persisting Question: Sociological Perspectives and Social Contexts of Modern Antisemitism, Current Research on Antisemitism*, ed. Helen Fein (New York: Walter de Gruyter, 1987): 67–85.

88. Pieter Bevelander, Mikael Hjerm, and Jenny Kiiskinen, *The Religious Affiliation and Anti-Semitism of Secondary School Swedish Youths: A Statistical Analysis of Survey Data from 2003 and 2009* (Bonn, Germany: Institute for the Study of Labor, 2013).

89. See William I. Brustein, *Roots of Hate: Anti-Semitism in Europe Before the Holocaust* (Cambridge: Cambridge University Press, 2003); Robert Chazan, *In the Year 1096: The First Crusade and the Jews* (Philadelphia, PA: The Jewish Publication Society, 1996); Henry Kamen, *The Spanish Inquisition: A Historical Revision* (4th Ed.) (New Haven, CT: Yale University Press, 2014).

90. Grace Hauck, "Jewish Groups Sound Alarm on Rise in Antisemitic Hate Crimes amid Tensions between Israel, Hamas," *USA Today* (May 22, 2021): A1. Retrieved on May 22, 2021 from https://www.usatoday.com/story/news/nation/2021/05/22/israel-hamas-conflict-jewish-groups-sound-alarm-antisemitism-us/5220334001.

91. TomDouglas, *Scapegoats: Transferring Blame* (New York: Routledge, 1995).

92. Neil J. Kressel, "Mass Hatred in the Muslim and Arab World: The Neglected Problem of Anti-Semitism," *International Journal of Applied Psychoanalytic Studies* 4, no. 3 (2007): 197–215. https://doi.org/10.1002/aps.140.

93. Christian H. K. Persaud, *Israel against All Odds: Anti-Semitism From Its Beginnings to the Holocaust* (Canbridge, OH: Christian Publishing House, 2019).

94. Norman C. Tobias, *Jewish Conscience of the Church: Jules Isaac and the Second Vatican Council* (New York: Palgrave Macmillan, 2017).

95. Flora Cassen, "Jews and Money: Time for a New Story?" *Jewish Quarterly Review* 110, no. 2 (2020): 373–82. https://doi.org/10.1353/jqr.2020.0007.

96. Rosemary Horrox, *The Black Death* (Manchester: Manchester Unversity Press, 1973).

97. Mark Clarfield, "The Soviet 'Doctors' Plot'—50 Years on," *The British Medical Journal* 325 (2002). https://doi.org/10.1136/bmj.325.7378.1487.

98. Neil J. Kressel, "Antisemitism, Social Science, and the Muslim and Arab World," *Judaism* 52, no 3 (2003): 225–45.

99. James Morcan and Lance Morcan, Debunking *Holocaust Denial Theories: Two Non-Jews Affirm the Historicity of the Nazi Genocide* (Papamoa, New Zealand: Sterling Gate Books, 2016).

100. William F. S. Miles, "Third World Views of the Holocaust," *Journal of Genocide Research* 6, no 3 (2004): 371–93. https://doi.org/10.1080/1462352042000265855.

101. Mortimer Ostow, "Commentary on 'Mass Hatred in the Muslim and Arab World: The Neglected Problem of Anti-Semitism' by Neil Kressel," *International Journal of Applied Psychoanalytic Studies* 4, no. 3 (2007): 221–34. https://doi.org/10.1002/aps.141.

102. András Kovács, "Antisemitic Prejudice and Political Antisemitism in Present-Day Hungary," *Journal for the Study of Antisemitism* 4, no. 2 (2012): 443–69.

103. Swaan van Iterson and Maja Nenadović, "The Danger of Not Facing History: Exploring the Link between Education about the Past and Present-Day Anti-Semitism and Racism in Hungary," *Intercultural Education* 24, no. 1 (2013): 93–102. https://doi.org/10.1080/14675986.2013.782735.

104. Katalin Halasz, "The Rise of the Radical Right in Europe and the Case of Hungary: 'Gypsy Crime' Defines National Identity?" *Development* 52 (2009): 490–4. https://doi.org/10.1057/dev.2009.63.

105. Norbert Pap and Viktor Glied, "Hungary's Turn to the East: *Jobbik* and Islam," *Europe-Asia Studies* 70, no. 7 (2018): 1036–54. https://doi.org/10.1080/09668136.2018.1464126.

106. Kovács, "Antisemitic Prejudice and Political Antisemitism," 446–8.

107. Juliet Johnson and Andrew Barnes, "Financial Nationalism and Its International Enablers: The Hungarian Experience," *Review of International Political Economy* 22, no. 3 (2015): 535–69. https://doi.org/10.1080/09692290.2014.919336.

108. Liz Fekete, "Hungary: Power, Punishment and the 'Christian-National Idea'," *Race & Class* 57, no. 4 (2016): 39–53. https://doi.org/10.1177/0306396815624607.

109. Emilia Palonen, "Performing the Nation: The Janus-Faced Populist Foundations of Illiberalism in Hungary," *Journal of Contemporary European Studies* 26, no. 3 (2018): 308–21. https://doi.org/10.1080/14782804.2018.1498776.

110. Péter Krekó and Zsolt Enyedi, "Explaining Eastern Europe: Orbán's Laboratory of Illiberalism," *Journal of Democracy* 29, no. 3 (2018): 39–51. https://doi.org/10.1353/jod.2018.0043.

111. Ibid, 41.

112. Patrick Kingsley, "A Friend to Israel, and to Bigots: Viktor Orban's 'Double Game' on Anti-Semitism," *The New York Times* (May 19, 2019): A1. Retrieved on April 12, 2021 from https://www.nytimes.com/2019/05/14/world/europe/orban-hungary-antisemitism.html.

113. Ibid, A1.

114. *Deutsche Welle*, "Rising Anti-Semitism in Hungary Worries Jewish Groups," *Deutsche Welle* (November 29, 2020). Retrieved on April 12, 2021 from https://www.dw.com/en/rising-anti-semitism-in-hungary-worries-jewish-groups/a-55978374.

115. Krekó and Enyedi, "Explaining Eastern Europe," 47–8.

116. Joshua Shane, "Netanyahu, Orbán, and the Resurgence of Antisemitism: Lessons of the Last Century," *Shofar* 37, no. 1 (2019): 108–20. https://doi.org/10.1353/sho.2019.0005.

117. Krekó and Enyedi, "Explaining Eastern Europe," 47–8.

118. Ibid, 47–8.

119. Palonen, "Performing the Nation," 317.

120. Julia Kristeva, *Desire in Language* (New York: Columbia University Press, 1980).

121. David Bloome and Ann Egan-Robertson, "The Social Construction of Intertextuality in Classroom Reading and Writing Lessons," *Reading Research Quarterly* 28, no. 4 (1993): 304–33. https://doi.org/10.2307/747928.

122. Kristeva, *Desire in Language*, 66.

123. James Braxton Peterson, "The Depth of the Hole: Intertextuality and Tom Waits' 'Way Down in the Hole'," *Criticism* 52, no. 3 (2010): 461–85. https://doi.org/10.1353/crt.2010.0050.

124. Margarete Landwehr, "Introduction: Literature and the Visual Arts; Questions of Influence and Intertextuality," *College Literature* 29, no. 3 (2002): 1–16.

125. Ivan Kalmar, "Islamophobia and Anti-Antisemitism: The Case of Hungary and the 'Soros Plot'," *Patterns of Prejudice* 54, no. 1 (2020): 182–98. https://doi.org/10.1080/0031322X.2019.1705014.

126. Cited in Shane, "Netanyahu, Orbán, and the Resurgence of Antisemitism," 112.

127. Ibid, 112.

128. Cited in Richard S. Levy, *Antisemitism in the Modern World: An Anthology of Texts* (Lexington, MA: D. C. Heath, 1991): 102.

129. Kalmar, "Islamophobia and Anti-Antisemitism," 188–90.

130. Chip Berlet, "Protocols to the Left, Protocols to the Right: Conspiracism in American Political Discourse at the Turn of the Second Millennium," in *The Paranoid Apocalypse: A Hundred-Year Retrospective on The Protocols of the Elders of Zion*, ed. Richard Landes and Steven T. Katz (New York: New York University Press, 2012): 186–217.

131. Kalmar, "Islamophobia and Anti-Antisemitism," 188–90.

132. Henry Ford, *The International Jew: The World's Foremost Problem* (Alexandria: Library of Alexandria, 1948).

133. Randall L. Bytwerk, "Believing in 'Inner Truth': The Protocols of the Elders of Zion in Nazi Propaganda, 1933–1945," *Holocaust and Genocide Studies* 29, no. 2 (2015): 212–29. https://doi.org/10.1093/hgs/dcv024.

134. Steven Erlanger, "Russia Court Calls 'Protocols' Anti-Semitic Forgery," *The New York Times* (November 27, 1993): A1. Retrieved on May 14, 2021 from https://www.nytimes.com/1993/11/27/world/russia-court-calls-protocols-anti-semitic-forgery.html.

CHAPTER 16

Antiterrorist Public Communication Campaigns

Although governments, law enforcement agencies, and nongovernmental organizations occasionally take reactionary approaches to terrorist attacks, they are becoming increasingly aware that they should rather be more proactive and act more preventively in order to wise up to the terrorism game. Those entities are keenly aware that hard security tools alone are inadequate to tackle violent extremism. Instead, their approaches should also include ways that grapple with the basic roots of extremism. Radical ideologies are the glue that bind extremists together and nurture their grievances. Governments, law enforcement agencies, and nongovernmental organizations must understand terrorism to the fullest extent and develop antiterrorist communication campaigns.[1] As explained in Chapters 13 and 14, terrorist organizations themselves clearly understand the power of communication campaigns.

Enter Al-Shabaab. **Al-Shabaab** is a Somali terrorist organization that uses diverse communication technologies to publish an online jihadist magazine called *Gaidi Mtaani*. Through this magazine, Al-Shabaab promotes jihad in Somalia and neighboring countries like Kenya. **Jihad** is holy war against the Infidels (i.e., non-Muslims) and Apostates (i.e., Muslim "traitors").[2] Defined as "Terrorist on the Street" in Swahili, Gaidi Mtaani is a propaganda magazine that is accessible online and that motivates Eastern and Central Africans to commit jihadist acts in their own regions by using improvised explosive devices (IEDs) and other weapons that they can get. A glossy, visually powerful, neatly written, and well-articulated magazine, *Gaidi Mtaani* allows Al-Shabaab to disseminate its communication campaign to the Swahili-speaking public in Africa and to the English-speaking **ummah** (i.e., the global Islamic community).[3] The terrorist group can also run its strategic communication campaign through organic websites, circulation of newsletters, and

Fundamentals of Public Communication Campaigns, First Edition. Jonathan Matusitz.
© 2022 John Wiley & Sons Ltd. Published 2022 by John Wiley & Sons Ltd.

international media conferences and interviews.[4] In fact, Al-Shabaab's success in reaching the ummah through its campaign has led to growing support from global jihadist networks like Al-Qaeda, as well as financing and volunteer recruitment from the Somali diaspora around the world.[5]

Under these circumstances, developing initiatives—in Somalia, Africa, and throughout the world—to counter communication campaigns like those of Al–Shabaab should be a priority. Many antiterrorist communication campaigns are interventions that use broadcasting persuasive messages with the mission of (1) raising awareness about the deleterious consequences of extreme violence and (2) changing people's behaviors and attitudes accordingly. Evidence suggests that those interventions are somewhat effective. The majority of them focus on the elements of a message's content that predicts its persuasive potential.[6] An antiterrorist communication campaign takes two main forms. It can focus on countering information; it can also develop a counterradicalization program, which goes deeper than the former. Naturally, it can also do both (and most of them do). A **counterinformation campaign**, in essence, seeks to "get the message out." The purpose is to increase awareness of true facts and develop positive relationships with key constituents.[7] No attempt is made at rewiring the mind or deradicalizing the target audience.

WINNING THE WAR OF IDEAS

Targeting the radical ideologies of terrorist campaigns can assist antiterrorist activists in winning the war of ideas. Upon exploring various options for countering violent messages, what is of relevance is the content and channel of countermessages. A significant challenge in setting this type of campaign into motion is to ensure that many voices be heard. This means providing key individuals with the toolkit and skills to craft appropriate messages and diffuse them to those who are susceptible to radicalization. The centerpiece of this chapter is that success depends on the ability to confront and, hopefully, inhibit terrorist ideologies. This is how we can win the war of ideas.[8] As the concept of counterinformation campaign was just defined, it would be useful to describe counterradicalization campaigns.

Counterradicalization Campaigns

A **counterradicalization campaign** provides an alternative picture of what life would be after renouncing extreme violence. It is a set of messages that attribute meaning to the actions it is requesting of the audience. The campaign must disprove and invalidate the terrorist discourse by (1) delegitimizing the violence that terrorists advocate and (2) making a strong case for resorting to nonviolent activism and civic participation.[9] A counterradicalization campaign uses alternative narratives, positive stories about social values, broad-mindedness, liberty, and democracy.[10] Schmid (2014)[11] avers that counternarratives can bridge the gap between "Us" and "Them" that is forged by extremists and unite human beings from all sides. They are more dedicated to "what we are for" and less on "what we are against." While strategic communication is the province of government, alternative narratives are designed by both government and civil participants and groups.

A **narrative** is defined as a "simple unifying, easily-expressed story or explanation that organizes people's experience and provides a framework for understanding events."[12] This perspective, deeply embedded within culture, can inspire positive forms of individual action.[13] Narratives are compelling because they can glue the pieces of the puzzle together and appear truthful to members of the target audience.[14] **Counternarratives** are efforts to directly or indirectly confront violent extremist messages. These initiatives can be done both online and offline, and many campaigns utilize both platforms. This approach is predicated on the old notion of winning the war of ideas. Counternarratives reveal the dangerous sides and effects of extremist ideologies, impugn assumptions, expose falsehoods, and debunk related conspiracy theories.[15] This is in line with Braddock and Horgan's (2015)[16] interpretation of counternarratives as the development and diffusion of "narratives designed to contradict potentially radicalizing themes intrinsic to terrorist narratives."

Counterradicalization vs. Deradicalization

A distinction needs to be made between counterradicalization and deradicalization. **Deradicalization** refers to the process of modifying an individual's belief system so that he or she can combat his or her own radical ideology and, in due course, adopt mainstream values.[17] The best synonym for deradicalization is disengagement. Disengagement initiatives have the priority of improving public safety from terrorist attacks, while helping communities and families by giving them opportunities to turn their back on violence and embrace more positive, law-abiding ways. Such programs typically underscore the importance of disengagement from violent organizations and deradicalization from personally held extreme beliefs. Experts who advocate deradicalization remark that a small percentage of people with prior extreme beliefs are no longer violent. For people who still engage in violence, other compelling factors may continue to persist apart from ideology.[18]

On the other hand, **counterradicalization** refers to (1) community-based programs aimed at preventing participation in extreme violence and (2) approaches that challenge radical beliefs and feelings for those who have not yet committed violence. The results of counterradicalization and deradicalization are comparable in their capacity to curtail radicalization in society and repudiation of the Other.[19] Although counterradicalization programs are often likened to deradicalization programs,[20] according to Horgan's (2009)[21] definition, these preventative proposals are neither deradicalization nor disengagement efforts. Rather, they exemplify counterradicalization strategies because they center a great deal on risk prevention. An ideology cannot be crushed by hard power only (see next section). Those who want to fight extreme ideologies advance the concept that its value—even if not always understood—is better than the risks of not taking the counterradicalization route.[22] As Koehler (2017)[23] explains, "those who care about the extraordinary social and psychological toll associated with terrorism cannot sit idly by while academics and politicians pontificate on whether we are using appropriate definitions, language, and terminology."

The "Soft Power" Approach

Antiterrorist campaigns invariably propose the soft approach, which presents stages that at-risk individuals should follow to divert themselves away from terrorism. For instance, in addition to counternarratives, this type of intervention includes counseling, mentoring, or mental healthcare[24] to repel the drivers that lead those individuals to participate in politically or ideologically motivated violence.[25] Developed by Joseph Nye (1990),[26] **soft power** is the ability to convince, co-opt, and be appealing, instead of coercing (i.e., hard power). In other words, soft power consists of influencing the preferences of others through charisma and attraction. A distinctive attribute of soft power is that it is noncompelling; it capitalizes on lifestyles, political values, and foreign policies. The concept has particular relevance in international politics, where power play can determine the outcomes of confrontations. **Power play** is a diplomatic or political maneuver in which power is displayed.[27] In the case of soft power, however, one side can try to be subtly more "powerful" than the other through noncoercive maneuvers.

Power, in and if itself, is the ability to influence others to obtain the outcomes desired. There are multiple routes to achieve this: to coerce people with threats; to induce them with financial compensation; or to attract and co-opt them to desire a new outcome. The last one here is soft power because it co-opts people instead of coercing them.[28] Soft power, then, seeks to shape the preferences of others. At the interpersonal level, the power of attraction and charm can go a long way. Political leaders are well aware that it can set the agenda and form the blueprint of negotiations. Soft power is the essence of democracy. The power to create preferences is contingent on intangible assets like charismatic personalities, culture, moral virtues and institutions, and policies that are perceived as fair or having moral authority. If one party can get the other party to desire to change, then no coercion is necessary.[29]

Whereas soft power is the ability to convince another to do what one wants,[30] **hard power** is the practice of forcing them to do something. "Hard power" approaches include military intervention, coercive diplomacy, and economic sanctions.[31] "Hard power" advocates, those with political and institutional power, can articulate their arguments inefficiently because they operate on the principle that they should ignore or simply integrate elements of national power that fall outside their traditional scope.[32] Lastly, **smart power** combines hard power and soft power approaches. This strategy underlines the importance of a strong military, but also devotes much time and energy in forming alliances, partnerships, and foundations of all levels to expand their reach and secure legitimacy of their actions.[33]

MOVING TO THE ONLINE SPACE

Antiterrorist communication campaigns have successfully moved to the online space and they, too, are in need of understanding and evaluation.[34] These campaigns—whether ran on YouTube, Facebook, or Twitter—have a wide assortment of analytics available on the social media platform that they employ. Such analytics can identify how many users view, like, share, or comment on the campaign. Some platforms even have at their disposal data on campaign audience demographics—a plethora of information that can significantly facilitate campaign implementation.[35] Moving antiterrorist communication campaigns online allows planners to use a networked approach where key individuals who act as hubs in their respective social networks can implement counterinformation and counterradicalization tactics. Interactive, interpersonal messages online can overcome barriers to traditional participation in such initiatives. Evidence shows that these messages online tend to be positively received when they pertain to broader community issues and priorities around the world.[36] Part of what this chapter will cover is how entities like governments diffuse narratives online in order to counter the propaganda of terrorist organizations and monitor or suppress messages that breed extremism.[37]

The Terrorists' YouTube Effect

The dangers of the YouTube effect are something to behold. The **YouTube Effect** is an overarching concept that describes how social networking sites like YouTube, Facebook, and Telegram—to name a few—have tactical advantages that television or radio do not have. As such, one of the most valuable tools of social media is that they constitute a platform to any individual trying to shape public opinion—which is why it is called "the YouTube Effect."[38] The expansion of the internet and online media channels like YouTube has greatly improved social influence exerted through traditional frameworks, where fewer people and entities can generate content for consumers, thereby emboldening any user to use these online media channels to share content.[39] Although terrorists tend to entrust their media personnel with propaganda production, even the killers and foot soldiers themselves can and do post gruesome content—e.g., beheading videos or any feat from "the battlefield"—for the world to see.[40] Readily available internet-based devices facilitate their propaganda creation and the organization of their campaigns to recruit as many would-be fighters as possible.[41]

Enter the **Islamic State of Iraq and Syria**, or **ISIS**, a global jihadist network that rose to infamy in 2014 when it launched a campaign solely focused on publicizing barbarous executions (e.g., beheadings, burning prisoners alive, etc.). These rituals of capital punishment were diffused online, along with their propagandistic messages that turned up on the screen of their videos.[42] The YouTube Effect enabled ISIS to co-opt mass-sharing sites to magnify their international reach.[43] To this point, by the summer of 2021, YouTube had over two billion users.[44] In their examination of YouTube videos, Huberman, Romero, and Wu (2009)[45] noticed a highly positive dependence on attention, as determined by the percentage of downloads. On the other hand, insufficient attention led to a decrease in both YouTube viewings and the number of videos watched (in addition to a subsequent reduction in productivity). The YouTube Effect is most valuable when videos are brilliantly advertised because they raise the level of attention.[46]

The role of Telegram in ISIS's public communication campaigns is also worth mentioning. **Telegram** is a free cross-platform that has rapid messaging applications so necessary for secure communications. Bloom, Tiflati, and Horgan (2019)[47] argued that Telegram is gradually—but only partially—replacing the terrorist group's activities on social media like Twitter because the latter can easily remove ISIS-linked accounts. After analyzing 16 Telegram chatrooms, the three scholars deduced that ISIS's campaigners were vigorously sharing propaganda (e.g., through links, online bulletin boards, and memes) and exchanging information with one another and new members. Some chatrooms had more than 300 members.

Strategies for Pushing Back

In recent years, antiterrorist communication campaigns have looked for both former terrorists and survivors of terrorism as they have more direct experience and can empower these campaigns by pushing back terrorist ideologies and preventing the recruitment of at-risk people—youths in particular. This process can be facilitated by using the online space to connect, exchange, and diffuse counterradical content and deter all types of violent extremism (e.g., whether from the far right or the far left). The online space can harness key lessons, experiences, and networks of participants who had first-hand encounters with extremism. Thanks to websites like Facebook and Twitter, participants can stay in contact, share ideas, cooperate, identify additional partners, and convey their messages to wider audiences.[48] Typically, antiterrorist communication campaigners can follow 10 key strategies described in similar ways throughout this book. As such, they can:

1. Conduct an in-depth analysis on target audience needs and behaviors in order to fully utilize the potential of social media advertising applications and, in so doing, escalate the impact of a campaign.[49]

2. Pilot-test a multitude of topics and communication styles with similar target audiences—as a form of A/B testing or **split-run testing**. This type of testing is a short and simple way of conducting a controlled experiment. The goal is to figure out what seems to work and, then, match the findings to the campaign.[50]

3. Focus specifically on at-risk audiences. Antiterrorist communication campaigns that seek to influence groups of actual or would-be terrorists are effective when the degree of support is high or such assistance is crucial to perpetrators of extreme violence. However, such initiatives should also target at-risk individuals through mentorship programs and vocational training—i.e., this should be done, to the extent possible, in main locations.[51]

4. Begin by allocating small amounts of funding in order to increment the reach and scope of antiterrorist communication campaigns. For example, it is not unusual for a Facebook-based campaign to use $3,000 to $4,000 to achieve a reach of more than half a million individual users.[52]

5. Understand the power of online advertising. Although complimentary methods for maximize the impact of campaigns are available, campaigners can also rely on paid advertising on social networking sites to reach their audience.[53]

6. Train members of staff and volunteers to become apt at applying social media and online marketing tools. Make sure that social media and marketing analytics be correctly applied and superintended during the campaign.[54]

7. Bolster counternarrative campaigns with user engagement tactics. This usually necessitates labor-intensive pursuits, like engaging in face-to-face with audience members.[55]

8. Resort to alternative media conduits in geographic areas where online access is restricted.[56]

9. Blend web-based campaigns with traditional ones (like events).[57]

10. Assess the overall campaign and share the assessment results with both campaigners and managers of online platforms that target at-risk audiences. Campaigners need to be fully aware of what went well and what did not.[58] As discussed in Step 10 of Chapter 2, to make progress in a communication campaign, it is imperative to measure the effects of that campaign (e.g., through analytics and metrics) to confirm whether it was successful.

Case Study 1:   Exit USA

Exit USA is a campaign launched by a Chicago-based nonprofit organization, Life After Hate, which is established to deter people from joining White supremacist movements and promote defection by offering a "way out." **Life After Hate** is an "exit program" organization that supports former White supremacists and far-right terrorists through disengagement and reintegration programs.[59] The organization also promotes loving oneself and accepting the Other, regardless of race, beliefs, and sexual orientation.[60] Life After Hate strategists perform outreach work to assist those who want to renounce membership of such extremist groups. It is important to note that Life After Hate was awarded a $400,000 grant from the Department of Homeland Security under their Countering Violent Extremism (CVE) program. However, the grant was allocated to another party in 2017. For unknown reasons, Life After Hate was excluded from the list.[61] Immediately after the grant was rescinded, donators gave over $500,000 to sustain the organization's activities. According to the Life After Hate website, since the deadly "Unite the Right" rally in Charlottesville, Virginia, in 2017, more than 150 individuals have contacted to the organization for help and support.[62]

Exit USA offers one-on-one assistance like therapy, career counseling, and social support to both men and women aspiring to abandon White supremacism and far-right extremism. In turn, participants in the program are asked to become formal or informal consultants for law enforcement agencies (e.g., by giving advice on right-wing recruitment strategies) and run seminars in schools around the United States. An important approach is their public communication campaign to help former extremists be rehabilitated in society. The staff of Exit USA themselves are former White supremacists and far-right extremists. Thanks to their unique experiences and journeys in and out of those dangerous movements, they are the best equipped to offer guidance to those who want to follow the same path or find enlightenment.[63]

During the course of the campaign, four videos have already been produced on the YouTube channel Exit USA. They were designed to "discredit far-right extremist groups," "sow the seeds of doubt" in "far-right extremist individuals, and promote their exit program." The four videos are titled *No Judgment Just Help*, *There Is Life after Hate*, *Oak Creek*, and *The Formers*.[64] These videos were shared on YouTube and, subsequently, other social media sites to engage with at-risk individuals in a thoughtful and positive fashion. For example, video administrators frequently interacted with users and responded to the comments and messages on both their videos and social media accounts.[65] This is the advantage of the aforementioned YouTube effect and, in this case, the campaign barely costs anything.

In a study conducted by Schmitt, Rieger, Rutkowski, and Ernst (2018),[66] results indicated that all four Exit USA videos were part of 25 video communities that comprised a wide variety of subjects. In addition to a significant amount of entertaining videos dealing with issues like lifestyles, celebrities, music, and movies, other videos dealt with political information and expressions of political views (without extremist information). Furthermore, results revealed that about 4.6% of the videos in those communities were directly tackling extremist propaganda. The remaining communities consisted primarily of entertaining videos, discussing subjects like animals and educational opportunities. The researchers located only four other communities addressing extremist content, including videos that challenged conspiracy theories and hate speech.

Case Study 2:   Exit Norway

Having no relation to Exit USA, **Exit Norway** is a campaign established in 1997 by two researchers at the Norwegian Police Academy College, including Dr. Tore Bjørgo, a professor of Police Science there. The campaign disseminates peer-to-peer messages and provides assistance to people linked to White supremacism and far-right extremism. Exit Norway also examines the fundamental rules of attraction to such movements and applies the results to help those people "exit."[67] The campaign purports to have three primary objectives:

> To establish local networks to support the parents of children embedded in racist or violent groups; to enable young people to disengage from these groups; and to develop and disseminate methodological knowledge to professionals working with youths associated with violent groups.[68]

To achieve these goals, Exit Norway runs its campaign at both the societal and individual levels.[69] The target audience is typically at-risk or radicalized youths who can be identified through proactive outreach measures.[70] As is the case for Exit USA, the campaign staff and volunteers also include "formers" (previous members of such violent organizations) who function as role models for youths. Since the mission is to get people to exit these organizations, campaign planners deem it important to be practical in their approach, for example by having the formers describe their own experiences to motive youths to get out.[71] Carried out by local agencies—like municipal agencies and other[72]—the campaign uses videos and flyers to inform their target audience about the consequences that they would face in the event of an arrest and trial for enacting risky behavior.[73] Exit Norway also demonstrates that the inclusion of change agents like parental network groups can be highly efficient in countering extremism because it improves information sharing among affected families.[74] The campaign promoters constantly bring up past research that indicates that members of extremist groups do not necessarily come from similar backgrounds or do not even have extreme attitudes before joining. Nor are they automatically attracted to these groups for ideological motives. This is why Exit Norway takes a deep look at the social conditions of youth extremism. This can facilitate disengagement from extremist groups.[75]

Although it started out as a small private agency, Exit Norway soon realized that the idea of facilitating such disengagement through the methods described earlier would become mainstream. Today, Norwegian law enforcement, the Security Service, and municipal social workers are applying Exit Norway's approach.[76] Its campaign has been considered "generally successful" and has percolated to other European countries.[77] The techniques developed by Bjørgo and his colleague are even used around the world.[78] A former neo-Nazi from Sweden, Kent Lindahl, has applied Bjørgo's idea. Lindahl sought to offer similar assistance to Swedish youths who aspired to leave the far right, but needed psychosocial reinforcement to do so. Unlike the counterradicalization campaigns developed in Saudi Arabia and Singapore (described later), this "exit" approach centers more on changing people's actions than their beliefs. This is founded on the premise that violence is the root cause, not belief systems.[79]

Case Study 3:   Building Community Resilience

The fight against terrorist ideologies requires the collaboration of federal and local governments with society in a growingly populated democracy. In the case of jihadists, they view their host society as a foe to exterminate. The supreme mission is to confront this antagonistic dogma by ensuring that it does not penetrate the minds of youths. This can be achieved through a social transaction process.[80] As such, during the second Obama administration, this approach to countering violent extremism (CVE) through a social transaction process was undertaken with public communication campaigns conducted with community partners. The overarching project was called "community resilience," which tackled CVE issues at multiple levels, in a sociocultural context, and with assistance from the community.[81]

Community Resilience

Community resilience is the potential of a community to employ resources at hand—mutual assistance, education, communication, transportation, etc.—to properly react to, endure, and recover from adverse circumstances.[82] Explained differently, communities are able to adapt and grow after being struck by a tragedy.[83] Community resilience can minimize the impact of any tragedy, attempting to make the return to normalcy as painless as possible. As one would expect from a public will campaign, by putting a community resilience plan into practice, a community can rise together and triumph over any catastrophe, while regaining physical, psychosocial, and economic strength.[84] Communities have long been used as critical means against a range of violence types.[85] **Resilience** is defined as "the process of, capacity for, or outcome of successful adaptation despite challenging or threatening circumstances."[86]

With respect to CVE, one daunting task is having to deal with the terrorists' obsession with killing innocent people. Not only can they recruit people who, in turn, engage in violence themselves but, also, these terrorists are often unstoppable in their ideologies. Hence, a successful campaign is one centered on the community, where people come together in such a manner that its members teach vulnerable youth to no longer pose a threat to society. In brief, one mechanism for becoming a resilient community hinges on decreasing possible vulnerabilities or risk factors and establishing protective measures. Social relations within and between communities will further alleviate risk factors related to violent extremism. "Within communities" refers to people who have similar social identities (called **social bonding**), and "between communities" refers to groups made up of people with different social identities, but who have a commonsense of community in other respects (called **social bridging**). By extension, the role of social relations between communities and governing agencies (called **social linking**) offers opportunities for tackling problems of social injustice and for constructing mechanisms for intervention with youths who are walking down the wrong path.[87]

Community resilience cannot support itself without community competence. **Community competence** is a phenomenon whereby resilient communities show their capability of working together effectively in order to identify and accomplish goals.

Community competence can encompass both **collective efficacy** (i.e., joining forces to accomplish a goal) and **empowerment**—the process of cutting through power differentials in order to lend a higher voice and agency to people generally in positions of lower power. Therefore, community competence bears some resemblance to the concepts of social linking, trust, and relationships between governing agencies and community members.[88]

Building Community Resilience

In 2014–5, the US Department of Justice launched the $1 million Building Community Resilience campaign to fight back against recruitment of Somali Muslims in the Twin Cities (i.e., Minneapolis–Saint Paul). Initially, US President Obama's plan was to select several key American cities to bring together community officials, public safety experts, and faith leaders to grapple with radicalization to violence.[89] The Twin Cities were eventually selected for this campaign because of the historic and solid relationships between the Somali Minnesotan community and local police forces. Since Al-Shabaab started recruiting Minnesota's boys and girls in 2006, the Twin Cities have remained a hotbed of terror recruiting by international terrorist organizations like ISIS. This is particularly true for Minnesota's Somali community, which led to convince Somali community leaders to collaborate closely with police forces and community change agents to apply the Building Community Resilience project locally.[90] The campaign included a program for assisting youths, mentoring sessions, higher education scholarships, new employment opportunities and training, and more collaboration between religious leaders and Somali youths. This large-scale initiative also brought together community-based groups and local affiliates (e.g., interfaith and nongovernmental organizations), and state, regional, and local governments. On top of government sources of funding, many Twin Cities corporations and foundations pledged to finance the Building Community Resilience campaign.[91]

It is important to observe that measures were taken to ensure that no Somali or Muslim communities were turned into "suspect communities." The reason is that campaigns that create "suspect communities" may weaken the pathway towards community resilience. In a study evaluating programs designed to reduce violent extremism in three European cities, Vermeulen (2014)[92] found that, when targeting entire communities, unanticipated consequences of heightened stigma and discrimination occur and pave the way for even higher risk of violent extremism. As the scholar noted, "viewing a whole group as inherently suspicious proved conducive to the severe stigmatization of an entire community."[93] "Suspect communities" lead to stigmatization, social rejection, and long-term marginalization, which not only has negative corollaries for the target group(s), but may also create breeding factories of future terrorists.[94]

On the other hand, empowering social identities within the ethnic or religious in-group represents a vital method for developing community resilience to violent extremism. In their study investigating attributes of Muslim–American communities that obviate radicalization to violence, Schanzer, Kurzman, and Moosa (2010)[95] recognized that the strengthening of Muslim–American identity is the best protective factor, particularly when harmonious with other identities (including American). They also found that "the creation of robust Muslim American communities may serve as a preventative measure against radicalization by reducing social isolation of individuals who may be at risk of becoming radicalized."[96]

Case Study 4:   Average Mohamed

The **Average Mohamed** campaign has diffused multiple animated videos and posted tweets that borrowed Muslim principles on peace to "counter the ideology of Islamist extremist groups."[97] The cartoons, which Ahmed publishes on his averagemohamed. com website and YouTube, feature a character named Average Mohamed, an outspoken Muslim believer who denounces the misinterpretations of his religion by terrorists. The unshaven and gap-toothed Mohamed says that ISIS is "about genocide" and cites Quranic verses to support the case that Muslims who witness dubious activities should inform authorities. The target audience are children ages 8 to 16. Mohamed Ahmed, a gas station overseer in Minnesota, created the Average Mohamed campaign. He wants Muslim Americans to have more trust in the US government to handle the radicalization problem.[98]

Targeting Muslim Youths

Average Mohamed appears to direct his message to youths all over the world by presenting an alternative identity of Muslims that he thinks has been tainted by both jihadists and the mainstream media. He seeks to construct a perception of what it means to be an Islamic devotee by offering a peaceful and democratic version of average Muslims. In terms of technicality, the Average Mohamed campaign is split into very brief animated cartoons—each video lasts for a few minutes, with simple, colorful animated graphics—that diffuse democratic messages on identity, freedom of speech, and the respect of women in Islamic culture.[99] In fact, viewers know when the issues of democracy and freedom in Islam are about to be brought up in the cartoons because images begin to change in texture—i.e., the images get stronger (more vivid and lively) and are lightened by the graphic style. At the end of each video, Average Mohamed and his friends repeat the same democratic values.[100] We can also observe that the campaign calls terrorists' arguments and propaganda about Islam into question and advance that they are, in no way, representative of Islam. Let us look at the excerpt:

> Average Mohamed asks: What do you think your job description is when you join Islamic State? Your job description is to commit genocide against Muslims, Christians, Yazidi, and Jews; terrorize innocent women, men, and children like your family into blind obedience; behead unarmed, innocent people you round up; destroy world heritage sites, mosques, tombs, and shrines; empower unelected, self-nominated, murderous, blood-thirsty, individuals as leaders. Not exactly Disney World, or action-film like the propaganda says it is, is it? Remember: peace up, and extremist thinking, especially Islamic State, out. This message is brought to you by averagemohamed.com.[101]

Of all the Americans who joined or attempted to join ISIS, the majority came from Minnesota. Getting advice from Minneapolis **imams** (i.e., worship leaders in mosques), Ahmed inserts religious messages in his cartoons to illustrate why ISIS's message is flawed. Because the short videos feature a protagonist whose name is arguably the most common name in the world today, Average Mohamed was designed to represent all nonviolent Muslims. This includes any Muslim man or woman—e.g., gas station operators, physicians, agricultors, and professors—who unequivocally condemns ISIS's dangerous interpretations of Islam.[102] To this day, no formal assessment or research has been done to determine whether the Average Mohamed campaign has managed to discourage youths from becoming jihadists. Nevertheless, the campaign is still running and continues to debunk fanatical interpretations of the Qur'an, as shown in the next excerpt:

> What does the Quran have to say about suicide bombing?—English," the eponymous narrator notes, "the Prophet Muhammad, peace be upon him, says: 'He who commits suicide by throttling himself will keep on throttling himself in the hellfire. And he who commits suicide by stabbing himself shall keep on stabbing himself in the hellfire" (Sahih al-Bukhari, Hadith, number 1365). What do you think happens to suicide bombers? You'll be made again, blown up again, be made whole again, blown up again, be made whole again, blown up again, eternally in the hellfire!' Average Mohamed often contrasts the horrific crimes committed by ISIS and other terrorists (rendered in cartoon explosions and vehicular homicides) with passages drawn from the Qur'an and Hadith. His content also draws extensive links between authentic Islam and Western citizenship in 'Family video', 'Identity in Islam' and 'A Muslim in the West', 'Be Like Aisha', and 'The Bullet or the Ballot' are examples of aspirational calls to action for Muslims.[103]

In spite of the lack of formal assessment or research, Average Mohamed has been hailed internationally as an ideal counternarrative campaign because it stands out as a well-developed production for child audiences. Into the bargain, these animated cartoons have been the inspiration for meetings with the US Department of State and a presentation at a counterextremism convention in London.[104]

Emphasizing the Self, Not the Other

It is remarkable that Mohamed does not devote a great deal of time and energy to attacking the terrorists themselves. Rather than emphasizing the Other, he focuses on the Self in order to curtail the power of the Other. In other terms, the protagonist reinforces and aggrandizes the Self into a better, value-laden identity. An "extreme and radical Other" in contrast to the "normal Self" emerges within a digital performative securitization. Average Mohamed stresses the importance of "we" by conjuring up shared values. He actually does not describe the Self *per se*. By making it open to interpretation, viewers can still absorb Mohamed's value-laden identity and find his core message relatable and applicable in real life. Such an approach can also elicit many of the same attributes of religious markers as deep common values.[105]

Sheikh (2012)[106] contends that "doctrines of secularism or freedom, as they are often represented in a Western context, draw on strong myths." Myths can be more easily accepted by the audience because they arouse a sense of identity and "who we are."[107] Considering the relational and relative aspect of identities, the Average Mohamed frame does exactly what a counterradicalization campaign wants to achieve: to open doors for negotiation on identity.[108] Aside from the cartoon videos, on Twitter Average Mohamed attempts to remove

488 Chapter 16   Antiterrorist Public Communication Campaigns

the monolithic nature of the typical Muslim identity (as has been portrayed in this era of social media).[109] He does so by eliminating the negative attributes of identity ascribed to Muslim men and women. Instead, he wants to construct a broader Self based on positive democratic markers like freedom and respect. Ultimately, Average Mohamed is a mixture of Western and Islamic selves that become one identity, one that is the total opposite of violent and extremist identities in his religion.[110]

Case Study 5:   Saudi Arabia's Prevention Campaigns

With a population of over 35 million people, the Kingdom of Saudi Arabia (KSA), the birthplace of Islam, is distinct in designating itself as an Islamic state established on a conservative and puritan interpretation of the Qur'an and **sunnah** (the traditions and practices of the Prophet Muhammad). The House of Saud, in a close relationship with the KSA's ultraconservative religious institutions, has ruled the Kingdom for over three hundred years and governs by **sharia** (a body of Islamic laws derived from Allah).[111] Though less obvious than in its neighboring countries, sectarian tensions still persist in the Saudi Arabian society, a problem which is becoming more manifest with the rise of Sunni radicalism and the tendency for religion to regulate social relations.[112] From 1995 to 2003, the KSA became beleaguered by a radical Islamist insurgency. Saudi armed forces successfully vanquished the radical Islamists with a fierce "hard power" campaign. At the same time, the Kingdom was not fully aware that they could not tackle violent Islamism exclusively with hard power,[113] even though Al-Qaeda in the Arabian Peninsula (AQAP) did not hesitate to use its hardest power, during its 2003–6 terrorist crusade in the KSA, to target foreigners, especially Americans.[114]

By and large, jihadists are not **mullahs**—Muslims who are well-versed in Islamic theology and sacred law.[115] Rather, they tend to be young products of contemporary educational institutions. Those with a college degree are usually more scientific than literary; they were raised in urbanized families or from the lower-middle classes. Islamist militants look at Islam as both a religion and a political doctrine. It is an ideology on which they capitalize and which remains antithetical to what the **ulamas** (Muslim clerical scholars) profess. Jihadists learn their political knowledge not in religious establishments but on college and university campuses, where they consort with militant Communists. The accent is placed on Islam as a religious structure or an organization, a framework evocative of Marxist–Leninist parties and extremist brotherhoods. For them, seizing control of a state like the KSA (among others) will facilitate the expansion of Islam in a Muslim society warped by Western modernity and principles and will facilitate the misappropriation of science and technology (e.g., to develop even more dangerous weapons). Not only do they advocate a return to the Golden Age of Islam, but they also want to reappropriate society and new technologies based on political violence.[116] Two counterradicalization campaigns have attempted to influence the hearts and minds of such (would-be) jihadists: (1) Prevention, Rehabilitation, and After Care (PRAC) and (2) the Sakinah Campaign.

Prevention, Rehabilitation, and After Care (PRAC)

Prevention, Rehabilitation, and After Care (PRAC) was a wide-ranging and well-funded campaign launched in 2004. It revolved around counterradicalization, rehabilitation, and disengagement programs. A centerpiece of the campaign is that incarcerated suspects should be treated as people who have had the misfortune of being misled by Marxist–Leninist demagogues who want to promote jihadism. These suspects, the campaign continued, were in serious need of advice, rather than condemnation or social disgrace for criminality.[117] Participants in PRAC included detainees who had traveled for holy war in Afghanistan, Iraq, Somalia, and Chechnya, as well as returnees from Guantánamo Bay.[118] Later, other rehabilitation centers were opened to rewire the minds of returnees from the Syrian conflict.[119]

The PRAC campaign was created after a long series of terrorist attacks in the KSA between the mid-1990s and early 2000s. As a result, Saudi Arabia's Ministry of the Interior (MOI) designed a counterradicalization campaign to supplement the Kingdom's "hard power" operations. The MOI designed this campaign to "combat the intellectual and ideological justifications of violent extremism by engaging an ideology that the Saudi Government asserts is based on corrupted and deviant interpretations of Wahhabi Islam."[120] PRAC employed an ideology-based strategy to counterterrorism inspired by a mix of Muslim theology and authority. The campaign assumed that it could challenge Islamist radicalism by defusing it and proving to them that their interpretations have warped true Islam. The ideological part of the campaign centered on key concepts of Islamic authority and the religious doctrine to discredit the theological foundations of Islamist radicalism. Through seminars, PRAC tried to improve the participants' understanding of Islamic theology, particularly as envisioned by the Saudis.[121]

The results of the campaign were mixed, though representing an improvement over the previous conditions of some of the incarcerated militants. PRAC itself reported a moderate success.[122] As part of the public campaign, Saudi newspapers devoted special pages, weekly, to confront the problems of extremism. Of equal relevance are the Saudi efforts (against terrorism) described both through traditional media and social media in the KSA. This large-scale campaign was meant to improve the lives of all citizens there.

The Sakinah Campaign

Translated from Arabic as "religiously-inspired tranquility," the **Sakinah Campaign** still operates today as an independent initiative financed by the Ministry of Islamic Affairs. Comparable to other counterradicalization and demobilization programs in the KSA, the Sakinah Campaign employs mullahs and professors to develop online interactions with people searching for religious knowledge. The objective is to lead them away from extremist sources.[123] More precisely, the campaign aids internet users who have visited radical ideological sites in communicating with legitimate mullahs and professors online, with a view to abandoning radicalism altogether.[124] Online users who are deemed potential targets of extremist indoctrination are paired with a counselor who can give them answers about Islam and discuss the true nature of jihadist organizations like ISIS.[125] Today, with a team of about 40 people from diverse religious, psychological, and social backgrounds, the Sakinah Campaign continues to use social media and internet chatrooms to (1) challenge extremists who spread deviant thoughts and ideas, (2) diffuse accurate and moderate religious precepts and interpretations about both old and new events, and (3) identify and engage with would-be radicals.[126]

According to a Sakinah self-evaluation, the campaign has managed to mitigate dangerous opinions and rectify the views of 1,500 of the total 3,250 radicals with whom mullahs and professors interacted either privately or publicly. Among those 1,500, 40% have abandoned all or virtually all of the radical thoughts that they used to embrace, while the remaining 60% have steered away from only the most dangerous ideas and thoughts. The participants of the Sakinah Campaign did not come from one country or region alone. About 50% came from the Gulf Cooperation Council (GCC) region, 30% from other neighboring Arab nations, and the remaining 20% from Europe and the United States. All of the interactions with mullahs and professors have been documented and archived by the campaign, which will be included in a film production called the "Sakinah Documentary," a mother lode for experts and researchers upon request.[127]

Case Study 6:   Antiterrorism through Entertainment–Education (EE) in the Middle East

Radicalization among youths is a difficult issue facing the Middle East. Reports in the late 2010s show that more than 20,000 Arab youths migrated to Iraq and Syria to join ISIS and another 5–15% of Millennials in seven Arab nations consider certain jihadist organizations to be on the right path. In response, Arab countries have included principles of entertainment–education (EE) in their antiterrorist communication campaigns. More specifically, they have used aspects of pop culture to tackle radicalization at the societal level.[128] EE is a valuable tool to reach large segments of the Arab population. Arab TV stations have broadcast antiterror videos, satirical productions, songs, movies, and drama series.[129]

For example, in Bahrain, the government is trying to quench a Shia revolt inspired by the events of the Arab Spring in 2011, but a possible reason for the insurgency is the preparation for terrorism. A public service announcement (PSA) that was diffused on the official Bahraini TV channel explains the negative consequences of the actions of young men resorting to violence and chaos. At the end of the PSA, a statement turns up on the screen, stating, "Together to extinguish the fire of terrorism."[130] Such content is meant to propagate prosocial narratives and educate the audience about the consequences of extremism in entertaining ways, a central component of EE programming.[131]

Another example is *al-Siham al-Marika*. Also an anti-extremism EE project, the *al-Siham al-Marika* (i.e., "The Piercing Arrows") is a television drama series that depicts life under ISIS's control. Thirty episodes were aired on YouTube in 2018–9. The focus of this series is the revelation of ISIS as a distinct threat to the Arab world, in comparison with previous jihadist threats that were of lower magnitude. The concept of *al-Siham al-Marika* came from coproducer Moez Masoud, a young, famous Muslim televangelist who has produced several TV series about Islam since the early 2010s. He contributes a degree of religiosity and education to anti-ISIS narrative campaigns. His television drama has not been sponsored by any government and is independent of any foreign production, which moderates the public's suspicions about the program's intent. The production crew for *al-Siham al-Marika* comes from all over the Arab world. They are Egyptian, Iraqi, Lebanese, Syrian, and Tunisian professionals, a collaboration that has boosted the show's appeal in the pan-Arab region. Lastly, the accessibility of all episodes on YouTube after being broadcast on Emirati and Egyptian TV stations in 2018–9 has also increased the audience size for the TV drama—i.e., 11.5+ million views on YouTube by May 2020—and, most importantly, allows campaign evaluators to better analyze audience reactions (e.g., in the comments section).[132]

In regards to the content, *al-Siham al-Marika* showcases positive role models (and transitional characters) in the script to communicate an anti-extremist and educational message. The story takes place in an undisclosed town in Syria that was previously controlled by ISIS. The positive role models are people who, despite living in the organization's territory, make a sharp distinction between ISIS and Islam. They denounce extremist ideologies and maintain their Muslim identity. The main protagonists either keep their beliefs to themselves (until they are able to leave) or join resistance units to combat ISIS and, in most cases, die as heroes. The negative role models are ISIS foot soldiers and leaders who are seemingly observant of the religion but, in reality, manipulate the sacred scriptures to rationalize their horrid crimes: rape, the abduction of women, theft, torture, and the killing of civilians. In some cases, the punishments for not following ISIS's version of Islam are graphic, such as civilians suffering grave injuries or committing suicide as a sign of desperation. In other cases, however, there is a silver lining: the storyline makes it explicit that an impending bad finale lies in wait for ISIS leaders because, for example, an increasing number of civilians and ISIS soldiers themselves are turning against them.[133]

Case Study 7:   Say No to Terror

Say No to Terror is a comprehensive communication campaign composed of a website, traditional media channels, and an online social media presence. The campaign uses a range of tools like short videos and posters to convey a counternarrative to certain aspects of the terrorist narrative.[134] Previous large-scale antiterrorist public communication campaigns were introduced in Iraq in 2004, with the first one being called "Terror Has No Religion." The purpose was to confront the threats of sectarianism and Al-Qaeda. After the disengagement of many US troops and coalition forces from the country in late 2010, the campaign was no longer in use. Later, Say No to Terror emerged as a new and fresh one—one whose advertisements mostly targeted the Arab Muslim public at large.[135]

The website, for instance, is written entirely in Arabic. It contains general information (Mission Statement and About Us), videos, chatrooms, posters, and links to social networking sites (Facebook and Twitter). New users who create an account can post comments about the videos and attach other materials. Say No to Terror is specifically aimed at an Arab Muslim audience because the campaign's slogan is "Terrorism. I am Muslim: I am against it" and its language is exclusively Arabic. According to the website, "Terrorism is a criminal act targeting innocent people, and it deserves to be fought by all means and to have its claims and its devastating effects on our society disclosed."[136] The "About Us" section on the main page designates the website creators as firm believers in true Islam and guardians of its greatness. Their mission is to "expose the claims of terrorist agitators and unveil their crimes, to encourage all those who have a conscience to reject their criminal acts and destructive ideas." As the mission statement continues, it is important "to fight them in order to protect our society from their wrongs and their destructive impact on all levels."[137]

Rejecting Violence

In contrast to Al-Qaeda's narrative that imposes a religiously and morally empowered obligation to wage a violent holy war, the Say No to Terror campaign borrows elements from Islamic cultural history to impose a religiously and morally empowered obligation to reject violence.[138] Its videos include Quranic passages and popular **hadiths** (records of the deeds or sayings of the Prophet Muhammad) and evoke Muslim traditions that prioritize family and collectivist values over individualism. The campaign wants to draw public attention to the fact that terrorists gather money through fundraising. This is why it calls on the audience to act responsibly by ensuring that charitable donations and zakat (almsgiving) do not indirectly fund terrorism. In many posts, Islamist radicals are unambiguously described as the real foes of Islam who invite even more Islamophobia.[139]

The Say No to Terror website is hosted in Montenegro in what could be a way to dodge attitudes of suspicion of American-sponsored communication in the Arab world. However, upon closer examination, we can see that the website content points to affiliations with or sympathies to Saudi Arabia. The campaign's videos posted on YouTube are frequently transmitted as PSAs on the Pan-Arab Middle East Broadcasting Center (MBC) and Al-Arabiya channels, both owned by the KSA. Posts that allude to particular religious principles or situations (e.g., the Syrian conflict) correspond to the KSA's stance on such matters. These posts express reverence to the Kingdom, "The Custodian of the Two Holy Mosques," and view them as the legitimate authority in Islam.[140]

Exposing Jihadism through Videos

A recurring theme in the website videos centers on the duty to unmask the agenda and manipulative strategies of jihadist organizations. Several videos portray them as criminal and warn the public against being swayed by the terrorist narrative, while others include the testimonies of terrorists-turned-activists to expose "the enemies of Islam." For example, "The Misguided Terrorist" video tells the story of a real person who perpetrated real atrocities. A young man relates an account of his arrest for participation in terrorism. "The Enemy Within" has similar themes denouncing jihadists for slaying innocent Muslims, while the "I am Innocent of Your Crimes," "The Scream," and "No Life Flourishes where there is Terrorism" videos include symbols of innocence juxtaposed against symbols of terrorism. These three videos include pictures of children and symbols of childhood to expose the deleterious effects of terrorism. "The Road of no Return" is more devoted to the dangers of sectarian violence, indicating that the video is directed at an Iraqi audience.[141] The video frames sectarianism as a weakening situation that terrorists exploit. As Aly, Weimann-Saks, and Weimann (2014)[142] explain,

> Sectarianism makes you enter the prison of extremism, and so you become a prey for agitators seeking to achieve their political goals. It is not through sectarian extremism that you defend your religion, but you defend your religion through protecting it from sectarian extremism.

Terrorists are framed—visually, rhetorically, and symbolically—as ominous characters who kill unarmed civilians, abduct them, and lead the ummah's youths to perdition. Aside from videos, a poster titled *Youth in the Hands of Preachers of Extremism* is accompanied by the text:

Who are these people who are misleading youth? They are a category of people who mix, in their methods and rhetoric, between old means of agitation and new ones. Sometimes they try to hide behind religious or ideological slogans and sometimes behind popular claims or appeals or slogans, in order to justify terrorism and call for more of it and incite young people to practice it. It has become clear that the misleading discourse of incitement uses a set of means and mechanisms.[143]

Case Study 8:   Reparation Campaigns in Australia

The author would like to end this book by describing a few reparation campaigns that have proved to be effective: ones that acknowledge the violence committed against Aboriginal Australians and that serve to protect their dignity. Also called **First Peoples**, **Aboriginal Australians** are made up of many different peoples who have moved across Australia for over 50,000 years. These peoples have a common, though complex, ancestry. It is only in the last few centuries that they have been labeled "Aboriginal Australians" and started to self-identify as such. In 1788, White settlers began to supplant or uproot them, from coast to desert, through strength in numbers, propagation of diseases, technology, and extreme violence.[151] The present-day population in Australia is over 25 million.

Aboriginal Australians Today

In the 2016 Australian Census, Indigenous Australians comprised 3.3% of the country's population, with about 90% of these identifying as Aboriginal only.[152] The same census records a high percentage of interethnic marriage. In fact, most Indigenous Australians have entered into official relationships with non-Indigenous Australians. Yet, anti-Aborigenism is still prevalent and has caused a myriad of health-related problems among Indigenous Australians. Studies report connections between racial discrimination, depression, and anxiety—in addition to smoking, drug use, and lower self-evaluated health status.[153]

The Aboriginal people of Australia should not be regarded as "simple hunter-gatherers" wandering the country in search of food and water. They constitute a people with an advanced "non-material" culture that combines individual and collective subjectivity into their milieu and environment. They should not be equated with individuals who are part of nature, but as intelligent beings who play a major contribution to the self-government of the exchanges between species and milieu. When an unwarranted separation is made between the Australian people and the Australian nation, both experience trauma and subsequent demise. The land would greatly benefit from the Aboriginal people if Anglo-Australians gave them more opportunities to develop it. Few government solutions and no "whitefella" (Anglo-Australian) scheme has proven to be highly effective.[154]

Racist Violence and Indirect Terrorism

Mellor's (2003) study points to the fact that, in the early 2000s, Aboriginal Australians experienced racist violence on a regular basis and that much of it was explicit or old-fashioned (e.g., racial slurs, mass beatings, etc.). Indigenous Australians are still disproportionately suffering from crime (i.e., in particular, assault). The aforementioned Australian Bureau of Statistics (2016)[155] report revealed that they experience assault 2.6 times as much as their non-Indigenous counterparts (in New South Wales), 6 times as much (in South Australia), and 5.9 as much (in Northern Territory). Indigenous women are even more represented in these statistics. Extreme violence is a social problem with long-term negative consequences. Former Australian Prime Minister Kevin Rudd (2016)[156] expressed his concerns about this undercurrent of racism. "It's like a cancer that eats away at the fabric of our society."

More importantly, state terrorism against Aboriginal Australians has also occurred. Involuntary sterilization of Aboriginal women and girls was and is still common in Australia. Already in the eighteenth century, Aboriginal women were seen as impure by British colonizers. This theory laid the groundwork for a vast sterilization crusade against Aboriginal women in the country. Even today, sterilizing them is a grave concern for international organizations, such as the United Nations, which declared in November 2015 that this practice in Australia is a total violation of Human Rights.[157] Numerous scholars[158] consider involuntary sterilization and racism as indirect terrorism. **Indirect terrorism** is organized and structural violence aimed at a specific group; it is inconspicuous, quasi-invisible, government-backed terrorism.[159]

Reparation Campaigns

A **reparation campaign** is a campaign that seeks to create awareness of past injustices committed against particular groups of people—such as African Americans and Native Americans in the United States, Africans in the Belgian Congo, and Jews during the Holocaust. Profound past injustices can rise to the level of genocide or crimes against humanity. Reparation campaigns communicate the importance of acknowledging historical offenses in order to make amends with those groups—and with oneself—and foster a general sense of moral and political obligation within contemporary audiences. Typically, they also seek to provide persecuted groups with financial compensations.[160]

In Australia, the **Sea of Hands** campaign symbolizes endorsement of land rights, justice, and reconciliation for Aboriginal Australians and Torres Strait Islanders. Each plastic or paper-made hand is planted in the ground to express solidarity with them. The desired outcome is a genuine representation of a united people, without any reservations. Since October 1997, the Sea of Hands campaign has successfully inculcated the idea of solidarity within Australian youths in particular. Today, about 400,000 Australians have put their signatures on a hand and installed countless of them across the nation.[161]

Another example is **National Reconciliation Week**. It was developed by Reconciliation Australia, an independent nongovernmental organization with the mission of fostering relationships, respect, and trust within the nation at large. National Reconciliation Week, too, promotes respectful relationships with Aboriginal Australians and Torres Strait Islanders. The week runs between May 27 and June 3 annually, and events are organized across the nation to cultivate reconciliation debates and activities.[162] At the beginning of National Reconciliation Week, Australians observe Sorry Day to express remorse for their historical and contemporary persecution of the First Peoples.[163]

Since the twenty-first century, there have been reenactments and rituals of peace and reconciliation called "Acknowledgment" and "Welcome to Country." These are direct responses to the perceived lack of social justice. "Acknowledgment," for example, is delivered by various people through public addresses at the beginning of public events. They involve brief statements of traditional belonging on the part of Aboriginal Australians and Torres Strait Islanders to the land in which the event is occurring.[164] The address is usually delivered by a person with a recognized or official status but who is not indigenous. The other ceremony of recognition, "Welcome to Country," is slightly more complex. An indigenous individual delivers a verbal statement of welcome in front of a gathering. This is sometimes accompanied by a dance or other types of performances like small rites of "smoking" (i.e., being cleansed with smoke).[165]

These rituals are examples of **recognition**, that is, a normative reaction to experienced neglect and injustice.[166] Recognition is designed to make an entire nation evolve from earlier hostilities and differences to greater hospitality that acknowledges the value and contributions of all peoples and cultures. Now, recognition is more than just a theme of apology and reconciliation. It is also part of a political agenda to make reparations an official policy that will seek to generate further compensations to groups that have been persecuted. Today, most reparation campaigns across the world are inspired by the post-World War II growth of Holocaust consciousness.[167]

Study by Donovan and Leivers

Donovan and Leivers (1993)[168] ran a research-focused communication campaign to assess the practicability of employing mass media to change racist or discriminatory beliefs towards Aborigines in a small town in Australia. The communication campaign designed by the two researchers used mostly paid advertising. The two-week campaign centered on Aboriginal employment week to motivate Aborigines to look for employment and, at the same time, motivate the community and employers to hire Aborigines on a fair basis. One of the main objectives of the study was to neutralize the racist or discriminatory beliefs about Aborigines and their employment. Three stereotypical beliefs were addressed and included on a measurement scale: (1) Very few Aborigines have real jobs; (2) most of those who work do it for a short period of time; and (3) most of those who work are not skilled. These beliefs were targeted because qualitative studies report that they constitute the reasons for believing that Aboriginal Australians are lazy, irresponsible, and incompetent, which unsurprisingly hinders their chances for employment. The two researchers used a pre-postindependent samples design. After the two-week campaign, the results indicated considerable changes in beliefs about the percentage of Aborigines in paid employment and in keeping their job for longer periods of time.

THE MIXED RESULTS OF ANTITERRORIST COMMUNICATION CAMPAIGNS

Although the campaigns described in all case studies in this chapter reveal massive efforts to counter terrorism, extremism, and radicalization through narratives and other strategies, they tend to produce mixed results—or, at least, some are more productive than others. For example, in regards to the last campaign described, Say No to Terror, Aly, Weimann-Saks, and Weimann (2014)[144] applied terms related to "noise" (i.e., visibility, persuasion, and impact) to determine whether the core elements of the campaign can be effectively used as a counternarrative approach against jihadists' appeal on the internet. The authors found that, although the messages of Say No to Terror are consistent with recommendations based on empirical research for the design of successful antiterrorist communication, the campaign itself has only fulfilled certain basic criteria for effective noise. By extension, Al-Rawi (2013)[145] reported that more than 350 other videos included counterarguments to Say No to Terror. As such, 60% of YouTube commentators did not consider the campaign in a positive light, raising concerns about its real intentions.

Scientific evidence on what works in countering terrorism, extremism, and radicalization remains limited. While studies on that matter are still being conducted, empirical analysis has produced two key conclusions: (1) No clear profile of a terrorist exists; the process by which people resort to using extreme violence fluctuates and depends on a range of personal, social, and political dynamics that sometimes interact with each other in mysterious ways; and (2) precisely because it can be a complicated interaction of factors that eventually contribute to terrorism, there is more than one path to terrorism. It is difficult to accurately determine who is more prone to committing terrorism within a population and who is not.[146]

Nevertheless, certain demographic attributes can still help guide the message, channel, and messengers themselves for the antiterrorist communication campaign. It is imperative that these attributes be taken into account when thinking about a target audience, as these assist planners in knowing whom they need to reach. One indicator for the identification of a would-be terrorist is his or her unwavering search and continuing interest in terrorism, extremism, or potentially dangerous subjects—i.e., when he or she is said to be in an intense exploration or soul-searching phase. A typical person who fits that profile could be anyone: a mother with young kids, an instructor, or a social worker who wants to acquire more information about the indoctrination process.[147]

To this crucial point, however, campaign planners have to be mindful of another reality: the danger of pushing would-be terrorists even further in the wrong direction. In a review of the literature on people's exit from violent extremist organizations, Dalgaard-Nielsen (2013)[148] borrowed elements from social psychology research to understand the opposition faced by persuasive strategies to deradicalization. When someone has internalized a radical belief that comes to shape his or her self-perceived identity, attempts to discredit that radical belief may backfire and produce a defensive posture that may exacerbate the situation. Both Dalgaard-Nielsen and Braddock (2014)[149] brought up the theory of psychological reactance developed by Jack Brehm in the 1960s to explain unintended consequences of deradicalization efforts. Brehm's (1966)[150] postulation is that arguments that threaten a person's freedom of thought can lead to even more extremist thoughts and a heightened desire to enact those in the real world.

NOTES

1. Katherine E. Brown and Tania Saeed, "Radicalization and Counter-Radicalization at British Universities: Muslim Encounters and Alternatives," *Ethnic and Racial Studies* 38, no. 11 (2015): 1952–68. https://doi.org/10.1080/01419870.2014.911343.
2. Taylor Armstrong and Jonathan Matusitz, "Hezbollah as a Group Phenomenon: Differential Association Theory," *Journal of Human Behavior in the Social Environment* 23, no. 4 (2013): 475–84. https://doi.org/10.1080/10911359.2013.772425; Jonathan

Matusitz and James Olufowote, "Visual Motifs in Islamist Terrorism: Applying Conceptual Metaphor Theory," *Journal of Applied Security Research* 11, no. 1 (2016): 18–32. https://doi.org/10.1080/19361610.2016.1104276; Jonathan Matusitz, "Brand Management in Terrorism: The Case of Hezbollah," *Journal of Policing, Intelligence and Counter Terrorism* 13, no. 1 (2018): 1–16. https://doi.org/10.1080/18335330.2017.141248 9; Jonathan Matusitz, "Understanding Hezbollah Symbolism through Symbolic Convergence Theory," *Journal of Visual Political Communication* 7, no. 1 (2021): 43–60. https://doi.org/10.1386/jvpc_00008_1; Kari Olechowicz and Jonathan Matusitz, "The Motivations of Islamic Martyrs: Applying the Collective Effort Model," *Current Psychology* 32 (2013): 338–47. https://doi.org/10.1007/s12144-013-9187-0; Sarah Ponder and Jonathan Matusitz, "Examining ISIS Online Recruitment through Relational Development Theory," *Connections* 16, no. 4 (2017): 35–50. https://doi.org/10.11610/Connections.16.4.02.

3. Jonathan Matusitz, Andrea Madrazo, and Catalina Udani, *Online Jihadist Magazines to Promote the Caliphate: Communicative Perspectives* (New York: Peter Lang, 2019).

4. Eloy E. Cuevas and Madeleine Wells, *Somalia: Line in the Sand-Identification of MYM Vulnerabilities* (Carlisle, PA: US Army War College, 2010).

5. Ibid, vii–viii.

6. Martin Fishbein, Kathleen Hall-Jamieson, Eric Zimmer, Ina von Haeften, and Robin Nabi, "Avoiding the Boomerang: Testing the Relative Effectiveness of Antidrug Public Service Announcements before a National Campaign," *American Journal of Public Health* 92, no. 2 (2002): 238–45. https://doi.org/10.2105/AJPH.92.2.238.

7. Jonas Becker, "Fighting at Home and Abroad," *Atlantisch Perspectief* 39, no. 5 (2015): 23–7.

8. Matusitz, Madrazo, and Udani, *Online Jihadist Magazines to Promote the Caliphate*, 269–72.

9. Katherine E. Brown, "Gender and Counter-Radicalization: Women and Emerging Counter-Terror Measures," in *Gender, National Security, and Counter-Terrorism: Human Rights Perspectives*, ed. Margaret Satterthwaite and Jayne Huckerby (New York: Routledge, 2012): 36–59.

10. Garth Davies, Christine Neudecker, Marie Ouellet, Martin Bouchard, and Benjamin Ducol, "Toward a Framework Understanding of Online Programs for Countering Violent Extremism," *Journal for Deradicalization* 6 (2016): 51–86.

11. Alex P. Schmid, *Al-Qaeda's "Single Narrative" and Attempts to Develop Counter-Narratives: The State of Knowledge* (The Hague: International Centre for Counter-Terrorism, 2014).

12. Schmid, 3.

13. Steven Corman, "Understanding the Role of Narrative in Extremist Strategic Communication," in *Countering Violent Extremism: Scientific Methods and Strategies*, ed. Laurie Fenstermacher and Todd Leventhal (Washington, D.C.: NSI, 2011): 36–43.

14. H. L. (Bud) Goodall, "From Tales of the Field to Tales of the Future," *Organizational Research Methods* 13, no. 2 (2010): 256–67. https://doi.org/10.1177/1094428109340039.

15. Schmid, *Al-Qaeda's "Single Narrative,"* 1–3.

16. Kurt Braddock and John Horgan, "Towards a Guide for Constructing and Disseminating Counter-Narratives to Reduce Support for Terrorism," *Studies in Conflict & Terrorism*

39, no. 5 (2015): 381–404, 385. http://www.tandfonline.com/doi/abs/10.1080/10576 10X.2015.1116277.

17. Anthony Richards, "From Terrorism to 'Radicalization' to 'Extremism': Counterterrorism Imperative or Loss of Focus?" *International Affairs* 91, no. 2 (2015): 371–80. https://doi.org/10.1111/1468-2346.12240.

18. Kelly A. Berkell, "Off-Ramp Opportunities in Material Support Cases," *Harvard National Security Journal* 8 (2017): 1–52.

19. Tom Pettinger, "De-Radicalization and Counter-Radicalization: Valuable Tools Combating Violent Extremism, or Harmful Methods of Subjugation?" *Journal for Deradicalization* 12 (2017): 1–58.

20. Donatella Della Porta and Gary LaFree, "Guest Editorial: Processes of Radicalization and De-Radicalization," *International Journal of Conflict and Violence* 6, no. 1 (2011): 4–10.

21. John Horgan, *Walking Away from Terrorism: Accounts of Disengagement from Radical and Extremist Movements* (London: Routledge, 2009).

22. Tom Pettinger, "De-Radicalization and Counter-Radicalization: Valuable Tools Combating Violent Extremism, or Harmful Methods of Subjugation?" *Journal for Deradicalization* 12 (2017): 1–58.

23. Daniel Koehler, *Understanding De-radicalization: Methods, Tools and Programs for Countering Violent Extremism* (New York: Routledge, 2017): xii.

24. Faiza Patel and Meghan Koushik, *Countering Violent Extremism* (New York: Brennan Center for Justice, 2017).

25. Owen Frazer and Christian Nünlist, *The Concept of Countering Violent Extremism* (Zurich: ETH Zürich, 2015).

26. Joseph S. Nye, *Bound to Lead: The Changing Nature of American Power* (London: Basic Books, 1990).

27. John M. Barry, *Power Plays: Politics, Football, and Other Blood Sports* (Jackson, MI: University of Mississippi Press, 2001).

28. Joseph S. Nye, *The Powers to Lead* (New York: Oxford University Press, 2008).

29. Joseph S. Nye, "Public Diplomacy and Soft Power," *The Annals of the American Academy of Political and Social Science* 616 (2008): 94–109. https://doi.org/10.1177/0002716207311699.

30. Ernest J. Wilson, "Hard Power, Soft Power, Smart Power," *The Annals of the American Academy of Political and Social Science* 616 (2008): 110–24. https://doi.org/10.1177/0002716207312618.

31. Kurt Campbell and Michael O'Hanlon, *Hard Power: The New Politics of National Security* (New York: Basic Books, 2006).

32. Wilson, "Hard Power, Soft Power, Smart Power," 110.

33. Richard L. Armitage and Joseph S. Nye, *CSIS Commission on Smart Power: A Smarter, More Secure America* (Washington, D.C.: Center for Strategic and International Studies, 2007): 7.

34. Louis Reynolds and Henry Tuck, *The Counter-Narrative Monitoring & Evaluation Handbook* (London: Institute for Strategic Dialogue, 2016).

35. Todd C. Helmus and Kurt Klein, *Assessing Outcomes of Online Campaigns Countering Violent Extremism: A Case Study of the Redirect Method* (Santa Monica, CA: RAND Corporation, 2018).

36. Talene Bilazarian, "Countering Violent Extremist Narratives Online: Lessons from Offline Countering Violent Extremism," *Policy & Internet* 12, no. 1 (2020): 46–65. https://doi.org/10.1002/poi3.204.

37. Patel and Koushik, *Countering Violent Extremism*, 1–5.

38. Naím, Moises, "The YouTube Effect," *Foreign Policy* 158 (2007): 103–4.

39. Bernardo A. Huberman, Daniel M. Romero, and Fang Wu, "Crowdsourcing, Attention and Productivity," *Journal of Information Science* 35, no. 6 (2009): 758–65. https://doi.org/10.1177/016555150.

40. Yonah Alexander and Dean Alexander, *The Islamic State: Combating the Caliphate without Borders* (Lanham, MD: Lexington Books, 2015); Sarah Ponder and Jonathan Matusitz, "Examining ISIS Online Recruitment through Relational Development Theory," *Connections* 16, no. 4 (2017): 35–50. https://doi.org/10.11610/Connections.16.4.02.

41. Maris Kulis, "Propaganda of Islamic State in the Digital Age," *Religiski-Filozoiski Raksti* 20 (2016): 98–114.

42. Jonathan Matusitz, "Islamic Terrorist Radicalization through Online Jihadist Magazines," *Journal of Communication & Religion* 43, no. 1 (2020): 26–39.

43. Neal Mohan, "VidCon 2018: Helping Creators Earn More Money and Build Stronger Communities," (June 21, 2018). Retrieved March 26, 2021 from https://youtube.googleblog.com.

44. Available at https://www.omnicoreagency.com/youtube-statistics.

45. Huberman, Romero, and Wu, "Crowdsourcing, Attention and Productivity," 758–65.

46. Daniel de Zayas and Jonathan Matusitz, "Understanding the Dissemination of ISIS Beheading Videos through the Diffusion of Innovations (DoI) Theory," *Journal of Policing, Intelligence and Counter Terrorism* 16, no. 3 (2021): 205–22. https://doi.org/10.1080/18335330.2021.1892168.

47. Mia Bloom, Hicham Tiflati, and John Horgan, "Navigating ISIS's Preferred Platform: Telegram," *Terrorism and Political Violence* 31, no. 6 (2019): 1242–54. https://doi.org/10.1080/09546553.2017.1339695.

48. Tanya Silverman, Christopher J. Stewart, Zahed Amanullah, and Jonathan Birdwell, *The Impact of Counter-Narratives* (London: Institute for Strategic Dialogue, 2016).

49. Ibid, 7–8.

50. Joseph Zubin and John G. Peatman, "Testing the Pulling Power of Advertisements by the Split-Run Copy Method," *Journal of Applied Psychology* 29, no. 1 (1945): 40–57. https://doi.org/10.1037/h0062358.

51. Martine Zeuthen, *Reintegration: Disengaging Violent Extremists* (The Hague: Policy and Operations Evaluation Department of the Ministry of Foreign Affairs, 2021).

52. Silverman, Stewart, Amanullah, and Birdwell, *The Impact of Counter-Narratives*, 7–8.

53. Henry Tuck and Tania Silverman, *The Counter-Narrative Handbook* (London: Institute for Strategic Dialogue, 2016).

54. Silverman, Stewart, Amanullah, and Birdwell, *The Impact of Counter-Narratives*, 7–8.

55. Ibid, 7–8.

56. Ibid, 7–8.

57. Ibid, 7–8.

58. Tuck and Silverman, *The Counter-Narrative Handbook*, 5.

59. Berkell, "Off-Ramp Opportunities in Material Support Cases," 19.

60. Christian Picciolini, *Breaking Hate: Confronting the New Culture of Extremism* (New York: Hachette Books, 2020).

61. Jay Price, "Trump Administration Rescinds UNC Grant to Fight Violent Extremism," *The News & Observer* (June 26, 2017). Retrieved on March 30, 2021 from https://www.newsobserver.com/news/politics-government/article158205859.html.

62. Victoria DeSimone, "From the Ground Up: Combatting the Rise of Right-Wing Terror," *New Perspectives in Foreign Policy* 18 (2019): 10–5.

63. Ibid, 10–5.

64. Cited in Josephine B. Schmitt, Diana Rieger, Olivia Rutkowski, and Julian Ernst, "Counter-messages as Prevention or Promotion of Extremism?! The Potential Role of YouTube: Recommendation Algorithms," *Journal of Communication* 68, no. 4 (2018): 780–808, 786–9. https://doi.org/10.1093/joc/jqy029.

65. Tuck and Silverman, *The Counter-Narrative Handbook*, 38.

66. Schmitt, Rieger, Rutkowski, and Ernst, "Counter-messages as Prevention," 793–5.

67. Keiran Hardy, "Countering Right-Wing Extremism: Lessons from Germany and Norway," *Journal of Policing, Intelligence and Counter Terrorism* 14, no. 3 (2019): 262–79. https://doi.org/10.1080/18335330.2019.1662076.

68. Cited in Simon Copland, "A Psychological Understanding of the 'Extremist Mindset' Is Essential to Combat Violence," *BBC News* (May 1, 2019). Retrieved on March 30, 2021 from https://www.bbc.com/future/article/20190501-how-do-you-prevent-extremism.

69. George Popp, Sarah Canna, and Jeff Day, *Common Characteristics of "Successful" Deradicalization Programs of the Past* (Cambridge, MA: NSI Reachback, 2020).

70. See Zeuthen, *Reintegration*.

71. See Copland, "A Psychological Understanding".

72. Arie W. Kruglanski and Shira Fishman, "Psychological Factors in Terrorism and Counterterrorism: Individual, Group, and Organizational Levels of Analysis," *Social Issues and Policy Review* 3, no. 1 (2009): 1–44. https://doi.org/10.1111/j.1751-2409.2009.01009.x.

73. Tore Bjørgo and Yngve Carlsson, *Early Intervention with Violent and Racist Youth Groups* (Oslo: Norwegian Institute of International Affairs, 2005).

74. Tore Bjørgo, Jaap van Donselaar, and Sara Grunenberg, "Exit from Right-Wing Extremist Groups: Lessons from Disengagement Programs in Norway, Sweden, and Germany," in *Leaving Terrorism Behind*, ed. Tore Bjørgo and John Horgan (New York: Routledge, 2009): 135–48.

75. Ibid, 135–8.

76. Jessica Eve Stern, "X: A Case Study of a Swedish Neo-Nazi and His Reintegration into Swedish Society," *Behavioral Sciences & the Law* 32, no. 3 (2014): 440–53. https://doi.org/10.1002/bsl.2119.

77. Popp, Canna, and Day, 5.

78. Stern, "X: A Case Study," 448.

79. Ibid, 448.

80. Maurice Blanc, "The Place of Islam Within a Secular France and Europe: How to Avoid the Traps of the So-Called Islamic Extremism?" in *Citizenship and Religion: A Fundamental Challenge for Democracy*, ed. Maurice Blanc, Julia Droeber, and Tom Storrie (New York: Springer, 2020): 203–30.

81. Stevan Weine, Schuyler Henderson, Stephen Shanfield, Rupinder Legha, and Jerrold Post, "Building Community Resilience to Counter Violent Extremism," *Democracy and Security* 9, no. 4 (2013): 327–33. https://doi.org/10.1080/17419166.2013.766131.

82. Lee Bosher and Ksenia Chmutina, *Disaster Risk Reduction for the Built Environment* (Hoboken, NJ: Wiley, 2017).

83. Fran H. Norris and Susan P. Stevens, "Community Resilience as a Metaphor, Theory, Set of Capacities, and Strategy for Disaster Readiness," *American Journal of Community Psychology* 41, no. 1 (2008): 127–50. https://doi.org/10.1007/s10464-007-9156-6.

84. Ayyoob Sharifi, "A Critical Review of Selected Tools for Assessing Community Resilience," *Ecological Indicators* 69 (2016): 629–47. https://doi.org/10.1016/j.ecolind.2016.05.023.

85. B. Heidi Ellis and Saida Abdi, "Building Community Resilience to Violent Extremism through Genuine Partnerships," *American Psychologist* 72, no. 3 (2017): 289–300. http://dx.doi.org/10.1037/amp0000065.

86. Ann S. Masten, Karin M. Best, and Norman Garmezy, "Resilience and Development: Contributions from the Study of Children Who Overcome Adversity," *Development and Psychopathology* 2, no. 4 (1990): 425–44, 426. http://dx.doi.org/10.1017/S0954579400005812.

87. Ellis and Abdi, "Building Community Resilience," 290.

88. Ibid, 292.

89. Ryan Schuessler, "Meet 'Average Mohamed', the Gas Station Manager Fighting ISIS," *The Guardian* (February 17, 2016): A1. Retrieved on March 26, 2021 from https://www.theguardian.com/world/2016/feb/17/meet-average-mohamed-gas-station-manager-fighting-islamic-state.

90. US Department of Justice, *Building Community Resilience* (Washington, D.C.: US Department of Justice, 2017).

91. Ibid.

92. Floris Vermeulen, "Suspect Communities: Targeting Violent Extremism at the Local Level: Policies of Engagement in Amsterdam, Berlin, and London," *Terrorism and Political Violence* 26, no. 2 (2014): 286–306. https://doi.org/10.1080/09546553.2012.705254.

93. Ibid, 288.

94. Ibid, 286.

95. David Schanzer, Charles Kurzman, and Ebrahim Moosa, *Anti-Terror Lessons of Muslim-Americans* (Washington, D.C.: National Institute of Justice, 2010).

96. Ibid, 2.

97. Helmus and Klein, *Assessing Outcomes of Online Campaigns*, 2.

98. Aamer Madhani, "Average Mohamed Tries to Thwart Islamic State," *USA Today* (February 3, 2015): A1. Retrieved on March 26, 2021 from https://www.usatoday.com/story/news/2015/02/03/average-mohamed-minneapolis-isis-countering-violent-extremism/22393287.

99. Sara Monaci, "Combating Extremism in a Public Sphere at Risk: Platforms' Affordances, Dilemmas and Opportunities of Social Media Campaigns," *H-ermes: Journal of Communication* 15 (2019): 229–48. https://doi.org/10.1285/i22840753n15p229.

100. Sara Monaci, "Social Media Campaigns Against Violent Extremism: A New Approach to Evaluating Video Storytelling," *International Journal of Communication* 14 (2020): 980–1003.

101. Cited in James Digby, *Cartoons vs. the Caliphate: The Scale of Counter-Narrative Campaigns and the Role of Religion* (2018): 1. Retrieved on March 28, 2021 from https://escholarship.org/uc/item/0v90p2gn.

102. Schuessler, "Meet 'Average Mohamed'," A1.

103. Cited in Digby, *Cartoons vs. the Caliphate*, 73.

104. Ibid, 74–8.

105. Anna Warrington, "Countering Violent Extremism via De-Securitisation on Twitter," *Journal for Deradicalization* 11 (2017): 258–80, 268–9.

106. Mona Kanwal Sheikh, "How Does Religion Matter? Pathways to Religion in International Relations," *Review of International Studies* 38, no. 2 (2012): 365–92, 398. https://doi.org/10.1017/S026021051100057X.

107. Ibid, 390.

108. Lene Hansen, "Reconstructing Desecuritisation: The Normative-Political in the Copenhagen School and Directions for How to Apply It," *Review of International Studies* 38, no. 3 (2012): 525–46. https://doi.org/10.1017/S0260210511000581.

109. Jonathan Matusitz, "Applying McLuhan's Tetradic Framework to the Effects of 9/11 on US Media Reports and Depictions of Muslims," *Journal of Arab & Muslim Media Research* 13, no. 2 (2020): 179–94. https://doi.org/10.1386/jammr_00018_1.

110. Warrington, "Countering Violent Extremism," 270–1.

111. Jonathan Matusitz, *Global Jihad in Muslim and Non-Muslim Contexts* (New York: Palgrave Macmillan, 2020).

112. Angela Gendron, "Confronting Terrorism in Saudi Arabia," *International Journal of Intelligence and Counter Intelligence* 23, no. 3 (2010): 487–508. https://doi.org/10.1080/08850601003780946.

113. William Sheridan Combes, "Assessing Two Countering Violent Extremism Programs: Saudi Arabia's PRAC and the United Kingdom's Prevent Strategy," *Small Wars Journal* 9 (2013): 10–21.

114. Abdullah bin Khaled al-Saud, "Deciphering IS's Narrative and Activities in the Kingdom of Saudi Arabia," *Terrorism and Political Violence* 32, no. 3 (2020): 469–88. https://doi.org/10.1080/09546553.2017.1378645.

115. Olivier Roy, *The Failure of Political Islam* (Cambridge, MA: Harvard University Press, 1994).

116. Ibid, 3.

117. Naureen Chowdhury Fink and Hamed El-Said, *Transforming Terrorists: Examining International Efforts to Address Violent Extremism* (New York: International Peace Institute, 2011).

118. Jason Burke, "Fighting Terrorism: Do 'Deradicalisation' Camps Really Work?" *The Guardian* (June 9, 2013): A1. Retrieved on May 6, 2021 from http://www.theguardian.com/world/2013/jun/09/terrorism-do-deradicalisation-camps-work.

119. Aaron Y. Zelin and Jonathan Prohov, "The Foreign Policy Essay: Proactive Measures-Countering the Returnee Threat," *Lawfare* (May 1, 2014). Retrieved on May 6, 2021 from http://www.lawfareblog.com/2014/05/the-foreign-policy-essay-proactive-measures-countering-the-returnee-threat.

120. Cited in Christopher Boucek, *Saudi Arabia's "Soft" Counterterrorism Strategy: Prevention, Rehabilitation, and Aftercare* (Washington, D.C.: Carnegie Endowment for International Peace, 2008): 1.

121. Ibid, 4.

122. Benjamin Barthe, "Saudi Correctional Centre Claims Success with Former Jihadists," *The Guardian* (September 27, 2014): A1. Retrieved on March 30, 2021 from http://www.theguardian.com/world/2014/sep/27/mohammed-bin-nayef-centre-rehabilitation-jihadists.

123. Christopher Boucek, "The Sakinah Campaign and Internet Counter-Radicalization in Saudi Arabia," *CTC Sentinel* 1, no. 9 (2008): 1–3.

124. Gendron, "Confronting Terrorism in Saudi Arabia," 497.

125. Dylan Gerstel, "ISIS and Innovative Propaganda: Confronting Extremism in the Digital Age," *Swarthmore International Relations Journal* 1 (2016): 1–9.

126. bin Khaled al-Saud, "Deciphering IS's Narrative and Activities," 469–88.

127. Cited in Abdullah bin Khaled al-Saud, "The Tranquillity Campaign: A Beacon of Light in the Dark World Wide Web," *Perspectives on Terrorism* 11, no. 2 (2017): 58–64, 59.

128. Cited in Kareem El Damanhoury, "Entertainment–Education Versus Extremism: Examining Parasocial Interaction among Arab Viewers of Anti-ISIS TV Drama," *Journal for Deradicalization* 24 (2020): 40–78, 40.

129. Heather Jaber and Marwan M. Kraidy, "Mediating Islamic State: The Geopolitics of Television Drama and the 'Global War on Terror': Gharabeeb Soud Against Islamic State," *International Journal of Communication* 14 (2020): 1868–87; D. Della Ratta, *Shooting the Revolution: Visual Media and Warfare in Syria* (London: Pluto Press, 2018).

130. *Bahrain TV*, "Together to Extinguish the Fire of Terrorism." Accessed on YouTube on March 26, 2021 from http://www.youtube.com/watch?v=1hoEYn3mMNw.

131. El Damanhoury, "Entertainment–Education Versus Extremism," 40.

132. Ibid, 47–8.

133. Ibid, 49.

134. Gabriel Weimann, *Terror on the Internet: The New Arena, the New Challenges* (Washington, D.C.: US Institute of Peace Press, 2006).

135. Ahmed K. Al-Rawi, "The Anti-Terrorist Advertising Campaigns in the Middle East," *The Journal of International Communication* 19, no. 2 (2013): 182–95. https://doi.org/10.1080/13216597.2013.833534.

136. Cited in Anne Aly, Dana Weimann-Saks, and Gabriel Weimann, "Making 'Noise' Online: An Analysis of the Say No to Terror Online Campaign," *Perspectives on Terrorism* 8 (2014): 33–46, 37.

137. Ibid, 37 for both quotes.

138. Jan-Jaap van Eerten and Bertjan Doosje, *Challenging Extremist Views on Social Media: Developing a Counter-Messaging Response* (New York: Routledge, 2020).

139. Rachele Cecchi, Claudia D'Agostini, Agnese Pacciardi, and Martina Turra, "Reframing the Fight against Terrorism: Can Counter-Narratives Write a New Story?" *Security Praxis* (April 17, 2019). Retrieved on March 30, 2021 from https://securitypraxis.eu/terrorism-counter-narratives.

140. Aly, Weimann-Saks, and Weimann, "Making 'Noise' Online," 37.

141. Ibid, 39.

142. Ibid, 39.

143. Ibid, 40.

144. Ibid, 33.

145. Al-Rawi, "The Anti-Terrorist Advertising Campaigns," 182–95.

146. Patel and Koushik, *Countering Violent Extremism*, 10.

147. Tuck and Silverman, *The Counter-Narrative Handbook*, 8.

148. Anja Dalgaard-Nielsen, "Promoting Exit from Violent Extremism: Themes and Approaches," *Studies in Conflict and Terrorism* 36, no. 2 (2013): 99–115. https://doi.org/10.1080/1057610X.2013.747073.

149. Kurt Braddock, "The Talking Cure? Communication and Psychological Impact in Prison De-radicalisation Programmes," in *Prisons, Terrorism and Extremism*, ed. Andrew Silke (New York: Routledge, 2014): 60–74.

150. Jack W. Brehm, *A Theory of Psychological Reactance* (New York: Academic Press, 1966).

151. Richard Broome, *Aboriginal Australians: A History since 1788* (5th Ed.) (Crows Nest, Australia: Allen & Unwin, 2019).

152. Australian Bureau of Statistics, *2016 Census Overview: The 2016 Census Was Australia's Seventeenth National Census of Population and Housing* (Canberra: Australian Bureau of Statistics, 2016).

153. Yin Paradies, Ricci Harris, and Ian Anderson, *The Impact of Racism on Indigenous Health in Australia and Aotearoa: Towards a Research Agenda* (Darwin, Australia: Cooperative Research Centre for Aboriginal Health, 2008).

154. Bruce Reyburn, "The Forgotten Struggle of Australia's Aboriginal People," *Cultural Survival Quarterly Magazine* 17 (1988): 10–8.

155. Australian Bureau of Statistics, *2016 Census Overview*.

156. Kevin Rudd, "The Apology and Beyond. How We Must Confront Racism in Australia," *The Huffington Post* (December 2, 2016): A1. Retrieved on April 1, 2021 from https://www.huffingtonpost.co.uk/kevin-rudd/the-apology-and-beyond-ho_b_9221102.html.

157. Bridie Jabour, "UN Examines Australia's Forced Sterilisation of Women with Disabilities," *The Guardian* (November 15, 2015): A1. Retrieved on April 1, 2021 from https://www.theguardian.com/australia-news/2015/nov/10/un-examines-australias-forced-sterilisation-of-women-with-disabilities.

158. For example, see Margaret Gonzalez-Perez, *Women and Terrorism: Female Activity in Domestic and International Terror Groups* (New York: Routledge, 2008); Philip R. Reilly, "Eugenics and Involuntary Sterilization: 1907–2015," *Annual Review of Genomics and Human Genetics* 16 (2015): 351–68. https://doi.org/10.1146/annurev-genom-090314-024930.

159. Alexander L. George, *Western State Terrorism* (Cambridge: Polity Press, 1991); Thomas H. Snitch, "Terrorism and Political Assassinations: A Transnational Assessment, 1968–80," *The ANNALS of the American Academy of Political and Social Science* 463, no. 1 (1982): 54–68. https://doi.org/10.1177/0002716282463001005.

160. Jo-Anne Wemmers, *Reparation for Victims of Crimes against Humanity: The Healing Role of Reparation* (New York: Routledge, 2014).

161. Available at https://antarvictoria.org.au/seaofhands.

162. Antonio Buti, "'Reconciliation': Its Relationship and Importance to Law," *University of Western Australia Law Review* 43 (2018): 107–17.

163. Michael Mullins, "Paul Keating and Sorry Day's Indulgence with a Purpose," *Eureka Street* 23, no. 10 (2013): 20–1.

164. Francesca Merlan, "Recent Rituals of Indigenous Recognition in Australia: Welcome to Country," *American Anthropologist* 116, no. 2 (2014): 296–309. https://doi.org/10.1111/aman.12089.

165. Ibid, 296–7.

166. Charles Taylor, "The Politics of Recognition," in *Multiculturalism: Examining the Politics of Recognition*, ed. Amy Gutmann (Princeton, NJ: Princeton University Press, 1994): 25–74.

167. Merlan, "Recent Rituals of Indigenous Recognition," 296–7.

168. Robert J. Donovan and Susan Leivers, "Using Paid Advertising to Modify Racial Stereotype Beliefs," *Public Opinion Quarterly* 57, no. 2 (1993): 205–18. https://doi.org/10.1086/269366.

Glossary

ABC behaviors   a concept employed by HIV/AIDS prevention scholars and practitioners to allude to the three behaviors believed to be crucial in lowering the sexual transmission of HIV/AIDS: abstinence, being faithful, and using condoms, respectively (Ch. 5).

Aboriginal Australians   Australia's First Peoples made up of different groups who have moved across Australia for over 50,000 years. These groups have a common, though complex, ancestry (Ch. 16).

Absolute rights   rights that enjoy the highest protection and cannot be denigrated in any form (Ch. 9).

Absorption–addiction model   a model that confirms real instances of celebrity worship, whereby a co-opted identity structure for some people enables psychological absorption with a celebrity in an effort to fashion an identity and a sense of self-actualization or gratification (Ch. 8).

Active video games   games that work through the player's movements. The movements are used to operate them (the games) (Ch. 8).

Aesopian language   language that contains a seemingly innocuous meaning while, in reality, there is a deeper meaning lurking inside the phrase (Ch. 13).

Affect   the energy invested in a particular situation or sphere. It is an investment made by a person to a cultural text and it depends on that person's mattering map (Ch. 8).

Agency   a method by which we employ our unique resources and talents, and exploit relevant opportunities, to attain our desired outcomes (Ch. 9).

Agenda-setting theory   a theory predicating that the media can influence or maneuver public awareness and concern of salient issues (Ch. 11).

All-channel networks   networks that allow individuals to communicate with each other or with those involved in the same process (Ch. 1).

Ally activism   collective action in support of, or in concert with, a disadvantaged group (Ch. 12).

Allyship   the process of supporting disenfranchised groups by promoting social justice, inclusion, and human rights by members of privileged groups (Ch. 12).

Fundamentals of Public Communication Campaigns, First Edition. Jonathan Matusitz.
© 2022 John Wiley & Sons Ltd. Published 2022 by John Wiley & Sons Ltd.

Al-Shabaab   a Somali terrorist organization that uses diverse communication technologies to publish an online jihadist magazine called *Gaidi Mtaani* (Ch. 16).

al-Siham al-Marika   a television drama series that depicts life under ISIS's control (Ch. 16).

Alt-Right   a comprehensive term to describe groups that surmise that European ancestry and White identity and principles (e.g., Judeo–Christian values and traditional gender roles) are under threat by political correctness, social justice reforms, and massive immigration (Ch. 14).

AM/FM Activism   an online platform that enables local activists to use published resources needed for responding to defamatory claims within their own communities (Ch. 11).

Ambiguity   in public communication, it is an attempt to elevate intrigue and make associations between variables that defy logic (Ch. 4).

Animal welfare initiatives   campaigns that promote healthier living conditions for animals during their treatment (Ch. 4).

Anomic suicide   a type of suicide caused by a rupture of social equilibrium, like a bankruptcy or after winning a lottery (Ch. 7).

Antisemitic canard   an anti-Jewish falsehood (Ch. 15).

Antisemitism   intolerance of, hatred of, or discrimination against Jews for motives linked to their Jewish heritage (Ch. 15).

Anti-vaxxers   people who oppose the use of vaccines for a multitude of reasons (Ch. 7).

Argumentum ad populum   an "appeal to the people" (Ch. 7).

Attitude accessibility theory   a theory postulating that attitudes towards more familiar objects are more developed and become more accessible than attitudes towards less familiar objects (Ch. 3).

Attitude object   the notion around which an attitude develops and can transform in due course (Ch. 3).

Attitudes   evaluative cognitive structures that prompt us to behave in certain ways. They are a function of perceived attractiveness and likelihood of anticipated outcomes (Ch. 3).

Audience   a chosen group of individuals that should be large for a public communication campaign and to whom frequent communication is directed (Ch. 2).

Audience adaptation   the process of tailoring a public communication campaign to the diversity, beliefs, values, and needs of the audience (Ch. 2).

Audience analysis   the study of the intended public for the communication campaign (Ch. 2).

Audience diversity   the analysis of the cultural, demographic, and individual characteristics that vary among publics (Ch. 2).

Audience perception   a phenomenon whereby the public filters and construes information from the five senses to conceive a meaningful picture of the environment in which they live (Ch. 2).

Autonomy   the ability to self-organize and regulate one's own behavior, which includes the tendency to work towards inner coherence and integration among regulatory demands and goals (Ch. 8).

Availability heuristic   the idea that a phenomenon is deemed recurrent or plausible to the degree that instances of it can be extracted from memory without difficulty (Ch. 4).

Average Mohamed   a campaign that has diffused multiple animated videos and posted tweets that borrowed Muslim principles on peace to counter the ideology of Islamist extremist groups (Ch. 16).

Axiom   a declaration that is believed to be true. It is employed as a premise or starting point for additional reasoning and arguments (Ch. 3).

Bandwagoning   an appeal to a popular trend; the observation that human beings generally follow a trend because many others do the same (Ch. 7).

Behavior Change Communication   a strategy that uses communication to motivate individuals or communities to change their behavior (Ch. 3)

Behavioral intention   the degree of likelihood that a person will perform a particular behavior (Ch. 3).

Behavioral risk factors   unfavorable social problems that can be reduced or solved by citizens or physicians (Ch. 5).

Being-in-the-world   the premise that we can understand an unfamiliar phenomenon if we put ourselves in the context of another person linked to that phenomenon (whether today or in the past) (Ch. 8).

Belief   an individual or group-based principle about the properties or peculiarities of an object (Ch. 2).

Belief bias   a pattern of reaching conclusions based on personal beliefs (Ch. 3).

Belief perseverance   the persistence of hanging on to one's beliefs in the face of evidence to the contrary (Ch. 3).

Beneficence   a situation that looks at the balance between benefits and risks (Ch. 3).

Benevolent sexism   the practice of taking a seemingly positive, yet patronizing, attitude towards women (Ch. 10).

Biased message processing   the selective use of information according to memory and experience, which may result in flawed subjective perception of information during the course of persuasion (Ch. 3).

Biomedicine   the medical practices and ideas stemming from Western scientific conventions, including studies of germs, biology, biochemistry, and biophysics. It mostly concentrates on determining physical causes for disease (Ch. 6).

Bite–snack–meal approach   an approach whereby the headline is the bite and serve as a hyperlink to a whole "meal" of a message. A "snack" underneath the headline provides the main points of the message in a few short sentences (Ch. 2).

Black Lives Matter (BLM)   a US decentralized sociopolitical movement denouncing White supremacy, particularly police brutality and racially motivated violence against African Americans (Ch. 12).

Blaming the victim   directing the causes of social problems at the person, not at the social environment (Ch. 3).

Blood libel   also called blood accusation, it is the myth that Jews abducted and killed the children of Christians, so they could use their blood for religious rituals during Jewish celebrations (Ch. 15).

Bolivarianism   principle of popular democracy, economic autonomy, fair redistribution of revenues, and an end to political corruption (Ch. 13).

Bolivarian populism   a left-leaning social movement in South America. It is named after Simón Bolívar, a nineteenth-century Latin American revolutionary leader born in Venezuela (Ch. 13).

Boomerang effect   a phenomenon whereby the response from the audience is contrary to the anticipated response of persuasion messages (Ch. 3).

Bottom–up change   change that comes from the grassroots (Ch. 9).

Brazil without Homophobia a campaign that became a hallmark for public policies in favor of the LGBTQ+ population in Brazil (Ch. 11).

Broken Windows an anticriminal initiative applied to clampdowns on petty crimes like graffiti and public urination, under the assumption that neighborhood disorder led to such offenses and attracted felons who would eventually perpetrate more dangerous offenses in these neighborhoods (Ch. 12).

Buzz campaigning a campaigning method that causes a stir and uproar about a product, service, or issue that pushed audiences to pay attention (Ch. 4).

Campaign a comprehensive and organized attempt at shaping the behavior, attitude, or decision-making status within a community of people (Ch. 1).

Campaign against Homophobia a Polish pro-LGBTQ+ campaign that operates as both an advocacy and political movement (Ch. 11).

Campaign Zero a campaign for American police reform launched in the summer of 2015 when BLM was denounced for demonizing police and having no plan to concretely end police brutality (Ch. 12).

Carriers of the misperception individuals with misperceptions that people engage in problematic or risky behaviors more than they actually do (Ch. 1).

Case definition a mechanism by which public health experts determine who is to be included as a case (i.e., a person directly impacted by an epidemic, pandemic, or outbreak) (Ch. 7).

Celebrities individuals who experience a large volume of media-related capital through their repeated presence in the public sphere (Ch. 8).

Celebrity culture a practice whereby the media influences publics by determining how they can be affected by the advice given by prestigious people (Ch. 8).

Central beliefs beliefs that are less resistant to change and come directly or indirectly from an authority (whether an object or a person) (Ch. 2).

Centralized networks networks in which centrality keeps the flow of communication smooth (Ch. 1).

Central route processing persuasion reached through the quality of the arguments in a message (Ch. 3).

Change agent a person who stimulates innovation decisions in a direction deemed appropriate by a campaign (Ch. 1).

Charisma a certain quality of an individual personality by virtue of which he or she is set apart from ordinary people and treated as endowed with supernatural, superhuman, or at least specifically exceptional quality (Ch. 8; Ch. 13).

Charitable orientation for a nongovernmental organization, it is a top–down structure with only a modicum of participation or input by beneficiaries (Ch. 9).

Charity principle the philosophy that more resourceful members of society help their less resourceful counterparts, including the jobless, the disabled, the diseased, and the elderly (Ch. 9).

Choice architecture a situation that occurs when construction of different frames gives the audience choices (Ch. 4).

Cisgender people whose gender identity and assigned-at-birth gender remain the same (Ch. 11).

Cisnormativity a phenomenon whereby we assume that all, or almost all, humans are cisgender (Ch. 11).

Citizen participation citizen action for increased public decision-making (Ch. 9).

Citywide organizations organizations like chambers of commerce, partisanships between business and educational groups, and leagues of community organizations (Ch. 9).

Civil society organization a nonprofit, voluntary citizens' group with many interests and ties and arranged on a local, national, or international platform (Ch. 11).

Clean India Mission a nationwide campaign launched by the Government of India in 2014 to eradicate open defecation and develop solid waste management (Ch. 5).

Clutter the infinite number of messages to which we are exposed every day (Ch. 2).

Cognitions about the universe subjective prospects that an object has a certain attribute, or an action will result in a specific outcome (Ch. 2).

Cognitive biases statements or decisions that systematically deviate from rationality in judgment (Ch. 3).

Cognitive capital social capital that includes norms, values, attitudes, and beliefs that influence factors like interpersonal or intergroup trust and readiness to exchange knowledge or resources (Ch. 1).

Cognitive dissonance a phenomenon whereby someone has contradictory beliefs, ideas, or values (Ch. 2).

Cognitive mobilization the way citizens' political participation is materialized. It is influenced by the fact that citizens tend to be more educated, with wider access to information (Ch. 9).

Collective efficacy joining forces to accomplish a goal (Ch. 16).

Collective identification sentiments of solidarity, collective efficacy, and common culture (Ch. 9).

Collective norms norms maneuvered at the social level or at the level of the social network (Ch. 1).

Collective victimhood a type of symbolic representation used by a campaign to associate the dead to advocates, demonstrators, and the movement through images of protest or photos of victims that speak to the values and objectives of the movement (Ch. 12).

Commons a place where no permission or registration is mandatory for entry; nor are people discriminated based on who they are (Ch. 1).

Communal mindset the need for collaboration within communities, not only for the entity or institution designing the campaign (Ch. 2).

Communication the process of conveying a message from a sender to a receiver (Ch. 1).

Communication channel the means by which a message gets diffused from people to people (Ch. 1).

Communicative health literacy a type of literacy that encompasses higher cognitive and literacy skills (that complement social skills to allow us to engage in diverse activities and utilize information to changing situations) (Ch. 6).

Community-based organizations organizations that emerge from people's own initiatives (Ch. 9).

Community competence a phenomenon whereby resilient communities show their capability of working together effectively in order to identify and accomplish goals (Ch. 16).

Community resilience the potential of a community to employ resources at hand—mutual assistance, education, etc.—to properly react to, endure, and recover from adverse circumstances (Ch. 16).

Compassion fatigue   a term explaining how repeated exposure to a message can cause the audience to "switch off" (Ch. 3).

Competence   the ability to engage optimal challenges and experience mastery or effectance in the physical and social worlds (Ch. 8).

Complete observation   watching people from afar (unlike participant observation) (Ch. 6).

Concepts   mental representations of the world (Ch. 6).

Conceptual mapping   the creation of a model or theoretical framework that helps understand how individuals within a culture think (Ch. 6).

Confirmation bias   a phenomenon whereby people are used to actively seeking out and placing more emphasis on information that confirms their hypothesis (Ch. 3).

Connotative meanings   the expressive and more subjective uses of a symbol, like flags symbolizing law and order, nationalism, chauvinism, national pride, and so forth (Ch. 6).

Conscientization   a social concept that seeks to impart an in-depth understanding of the world by exposing social and political contradictions and inequalities, and by describing how common citizens feel about them (Ch. 9).

Consensus reality   a way for us to address the question "What is real?" (Ch. 6).

Consequentialism   a worldview postulating that the outcomes of a specific action become the foundation for any viable moral judgment about that action (Ch. 4).

Consumer aperture   a concept that tackles the question, "When, where and under what circumstances is the audience's mind most receptive to the message?" (Ch. 2).

Containment   a conscious attempt at limiting the length of a crisis or preventing it from propagating to other regions that have afflicted a country (Ch. 7).

Content strategies   the type of informational content on which campaign messages should focus (Ch. 1).

Continuous change   a category of social change that is cultivated mainly for the sake of change (Ch. 9).

Coping self-efficacy   the confidence that we have when performing a task during taxing circumstances (Ch. 7).

Copyright   a form of intellectual property, including original designs, patents, and trademarks (Ch. 2).

Core beliefs   beliefs that are the least likely to change (Ch. 2).

CoronaJihad   an Islamophobic hashtag propagated immediately after the news that COVID-19 allegedly originated from a Muslim missionary group (i.e., Tablighi Jamaat) (Ch. 15).

Corporate social responsibility   the notion that organizations, particularly (but not only) corporations, have a moral duty to care for the interests of consumers, staff, shareholders, communities, and the environment at large in all parts of their activities (Ch. 9).

Cosmic Justice   the existential *raison d'être* of social justice. This ethos is shared by every person who has the goal of achieving a social balance on a large scale (Ch. 9).

Cosmopolite channels   communication channels that connect potential adopters with sources external to their social system (Ch. 1).

Counterinformation campaign   a campaign that seeks to "get the message out." The purpose is to increase awareness of true facts and develop positive relationships with key constituents (Ch. 16).

Counternarratives   efforts to directly or indirectly confront violent extremist messages (Ch. 16).

Counterradicalization   community-based programs aimed at preventing participation in extreme violence and approaches that challenge radical beliefs and feelings for those who have not yet committed violence (Ch. 16).

Counterradicalization campaign   a campaign that provides an alternative picture of what life would be after renouncing extreme violence (Ch. 16).

COVID-19   a contagious disease produced by a severe and acute form of the respiratory syndrome coronavirus 2 (SARS-CoV-2) (Ch. 7).

Credibility   the attitude towards a source of communication held at a given time by a receiver (Ch. 13).

Crisis communication   a discipline that deals with the public relations side of communication and attempts to strategically manage and frame audience perceptions of a crisis—i.e., to make sure that harm is alleviated for both the state and those who are impacted (Ch. 7).

Critical consciousness   see **Conscientization** (Ch. 9).

Critical health literacy   a type of literacy that consists of high-quality cognitive and social skills that we can employ to wield more control over our lives (Ch. 6).

Critical mass   the moment in the diffusion process at which the increase in new adopters is magnified by communication within the aforementioned social system (Ch. 1).

Critical questioning   a technique of coaching and "problematization" used by social theorists to expose the dominant social narratives that uphold oppression (Ch. 9).

Critical race feminism   an academic approach that provides an in-depth examination of the legal status and rights of women of color across the world (Ch. 10).

Critical race theory   a theoretical framework for understanding systemic racism. Its precepts shine a light on the immersion of racism within US society and the mechanisms through which presumably race-neutral establishments, systems, policies, and practices uphold White supremacism (Ch. 12).

Critical social analysis   an academic discipline that identifies both manifest and hidden social inequalities and that constructs a framework for explaining the unfair exercise of sociopolitical power that engenders them (Ch. 9).

Critical social justice   a theoretical framework that approaches the phenomenon of social justice by describing inequality as deeply entrenched within the fabric of society (Ch. 12).

Cross-cultural trainers   trainers who teach organizational members how to identify and honor other cultural norms, and to maximize the efficiency of their interactions with those of different domestic and international backgrounds (Ch. 6).

Crowd manipulation   the deliberate use of techniques based on the tenets of crowd psychology (Ch. 3).

Cuckservatives   conservatives accused of having been disloyal to conservativism by cowardly embracing hegemonic liberal philosophies like equality and multiculturalism (Ch. 14).

Cultural awareness   the intentional and cognitive process by which we come to appreciate and become receptive to the values, lifestyles, practices, and problem-solving approaches of people from other cultures (Ch. 6).

Cultural barriers   visible and/or invisible differences that separate cultures, regions, traditions, habits, understandings, interpretations, and opinions (Ch. 6).

Cultural blueprint   a concept explaining how culture creates a blueprint that shapes the way we think, feel, and behave in our environment (Ch. 6).

Cultural capital   the type of education, general knowledge produced by the culture, communication skills, identity, dress, and the kinds of groups (Ch. 6).

Cultural competency   the ability of people to understand and cope with cultural phenomena, like language, beliefs, and traditions, in a manner that does not interfere with the exchange or communication with such cultural phenomena (Ch. 6).

Cultural determinism   the belief that our culture shapes who we have become from an emotional and behavioral perspective (Ch. 6).

Cultural diversity   the manifold cultural dimensions within the target audience. Examples are power distance, collectivism vs. individualism, femininity vs. masculinity, uncertainty avoidance, long-term vs. short-term orientation (Ch. 2).

Cultural domain of power   social institutions and practices that generate hegemonic ideas for preserving social inequalities or counterhegemonic ideas to denounce inequitable social relations (Ch. 12).

Cultural fundamentalism   a vehement adherence to a particular set of beliefs, even when these beliefs defy logic or are seen as extremely unpopular by other countries (Ch. 6).

Cultural hijacking   the practice whereby the symbols and discourse of civil rights advocates are reframed to further far-right narratives (Ch. 14).

Cultural knowledge   the practice of actively searching for information about other cultural and ethnic groups (Ch. 6).

Cultural immersion   a process whereby the ethnographer may live within the culture for a few years (Ch. 6).

Cultural literacy   the ability to comprehend and participate confidently in a given culture (Ch. 6).

Cultural norms   the system of values, beliefs, practices, and the like of a target audience (Ch. 6).

Cultural patterning   the observation of cultural patterns involving both physical and nonphysical symbols (Ch. 6).

Cultural politics   the way that culture—including citizens' attitudes, opinions, beliefs, and perspectives, as represented in civic life, the media, and the arts—shapes society and political opinion, and forms the basis of social, economic, and legal realities (Ch. 9).

Cultural skill   the skill and talent to perceive values, beliefs, and customs in interpersonal encounters and knowing how to interpret cultural or group variations in clinical statistics and program data (Ch. 6).

Culture   a historically transmitted pattern of meanings embodied in symbols by means of which men communicate, perpetuate, and develop their knowledge about and attitudes towards life (Ch. 6).

Culturespeak   a term denoting the myriad of ways in which human beings talk about culture (Ch. 6).

DanceSafe   a not-for-profit organization in the United States of which the mission is to support health and safety at raves and nightclubs (Ch. 5).

Dasein   a German word for existence ("being there"). It is a being made up by its temporality; it clarifies and construes the meaning of being at a particular time (Ch. 8).

Decentralized networks   networks with the most efficiency because they not only consist of numerous direct communication lines among nodes; they also manage to balance the need to operate cooperatively and the need to maintain trust and secrecy within collaborative undertakings (Ch. 1).

Deep State   a form of governance that consists of secret and illicit networks of power that act separately from a state's political leadership. They have an agenda and objectives of their own (Ch. 14).

Deficiency needs   fundamental human needs that must be fulfilled before higher-order needs can be satisfied (Ch. 2).

Demographic diversity   the age, gender/sex, race, country or region of origin, socioeconomic status, education, occupation, religion, or language of an audience (Ch. 2).

Denizen   citizen (Ch. 14).

Denotative meanings   the direct and more objective uses of a symbol, like a flag that represents a nation, institution, university, sports team, and so on (Ch. 6).

Deradicalization   the process of modifying an individual's belief system so that he or she can combat his or her own radical ideology and, in due course, adopt mainstream values (Ch. 16).

Descriptive beliefs   perceptions or hypotheses about the environment in which we live and that are anchored in our heads (Ch. 2).

Descriptive social norms   norms that influence perceptions of the behaviors performed by individuals with whom one has affinities. They are efficient because they "describe" the desired behavior (Ch. 1).

Desensitization   a cognitive process that happens when lengthy exposure to violent messages can have a deadening or suppressing effect on the audience's compassion towards other groups, thereby creating insensitivity or the lack of desire to feel sorry for enemies (Ch. 13).

Dialogic communication   a form of two-way communication where audience members share their opinions or provide feedback to campaign communicators (Ch. 2).

Diffusion of Innovations   a theory that describes how innovations (i.e., ideas, movements, or inventions) are diffused via selected channels over time across communities and cultures (Ch. 1).

Digital divide   the gap in access to communication technologies or training in how to use them (Ch. 6).

Digital games   games played with the assistance of digital devices like computers and phones (Ch. 8).

Digital storytelling   a communication technique whereby a person appears in a video or a social media platform to diffuse a message (Ch. 8).

Digitization   a combined growth of social media and internet use (Ch. 7).

Disciplinary domain of power   agency and actions assumed by citizens to apply rules, regulations, and public policies daily to sustain social hierarchy or resist it (Ch. 12).

Distinctiveness   in public communication, it is the ability to raise the audience's level of attention (Ch. 4).

Distorted assimilation   the selective acceptance of message content (or rejection of it) and prejudiced application of such content in ensuing message processing (Ch. 3).

Diversification   the use of a wider and more diverse spectrum of frames within a movement—one that can include both rigid and flexible frames (Ch. 11).

Diversity in School   a campaign that raises consciousness, understanding, and honor of sociocultural differences by offering traditional and online courses on ethnic relations and LGBTQ+ rights for students, teachers, and school administrators in the Brazilian public school system (Ch. 11).

Diversity training   a type of training with the aim of making diversity a rationale for personal growth and allowing people from various backgrounds to effectively collaborate and make a significant contribution to the mission of the organization (Ch. 6).

Domestic violence   a comprehensive term that includes various forms of abuse perpetrated by a current or ex-partner (Ch. 10).

Downstream social marketing   a social marketing approach that functions at the micro level to influence and change an individual or small group (Ch. 1).

Dramatic social change   a situation in which a rapid event evolves into a deep societal transformation and provokes a breakdown in the stability of the socionormative structures and also jeopardizes the cultural identity of certain groups (Ch. 9).

Duality of structure   a theoretical concept according to which structures consist of both the means and the products of the practices which make up social systems (Ch. 6).

Dyad   two best friends (Ch. 1).

E-blasts   mass emails sent out to a targeted list of addressees (Ch. 2).

Ecological responsibility   the philosophy that organizations devoted to environmentally responsible causes have higher accountability for the ecological footprint that they carry on their environment, its citizens, and the organizations' own stakeholders (Ch. 9).

Effect evaluation   evaluation that considers the actual outcome of a campaign (Ch. 2).

Ego   self-concept or the view that one has of one's self (Ch. 3).

eHealth   the use of available or remote communication technologies in the healthcare environment and the application of highly developed information and communication technologies to fulfill the needs of citizens, patients, healthcare providers, and practitioners (Ch. 6).

E-inclusion   a philosophical movement to bring to an end to the digital divide, given that the world is somewhat divided into groups that do and groups that do not have access to—or the capability of using—modern technological media (Ch. 6).

Elaboration   the level at which the audience scrutinizes a message (Ch. 3).

Elaboration Likelihood Model   a theory based on the premise that people with motivation and ability are more prone to initiating elaborative processing (Ch. 3).

Empathy   a communicator's indirect experience of others' feelings in dialogic communication (Ch. 2).

Empowering orientation   for a nongovernmental organization, it is an attempt to assist disadvantaged or disenfranchised groups in the formulation of a better understanding of the social, political, and economic problems overwhelming them (Ch. 9).

Empowerment   the process of cutting through power differentials in order to lend a higher voice and agency to people generally in positions of lower power (Ch. 16).

Endemic   something that stays in (or within) a population (Ch. 7).

Entertainment–Education   a communication strategy that aspires to ease a social problem or educate the public through a customized type of entertainment (Ch. 8).

Epidemic   a category of disease that emerges as new cases in a human population, during a specific time frame, at a fast-paced rate, and based on recent experience (Ch. 7).

Epidemic of apprehension   an unnecessarily high concern on the part of the general population, thereby chipping away at their sense of well-being (Ch. 3).

Epidemiology   the actual study of pandemics, epidemics, and outbreaks (Ch. 7).

Epistemic injustice   a theoretical concept that explains how the fight against injustice stems from a disenfranchised group's lack of representation in the realm of knowledge (Ch. 10).

Ethical egoism   the idea that people should behave in their own self-interests (Ch. 4).

Ethical investing   an investment strategy to create both financial return and social good (Ch. 9).

Ethics   a branch of philosophy that concerns itself with resolving issues of human morality by addressing concepts such as good and evil, and virtue and vice (Ch. 3).

Ethnic cleansing   a euphemism for genocide (Ch. 13).

Ethnocracy   an ethnic democracy where primacy is placed on protecting one's own people (Ch. 14).

Ethnography   the direct observation, reporting, and description of people's behaviors within a culture. The ethnographer lives within the culture, or goes back there every day (or very frequently), for several months to several years (Ch. 6).

Ethnomedical belief systems   culturally distinct beliefs and knowledge about health and illness (Ch. 6).

Ethnopluralism   a philosophy that sees cultures as equal but distinct and, thus, not reconcilable (Ch. 14).

Ethos   an appeal to credibility (Ch. 3).

Euphemism   a substitution of a good-natured or less unpleasant phrase for one that expresses something distasteful to the audience (Ch. 13).

Evaluation   the passing of judgment about the value and relevance of findings and results within a framework and with respect to objectives set, and it puts these judgments into operation to both reporting and planning of future approaches (Ch. 2).

Exclusionary populism   a philosophy that describes "the people" in a much narrower sense, centering on a specific sociocultural group and disregarding minority groups (Ch. 14).

Executional strategies   assessments about the presentation of the informational content of campaign messages so that they get positively received by the target audience (Ch. 1).

Exemplary victimhood   a type of symbolic representation that appears when a handful of those victims become known figures that embody the entire collective of the dead (Ch. 12).

Exit Norway   a campaign established in 1997 that disseminates peer-to-peer messages and provides assistance to people linked to White supremacism and far-right extremism (Ch. 16).

Exit USA   a campaign established to deter people from joining White supremacist movements and promote defection by offering a "way out" (Ch. 16).

Expectancy   the person's belief that efforts will lead to a desirable performance (Ch. 3).

Expectancy theory   a theory that rests on the predication that individuals' behaviors or actions are guided by their motivations to choose a particular behavior of action over others (Ch. 3).

Expectancy-value equation   a theory positing that attitudes are predicted by beliefs about the probability that a behavior results in consequences, amplified by one's assessment of those consequences (Ch. 1).

Experiential identity   a type of identity that constitutes the characteristics of a person with respect to his or her culture of origin, language, age, and gender, along with life experiences and culture (Ch. 1).

Explanatory uncertainty   a phenomenon whereby we cannot explain why others behave the way they do (Ch. 6).

Extended Parallel Process Model (EPPM)   a theory that explains how people's attitudes can be modified through fear appeals; that is, when fear is exploited as a reason for persuasion (Ch. 4).

External threats   threats that emerge either from impersonal situational circumstances that accidentally form an obstacle to a person's freedom or from social influence attempts aimed at a specific person (Ch. 3).

Extragenetic   an element of culture that is not in our DNA (Ch. 6).

Extrasomatic   an element of culture that is nongenetic and nonbodily (Ch. 6).

Extremely Online   being an active participant in internet culture (Ch. 14).

Extrinsic motivation   motivation guided by the desire to accomplish a task so as to receive some type of reward (Ch. 3; Ch. 8).

Fabian change   progressive and reformist incremental advancement in society according to the method of the Fabian Society (Ch. 9).

Fabian society   a British institution with the mission to promote the golden rules of democratic socialism through gradualist and reformist endeavor in democracies, instead of revolutionary overthrow (Ch. 9).

Faith-based organizations   organizations driven by their faiths and beliefs to make society a better place by, for instance, converting locals into their religions and improving the overall well-being of the underprivileged (Ch. 9).

FARC   a Colombian Marxist–Leninist terrorist organization that has targeted the Colombian government and innocent civilians since the 1960s (Ch. 13).

Fascism   a philosophy that combines extremism, nativism, and exclusionary populism. It promotes a national rebirth and the violent overthrow of the liberal democratic régime (Ch. 14).

Fatalism   the philosophy that health issues are designed or brought about by supernatural forces (Ch. 6).

Fear   an unpleasant emotion that emerges in situations of seeming threat or danger to individuals or their environment (Ch. 4).

Fear appeal   a persuasive message that tries to stimulate fear in order to direct or switch our behavior through the threat of looming danger or harm (Ch. 4).

Fear mongering   using fear to leverage the attitudes of the audience towards an agenda (Ch. 4).

Female genital mutilation   a technique of severing the partial or total external female genitalia for nonmedical aims (Ch. 9).

"Finish It"   a revamped "truth" campaign advocating that youths be the first generation to eliminate the concept of smoking (Ch. 5).

Focal segments   subgroups who benefit more from the campaign because they were targeted based on their at-risk situations or their need of assistance or improvement (Ch. 1).

Framing   a form of social construction of an issue; framing can be done by media outlets, political or social movements, lawmakers, and other players and entities (Ch. 4).

Framing theory   a theory based on the assumption that communicators employ schemas, mental images, or symbolic representations to describe what exists, what happens, and what matters (Ch. 4).

Free & Equal Campaign   an international public awareness campaign led by the United Nations Human Rights Office (Ch. 11).

Full participant observation   blending in a group without revealing one's true identity/ purposes (Ch. 6).

Functional health literacy   a type of literacy that encompasses the fundamental level of reading and writing necessary to function properly in daily life (Ch. 6).

Functional literacy the aptitude and skill to (1) understand the content of reading material or arithmetic questions, (2) communicate and resolve issues by gaining general information, and (3) apply the content to definite circumstances experienced on a daily basis (Ch. 6).

Gaidi Mtaani a propaganda magazine that is accessible online and that motivates Eastern and Central Africans to commit jihadist acts in their own regions by using improvised explosive devices (IEDs) and other weapons that they can get (Ch. 16).

Gain-framed messages messages that highlight the benefits or gains of abiding by messages. They accentuate the advantages of either following or not following a course of action (Ch. 4).

Game a rule-based type of play that involves a challenge to attain an objective and offers feedback on the player's progress towards that objective (Ch. 8).

Game fiction the incorporation of a fictional game universe or story (Ch. 8).

Games for Change digital or hybrid games used as a viable educational and persuasive platform thanks to their entertaining and motivating dispositions (Ch. 8).

Game mechanics a certain level of interaction with the game or the other players participating in the game activity (Ch. 8).

Gamification gaming features available outside games (Ch. 8).

Gaming culture a situation where digital and analog games function as intermediaries for diverse types of relationality (Ch. 8).

Gender a construct that refers to how women, men, and nonbinary people conduct themselves based on feminine, masculine, or fluid features of men and women (Ch. 11).

Gender expression an individual's behavioral signs towards masculine, feminine, or other variant clothing, appearance, voice, and body properties (Ch. 11).

Gender identity a conception of oneself as male, female, or other gender-related construct. We can change gender identity in our lives (Ch. 11).

Genderqueer any person who resists the idea that each human being falls in one of two fixed categories: male or female (Ch. 11).

Generation Z the age bracket that includes people born between the mid- to late 1990s and the early 2010s (Ch. 9).

Genocide an organized practice of exterminating a group, or a certain percentage of people from that group, within a specific time frame. The victim group is considered to have different ethnic, racial, or otherwise organic attributes (Ch. 13).

GLAAD an organization that stands for Gay and Lesbian Alliance Against Defamation. It is an advocacy group that specializes in disseminating accurate media depictions of the LGBTQ+ community—whom GLAAD used to call "queer" community—and monitoring the media establishment (Ch. 11).

Global divide the gap that falls along what has been called the north–south divide (between northern wealthier countries or regions and southern poorer ones) (Ch. 6).

Global media effect a situation in which no single actor will have total control over the effects of other individuals or actions (Ch. 1).

Glocalization strategies of adaptation used by organizations when venturing in foreign cultures (Ch. 6).

Goals broad targets (Ch. 2).

Goal setting the desired outcome. It helps enhance self-regulation, which has an effect on self-efficacy (Ch. 7).

Google Analytics   a free service that observes, measures, and gives an account of website traffic (Ch. 2).

Governance   "conduct of conduct." It motivates people to govern themselves in a novel manner (Ch. 1).

Grassroots activism   a method that people use when pursuing social change from the ground up; it is the most basic level of activity that galvanizes the huddled masses to make decisions that favor change (Ch. 9).

Gratifications obtained   gratifications that we actually feel through the use of a specific medium (Ch. 2).

Gratifications sought   usually known as "needs" or "motives," those are gratifications that we expect to gain from a medium before we even have come into contact with it (Ch. 2).

Great Lockdown   the idea that world economies could have faced the worst recession, since the Great Depression, as a result of the lockdowns during the COVID-19 pandemic (Ch. 7).

Green audiences   audiences who base their behavior on environmentally sound conditions and products and who are ready to make more effort or pay more money for bettering the environment (Ch. 9).

Green campaigns   campaigns that comprise all activities responsible for creating and facilitating any exchanges meant to fulfill individual and social needs—in order to make the satisfaction of these needs occur—with the lowest adverse impact possible on the natural environment (Ch. 9).

Grounding   a mutual orientation of interactants to find common ground (Ch. 2).

Group polarization   the proclivity of a group of individuals to make decisions on the basis of what they believe or see other people doing (Ch. 14).

Groupthink   a phenomenon whereby group members make decisions that are more extreme than their individual inclinations, generally due to the desire to belong and adapt to group norm (Ch. 14).

Growth needs   higher-order human needs which can be gratified only after deficiency needs have been satisfied (Ch. 2).

Guerrilla "on-the-street" marketing   an advertisement approach in which a corporation relies on surprise and/or *avant-garde* interactions to promote a product, brand, or service (Ch. 5).

Habitus   the notion that human beings live in a social sphere (Ch. 6).

Hadiths   records of the deeds or sayings of the Prophet Muhammad (Ch. 16).

Hard power   the practice of forcing them to do something. "Hard power" approaches include military intervention, coercive diplomacy, and economic sanctions (Ch. 16).

Harm reduction   an approach to public health intended to be a progressive substitute for the ban of particular hazardous dangerous lifestyles (Ch. 5).

Hashtag activism   a phrase that sprung up from several media outlets to denote the use of Twitter's hashtags for online activism (Ch. 10).

Health   the absence of disease (Ch. 5).

Health Belief Model   a theory positing that two main factors increase the likelihood that people embrace a proposed health-protective behavior change. First, people must fear that an illness or grave health consequences could afflict them. Second, they must believe that the benefits of following the proposed action prevail over the perceived hurdles to (and/or costs of) adhering to the preventive action (Ch. 5).

Health communication   the discipline and application of communication strategies to inform and sway personal and community decisions that improve health (Ch. 5).

Health communication campaigns   approaches designed to convince or encourage audiences to modify their behavior so as to improve their health (Ch. 5).

Health literacy   the extent to which people have the ability to acquire, process, and grasp basic health information and services required to make proper health decisions (Ch. 6).

Hegemony   the practice of a group to exert unreasonable dominance and power over other groups (Ch. 14).

Herd behavior   a situation in which people follow the herd and abandon their sense of autonomy (Ch. 14).

Herd immunity   the indirect protection that occurs for people whose immunity may be compromised and who cannot be vaccinated because a slight dose of it would harm them (Ch. 7).

Heroes   the real or imaginary individuals used as role models within a culture (Ch. 2).

Herstory   Alicia Garza's campaign that seeks to expand the discourse of social justice and racial equity by including Black lives and accentuating BLM's vehement commitment to intersectionality (Ch. 12).

Heuristics   any methods of problem-solving that may not be ideal or rational, but that are nevertheless adequate enough for reaching instant, short-term objectives or approximations (Ch. 3).

High-sensation seekers   people who express a longing for freshness and stimulation, a personality feature that increase their chances of engaging in risky health behaviors like cannabis use (Ch. 4).

Hindutva   sometimes referred to as the Hindu right or Hindu nationalism, Hindutva (which means "Hinduness" in English) is the most prevalent form of Hindu nationalism in India (Ch. 15).

Holocaust   the genocide of Jews during World War II in Europe. Six million Jews were annihilated by the Nazis in a manner that is hard to imagine except in the minds of the perpetrators (Ch. 15).

Holocaust denial   the act of denying, minimizing, or ignoring the Holocaust (Ch. 15).

Holocaust parallelism   reparations claims for other groups' historical persecutions that derive their moral authority and approaches from official decisions made in support of Holocaust victims (Ch. 15).

Homophobia   the expression of biased attitude and action against nonheterosexual orientation (Ch. 11).

Honor killing   the killing of a family member because the executor thinks that (1) the victim caused shame to the family and/or (2) the victim dishonored the moral values of a community or religion (Ch. 9).

Host desecration   the myth that, in the Middle Ages, Jews stole hallowed or sacred hosts (i.e., communion wafers or sacramental bread) and desecrated them to reconstruct the crucifixion of Jesus by piercing or setting the host on fire (Ch. 15).

Hubs   the key nodes in a network (Ch. 1).

Human Needs Theory   theory positing that people turn to violence when their fundamental human needs are insufficiently met, totally denied, or taken away from them (Ch. 2).

Human rights   moral codes or norms for fundamental principles of human behavior and are expected to be protected in domestic and international law (Ch. 9).

Identities for critique   symbolic representations that stress the importance of difference (Ch. 11).

Identities for education   symbolic representations that insist on similarity with the dominant society and on heteronormativity (Ch. 11).

Identification   an emotional and cognitive process whereby members of the audience assume the roles of characters in a storyline (Ch. 8).

Identity   a construct whereby people negotiate their own (and others') category memberships across a multiplicity of situations, via rhetorical and other social practices (Ch. 14).

Identity politics   a political approach by which people of a particular race, gender, religion, social status, or other category develop political agendas based on core characteristics of such categories (Ch. 12).

Ideology   a one-sided perspective or worldview limited by preconceived notions of the world, mental representations, convictions, attitudes, and evaluations (Ch. 14).

I–It relationship   type of dialogue/relationship of divisiveness and detachment (Ch. 2).

Illocutionary acts   acts designed to say something—which implies doing something as well (Ch. 13).

Imagined communities   real or imagined relationships grounded in the "politics of identification" (Ch. 8).

Imams   worship leaders in mosques (Ch. 16).

Impact knowledge   general information about a topic with the inclusion of facts and figures (Ch. 1).

Implicit bias   an unconscious attribution of negative qualities or characteristics to all members of particular groups—i.e., usually members of long-established disenfranchised groups (Ch. 12).

Incidence rate   the percentage of new cases in a human population during a given time frame (Ch. 7).

Inclusionary populism   a philosophy that makes requests that physical benefits and political rights be granted to historically disenfranchised groups (Ch. 14).

Incremental social change   a situation in which a slow event evolves into an incremental but deep societal transformation, which gradually reshapes the social and/or normative apparatus (Ch. 9).

Indicated prevention   prevention that targets people who already show signs of a problem (Ch. 1).

Indirect terrorism   organized and structural violence aimed at a specific group; it is inconspicuous, quasi-invisible, government-backed terrorism (Ch. 16).

Individual behavior-change campaigns   campaigns that attempt to change individual behaviors that create problems in society or promote behaviors that better individual or social well-being (Ch. 1).

Individual diversity   the belief systems, values, self-drives, attitudes, knowledge, expectations, and needs of an audience (Ch. 2).

Indoctrination   the operation of inculcating ideas, attitudes, beliefs, or cognitive approaches within the mind of a person (Ch. 13).

Inertia   a tendency not to change our attitudes, behaviors, or beliefs (Ch. 3).

Infibulation a technique that requires the surgical removal of the clitoris and labia of a female and sowing together the contours of the vulva to guarantee that no sexual intercourse occurs (Ch. 9).

Infodemic a process that occurs when blatantly erroneous or misleading information is diffused in both online social media and physical environments during an epidemic, pandemic, or outbreak (Ch. 7).

Infodemic management an approach that seeks to methodically use risk communication, risk-based assessments, and evidence-based approaches to manage the infodemic and decrease its effects on health attitudes during crises and emergencies (Ch. 7).

Information density the ability of a medium to bear the information load and distribute the same successfully (Ch. 5).

Information hubs online media like popular websites (Ch. 1).

In-group norms norms used when people come together in groups to cultivate a notion of what they share in common and the characteristics that differentiate them from other groups (Ch. 1).

Injunctive social norms norms that influence perceptions of what behaviors should be approved or disapproved by an individual's in-group (Ch. 1).

Innovation the idea, movement, or invention regarded as new by a person or unit of adoption (Ch. 1).

Inoculation theory a theory postulating that persuasive arguments can inoculate (immunize) the audience to the influence of messages (Ch. 4).

Institutionalization a process whereby our knowledge and perception of reality become ingrained in the social fabric of our culture (Ch. 6).

Institutional racism see **Systemic racism** (Ch. 12).

Institutional theory a theory suggesting that the survival of an organization depends not only on physical resources and technical knowledge, but also on the organization's legitimacy in the eyes of the public (Ch. 13).

Instrumentality the belief that we will get a reward if we perform as anticipated (Ch. 3).

Intellectual property the practice that enables the originator or owner of an invention (material or immaterial) or original work to make use of, reproduce, and distribute it (Ch. 2).

Interdisciplinary approaches approaches where individual disciplines collaborate to produce input, but participants remain within their respective disciplinary boundaries (Ch. 1).

Internal threats self-inflicted threats that come from choosing particular alternatives and discarding others (Ch. 3).

Interpersonal domain of power the manifold experiences that citizens live within outright distressing interactions with people of authority (Ch. 12).

Interpretivists researchers who stress the role of interpretation and context (Ch. 2).

Intersectionality an analytic frame of reference that seeks to identify how interlocking mechanisms of power affect communities who are most disenfranchised in society (Ch. 12).

Intertextuality the practice of taking separate texts in order to find shared meanings. Intertextuality entails a relationship between juxtaposed texts (Ch. 15).

Intimate partner violence mistreatment or assault that takes place in close relationships (Ch. 10).

Intimate publicity a theoretical concept that traces how various audiences unite around common affective intensities and do so intimately (Ch. 10).

Intrinsic motivation   motivation guided by an internal desire to perform a task (Ch. 3; Ch. 8).

Inverted pyramid   a method whereby "who, what, when, where, and why" questions are the pillars of any serious enterprise and the launchpad for any meaningful campaign (Ch. 2).

Invitational rhetoric   a type of rhetoric whereby the situation fosters an invitation to understanding as a means to create a relationship rooted in equality, immanent value, and self-determination (Ch. 2).

Iron Curtain   a political barrier dividing Europe between the Western and Eastern areas (Ch. 11).

Irrational fear   fear based on a nonexistent threat or reality (Ch. 4).

Islamic State of Iraq and Syria (ISIS)   a global jihadist network that rose to infamy in 2014 when it launched a campaign solely focused on publicizing barbarous executions (Ch. 16).

Islamophobia   the stereotypical oversimplification of Islam and/or Muslims that can lead to the discrimination or harassment of Muslims (Ch. 15).

I–Thou relationship   a type of dialogue/relationship in which communicators have the orientation of mutuality, considering other parties as being part of a grand unity (Ch. 2).

"It's Okay to Be White"   a campaign initiated by the website 4chan, more specifically its forum /pol/, in 2017 (Ch. 14).

Jewish deicide   the wrongful attribution of responsibility for the death of Jesus to the Jewish people as a collective (Ch. 15).

Jihad   holy war against the Infidels (i.e., non-Muslims) and Apostates (i.e., Muslim "traitors") (Ch. 16).

Kaiser Family Foundation   a California-based philanthropic institution that specializes in healthcare issues facing the nation. It operates and supervises its own research and communications projects, ordinarily in alliance with external organizations (Ch. 8).

Knowledge gap   a phenomenon whereby people do not necessarily make decisions on the basis of what they know (Ch. 2).

Knowledge-gap hypothesis   a model that rests on the premise that each new technology widens the gap between the information-rich and information-poor, due to disparities in access to the medium, and regulation over its use, among other reasons (Ch. 6).

Kulturbrille   "cultural glasses;" i.e., entrenched beliefs and attitudes (Ch. 6).

Language intensity   language that includes tropes, strong and vivid language, and emotionally charged phrases (Ch. 13).

Latitude of acceptance   the scope of acceptable positions (Ch. 3).

Latitude of noncommitment   the range of viewpoints that are neither acceptable nor unpleasant (Ch. 3).

Latitude of rejection   the breadth of objectionable positions (Ch. 3).

La Voz de la Resistencia   the most prominent station of the FARC's Bolivarian Radio Network (Ch. 13).

Leaderless resistance   a social resistance approach in which small, autonomous groups of people go up against an established institution (Ch. 14).

Learning processes   processes that assist ethnographers in understanding how a culture conveys practices, content, and symbols that it deems important for next generations (Ch. 6).

Learning through imitation   learning by modeling oneself on others who are regarded as upright and worthy of admiration (Ch. 8).

Learning through interaction   learning inspired by observation of, or connection to, others. It can be made possible through social interaction or social information (e.g., online) (Ch. 8).

Learning through reinforcement   learning both through direct conditioning and replication of others' behaviors (Ch. 8).

Lede   the hook; the first sentence that determines whether the whole text will be read, remembered, and acted upon (Ch. 2).

Lexical ambiguity   a linguistic technique that allows two or more possible meanings (Ch. 13).

LGBTQ+   an acronym that stands for lesbian, gay, bisexual, transgender, queer, and others (Ch. 11).

Life After Hate   an "exit program" organization that supports former White supremacists and far-right terrorists through disengagement and reintegration programs (Ch. 16).

Lifestyle marketing   a type of marketing that involves creating a resemblance or emotional attraction to a certain product or service by associating it with the favorite lifestyles of potential consumers (Ch. 1).

Likeability heuristic   a principle that explains how audiences put more confidence in those whom they like (Ch. 8).

Liking   positive appraisals of a character (Ch. 8).

Localite channels   communication channels that connect potential adopters with sources inside their social system (Ch. 1).

Locutionary acts   the referential attributes of utterances; each declaration has to be meaningful, grammatically and communicatively, in a speech (Ch. 13).

Logos   an appeal to facts (Ch. 3).

Loss-framed messages   messages that emphasize the risks or costs of not following messages. They draw attention to the disadvantages of either following or not following a course of action (Ch. 4).

Low external locus of control   a situation in which people believe outside factors are beyond their influence and control, which deters them from considering the issue or trying to tackle it, notwithstanding powerful or factual campaign messages (Ch. 3).

Manosphere   a network of groups and websites that espouse male supremacy and subjugation of women (Ch. 14).

Manufacturing consent   a concept describing how the mass media are effective and powerful ideological institutions that carry out a system-supportive propaganda function (Ch. 7).

Marginal literacy   a level of literacy that allows people to understand the content of plain reading material for solving problems experienced daily, such as completing a form or applying basic arithmetic and quantitative measures (Ch. 6).

Markers   distinct identifiable components of messages like new words, phrases, or behaviors that ideally mimic new realities to disrupt the oppressive power structures within cultures (Ch. 8).

Marquetalia Republic   a term used to informally refer to one of the territories in rural Colombia which Communist peasant militants controlled in the wake of *La Violencia* (1948–58) (Ch. 13).

Mass communication   a process that diffuses information from a major source via consolidated media, like TV, newspapers, and radio (Ch. 1).

Mattering map   the person's appreciation or willingness to invest in a certain cultural text (Ch. 8).

Media   the vehicles of communication, as TV, radio, newspapers, etc., that influence or get a message to audiences widely (Ch. 2).

Media advocacy   the planned use of mass media in conjunction with community organizing to promote public policies (Ch. 2).

Media ecology theory   a theory that describes how media, technology, and communication impact the human environment (Ch. 2).

Media kit   a broad-based news release that includes backgrounders, leaflets, photo shoots, fact sheets, and any other germane information on a subject (Ch. 2).

Media system dependency theory   a theory positing that the more we rely on the media to fulfill our needs, the more important the media becomes in our lives, and therefore the more impactful the media will be on us (Ch. 13).

Mediated campaigns   campaigns that include at least one category of media to diffuse messages (Ch. 1).

Meme   unit of cultural transmission (Ch. 2).

Men Going Their Own Way   a supremacist manosphere-based group that has launched a campaign based on principles from the Men's Liberation Movement (Ch. 14).

Mental health issue   a behavioral or mental pattern that provokes considerable distress or harm of personal functioning (Ch. 8).

Message   a statement of a certain scope that tends to contain only one central idea and relates to the objectives stipulated by a specific communication intervention (Ch. 1).

Messaging   a practice of sending messages through community-based or interpersonal channels (Ch. 1).

MeToo   a social movement that exposes sexual harassment and sexual violence after victims make allegations of sexual misconduct public (Ch. 10).

Microaggressions   subtle, indirect, or unintentional discriminatory or derogatory actions towards marginalized groups. They can be verbal or behavioral, are usually brief and commonplace, and occur on a frequent basis (Ch. 12).

Midstream social marketing   a social marketing approach that targets social groups, opinion leaders, business owners, or municipal employees for causing change of individual behaviors and attitudes within their own communities (Ch. 1).

Millennials   those generally born between 1981 and 1996 (Ch. 9).

Monologic communication   a form of communication that tries to command, compel, manipulate, defeat, confuse, misinform, or exploit (Ch. 2).

Motivation   a phenomenon whereby choices are governed by various forms of voluntary activities (Ch. 3).

Mullahs   Muslims who are well-versed in Islamic theology and sacred law (Ch. 16).

Multidisciplinary approaches   approaches that integrate involvement from disciplines independently. The result may be an array of nonintegrated interventions, which could clash with each other (Ch. 1).

Muted group theory   a theory hypothesizing that, within many cultures, the dominant group contributes the most to the language system, while subordinate groups feel obligated to employ the dominant language system to be heard or taken seriously by mainstream society (Ch. 10).

Myth   a morality in story form which has profound explanatory or symbolic power for a culture (Ch. 2).

Narrative   a simple unifying, easily expressed story or explanation that organizes people's experience and provides a framework for understanding events (Ch. 16).

Narrative exchange   the practice of producing and circulating content around a specific narrative (Ch. 1).

Narrative involvement   the degree to which audiences follow events as they develop in a story (Ch. 8).

National Reconciliation Week   a campaign that promotes respectful relationships with Aboriginal Australians and Torres Strait Islanders (Ch. 16).

Natural rights   the prepolitical rights that we have when official political authority is lacking; that is, it is natural for us to benefit from such rights (Ch. 9).

Need   a state in which a person, animal, or object must do or have something (Ch. 2).

Neo-Marxism   a school of thought that seeks to identify and tackle sociocultural and political problems within modern society (Ch. 12).

Neopronouns   words created to replace long-established pronouns like "he" or "she" that serve as pronouns without showing any sign of gender (Ch. 11).

Networked communication   a process that sends information from a wide array of sources, including nontraditional ones (e.g., average citizens on the street) and, as such, reflects many different views (Ch. 1).

Networked framing   influencing the process of online conversations (Ch. 2).

Network effect   an effect that develops when individuals are more willing to use a particular medium of communication if other people have done it successfully (Ch. 1).

New Left   a broad spectrum of left-wing intellectual currents that advocates for social justice issues like civil rights, political rights, legal reform, feminism, gay and lesbian rights, abortion rights, gender emancipation, and pro-drug attitudes (Ch. 12).

New public health   a branch of health studies that focuses on the manners by which lifestyles and living conditions establish health status (Ch. 5).

Nodes   people in a network (Ch. 1).

Nonbinary   the phenomenon whereby a person resists the idea that each human being falls in one of two fixed categories—male or female (Ch. 11).

Nonconsequentialism   a worldview according to which the end never justifies the means (Ch. 4).

Nongovernmental organizations   nonprofit, self-governing local, domestic, or international groups—which could nevertheless be funded by governments—that charge themselves with solving charitable, philanthropic, human rights, social, educational, healthcare, public policy, environmental, or other issues, usually to create long-lasting changes in accordance with their objectives (Ch. 9).

Normative knowledge   knowledge that focuses on the norms of audiences, at a larger level (Ch. 1).

Numeracy skills   the skills that we possess to apply arithmetic techniques and the way we use numerical information in printed materials; it is also called quantitative literacy (Ch. 6).

Nutgraf   a paragraph after a lede that explains why the issue is worthwhile. It is informative (Ch. 2).

Objectives   unlike goals, objectives are more specific and open to actual assessment (Ch. 2).

Objective victimhood   an indexical symbolization of the dead during a campaign against police brutality (Ch. 12).

Occasion   the purpose and setting of a public communication campaign (Ch. 2).

Opinion leadership   the practice of using influential individuals to change people's beliefs, attitudes, or behaviors in a desired manner with relative frequency (Ch. 1).

Opportunism   taking advantage of an event to get something out of it (Ch. 8).

Oppression Olympics   the aspiration to have one identity (not necessarily our own) or one type of subordination seen as more important or essential than others (Ch. 12).

Optimism bias   a type of bias that occurs when communicators give the impression of being too optimistic about a certain subject (Ch. 3).

Oral culture   a genre of human communication in which knowledge, talent, thoughts, and cultural material are imparted, maintained, and transmitted orally from one generation to the next (Ch. 6).

Orbán, Viktor   the leader of the center–right Fidesz party, which won Hungary's parliamentary elections by a wide margin in 2010 (Ch. 15).

Organizational legitimacy   consistency between systemic norms and social values related to or implied by an organization's activities (Ch. 13).

Othering   a philosophical concept that denotes the practice of producing an "Us vs. Them" dichotomy, thus making efforts to antagonize certain "others" from one's in-group and, in broader terms, the entirety of the society (Ch. 15).

Outbreak   a swift increase in occurrences of a disease within a small, localized group of individuals or agents infected with a virus or illness (Ch. 7).

Outcome evaluation   a type of evaluation that seeks to determine whether a campaign created its desired impact (Ch. 2).

Outcome expectancy   the beliefs associated with a particular behavior, which leads to a definite outcome (Ch. 7).

Pandemic   a global epidemic that can affect all (*pan*) people (*demos*) on the globe or, at least, across large regions (Ch. 7).

Parasocial interaction   the relationship between a viewer and a media figure, which reaches such a point that a pseudorelationship develops (Ch. 8).

Participant observation   the process by which an ethnographer builds and upholds many-sided and comparatively long-term relationships with individuals in their environment in order to provide a cultural interpretation of that association (Ch. 6).

Participatory orientation   for a nongovernmental organization, it is a set of initiatives involving local people in the execution of a project by donating money, appliances, land, materials, and labor (Ch. 9).

Passive empathy   a type of empathy that allows perpetrators, and even victims, to display sentiments of common ground, understanding, as well as fear and remorse, instead of making the effort of being self-reflexive (Ch. 10).

Pathos   an appeal made to people's emotions (Ch. 3).

Patois   the English-lexicon Creole that remains the colloquial dialect in Jamaica (Ch. 6).

Peer cluster a small clique of friends with similar values, beliefs, attitudes, and behaviors (Ch. 1).

Peer cohort people who are in the same age group (Ch. 1).

Peer group group of people who share similarities with each other (Ch. 1).

People for the Ethical Treatment of Animals (PETA) an American animal rights organization that has laid out four principal issues: resistance to factory farming, fur farming, animal testing, and the exploitation of animals in entertainment (Ch. 4).

Perceived control a situation that increases a person's assessment of the controllability of a situation to bring out the necessary coping strategy (Ch. 2).

Perceived message sensation value the degree to which people view a message as possessing high-sensation-value traits (Ch. 4).

Perceived norms norms used at the individual level (Ch. 1).

Perceptions of effectiveness perceptions that pertain to evaluations of the usefulness of actions (Ch. 2).

Perceptions of self-efficacy perceptions that have to do with confidence in one's own capacity to realize a behavior outcome; these perceptions are good at predicting behavior (Ch. 2).

Perceptual defense the propensity for people to shield themselves from ideas, objects, or circumstances that are threatening (Ch. 4).

Perceived similarity the degree to which a person perceives that he or she shares things in common with a character (Ch. 8).

Peripheral beliefs the least important beliefs and the most likely to change (Ch. 2).

Peripheral route processing the influence of a message from factors external to the quality of the message (Ch. 3).

Perlocutionary acts acts that materialize by saying something and that bring about certain outcomes (Ch. 13).

Persuasion an attempt to manipulate a person's beliefs, attitudes, objectives, or behaviors (Ch. 3).

Persuasive games video games that open new avenues for persuasion through their representational method of procedurality (Ch. 8).

Phobia an exaggerated or illogical fear of a specific object, class of objects, concept, or event (Ch. 15).

Planned diffusion active interventions that seek to change behavior by disseminating programs to targeted populations (Ch. 1).

Pluralism a philosophy that considers society as a large entity made up of multiple communities whose dissimilar interests must be bridged through a process of bargaining (Ch. 15).

Pluralistic ignorance a situation in which individuals continue to believe that their peers' behaviors are different from their own (when, in reality, it is not the case) (Ch. 1).

Pogroms organized massacres of a targeted religious group (Ch. 15).

Political demonology the inflation, stigmatization, and dehumanization of political foes (Ch. 9).

"Politically Incorrect" (/pol/) a social media platform introduced in 2011 as a sphere for repugnant views that, by that year, had begun to monopolize most of the boards on 4chan (Ch. 14).

Political radicalism   the aspiration to reshape or replace the fundamental principles of a culture or political system (Ch. 9).

Political self-efficacy   an approach that helps individuals develop a sense of confidence to take steps to improve their plight (Ch. 9).

Polity   a gathering of citizens who took part in the political process in many Greek city-states (Ch. 1).

Populism   a philosophy that considers society as distributed between two homogeneous and incompatible groups: "the pure people" and "the corrupt élite" (Ch. 15).

Positivists   researchers who champion quantitative methods where randomized, controlled trials are viewed as the "gold standard" (Ch. 2).

Postmodernism   a comprehensive theoretical paradigm that denounces knowledge claims and value systems as socially conditioned and historically steeped, conceptualizing them as the fruits of political, historical, and sociocultural discourses and structures (Ch. 12).

Power   the ability to influence others to obtain the outcomes desired (Ch. 16).

Power play   a diplomatic or political maneuver in which power is displayed (Ch. 16).

Precontemplation   the stage during which we do not intend to change behavior in the immediate future (Ch. 3).

Preproduction research   a type of research where information on audience characteristics, the behavior in question, and message channels are acquired (Ch. 2).

Prescriptive beliefs   "ought"/"should" principles reflecting interpretations of preferred end-states (Ch. 2).

Press release   a brief news item that broadcasts events to newspapers, magazines, or social media outlets (Ch. 2).

Prevention, Rehabilitation, and After Care (PRAC)   a wide-ranging and well-funded Saudi campaign that revolved around counterradicalization, rehabilitation, and disengagement programs for people who were misled by Marxist–Leninist demagogues who want to promote jihadism (Ch. 16).

Priming   a phenomenon whereby exposure to one stimulus inspires a reaction to another stimulus later, without intention or deliberate guidance (Ch. 3).

Print literacy   the capacity of understanding and handling written content, including text (prose literacy), and of identifying and using information in documents (Ch. 6).

Procedurality   rule-founded representations and interactions (Ch. 8).

Procedural knowledge   knowledge that occurs when campaigns want to prompt action (Ch. 1).

Procedural rhetoric   a form of rhetoric that originates in the essential affordances of computers: running processes and operating rule-based symbolic manipulation (Ch. 8).

Process evaluation   a type of evaluation that seeks to regulate and gather data on fidelity and execution of campaign activities (Ch. 2).

Process research   a technique that evaluates the campaign as it develops to guarantee that the messages get across the target audience through the media (Ch. 2).

Production testing   a type of pretesting where initial messages are tested with target populations in order to obtain their perceptions regarding the suitability and persuasive effects of those messages (Ch. 2).

Propaganda   intentionally deceptive communication. It is public communication directed at a large collective of people and conceived to shape attitudes and behavior in times of crisis (Ch. 13).

Prospect theory   a theory describing how we choose between the likelihood of gains and losses (Ch. 4).

Protocols of the Elders of Zion, The   published in 1903, it was a widespread and seemingly believable Russian fake text against the so-called Zionists (Ch. 15).

Proud Boys   a White supremacist and neo-Fascist group of men that encourages and enacts political violence in North America (Ch. 14).

Provocation   the process of inciting people (not) to take actions on the basis of powerfully elicited emotions, such as anger, shock, and disgust, as a result of certain types of norm transgressions (Ch. 4).

Psychological reactance theory   a theory predicating that people become defensive when they feel that they are manipulated; they want to make decisions independently from others (Ch. 3).

Public   a particular body or aggregation of people. It could also be the overall entity of humankind (Ch. 1).

Public communication   the discipline that relates to the production and management of messages in public settings. It is the practice of delivering a message from which audiences can learn (Ch. 1).

Public communication campaign   a set of coordinated messages or communicative efforts to accomplish predetermined goals and objectives: to sway people's beliefs, attitudes, and behaviors (Ch. 1).

Public connection   when individuals' shared orientation to a public world where matters of shared concern are addressed (Ch. 2).

Public health   a branch of health studies that pertains to population health, sanitation, epidemiology, disease prevention (including mental disorders), access to healthcare, and overall well-being (Ch. 5).

Publicist   an expert whose task is to create and manage publicity for a product, public figure (like a celebrity), or a work such as a book or film (Ch. 1).

Publicity   a deliberate attempt at manipulating the public's perception of one's products (Ch. 1).

Publics   particular audiences who are the intended target of a message (a distinction from the general public) (Ch. 1).

Public service announcement   a free, nonpolemical, broadcast communiqué—e.g., to reduce alcohol-related birth defects, pregnant women should abstain from drinking alcohol (Ch. 8).

Public space   a place open to anyone without exclusion, even if this may not necessarily be the case in the real world (Ch. 1).

Public sphere   the aspect of life in which a person interacts with others in society (Ch. 1).

Public will   a manifestation of how the community feels and acts (Ch. 1).

Public will campaigns   campaigns that serve to muster public action for policy action and change (Ch. 1).

Pull social marketing   a promotional strategy that targets audiences by allowing them to pull the product/service/ideas (Ch. 1).

Push social marketing   a promotional technique that vigorously advocate products/services/ideas to audiences through adapted distribution channels (Ch. 1).

QAnon   a US far-right conspiracy theory according to which a dark league of Satan-worshipping, cannibalistic pedophiles was operating an international child sex-trafficking network and planned to knock down President Donald Trump while in office (Ch. 14).

Queer　a construct that entails an opposition to fixed identity categories (Ch. 11).

Queerbaiting　a marketing ploy in which entertainment producers only "hint" at LGBTQ+ romance or representation—rather than giving a genuine depiction of it—in television series (Ch. 11).

Quid pro quo　the uninvited or improper assurance of rewards in exchange for sexual favors (Ch. 10).

Racism　any action, deliberate or unintended, based on race or skin pigmentation that subjugates a group or individual based on their race or skin pigmentation (Ch. 12).

Radical change　deep-rooted change of features and parameters of certain aspects of society, usually in the style of political radicalism (Ch. 9).

Radicalization　a gradual path towards attitude and behavior change through a process of persuasion and socialization into extreme beliefs. These extreme beliefs can translate into violent actions (Ch. 13).

Radical traditionalism　an aspiration to regain the natural order of things and wield domination is termed, by members (Ch. 14).

Radio Machete　the moniker of the Radio Télévision Libre des Mille Collines (RTLM), a radio station established by Hutu extremists in the Rwandan government in 1993, which facilitated the Rwanda Genocide (Ch. 13).

Rape culture　a pervasive ideology that effectively supports or excuses sexual assault (Ch. 10).

Reactance　a disagreeable motivational arousal that appears when we face a threat to or a decrease in our free behaviors (Ch. 3).

Receiver　recipient of that message (Ch. 2).

Recognition　the practice of making an entire nation evolve from earlier hostilities and differences to greater hospitality that acknowledges the value and contributions of all peoples and cultures (Ch. 16).

Redlining　denying people adequate services because they reside in a racially associated area (Ch. 12).

Red pill　a phrase used to describe an awakening to the importance of fighting to maintain such traditional gender roles (Ch. 14).

Reference group　a group with whom members have the most affinities (Ch. 1).

Reference point　a new idea ranked on an attitude scale in a person's mind (Ch. 3).

Reform　action that improves society or the lives of individuals (Ch. 1).

Reframing　a communicative technique like commenting, reposting, or even parodying (Ch. 2).

Refutational preemptions　tactics that aid in the inoculation process by offering arguments and/or evidence to reject arguments included in attitude attacks, and by giving message receivers practice at defending their positions through counterarguing (Ch. 4).

Reimagine Education　a UNICEF campaign designed to transform and modernize learning and skills development for high-quality education for every child (Ch. 6).

Relatedness　a concept that increases the likelihood of intrinsic motivation and helps understand one's willingness of being connected to others (Ch. 8).

Relative weighting　a prioritization tactic that takes both the advantages and the disadvantages of an action into account (Ch. 3).

Reparation campaign　a campaign that seeks to create awareness of past injustices committed against particular groups of people—such as African Americans and Native

Americans in the United States, Africans in the Belgian Congo, and Jews during the Holocaust (Ch. 16).

Repeated exposure   a technique that uses constant repetition of a message; also called argument from repetition, *argumentum ad nauseam*, or *argumentum ad infinitum* (Ch. 3).

Resilience   the process of, capacity for, or outcome of successful adaptation despite challenging or threatening circumstances (Ch. 16).

Respectability politics   the philosophy that oppressed groups can gain support for their cause by following simple standards of decency or etiquette (Ch. 12).

Response efficacy   information regarding the effectiveness of the proposed action (Ch. 4).

Responsive chord   a theory that rests on the premise that the communication process is contingent on information with which people are already familiar (Ch. 4).

Revolutionary change   rampant, radical, and far-reaching change, with inclusion of violence and longing for starting afresh (Ch. 9).

Rhetoric   a process of communicating effectively through language (oral and written) (Ch. 2).

Rhetorical strands   rhetorical dimensions that form among people through public communication (Ch. 1).

Rights-oriented approaches   initiatives concerned with both the quality of lives that animals enjoy and whether they benefit from autonomy and other rights adapted to their capacities and needs (Ch. 4).

Risk assessment   the evaluation of the risk from data to generate a risk probability (Ch. 7).

Risk communication   the exchange of real-time information, suggestions, and educated opinions between experts and audiences experiencing risks to their health or socioeconomic well-being (Ch. 7).

Risk evaluation   the process of producing a measurable perception about the risks that a society faces and what measures can be taken against those risks (Ch. 7).

Risk management   the evaluation of the magnitude of a particular risk and an estimation of how serious the risk is (Ch. 7).

Robber barons   businesspeople who used exploitative maneuvers to get rich in the nineteenth century (Ch. 9).

Rose's Theorem   a model postulating that a large percentage of individuals at small risk may cause more new cases of a disease than a small percentage at high risk (Ch. 7).

Rwanda Genocide   a genocide committed in Rwanda in 1994 that killed between 700,000 and 1,000,000 people (predominantly the minority Tutsi population) (Ch. 13).

Sabido, Miguel   a Mexican writer and producer who took advantage of the insights of Albert Bandura to forge a genre of media that later became known as Entertainment–Education (Ch. 8).

Sabido methodology   a methodology that pushes audiences to embrace desired behaviors by displaying role model characters who are rewarded for enacting those behaviors. The postulation is that viewers pair the TV characters with positive outcomes (Ch. 8).

Sakinah Campaign   a Saudi campaign that employs mullahs and professors to develop online interactions with people searching for religious knowledge. The objective is to lead them away from extremist sources (Ch. 16).

Salience effect   the idea that, when individuals' attention is aimed at one aspect of the environment, they tend to remember and maintain it as central when making subsequent decisions (Ch. 4).

Saliency   the degree of significance of an issue. Without a nutgraf, it can be ignored even if the issue is salient (Ch. 2).

Salt   an angry Leftist reaction on social media or sensational news segments in the mass media (Ch. 14).

Sanctioning processes   processes that explain how certain elements of a culture are both formally and informally sanctioned or prohibited (Ch. 6).

Satyagraha   a form of nonviolent resistance or civil resistance. It became a catalyst for the Indian independence movement to end the British Crown rule in India (achieved in 1947) (Ch. 5).

Say No to Terror   a comprehensive communication campaign composed of a website, traditional media channels, and an online social media presence. The campaign uses a range of tools like short videos and posters to convey a counter-narrative to certain aspects of the terrorist narrative (Ch. 16).

Scapegoating   the practice of victimizing an exclusive person or group for undeserved blame and resultant antagonistic treatment (Ch. 15).

Sea of Hands   a campaign that symbolizes endorsement of land rights, justice, and reconciliation for Aboriginal Australians and Torres Strait Islanders (Ch. 16).

Search Engine Optimization   a method of improving the visibility of one's website in a search engine's "unpaid," "organic," or "earned" results—i.e., as opposed to paid advertising (Ch. 2).

Second party   the immediate receiver of the message (Ch. 2).

Sedentary games   games that include a control scheme enabled by the game controller or keyboard and mouse (e.g., as we see in traditional PC games) (Ch. 8).

Sedition   rebellion against the state (Ch. 10).

Segmented communication   communication that is tailored based on the type of audience (Ch. 1).

Segmented marketing   a type of marketing in which advertisers focus on the lifestyle approach (Ch. 1).

Selective perception theory   a theory positing that people perceive whatever they wish to in mediated messages, at the same time paying no attention to opposing viewpoints (Ch. 4).

Selective prevention   prevention that targets all members of a community who are at risk for a precarious behavior (Ch. 1).

Self-affirmation theory   a theory hypothesizing that people's contemplations of values that are personally dear to them will make them less likely to undergo distress or react in a defensive manner when faced with information that challenges or jeopardizes their self-concept (Ch. 3).

Self-concept   a set of beliefs about oneself. Put simply, it is a cognitive or descriptive part of one's self. It also includes past, present, and future selves (Ch. 3).

Self-determination theory   a theory hypothesizing that people can be driven by intrinsic and/or extrinsic motivation and explains how basic psychological needs are indispensable for well-being (Ch. 8).

Self-efficacy   the belief that we have the skills and aptitudes required to accomplish the behavior under various circumstances (Ch. 4; Ch. 7).

Self-efficacy information   a set of arguments that the person needs to perform the recommended action (Ch. 4).

Self-efficacy theory a theory predicating that all courses of psychological change operate through the modification of the person's expectancies of self-mastery or individual efficacy (Ch. 4).

Self-integrity one's perception of oneself as a good, moral human being, who acts in a manner consistent with cultural and social norms (Ch. 3).

Sender the source of the message (Ch. 2).

Sensation seeking a personality attribute characterized by the search for experiences and feelings that are diverse, new, complex, and intense (Ch. 4).

Sensation seeking targeting (SENTAR) a prevention method in the conception and placement of campaign messages, particularly resulting in a successful lessening in cannabis use among high-sensation seeking teenagers (Ch. 4).

Sensation value the degree to which formal and content audio–visual features of a televised message elicit sensory, affective, and arousal responses (Ch. 4).

Serious fear fear that permeates our psyche when facing immense peril (Ch. 4).

Serious game game that provides an opportunity for investigating the premise that playing games paves the way for a form of learning that is meaningful, perpetual, and transferable to the real world (Ch. 8).

Serious game assisted learning a phenomenon whereby educational components can be mixed with the gameplay, which are subconsciously absorbed by the players during the course of the play (Ch. 8).

Service orientation for a nongovernmental organization, it is a set of activities like providing health, family planning, or education services for which the project is developed by the organization (Ch. 9).

Severity information information about the depth or magnitude of the danger (Ch. 4).

Sexual attractiveness sex appeal; it is a person's ability to magnetize the sexual or erotic interests of others, and it is a driver for sexual selection or mate choice (Ch. 11).

Sexual harassment a category of harassment that contains some form of explicit or implicit sexual overtones, like the uninvited or improper assurance of rewards in exchange for sexual favors (Ch. 10).

Sexual misconduct an overarching term for misconduct of a sexual nature that is based, to some level, on personal power or authority—which renders the occurrence inappropriate or even criminal (Ch. 10).

Sexual orientation a construct that encompasses the four elements of sexual attraction, identity, conduct, and relationships with other people (Ch. 11).

Sharia a body of Islamic laws derived from Allah (Ch. 16).

Shock tactics powerful emotional appeals through both verbal and nonverbal communication (Ch. 4).

Shockvertising a type of advertising that deliberately, rather than inadvertently, startles and offends its audience by violating norms for social values and personal ideals (Ch. 4).

Signaling the practice by advocacy groups to convince audiences to publicly support lawmakers (Ch. 11).

Slacktivism the practice of endorsing a political or social cause through communiqués on social networking sites or online petitions (Ch. 12).

Smart power a strategy that underlines the importance of a strong military, but also devotes much time and energy in forming alliances, partnerships, and foundations of all levels to expand their reach and secure legitimacy of their actions (Ch. 16).

Soap operas   popular entertainment programs that portray real-life circumstances like friendships, love affairs, and family life (Ch. 8).

Social bonding   social relations for people who have similar social identities (Ch. 16).

Social bridging   social relations for people with different social identities, but who have a commonsense of community in other respects (Ch. 16).

Social capital   the social norms, networks of reciprocity and exchange, and relationships of trust that enable people to act collectively (Ch. 1; Ch. 6).

Social change   the process of reshaping the social order of society (Ch. 9).

Social choice theory   a theory that can explain social good by highlighting the procedures by which social good may or may not be achieved in societies (Ch. 1).

Social cognitive theory   a theory that rests on the premise that we are more likely to embrace new behaviors when we observe others performing them (Ch. 7).

Social construct   the way we interpret reality (Ch. 6).

Social construction of reality   a theoretical concept that explains how concepts are created through our interactions in society (Ch. 6).

Social determinants of health   the conditions in the areas where people are born, reside, interact, learn, work, play, worship, and grow old (Ch. 5).

Social distancing   keeping a physical separation by decreasing the number of instances we come into close contact with others (Ch. 7).

Social glue   a concept explaining how what binds us together not only maintains values for future generations to come, but it also constructs what education and learning should be (Ch. 6).

Social good   what is common and beneficial for all or most people within a community, or what is attained through citizenship, collaboration, and active participation in politics and public service (Ch. 1).

Social hygiene movement   a massive-scale campaign in Europe and the United States to control sexually transmitted infections, regulate prostitution and sexual perversity, and diffuse sex education by including scientific research methods and modern media approaches (Ch. 3).

Social identity theory   a theory that rests on the premise that identification with a group shapes individual and group behaviors, attitudes, and norms (Ch. 10).

Social impact entertainment   an alternative to conventional entertainment, like movies and television, that intends to create huge entertainment value to have an impact on social attitudes (Ch. 8).

Social judgment theory   a theory that rests on the premise that an idea is interpreted and deduced after comparing it with existing attitudes (Ch. 3).

Social justice   the relation of balance between people and society that is determined by comparing distribution of disparities, from individual freedoms to possibilities for equal privilege (Ch. 9).

Social justice seeker   an activist committed to a particular cause because he or she genuinely wants to see transformation in certain aspects of culture, like the elimination of homelessness and poverty, feeding the poor, fighting against gentrification, and alleviating racial tensions and racist mindsets (Ch. 9).

Social justice warrior   a pejorative term for an activist who vouches for socially progressive ideas—like feminism, equality, and multiculturalism (Ch. 9).

Social learning theory a theory postulating that on-screen characters are potential role models and may improve viewers' self-efficacy for following new behaviors (Ch. 8).

Social linking social relations between communities and governing agencies (Ch. 16).

Socially responsible investing see **Ethical investing** (Ch. 9).

Social marketing the process of designing, implementing, and controlling programs to increase the acceptability of a prosocial idea among population segments of consumers (Ch. 1).

Social movement a peaceful or bellicose performance, display, or campaign by which common citizens make collective claims on certain issues or groups (Ch. 9).

Social movement theory a theory describing the social production and propagation of meaningful ideas from united groups and how they act and communicate as a collective (Ch. 9).

Social Network Analysis an approach that predicates that nodes are connected to each other via clear or unclear relationships (Ch. 1).

Social norms norms that guide individual behavior by advising members of a community what behaviors the group expects from and requires of them (Ch. 1).

Social norms marketing an approach in social sciences that postulates that, after people correct the perceived norm to match the actual norm, they will modify their behavior accordingly (Ch. 1).

Social privilege special treatment or favoritism in society. It clearly benefits certain groups to the detriment of others (Ch. 12).

Social reproduction a phenomenon whereby public communication campaigns perpetuate current social distributions of knowledge, attitudes, and behaviors (instead of reform or improvement) (Ch. 3).

Social risk factors the unfavorable social conditions caused by poor health, such as lack of food and housing instability (Ch. 5).

Social structure a structure that embodies an apparatus of socioeconomic stratification, social institutions, establishments, national policies, and legislation that help crystallize the rules, roles, behaviors, and values of societal members (Ch. 9).

Social system a set of interrelated units integrated into a collective problem-solving task to attain a common goal (Ch. 1).

Soft power the ability to convince, co-opt, and be appealing, instead of coercing (Ch. 16).

Software of the mind our way of thinking, our thinking pattern, or our mental program (Ch. 6).

Solidarity the state of sharing interests, goals, principles, and sympathies to develop a sociopsychological sense of unity of groups or classes (Ch. 9).

Speech act theory a theory predicating that communicators speak to accomplish intended actions and, in that process, the public concludes or interprets intended meaning based on what those communicators uttered (Ch. 13).

Spiral of silence a theory positing that societal institutions like the government, the media, or the academic world impose opinions onto mainstream life. For this reason, people tend to avoid voicing their true opinions out of fear of being ostracized (Ch. 10).

Split–run testing a type of testing that consists of conducting a controlled experiment (Ch. 16).

Spontaneous diffusion a type of diffusion that occurs when the proliferation of messages within a specific population is not planned (Ch. 1).

Stakeholders individuals or groups who have a vested interest in a public communication campaign or the entity that organizes it (Ch. 1; Ch. 5).

Stalking a pattern of constant, undesired attention and contact by a partner that triggers fear or concern for his or her own safety or the safety of a third party (that is either close to the victim or the perpetrator, or both) (Ch. 10).

Standpoint a mental position or angle regarding certain issues, principles, or objects, often emerging from our circumstances or beliefs (Ch. 12).

Standpoint feminism a critical approach postulating that feminist social science should be applied from the standpoint of women or specific groups of women because they are more qualified or experienced to understand certain characteristics or dimensions of the world (Ch. 12).

Standpoint theory a theory predicated upon the idea that our knowledge creates some degree of authority and the power from such authority molds our opinions in everyday life (Ch. 12).

Strategic communication an approach that comprises a range of communication-related specialties, such as risk communication, public relations, brand management, and corporate communication (Ch. 7).

Structural capital social capital that includes social networks (Ch. 1).

Structural domain of power public policies that develop and control the social institution (Ch. 12).

Structural racism see **Systemic racism** (Ch. 12).

Structure an entity that employs both systems (of rules and norms for group activity) and resources (to cement power or attain objectives) in an interactive context (Ch. 6).

Subjective soaking the process that occurs when the ethnographer relinquishes the idea of pure objectivity or scientific neutrality (Ch. 6).

Summative evaluation the practice of answering questions in regards to exposure of the intended audience (size and features), as well as acceptance and assessment of campaign messages and effects (i.e., on knowledge, attitudes, and behavior) (Ch. 2).

Sunnah the traditions and practices of the Prophet Muhammad (Ch. 16).

Susceptibility information information about the likelihood that threatening results will happen (Ch. 4).

SWOT analysis a strategic planning approach to help a person or institution identify strengths, weaknesses, opportunities, and threats with respect to any key endeavor or project planning (Ch. 2).

Symbol a physical or nonphysical entity that represents something else—i.e., a material item, a concept, a behavior, or an event that stands for something else (Ch. 6).

Symbolism the language of symbols or a system of representing semantic units (both verbal and nonverbal) through symbols (Ch. 6).

Systemic racism a category of racism that is established as common practice within society, a cultural group, or an organization (Ch. 12).

Tablighi Jamaat a Muslim organization whose mission is to beseech Muslims and fellow members to return to traditional Islam in regards to ritual, dress, and personal behavior (Ch. 15).

TablighiJamatVirus an Islamophobic hashtag propagated immediately after the news that COVID-19 allegedly originated from a Muslim missionary group (i.e., Tablighi Jamaat) (Ch. 15).

Tagging content a process that entails embedding metadata in content. It enables to identify what online content has been accessed and for how much time (Ch. 2).

Tailoring a communication strategy in which messages are designed in relation to the audience's knowledge, beliefs, circumstances, and past experiences on certain issues (Ch. 1).

Targeted Community Intervention an innovative approach that offered support to residents of low-income districts in Jamaica (Ch. 6).

Teen dating violence intimate partner violence that occurs in adolescence (Ch. 10).

Telegram a free online cross-platform that has rapid messaging applications so necessary for secure communications (Ch. 16).

Telelogic communication computer-mediated dialogue (Ch. 2).

Telenovelas Latin America's popular soap operas (Ch. 8).

Temperance fountain a fountain usually built by a private donor and inspiring citizens not to drink alcohol by the provision of free, clean water (Ch. 1).

Temperance movement a movement that campaigned against the recreational use and sale of distilled spirits and advocated total abstinence in Anglo-Saxon countries in the nineteenth and twentieth centuries (Ch. 1).

Terrorism an intentional and insensible form of violence, making it uncontrollable and, in the eyes of many, transcending the mere concept of warfare (Ch. 13).

Terror Management Theory a theory predicating that all human motives fundamentally come from a biologically based need for survival or self-preservation (Ch. 15).

Theory of Planned Behavior a theory that presents norms as an indicator of personal behavior in addition to personal attitudes and perceived behavior control (Ch. 1).

Thick description an in-depth observation (and subsequent report) of a cultural site. The description includes many details; a high volume of notes are taken (Ch. 6).

Third party the receiver beyond the immediate receiver of the message (Ch. 2).

Third-person effect a theory positing that individuals have a tendency to perceive that mass media messages are more impactful on others than on themselves, because of personal biases (Ch. 1).

Time the amount of time needed for an innovation to diffuse and be accepted (or not) by people (Ch. 1).

Top–down change change that comes from leadership (Ch. 9).

Topical relevance the extent to which information meets the needs of the public (Ch. 2).

Toxic masculinity a type of machismo that advocates cultural norms like patriarchy and male social dominance (Ch. 10).

Transdisciplinary approach an approach that is synergistic through its employment of models, theories, research methods, analytical tools, and strategies for the explanation of findings (Ch. 1).

Transformational change a New-age perspective on social change, with fewer negative connotations or ramifications. It is a process of causing substantial change in the culture and work (or functioning) mechanisms of a society (Ch. 9).

Transformative empathy a type of empathy that recommends listening instead of distancing or looking at an individual as the Other (Ch. 10).

Transgender any person whose gender identity differs from the gender that a person was assigned at birth (Ch. 11).

Transportation   a convergent process, where all mental systems and capacities become focused on events occurring in the narrative (Ch. 8).

Transtheoretical Model   a model of behavior change that emphasizes the decision-making of a person (Ch. 3).

Traveling theory   a theory describing how people and ideas travel from one area to another (Ch. 9).

Treatment Action Campaign (TAC)   a South African patient-driven, rights-based activist campaign that grew predominantly from the late apartheid and transition-to-democracy era in the late 1990s (Ch. 5).

Trifling fear   fear that emerges when experiencing harm of inconsiderable dimensions (Ch. 4).

Tropes   figures of speech (Ch. 13).

truth   a long-standing antismoking campaign designed for youths in the United States. It is run by the American Legacy Foundation and funded by diverse tobacco companies (Ch. 5).

Two-step flow of communication   a two-step model that works on human agency. According to the model, mass media messages are diffused to the "masses" by way of opinion leadership (Ch. 1).

Ulamas   Muslim clerical scholars (Ch. 16).

Ummah   the global Islamic community (Ch. 16).

United Nations Children's Emergency Fund (UNICEF)   a United Nations program charged with providing humanitarian and developmental assistance to children around the world (Ch. 6).

Universal prevention   prevention that targets all members of a community without specifying who is at risk of abuse (Ch. 1).

Upstream social marketing   a broader approach to social marketing that operates at the macro level and that can influence policymakers (Ch. 1).

US Capitol riots   also called the 2021 storming of the United States Capitol or the 2021 Capitol insurrection, the US Capitol riots were a forceful attack against the US Congress in Washington, DC, on January 6, 2021 (Ch. 14).

User-Generated Content   a term that most people use to designate any type of content created by users in digital networks (Ch. 10).

Uses & Gratifications theory   a theory assuming that (1) audiences are not passive consumers of media, (2) they have power over media consumption, and (3) they are responsible for selecting media that fulfill (i.e., gratify) their desires and needs (Ch. 2).

Utilitarian genocide   self-serving mass killing (Ch. 13).

Utilitarianism   the end justifies the means (Ch. 4).

Vaccination   the act of injecting a vaccine to assist the immune system in developing protection from a disease (Ch. 7).

Vaccine hesitancy   postponement in acceptance or refusal of vaccination regardless of availability of vaccination services (Ch. 7).

Valence   the value that we attribute to the expected reward (Ch. 3).

Values   our most cherished beliefs about right and wrong (Ch. 2).

Vanity metrics   the measurement of how successful one is in the realm of social media (Ch. 2).

Violent extremism   a form of extremism that consists of many types of dangerous actions, including those who support or commit ideologically motivated violence to further political goals (Ch. 13).

WebMD.com   a healthcare website that offers top services to assist healthcare providers, patients, and other visitors in making their way through the complex healthcare system (Ch. 6).

Well poisoning   a conspiracy against "Jewish poisoners" that became standard antisemitism (Ch. 15).

Whiteness   the societal privilege that benefits White people over non-White people in certain areas, especially White people who find themselves in similar social, political, or financial situations (Ch. 12).

White supremacism   an ideology advancing that the White race is superior to other races and, as such, should dominate or exterminate them. White supremacism is rooted in the widely debunked theory of scientific racism and its pseudoscientific assertions (Ch. 14).

White supremacist terrorism   a class of terrorism carried out by non-state actors whose objectives include, but are not limited to, (1) racial dominance, (2) hostility towards government authority, and (3) virulent disapproval of abortion (Ch. 14).

Wishful identification   a phenomenon whereby a viewer aspires to be like the character, feels a dynamic yearning for emulating the figure, and expresses undue respect for the character (Ch. 8).

Wokeism   also called wokeness, it it a term denoting the awareness of racial prejudice and discrimination (Ch. 12).

YouTube Effect   an overarching concept that describes how social networking sites like YouTube, Facebook, and Telegram—to name a few—have tactical advantages that television or radio do not have (Ch. 16).

4chan   an online message board composed of threads and related comments; the movement migrated to 8chan in November 2017 (Ch. 14).

8kun   formerly known as 8chan, it is an online image board made up of user-created message boards. Each board is moderated by an owner, allowing a modicum of interaction from site administration (Ch. 14).

Index